C000072513

Access 97
Unleashed

SECOND EDITION

Dwayne Gifford, et al.

SAMS

Unleashed

Access 97 Unleashed, Second Edition

Copyright ©1998 by Sams

International Standard Book Number: 0-672-31271-9

Library of Congress Catalog Card Number: 97-80844

Printed in the United States of America

First Printing: May 1998

00   99   98   4   3   2

Trademarks

EXECUTIVE EDITOR
Rosemarie Graham

ACQUISITIONS EDITOR
Corrine Wire

DEVELOPMENT EDITORS
Richard Alvey
Tony Amico
Marla Reece-Hall

MANAGING EDITOR
Patrick Kanouse

PROJECT EDITOR
Rebecca Mounts

COPY EDITOR
Sean Medlock
Tonya Maddox

INDEXERS
Christine Nelsen
Bruce Clingaman

TECHNICAL EDITOR
Damon Darling

SOFTWARE DEVELOPMENT SPECIALIST
Andrea Duvall

PRODUCTION
Michael Henry
Linda Knose
Tim Osborn
Staci Somers
Mark Walchle

Overview

Contents

Dedication

This book is entirely dedicated in memory of the greatest man I have ever met:

Dr. Hernan Barrientos Urquieta.

To his gifted wisdom, integrity, charisma, and altruism. To his unmatched virtues, which led him to grow to distinction and excellence even in youth. He was an exceptional human being who deeply cared about people. He brought greater fulfillment and joy to all individuals who were lucky enough to know him.

His devotion and constant demonstration of magnificent wisdom, excellence, love, and commitment to higher achievements made him the finest University Professor of Law.

Throughout his brilliant career, he delivered the law with justice and moral strength. Integrity was the mirror of his soul and his actions. His remarkable professionalism, decisive leadership, outstanding background, and sense of fairness were the keys to his success, and he was a master of them.

This is a token of my admiration, reverence, and respect to my beloved father in-law, who was like a father to me and who I have loved dearly. Heaven has gained an angel of justice; he is that beautiful force of love and gentleness that constantly protects his beloved ones.

Dad, our hearts are blossoming full of beautiful and tender memories that we deeply treasure. You have been our greatest inspiration. You have taught us the important values in life that made us confident and strong, yet sensible and wise. Through your unconditional love, you showed us the precious essence of the family values that promptly turned into golden threads of our now strong foundation. You have set a fine example throughout your impeccable life.

We are so proud of you. Thank you for your delightful presence in our lives and thank you for all you have been to all of us. We love you so much. There are no words capable of conveying all that we feel for you.

May your gentle soul enjoy the presence of God.—Dwayne Gifford

Acknowledgments

It would be perhaps impossible for one person alone to create this valuable resource, which is the outcome of great teamwork, commitment to excellence, and dedication.

This book was made feasible by the vast efforts of many skilled people, and it is with great pleasure that I take this opportunity to thank each of them, not only for their significant contributions to the implementation and completion of this book, but also for their dedication.

I would like to also express appreciation to some very special friends: Kim Spilker, who initiated my writing career; Steve Straiger, who wisely guided me through a number of situations, putting them into perspective and then challenging me to new heights; and Tom Eaves, for showing such professionalism, support, and confidence in me, and for giving me the unique opportunity to make things happen.

Furthermore, I would like to thank some very good friends who have earned my trust, affection, and respect: Gonzalo Barrientos, Amrik Bhogal, Bruce Gillispie, Eric Borrows, Robert Atlinger, Marco Peredo, Hernan Barrientos, Juan Carlos Roman L., Craig Longman, Bruce McAuley, Karen Alajica, Jan Osborne, Lance Lindburg, Aaron Carta, Kwing Ng, Tom Buser, and a special thanks to Mike Murphy for his assistance throughout the writing of this book.

To my loving Mamita, the best example of kindness, sensitivity, understanding, and love humanly possible. Thank you for being my angel.

To my parents for their assiduous support and endless love, a gratitude I may never truly express.

It would be unfair to give acknowledgments without showing my appreciation to my three sister-in-laws: Mirnita, Jimenita, and Silvita, who are very special to me.

I can never say enough about the love, support, and genuine caring that I receive from my beautiful wife Iris, and my three lovely and gorgeous children, Kevin, Monica Michelle, and Jason, who gently overflow my heart. Kids, I love you more than you will ever know.

Irisita, you are a dream come true, my blessing and inspiration, the gift that furnishes ecstasy and magnificence to each of my days.—Dwayne Gifford

I would not be where I am without my family, friends, and teachers who helped me so much along the way.—Alex Feinberg

About the Author

Dwayne R. Gifford is a Programmer/Analyst in Access, Visual Basic, MS SQL Server, and Visual C++, a hobby that he has enjoyed for the past seven years. In addition, he is the author and co-author of several books on Access, Visual Basic, SQL Server, and Office. Throughout his career, he has delivered a number of seminars, workshops, and training courses to industry professionals worldwide. However, one of his favorite hobbies is to pass on his knowledge to anyone who shows the slightest desire to learn. His current position is Information Engineer Manager for a exciting young company, Star Software Systems. He began his professional career in Canada, where he worked for Labatt Breweries, following which he consulted for Microsoft as a lead analyst for its largest volume licensing. As his career grew, he became the lead architect for Homeside Lending. He is a true professional—a combination of hands-on experience, solid education, and a desire driven by knowledge not just for himself, but for others as well. He can be reached at dgifford@starsoftware.com.

Daniel Carollo was born and educated in France, with a university degree in physical sciences and mathematics, a college education in electronics, and various specialty programming courses. Daniel wrote (and passed) the Microsoft Access exam in 1997. He has his own company that specializes in software development and consulting, mainly in Access and Visual Basic. Daniel's customers include both small and large companies in South Africa, France, and Switzerland. Daniel has been working with Access since version 1.0 and has been designing various applications since version 1.1. These applications include a billing/stock control system, a multiple-level industrial recipe database, a Web site document management system for a labor law firm, and many others.

Alex Feinberg emigrated from Odessa, Ukraine in 1991. He graduated from Pace University, New York in January 1998. Currently, Alex is working as an independent consultant to L&T Incorporated, specializing in Payroll Tax software. Alex has been developing with Access since version 2.0 and with Visual Basic since version 3.0. He also participates in the NYC Access/Visual Basic User Group.

Stephen Forte owns the Aurora Development Group, a NYC consulting firm specializing in ActiveX technologies (http://www.auroradev.com). Stephen also serves as the President of the NYC Access/Visual Basic User Group (http://www.nycaccessv.com). He also travels around the world, speaking at professional developer conferences.

Joel Goodling designs client/server and Internet/intranet applications for clients of ETI. Currently, Joel is designing a multi-tier e-commerce application that is designed to be used over the Internet and intranets. The application is designed to be able to use any

ODBC-compliant database as a backend, including Access 97. Joel has built several commercial applications using Access 97, often tying Access as a front end to a Microsoft SQL Server back end.

Brett Herrmann, P.E., graduated from California State Polytechnic University, Ponoma, with a degree in Mechanical Engineering. He has worked with Microsoft Access since version 1.0, in 1993, and has also consulted in Southern California. He enjoys combining his technical, business, and people skills to develop exciting new products for individual business needs. Some of Brett's projects and experience include an environmental test results database, cancer specimen analysis, electronic approval and document release, business process analysis, data modeling, and database design. In his leisure time he enjoys cycling and spending time with his wife and three kids (golden retrievers). You can reach Brett at BretinCA@aol.com.

Stephen Holland is a full-time professor in the Computer Information Systems department at New Hampshire Technical Institute in Concord, New Hampshire. While at NHTI, Stephen has developed and taught many courses in Visual Basic and introductory/advanced Access. He brings to the classroom over sixteen years of business experience in the information systems field as a programmer and system analyst. He enjoys attending the Visual Basic/Access user group meetings held in New Hampshire. He can be reached via email at stwh@gsinet.net.

Jay Holovacs is a system administrator, software developer, and consultant specializing in Access and C++ applications. Database applications that he has developed include purchase and inventory systems, travel reservations, mass mailing billing, and construction job management. Jay can be contacted at holovacs@idt.net.

Jon Price has worked with Microsoft Access databases since Access 2.0. Projects Jon has completed include a sales force automation database for a communications company, a customer courtesy desk database for a small grocery chain, an ordering and cataloguing database for a small computer firm, a project and clientele tracking for an engineering firm, a loan history and forecasting database for a major banking company, a production reporting database for a major insurance company, and an insurance policy generator, tracker, and forecasting database for a major insurance company. Jon is currently employed, under contract, with United States Automobile Association (USAA) in San Antonio, TX. At USAA, he is part of the Office Support Tools Team Project, which is involved in converting all legacy applications, used by more than 12,000 employees, over to the Microsoft Office suite of tools. Jon is currently pursuing the Microsoft Certified Solutions Developer (MCSD) certification. He lives in San Antonio with his wife and two children.

Kent Waldrop is a database consultant with Computer Management Sciences, Inc. in Jacksonville, Florida. He has worked with Microsoft SQL Server, Access, and Sybase SQL Server over the past nine years. Much of this work has consisted of designing, implementing, and optimizing SQL databases. Other work includes document imaging, workflow, and OCR applications. Kent is currently assigned to Homeside Lending, Inc. as a database administrator and SQL specialist.

About the Technical Editor

Damon Darling is the Senior Windows Developer at Digital Lava, Inc. in Los Angeles. Digital Lava is the pioneering developer of video publishing software for corporate training, communications, distance learning, research, and other applications. Digital Lava provides business with the next step in video technology, transforming cumbersome linear video into easily accessible and manageable digital information. Darling specializes in ActiveX COM development, Win32 API, and Internet technologies. He develops video management, multimedia, Internet, and client/server applications in Visual Basic and Access. Visit Digital Lava at `http://digitallava.com`.

Introduction

Microsoft Access 97 is a true 32-bit application that gives you not only power and robustness, but also ease of use. This new version of Access offers you the same look and feel as other Microsoft Office applications, as well as some new features:

- Class modules
- Improved tab control
- The ability to remove source code from the database
- Partial replication
- Replication across the Internet
- Command bars
- Hyperlinks
- The ability to publish Access objects to the Web

Access 97 Unleashed, Second Edition will take you from beginner to expert level as you master this professional database tool, and is filled with tips, shortcuts, and real-world examples. This book reveals the ins and outs to help you release the full power of Access 97.

Special Features of This Book

➡ Sometimes a line of code will not fit within the margins of this book. When that happens, the line will be broken and this code continuation character will be placed on the second line. This icon indicates that you should type the code as a single line.

NOTE

Notes present supplemental information to the text. Sometimes these can be real-world experiences with Access 97.

TIP

Tips are suggestions to help you in real-world situations. These can often be shortcuts or information to make a task easier or faster.

> **WARNINGS**
>
> Warnings provide information about detrimental performance issues or dangerous errors that can occur. Pay careful attention to Warnings.

Where to Find Author Source Code and Sample Databases

Throughout this book you are referred to the book's Web site. You can locate this information by going to www.mcp.com/info. When you get to this page, you will be asked to provide the ISBN for this book. Enter in 0-672-31271-9 and there you should be able to locate the appropriate files.

Planning for Data Population Databases and Tables

IN THIS PART

Essentials for Creating New Databases

CHAPTER 1

Database Wizard

The Database Wizard (see Figure 1.1) was introduced in Access 95 and has been retained in Access 97, bringing database development within reach of users without prior database experience. The Database Wizard creates all the tables, forms, and reports for the predefined database you specify in one operation. The predefined database types vary from address books and contact management to wine lists and workout databases. Each predefined database type has its own characteristics that are unique to the type of application it's supposed to be building. A blank database type is also included that creates an empty database where you can add tables, forms, reports, macros, and code modules.

FIGURE 1.1.

The Database Wizard.

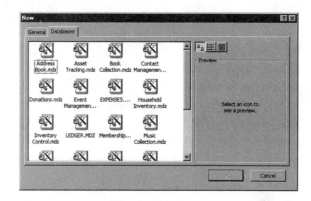

Database Properties

With Access 97, you can change, view, and define database properties, as well as define your own database properties to identify the characteristics of a database. You can do a search using these properties as criteria to get a list of databases. Some of the properties include the author, title, and subject of the database, as well as statistics such as creation date and time and the last user to access the database. You can also obtain a list of all the objects in the database.

The database properties are grouped into categories accessible via different tabs of the Database Properties dialog box. Some of these properties are read-only, while others can be changed by the user, either directly in this dialog box or through Visual Basic code in a module.

To see the Database Properties dialog box, shown in Figure 1.2, choose File | Database Properties.

FIGURE 1.2.

The Database Properties dialog box.

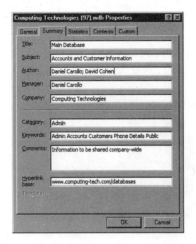

The first tab, General, gives information about the database object, including its name, location, type, size and attributes. None of that information can be changed by the user at this point.

The second tab, Summary, lists user information that can be used in search criteria within Windows Explorer. With Microsoft's great emphasis on the Internet, Access 97 has added the Hyperlink Base setting. You use it to create the base hyperlink path that is appended to the beginning of relative `HyperlinkAddress` property settings. Access 97's Internet capabilities are discussed in detail in Chapter 24, "Configuring a Web Site for Access," and Chapter 25, "Using Access 97 with Static HTML Pages."

The next tab, Statistics, shows information about the database that obviously cannot be changed by the user.

Contents, the fourth tab, gives a list of all objects in the database. When you elect to see system and/or hidden objects in the database window (controlled by the Tools I Options I View settings), these objects are also listed in the Properties I Content tab.

The fifth tab, Custom, is the one that is very exciting for developers. It enables the user to store and retrieve properties available throughout the database via code. Popular uses range from storing global tax rates to storing version numbers and other global use values.

The Startup properties enable you to create customized applications that specify different options. Some of these options include toolbar customization, status bar and database window display, and what form is displayed when a database is opened. They also enable you to set whether the user can view the code after an error occurs or whether the Access 97 special keys—such as Show Database Window, Pause Execution, and Display Code Window—are active. To see the Startup dialog box, shown in Figure 1.3, choose Tools | Startup.

FIGURE 1.3.

The Startup dialog box.

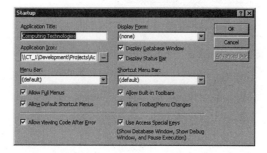

Creating a Database

Access 97 has two convenient methods for creating databases. The more user-friendly approach is to use the Database Wizard, which creates all the tables, forms, and reports for the database type you choose. The other, more work-intensive method is to create a blank database and add the tables, forms, and reports separately. This method leads to more flexibility for the developer; however, it means that each element must be defined separately. In either case, you can extend and modify your database definition anytime after it has been created.

Creating a Database Using the Database Wizard

Experienced developers might choose to let the wizard create a database as the starting point for a new project development, and then modify what the wizard has created to suit the project's requirements. When Access 97 starts, a dialog box appears that enables you to open an existing database or create a new one, as shown in Figure 1.4. From this dialog box, select Database Wizard and click OK. If you have already been working in Access 97, you can click the New Database button in the main toolbar—if you haven't customized it.

From here, select from the list the type of database you want to create. If the exact type you want is not in the list, either create a blank database or select the type that is the closest match, and you can modify it later. For this example, create a Wine List database, selecting it from the list of choices.

FIGURE 1.4.

*The opening
selection dialog
box.*

You must then specify a name and location for the database in the File New Database
dialog box. Note that Access 97 uses the Windows 95 common file dialog box, so you
don't have to specify an extension. Access 97 databases are registered in the Registry, so
Windows 95 knows to add the .MDB extension.

After you click Create to define your database, Access 97 begins to create the database.
You are first shown some summary information about what kind of data your selected
database will store. Click Next to move forward. You are then prompted as to whether
you would like to include any extra fields or sample data to help you learn to use the
database, as shown in Figure 1.5. If this is your first experience with Access, including
the sample data is a good way to help you learn the various features of the database you
created.

FIGURE 1.5.

*Prompting for
additional fields
and sample data.*

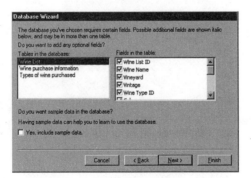

The Database Wizard then prompts you for the type of screen display you want to use, as
shown in Figure 1.6. You can choose from several types, and choosing an uncluttered
background will help improve readability. The Standard style is especially recommended
for users with monochrome VGA or with systems that only support 16 colors.

FIGURE 1.6.

Prompting for the screen display type.

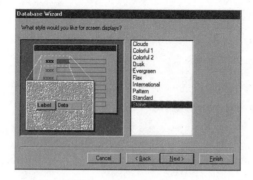

After you choose a screen display type, you are asked to choose a report type. You can see what each report type looks like in the preview window before you decide which type you want to use.

You are then prompted for the title of your database, as shown in Figure 1.7. Enter a title or just use the default title. You can also add a picture to the background of the forms and reports onscreen. Do so by clicking the check box with the caption "Yes, I'd like to include a picture." Then click the Picture button and locate the picture you want to use. Or you can provide the filename for the picture.

FIGURE 1.7.

Prompting for the title and picture.

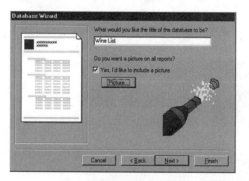

After you click the Next or Finish button, the Database Wizard creates the database based on the parameters you have provided. Depending on what kind of system you have, the RAM it contains, and so forth, this process could take a few minutes. When the Database Wizard is finished, your new database switchboard is shown in the Database window. Congratulations! You have just created an Access 97 database application!

Creating a Database Without Using the Database Wizard

If you're just starting Access 97, you're presented with options to create a new database or open an existing one. See Figure 1.4 for an example of this dialog box. To create a database manually, select Blank Database and then click OK.

If you have been working in Access 97 and want to create a new database, select the New Database button from the main toolbar and select the Blank Database icon in the New Database dialog box.

You then see the Database window with your blank database in it, as shown in Figure 1.8. The blank database is similar to an empty container, waiting for you to put something into it. You need to add objects such as tables, forms, and reports to the database.

FIGURE 1.8.
The Database window with a blank database.

Maintaining Databases from the Tools Menu

You can do most database maintenance, if not all, from the Tools menu when you don't have any databases open. The Tools options of particular note for maintenance are Database Utilities, Security, and Custom Controls. The other options, Macros, Options, ActiveX, and AutoCorrect are not directly related to database maintenance and will not be discussed in this chapter.

Database Utilities

The first menu option discussed here is Database Utilities, which contains several useful options. The Convert Database option takes an Access 1.*x*, 2, or 95 database and converts it to Access 97, thus allowing it to take advantage of the new features of Access 97. The

Compact Database option enables you to compact the database so that it uses disk space more efficiently; using this option should aid performance if you haven't compacted the database for some time. The Repair Database option attempts to repair a damaged database. Access 97 usually detects damaged databases, but you can attempt to repair any database you think might be damaged. The Make MDE File option is a new utility in Access 97.

> **WARNING**
>
> If you need to share your database with users of previous versions of Access, do not convert it to the Microsoft Access 97 format.

What is an MDE file? If your database contains Visual Basic code, saving it as an MDE file compiles all modules, removes all editable source code, and compacts the destination database. Your Visual Basic code continues to run, but it can't be viewed or edited. The database is considerably smaller because of the removal of the Visual Basic code. Memory use is also optimized, which improves performance.

Saving your database as an MDE file prevents the unauthorized maintenance of your project by not allowing the following:

- Viewing, modifying, or creating forms, reports, or modules.
- Adding, deleting, or changing references to object libraries or databases.
- Changing code using the properties or methods of the Access or VBA Object models. An MDE file contains no source code.
- Changing your database's VBA project name using the Options dialog box.
- Importing or exporting forms, reports, or modules. However, you can export or import tables, queries, and macros to or from non-MDE databases. You can export any tables, queries, or macros in an MDE database into another database, but you cannot export forms, reports, or modules into another database.

> **TIP**
>
> The MDE database is created as a separate file from your original MDB. Do not delete the MDB because you'll need it if you want to change anything in the design of the database. If you need to modify the design of forms, reports, or modules, open the original MDB database, modify it, and then save it as an MDE file again.

For more details on the MDE file utility, please see Appendix B, "Access 97 Specific Features."

Database Security

The next option on the Tools menu is Security, which contains options to maintain user and group accounts, as well as the capability to encrypt or decrypt a database.

The User and Group Accounts option enables you to administer workgroup accounts by adding, deleting, and modifying various users and group accounts.

In a workgroup environment, the concept of permissions and who has which type of permission is critical. Two types of permissions exist: explicit and implicit. Permissions can be granted either to a single user (a user account) or to a group of users (a group account). Granting permission to a user account is called *explicit permission;* granting permission to a group account is called *implicit permission.* If a user is a member of a group, he or she has that group's permissions. Therefore, by adding or removing users from a group, you can change permissions for a user (or group of users). The topics of assigning and removing permissions for a database and database objects, as well as the types of permissions available, are discussed in Chapter 23, "Security."

The Encrypt/Decrypt option either encrypts a database so that it can't be read by a general utility program or word processor, or decrypts the database and removes the previously applied encryption. Sometimes, for example, you may want your database to be read only by Access 97. The encrypt function prevents your database from being read by any other program except Access 97. As part of the encryption process, Access compacts the database as well. To compact a database without encrypting it, see "Compacting an Access 97 Database" later in this chapter.

Whereas the encryption process makes your database indecipherable to a word processor or utility program, the decryption process removes the encryption and reverses its effects. Encryption and decryption, and their advantages and disadvantages, are discussed in more detail in Chapter 23.

With a database open, three other options on the Tools menu are enabled. By selecting User and Group Permissions, you can assign permissions by user or group to any object in the database. You can also change the database owner. The User-Level Security Wizard creates a new secured database from your unsecured database. Your existing database is not modified.

Set Database Password is also enabled. Using this option, you can assign a single password to control who can open a database instead of, or in addition to, implementing user-level security.

Database Replication

Replication, which is available only if a database is currently open, contains an option that enables you to convert a database into a replica. This capability is necessary if you want to use Access 97's Briefcase Replication feature.

So, what exactly is database replication? It's a method of creating synchronized copies of a database with different users over a network or the Internet. When you're using replication, you create a replica set consisting of your original database and one or more identical copies of it.

While giving you centralized control of the structure of your database, replication allows free exchange of data between members of the replica set. By placing the replicated databases on users' computers, you create a multiuser environment with much less associated network traffic than if your database were located on a network server.

You should definitely consider replication if you have multiple users in different locations working on the same database. More details can be found in Chapter 21, "Replication."

Converting to an Access 97 Database

In Access 97, you can work with databases from older versions of Access. You can't change the design of the objects in the older database or take advantage of all the new features, however, until you convert the database to Access 97. You also can't add new objects to the older database under Access 97. Note that the conversion is a one-way ticket, however: after you convert the database to Access 97, you can't open it in an older version of Access, and you can't convert it back to the older version.

With all the benefits of the new version, is there a reason you shouldn't convert a database to Access 97? The primary reason is that if you have users who can't upgrade or haven't upgraded to Windows 95 or Windows NT 3.51 build 1057 or later, they can't open an Access 97 database and thus can't use your application. Also, if a database was created or is being used in Visual Basic 2 or 3, you shouldn't convert the database. Visual Basic 2 and 3 can't open or use Access 97 databases. Visual Basic 4 can use an Access 97 database using DAO 3.5, however, so you should wait to convert the database until your VB application can be upgraded to Visual Basic 4.

Converting a database is straightforward and easy. First you should back up the database you're going to convert so that you can still use it until you're comfortable using Access 97. You should also ensure that any linked tables or databases are still in the directory where your database refers to them. Then close the database you're going to convert; if the database is located on a server or is shared, make sure that no other users have it open. If you're using a secure workgroup, make sure that you have Modify Design or Administer permissions on all tables in the database before you proceed. Otherwise, you will be unable to convert the database. If you have successfully completed the preceding steps and have the proper permissions, you're ready to convert the database.

> **NOTE**
>
> If you are converting from a database created in a version prior to Access 2.0, you should rename all objects that used the quote character (') in their name. This is not allowed in Access version 2.0 and after.

Choose Tools | Database Utilities, and then select Convert Database. From here, select the database you want to convert, as shown in Figure 1.9.

FIGURE 1.9.

Selecting the database to convert.

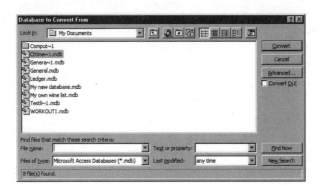

You are then prompted for the name of the file you would like to save the converted database in, as shown in Figure 1.10. To keep the same name, change to another directory. Otherwise, type in a new name without the .MDB extension and click Save. Access 97 then converts the database. Depending on the size of your database, this process could take several minutes. Note that, depending on the size of your forms, reports, and modules, this conversion could be as much as twice the size of your original database due to storing as Visual Basic for Applications instead of Access Basic. All Access Basic objects, and the objects they refer to, are converted to Visual Basic for Applications. You should also be aware that you have to convert any 16-bit API calls to their 32-bit counterparts manually because the conversion process does not handle this change. Otherwise, a runtime error will occur.

FIGURE 1.10.

Selecting the database to convert to.

> **NOTE**
>
> If your database uses linked tables, you also have to convert the database in which the linked tables reside.

> **NOTE**
>
> Access 97 is generally compatible with version 1.*x* databases. However, Access 97 might change the behavior of some database objects.

Compacting an Access 97 Database

As time goes by and you delete tables and records, your database file becomes fragmented on the disk, thus using disk space inefficiently and causing performance degradation. Compacting the database makes a copy of the database, removing the fragmentation so that the database uses disk space better. You must have Modify Design or Administer permission for all the tables in the database, if you are in a secure workgroup. To compact the database, you should first close it on your system. If the database is shared or on a server, make sure that no other users are using it; otherwise, you will be unable to compact the database. If you have successfully closed the database and you have the proper permissions, you are ready to compact the database.

> **WARNING**
>
> If you're compacting an Access 1.*x* database and an object in it has the backquote character (`` ` ``) in its name, you must go into Access 1.*x* and rename the object. You then have to change all references to the old object to the new object name in the forms, queries, reports, macros, and code. If you fail to take this step, you will be unable to compact the database.

TIP

If the database is replicated, you should compact it twice. On the first pass, Access reclaims some free space and flags some of it a reclaimable, but without reclaiming it. On the second pass, the flagged space is reclaimed. There is no benefit in running the procedure a third time.

Choose Tools | Database Utilities and then select Compact Database. From here, select the database you want to compact, as shown in Figure 1.11.

FIGURE 1.11.

Selecting the database to compact.

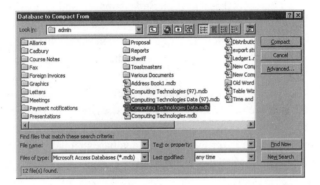

You are then prompted for the name of the file in which you would like to save the compacted database, as shown in Figure 1.12. To keep the same name, change to another directory. Otherwise, type in a new name without the .MDB extension and click Save. Access 97 then compacts the database. This process could take several minutes.

FIGURE 1.12.

Selecting the database to compact to.

> **WARNING**
>
> Make sure that you have enough disk space for both the original and compacted versions of the database, even if you save the compacted version with the same name as the original. If you don't, delete any unneeded files and then try to compact the database. Otherwise, you will get an error.

Repairing an Access 97 Database

On rare occasions, your Access 97 database might become damaged or corrupted. In most cases, Access 97 detects that the database is damaged and gives you the option to repair it. Sometimes, however, Access 97 can't detect database damage and you must repair it yourself. For example, you might have to repair the database if it's behaving unpredictably. A good first step is to repair the database and see whether that remedies the problem. To repair the database, you should first close it on your system. If the database is shared or on a server, make sure that no other users are using it; otherwise, you will be unable to repair the database. If you have successfully closed the database, and you think a repair is warranted or Access 97 prompts you to repair it, you're ready to do so. The following procedure is for repairing the database manually. If Access 97 prompts you to repair the database, it handles the procedure automatically.

Choose Tools | Database Utilities and then select Repair Database. From here, select the database you want to repair, as shown in Figure 1.13.

FIGURE 1.13.

Selecting the database to repair.

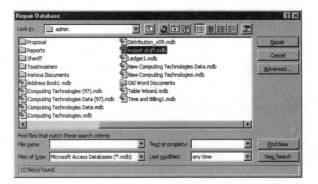

After you select the file, click Repair. Access 97 attempts to repair the database. This process could take several minutes. Note that not all databases can be repaired if the damage is severe enough.

WARNING

Before you attempt to repair the database, make a backup copy of it. If your data is valuable and you can't repair the database, you'll want to send that copy to one of the companies that specialize in retrieving data from corrupted Access databases, and most of them prefer working on a database in which Access hasn't attempted the repair yet.

Planning for Success

Success seldom happens by chance. If you are developing databases for use by third parties, taking the next points into consideration will help you plan a successful rollout of your application.

Configuring Windows

When you're installing Access 97 ODE to create setup disks, keep in mind that Setup will create disks that contain the DLLs and OCX files that are in use on the current machine. If the target machine has a different operating system, the status of the target machine after installation will be, at best, unpredictable.

When you're developing for a different target (for example, when you're using an NT workstation as a development machine, and targeting Windows 95 as a user platform), it is best to move the database to the user platform and use the Setup Wizard in that environment.

Network and Client/Server Considerations

Access 97, or rather the Jet engine, is a file-based database, and the creation of recordsets takes place on the client machine. This is as opposed to SQL Server, where the server returns recordsets to the requesting client.

When you're developing a database that will be used on a network, keep a few points in mind. It has become customary to split the database into a front end, which contains reasonably static objects and resides on the user's machine, and a back end, which contains the changing data and is on a path that's accessible to all users. This is done to minimize network traffic—forms and other objects that seldom change are opened on the client machine, generating no network traffic. The preoccupation of the developer is then to implement a scheme to keep all the front ends up to date. Replication is a viable solution in this case.

> ### TIP
>
> When you're naming the objects in your database (tables and fields), type the names without imbedding spaces in them because this character is not allowed in SQL Server. You can use the underscore character instead. The conversion of your application to SQL Server later on will be simplified.

The Art of Normalizing Databases

Creating a sound design from the beginning is important. Modifications and additions to the database are made easier when the right steps were taken at design time. Normalization goes a long way towards ensuring that the storage of data is optimized.

Normalization Goals

Normalization is the attempt to structure the database and design its schema to eliminate the duplication of information. If data in a field needs to be copied into another field, ideally this data should be contained in a separate table, and pointers to the data in the new table will be kept in the original fields.

Data integrity is enforced by using different types of relationships between the tables. This will be discussed in a later paragraph.

Normal Forms

A normal form for a database implies that every table has a unique index, and that each item of data is present only in one place in the database so that any change to the data need happen only once.

Getting Normal

You can run the Table Analysis Wizard to check whether your table should be split up and a one-to-many relationship established. The goal is to eliminate the duplication of information in records. If an element of information is common to several records, chances are that the relevant field belongs to a table at a higher level than the one concerned.

Integration

Integration requires that all the information relevant to an item is kept in the table describing that item.

Decomposition

All items in the database are decomposed to the lowest level, so the tables have fields pertinent to the simplest elements.

Trade-Offs

The downside of normalization is that for you to know all there is to know about a single item, several tables need to be queried. This is really a small trade-off when you consider the advantages in data integrity and the elimination of redundancy.

Matching Relationships to Business Objects

Sometimes, database relationships are not obvious at first, but inevitably they outline characteristic relations between the objects stored in the database. Understanding the objects described by the tables and how they relate to each other is key to designing the database relationships.

One-to-Many

A one-to-many relationship often reflects a hierarchy of details, with a parent record that contains information about a group of items and each item having details stored in a separate table.

An examples of this is company and employee data. There is no need to enter company data repeatedly for each employee. A one-to-many relationship ensures that the company details are stored in a parent record, and each employee record points to the relevant record from the company table.

Invoice and customer data also uses this type of relationship. An invoice being drawn against a customer account doesn't need the repetition of the company data already on record.

Many-to-Many

A many-to-many relationship can only be implemented in Access by introducing a third table in the middle, thereby replacing the relationship with two one-to-many relationships.

An example of this would be when a company uses parts to make up assemblies, and some parts are used in more than one type of assembly. A third table is used between the assembly table and the part table to describe fully what gets used where.

For example, let's say you have a business that receives items of furniture from several manufacturers and then ships crated packages to customers. The first table, shown in Figure 1.14, gathers all the details pertinent to the parts that go in a crate, such as a description and a purchase price.

FIGURE 1.14.

The tblPart table.

The second table, shown in Figure 1.15, stores information about the crates, with fields for a description and the assembly cost.

FIGURE 1.15.

The tblAssy table.

The third table, shown in Figure 1.16, links the first two and adds fields to qualify each element. The first field is unique to the tblAssyItems table and is used to provide a unique reference to each record. The second and third fields are linked to the tblAssy and tblPart tables, respectively. Access shows the descriptions in these fields, but the only key field is stored. There's also a Qty field (there's usually more than one chair in a given package), an order field to specify in what order the elements should be assembled, and some remarks pertinent to the items being added.

FIGURE 1.16.

The tblAssyItems table.

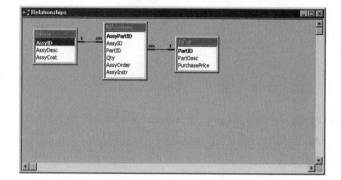

	AssyPartID	AssyID	PartID	Qty	AssyOrder	AssyInstr
	2	Economy Lounge suite	Armchair	4	1	Match seat colors
	4	Economy Lounge suite	Table	1	2	
	5	De Luxe Lounge Suite	Armchair	6	1	Carefully match color
	6	De Luxe Lounge Suite	Table	1	2	
	7	Fancy Dining-Room	Chair	6	1	Select comfort models
	8	Fancy Dining-Room	Table	1	2	Match wood color to chairs
	9	Dream Bedroom	Wardrobe	1	1	
	10	Dream Bedroom	Bedside Table	2	2	
	11	Dream Bedroom	Single Bed	2	3	
▶	AutoNumber) 0		0	0	0	

Record: 10 of 10

Figure 1.17 shows the example we've been discussing, with the tblAssy and tblPart tables on the "one" side of the relationships, and the tblAssyItems on the "many" side.

FIGURE 1.17.

A many-to-many relationship.

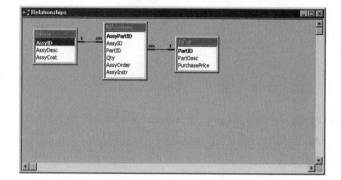

One-to-One

The one-to-one relationship is used when a lot of information has to be kept for each record, usually in numerous fields. Access has a limit of 255 fields per table, but you'll probably want to split the data into several tables before you reach that limit. The fields that uniquely identify the records are kept in a table, as well as any other indexed fields that are used in searches. This table is then linked in a one-to-one relationship to a second table, which contains all the other fields. When you're retrieving recordsets, the selection criteria can be applied against the first table, thus reducing the number of retrieved records, and the necessary data from the second table can then be retrieved faster, using only the small recordset from the first table.

A one-to-one relationship is also used in cases where record fields are split between two separate tables, or even databases, for security or access reasons. For example, personnel and salary data might both have the same primary key (the employee ID), and separating the general information from the salary data simplifies controlling the access to sensitive information.

Relationship Properties

In the Relationships window, right-clicking on the Relationship line and choosing Edit Relationship will bring up the dialog box shown in Figure 1.18.

FIGURE 1.18.

The Relationships dialog box.

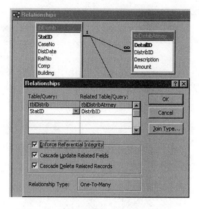

Cascading Updates

With Enforce Referential Integrity selected, there are several user events that need to be handled. One such event is a change of the field on the "one" side. With Cascade Update Related Fields selected, this change is propagated to the "many" side, so the records in the detail table are not left orphaned.

Cascading Deletes

The other event that needs to be considered is the deletion of the parent record. When Cascade Delete Related Records is selected, the deletion of the record on the "one" side forces the deletion of the records on the "many" side.

When warnings are enabled (the default on installation) and the user deletes a record on the "one" side, he sees the warning message shown in Figure 1.19.

FIGURE 1.19.

The cascading deletes warning.

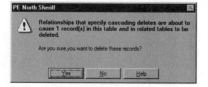

Validation Rules—"Garbage In, Garbage Out!"

There are many opinions regarding the validation of data. One school of thought favors checking at the field level so that any error is signaled to the user as soon as possible, reducing the time to check that information. This is not always possible because the data in one field may depend on another field. It would then be the duty of the front end to check all the fields in a form before committing the changes to the database. Whatever your strategy choice, Access has several features in place to help you validate data.

Validation rules can be implemented at the table level or at the form level. Implementing the rules at the form level is very flexible and can be very powerful, but it is also a lot of work to make sure that all forms stay consistent with the data. The usage of field validation rules is the same in both forms and tables. Obviously, you can't implement a table validation rule in a form.

Field Level

Access automatically validates values based on a field's datatype. For example, Access doesn't allow text in a numeric field. You can set rules that are more specific by using the ValidationRule property.

You can use the ValidationRule property to check the validity of data entered into a record, field, or control. When data is entered that violates the ValidationRule setting, you can use the ValidationText property to specify the message displayed to the user by Access.

The maximum length for the ValidationRule property setting is 2,048 characters. The maximum length for the ValidationText property setting is 255 characters.

For field and record validation rules, the expression you set as ValidationRule can't contain user-defined functions, domain aggregate or aggregate functions, the CurrentUser or Eval function, or references to forms, queries, or tables. In addition, field validation rules can't contain references to other fields.

If you set the ValidationRule property but not the ValidationText property, Access displays a standard error message when ValidationRule is violated. If you set the ValidationText property, the text you enter is displayed as the error message, as shown in Figure 1.20.

FIGURE 1.20.

Validation rule on a field.

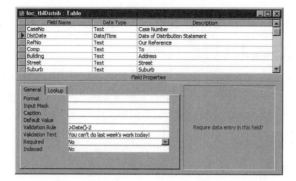

If you create a validation rule for a field, Access doesn't normally allow a Null value to be stored in the field. If you want to allow a Null value, add `Is Null` to the validation rule, as in `> #1/1/1998# Or Is Null`, and make sure the `Required` property is set to No.

> **NOTE**
>
> You can't set field or record validation rules for linked tables from databases of a different type to Access (for example, dBASE, Paradox, or SQL Server). For these kinds of tables, you can create validation rules for controls only.

Table Level

The usage is the same as for a field validation rule, with the addition that Access will let you reference other fields in the rule (see Figure 1.21).

FIGURE 1.21.

Validation rule for a table.

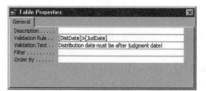

Using the Microsoft Add-In: How to Print Relationships

The Print Relationships Wizard is a late addition to Access, and how welcome it is! Whereas in the past countless developers had to juggle the Print Scrn key, Paint, and a lot of patience, this wizard makes the whole exercise very simple.

The file `Prels80.exe` is available on Microsoft's Web site, and on Microsoft Technet CD, among others. Executing the file will launch the Print Relationships Wizard installation, which is straightforward.

To use the wizard, first lay out the tables you want to see on the printout using the Relationships window, accessible via Tools | Relationships. When the layout looks the way you want it, close the Relationships window.

Open the Print Relationships Wizard by going to Tools | Add-Ins | Print Relationships. This will create a report showing the tables and relationships you laid out earlier (see Figure 1.22).

FIGURE 1.22.

Output from the Print Relationships Wizard.

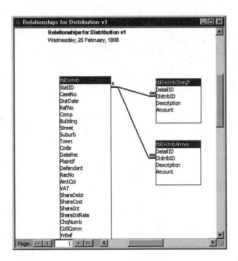

This wizard has the peculiarity of not having a visible interface, aside from an error message, shown in Figure 1.23, when the relationships haven't been defined or the layout is not saved in the Relationships window.

FIGURE 1.23.

Error message from the Print Relationships Wizard.

The output of the Print Relationship Wizard, shown in Figure 1.24, is a report. I do not advise saving this report because the relationships drawn on it are not dynamic. It's a snapshot of the relationships at the time the report was created, and it isn't run, so any change to the relationships after the creation of the report will not be reflected when you run it a second time. To get another printout, run the wizard again.

FIGURE 1.24.

Output from the Print Relationships Wizard.

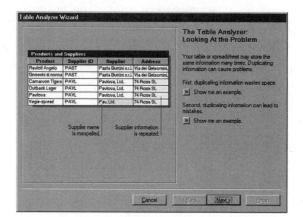

The Table Analyzer Wizard

Microsoft has made it easier for you to create normalized databases by including the Table Analysis Wizard with Access.

You run the wizard by selecting Tools | Analyze | Table. The opening screen contains valuable information if you are new to database design.

After another informative introductory screen, the wizard prompts you for the name of the table to analyze (see Figure 1.25).

There are two choices you can make at this point: let the wizard decide, or drive the analysis process yourself. Even when you let the wizard decide, it might not be able to optimally split the table, as shown in Figure 1.26.

FIGURE 1.25.

Choosing a table to analyze.

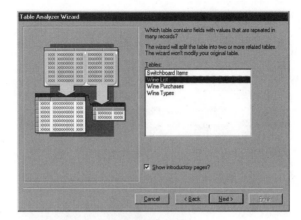

FIGURE 1.26.

A puzzled wizard.

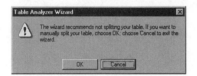

In this case, go back one step and select "No, I want to decide." After clicking Next, you'll be presented with a screen that lets you create tables and set the correct relationships by just dragging fields out of the main table onto the background. Give the new tables and fields meaningful names.

After editing, your screen might look similar to Figure 1.27.

FIGURE 1.27.

Modifying the database structure.

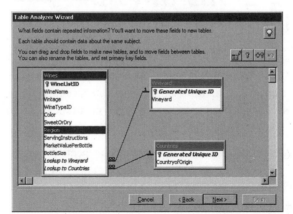

In the next step, shown in Figure 1.28, the wizard will attempt to match similar-looking field entries. The wizard might suggest a value. You can override this choice by choosing another value from the combo box.

This step will be repeated for each new table that was created.

FIGURE 1.28.

Editing the data.

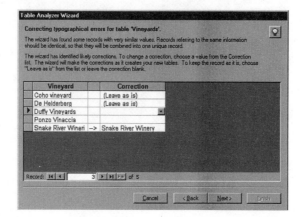

When all the tables are created, the wizard offers to create a query that will simulate the original table. The original table's name will have _OLD appended to it, so any reference to it in forms, reports, and other objects will point to the query fields instead of the table. This makes changes transparent for the other database objects.

Warning Signs of Poor Normalization

Duplicate information usually indicates poor normalization. You shouldn't have to enter the same information in different places. In an invoice, for example, the address of the customer should be entered in a form that describes the customer. The shipping address and mailing address will not need to be reentered the next time this same customer places another invoice with your company.

Some subtler signs of poor normalization might be unexpected results in queries. When you're summarizing results in a query for a report by state, you might have difficulties obtaining the right results if half the purchases were written for "Washington" and the other half for "WA," not counting the ones for "Wash." and other creative spellings.

ActiveX Controls

Using the ActiveX controls (also called *custom controls* or *OLE custom controls*) option, you can register or unregister ActiveX controls. Access 97 and Windows 95 use ActiveX controls (commonly called *OCX controls* for the file extension with which they are named), which are an upgrade to the immensely popular VBX control. Aside from being true 32-bit, ActiveX controls provide several advantages over VBX controls. The least of these advantages is that ActiveX controls are designed from the ground up, meaning that they are not dependent on the Visual Basic environment and that they are extensible. The more you develop in Access 97, the more apparent the advantages of ActiveX controls will become.

Access 97 includes this functionality to use ActiveX controls and is much the better for it. ActiveX controls are a powerful item in the move toward component software and reusability. This means that you can buy a control that does something unique. For example, the control could create an outline of your data. You could drop the control on your form or report and have it do the data outline for you. You wouldn't have to write that functionality yourself every time.

The ActiveX option enables you to register ActiveX controls in the Windows 95 or Windows NT Registry. Controls that aren't included in Access 97 (or if you didn't check the register controls option during setup) need to be registered so that Access 97, as well as your other applications that can use ActiveX controls, can use the functionality of the control.

Summary

This chapter covered several features of Access 97 databases. With the appearance of the MDE file format, notable improvements have been made in database application security. Most of the functions from previous versions of Access are still present but are now easier to use, such as compacting and repairing a database. The addition of wizards has made Access an easier tool to use for building database solutions.

Using Alternate Data Sources

In today's business world, most database applications rely on giving data to or getting data from other applications. The first step in doing this is to make the data available. One of the ways to make data available is to export the data from another application and import it into the current application. If the current application needs to share its data, it needs to export the data in a format that other applications can import. The goal of this chapter is to explain how to import and export data to and from Access. In this chapter, you use the graphical user interface (GUI) tools that Access makes available.

The Import and Export Interfaces

Access supplies many GUI tools to help you import and export data in many different formats. These tools have many similarities, so none of them should seem too unfamiliar to you.

The Import Interface

To get to the Import tool, you can either choose File | Get External Data | Import or right-click the Database object tabs. When you click Import, the dialog box shown in Figure 2.1 appears. In this dialog box, you select the appropriate file to import.

FIGURE 2.1.

Selecting a file for import.

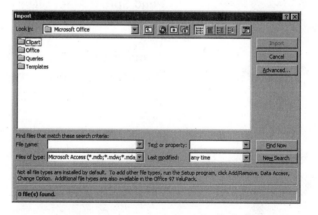

In the Import dialog box, you can navigate your way through the file folders until you locate the file you want to import. First, select the type of file you want to import; the Import dialog box limits the file list to the type selected. You select the type of file from the Files of Type list box. After selecting the type, you need to navigate your way to the correct folder. To change drives, click the Look In list box. To change to a folder other than the current one, click the Up One Level button, which has an arrow pointing up inside a folder. After you select the file you want to import, click OK.

Depending on the format you've chosen, you're presented with appropriate dialog boxes and selections.

The Export Interface

Access gives you the flexibility to export all database objects. You must remember some rules, however, when exporting any of the objects:

- When exporting a table or a query, you can save the object to a new file or database, or a new table or query within the current database.
- When exporting a form or a report, you're limited to Access, Excel versions 5 through 7, text files, rich text format, HTX, and HTML. In all cases except the Access format, the data that makes up the form or report is exported. Access actually exports the form or report, not the data.
- When exporting a macro, you're limited to an external file or database, a Visual Basic module, or a new macro within the current database.
- When exporting a module, you can export into Access and text files.

After you decide what to export, choose File | Save As/Export to start the export process. You're presented with a dialog box that asks if you want to save within the current database or to an external file or database. If you select an external file or database, the Save Form dialog box, shown in Figure 2.2, appears.

FIGURE 2.2.

Using the export interface to export data.

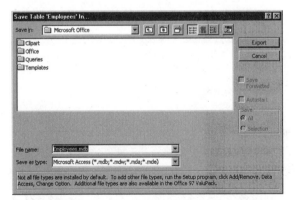

In this dialog box, you can navigate your way through the file folders until you locate the folder in which you want to export the file. First, select the type of file you want to export so that only that type of file appears in the list. You do so by using the Save As Type list box. After you select the type, navigate your way to the correct folder. To change drives, click the Save In list box. To change to a folder other than the current folder, click the Up One Level button, which has an arrow pointing up inside a folder. After you set the name of the new file and you locate the correct folder, click Export or press Enter.

Depending on the format you choose, you're presented with different interfaces. These interfaces are covered in the following sections.

Standard File Formats

Access has more than 10 different formats available for export and more than 8 formats available for import. Import has fewer formats because the available Text Import Wizards group all text files as one format. In export, the text files are separated into the following groups: delimited and fixed-width, rich text format, and Word merge format.

Microsoft FoxPro

Versions 2.x and 3.0 of Microsoft FoxPro file formats are available to you for importing or exporting. When exporting to any of these formats, you're prompted for the location and filename. When importing, you need to locate the file, highlight it, and click OK. If the file is imported successfully, a prompt is displayed, giving you the table name. These files usually have a .DBF extension.

dBASE

dBASE III, IV, and 5 are all supported. These files usually have a .DBF extension, the same as Microsoft FoxPro. The Import and Export tools work the same as they do for FoxPro.

Paradox

Versions 3.x, 4.x, and 5.0 of Paradox are all supported. These files usually have a .DB extension. The Import and Export tools work the same as for FoxPro. To get the Paradox driver, you need to get the Office 97 ValuePack.

SQL Tables and Databases Supported by ODBC

For Access to import or export a table from or to Microsoft SQL Server, Sybase SQL Server, Oracle Server, and other formats, you need to have an installed ODBC driver. Click the Save as type list box and choose ODBC Databases. You are presented with an Export dialog box allowing you to name your Access object something else when it is exported to the ODBC database. Once you have changed the name or agreed to keep the current name, click OK. At this point, you are presented with Figure 2.3.

FIGURE 2.3.

Select Data Source.

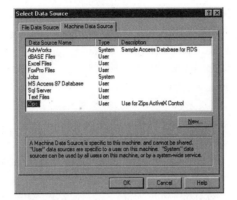

You have two tabs on this dialog box. The first is File Data Source, and the second is Machine Data Source. The File Data Source tab allows you to connect to shared data sources that are located either on your machine or on the network. The Machine Data Source is made up of two types. The first is System Data Source, and the second is User Data Source. A System Data Source is available to all users who sign in on the current machine, and the User Data Source is available only to the currently signed-in user. In this example, we are going to be concerned with the Machine Data Sources. As you can see in Figure 2.3, you will see all available data sources to the machine and to the current user. If the data source you wish to use is in the current list, select it by clicking the Data Source Name and then clicking the OK button. If it's not in the list, you can create a new source by clicking the New button.

> **WARNING**
>
> If you select ODBC Database and you receive the error message `Unable to locate ODBC32.DLL`, you need to either reinstall Access or add the option Microsoft SQL Server ODBC Driver, which is located under Data Access. When reinstalling, you need to select the custom installation option and make sure that the option Microsoft SQL Server ODBC Driver is selected.

To create a new SQL Server data source, follow these steps:

1. Select the type of data source you want to create. Your choices are System and User.

2. Choose the type of ODBC driver on which the source will be based.

Here you are presented with the information you selected from the previous prompts and are told that the driver may ask you more questions if it requires more information to create the data source. In this case, since I am explaining the setting up of an SQL Server data source, you will need to fill in two more screens before you are done.

3. Set up the Data Source Name (DSN), Description, Server (the name of the host machine), Network Address, and Network Library.

If you want to set up further options, click the Options button. This way, you can set up the database name, the language name, an option to have the stored procedures generated for prepared statements, and an option to convert OEM to ANSI characters, or you can click Select and choose another available translation type. After you enter all the information, click OK. If you have any questions regarding this section, click the Help button.

> **NOTE**
>
> If you select an installed ODBC driver other than SQL Server, you are prompted for the DSN and the description. After that, each of the available drivers has different requirements.

4. You're returned to Figure 2.3 with your new entry as the active item. To use this new source, click OK.

Now that you have either selected your data source or created a new one, you're asked to sign into the source. DataSource is defaulted to the DSN you selected in the previous dialog box. Login ID is blank, or if you're using Windows NT, it defaults to the name you used to sign into Windows NT. The password is left blank. If you click the Options button, you're presented with four new choices. The first is a drop-down list of Database names; it defaults to the database name that was typed in the database option field in the previous window. If it was blank there, it is blank now. The next choice you have is Language, and the last two choices are Application Name and Workstation ID. Both of these fields are filled in with the appropriate information. The Application Name is made up of Microsoft Access; the Workstation ID is the name used to identify your computer.

> **NOTE**
>
> If an invalid username or password is entered, you receive an ODBC error when you try to click the Database list box or the Language list box.

If you're exporting, you're returned to the Database window unless there was a problem with the export. If you're importing, you have two more steps.

5. After you type in a valid username and password (if required), the Import Objects dialog box, shown in Figure 2.4, appears. This dialog box includes a list of available tables that can be imported.

FIGURE 2.4.

The Import Objects dialog box.

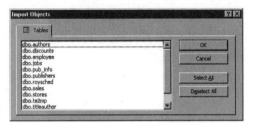

6. With the new Import engine, you can import one table or multiple tables. To select all the tables, click the Select All button. To select multiple tables, either Shift+click or Ctrl+click the tables you want to select. Shift+clicking selects all the tables between the first and last that you highlight, and Ctrl+clicking selects the table(s) you click. If you want to start the selection process over, click the Deselect All button. When you're satisfied with your selection, click OK. The dialog box appears, giving you an import status. If no problems occurred with the import, you're returned to the Database window.

Microsoft Excel

Versions 2.0 through 7.0 and 97 of Excel are supported by Access 97. When you select a spreadsheet file from the Import Objects dialog box, as shown in Figure 2.1, or the Export dialog box, you're presented with the Import Spreadsheet Wizard or the Export Spreadsheet Wizard. These wizards are fully covered in the section "Using the Word Merge, HTML, Text, and Spreadsheet Wizards."

Lotus 1-2-3 Spreadsheets

Three formats are supported by Lotus 1-2-3: WKS, WK1, and WK3. When you select any of these formats, you are walked through the Import Spreadsheet Wizard or Export

Spreadsheet Wizard just like you are in Excel. These wizards are fully covered in the section "Using the Word Merge, HTML, Text, and Spreadsheet Wizards."

Text Files

After you select Text from the Files of Type list box in the Import or Export dialog box and locate your file, click OK. You're presented with the Text Import Wizard or the Text Export Wizard. The Text Wizards help you import or export the text file. They are fully covered in the section "Using the Word Merge, HTML, Text, and Spreadsheet Wizards."

Access

Selecting an Access .MDB file to import or export is much like importing or exporting from an SQL Server source. When you select an .MDB file for import and click OK, you see the dialog box shown in Figure 2.5. Instead of just the Tables tab, it also includes tabs for queries, forms, reports, macros, and modules. Inside this dialog box, you can select multiple items in each of the tabs. You also can click Select All to select all entries for the current tab. If you click Deselect All, the items that are selected for the current tab are deselected.

FIGURE 2.5.
*The Import
Objects dialog
box.*

After you select the items you want to import, click OK. The dialog box changes from the one shown in Figure 2.5 to the one that shows you the progress of import. You can watch it go through the items that were selected. Upon completion of the import, you're returned to the Database window.

When you select an .MDB file for export, you can export only one table at a time. Your only options are Definition and Data, and Definition Only.

HTML/HTX Files

The data format of HTML is available for tables, queries, forms, and reports. HTX, on the other hand, is available only when you export tables, queries, or forms. When you import an HTML file, it always becomes a table, and the HTML Import Wizard is used. This wizard is fully covered in the next section.

Using the Word Merge, HTML, Text, and Spreadsheet Wizards

Access has three wizards available to help you import data—the Text Import Wizard, the HTML Import Wizard, and the Import Spreadsheet Wizard. It also includes two wizards to help you export data to Word. When you are importing, all you need to do is select one of these formats, and the corresponding wizard starts up. To export data to Word, however, you need to select the table or query you want to use and then select the Tools menu or the command button that has the Word icon on it.

The Text Import Wizard and the Import Spreadsheet Wizard

Because the Text Import Wizard and the Import Spreadsheet Wizard have the same last steps, this section will cover the unique steps from each wizard before covering the common steps.

The Text Import Wizard asks whether the file is delimited or fixed-width. As you change between the two options, you see the sample window change to the new choice.

When you click the Advanced button, the dialog box shown in Figure 2.6 appears. In this dialog box, you can change the file specifications for import. The options are File Format, File Origin, Date Order, Date Delimiter, Time Delimiter, Four Digit Years, Leading Zeros in Dates, and Decimal Symbol. You can also change the size of the column by adjusting the Field Information. If you've already set up your own import specifications, you can load them by clicking the Specs button. If you like these specifications and want to use them again, you can click Save As and give them a name to be used later.

FIGURE 2.6.

The Employees Import Specification dialog box.

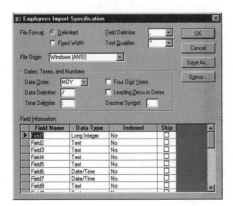

If you select Fixed Width, you're prompted to tell the wizard where the breaks occur. A break is the place where you think one column of information stops and a new column starts. The default for Fixed Width is best guess, meaning that the wizard tries to decide for you. If you select Delimited, you need to tell the wizard what type of delimiter it is and whether the first row contains the header information. The default for delimited files is best guess; if the delimiter being used isn't one of the common delimiters, it is still best guess from the common delimiters. If you're importing a file that isn't using a common delimiter, don't click Finish before you complete this step.

Now that you've told the wizard how to divide the text into columns, it needs to know if it should append the text to an existing table or place it in a new table. The default is a new table.

The Import Spreadsheet Wizard, shown in Figure 2.7, gives you two options. The first option is Show Worksheets, and the second option is Show Named Ranges. Depending on which item you select, you're given a list of available items. By default, the first item in the list is selected. This list item tells the sample data window what to display. As you change between items in the window, the sample data is changed to the correct data.

FIGURE 2.7.

The initial Import Spreadsheet Wizard dialog box.

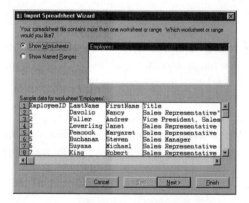

If you select a worksheet in the initial dialog box, the wizard asks which line to start the import from and whether the first line contains the header information. If you select a named range, the wizard asks only whether the first line contains the header information. The default is to start with line 1 and leave the Include Field Names option unchecked.

The following information is the same for the Text Import Wizard and the Import Spreadsheet Wizard.

If you choose to append to an existing table from the Text Import Wizard, you skip the next prompt. Otherwise, both wizards ask whether each column has an index. If you're running the Text Import Wizard, it also lets you change the data type. Figure 2.8 shows the Text Import Wizard. Here you can set the data type for each column. It does a best guess for all columns. After you check each column and verify that the column is the way you want it, click the Next button. The default is no index for all columns and best guess on the datatype.

FIGURE 2.8.

The Text Import Wizard with Data Type enabled.

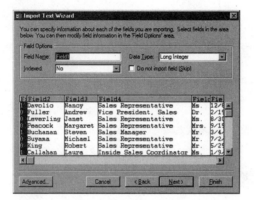

If you choose to append to an existing table from the Text Import Wizard, the next step is bypassed. You have three options: allow Access to add an index, identify the index from the columns that are being added, or import the file as is. Figure 2.9 shows this dialog box with the Choose My Own Primary Key option selected. Notice that Access has added a new column called ID to the sample window.

FIGURE 2.9.

The Text Import Wizard with Primary Key selected.

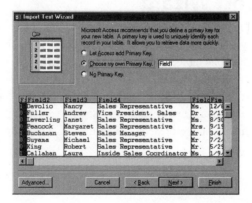

Access recommends that all data being added have an index. By default, Access assumes that you want it to add an index for you.

For the last step of the Import Wizards, type in a name for the new table and choose whether you want to have Access analyze the structure after the table has been imported. The defaults are table1 for the name and No for the Analyze My Table After The Import Is Over option. If you don't click Analyze table, you see the Import Wizard Success dialog box when the table is imported. You see this dialog box only if no errors were encountered in the import.

If you select to analyze the table after import, you're presented with the Import Text Wizard message box, shown in Figure 2.10. It tells you that the import was successful and asks whether you want the wizard to analyze the table. If you click Yes, you are placed in the Table Analyzer Wizard (covered in Chapter 1, "Essentials for Creating New Databases").

FIGURE 2.10.

The Import Text Wizard message box.

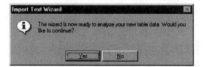

At any time during the Import Text Wizard or Import Spreadsheet Wizard process, you can click the Finish button, and the wizard supplies the default answers for the remaining questions and imports the data. After it imports the data, you're presented with the Import Wizard Success dialog box.

The HTML Import Wizard

The HTML Import Wizard is designed to help you import HTML files more effectively. When you use the wizard, you may go through six different steps. The first step appears only if your file has more than one table. In this case, the first five steps are exactly the same as with the Import Spreadsheet Wizard discussed previously. The last five steps appear if you do have more than one table. Remember that the HTML Import Wizard imports only HTML files that contain either tables or lists. If you try to import an HTML file that does not contain either, you are presented with the message shown in Figure 2.11.

FIGURE 2.11.

The No Data to Import Error message box.

To get back to the Database window, you need to acknowledge the error message by clicking OK. After you select an HTML file from the Import dialog box, and if it has more than one table or list, you are presented with the dialog box shown in Figure 2.12.

FIGURE 2.12.

The HTML Import Wizard.

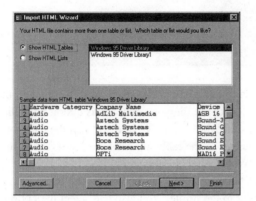

In this dialog box, you can tell the wizard which table or list you want to import. Keep in mind that when trying to import an HTML file that contains more then one table or list, you can import only one of these items at a time. The tables will be named according to the captions specified between the <CAPTION> and </CAPTION> tags. If the captions are missing, the title between the <TITLE> and </TITLE> tags is used. The tables will have the same name as the title with a number starting with a 1 added to the name of the second table. So if the title of the HTML document is "Look at my Table," the first table will be assigned the name "Look at my Table," while the following table will be named "Look at my Table1." Otherwise the tables are named "Table," "Table1," and so on. After you select the item that you want, click the Next button. This will bring you to the next step in the process, which is also, the same step that the Import Spreadsheet Wizard uses.

The Word Merge and Publish Wizards

If you select a table or a query, you can export that data to Word. You have two choices. The first is to do a mail merge with Word, and the second is to publish the data in Word using a table. If you select a form or report, you can only publish it with Word. If you choose to publish it with Word, Microsoft Word is opened and the data is copied from Access to Word. It is then placed in a table in the new Word document. If you choose to merge the data with Word, a dialog box opens, as shown in Figure 2.13, asking if you want to link your data to an existing document or create a new Word document.

If you select Link Your Data to an Existing Microsoft Word Document, the Find File dialog box appears. After you locate the file you want in this dialog box, click Open. Word then opens, and Access runs the Mail Merge Wizard and sets the data source to the current table. As you make changes to the table, the changes are reflected in the Mail Merge document. Once you're in Word, you can insert the fields from the table into the document or type the document from scratch. After you set up the document, you can print it to a new document or send it to the printer. You also can select the options Find Errors, Merge it, Find Records, or Edit Data Source. If you select Edit Data Source, you are taken into the database, and the table is opened for you to edit.

Outputting Reports to ASCII .TXT Files

One of the features missing in older versions of Access is the possibility to export the reports into text files. Access 97 allows you to preserve the relative position of the fields on the report when exporting them to test files using the Export to Text Wizard. The wizard also preserves the formatting of the fields, putting in $, %, and dots as necessary. The number of characters that fit in the text fields approximately equals the number of characters displayed on the status bar as you resize the text box or the label in Design view of the report with the font set to 9-point Arial as shown in Figure 2.14.

Linking Data to Access

While importing provides total control of data from different sources, linking allows you to use the data from various sources in Access applications. Because most of the world's data is not stored in databases, but is rather saved in miscellaneous other formats, Access's link feature comes in handy when it is necessary to that data.

TIP

Linking is better than importing when:

- Data is in constant use by other applications.
- In Access data will be used read-only or as look-up.
- Data changes often.
- The structure of the data does not change.

FIGURE 2.14.
Report Design view.

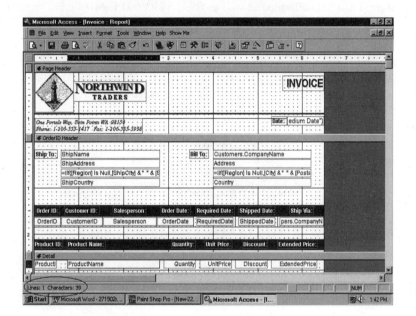

In spite of its attractiveness, linking carries a number of drawbacks, though:

- Some formats place restrictions on updates, deletes, and appends of the data.
- Because data is not stored in a database, some formats will not allow indexes or keys to be used.
- Once the structure of the file changes, it becomes inaccessible, or will contain errors.
- When the linked table is open, the file is exclusively locked, so nobody else can open it (with non-database file formats).

The formats available for linking are the same as the formats available for importing, with one subtle difference: There is only one FoxPro format available, which works with all FoxPro tables. To get to the Link tool, you can either choose File | Get External Data | Link Tables or right-click the Database object tabs. The dialog box, which comes up as you do it, is similar to the one in Figure 2.1. It allows you to select a file to link. Selecting different formats will display the files of the appropriate type. Because linking involves steps similar to importing, these will not be repeated here. A list of the restrictions of tables linked to files of each datatype will be presented instead.

Linking Text Files

Access can link delimited as well as fixed-width text files. Linking fixed-width files will not let you use the top row as field names. Fixed-width files should not contain line breaks within potential records. Once linked, opening the table will exclusively lock the corresponding text file, preventing any kind of access by anyone else. The Text ISAM (a driver used to import and link text files) will prevent edits to existing records and/or their deletion. Trying to do so will result in the message seen in Figure 2.15. You can add new records, though.

FIGURE 2.15.

The linked table restriction message box.

Linking HTML/HTM Files

Similar to the Import Wizards, the Link Wizards let you select the table or list you want to link, giving you a choice to use the values in top row as field names. Once linked, you can only view the data in the table.

Linking Excel Files

After selecting the Excel file for linking, the wizard presents you with a screen similar to the one on Figure 2.7. After completion of the process you can open a newly linked table, which will lock the associated Excel file. Access will allow you to edit existing data, and add new records, but will prevent you from deleting existing records. The table will behave as though you are using a spreadsheet, thus, in some cases, after you clear all fields in the last record, and close the table, the record will be gone when you reopen it.

Linking dBASE and FoxPro Files

You can only link files saved and named in 8.3 format. Even though you can select a longer name file, you will not be able to open the table upon completion. Linking dBASE III files will only allow you to select NDX files as index files, while linking dBASE IV and 5 files will let you select MDX files as well. FoxPro files of all versions until 3.0 can be linked using the same driver. After selecting a DBF file to link, you will be prompted to select an index file. You can select many files one-by-one. When you click Close, you will be prompted to choose the unique record identifier as shown in Figure 2.16. Here you select the primary key.

FIGURE 2.16.

*The Select Unique
Record Identifier
dialog box.*

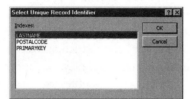

If you are linking to the table previously exported from Access, the Wizard will try to use the INF file created during export, prompting you with the message pictured in Figure 2.17. Select No to use default values, Yes to select a different index.

FIGURE 2.17.

*dBASE and
FoxPro index mes-
sage box.*

NOTE

Since FoxPro and dBASE create files to represent each of their objects, each index is stored as file as well. In later versions of both programs, multiple index files were devised, allowing you to store more than one index in one file.

dBASE uses the following file extensions:

- NDX for single index
- MDX for multiple index

FoxPro uses the following file extensions:

- IDX for single index
- MDX for multiple index

Analyzing the Existing Data Source for Access 97 Compatibility

Before linking or importing data to Access, it is important to know whether Access will accept the data without any unpleasant surprises. People who are moving from spreadsheets to Access for better and easier data management will probably experience a bit of a shock once acquainted with the numerous rules and restrictions Access imposes on the data it contains. Suddenly normalization rules come into play. Adding an extra column of data, a trivial task in any spreadsheet, now requires a careful analysis of the data. One has to make sure whether that extra field is really needed or not.

Like spreadsheets, text files require special setup routines before importing or linking. Thanks to Access's wizards, the task of setting up the process is quite easy. Here are the things to consider.

Delimiters in ASCII Files

By default Access assumes that the text file is comma-delimited and that the string fields are surrounded by quotes. Unless carefully handled, quotes, as sub-strings of some data, will confuse the wizard, producing unexpected results. You can define another character as a string delimiter, but during importing or linking you must type it into the Text Qualifier combo box of the wizard. The wizard can accept any value. If you want to use a non-printing character, you can accomplish it by holding on the Alt key while punching the ASCII value of the character on the keypad, and then releasing the Alt key.

Access can also automatically assign field names if you decide to import the data to a new table or link it. In case of conflicts or errors you will be prompted with the message seen in Figure 2.18. Acknowledge the warning and continue.

FIGURE 2.18.

Import Text Wizard warning about field names.

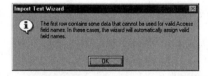

Appending into Existing Tables

Appending to existing data in tables requires extra consideration. Since the rules were already setup for the records in the target table, the newly imported data cannot break them. Conflicts due to unique index or primary key violations may occur if records containing repeated data are being imported. In such situation occurs you will receive a message similar to the one shown in Figure 2.19. If you decide to continue, the wizard will only import the records that do not break the rules. If you click No, you will be warned about failure of the import and brought back to the last step of the wizard.

FIGURE 2.19.

The import failure message box.

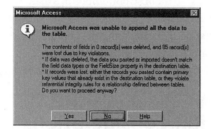

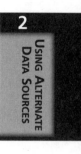

Another type of error can occur when the wizard cannot properly convert a field of one data type to another. If such a situation occurs, the wizard will still try to import the record, leaving the field blank. If the field can contain a blank value, the record will be imported. The wizard will also create a table named after the file you are trying to import with _ImportErrors appended to its name. So if you are trying to import a file called Employees.txt, the error table will be called Employees_ImportErrors. The table will look something like the one pictured in Figure 2.20. You will also get a warning announcing the failure and specifying the table where the error information resides.

FIGURE 2.20.

The Employees_Import Errors table.

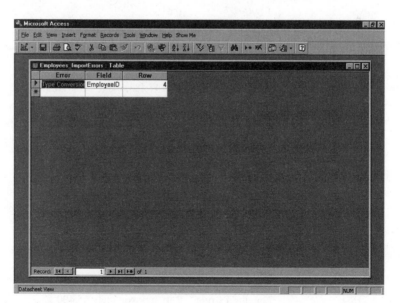

If the data cannot be left blank in the offending field, the import will fail because of the index conflict and the import errors table will also be created.

Another problem occurs when importing data into an AutoNumber type field. Since Access takes full control of what goes into the fields of AutoNumber type, it cannot allow data from any other source to be put into them. Upon importing data, the Wizard does not consider the AutoNumber fields as possible destinations, thus thinking that the source data contains extra fields of data that do not match any destination. Since the number of source fields is greater than the number of the destination fields, the import fails. You must eliminate the columns from the text file, which would otherwise attempt to go into the AutoNumber type fields.

Field Type Conversion Considerations

Importing into a table also requires field type compliance on the side of the source file. If attempting to import produces a large number of Field Type Conversion errors, you are probably mismatching the fields in the file with the table design. An occasional error is a definite candidate for a review of the source data. Table 2.1 lists the Jet 3.5 data types and the range of allowed values.

TABLE 2.1. ACCESS DATATYPE SUMMARY.

Datatype	Storage size	Range
Byte	1 byte	0 to 255
Boolean	2 bytes	True, 1, −1 as TRUE False, 0, null as FALSE
Integer	2 bytes	−32,768 to 32,767
Long(long integer)	4 bytes	−2,147,483,648 to 2,147,483,647
Single (single precision for floating-point)	4 bytes	−3.402823E–38 to −1.401298E–45 for negative values; 1.401298E+45 to 3.402823E+38 for positive values
Double (double precision floating-point)	8 bytes	−1.79769313486232E–308 to −4.94065645841247E–324 for negative values; 4.94065645841247E+324 to 1.79769313486232E+308 for positive values
Currency (scaled integer)	8 bytes	−922,337,203,685,477.5808 to 922,337,203,685,477.5807
Date	8 bytes	January 1, 100 to December 31, 9999
String	Length of string	1 to approximately 65,400

For more information on datatypes, you can search MS Access online help for "Data Types."

Summary

Access tries to give you the easiest way to get at data, no matter what its format. Access also tries to make sure that this data comes across without errors. For these reasons, Access provides several wizards to help you through difficult tasks and offers several default formats.

Accessing Data with Queries and SQL

PART
II

Creating Sophisticated Queries

You can find the capability to use relational information all around. One of the most common examples of a relational database is your telephone book. You can think of every person and business telephone number as an individual record. The white pages list these records in alphabetical order. The yellow pages show a relationship between the individual number and the type of business in which the company can be grouped. For example, Acme Flyers can be listed under airlines, transportation, travel, and/or recreation.

The Queries module in Access—whether it's Access 2.0, Access 95, or Access 97—enables the user to view information about records, just like in the white pages. These records can be in one table or in multiple tables, in one query or multiple queries. They do not even have to be in the current database (meaning that a table can be attached to another database). They can be viewed or manipulated.

Queries actually perform a number of different functions. They can be used to look at data or to add, edit, or delete data, as well as perform calculations. They can also be used as a record source for a form or report. For these reasons, queries are considered the brain of a relational database system.

Setting Query Properties

Every object has properties. This fact also holds true for objects within other objects, like database containers. You can set query properties to the query object as a whole or on the individual objects within the query. This section covers setting properties to the query object as a whole, followed by information on setting properties to the individual tables and fields within a query.

When the Queries module of the database container is active, a list of all the queries is visible. In Access 97, every individual query object can have properties assigned to it. To assign properties, highlight a query and click the Properties button on the toolbar. The properties sheet appears, as shown in Figure 3.1. You can also access the properties sheet by highlighting a query and right-clicking.

For every object, you can assign a description up to 255 characters long. The properties sheet shows when the query was created, when it was modified, and who owns it. Notice that there are two check boxes at the bottom of the sheet. They pertain to the attributes of the object—in this case, a query. When the Hidden check box is selected and applied, the query object is no longer visible in the database container window. This way, you can set security in the database on an object-by-object basis.

FIGURE 3.1.

Every object in a database container window can have properties assigned to it, even queries as a whole.

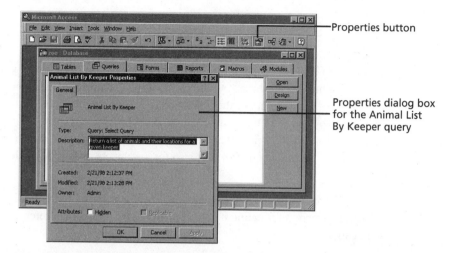

Properties button

Properties dialog box for the Animal List By Keeper query

NOTE

If the letters USYS appear in front of an object name, that object does not appear in the database container window. USYS means *User System* objects. You can unhide the object by viewing the system objects.

To view objects that are hidden, choose Tools | Options. Choose the View tab and select Hidden Objects to unhide all the objects that were hidden in the properties sheet. Notice the System Objects check box. It unhides any objects with the prefix USYS or MSYS.

WARNING

USYS objects are created by the developer and hidden from the end user by that prefix. MSYS objects are created by Microsoft and hidden from the developer by that prefix. It is not recommended that a user be given access to any system objects. Users could inadvertently corrupt the database.

The other attribute in the Attributes section of the query object's properties sheet is the Replicable check box. When it's selected, modified versions of this object can be updated. This option is helpful when there is more than one developer or more than one development site. For example, if a developer is developing a contact management system, he

3

CREATING SOPHISTICATED QUERIES

or she might develop not only at work, but also at home or on the road. As the developer makes changes to copy, new modification dates are set for each object modified. When the developer dials in or brings the contact management system back to work, these databases need to be synchronized. Instead of copying over the old version, the developer can synchronize the two databases. Any object that is replicable and has a modification date that is greater than the date of the object in the master database is updated. Any object that is not replicable and has a modification date that is greater than the date of the object in the master database is not updated. This is true not only for objects in the Queries module of the database container, but also for all objects in every module of the database container.

If the Replicable check box is inactive, the database as a whole has not had a replica created yet. For more information on creating and using replication, refer to Chapter 21, "Replication."

Everything I've discussed on setting properties so far has dealt with the whole query as an object. Within each and every query, there are also objects. Every object—like tables, fields, and even joins—has properties. To access the properties for an object, highlight it and choose View | Properties. You can also highlight the object and either right-click or click the Properties button on the toolbar. Yet another way to get to the properties of some of the objects is to double-click the joins or the table pane itself in the query window.

TIP

If you double-click the table, all the fields in that table are highlighted. If you double-click one of the fields in a table, that field is automatically placed in the query grid below. The only objects that you can double-click to view their properties are the join lines and the table pane.

Right-click anywhere in the table pane of the query window and bring up its properties, as shown in Figure 3.2.

You can manipulate several different items of a query. In the following list, I describe all the items available on the Query properties sheet:

- Description—If a description line is entered in the Properties dialog box of the query through the database container, it is visible here. If not, you can enter up to 255 characters for a description of a query.

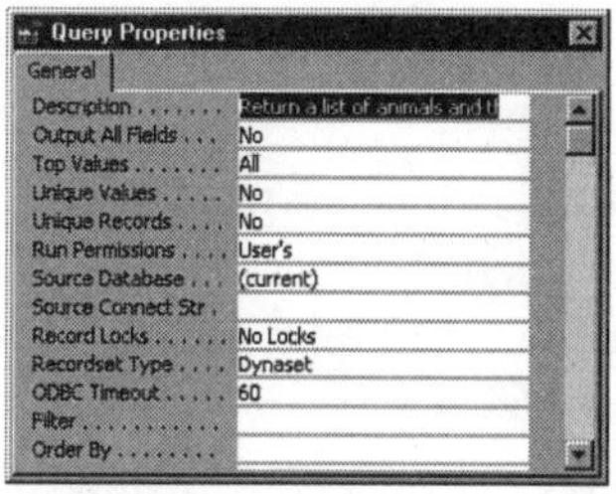

FIGURE 3.2.

You can open detailed query properties by clicking the query title bar and choosing View | Properties.

- Output All Fields—The fields placed on the QBE grid produce values when the query is run. Setting this feature to Yes means that every single field on the QBE grid is visible when the query runs. Setting this option is the same as placing a check mark in every Show box in the QBE grid. This option also dictates if the fields in the QBE grid are available when you're working with a form's or report's `Record Source` property.

- Top Values—This option enables you to query the top 5, 25, or 100 records in the query, or the top 5 percent or 25 percent. It actually calculates the top number or top percentage on the leftmost sorted field. For example, say you have 27 records in the query, and the third field from the left contains Last Names. The Last Names field has a Descending sort, and the top 5 is based on the Last Names field. Because the sort order is Descending, the query will return the bottom 5 records. Because the field is a text field (as opposed to a numeric field), the 5 records returned will be from the bottom of the alphabet. If no fields in the query grid have any sorting attributes, Access 97 gives the top 5 of the 27 records as they appear when the query is executed without any top value impositions.

- Unique Values—This option enables you to return only records that are unique. For example, say you have a contact management database. You need to know how many different countries are represented in the database. A Contact table is in the query, and the only field in the QBE grid is Country. If thousands of records appear in the database, the recordset shows all the records when the query is executed. If Unique Values is set to Yes, only three records may appear in the set: Canada, Mexico, and the United States.

- Unique Records—Unique Record is similar to Unique Values. The major difference is that with Unique Values, you get the unique values for the fields listed in the QBE grid. With Unique Record, you get the unique records based on all fields in the underlying data source, not just those fields present in the QBE grid.

- Run Permissions—This option enables you to give an end user authorization to perform an action that he or she would otherwise not be allowed to execute. An end user may have Read-Only authorization, but if the developer gives him or her

Owners authorization on a query, the end user can append to this query. This way, you can turn on and off security for an end user on an object-by-object basis.

- Source Database—The default for this option is (current). With this property you can specify, in a string expression, an external database where the tables or queries for the current query remain. This option is helpful for databases that are created in applications that do not use attached tables.

- Source Connect Str—This option works in conjunction with the Source Database item. It is the name of the application in which the external database was created.

- Record Locks—This feature is used for multiuser systems. It determines how the records are locked while the query is being executed by a user. This item has only three options: No Locks, All Records, and Edited Record. No Locks means just that. In a multiuser system, two or more users can access and edit the same record at the same time. He who saves first, wins. The other users who try to save the record are prompted that the record has been changed. They can reject the changes that they have made, overwrite the saved changes, or copy their changes to the Clipboard and view the saved record.

- Recordset Type—This option allows you to decide whether the data available to a form or report will be a dynaset or a snapshot.

- ODBC Timeout—This item is only important when the database is or will be networked. It sets how long this workstation checks the network connection for a response before telling the user that the network station is no longer connected to the network. The default is 60 seconds. You may wonder why the time limit isn't shorter. Wouldn't the user want to check for a response every five seconds? Maybe. However, if the user runs a query on data located on the server, the workstation waits for a response from the server. If that response does not come in five seconds, the workstation assumes that the network connection has been dropped, and the user gets an error. If heavy network traffic occurs at the time the query is run, response may also be slower than expected. If no response occurs in however many seconds, the user still gets a message stating that the connection has been dropped. However, the timeout should not be too long (such as 10 minutes) because the user would have time to perform several operations before realizing that the network connection had been dropped.

NOTE

The time range for the ODBC Timeout is entered in seconds, starting at 1 second. If a zero is entered, the workstation does not continuously check for connection. Zero is a special number to the ODBC Timeout. Entering a 0 is like turning the ODBC Timeout feature off, and no timeout errors occur.

- Filter—This item is a great novice developer's tool. It functions similarly to the Criteria section of the QBE grid. This line is automatically filled in for you after specifications have been made to the query during a run. When the query is run, all the records are shown. On the toolbar, the user has access to the filtering buttons. When the Filter by Form button is selected and criteria are applied, those criteria should appear in the Filter property of the query. The difference between Filter in the properties sheet and Criteria in the Criteria section is that you must know the correct syntax before the query will be performed. A novice developer or user can run the query and execute the Query by Form, and Access automatically fills in the Filter line of the query's properties based on the criteria given. The expanded view of the Filter property line for the query is visible in Figure 3.3.

FIGURE 3.3.

When criteria are selected from the Filter by Form button after the execution of a query, those criteria are automatically entered into the Filter property line.

- Order By—This item is another novice developer's tool. It functions similarly to the Sort section of the QBE grid. This line is filled in for you by Access when the query is run and specifications have been made. When the query is run, all the records are shown. On the toolbar, you have access to the Sort Ascending and Sort Descending buttons. You can select a column of data and sort that data in ascending or descending order.

- Max Records—This option determines the maximum number of records returned by an ODBC database. The datatype is Long, and the default of 0 means that it will process all the records. If you specify a number, Access executes the query until the number of records processed matches the number in the `Max Records` property. No more records are returned into the recordset by Access, even if additional records would qualify.

So far, you've learned about properties concerning the query as a whole object. Each query object is composed of several objects. These objects are tables, other queries, and fields. You can observe the properties for each object by clicking the object you want and choosing View | Properties while the query is in Design view.

TIP

You can select the properties for an individual object within a query by high-lighting the object you want and right-clicking.

Figure 3.4 shows the properties for a table. The two properties shown for this table are Alias and Source. Alias allows you to name a table. Normally, this capability is not important, but in some situations it may be helpful. If you have two copies of the same table in one query, this feature would be helpful. For example, you might need a list of companions for a given animal in your zoo. These companions are animals that reside in the same location at the zoo. For this list, you need to display the name of the particular denizen, what kind of animal it is, and the location where it lives. Companions are iden-tified as having the same keeper location. This means that the KEEPER table must be joined with itself to find other KEEPER records that have the same location. Companions are identified as DENIZEN records that are contained in the second set of KEEPER records. Because all tables in the query are used twice, it is essential to use aliases to reduce con-fusion. Making a distinction between two tables with different names, as opposed to two tables with similar names, makes it easier to understand.

FIGURE 3.4.

The view of the properties for a table object in a query.

The other property for the tables in a query is called Source and is also visible in Figure 3.4. This line shows where the table comes from. If the table comes from the current database, this line is blank. However, if the table comes from another Access database or another back-end database such as Oracle, the property reflects the source of the table.

The purpose of queries is to extract data and make it available to the user. Data is made available by running queries. Queries cannot be run unless at least one field appears in the QBE grid. Each individual field in the QBE grid has properties, which you can see in Figure 3.5.

The Properties dialog box for a field is a two-tabbed box. The first tab, General, has four attributes. The Lookup tab has one attribute. The following list describes the five attrib-utes for the field properties:

- Description—This feature functions exactly like the description feature found in the Design view of a table. You can enter up to 255 characters, which will appear in the status bar when a form is created. If the field is not from a table in the current database, the description is automatically filled in by Access with the connection information used for the field.

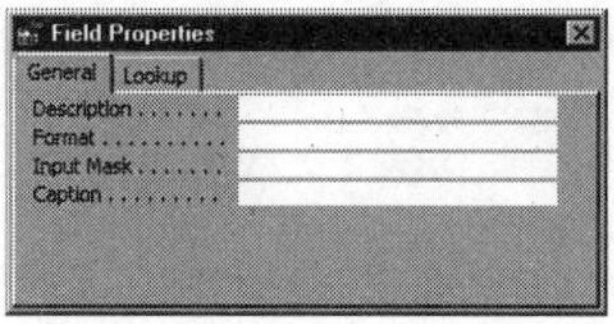

FIGURE 3.5.

The properties for a field in the QBE grid.

- Format—Format allows you to customize the way datatypes are displayed and printed. Usually, either the Format or Input Mask of a field is filled out when you want to control the display of a field. If both happen to be filled out at the same time for the same field, the Format line takes precedence.

- Input Mask—Input Mask is similar to Format in that it controls the way you display data. In fact, you can access a wizard that builds the code in correct syntax based on the type of output you select.

  The difference between Format and Input Mask is that the Input Mask can control how the data is entered. You can use certain symbols in a mask that make the field mandatory. If a form is created based on a query that has a mandatory field, the user must enter information that conforms to the input mask. For example, you could set the Input Mask of the Postal Code field to 00000. When a form is built based on this query, the user cannot enter only three digits in the postal code field, but must enter a five-digit postal code.

- Caption—Caption functions in the exact same way as it does in the Design view of a table. The caption is the text that appears in the label of a field. Even though a caption can be 2,048 characters long, if there is not enough room for the caption to appear, it is truncated.

- Display Control—You can find the Display Control on the Lookup tab of the properties for a field in the QBE grid. Three types of controls are available: a text box, a list box, and a combo box. Each control has its own attributes, which become visible when the control is selected. When a form is based on a query in which a lookup control has been set, all the configurations for that control stay with the field. When that field is pulled from the field list onto a form, the lookup control with all the appropriate properties remains with the field. For example, say that the Customer Type field is set to combo box. When a form is based on this query and you pull the Customer Type field onto the form, it appears as a combo box with all the properties already set.

3

CREATING SOPHISTICATED QUERIES

> **NOTE**
>
> All the field properties in a query can be found in a table. If you set a single fields' properties to perform an action in the table and have a query based on that table, the properties for that single field do not follow through to the query. You can have different properties for the same field in several different queries. The attributes for a field in a form are based on the record source of the form. If the form is based on a table, the attributes for the field are the same as they are in the table. If the form is based on a query, the attributes for the field are the same as they are in the query.

Different Types of Query Joins

Query joins are the lines that are visible between two or more tables. They relate the tables and queries in the table pane of the grid to each other. These lines can either be created manually or automatically. To create a join line, simply click one field in one table and drag it to a field in another table. Actually, there is more to a query than dragging any field to another field, but the join line itself is produced by dragging a field from one table to another table.

Microsoft Access can automatically create join lines between tables, provided the AutoJoin option is turned on. Access uses one of two sources of information that the developer may have already provided. The first way Access can automatically create a join line is based on a relationship that already exists. If the developer has already created a relationship, Access uses the relationship schema when automatically creating a join between two or more tables or queries. The other way that Access instinctively creates joins is based on the naming conventions used to create the fields in a table. If two tables have the exact same name and comparable datatypes, Access automatically joins the two tables by the fields that have the same name.

> **NOTE**
>
> Whether the join line is automatically drawn when two or more tables or queries are placed in the table pane of the query, or you draw the line by dragging one field in one table to the matching field in another table, the line may have symbols attached to it. Only two types of symbols can exist: a 1 or an infinity symbol, which looks like the number 8 lying on its side. You can have only three relationship types: one-to-one, one-to-many, and many-to-one.

You can access the Join Properties dialog box, shown in Figure 3.6, in a number of different ways. You can double-click an existing join line, or you can highlight an existing join line and right-click to show the Join Properties line item. You can highlight an existing join line and choose View | Join Properties. Or, if no join line is available, you can create one by dragging a field from one table to the field of another table. With the line created, you can perform one of the previously mentioned methods for accessing the Joins Options dialog box. In the same way, you would create and classify joins in the Relationships window, which is available by opening the database container and choosing Tools | Relationships.

FIGURE 3.6.

You can open the Join Properties dialog box by highlighting a join and choosing View | Join Properties.

An Access query can have only three types of joins: inner join, left outer join, and right outer join.

- Inner join, the first option, is usually the default. This join selects records from the two tables where only the values of the joined field are equal in both tables. The join does not have an arrow on either end of the line.

- Left join, the second option, is also commonly known as a left outer join (these words are reserved for Microsoft Access). Left outer joins include all the records from the table on the left of the join, even if no matching record values in the table appear on the right side of the join. Records from the right table are combined with records from the left table only when they match.

- Right join, the third option, is also commonly known as a right outer join (these words are reserved for Microsoft Access). The join includes all the records from the table on the right and all the records that have a matching value from the table on the left. Records from the left table are combined with the records from the right table only when they match.

As stated earlier, when two or more tables are added to a query, joins are automatically drawn based on a relationship that already exists or based on fields with the same name, if the AutoJoin feature is turned on. If lines are not automatically drawn, you can draw them by clicking one field in a table and dragging it to another field in another table. Properties for the join are set when you click the join line and open the Join Properties dialog box. If you select option 1 in this dialog box, the join becomes an inner join and includes only the records from both tables where the fields by which they are joined have the same value. If you select option 2, the join becomes a left outer join, and if you select option 3, the join becomes a right outer join. In Figure 3.7, both queries appear to be right outer join queries (because they have arrows pointing to the right), but they are not. Only the one on the right is a left outer join query.

FIGURE 3.7.

Both queries appear to be right outer join queries, but only the right one is.

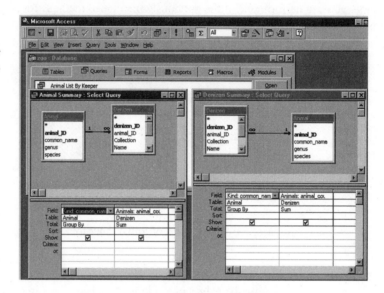

When the queries in Figure 3.7 are run they do not produce the same results, as shown in Figure 3.8.

FIGURE 3.8.

Just because both queries have the same tables and have arrows pointing to the right does not mean that they produce the same results.

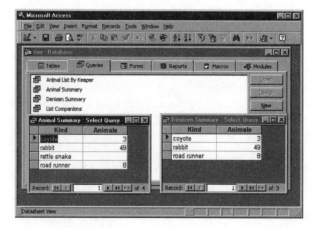

Just looking at which way an arrow is pointing is not a reliable indicator of whether a join is a left outer join or a right outer join. Sometimes it is hard to remember which option means left and which means right. One of the best ways to find out if the query is using a left or right outer join is to view the query in its SQL form. Choose View I SQL. As you can see in Figure 3.9, even though both queries look similar in Design view, they are different in SQL view.

FIGURE 3.9.

By looking at queries in SQL view, you can easily determine whether the query contains a left outer join or a right outer join.

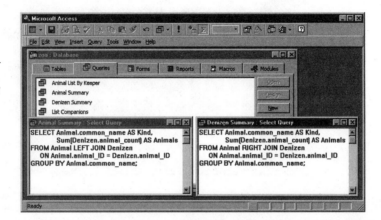

> **NOTE**
>
> It is helpful if the joined field names are the same, but they do not have to be. However, they must be of the same or comparable datatype. Each field must also have the same kind of data. For example, say you have two tables, and each table has a field called FieldX. FieldX in table 1 is a Text datatype; FieldX in table 2 is a Date/Time datatype. Only a left outer join works in this scenario. An inner join or a right outer join does not work because of the datatype conflict. A date/time value can go into a text field, but a text value cannot go into a date/time field.

So far, you have learned about the three different types of joins. Knowing the different types of joins is only half the battle. Knowing when to use each join is the other half. Figure 3.10 shows the three different types of joins. Each query contains the same two tables (Orders and Employees), is joined by the same field (Employee ID), and has only one output field (Customer ID).

FIGURE 3.10.

Left outer join, inner join, and right outer join queries in Design view.

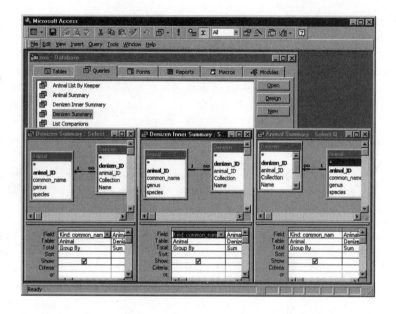

In this figure, each query uses the same data tables and is joined by the same fields, yet each query is joined differently. The SQL view of each query is shown in Figure 3.11. The type of join is defined by the words LEFT, INNER, and RIGHT.

FIGURE 3.11.

You can easily determine whether the query contains a left outer join, inner join, or a right outer join in SQL view.

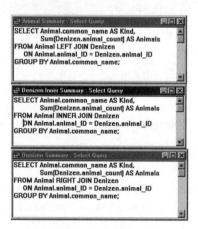

Even though all three queries in this figure have the same tables, are joined by the same fields, and have the same field in the QBE grid, the output is different for each. In Figure 3.12, you can see the data output for each query.

FIGURE 3.12.

The queries may look the same, but the joins cause the outcome to differ.

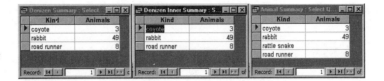

Left outer joins are usually illustrated by a join line arrow that goes from the left table to the right table. This visual representation of a left outer join query is necessary to the description of the effect of the join. In Figure 3.10, the left outer join actually has an arrow that points to the right. It is not important where the arrow points, but from where it originated. All the records from the left side of the join are added to the query's results, even if no matching records from the table appear on the right. However, if records do match the join field from the table on the right, they are added to the results.

An inner join is depicted by a line drawn between two tables without an arrow on either end, as you can see in Figure 3.10. As I stated earlier, this join is usually the default between objects in the table pane of the query. It takes only the records from each table when they match the joining field.

A right outer join is a mirror image of the left outer join in that the join line arrow goes from the right table to the left, as shown in Figure 3.10. The arrow actually points to the left and originates from the right, and that is what makes this a right outer join. All the records on the right side of the join are added to the query's results, even if no matching records from the table appear on the left. Yet, if records do match the join field from the table on the left, they are added to the results.

3

CREATING SOPHISTICATED QUERIES

NOTE

A left outer join and a right outer join may appear the same because the arrows may both point to the left or the right. After the join is established, you can move the objects in the table pane of the query anywhere you want. The way to tell if the join is left or right is to either double-click the join line to open the Join Properties dialog box and see which option is selected, or view the query's SQL statement. In the Join Properties dialog box, if option 2 is selected, the join is a left outer join. If option 3 is selected, the join is a right outer join.

Relationships and Referential Integrity

When you're establishing relationships, you should understand that they are not created in the Queries module of the Database container. A relationship is not a query, even though it looks similar to a query. It is actually created from the database container and affects the database as a whole.

You can create relationships based on queries, but referential integrity isn't enforced. Referential integrity ensures that relationships between records in related tables are valid. This prevents the user from accidentally deleting or changing related data.

I often receive requests from application managers to transfer records from one version of a database to another. In many cases these requests are for tables that have dependent relationships to other tables. Often I have attempted to insert requested data into a table, only to find that referential integrity checks would not allow the update because the foreign keys did not exist in the referenced table. Referential integrity checking has saved me many times from damaging tables with bogus record insertions.

Changing the AutoJoin Option

Relationships are logical joins, or lines drawn between tables for the database as a whole. Joins in a query are the lines drawn between tables and pertain only to the query itself. After the query is closed, the joins are no longer relevant.

You have access to an option called AutoJoin, which you can see in Figure 3.13. You access AutoJoin by choosing Tools | Options under the Tables/Queries tab. When this option is enabled, Access automatically creates an inner join between two tables under two conditions. The first condition is that the fields have the same name. The second condition is that one of the fields must be a primary key.

If the AutoJoin feature is not activated, you can create a join between two tables manually by clicking one field in the first table and dragging it to another field in the second table. If the AutoJoin feature is turned on, you can have another join between the same two tables. If you don't want the join created by the AutoJoin for the current query, you must delete it by highlighting the join line and pressing the Delete key. If you want to keep the join and a second join is required, you can create the second join by dragging one field from the first table to another field in the second table.

FIGURE 3.13.

The AutoJoin option is available in the Options dialog box.

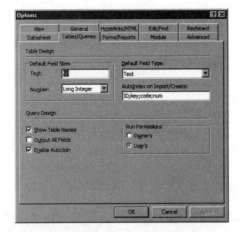

Because the join created by the AutoJoin option is an inner join, you can change the join at any time. To do so, highlight the join line and right-click to open the Join Properties dialog box. Select the join you want—either 2 (left outer join) or 3 (right outer join)—and click OK to save.

Using Each of the Standard Query Types

A finite number of queries is available. They're like colors. Even though several thousand different colors are available, each and every color is derived from the three primary colors—red, blue, and yellow. Even though several different variations of queries may be created, there are only two types of queries: queries that are acted on, or *action* queries, and queries that are viewed, or *select* queries. The following sections describe the different types of action and select queries and when to use them.

Action Queries

Action queries are different from select queries in that they perform an operation. The four different types of action queries are MAKE TABLE, UPDATE, APPEND, and DELETE.

> **TIP**
>
> Access cannot perform an AutoForm or AutoReport operation on any of the action queries. They are not considered valid queries for the basis of an AutoForm or AutoReport.

SELECT

SELECT queries are those in which the data resulting from the query is viewed. There are two types of SELECT queries: simple select and crosstab.

Simple Select

Simple select queries are the most common of all the queries. They enable you to extract data from different tables and view it. Limited manipulations can be made with simple select queries. They're so common that a Select Query Wizard is available. The wizard lists all the existing tables and queries and asks for the fields that should appear in the query. From that information, it creates the simple select query.

> **TIP**
>
> For the Query Wizard to work flawlessly, the relationships for all the tables may have to be established already. If no relationship exists between the tables needed in the wizard, the query can still be created if a standard naming convention was used when the table fields were created.

To create a simple select query without the wizard, open a new, blank query and add the table or tables you want for the query. If a relationship does exist between the tables, a line is added between the fields that make up the relationship. If the relationship is not automatically established when the tables are entered into the table pane of the query, either the table fields do not adhere to a standard naming convention or no relationship was established in the relationship window of the database. You can establish a relationship for this query by dragging a field from one table to a related field in the other table. This kind of relationship appears only in this query.

You build a simple select query by dragging fields from the tables down to the QBE grid, as shown in Figure 3.14. Criteria can be set on them, and they can calculate sums, averages, counts, and other types of totals on one or more tables.

Crosstab

The second type of SELECT query is the crosstab query. It is somewhat like a simple select query in that it can calculate sums, averages, counts, and other types of totals on one or more tables. It differs from a simple select query in that it displays information not only down the left column of the datasheet, but also across the top. A crosstab query is similar in appearance to a PivotTable; it has row headings as well as column headings. A simple select query can produce the same information as a crosstab query, but the crosstab query produces a more concise datasheet.

FIGURE 3.14.

A simple select query.

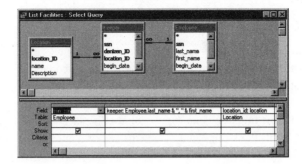

To create a crosstab query without the help of a wizard, open a new, blank query and add the tables needed for the result you want. Add the fields from the table or tables into the QBE grid. Choose Query|Crosstab or click the Query Type button on the design toolbar, as shown in Figure 3.15.

FIGURE 3.15.

You can create a crosstab query by selecting Crosstab Query from the Query Type list.

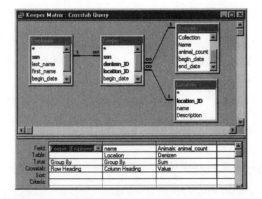

3

CREATING SOPHISTICATED QUERIES

> **TIP**
>
> When you create a crosstab query, you must have at least three output fields. One field must be a row heading, one field must be a column heading, and one field must be a value.

When the crosstab query is selected, Access automatically adds a Total row and a Crosstab row to the QBE grid.

On some occasions, data may be missing, or data that has been appended to the table or query in the crosstab and fields may be missing. This missing data may be data in the row or column headings of your crosstab query. When data for headings is missing, Access returns a "< >" sign, which means that this field is null. You can prevent a null sign from appearing in a heading by typing "Is Not Null" in the Criteria cell in the design grid for that field. This means that any time a heading comes across a null field, that record will not be considered for the crosstab query. However, if you need to know that records should be visible in the query even if you have a null heading field, you can use the Nz function. This function is an expression that is placed in the Criteria cell of the heading field and returns the string "Unknown" instead of a null.

> **NOTE**
>
> Data in crosstab queries cannot be edited.

Action Queries

Action queries move or change data. Through Access action queries, you can make bulk changes to tables of data. The unique facet of an action query is that it makes these bulk changes in one operation. Only four types of action queries exist: MAKE TABLE, UPDATE, APPEND, and DELETE. In some circles, a SQL passthrough query can also be considered an action query. It's important to remember that the AutoForm and AutoReport wizards can't be based on an action query.

The MAKE TABLE Query

MAKE TABLE queries actually do exactly what their name implies. They make tables based on one or more other tables by utilizing all or part of the data from each preexisting table.

There are several reasons why a developer would use the MAKE TABLE query. MAKE TABLE queries allow for creating tables to export data to other Access databases. With the creation of a MAKE TABLE query, you can control exactly what is exported. For example, a department might need to send a mailing to all of its employees. The mailing information is contained in the Employee table, along with other information that is considered confidential. Instead of exporting the entire Employee table, you can create a MAKE TABLE query that transfers only the information needed for a mailing to the department.

You also can use the MAKE TABLE query to create a query of historical information. It can retain all the information on a table or group of tables up to a specific date. Because the MAKE TABLE retains the information, it could be considered a backup table. MAKE TABLEs that are used to hold historical information have a two-pronged benefit. First, they enable you to retain all the information in smaller groups—say, yearly. Any information you need is quickly generated based on a yearly MAKE TABLE. Second, with a MAKE TABLE containing the historical information from years gone by, you can actually delete those records from the real tables, thus increasing the speed of any forms or reports based on those tables. You do not move old records, as you might in the Explorer. You simply copy the older records to another table and then delete the older records from the main table.

MAKE TABLE queries can be used for creating a backup copy of a table. Granted, the table resulting from a MAKE TABLE query isn't very helpful if the hard drive crashes, but that isn't its intended purpose. A backup copy of data is very useful to developers who are working with existing data and need to tinker with other queries. This backup copy allows the existing data to remain intact while you fine-tune different queries, forms, and reports based on a MAKE TABLE query or table.

MAKE TABLE queries can accelerate the performance of forms and reports that are based on multitable queries. Suppose that a number of forms and reports are based on the same three tables, and those forms and reports include totals. With a MAKE TABLE query, all the information and totals needed are retrieved and stored in one table. The query isn't rerun for each form or report. Speed isn't increased the first time the MAKE TABLE query is run; however, forms or reports based on the table resulting from a MAKE TABLE query will be faster than the original three-table query. All the data for the form or report is now in one table, and all the form or report has to do is read it.

To create a MAKE TABLE query, create a new, blank query with the tables that you want. Pull the fields down into the QBE grid and set the criteria, if any. Choose Query | Make Table, or click the Query Type button on the query's design toolbar and select Make Table. The Make Table dialog box appears, as shown in Figure 3.16. Type the name of the new table that you are creating in the Table Name text box.

FIGURE 3.16.

*When you're cre-
ating a* MAKE
TABLE *query, type
in the name of the
new table here.*

If the MAKE TABLE is to appear in another database, click the Another Database button. If the other database is an Access database, type the name of the database. It might be necessary to type the entire path of that database. If the database isn't an Access database, follow the name of the database with the name of the other database in quotation marks—

·for example, `C:\MyDocuments\db1d"Paradox;"`. After the name of the other database has been entered, click OK.

Click the Datasheet view of the query to make sure that the results are what is needed before the MAKE TABLE query is created. The MAKE TABLE is created when the query is actually run. After the query is run, check the Tables module of the database container. The new table should be there, as it is in Figure 3.17. Open the new table to see the records. As new records are added to the original table, they do not appear in the MAKE TABLE unless the MAKE TABLE query is run again. If it is, new records that match the criteria set by the query are added to the new table.

FIGURE 3.17.

When the MAKE
TABLE query is
run, the new table
appears in the
Tables module of
the database con-
tainer.

> ### WARNING
>
> Check MAKE TABLE queries before they are executed by viewing the Datasheet view of the query. If the output is correct, run the query. If it isn't correct, return to Design view and make modifications.

> ### NOTE
>
> Any field properties from the tables used in the MAKE TABLE query are not going to follow through. If you have Default Values or Input Masks set, those properties are not duplicated in the new table.

To update a table of a MAKE TABLE query to reflect the changes in the data, simply reexecute the query by opening it from the Database Container window or selecting Query | Run. When this happens, Access displays a message stating that a MAKE TABLE query is about to be run and that the data in the current table will be modified.

Access displays a message offering a last chance to preserve the data in the first MAKE TABLE. The default is set to No.

Remember, a MAKE TABLE query is just a snapshot of the data available at the time of creation. The data in that table can be edited without affecting the real data. It's even possible to create a MAKE TABLE query on an existing crosstab query. To do this, use the crosstab query as the basis for a new MAKE TABLE query. This can be useful for complex reports. If a MAKE TABLE query is the source for a form or a report, it might be wise to create an AutoNumber field for the new table because one isn't generated at the time of creation.

> **WARNING**
>
> When naming the new table for the MAKE TABLE query, remember not to give it the same name as the table being used as the source. The reason is that when you execute the query, the table is deleted and then the data is added. So if the new table has the same name as the original table, your new table will be built with no data.

The UPDATE Query

UPDATE queries enable you to change data on a global scale. For example, if all the employees in a company get an annual raise of five percent, their salaries are increased five percent through an UPDATE query. Or, if all the customer area codes in the Charlotte area are changed to 701, you can make the change through an UPDATE query. The UPDATE query is different from the MAKE TABLE query in that it actually makes changes to the real data, whereas the MAKE TABLE query makes a copy of the data and creates a new table based on that data.

Suppose we want to move all denizens of a zoo from one location to another. This is a good situation in which to use an UPDATE query. The records are stored in the Keeper table, we don't know in advance which denizens we want to move, and we want the move handled in a concise, consistent manner. We will call our UPDATE query Transfer All Denizens.

Before creating the query, run the MAKE PREVIOUS KEEPER query. This gives us a backup of the Keeper table, and it also gives us the ability to compare the contents of the Keeper table after the UPDATE query is run to its contents before the UPDATE query was run. After the MAKE PREVIOUS KEEPER query is completed, create the new Transfer All Denizens query.

In this example, we want to provide the ability to designate from where and to where the denizens are transferring. For this reason, this UPDATE query uses two parameters— arg_from_location_id and arg_to_location_id—to provide additional flexibility. Most UPDATE and DELETE procedures should include parameters for this same reason. Parameter queries will be discussed in a later section.

To create an UPDATE query, open a new, blank query and pull in the tables desired—in this case, the Keeper and Location tables. In this example, we want to update Keeper records that have location IDs matching the From Location ID argument, and each record's Location ID is set to the To Location ID argument. In addition, the Location table is used to verify that the To Location ID argument is a valid location.

LISTING 3.1. THIS UPDATE QUERY IS USED TO TRANSFER DENIZENS FROM ONE ZOO LOCATION TO ANOTHER.

```
PARAMETERS [arg_from_location_id] Text, [arg_to_location_id] Text;
UPDATE Keeper, Location SET Keeper.location_ID = [arg_to_location_id]
WHERE (((Keeper.location_ID)=[arg_from_location_id]) AND
((Location.location_ID)=[arg_to_location_id]));
```

To accomplish our goal of updating both the Discount and UnitPrice columns, we must add the [Discount] + .10 expression to the UnitPrice calculation. In design mode, we need to select the UnitPrice and Discount columns. Then, to make this an UPDATE query, select Query|Update, or click the Query Type button and select Update. In the query grid, the Update To row is added, as shown in Figure 3.18.

FIGURE 3.18.

The Update To row is added to the query grid for an UPDATE query, and the desired values have been inserted.

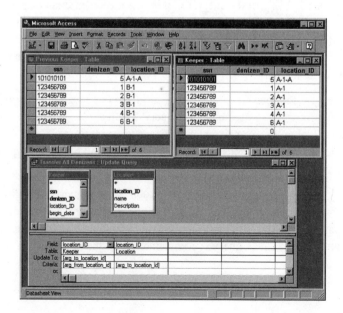

Executing an UPDATE query is uneventful. The records being changed don't fly past the screen. No meter or gas gauge shows that an action has taken place. The only way to tell whether the update has taken place is to open the table where the data was being updated. In Figure 3.18, you can tell that an UPDATE query has taken place by the difference in values on the right. The table on the left contains the actual data. The table on the right was created earlier by the MAKE TABLE. It is provided so that you can see the difference.

Many different expressions can be entered into an UPDATE query. They don't even have to pertain to numeric or currency datatype fields, as shown in the preceding code example. Table 3.1 shows some of the most common expressions. Use expressions in the Update To cell in the query-design grid for the field you want to update.

TABLE 3.1. COMMON UPDATE QUERY EXPRESSIONS.

Desired result	Expression to enter in the Update To cell
Need a field to read "Completed"	`"Completed"`
Need to change the date to Dec. 31, 1995	`#12-31-95#`
Need to change all the No fields to Yes fields	`Yes`
Need the last name and first name to appear as one field	`[last_name] &` `", " & [first_name]`
Need to calculate the total number of animals	`Sum (animal_count)`
Need to increase salaries by five percent	`[Salary]*1.05`
Need to keep only the first eight characters	`Left([FieldName], 8)`

It's important to remember that there are certain limitations to UPDATE queries. When certain situations occur, Access returns error messages that prevent the UPDATE query from firing. Table 3.2 shows some of the errors Access can return.

TABLE 3.2. SOME ACCESS ERRORS.

Error	Description
`Query Not Updatable`	This error occurs when an UPDATE query is being executed on another query that contains totals. Queries that contain totals usually can't be updated.
`Key Violations`	The UPDATE query can't be executed because of referential integrity rules that are already established.

continues

TABLE 3.2. CONTINUED

Error	*Description*
Lock Violations	These occur on fields or records that have been locked by the developer (on a form) or by another user (in a multiuser environment).
Validation Rule Violation	This error occurs when the UPDATE query is trying put data into a field where the validation rule has been set back at the table level for that field.
Type Mismatch Error	This refers to the datatype established for a field. If the UPDATE query tries to put text in a date/time field, this error occurs.

Usually, UPDATE queries based on one table are updatable. If the UPDATE query contains two tables with a one-to-one relationship, it usually executes. If the UPDATE query is based on three or more tables having a one-to-many relationship, it won't work. The reason might be that the Cascading Updates option has been checked. As a rule, queries containing three or more tables aren't updatable. Likewise, crosstab queries, passthrough queries, and union queries can't be updated.

You might want to consider using criteria for the UPDATE query to control which records are updated. This allows you to update only data that meets specific criteria.

The APPEND Query

The third action query is the APPEND query. It adds a group of records from one or more tables to the end of one or more other tables. The benefit of an APPEND query is that it saves the user time. Instead of the user typing each new record (and there could be hundreds), the developer can create an APPEND query. The APPEND query simply takes the new records and adds them to the end of an existing table.

The Arrival table contains records on animals that will be added to the Denizen table once the animals are received. The Receive Arrivals query is used for processing animals in the Arrival table that have not been received and adding this information to the Denizen table.

To create the Receive Arrivals query, press the New button in the Query tab. Make the query an APPEND query by selecting Query | Append. Access displays a dialog box like the one shown in Figure 3.19.

FIGURE 3.19.

*The Append dia-
log box.*

The first field, `Table Name`, is the name of the destination table that the field or fields in the query grid will be appended to. If the destination table isn't located in the current database, the name of the database must be entered into the `File Name` field.

> **NOTE**
>
> It might be necessary to enter the entire path of the database that contains the destination table—for example, `D:\MyDocuments\db1.MDB`.

The purpose of this query is to transfer the following information from the `Arrival` table to the `Denizen` table: 1) animal ID, 2) animal name, and 3) animal count. In addition, the `Collection` field is set to C and the begin date is set to the current date and time. Figure 3.20 shows the query after these fields have been set for the APPEND query. Listing 3.2 contains the SQL syntax for this same query.

FIGURE 3.20.

*The Receive
Arrivals query.*

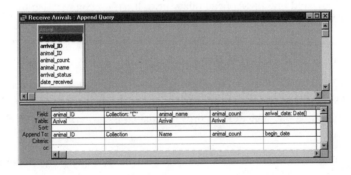

LISTING 3.2. THE RECEIVE ARRIVALS QUERY USED TO TRANSFER INFORMATION FROM THE ARRIVAL TABLE TO THE DENIZEN TABLE.

```
INSERT INTO Denizen ( animal_ID, Collection, Name, animal_count,
➥begin_date )
SELECT Arrival.animal_ID, "C" AS Collection, Arrival.animal_name,
Arrival.animal_count, Date() AS arrival_date FROM Arrival;
```

> **NOTE**
>
> The field matched in an APPEND query must be of the same datatype. Otherwise, a type mismatch error will occur. Match text to text fields, numbers to number fields, and so on.

How do you know whether an APPEND query has executed? Check the destination table to see whether the records have been appended to the bottom of the list.

> **NOTE**
>
> Access fills in the names in the Append To row automatically only if the destination table is in the same database as the source table.

Another concern crops up if you append all the records from one table to another table and have included the AutoNumber field in the APPEND query grid. If the destination table has an AutoNumber field and it's the primary key for that table, any duplicate AutoNumber records won't be appended.

Access renumbers the AutoNumber fields from the source table if you don't bring the AutoNumber field into the Append query grid. It isn't recommended that you include the AutoNumber field in the query grid when creating the Append query.

The DELETE Query

The DELETE query enables you to delete records from one or more tables in a single action. As helpful as this capability can be, it can also be very dangerous. If the DELETE query is based on one table, the records that match the criteria are deleted when the query is run.

The example we'll use to illustrate this point is a DELETE query that purges Arrival records based on the arrival_status field. The Purge Arrival query accepts the arg_status parameter. It then deletes all records from the Arrival table that have an arrival_status field matching the parameter.

> **WARNING**
>
> Before executing a DELETE query, always check the records that will be deleted by running a SELECT query based on the same criteria as the DELETE query. Make sure that the right information is being deleted. After a DELETE query has been executed, the Undo command won't be available.

Don't be intimidated by DELETE queries. They're easier than you might think. To create a DELETE query, open a new, blank query. Bring in the table containing the fields that will be used for the DELETE query. Select Query | Delete or select Delete from the Query Type button on the toolbar. Access automatically adds a Delete row to the query grid, as shown in Figure 3.21.

FIGURE 3.21.

The DELETE *query in Design view.*

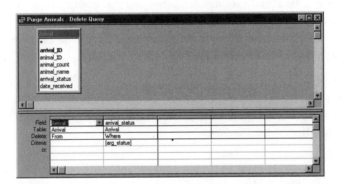

The Delete row of the query grid gives you only two options: From and Where. These clauses work together. The entire table is brought down to the grid. A single asterisk (*) denotes "all fields." This is the From part of the DELETE query. The individual field, Region, is the Where part of the DELETE query. It is here that a criteria is entered for the DELETE query. In this example, the user is allowed to enter the state where all the customers will be deleted. Allowing the user to enter the criteria makes a query more flexible.

Make sure that the DELETE query is always checked in Datasheet view before it's executed. The records that appear in the Datasheet view of a DELETE query are the same records that will be deleted. Figure 3.22 shows the parameter expression that was entered into the Criteria field for Region.

FIGURE 3.22.

An expression in the Criteria *field gives the* DELETE *query more flexibility.*

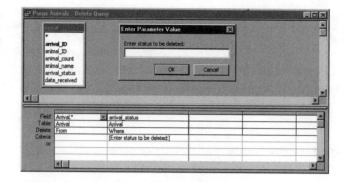

The criteria typed into the dialog box is then used to determine the desired records to be deleted. Select Query | Run or click the Run button (the red exclamation mark) on the design toolbar. This action executes the query, and the records that were returned in the Datasheet view are removed from the Arrival table. When the query is executed, Access displays a message informing you that *x* number of records will be deleted. This is your last chance to cancel the DELETE query.

The following is the SQL statement that actually performs a DELETE query. The DELETE statement is the creation of the DELETE query. The field where the criteria will be entered follows the name of the table. In this case, it is the arrival_status field from the Arrival table. Here is the statement:

```
PARAMETERS [arg_status] Text;
DELETE Arrival.*, Arrival.arrival_status FROM Arrival WHERE
(((Arrival.arrival_status)=[arg_status]));
```

The last line of the DELETE statement deals with the criteria specified by the developer. The WHERE clause works with the FROM clause, and in this example, users are allowed to type the criteria themselves.

Some restrictions in creating DELETE queries need to be mentioned here. Deleting records from one table isn't hard; however, when dealing with two tables, you must look at the relationship between those tables. One-to-many relationships must have the Cascading Delete option turned on for a query to work. All the records in the table on the "many" side will be deleted when the "one" side's corresponding record is deleted. Also remember that DELETE queries remove the entire record from the database, not just the specified fields.

Parameter Queries

Parameter queries give the user more flexibility. When a Parameter query is run, Access displays a dialog box prompting the user for more information. In the previous DELETE query, a parameter was used. It required the user to "Enter status to be deleted." The parameter declaration in SQL view appears at the end of the WHERE statement:

```
WHERE (((Arrival.arrival_status)=[Enter status to be deleted:]));
```

The section in brackets is the parameter.

Parameters can be set on just about all queries, including action and select queries. Perhaps the best use for parameter queries is in specifying date ranges or any other limiting criteria when running reports. Parameters should be used liberally.

You can create parameter type queries for a report in three ways. The first method is to use a query as demonstrated in the Purge Arrivals query. The second method is to build the query straight into the Data.RecordSource property of the report. The last method is much more difficult and involves the use of programming code in the report.

Union Queries

Union queries combine the results of two or more queries. There is a catch to creating a Union query: the entire query must be written in code. It can't be done from the Design view of a query.

To create a Union query, open a new, blank query. When the Show Table box appears, select the first table and whichever columns you plan to show in the first clause in the union. This builds the first SELECT statement for you. For our example, choose the Animal table and then the animal_id and common_name columns. The rest of the work will have to be done in SQL view. Listing 3.3 shows the SQL used to create the union displayed in Figure 3.23.

LISTING 3.3. A SELECT...UNION STATEMENT USED TO CREATE AN EXAMPLE UNION QUERY.

```
SELECT Denizen.animal_ID, common_name, sum(animal_count) as animals, "D"
as Arrival FROM Denizen, Animal WHERE Denizen.animal_ID = Animal.animal_ID
GROUP BY Denizen.animal_ID, common_name
UNION SELECT Arrival.animal_ID, common_name, sum(animal_count) as animals,
"A" as Arrival FROM Arrival, Animal WHERE Arrival.animal_ID =
Animal.animal_ID AND arrival_status = "O" GROUP BY
Arrival.animal_ID,common_name;
```

3

CREATING SOPHISTICATED QUERIES

FIGURE 3.23.

An example of using UNION *to join rows from the* Denizen *and* Animal *tables with rows from the* Arrival *and* Animal *tables.*

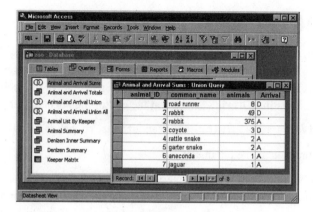

In a Union query, all the fields being combined must have the same data type, with one exception: a number field can have a corresponding Text field. Access then takes the column headers from the first SELECT statement and places each of the fields in the first SELECT and the second SELECT under the same placeheaders. This is why the literal string A or D is being placed under the Arrival header.

> **NOTE**
>
> A Union query allows different SELECT statements to be unioned together. The column headings used in the first SELECT statement are the placeheaders for all the unioned SELECT statements. If differing datatypes are used between the first and following SELECT statements, Access determines which datatype to use based on which type is compatible with both.

By default, the UNION operator unions all rows in both statements into a DISTINCT recordset. In other words, it does not return duplicate results. If you want your dataset to return duplicate results from the combining of the two SELECT statements, you need to use the UNION ALL operator. Figure 3.24 shows two very simple Union queries that clearly show the difference between the UNION and UNION ALL statements.

The last thing to note about Union queries is that there is no theoretical limit to how many SELECT statements you can union together. The only limit is the internal amount of memory that Access has available to process queries.

FIGURE 3.24.

Examples of the UNION *versus* UNION ALL *clauses.* UNION ALL *returns all rows, including duplicates.*

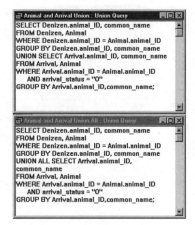

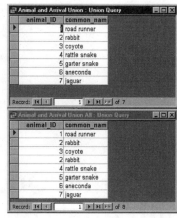

Nesting Queries

It's a fact that a query can be based on another query. This process can be several levels deep. When one query is based on the existence of another query, it's called a nested query. Why would a developer have a nested query? They're more manageable. Instead of having 10 different tables in one query, it's easier to break the query into several smaller, more manageable queries. Another benefit to having nested queries involves the SQL statement. A SQL statement can hold only about 64,000 characters. After it's reached this limit, Access displays an error message stating that the SQL statement is too large. At that point, Access attempts to fix the SQL statement by removing sections from the end of the statement, but you aren't informed of this attempt. Not until you examine the statement will you notice that sections of the SQL have been removed. With nested queries, there are fewer characters in the SQL to perform the same action.

The Animal and Arrival Sums query is a Union query that lists animals and counts of animals, and classifies these counts according to whether the animals are denizens or future arrivals. Suppose you also want to list totals of all animals and denizens. One way to accomplish this query is to base this query on the preexisting Animal and Arrival Sums query. Figure 3.25 shows the information used to create this query.

The trade-off of having several nested queries is speed. Nested queries are slower than one giant query because Access must run both the nested query and the main query.

Nested queries have been compared to subqueries, but they aren't the same. An example of a subquery is when you take the SQL statement from one query and place it in the Criteria cell of a field in another query. This is slower than a nested query, because each field's Criteria cell has to be run before the query itself can run.

3

CREATING
SOPHISTICATED
QUERIES

FIGURE 3.25.

An example of a nested query that is used to total all of the denizens and new arrivals for the zoo.

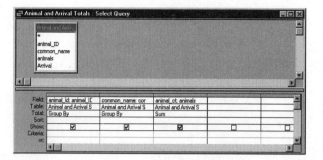

Analyzing Query Performance with Analyzer

Because the query is considered the brain of the database (without queries the database would be a flat file), you can spend a lot of time working queries. Queries can be accessed from the database container or the record source for a form or report. Often you may develop a query but won't be satisfied with it. The query may be sluggish or doesn't perform to your satisfaction, so what are you to do? Access 97 has come up with a way to analyze not only the query but also all the objects within that database to give you suggestions. This tool is called the Performance Analyzer.

You can access the Performance Analyzer by choosing Tools | Analyze from the Database container and then clicking Performance. After the Performance Analyzer is launched, a dialog box like the one shown in Figure 3.26 appears. You then can choose one object in the database or all objects in the database.

FIGURE 3.26.

The Performance Analyzer enables you to choose one object or all the objects in the database.

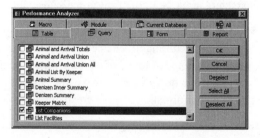

You can select an individual object type or select all objects from the drop-down list. By selecting them all, you can see every object created for this database. All the objects appear in Object Name list. You can then pick and choose the individual objects to be analyzed by selecting the box associated with each object. If you want the entire database to be analyzed, click Select All.

Depending on the size of the database and the complexity of its objects, the analyzing process can take anywhere from under one minute to more than five minutes. After the process finishes, Access displays a dialog box like the one shown in Figure 3.27.

FIGURE 3.27.

The Performance Analyzer offers suggestions on how to increase the speed of a object within a database or the entire database itself.

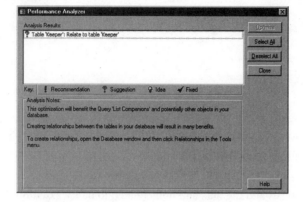

When the Performance Analyzer is finished grinding away, it returns a list of suggestions broken down into four categories: Recommendations, Suggestions, Ideas, and Fixed. Recommendations have red exclamation marks for icons. Suggestions have green question marks, and ideas have yellow light bulbs as icons. Objects that were fixed have a blue check mark. The Suggestion list shows the icon, the object module, the name of the object in question, and a suggestion on how to improve it.

If you click a recommendation or suggestion, Access proposes how to increase its performance. When an item is highlighted, the Optimize button is enabled. Access can make the changes to the database automatically. All the advice with a light bulb icon are ideas, and Access cannot optimize the object if the advice is only an idea. You must perform the Idea optimizations yourself.

In this particular case, the Keeper table is joined to itself according to location_id. The analyzer suggests relating the Keeper table to the Keeper table; however, there is no real relationship between this table and itself. The performance of this particular query could be improved, however, by adding an index to the Keeper table based on location_id.

> **WARNING**
>
> The Performance Analyzer can make some changes automatically, but be careful. Some recommendations and suggestions may not be what you intended for the database.

> **NOTE**
>
> The Performance Analyzer is a wonderful tool for developers. However, it can't provide suggestions on how to improve the performance of the machine on which it is running, nor does it provide recommendations on how to improve Microsoft Access itself.

Summary

This chapter covered many of the details involved with creating Access 97 queries. It started with the prerequisites of queries—including relationships, query joins, and referential integrity—and finished with details related to the various kinds of action and select queries.

Once these query types and the nuts and bolts related to query assembly were firmly established, you looked at query nesting, union queries, and using the Query Performance Analyzer to introduce a tool for optimizing query performance. At this point, you should be capable of creating the kinds of queries necessary to create solid applications.

Access 97 and Programming in SQL

CHAPTER 4

IN THIS CHAPTER

SQL Defined

Structured Query Language, or SQL (usually pronounced "sequel"), is the most popular relational database query language in use today. It was developed at IBM laboratories in the early 1970s to implement the relational model introduced by Dr. Edgar F. Codd in 1970.

Although it's certainly a query language, SQL is much more because of its powerful data-definition and data-access capabilities. SQL is known as a transform-oriented language. The user inputs English-like requests for data using a defined structure—hence the word "structured" in the language's name. The requests are then transformed by the relational database management system (RDBMS) into the requested output.

Some of the data access commands of SQL are SELECT, UPDATE, INSERT, and DELETE. The SELECT command forms the basis for retrieving data from a database. UPDATE, INSERT, and DELETE allow you to modify the data according to the parameters you supply. These commands are self-explanatory. An UPDATE command updates records in the database, INSERT inserts or creates a new record in the database, and DELETE deletes a record from the database.

SQL Language Constructs

Jet SQL is a mixture containing elements of the ANSI SQL-89 and SQL-92 language standards, although it doesn't completely implement either standard. In addition, Jet SQL enhances ANSI SQL with additional commands not found in the ANSI SQL standard. Some of the major differences are described in the following sections.

The BETWEEN...AND Construct

One difference between Jet SQL and ANSI SQL is how Jet SQL treats the BETWEEN...AND construct. This construct is used to specify a range of values *between* two values. It has the following syntax:

```
expression1 [NOT] BETWEEN expression2 AND expression3
```

The difference is that in Jet SQL, *expression1* can be greater than *expression2*; in ANSI SQL, *expression2* must be equal to or less than *expression3*. This is to your advantage if you're using Jet SQL, but you need to beware when using this construct with other SQL databases.

For example, in Jet SQL, the following two queries would return the same number of records from the Invoices table. (Notice that the dates are reversed in the second query.)

In ANSI SQL, the second query would return either an error or an empty recordset, depending on the database you're requesting data from.

Query 1:

```
SELECT DISTINCTROW Invoices.*
FROM Invoices
WHERE (((Invoices.[Order Date]) Between #1/1/93# And #1/31/93#));
```

Query 2:

```
SELECT DISTINCTROW Invoices.*
FROM Invoices
WHERE (((Invoices.[Order Date]) Between #1/31/93# And #1/1/93#));
```

Access 97 uses different wildcard characters than does ANSI SQL. Table 4.1 shows the differences.

TABLE 4.1. JET SQL WILDCARD CHARACTERS.

Jet SQL	ANSI SQL	Description
?	_ (underscore)	Matches any single character
*	%	Matches zero or more characters

Enhanced Features of Jet SQL

Many of the SQL databases in use today contain a mixture of ANSI SQL and proprietary commands specific to that product. This helps build a loyal following of customers for a certain product and allows software designers to improve the features that they or their users feel are important to enhance.

As mentioned earlier, Jet SQL contains commands and features of ANSI SQL-89 and SQL-92, as well as some features that are proprietary to Access 97. Some enhancements that aren't found in ANSI SQL are the TRANSFORM statement and the PARAMETERS declaration. (See "Structuring SQL-92" in this chapter for examples and more details on these.)

ANSI SQL Features Not Supported in Jet SQL

In addition to the enhancements in Jet SQL, more than 200 ANSI SQL keywords are *not* supported by Jet SQL. Because of the large number, it's beyond the scope of this chapter to detail all of these keywords, but here are a few of the more noteworthy features of ANSI SQL that you won't find in Jet SQL:

- Data-definition language (DDL) statements (other than Jet database's)
- Database security statements, such as `COMMIT`, `GRANT`, and `LOCK`

Why Use Jet SQL?

With Access 97, Microsoft has introduced many timesaving features that enhance and simplify management of an RDBMS. Access 97 has new and improved wizards and builders that make it much easier to create quite large and complex queries. These tools have limits, however, and as excellent as they are, some things still can't be done with them or simply won't work outside a native Access 97 environment (for example, using SQL pass-through to query data on an SQL database server).

One of the most common implementations of SQL in Access is to use a SQL `SELECT` statement as the source of records for forms, reports, and controls. You could create a standard query to use as the record source, but by using a SQL string as the record source, you have one fewer object to create and maintain in your database. For example, you might have a form that contains a combo box. For the `Row Source` property for the combo box, you could enter a SQL string such as the following:

```
SELECT DISTINCTROW CompanyName
FROM Customers;
```

This would display a list of all the company names when the combo box's down arrow is selected. List boxes and combo boxes based on SQL statements are slower than list boxes and combo boxes based on saved queries, however, so you should weigh this fact against the benefit of having fewer query objects in your database.

Some types of queries can be run only using SQL statements (as opposed to using the Query Designer). Following is a list of SQL-specific queries that are possible only with Jet SQL. (These are explained in more detail in the "Structuring SQL-92" section later in this chapter.)

- Union queries combine fields from tables or queries into one field.
- Data-definition queries are used to create new or modify existing data objects.
- Pass-through queries are used to communicate with external (ODBC) database sources.

Writing Queries with SQL

Two methods of writing SQL queries in Access 97 are available to you. The first method involves embedding SQL statements directly in your application's code. This method is often used when one is working with ODBC databases.

The second method is to write SQL by selecting the View | SQL option while in Query Design view. This brings up a text window that displays your query in SQL language. All the examples in this chapter were written by using this method.

SQL Conventions

SQL is rigid about certain aspects of your query, such as the order of statements, when you can and can't use particular clauses, and so on. For the most part, however, the appearance of your code is pretty much left up to you. You can, for example, enter a statement like the following:

```
select distinct [first name],[last name] from employees where [hire date]
➥>1/1/93
```

The following alternative makes the code much easier to read and understand:

```
SELECT DISTINCT FirstName,LastName
FROM employees
WHERE HireDate > 1/1/93
```

Using uppercase for the SQL keywords, lowercase for the names of the data elements, and entering each command on a separate line makes it easier for you and for others who might be required to use or maintain your code later to decipher it.

The SQL examples in this chapter use the following conventions:

- Square brackets ([ ]) indicate optional items:

  ```
  SELECT [predicate]
  ```

- Curly braces ({}) combined with vertical bars (¦) indicate a choice:

  ```
  { * ¦ table.* ¦ [table.]field1 [, [table.]field2.[, ...]]}
  ```

- Ellipses (...) indicate a repeating sequence:

  ```
  FROM tableexpression [, ...]
  ```

The SELECT Command

The SELECT statement is the most important statement in SQL. With its powerful options, there are many ways to retrieve your data and to perform complex data calculations.

Jet SQL SELECT queries select rows of data and returns them as a dynaset (an updatable) recordset.

The basic form of a SELECT query is as follows:

```
SELECT [predicate] { * ¦ table.* ¦ [table.]field1 [, [table.]field2.
➥[, ...]]}
[AS alias1 [, alias2 [, ...]]]
FROM tableexpression [, ...] [IN externaldatabase]
[WHERE... ]
[GROUP BY... ]
[HAVING... ]
[ORDER BY... ]
```

A simple SELECT query might look like this:

```
SELECT *
FROM customers
WHERE City = 'Seattle';
```

Figure 4.1 shows the results of this query.

FIGURE 4.1.

A simple SELECT *query.*

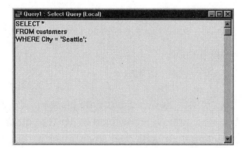

The SELECT command in this query followed by an asterisk (*) indicates that all columns from the selected table or tables are to be returned. This is a quick and easy way to specify all columns without having to enter them all. The columns are returned in the same order in which they were created in the table, and the column names are displayed as headings.

> **TIP**
>
> If performance is a priority, it is highly recommended that you do not use * in your SELECT statements. The reason is that Access first needs to examine the table structure to build the column name list before any records can be returned.

The FROM command tells the query engine from which tables or queries to select the records.

The WHERE command allows you to specify which records you want to return based on the criteria you enter; in this case, all columns from the Customers table will be returned in which the city matches "Seattle."

As another example, what if you wanted to see only the contact name, phone number, and postal code of those customers who live in Seattle in the 98128 zip code area?

```
SELECT ContactName, Phone, PostalCode
FROM customers
WHERE City='Seattle' AND PostalCode = '98128'
```

This time you get only the three columns you specified—contact name, phone, and postal code—from the Customers table in which the city matches 'Seattle' and the postal code matches '98128'.

The Predicate Options

You can use four options immediately following the SELECT statement to restrict the number of records returned either for unique values or records or to get the top values or percentages of the records returned. These four predicates—ALL, DISTINCT, DISTINCTROW, and TOP—are described in the following sections.

ALL

This is the default for a SELECT query. You would use it to return an unrestricted record-set. The following two queries produce the same results and return all the records from the Customers table.

```
SELECT ALL *
FROM Customers;

SELECT *
FROM Customers;
```

DISTINCT

DISTINCT is used when you want to restrict the output to single instances of each record.

> **NOTE**
>
> When you're using the DISTINCT predicate, the recordset that is returned is non-updatable and doesn't reflect subsequent changes made by other users.

For example, to return only unique last names from the Employees table, use the following query (see Figure 4.2):

```
SELECT DISTINCT [LastName]
FROM Employees;
```

FIGURE 4.2.

An example of using the DISTINCT *clause.*

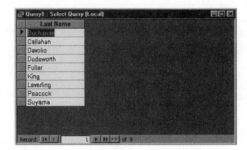

This returns one record for each unique last name. If there are two employees named Jones, only one record is returned.

WARNING

By using the DISTINCT clause, you're omitting records that you might have expected to be included. Keep in mind that by using this predicate, you're specifying that the values for each field listed in the SELECT statement are to be unique.

If your query includes more than one field, the combination of all fields must be unique to be considered a DISTINCT record. For this reason, the more fields you include, the fewer unique records will be returned.

TIP

When you're querying large databases, try to limit the number of fields in your SELECT string. Having too many fields returned can dramatically affect the performance of the query, particularly if the database is located on a network (either local or wide area).

Assume you have two employees named Bob Jones and one employee named Brenda Jones. Enter this query:

```
SELECT DISTINCT [LastName], [FirstName]
FROM Employees;
```

The result would return the record of only the first Bob Jones and the record of Brenda Jones.

DISTINCTROW

DISTINCTROW is used to restrict data to unique records for a multitable query. For example, the Customers table contains one unique record for every customer; each customer, however, can have many records in the Orders table (an example of a 1-M or one-to-many relationship). If you wanted a list of unique names of customers who have placed an order, you would enter a query such as the following (see Figure 4.3):

```
SELECT DISTINCTROW [CompanyName]
FROM Customers INNER JOIN Orders
ON Customers.[CustomerID] = Orders.[CustomerID]
ORDER BY [CompanyName];
```

FIGURE 4.3.

The result of using the DISTINCTROW *clause.*

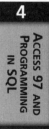

> **NOTE**
>
> Using the DISTINCTROW predicate in a SQL query is equivalent to setting the Unique Records property to Yes in the query property sheet in a query's Design view.

TOP

The TOP predicate is used to restrict the output to a certain number or percentage of records. It takes the following form:

```
SELECT TOP nn [PERCENT]
```

Suppose that you wanted to see the top 20 most expensive products in your Products table (see Figure 4.4):

```
SELECT DISTINCTROW TOP 20 Products.[ProductName], Products.[UnitPrice]
FROM Products
ORDER BY Products.[UnitPrice] DESC;
```

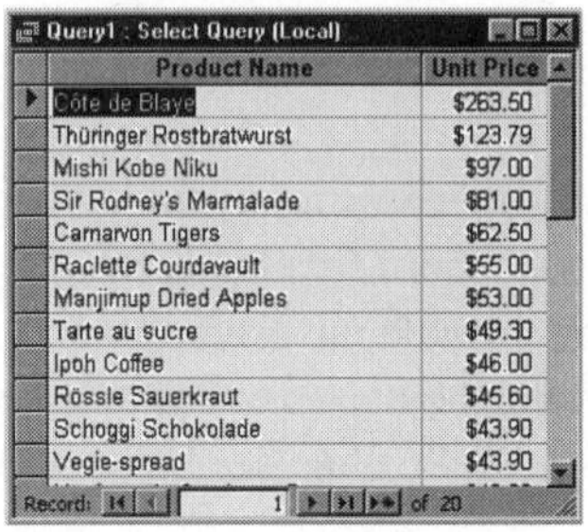

FIGURE 4.4.

A query result using the TOP *clause.*

This returns a list of the 20 most expensive products, with the list sorted in descending order from highest to lowest.

NOTE

Note the use of ORDER BY Products.[UnitPrice] DESC. This line tells Access that you want to output a descending sort (highest to lowest) by unit price. If you don't make this indication, an ambiguous set of records is returned.

To reverse this query and get the top 20 *least expensive*, just remove the DESC clause at the end of the ORDER BY statement.

What if instead of the top 20 most expensive products, you wanted a list of the top 10 percent of products, sorted by the quantity of units in stock? This is how you would do it (see Figure 4.5):

```
SELECT DISTINCTROW TOP 10 PERCENT ProductName, UnitsInStock
FROM Products
ORDER BY UnitsInStock DESC;
```

FIGURE 4.5.

A query result using the TOP *nn* PERCENT *clause.*

The SELECT...AS Option

The SELECT...AS option enables you to change the name of the output column in your query. This option can be used to shorten a long name or to create a calculated or compound column. For example, to create a single employee-name column that is a combination of first name and last name, you would use this (see Figure 4.6):

```
SELECT DISTINCTROW LastName & ", " & FirstName AS Employee
FROM Employees;
```

FIGURE 4.6.

Using the SELECT...AS *option.*

If your query includes more than one table or query that contains fields with the same name, you must enter the entire table and field name so that the query engine knows which fields you want to work with. For example, to indicate the `EmployeeID` field in `tblEmployee`, you would enter this:

```
SELECT tblEmployee.[EmployeeID]
```

The FROM Command

This is the format for using the `FROM` command:

```
FROM tableexpression [IN externaldatabase]
```

The `FROM` command indicates the tables or queries from which you want to select records. If more than one table or query is specified, you must also include a `JOIN` command that joins the tables or queries on specific fields. (See "Structuring SQL-92" later in this chapter for more information on using joins.)

> **NOTE**
>
> Access 97 uses the SQL-92 method of applying joins for multitable queries in the FROM clause. This differs from ANSI SQL, in which you specify joins in the WHERE clause.

The WHERE Command

The syntax for the `WHERE` command is this:

```
WHERE criteria
```

The `WHERE` command is the heart of any good SQL query. It is the means by which you can create simple or complex criteria that identifies which specific records you want returned. The `WHERE` command must include an operator and two operands. Here's an example (see Figure 4.7):

```
SELECT ShipName, ShipCountry
FROM Orders
WHERE ShipCountry="USA";
```

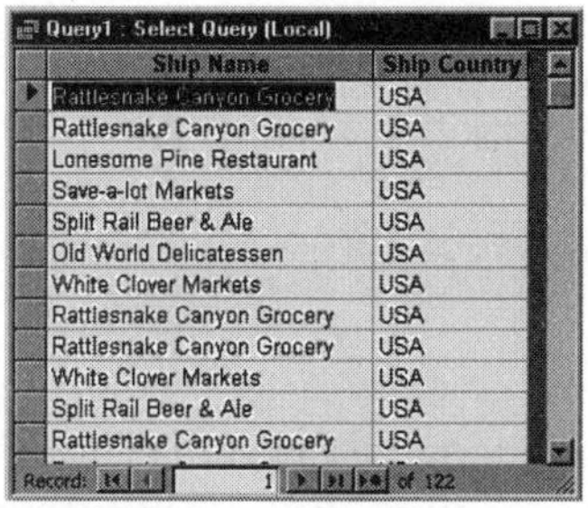

FIGURE 4.7.

A query using the WHERE *command.*

This produces a list of all customers within the United States who have placed orders. If you want to return all customers *except* the ones in the United States, simply add the NOT clause before the criteria for ShipCountry. Your query now looks like this (see Figure 4.8):

```
SELECT ShipName, ShipCountry
FROM Orders
WHERE NOT ShipCountry="USA";
```

FIGURE 4.8.

The same WHERE *query using the* NOT *option.*

Using Wildcard Characters

Any query language would be incomplete without special characters that function as placeholders for unknown characters. As mentioned earlier, Jet SQL uses a ? to match any single character and an * to match zero or more characters.

Suppose that you wanted to find all customers whose names start with Paul. You would use the asterisk as shown here:

```
SELECT DISTINCTROW Customers.[Contact Name]
FROM Customers
WHERE ((Customers.[Contact Name] Like "Paul*"));
```

The following query returns all customers who live in a city that begins with the letters "Ber" and is followed with any three other characters:

```
SELECT DISTINCTROW Customers.City
FROM Customers
WHERE ((Customers.City Like "Ber???"));
```

SQL Aggregate Functions

Using SQL aggregate functions, you can perform statistical calculations on your data. These queries can range from simple count or sum queries to complex variance and standard-deviation queries.

These are the SQL aggregate functions:

- `Avg`   Calculates an average of a specified field

- `Count`   Calculates the number of records

- `Min, Max`   Calculates minimum or maximum

- `StDev, StDevP`   Estimates the standard deviation

- `Sum`   Calculates the sum of a given field

- `Var, VarP`   Estimates the variance

The following example produces a count of all employees' orders that have an Order Date between 9/1/94 and 12/31/94 (see Figure 4.9):

```
SELECT Orders.EmployeeID, Count(Orders.EmployeeID) AS [Number of Orders]
FROM Orders
WHERE (((Orders.OrderDate) Between #9/1/94# And #12/31/94#))
GROUP BY Orders.EmployeeID
ORDER BY Count(Orders.EmployeeID) DESC;
```

Figure 4.9.

Using the Count *function.*

The next query shows an example of the `Avg`, `Min`, and `Max` functions. It queries the `SupplierID` field for an average, minimum, and maximum (see Figure 4.10):

```
SELECT Products.SupplierID, Avg(Products.UnitPrice) AS [Average Unit
➥Price], Min(Products.UnitPrice) AS [Minimum Price], Max(Products.Unit
➥Price) AS [Maximum Price]
```

```
FROM Products
GROUP BY Products.SupplierID
ORDER BY Avg(Products.UnitPrice) DESC;
```

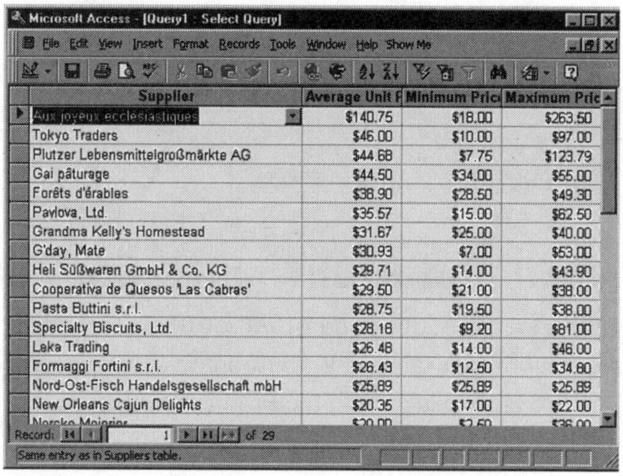

FIGURE 4.10.

Using the Avg,
Min, *and* Max
functions.

Structuring SQL-92

As explained at the beginning of this chapter, Access contains elements of the SQL-92 language. This section looks at some of the SQL-92 commands and demonstrates some ways to use this robust dialect.

The INNER JOIN Command

Following is the syntax for the INNER JOIN command:

```
FROM table1 INNER JOIN table2 ON table1.field1 = table2.field2
```

In Jet SQL, the INNER JOIN (also know as an *equi-join*) command is used after the FROM command in a multitable query. It's used to specify how and where Access 97 should attempt to join tables on a common field or fields. The query returns a record wherever the fields match in the indicated tables. The fields don't need to have the same name, but they do need to be of the same datatype; for example, a field that has a datatype of Text can join only with another text field. It can't join with a field that has a datatype of Number.

The following query selects all combinations of Categories and Products records that JOIN on Category ID (see Figure 4.11):

```
SELECT DISTINCTROW CategoryName, ProductName
FROM Categories
INNER JOIN Products ON Categories.[CategoryID] = Products.[CategoryID];
```

4

ACCESS 97 AND
PROGRAMMING
IN SQL

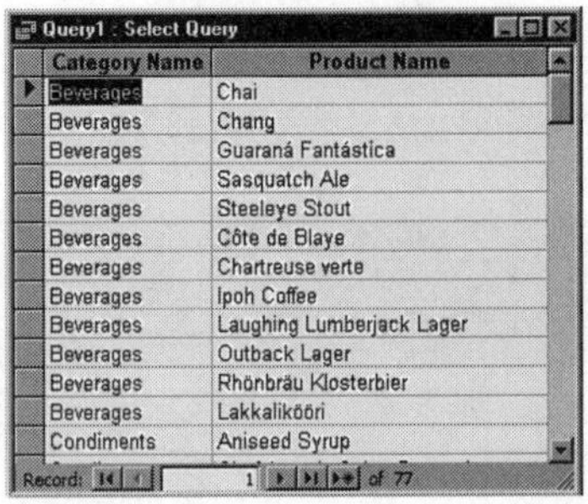

FIGURE 4.11.

A query showing the use of INNER JOIN.

The LEFT JOIN and RIGHT JOIN Commands

Two other types of joins are LEFT JOIN and RIGHT JOIN. These types of joins result in what is called an *outer join*. For example, if you wanted to return all records from Categories, even if there is no match with the Products table, you would enter this:

```
SELECT DISTINCTROW Categories.[Category Name], Products.[Product Name]
FROM Categories
LEFT JOIN Products ON Categories.[Category ID] = Products.[Category ID];
```

If you wanted the opposite—that is, to return all the records from Products, even if there is no match with the Categories table—you would use a RIGHT JOIN, as shown in the following:

```
SELECT DISTINCTROW Categories.[Category Name], Products.[Product Name]
FROM Categories
RIGHT JOIN Products ON Categories.[Category ID] = Products.[Category ID];
```

Using Expressions

The capability to use expressions in SQL statements is a very powerful feature that enables you to perform analysis and calculations within the statement itself.

The syntax of the statement and the placement of the expressions vary with the type of expression or the calculation you're trying to perform.

The following example returns the company name and dollar amount of items ordered in which the sum is greater than $1,000 (see Figure 4.12):

```
SELECT CompanyName, Sum([UnitPrice]*[Quantity]) AS OrderAmount
FROM Customers
INNER JOIN (Orders INNER JOIN [Order Details] ON Orders.OrderID =
➡[Order Details].OrderID)
ON Customers.CustomerID = Orders.CustomerID
GROUP BY Customers.CompanyName
HAVING (((Sum([UnitPrice]*[Quantity]))>1000));
```

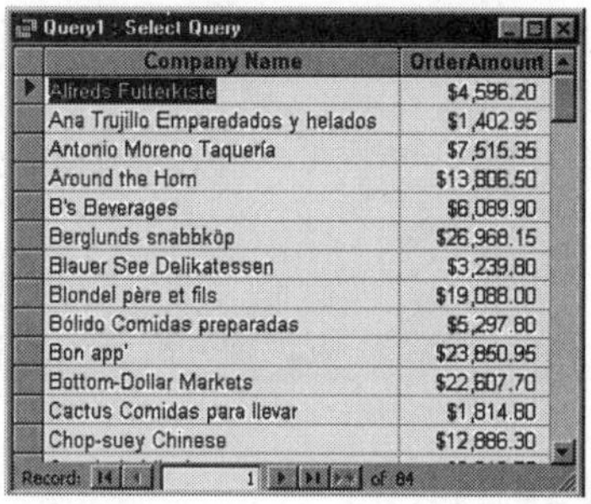

4

ACCESS 97 AND
PROGRAMMING
IN SQL

FIGURE 4.12.

A query result using expressions in a SQL statement.

The TRANSFORM Statement

The TRANSFORM statement is used to create crosstab queries. It's a very effective tool for summarizing data that compacts and groups your records in a spreadsheet-style format.

This is the syntax for the TRANSFORM statement:

```
TRANSFORM aggfunction
selectstatement
PIVOT pivotfield [IN (value1[, value2[, ...]])]
```

The TRANSFORM command must be the first statement in your SQL string. The TRANSFORM statement is followed by an aggregate function, such as Avg, Count, or Sum. Next is the SELECT statement, which can be any standard SELECT statement with optional WHERE and GROUP BY clauses. Following the SELECT statement is the PIVOT statement. The *pivotfield* value is where you specify a field to be used for creating column headings used in the returning recordset. If, for example, you wanted a crosstab showing a sum of all employees' sales for the year summed by quarter, you would pivot on the OrderDate field, which would create four columns, one column for each quarter. If you wanted to show a sales sum for only those employees hired in a specific month or two, you could restrict the *pivotfield* value to create headings from fixed values (*value1*, *value2*) listed in the optional IN clause.

The following query shows quarterly sales for each employee, with a column totaling all sales by employee (see Figure 4.13):

```
TRANSFORM Sum([Order Details].[UnitPrice]*[Quantity]) AS [The Value]
SELECT Employees.LastName, Sum([Order Details].[UnitPrice]*[Quantity])
AS [Total For Year]
FROM (Employees INNER JOIN Orders ON Employees.EmployeeID =
➡Orders.EmployeeID)
INNER JOIN [Order Details] ON Orders.OrderID = [Order Details].OrderID
GROUP BY Employees.LastName
PIVOT "Qtr " & Format([OrderDate],"q");
```

FIGURE 4.13.

A crosstab query result using the TRANSFORM *statement.*

Last Name	Total For Year	Qtr 1	Qtr 2	Qtr 3	Qtr 4
► Buchanan	$75,587.75	$32,010.00	$10,616.50	$14,978.20	$17,963.05
Callahan	$133,301.03	$38,003.95	$48,563.56	$21,568.45	$25,165.07
Davolio	$202,143.71	$55,769.48	$60,424.25	$39,255.33	$46,694.65
Dodsworth	$82,964.00	$28,268.65	$19,589.70	$10,672.80	$24,432.85
Fuller	$177,749.26	$49,729.00	$70,719.11	$20,426.10	$36,875.05
King	$141,295.99	$31,927.95	$58,712.30	$16,559.05	$34,096.69
Leverling	$213,051.30	$88,685.59	$73,193.85	$19,417.95	$31,753.91
Peacock	$250,187.45	$96,788.80	$52,791.75	$43,763.39	$56,843.51
Suyama	$78,198.10	$20,562.91	$22,246.64	$14,694.85	$20,693.70

Record: |◄ ◄ | 1 | ► | ►I | ►* | of 9

The PARAMETERS Declaration

The PARAMETERS declaration makes a query more reusable by allowing the user to enter parameter values for certain fields in the query. This can dramatically reduce the number of queries the developer needs to create and maintain.

Here is the syntax for the PARAMETERS declaration:

```
PARAMETERS name datatype [, name datatype [, ...]]
```

Like the TRANSFORM command, the PARAMETERS declaration must be the first statement in your SQL string. Following the declaration, enter a unique but meaningful name variable and a datatype, such as Text or DateTime. You can specify additional parameters by using a comma between them.

For example, if you have queries that are used to create mailing lists of customers but you want to specify which city the customers live in, instead of creating a query for every city (even if you did know them all), you could create a single PARAMETERS query like this (see Figure 4.14):

```
PARAMETERS [Enter City] Text;
SELECT *
FROM  Employees
WHERE City=[Enter City];
```

FIGURE 4.14.

A PARAMETERS *query result.*

Now each time this query is run, a parameter will be inserted, either from within your code or by a parameter-input dialog box, and the recordset returned will include only the records you specified.

The UNION Query

UNION queries combine fields from tables or queries into one field. This is actually an operation rather than a command, and it is performed on two or more tables or queries. The combined tables or queries must contain an equal number of fields. (They can be of different datatypes, however.)

This is the syntax for a UNION query:

[TABLE] *query1* UNION [ALL] [TABLE] *query2* [UNION [ALL] [TABLE] *queryn*
➥[...]]

> **TIP**
>
> UNION queries, by default, return unique records only. (This is similar to using DISTINCTROW in a SELECT query.) If you want your query to include *all* records, you must include the ALL predicate.

If you wanted to create a list of names and phone numbers, including the type of contact, for all companies in the Shippers and Suppliers tables, you would enter the following statements (see Figure 4.15):

```
SELECT CompanyName, Phone, "Shipper" AS [Contact Type]
FROM Shippers
UNION SELECT CompanyName, Phone, "Suppliers"
FROM Suppliers
ORDER BY CompanyName;
```

FIGURE 4.15.

A UNION query result.

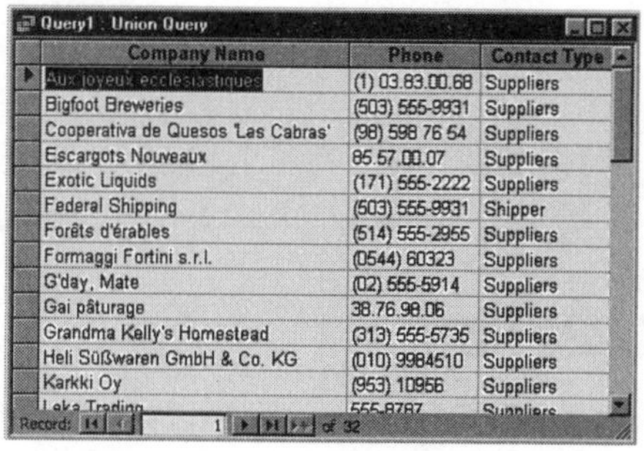

Company Name	Phone	Contact Type
Aux joyeux ecclésiastiques	(1) 03.83.00.68	Suppliers
Bigfoot Breweries	(503) 555-9931	Suppliers
Cooperativa de Quesos 'Las Cabras'	(98) 598 76 54	Suppliers
Escargots Nouveaux	85.57.00.07	Suppliers
Exotic Liquids	(171) 555-2222	Suppliers
Federal Shipping	(503) 555-9931	Shipper
Forêts d'érables	(514) 555-2955	Suppliers
Formaggi Fortini s.r.l.	(0544) 60323	Suppliers
G'day, Mate	(02) 555-5914	Suppliers
Gai pâturage	38.76.98.06	Suppliers
Grandma Kelly's Homestead	(313) 555-5735	Suppliers
Heli Süßwaren GmbH & Co. KG	(010) 9984510	Suppliers
Karkki Oy	(953) 10956	Suppliers
Leka Trading	555-8787	Suppliers

4

Data-Definition Queries

Data-definition language (DDL) queries are used to create new data objects or to modify existing ones. With the various DDL commands, you can create new tables and indexes or change (ALTER) an existing table by adding fields. You can also delete (DROP) tables and indexes.

> **NOTE**
>
> Access 97 implemented DDL with its own Jet database engine only. You can't use DDL queries in database types other than Access. For other databases, you can use the DAO method of creating and modifying data objects.

How to Write a DDL Query

Writing a DDL query is a little different from writing a normal SELECT query. This process requires a couple of extra steps:

1. Open a new query by clicking the Queries tab in the Database window, and then clicking New.
2. In the New Query dialog box, click Design View, and then click OK.
3. Click Close in the Show Table dialog box. (Don't add any tables or queries.)
4. Select Query | SQL Specific | Data Definition.
5. Enter the SQL statement for your data-definition query.
6. When you've finished, run the query by clicking the Run (!) button on the toolbar. (You can't use Datasheet view when using a DDL query; doing so produces an error dialog box.)

Here is an example of using the DDL statement to create a table:

```
CREATE TABLE UnleashedDemo
(Field1 TEXT,
Field2 TEXT,
Field3 INTEGER
CONSTRAINT PrimaryKey
PRIMARY KEY);
```

Crosstab Queries

Crosstab queries were discussed briefly in the preceding chapter. This chapter takes the discussion of crosstab queries to the next level.

The purpose of a crosstab query is to perform a consolidation process on sections of data that intersect and to give summary information on that data. The data appears in a two-dimensional array or matrix with mathematical operations being performed at each intersection. The word *crosstab* comes from the phrase *cross tabulation*, which is the action executed by the crosstab query. Basically, a crosstab is the method by which a relational database can display data in a spreadsheet-like manner.

In the past, crosstab queries were difficult for a novice user to understand and execute. Today, the Crosstab Query Wizard gives the novice the ability to create complex crosstab queries very easily. In this chapter, you will use the Crosstab Query Wizard to create simple crosstab queries, you will create crosstab queries without the wizard, and lastly you will add some complexity to the crosstab query quickly and easily. By the end of this section, crosstab queries shouldn't pose any problems for the developer who wants to create crosstabs without the guidance of the wizard. For all the examples in this chapter, you will use the sample Northwind database that ships with Access 97.

For the first example, say that you want to create a query that shows employee sales by month for 1995. To do this, you need to get the order date from the Orders table as well as the unit price and quantity data from the Order Details table.

NOTE

Only one table or query can be accessed from the Crosstab Query Wizard. If two or more tables are needed for a crosstab query, you have two options. First, you can cancel the wizard and create a query based on the number of tables needed for a crosstab and then run the wizard again and base it on the newly created query. Second, you can go directly into a blank query and create the crosstab from there.

To get around this, you first have to create a simple query that joins both tables—or in this case, you can leverage off of an existing query. Open the Orders Details Extended query in design mode. Choose Query | Show Table and add the Orders table. Next, double-click the fields OrderDate and CustomerID in the field list for the Orders table. This action adds these two columns from the Orders table to the query. Next, save the query and exit from query design mode.

Now you're ready to get started. To start the Crosstab Wizard, choose Query | New | Crosstab Query Wizard.

The wizard, displayed in Figure 4.16, shows an example layout of the final crosstab. A crosstab has three major parts: Row Headers, the Column Header, and the Value. The Value is simply the result to be calculated at the intersection (that is, total/sum of sales). At least one field or function must be chosen for the Column Header, the Row Header,

4

ACCESS 97 AND
PROGRAMMING
IN SQL

and the Value. Up to three fields can be chosen for the Row Headers, and only one field can be chosen for the Column Header and the Value.

FIGURE 4.16.

The Crosstab Query Wizard.

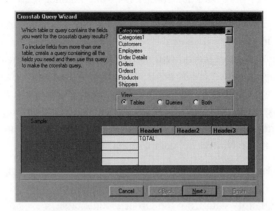

> ### TIP
>
> If more than one output field is listed as a Row Header, the fields should appear in the grid the same way they are to appear in the datasheet. For example, if the desired result were to show monthly sales by employee, customer, and product, these would be the three Row Headers, and they would have to be chosen in the order from the topmost grouping to the lowermost. The Datasheet view of that crosstab query would list all the employees in the left-most column of the array. For each employee, all of his customers would be listed. For each customer, all of her products would be listed.

To produce the desired results, the employee names will be placed in the Row Header section, the month will be placed at the Column Header, and the Value will be the extended price (see Figure 4.17). Moving forward, choose the Orders Details Extended query. The wizard then asks for up to three fields to use at the row level. Choose the EmployeeID field. Next, the wizard asks for the column field. Because the order date will determine which month should be displayed in the Column Headers, choose the OrderDate field. Because OrderDate has a date data type, Access then asks for the interval you want to use. The possible intervals are Year, Quarter, Month, Date, and Date/Time. Choose Month and then click Next. Finally, you need to choose the data to be summarized at the intersection and decide whether to add a grand total column. Go ahead and choose the SUM aggregate function, choose the Extended Price field, leave the Yes, include row sums box set to Yes, and click Finish. (Aggregate functions are described later in this chapter.)

FIGURE 4.17.

The crosstab result displays customer sales by month.

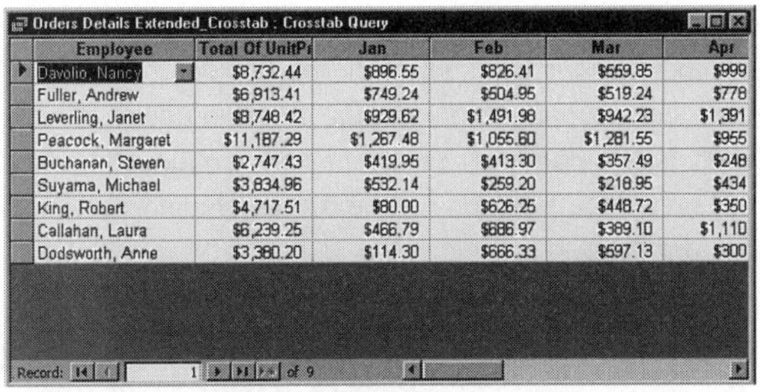

Employee	Total Of UnitP|	Jan	Feb	Mar	Apr
Davolio, Nancy	$8,732.44	$896.55	$826.41	$559.85	$999
Fuller, Andrew	$6,913.41	$749.24	$504.95	$519.24	$778
Leverling, Janet	$8,748.42	$929.62	$1,491.98	$942.23	$1,391
Peacock, Margaret	$11,187.29	$1,267.48	$1,055.60	$1,281.55	$955
Buchanan, Steven	$2,747.43	$419.95	$413.30	$357.49	$248
Suyama, Michael	$3,834.96	$532.14	$259.20	$218.95	$434
King, Robert	$4,717.51	$80.00	$626.25	$448.72	$350
Callahan, Laura	$6,239.25	$466.79	$686.97	$389.10	$1,110
Dodsworth, Anne	$3,380.20	$114.30	$666.33	$597.13	$300

Here are a couple of quick things to note from the crosstab result in Figure 4.17. Although you didn't choose to sort the Column Headings, the wizard went ahead and did it for you. Finally, the wizard didn't give you the option of limiting the data you needed, so you ended up with all sales from 1994 to 1996. All of these problems will be corrected shortly. Because everything you do from this point forward will be done from the query design form. Go back and see how this same crosstab result would be created without the wizard.

When you use the Select Query Design view, you won't have the same two-table limitation, so an entirely new query will be created. Create a new query and go into the Design view. Add the Orders table and the Order Details table to the query. Next, add the EmployeeID and the Order Date fields to the grid. For the last column, you want to sum the Quantity and UnitPrice fields to get the extended price. On the empty third column, type the following:

```
ExtendedPrice: (UnitPrice*Quantity)
```

At this point, this is still only a SELECT query. If it is executed, it will print a long, simple list of all items in the Order Details table with the extended prices. To turn it into a crosstab query, choose Query | Crosstab Query, as shown in Figure 4.18.

Once the query is converted to a SELECT query, the design views will be almost identical with the one exception that the Show section will be replaced by Crosstab (an example of the Crosstab Query Design view is displayed later in Figure 4.20). Because Access knows that it will have to group data to produce the desired results, it assumes that all fields need to be grouped. For this example, the ExtendedPrice field should be summed and not grouped. The drop-down box on the Total property now has all the aggregate functions added to it in addition to the GROUP BY value. Go ahead and select [Sum].

4

ACCESS 97 AND PROGRAMMING IN SQL

Next, change the crosstab properties of each of the fields to their respective values (EmployeeID = Row Header, OrderDate = Column Header, ExtendedPrice = Value). The last step to make this identical to the crosstab created with the Crosstab Wizard is to add the grand total column. Move to the empty fourth column and enter [TotalExtended: ExtendedPrice]. Then choose SUM for the total property and [Row Header] for the crosstab property. Now run the crosstab query. (Choose the ! icon.) This should return the error Too many crosstab header columns. This error occurred because you didn't create the function for the order date and because there were more than 483 distinct order dates.

FIGURE 4.18.

Preparing to turn the SELECT *query into a crosstab query.*

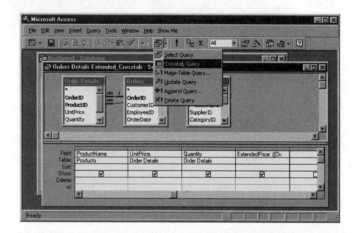

NOTE

Although it would be almost impossible to read a crosstab result with more than 50 Column Headers, Access allows you to have as many as 483 Column Headers.

To correct this problem, go back to Design view and modify the field property for order date and enter the following:

[Month: FORMAT(order date,'mmm')]

Run the query again. Now the result looks almost identical to the result obtained with the Crosstab Wizard, with the exception of the sorting of the months. Getting the months to display in their correct order is a little tricky.

Simply changing the sort property to [Ascending] will not help because this change sorts the month in alphabetical order. To get the desired sort order, go back to the Design view and highlight the entire Month column. Then choose View | Properties, or right-click to bring up the properties window (see Figure 4.19). Enter the following value in the Column Headings property:

["JAN","FEB","MAR","APR","MAY","JUN","JUL","AUG","SEP","OCT","NOV","DEC"]

FIGURE 4.19.

Column Headings can have a specific sort order.

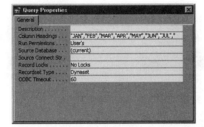

Now you have completed everything needed to turn a select query into the same results as the Crosstab Wizard provided. As you can see from all the modifications needed to turn the select query into a crosstab query, it is much more efficient to use the Crosstab Wizard to begin all crosstab queries. The only time the SELECT query should be used to do the initial crosstab design is when you want join one or more tables to produce the desired results. Figure 4.20 shows the completed crosstab query in Design view.

FIGURE 4.20.

The completed crosstab query screen and the result of the query.

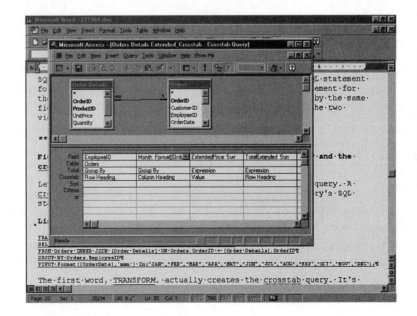

4

ACCESS 97 AND
PROGRAMMING
IN SQL

You might ask, "What really makes a crosstab query work?" To answer that question, it's necessary to look at the SQL statement that is created during a crosstab query. Figure 4.21 shows two views of the SQL statement for the query. The view on the left is the SQL statement for the select query. The view on the right is the SQL statement for the crosstab query. Both views have the same tables joined by the same field with the same output. The major differences between the two views are the words TRANSFORM and PIVOT.

FIGURE 4.21.

The major differences between the select query and the crosstab query can be seen in the SQL statement.

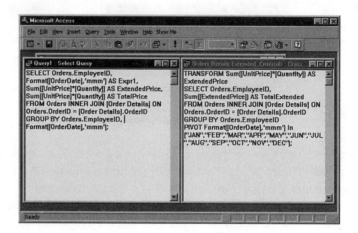

Look at and dissect the SQL statement for a crosstab query. A crosstab query has several distinct parts. The crosstab query's SQL statement is shown in Listing 4.1.

LISTING 4.1. THE CROSSTAB QUERY SQL STATEMENT.

```
TRANSFORM SUM([UnitPrice]*[Quantity]) AS ExtendedPrice
SELECT Orders.EmployeeID, SUM([ExtendedPrice]) AS TotalExtended
FROM Orders INNER JOIN [Order Details] ON Orders.OrderID = [Order
Details].OrderID
GROUP BY Orders.EmployeeID
PIVOT Format([OrderDate],'mmm') In("JAN","FEB","MAR","APR","MAY","JUN",
"JUL","AUG","SEP","OCT","NOV","DEC");
```

The first word, TRANSFORM, actually creates the crosstab query. It's followed by the aggregate function. The aggregate function is the meat of the crosstab query. In the crosstab query's Design view, the aggregate function would be the field where the word Value appears in the Crosstab row of the query grid. In Listing 4.1, the aggregate function is SUM, followed by a reference to a field and its table—in this case, the result of

`Quantity * UnitPrice` from the Order Details table. The most important thing to remember is that because there is only one possible intersection in a crosstab, only one column or aggregate function can be used in the Column Header, whereas many aggregate functions can be used as Row Headers.

Summary

This chapter has given you a glimpse of the power and possibilities available to you using Jet SQL. In deciding how to make the best use of Jet SQL, the bottom line is this: If you're creating SQL Pass-through queries to an ODBC database, or queries that might be transferred to another SQL database, you must limit your queries to ANSI SQL. If, however, you're writing queries that will remain entirely in Access 97, the power and flexibility of Jet SQL with its enhanced SQL-92 features make it an excellent choice.

Optimizing Queries

CHAPTER 5

Expectations are made for every software application that's developed—expectations such as stability, ease of use, response in a certain amount of time, and so on. Sometimes, during the process of developing software, it is found that response-time expectations are not met. It becomes necessary to optimize an Access 97 query when it does not return results fast enough to meet the response-time expectation.

Most users want answers to their questions in a second or less. Waiting while the computer processes a query is often viewed as simply wasting time. This is often not a factor when a small amount of data is stored. However, it is a fact that queries take more time as more and more data is stored in a database. It is for this reason that optimizing queries is such an important issue—especially with larger databases.

> **NOTE**
>
> The more indexes you add, the longer your action queries can take. The other problem you can run into when working in a multiuser environment is record locking. The best way to add an index to a table is to play a little with the index and see which types of performance increases and decreases you start to see.

Using Indexes for Faster Queries

Two things that greatly affect the performance of queries are the design of the database schema and the selection of indexes that are used on each table. Although in many cases changing the schema may provide the greatest performance improvements, it's often too costly to change an application to reflect the schema change. This means that the only option you have left that can make an impact is to use indexes. By using an index on a table, the query now gains assistance from the index to sort the results.

Table indexes are usually relatively easy to add, modify, and remove. The main tasks involved in deploying indexes are analyzing query requirements and deciding which indexes are and are not necessary to provide the desired performance. Usage of indexes therefore provides the best way to tune database tables and queries for data access.

You can improve data access in your Access database by following these basic guidelines for indexing:

- All database tables must have a primary key. This is good practice for a number of reasons: Relational modeling theory mandates it, it makes clear the properties of a row that uniquely identify each row of a table, and it provides the fastest path to locate any record when its identifying properties are known in advance.

- Fields that are not part of the primary key and are frequently used for selecting records should be indexed. This is not important when only a few dozen records or less are present in a table, but it's critical when records in a table number in the thousands or more.

- Use direct comparisons of primary keys and indexed fields. This means that the Field designator of a search criteria must contain only the name of the field and cannot contain a computed value.

- Do not "automatically" add indexes other than the primary key to a table. Indexes cost computer time and power to maintain, and it is possible to over-index a table.

- Absorb one index into another whenever possible. For instance, a `Customer` table may require rows to be selected based on STATE in one instance, and STATE and COUNTY in another. There is no need to create the STATE index because the STATE and COUNTY index can be used to satisfy both requirements.

- A field that is part of a multi-field index can only be used as part of the index if the fields that precede it in the index are also designated. For instance, if an index contains a `callback_flag` and a `callback_date`, this index cannot be used if only the `callback_date` is used as a selection criteria.

- All records that are accessed for a single record SELECT, UPDATE, or DELETE should be addressed by the primary key. This is done to establish standards to provide online transaction processing that executes in a few dozen milliseconds or less.

- When a dependent table is joined with a referenced independent table, the independent table should be referenced by its key. It's simple: Primary keys have been created on all tables, and all you have to do is take advantage of them.

- Records that are selected as part of a frequently used single table list or grid should be accessed through an index. Again, this is not important when only a few dozen records or less are present in a table, but it's critical when records in a table number in the thousands or more.

- When filtered records are selected from the join of a dependent and an independent table and the filtering is based on information contained in the independent table, the dependent table should be indexed on its reference to the independent table.

- Each query that involves the joining of four or more tables should be carefully analyzed for indexing and joining. Keep in mind that the number of join combinations available for a query is the factorial of the number of tables being joined. When two tables are joined, there are only two ways to join them. When three tables are joined, there are six ways to join them. When a query joins six tables, it means that there are 720 different ways to join these tables! What is worse is that when several of these tables are large, there are probably more than 700 inefficient ways to join the tables and only a few efficient ways to join them. It pays to be careful!

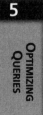

- When two non-related tables are joined based on common elements, both tables should be indexed based on these same common elements. This type of join is particularly dangerous to performance because the number of logical records processed is the cross-product of records selected from each.

The Callback Database

The Callback application provides the capability to schedule and log calls to customers or individuals. The application is centered around the Callback table and the queries shown in Figure 5.1. The other tables—IDList, callback_comments, callback_dates, first_names, and last_callback—are only used for populating the Callback table with test data.

FIGURE 5.1.

The Callback *table.*

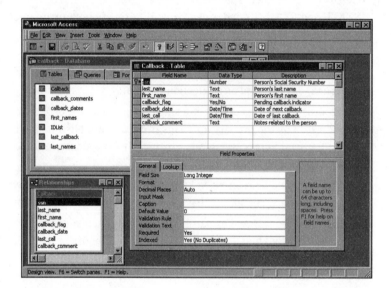

The general requirements of the Callback application are

- All callback records will be assigned with customer identifiers, which range from 100000000 through 1999999999.
- The Callback table will hold up to one million records.
- All queries should respond in one second or less.
- The Callback database size may be up to 120MB.
- All records with a pending callback have Yes in the pending_callback field.
- All records with a pending callback have a non-null callback_date field.

Preparing Response Time Test

The first step in preparing a proper test of the Callback application is to load the callback table with 1,000,000 records so that the response time can be simulated for a full database load. Several queries have been created to provide the capability to load simulation records into the database.

The second step in preparing the Callback database is to run the genIDList query several times until enough records are created that can be used for loading the Callback table. This query starts with one record and keeps the IDList table doubling until the proper number of records have been created.

Next, the genCallback query is run to append records to the Callback table. This query prompts for the total number of records to be created. One million records will fit in approximately 100MB of disk space. If this is too much disk space, simply scale back the test.

After genCallback creates the Callback table, the setLastCallback and setCallback records complete the test data by updating a few dozen of the callback records to contain callback and last callback information. Once this is done, the Callback table is ready for testing.

The first query in the Callback application needs to meet the following requirements:

- The getCallback query needs to provide the capability to retrieve callback records by customer ID.

- The query must return all Callback table information for the record that exactly matches the designated customer ID.

- Although most users have to deal with all of the customers, certain users only deal with customers with keys in the range of 100000001 through 100000999. These customers only want to enter 1–999 for their keys.

- It is acceptable to use a separate query for the group that wants to use the abbreviated keys. (We will name this query getCallbackByID.)

- Both of these queries will be used on a more-or-less constant basis to retrieve callback records.

Figure 5.2 shows the getCallback and the getCallbackByID queries. Try executing getCallback with a Customer ID of 100000001. This query returns its results immediately. Now try getCallbackByID with a Customer ID of 1. If only a few hundred records are present in the table, this query will also return its results immediately. However, with one million rows, this query may take a minute or several minutes. The second query is not optimized.

FIGURE 5.2.

The getCallback
and
getCallbackByID
queries.

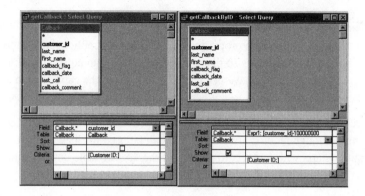

Sometimes the Performance Analyzer tool will provide suggestions to improve query performance. In this case, the Performance Analyzer has no suggestions. We must look elsewhere for answers.

The first step in improving the performance of a query is to inspect the query and look for potential problems. The Index Guidelines or some other troubleshooting guidelines can serve as a checklist for finding problems with queries. This is how we will proceed to review queries for optimization.

First, our table has a primary key that we are using for both of our search criteria. The second guideline does not apply because we are dealing with the primary key. However, note that in the getCallback query, the customer_id is isolated as the search field. This is not true for the getCallbackByID query, in which the search field is a computation of customer_id minus 100000000. This means that the primary key is indirectly referenced, which is why the query is slow.

Now change the getCallbackByID query so that the search field is customer_id and the criteria is 100000000 + [Customer ID:]. After this change is made, try running the query. It returns the data instantly.

The next requirement for the Callback application:

- The listByName query must provide the capability to retrieve callback records by name.
- This query must return all records that have exact matches on both last and first name.
- The list must be sorted according to last name and then first name.
- This query will be used on a more-or-less constant basis to retrieve callback records.

Figure 5.3 shows the `listByName` query. Try executing this query with a last name of Adams and a first name of Jennifer. It can take up to several minutes to retrieve the information. How can this query be optimized? As before, the query analyzer has no suggestions to improve performance, so let's inspect the query and proceed down the Index Guidelines.

FIGURE 5.3.

The `listByName` *query.*

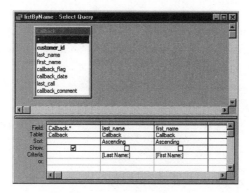

The first guideline does not apply because we already have the primary key based on the customer ID. The second guideline is for frequently used queries. Because `listByName` is used on a more-or-less constant basis, we will add a non-unique index to improve the performance of this query.

Create the `nameIndex` on the `Callback` table, as shown in Figure 5.4. Try running the query again after the index has been built. Adding `nameIndex` to the `Callback` table allows records to be returned by the `listByName` query almost instantly.

FIGURE 5.4.

The Callback index.

The next requirement to be implemented for the Callback application is

- The `listAllCallbacks` query lists all callback records that have pending callbacks.

- The first thing that designates that a Callback record has a pending callback record is that the Callback Flag is set on.

- The second thing that designates that a Callback record has a pending callback is that the `Callback Date` field is non-null.

- Records listed by the `listAllCallbacks` query should be sorted according to the date of the callback.

- This query is used on a more-or-less constant basis to retrieve callback records.

Figure 5.5 shows the `listAllCallbacks` query. This query initially takes about 10 to 20 seconds. It needs to be optimized. Because this query is used often, it needs a non-unique similar to the previous requirement. Figure 5.6 shows the addition of the `callbackIndex`.

FIGURE 5.5.

The `listAllCallbacks` *query.*

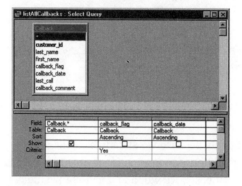

FIGURE 5.6.

The creation of `callbackIndex`.

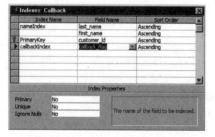

Retry the `listAllCallbacks` query after the new index is created. Information should now be displayed instantly. This query is now optimized and meets the requirements.

Let's now consider the requirements for the `listCallbacksByDate` query:

- The `listCallbacksByDate` query is to return callback records based on a given date.

- This query is to return all records on or before the input date.

- Records are to be displayed by the callback date.
- This query is used on a more-or-less constant basis to retrieve callback records.

Figure 5.7 shows the `listCallbacksByDate` query. You've probably already guessed that this query initially does not run fast enough and needs to be optimized. This is correct. You also might have guessed that you need to add an index based on the callback date—after all, that is what we are working on, right? Wrong.

FIGURE 5.7.

The
`listCallbacksBy-`
`Date` *query.*

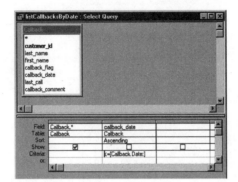

Look a little farther down the Index Guidelines and find where it talks about not automatically creating indexes, and also where it talks about absorbing indexes into other indexes whenever possible. Next, reexamine the general requirements given for the Callback application. Look at the last two general requirements. Because there is some overlap in these two statements, it is possible to combine the index requirements of the `ListAllCallbacks` and the `ListCallbacksByDate` queries into a single index.

The modification to `callbackIndex`, shown in Figure 5.8, consists of simply adding the `callback_date` field to the index. This index should not be capable of providing the required response time for the `listCallbacksByDate` query. However, first we have to make sure that the `listAllCallbacks` query still works! This is simply a matter of good discipline. Never assume that something is going to work. *Test it!*

After retrying the `listAllCallbacks` query and verifying that it still works properly, we proceed with completing the optimization of `listCallbacksByDate` (see Figure 5.9).

FIGURE 5.8.

Modifications to
`callbackIndex`.

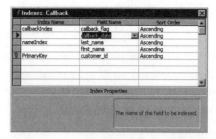

FIGURE 5.9.

Modifications to
`listCallbacksBy-`
`Date` *query*.

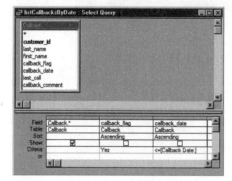

The most important point to remember about this query work is that the query must include the `callback_flag` criteria. If this criteria is omitted, performance will not be improved because a piece of the index that is more important than the callback date has been omitted.

NOTE

One of the features of running on a Windows NT workstation using the NTFS file format is that compressed files can be used for the databases. Database queries run noticeably slower when you use compressed files. If the space saved is significant, it might be worth it to take this modest performance hit.

A side effect of using a compressed database under NT is that when the database is compacted, a new copy of the database is created that is not compressed. This can cause surprise situations in which the database takes up more space after compacting than before it was compacted. It also means that if you want to keep the file compressed, you need to manually recompress the file anytime the database is compacted. In general, *compressed files should not be used*.

The next application that we will look at is the Customer Credit application, shown in Figure 5.10.

FIGURE 5.10.

The Customer Credit data model.

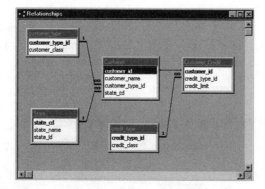

General requirements for the Customer Credit application are

- There are approximately two million customer records on file.
- Associated with the two million customer records are about 600,000 credit records.
- Customers are divided geographically into the 50 states and the District of Columbia.
- Customers are also divided into approximately 11 customer classes.
- Credit records are divided into approximately 13 credit classes.
- All customer credit transactions should be processed in one second or less.
- There are a number of maintenance, operational, and report functions included in the Customer Credit application. All of these meet performance objectives except for the `listCreditCustomers` query, which at times is somewhat sluggish.
- The Customer Credit application presently takes a little less than 300MB of disk space.

WARNING

The Customer Credit application takes up approximately 300MB of disk storage. It also takes a considerable amount of virtual memory and time to set up the Customer Credit database. It may be best to scale back the following application simulation and just get the flavor of it.

The procedure for setting up the Customer Credit database records is similar to the procedure used in the Callback application. First, run the genIDList query a number of times to create the proper number of identifiers for the Customer Credit table. In this example, a little over two million rows were created. Next, run the genCustomers query to load records into the Customer table. Finally, run the genCustomerCredit query to load the Customer Credit table records. This takes 25–50 minutes for two million customer records. Once this is completed, the database is ready for testing.

The listCreditCustomers query is shown in Figure 5.11.

FIGURE 5.11.

The listCredit-Customers *query.*

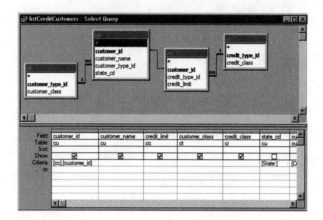

The requirements for this query are

- The listCreditCustomers query is to select records according to state, customer class, and credit class.

- The listCreditCustomers query is to display a list of all records that exactly match the selection criteria.

- Fields displayed by the listCreditCustomers window include the customer ID, the customer name, the credit limit, the name of the customer class, and the name of the credit class.

- Records should be displayed in order of customer name.

- This query should return its information in a second or less. Presently, it takes two to 10 seconds for this query to execute.

- This query is used about only a few dozen times per day.

Try executing the listCreditCustomers query with CO for the state, 7 for the customer class, and 2 for the credit class. The first time the query is executed, it takes about 10–13 seconds. Subsequent requests for the same Credit Customer list take only 1–3 seconds. This is frequently observed because the data becomes cached. Now look at the information being returned. Notice that the Customer Class and Credit Class information is all the same. It is more efficient to remove this repeated information from the query and retrieve it through some other means. This might or might not cure the performance problem, but it is still a good idea to modify the query in this fashion.

Figure 5.12 shows the `listCreditCustomers` query after modifications have been made. Because we no longer need to display the Customer Class and Credit Class columns, we can remove the joins to the tables associated with these columns. Retry the query after the modifications are complete. The query is still inconsistent and not quite fast enough. But now where do we go to improve performance? The Performance Analyzer offers no suggestions. It sure seems like you ought to be able to display these records faster.

FIGURE 5.12.

The modified `listCredit-Customers` *query.*

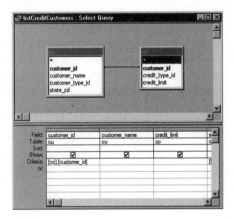

There *is* a way to improve the performance of this query. If you modify the data model such that the three filtering criteria—state, customer type, and credit type—all reside in one table, you can provide enough of a performance improvement to allow the query to execute instantly. However, this may not be an option that you can dictate. Times like these will typically require a trade-off. Typically, there will be a number of changes that will be required outside of the scope of the `listCreditCustomers` query—often, changes imposed on users who might not have any interest in the `listCreditCustomers` query or similar queries. The users have to decide if it is worth the performance improvement to force modifications onto other modules. Here we will assume that the changes are approved so that we can continue.

5

OPTIMIZING
QUERIES

The initial `Customer` table record population is 2,000,000 records. Of these, 1 in 51 will be retained based on the state. This reduces the record population by 2,000,000/51=39,216. Of these 39,216, 1 in 11 will be retained based on the customer type designation. This further reduces the Customer record population by 39216/11=3,565. Because no further filtering takes place based on `Customer` table information, this means that 3,565 Customer records must be processed.

Next, these 3,565 Customer records are joined with the associated Customer Credit records. However, only one of three Customer records have associated Customer Credit records. This means that the 3,565 Customer records will be joined with 3,565/3 =1,188 Customer Credit records. Of these 1,188 Customer Credit records, only one of 13 will be retained based on the credit class. This means that we will end up with a record population of 1,188/13=91. These 91 records will be joined with 91 Credit Type and 91 Customer Type records. The total number of records read is on the order of 3,565+1,188+91+91=4,935. About 5,000 records were read.

Next, we eliminated the join and the columns associated with the Credit Type and Customer Type records. However, this was not really much of a reduction because we still have to go through the entire process of filtering through the Customer and Customer Credit records. Eliminating the Credit Type and Customer Type records reduces our record population to 3,565+1,188=4,753. A rather modest reduction.

Let's suppose that we move the credit type information from the `Customer Credit` table to the `Customer` table. We store a value in the `Credit Type` field when the Customer has an associated Customer Credit record, and we store null when there is no associated Customer Credit record. I freely admit that this is a design compromise, but I also submit that this compromise will improve performance.

If all three filtering criteria are contained in the Customer record, filtering takes place only in the `Customer` table and we will be joining far fewer Customer records with far fewer Customer Credit records. The initial Customer record population is still 2,000,000. This is reduced by one in 51 due to state filtering. This reduces the record population by 2,000,000/51=39,216. This record population is reduced by one in 11 due to customer type filtering. This reduces the record population by 39,216/11=3,565. This record population is reduced by one in 13 due to credit type filtering. This reduces the record population by 3,565/13=274. These 274 Customer records will be joined with Customer Credit records. However, only 1 in 3 Customer records has an associated Customer Credit record. This means that 274/3=91 Customer Credit records will be read. The total number of records read is 274+91=365. We are reading only 1/13th the number of records that we were before. In fact, if our filtering were done on the Customer Credit record, we would only be reading 91+91=182 records. However, this would probably mean that we would duplicate data in both the Customer and Customer Credit tables. This is a much bigger design compromise than moving the credit class data to the Customer table. Therefore, we will stick with containing the filtering criteria in the Customer table.

Figure 5.13 displays the modified Customer Credit database. The Customer Credit table is no longer included because its data has been absorbed into the Customer table. We have denormalized in order to improve performance.

FIGURE 5.13.
*The modified
Customer Credit
database.*

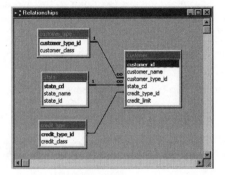

Figure 5.14 shows the new version of the listCreditCustomers query. This query has been completely stripped down. Initially, this table was the product of a four-table join. Now this query is basically just a table search based on three fields with the desired information being selected.

FIGURE 5.14.
*The modified
listCredit-
Customers query.*

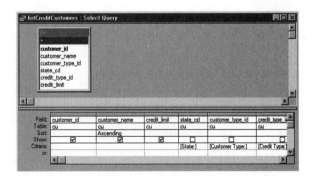

> **Warning**
>
> This database takes more space than the previous database and is even more tedious to load. It took me about 75 minutes to load this database, and it takes up about 330MB of disk space! In addition, I did not have enough memory to run the @ query without segmenting it into pieces. You may want to scale this down just out of self-preservation. Be on guard.

The process for populating the Customer database is similar to the previous process. First, run the genIDList query a number of times to create the desired number of key identifiers. Next, run genCustomers to create the Customer table records. Finally, run setCreditLimits to update the Customer table with credit information. The setCreditLimits query expects two parameters—Low ID Limit and High ID Limit. These parameters allow this procedure to be run in segments. This process takes a considerable amount of time.

How the Jet Engine Processes Queries

Technically, the Jet does not have a user interface. You use it via Microsoft Access. The Jet is a database engine and query processor with security and remote access. It is composed of a series of Dynamic Link Libraries (DLLs) that work together. The DLLs are as follow:

- The Jet DLL—The main engine program that executes requests for data.
- The Access Objects DLLs—A Jet component that gives a programmer access to the Jet engine in the form of Data Access Objects (DAOs).
- The External ISAM DLLs—Entry to Indexed Sequential Access Method (ISAM) format files.

The Jet Query engine, which is a component of the Jet engine, is a complex query processor that interprets and executes queries. It has four sections:

- Query Definition—Queries are defined through several different devices. The most common device is the QBE interface, which is available through the Query module of the Access database container. Another device is the SQL window, which is also available through the Query module of the Access database container. It can also be used as the control source for different controls on a form. The final device is the DAO language. It is better known as QueryDefs and uses standard SQL statements. However the query is devised, the SELECT statement is passed to the Jet Query Optimizer for compilation and optimization of the query.

- Query Compilation—In this section, the SQL string is compiled into an internal query object definition format. The parts of the string are parsed out, and the common parts are replaced with tokens.

- Query Optimization—This section takes the components of the compilation and chooses an optimum query execution strategy via algorithms. The parts of the query that are subject to optimization are the tables and joins. Here, *Rushmore* technology comes into play. Rushmore technology can work with one or more indexes, of which there are three types: the Index Intersection, the Index Union, and the Index Counts.

- Query Execution—After the query has been optimized and compiled, it is executed to return a dynaset or a snapshot. The difference between dynasets and snapshots is that dynasets can have their records edited, whereas snapshots are usually read-only recordsets.

The Jet Query engine processes the query by defining it, compiling it, optimizing it, and then executing it to return the desired result set.

Improving the Performance of the Jet Engine

The new Jet engine allows large queries to run faster. By taking the following steps, you can improve the performance of your queries while developing the database:

- Index all columns used in query joins.

- Use the primary keys instead of unique indexes because the primary key indexes disallow nulls. This way, the Jet Query Optimizer has additional join choices internally.

- Use unique indexes when primary keys are not possible. Non-unique indexes are not as accurate, statistically speaking, from the Jet's point of view.

- Reduce the number of columns in the resultset. Fewer columns are returned faster.

- Stay away from using complex expressions—for example, Immediate If (IIF) functions. When you're using nested queries, move any query that contains expressions to the last (highest) query.

- When counting records, use `Count(*)` as opposed to `Count ([ColumnName])`.
- Use `Between` operators rather than open-ended operators. For example, use `Between $1000 and $1500` rather than `>= $1000`.
- Table normalization causes the join strategies to execute more quickly.

Debugging Queries

Debugging is a software development activity that begins when the code of the first application module is completed, and continues until after an application is moved into production. The objective of any good development effort is to deliver a product that has no defects. The only way to do this is to have a solid systematic approach to testing and debugging.

All applications must be debugged. One of the biggest problems that I frequently encounter is timing when debugging is to take place. Remember this: The development of all applications takes time and therefore money, even if the application is just a simple game for you or your children to enjoy. Fixing software problems is a fact of life. The earlier in the life of an application that problems are detected through testing, the lesser the costs of debugging and correcting code. The best time to fix problems is during the design phase of an application, so that problems are fixed before any code is produced.

The most frequent source of query problems that I find on a day-to-day basis are

- System requirements that were omitted from the design and later turned out to be necessary—*scope creep*.
- Problems associated with the database model. Often this is a problem associated with some kind of scope creep.
- Problems associated with properly providing an environment that supports some of the more difficult query requirements of an application. The most frequent example of this is that report requirements are not accounted for when the data model is being developed. Joins associated with queries should not be much more than a handful of tables. Remember: If you have a query that has a 15-table join, there are about 15 factorial ways that these tables can be combined incorrectly—which is a huge number! Avoid this situation like the plague.
- Incomplete or no testing. This happens all the time. The good news is that many times you can simply look over someone's shoulder and have him step through a query, and he realizes on the spot which problems exist. This often is a management problem in which you need to complete code to meet a deadline.

- Not understanding the requirements. Often the requirements are documented poorly or not at all. I am presently working on a nightmare set of queries, in which I am supposed to improve the performance of a query for which I have no documentation, just code. How am I supposed to figure out what is wrong with it?

There are many other sources of problems. If you can think of it, it will probably happen. Regardless of why problems occur, it is your job as a developer to minimize these problems. Here are the suggested debugging strategies:

- Be single-minded about debugging. Every inch of code must be debugged. Nothing must remain untested. During unit development, use debuggers and print functions liberally.

- Make sure that all interfaces are debugged. This is the basis of integration testing. It is fine if a piece of an application works as a single unit, but each unit must be capable of talking to all of the other units. You must not only debug the code, but also the seams that exist between the various units of code.

- Make sure that all of the functions of the application work as a whole. This is the basis of systems testing.

- Never assume anything works. Test it! If there is any doubt about something, test it again!

- Seek help whenever you need it. The flipside of this is that you also need to be willing to give help. Promoting good teamwork makes any development better. It is better to take a few minutes of someone else's time than to spend hours on something with which you are not familiar. It helps to have some documentation prepared in advance if you are going to ask for someone else's help.

- Have a documented test plan. Develop test data and test cases wherever possible.

- Make sure that the target load of an application is understood and that the application is tested under circumstances that simulate that load.

- Document test results. Facts are your friends. When discussions about problems break out—and in any development effort, they will—it's much easier to find solutions when the participants have significant facts related to tests and debugging at their command.

- Strive to keep debug versions of all code. It can save your night, week, month...

Summary

This chapter covers information used for optimizing the performance of Access 97 queries. The Index Guidelines were introduced to serve as a basis for analyzing query performance and providing a standard query preflight checklist. Two applications were discussed in the light of these Index Guidelines to provide a model of analyzing application requirements, comparing the application requirements to actual performance measurements, and making modifications to database tables and queries where necessary to provide performance that meets performance objectives.

Also discussed was how the Jet SQL engine processes queries and how to improve the performance of the Jet engine. It was with these two topics in mind that the Index Guidelines were developed. The Index Guidelines provide the glue necessary to keep queries and the Jet engine working in harmony.

The earlier sections of this chapter emphasized analysis and testing, and the rest focused on debugging and testing. It was emphasized that the objective of all application development is to provide a bug-free application. The only way to accomplish this is to have a testing and debugging plan. Finally, only through testing, debugging, and analysis can a developer or a development manager form an opinion on an application's production-worthiness. These same facts also can be used to provide measurements of quality. After all, that is the central objective of query optimization: quality.

Creating a Powerful User Interface

PART

III

IN THIS PART

Creating
Interactive Forms

CHAPTER 6

This chapter discusses the range of form features, from the simple AutoForm Wizards through customization, controls and their uses, using Visual Basic code, handling multiple users, and using the Office 97 enhanced capabilities (Pivot Tables and Charts).

What's New in Access 97

Several new features are included in Access 97. These features are visible not only in the Toolbox, but also in the pull-down menus and the properties of objects for forms. The following list highlights some of those new features that will soon become commonplace for you:

- Hyperlinks. Allow users to jump to other objects, such as databases, word processors, and spreadsheets, via an intranet or the Internet.
- Tab control. Allows you to create tabbed forms. This is now integral to Access 97 and not the tab OCX.
- `Multi Row` property. Allows you to create multiple rows for tabbed forms.
- Tab fixed width and height. Allows you to control the width and height of tabbed forms.
- Style. Allows developers to choose whether their tabbed forms are actually tabs or buttons.
- Enhanced Toolbox. Displays more than 50 additional ActiveX tools available.
- ActiveX controls. Enhance a user's interaction with the form. In Access 95 and 2.0, these controls were referred to as OLE controls.
- Web toolbar. Allows you to place the Web toolbar on a form that launches the user to a Web page.
- `Has Module` property. States whether the form has a class module and is a new addition to the form's property sheet.
- `Toolbar` property. Allows you to display custom toolbars on forms.
- `Triple State` property. Is a new property found on an option button that allows for Yes, No, and Null state values.
- Datasheet backcolor and forecolor. Allows you to determine the colors for a form in datasheet view.
- `PageIndex` property. States the active page within a number of pages on a tabbed form.
- `Mouse Pointer` property. Allows you to change the pointer to reflect that the system is busy or to change appearance when positioned over a control.

An Introduction to Forms

Forms should constitute the fundamental interaction between the Access database and the end user. Forms guide the user through the operation of the application, protect the underlying data from accidental damage, and provide a level of security control if necessary. Properly designed forms are the difference between a crude, error-prone application and an efficient, professional one. The range of form features available through Access 97 enables you to emulate many of the user-friendly interface features of professionally developed programs.

This chapter will use the Northwind database as a basis for experimentation with different form styles. You may want to create an extra copy and use that for your experiments.

> **NOTE**
>
> To differentiate between the programmer who's designing Access forms and the user who will eventually be using them to enter data, the term "user" in this chapter refers to the end user.

The Access object-oriented form model is based on objects (forms and controls) that can be significantly customized by modifying their properties. The form and control properties are discussed in greater detail later in this chapter.

How to Create New Forms

Simple forms can be created through Access wizards. By taking the developer through the initial steps of form generation, wizards provide the initial skeleton upon which to build. The AutoForm type wizards (Columnar, Tabular, and Datasheet) are very simple and self-explanatory. The general Form Wizard is more flexible.

> **NOTE**
>
> You will rarely, if ever, use a form exactly as the wizard generates it. But it does save you the work of creating each individual control and assigning their fields. It is then a simple (and often enjoyable) matter to modify the form and control properties to get it to look just right.

AutoForm Wizards

The AutoForm feature in Access enables you to quickly create fully functional data entry forms. AutoForms are fast and ask no questions of you.

> **Tip**
>
> You can set some default form properties: background, font, and border. Open a form in design view, then select the menu Format I Autoformat. The choices you make here will be applied to subsequent AutoForm invocations (only those from the Database container, not those invoked from the menu Insert I Form).

Tabular Wizard

The AutoForm Tabular Wizard takes the fields for the selected table or query and places them in a horizontal strip, in a series of scrollable repeated forms. The fields need not be left in this straight horizontal strip, however, and can be arranged in a more coherent display for the user. This is a good choice for instances where the data for each record is small, taking up little screen space.

Datasheet Wizard

The AutoForm Datasheet Wizard takes every field for every record in the record source and displays it in a datasheet format, very much like the Access table display format. Datasheet forms are most often used as subforms embedded in a larger form. A purchase order main form, with the individual line items in a datasheet, is a typical application (see the example in Figure 6.1).

> **Tip**
>
> There are somewhat counterintuitive aspects to customizing datasheet views. First of all, the headings of the columns in the datasheet layout are initially the field names in the underlying table or query. To change a heading, you might be inclined to change the alias in the query or the field names in the table, but these won't do it.
>
> During the original generation of the form, the individual text box fields are named after the data field names. Thereafter, however, it is the text of the

associated label (in form view), if such a label exists; otherwise, the actual text box name is displayed as the column heading. The label inserted by the Datasheet Wizard is not associated with the text box, so it does not affect the column heading. However, any text boxes you add, by default, have an associated label that controls the column heading, unless you delete it. To change a text box name, switch to design view. Highlight the text box field (not the label field associated with the text box). If the Properties box is not displayed, right-click the mouse and select Properties. Click the Other tab in the properties box and change the name to your desired heading (spaces and many punctuation marks are acceptable). More information on properties and their uses is provided later in this chapter.

Also, and perhaps equally unexpected, the display order of the columns is changed by altering the tab order of the form, not the order in the table or query. To change the tab order, switch to design view. Select the menu View | Tab Order. The list of text box names is displayed in the Tab Order dialog box. To move a text box or boxes, click the left pane by the named box (it will be highlighted). If you are moving a group at a time, hold down the Shift key and select the additional text boxes. Release the Shift key, left-click on one of the highlighted choices, and drag it to the desired location.

Form Wizard

The Form Wizard takes the form designer through several different steps. The real power of the Form Wizard comes into play with multiple data sources (for which relations have previously been defined). Depending on the relation (one-to-one, one-to-many), you can choose a form/subform view or a form/linked form view (the linked form can be invoked by the user for additional information). Figure 6.1 shows a form/subform created with a one-to-many relationship.

FIGURE 6.1.

A form/subform created by Form Wizard.

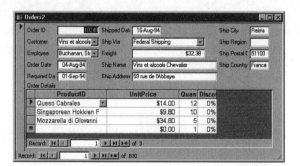

The first page of the wizard inquires about the desired information sources and determines the SQL statement that will appear on the Record Source property of the new form. Different fields can be extracted from multiple tables and queries only if you have properly established relations between those tables.

Two tables were selected for this example: the Orders table and the Order Details table. All the fields for each table were moved into the Selected Field box. The next step of the wizard is shown in Figure 6.2. This step lets the form designer decide how to view the multiple object form by listing all the objects. The designer can also decide whether the form is viewed in a Main Form/Subform format or a Linked Form format.

FIGURE 6.2.

The designer can determine how the data in the form is viewed.

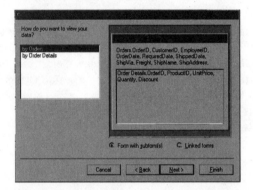

> **WARNING**
>
> Be careful when you're selecting multiple tables and queries. Duplicate fields might cause an error to occur.

> **TIP**
>
> The Linked Form option might not be available, depending on the object selected in the View Data box. The Linked Forms option is directly dependent on the relationship established between the objects.

In the final step, the Form Wizard requests names for the forms being created (Figure 6.3). Form designers can open the form in design view or form view, and can even request that the Help system be opened from this screen. Clicking the Finish button creates and saves the forms.

PivotTable Wizard

A PivotTable form is simply a convenient gateway to getting Access database information into Excel for analysis. PivotTables themselves are a Microsoft Excel function, not a part of Access. Users can choose from all the tables and queries that currently exist, but it is advisable to generate a query with the specific data you want to include. This gives you much more control than letting the Access and Excel wizards interpret the data. In Figure 6.4, a query has been created using data from Northwind.

FIGURE 6.3.

The final step in the Form Wizard.

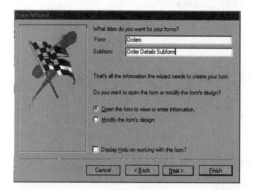

FIGURE 6.4.

Query for a sample PivotTable. All fields from this query are selected in the Pivot Wizard. At this point, the Pivot Wizard invokes Excel with Excel's own wizard.

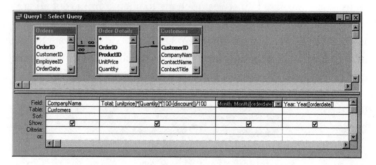

After the PivotTable has been generated, it looks like any other Access form. It is just a static snapshot, however. Even changing the underlying data will not change the data displayed. To update the data, as well as to do any other manipulation with the table, you must click the Edit PivotTable button.

WARNING

PivotTables cannot be used on machines without Excel.

Chart Wizard

Like the PivotTable, the Chart requires an external program, in this case Microsoft Graph 97. (This is the same graphing product used by Excel and other Office 97 products.) The Chart Wizard requires a single data source. (Again, as with PivotTables, it is advisable to create a suitable query to prepare the data.) Figure 6.5 shows a chart derived from the same query used for the PivotTable example.

FIGURE 6.5.

A chart view of the PivotTable data.

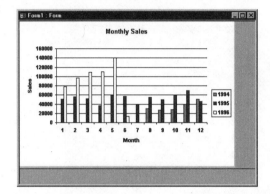

Initially you are offered 20 styles of charts to choose from (not all are suitable for all types of data), but the real power of Chart is revealed once your initial chart is created. Double-click on the chart area in Form Design mode to activate the chart editor. The chart editor offers a far more extensive array of chart styles, with considerable control over font, labeling, 3D effects, colors, and so on.

> **TIP**
>
> While in the chart editor, your data is back in Access, so the chart samples you see and the data table presented are just for demonstration purposes. To actually see your chart, you must close the chart editor and return to Access. In Access, dummy data is used for the form design mode view.

Under the Hood

The forms generated by wizards are already fully functional. This is just the beginning, however. You can make extensive changes to a form's appearance and behavior that are not possible through the wizards. Individual controls on a form can be customized through Visual Basic and macro procedures to provide the functionality your application requires.

The Property Model

As mentioned before, the core of form design is the concept of objects and their properties. Properties for each item are different, although many objects share properties such as size, color, and location. There's detailed coverage of which properties apply to which types of objects later in this chapter.

An object has properties, and properties have values. All objects of the same type have identical properties. For example, all labels have a property called Caption. But each instance of a label will have a different value for Caption: the text that is displayed on the label. Sometimes in casual discussion the terms "property" and "property value" are used almost interchangeably, but usually the meaning is clear from the context.

With a form displayed, select the View | Design View menu. If your screen does not display a Property sheet, select View | Properties to bring it up. At the top of the property sheet is the name of the object the sheet is referencing (typically "Form" if it has just been invoked). As you click on different objects on the form, notice that the property box title changes and the list of properties changes somewhat. To get the property sheet back to the underlying form, click on the small box in the upper-left corner of the form view frame or on the design window somewhere off the form itself.

Property values can be viewed and changed on this sheet. Some properties accept any string value, some are numeric, and some will only accept values from a pull-down list. Not all the changes are immediately visible in design view, but changing back to View/Form View will show the effects.

The Record Source Property

The form's Record Source property (in the Data section) controls the underlying data source for the form. This property value can be a named table, a named query, or a SQL statement extracting the data from an underlying table or query. This property value can be changed or fine-tuned as required. Selecting this property on the property sheet offers a choice of a pull-down lists of other tables and queries by name, and clicking on the ellipsis button to the right of the value field will open the SQL Builder window, essentially like the Query Builder (see Chapter 3, "Creating Sophisticated Queries").

Only those forms with fields bound to data fields in the database require a data source. A form that is informational or is used as a dialog box would not necessarily have a record source. Also, forms that interact with the data entirely through Visual Basic would not necessarily have a record source in the properties.

SQL Builder

Clicking on the ellipsis button to the right of the `Record Source` property opens the SQL Builder. Using the same techniques you used when creating a query, you can precisely select the data necessary for the form. If the underlying table has many columns and you are using only a few for this form, selecting only the required columns will greatly reduce network traffic when users are running the form.

WARNING

If you open a SQL Builder on a table, you will be offered the opportunity to create a new (unnamed) query based on the table. This is safe because no changes to the table or underlying data will occur. However, if you open a SQL Builder on a named query and you make changes, they will be saved to the query when you are done. This can affect any other forms, reports, or queries that reference this query.

If a form exists with fields on it and the record source is changed, all the fields that are no longer present in the new or modified record source display an error to the end user in the form view. This error is shown in Figure 6.6. The record source for Required Date was deleted. The error appears as #Name?.

FIGURE 6.6.

A missing field error shows in form and datasheet views, but not design view.

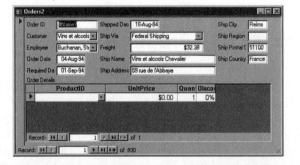

TIP

If you are in SQL Builder and you decide you would like to save the result as a query, simply invoke the Save button or File | Save menu. If you then return to your form design view, saving this change, the form's record source will be changed to this newly named query.

TIP

If you have made some changes in SQL Builder and would like to confirm that you are actually getting the data in the form that you want, simply select Query | Run from the menu. The query will display the data in a table format.

In SQL Builder, most of the features available to a query are available. Query building is described in greater detail in Chapter 3. Each field can have its own set of properties. Right-click on a field name to bring up the property sheet. (See Figure 6.7.) The properties your users will more often see, however, are those associated with the controls on the forms.

FIGURE 6.7.

*The SQL
Statement Query
Builder's fields
have properties.*

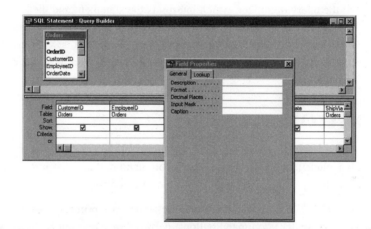

NOTE

The Input Mask property is visible on all the field properties, but it's usable only on text fields or date fields.

To add other tables or queries to the SQL Builder, select Show Table from the Query pull-down menu or click the Show Table button on the toolbar.

> **NOTE**
>
> You can join additional tables to display fields from them as well. If there is no established relation for these tables, however, the resulting dataset may not be editable.

If no fields are in the QBE grid, the SQL Builder statement will fail. At least one field must be in the query grid for the SQL statement to be accepted as a record source for the form.

Which is faster, a form based on a query or a form based on a SQL statement? The technically correct answer is a form based on a query because the SQL statement must be passed to the query optimizer, which interprets the statement and then runs it. The stored query has already been parsed; all that is left to do is run it. Keep in mind that parsing the query is still relatively fast. The running of the query can be a different matter, however, sometimes taking many seconds. So the perceived difference to the user may not be that significant.

Controls

Controls are graphical objects that allow the user to view data or perform an action. Controls include text boxes, check boxes, command buttons, and just about anything visible on the form. Even rectangles and lines are controls.

Some controls, such as labels, lines, and rectangles, are primarily passive visual elements. Others, such as command buttons, perform an action but are not associated with any data. Field type controls, including text boxes, combo boxes, check boxes, and so on, display data and often can also perform actions.

Displaying Data in Controls

On a form created with a wizard, field controls already exist for all the fields at the time of form creation. Just as the Record Source property determines the form's underlying data, so the Control Source property determines which field in the underlying data is associated with that control. To add new fields to the form, first make the changes in the underlying record source, then create new controls with the Control Source set to these new fields.

TIP

The easiest way to insert a new field into a form (after it has been added to the underlying record source) is from the field list. If the field list is not visible, select the menu View | Field List. Select the field desired, left-click, and drag it over to where you want it.

Adding new controls is often best done with the Toolbox (if the Toolbox does not display in your design view, select the menu View | Toolbox).

The Toolbox

Every item appearing on a form is a control of some sort. You can most easily add controls to a form in design view by using the Toolbox. Figure 6.8 shows the Toolbox and lists the function of each button. To view the ToolTip that displays the type of control or setting each button represents, let the mouse rest over the button for a few seconds.

FIGURE 6.8.

The Form Design Toolbox explained.

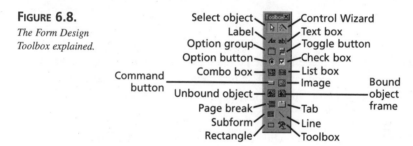

Most of the buttons on the Toolbox represent controls that you can add to a form. The top two items are special, however. You can restore the selection arrow by clicking the button with the arrow on the top left. Restoring the selection arrow deselects any selected control. You turn the Control Wizard on and off by clicking the Control Wizard button on the top right. (Control Wizards are available for some controls and are discussed later in this chapter.)

Adding Controls to a Form

To add a control to a form, click the Toolbox button for the control you want. The button changes to its clicked state, and the cursor changes to resemble the button you just clicked. If you want to add several controls of the same type to a form, you can "lock down" the Toolbox button by double-clicking it. This way you can add several labels to the form without having to reselect the label tool each time. To release the lock, click the button again, press the Esc key, or select a different tool from the Toolbox.

If the Control Wizard mode is active, adding a control launches the wizard (if the control has one).

To make a copy of a selected control (or group of selected controls), choose the menu Edit | Duplicate or the menus Edit | Copy (Ctrl+C) and Edit | Paste (Ctrl+V). Most of the properties, including the all-important Control Source, are copied to the new control, but any underlying event code is not. The name is changed, however, because Access doesn't allow for duplicate control names on a form.

TIP

Access, outside the Form Wizards, displays no originality in assigning names to controls (such as Text55). Immediately rename them to something descriptive. It will pay off when you start refining your forms later. It is helpful to use a consistent prefix for easier identification, such as TbxName for a text box.

You can select a group of controls in several ways. The first is to "lasso" the desired controls by clicking and holding the left mouse button on an unused portion of the form and then dragging the cursor in any direction. Use this method to surround the control you want to select. When the controls are selected, release the mouse button.

The second method can complement the first. Position the cursor over a control and Shift+click (hold down the Shift key while clicking the left-mouse button). This combination toggles the selection state of the control. If you have previously selected a control with the lasso technique and don't want it to be selected, simply Shift+click to deselect it.

TIP

Properties that multiple controls have in common can be set to a common value while they are all selected. For instance, if you select a group of controls that all have a font property, you can set them to a common font and point size in a single operation. Select carefully, however, because including a control without the desired property makes it unavailable for setting in the selected set.

Sometimes you need to cancel a selection. To do so, simply click an empty area of the form. Now no controls are selected.

The Text Box Control

The Text Box control, the most used field control, is used to display and edit text or numeric values. The control can be bound to a field in the database or can be used for entering other necessary information in a form. If the text box is not bound, the data entered into it will be accessible only with additional programming.

The Label Control

You use the Label Control to display textual information. The users of the form cannot edit the text displayed in the label.

Combo Boxes and List Boxes

Combo Boxes and List Boxes provide an easy way for a user to make a selection, as well as an alternate method of displaying rows from a database. The wizards for the Combo Box and List Box are similar, and are particularly useful for configuring these controls.

A List Box is a fixed-size rectangular control that displays one or more rows of data (typically scrollable if there are more rows than are visible in the control). A Combo Box looks similar to a List Box when active, but otherwise appears more like a Text Box when not in focus. Of the two, only the Combo Box permits the user to type in a value not on the list. (See Figure 6.9.)

FIGURE 6.9.

Combo Box and List Box.

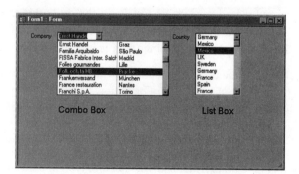

Combo Boxes and List Boxes each have two data sources, which is sometimes a bit confusing. The `Control Source` is the field to which the control is bound (as with a Text Box or other bound control). Changes made in the value of the control will be reflected in the data.

The other data source is the Row Source. This is the source for the list of values to pick from. Row Source can be either a table/query or a list of values entered into the Row Source property. The Row Source data is never directly altered by the control.

For example, a List Box may be arranged so that the user can select an employee name for the commission field of a sales order. The table of employee names is the Row Source. The commission field in the order table is the Control Source.

The Combo Box and List Box Wizards

To create a Combo Box, make sure that the Toolbox is visible and that the Control Wizard feature is enabled. (List Boxes are similar, but with fewer choices.) Click the Combo Box button on the Toolbox and place a Combo Box on a blank form. The Combo Box Wizard appears.

The first three choices determine where the list data comes from:

- "I want the combo box to look up the values in a table or query." Use this when there will be a large number of choices, or when the list of choices will vary periodically (such as an employee list or customer list).

- "I will type in the values that I want." Use this when the number of choices is small and will not normally change (such as Respond by: Fax, Phone, Letter).

- "Find a record on my form based on the value I selected in my combo box." This is a particularly useful option that creates a Combo Box or List Box as a navigational aid for your form. Specify a field that is useful to identify individual records (such as customer name). The wizard adds a short Visual Basic routine that will move the form to the desired record once the user makes a choice. In this case there is no bound field, so the Combo/List Box does not actually change any underlying data. This option does not appear if the Combo Box is inserted into an unbound form.

Next, choose which fields should be included in the Combo Box. You can include multiple fields for the convenience of your users. For example, a customer list might include the city and state fields in addition to the customer name and ID, so users can be comfortable that they are picking the correct row.

If there is a key field defined for the underlying table, the wizard will automatically include that as well. On the other hand, had you opted to type in the values, the wizard would instead have provided you a blank table to enter your desired values.

The next dialog box determines how the columns will look in the Combo Box. Note the Hide Key Column check box. By default, the wizard hides the key field, but you can choose to display it nonetheless. Also, at this point you can use your mouse to set the respective sizes of all the fields.

In the next dialog box, you specify how the data that the users enter is stored. You have two choices:

- "Remember the value for later use." This is normally selected for unbound Combo and List Boxes when you plan to process the information behind the form using Visual Basic.

- "Store the value in this field." This is the normal choice for a bound field control. Whatever value the user selects will be stored in the indicated field of the current record underlying the form.

In the final dialog box, you specify the text for the label to be placed next to the new combo box.

Combo Box and List Box Customization

There are several useful properties that apply specifically to Combo Boxes and List Boxes.

- Row Source—As discussed earlier, this defines the displayed data. Unless it is explicitly a table, named query, or typed list, it is a SQL statement and can be edited with SQL Builder just like the Record Source underlying a form. You can add, delete, or rearrange columns or control sort order.

- Bound Column—The Combo or List Box has a value associated with it specifying which row is selected. If Bound Column=0, the value returned by the control is a row number (starting with 0) rather than any of the values displayed. In Combo Boxes, the text from the first visible column is displayed to the user when the box is closed, regardless of the bound column. This can cause some unexpected behavior, as described later in this section.

- Limit to List (Combo Box only)— If this is set to True and a user types in a value that is not on the list, an error message is generated and the user must fix the entry before proceeding. Because of potential ambiguities, Limit to List is always Yes if Bound Column is not the same as the first visible column (non-zero column width).

- Auto Expand (Combo Box only)—If this is Yes, as the user types in characters, the combo box attempts to scroll down to match the entry fragment currently being typed in. This can be much faster than forcing the user to scroll through a large list. With very large lists, however, it can introduce noticeable delays in keyboard response.

- Column Count—Specifies the number of columns displayed. If you increase the number of fields in Row Source, you must adjust Column Count to make the additional columns visible.

- `Column Widths`—This property is closely associated with `Column Count`. Widths of all columns, except the last one, must be specified. If you have a column that you don't want to display, specify its width as 0″. Even invisible columns are included in `Column Count` and can be the bound column for the control.

- `Column Heads`—If this is Yes, column headings are displayed. These headings are derived from the `Row Source`. You can change the headings by aliasing the column names in SQL Builder. In the field row of SQL Builder, insert the new name followed by a colon before the entered field name (`newname: [fieldname]`).

- `List Rows` and `List Width` (Combo Box only)—These specify behavior of the drop-down box associated with the Combo Box. If `List Width` is set to Auto, the drop-down list is the same width as the displayed box.

If you choose a bound column that is not the same as your displayed column (particularly on a bound control), be sure that the bound column values are unique. Otherwise, when a user returns to that record, the control will display the first row in which the bound column matches the field value. This could be confusing if a different row is displayed.

Option Groups

Option Groups are a good way to display limited multiple choices to users. Normally, Option Groups display situations where only one choice at a time is valid, like the buttons on a car radio. (If you have a situation where combinations of options could be chosen, standalone checkboxes are a better choice.)

The Option Group Wizard is quite straightforward, if you keep the following points in mind:

- Be sure to assign a unique value to each user choice.
- It's almost always advisable to assign a default.
- Avoid using check boxes. Users are (rightly) conditioned to expect that check boxes represent independent options.

In using Option Groups, remember that it is the `frame` object that returns the selected value, so it is the frame that should be bound to a field or be read for value in Visual Basic. Each individual button has an `Option Value` property, but no valid `Value` property.

6

CREATING
INTERACTIVE
FORMS

The Tab Control

You use the Tab control to separate the controls on a form into multiple pages. The Tab control is similar to a traditional card file. You can click a tab to display the controls contained on its page. Each tab has a caption that describes the contents of that tab. If the Tab control's `Multi Row` property is set to Yes, an additional row is created as needed when more tabs are added.

TIP

The built-in Tab control is one of the best new features of Access 97. Properly used, it enables even complex forms with many fields to be easily understood by users.

The Tab control, in many places, can replace paged forms and linked forms while doing a better job of helping the user. In Figure 6.10, notice how the Northwind Employees form could be streamlined as a tabbed form (as compared to the original untabbed version supplied with Nwinds.mdb).

FIGURE 6.10.

Personal information is segregated from general information.

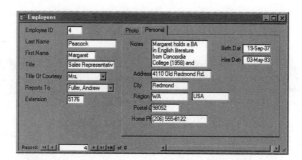

Tab controls, unlike linked forms, are part of the form upon which they reside. They have access to the same underlying data, and they see the same events. Controls on tab controls are children of the form, just like any other control.

There is currently no Tab Wizard. Simply click the Tab Tool button and place the control on the form. By default, the Tab control is created with two pages. You can add or delete pages at any time. For layout purposes, there are two types of borders associated with

Tab controls. When the border is first inserted, or if you click the outer edge in Form Design mode, the Tab control border is selected. This can be moved and resized in the normal manner. When you click on an individual tab in Form Design mode, the page border is highlighted. This can be resized independently of the Tab control border, but must always fit within it. Each page has a separate border.

To insert controls into a tab page, first select the tab page by clicking the tab (the page boundaries should become highlighted). Then, insert the control in the normal manner within the boundaries of the page. If you want to move a control from the form itself to a tab page, or from one tab page to another, select the control, cut it, select the page, and paste the control. If you simply drag the control, it will reside physically in front of the tab control, but will not respond to tab selections.

Tab pages themselves have properties just like any other control. Simply click the tab. To access properties of the Tab control, click the outer edge of the control. While a Tab control or page is selected, additional tabs can be inserted from the menu Insert | Tab Control Page. The order of the tabs can be changed from the menu View | Tab Control Order.

Adding an ActiveX Control

You also can add any ActiveX control to your form. Simply choose the menu Insert | ActiveX Control. You are presented with a list showing all the ActiveX controls available on your system.

> **NOTE**
>
> Although you can use ActiveX controls much like any other control in Access, they are actually external components and must be installed on each machine using your database. Microsoft supplies a range of them for installation with Office 97, and additional ActiveX controls can be obtained from other sources. If you plan to share your database with others (or use it in a network environment), you will need to be sure all users have the appropriate ActiveX controls installed.
>
> A note of caution: ActiveX is an interface standard for components, from a variety of vendors, for a wide variety of applications. ActiveX components that are not specifically designed to work with Access 97 may not perform as expected.

Adding a Hyperlink to a Form

Using Access 97, you can add a hyperlink to another document to your forms. The document you link to can be on the Internet or on a corporate intranet, or it can be a file accessible through the Windows file system. You can add a static link or use a Hyperlink type field to add the hyperlink to the form.

The hyperlink can also reference a different form within your database (select the form name under "Named Location in File") or even a form in another Access database (select the `.MDB` file under "Link to File or URL"). In this case, a second copy of Access will be invoked.

To add a static link to a form, you can either add a picture to the form or use the Hyperlink toolbar button to add a hyperlink label to the form. To add a picture for use as a hyperlink, follow these steps:

1. Add an image control to the form. In the Insert Picture dialog box, select the picture you want to use.

2. Select the image control and open the property sheet. On the Format tab of the property sheet, you'll find the `HyperlinkAdress` property.

3. You can either enter the URL for the document directly or load the Edit Hyperlink dialog box by clicking the Build button for the `HyperlinkAddress` property.

4. To test the hyperlink while in design view, right-click the image control. Select the Hyperlink shortcut menu and then choose Open.

To add a label that will serve as a hyperlink, follow these steps:

1. In form design view, choose Insert | Hyperlink.

2. The Insert Hyperlink dialog box appears. You can enter the URL directly, select the URL from the drop-down list box, or use the Browse button to locate the file.

3. If you want to open the document or file at a specific location, use the Named Location in File text box. This location can be a table in a database, a cell in a spreadsheet, or a bookmark in a Word document, for example.

4. Click the OK button. The hyperlink label is added to the form. The `Caption` property is initially set to the hyperlink address. To change the caption, open the property sheet and modify the `Caption` property.

5. To test the hyperlink while in design view, right-click the label control. Select the Hyperlink flyout menu and then choose Open.

If you're using a table that contains a Hyperlink field, you can insert the hyperlink by dragging the field's name from the Field List window onto the form. This hyperlink operates just like any other hyperlink, but changes as the current record changes.

Working with Hyperlinks

Access 97 provides several tools for working with hyperlinks after you've added them to a form. You can edit the hyperlink using the Edit Hyperlink dialog box (which is identical to the Insert Hyperlink dialog box), copy the hyperlink to the Clipboard, or open the hyperlink using your default Web browser.

All these features are available from the shortcut menu for the label and image controls while you're in design view. They are available for the hyperlink field while you're in data view. In addition, while you're in data view, you can add the current hyperlink field's value to your favorites list.

Linking OLE Documents to a Form

You can add objects created in other Windows applications to an Access form. For example, you can add a picture created with Microsoft Paint, a worksheet created with Microsoft Excel, or a document created with Microsoft Word.

> **NOTE**
>
> If you simply want to place a bitmap (`.bmp`) graphic on the form, there is less overhead involved in using the `Image` control (see "Adding Graphics to a Form" later in this chapter). An OLE control actually calls Paint to do the creating, so the program must also reside on the computer.

The type of control used to display the OLE document depends on whether you want the object to be bound or unbound. A bound object is stored in a field of the table. As you change records, the object displayed in the form changes to match the data stored in the field. The Northwind database, for example, stores a picture of each employee in the company. This field is displayed using a bound OLE control. Unbound objects are stored in the design of the form. Changing records has no effect on the object. For example, you might want to add a logo that you create with Microsoft Paint.

Both controls have an important property called `SizeMode` that affects how the data in the object is displayed within the control. The operation of the `SizeMode` property is identical to the `SizeMode` property for an image control. Refer to the section "Adding Graphics to a Form."

> **TIP**
>
> If you set the OLE object's `Enabled` property value to Yes, double-clicking the object will activate the creating program within the object's frame. A fully OLE-compliant program (such as Word 97) will actually place its own menu structure below the Access title bar. If `Locked` is set to No, the object can actually be edited and saved.
>
> Obviously, this will only work if the target computer has the appropriate OLE programs properly installed.

Unbound OLE Objects

You add unbound objects to the form by using the Unbound Object Frame control. Unbound objects can be either embedded into the form or linked to the original file. The difference is that an embedded object doesn't change if the source file changes. It's stored in the form and is always available. A linked object is updated when the source file changes because the data for the object isn't stored in the form—it's stored only in the source file. Therefore, the source file must be available to Access in order to display the contents of the object.

To add an unbound object to a form in design view, click the Unbound Object control in the Toolbox. Click on the form where you want the object to be placed, or choose Insert | Object.

If you want to create a new object, select the Create New radio button (it's selected by default) and then select the object type from the list box. This list box displays all the available OLE objects on your system. On the form, you can display either the contents of the object or an icon representing the object. The object is activated when the icon is double-clicked. To show the object as an icon, check the Display As Icon check box. When you click OK, the OLE server for the object you selected opens, thus enabling you to create the new object. After you create the object, exit the server application and you are returned to Access with the object shown on the form. This object is embedded by default because you created it within the design view.

To embed or link an object from an existing file, follow the same steps to get to the Insert Object dialog box. Select the Create From File radio button. The list box is replaced by a text box and a Browse button. You can enter the filename in the text box directly or use the Browse button to locate the file on your system. To link the object to the source file, check the Link check box. Again, you can select Display As Icon to display the object as an icon instead of its contents.

Bound OLE Objects

To create an OLE object that is bound to a field whose data type is OLE Object, open the Field List in design view. (The form's Record Source property must be set to a table or query that has an OLE Object field.) Select the OLE Object field and drag it to the form. Position the drag box where you want the object frame to be displayed. A bound object frame is created on the form. You can then size and position the frame to fit on the form and set necessary properties.

To add data to a bound OLE control, open the form containing the control in form view. Right-click the control and choose Insert Object from the shortcut menu. The standard Windows Insert Object dialog box appears. Here you can select whether to create a new object or create the object's data from an existing file. The types of objects in the list box (when Create New is selected) depend on which OLE server applications are registered on your system. Selecting an object type and clicking OK launches the object's server application, thus enabling you to enter data as you normally would in that application. If you select Create from File, you can specify the file that contains the data to be placed in the control. Again, the server application that created the file must be registered on your system to use the data. Also, if you've copied data to the Windows Clipboard from an OLE server application, you can insert it into the control by right-clicking and choosing Paste. This method is often the quickest way to add data to an OLE control.

Good Form Design Using the Form Design Editor and Control Properties Sheet

The Access 97 form design editor provides an ideal environment for polishing your forms. The visual layout, interactive testing, and wide range of form and control properties can meet just about any user form requirement. Because many of the controls share similar properties, the following section highlights efficient use of the form design view and general use of properties to enhance the functionality of forms.

Formatting Data in Controls

You can format data presented on a control in a variety of ways. The Format property is one of the properties that a bound control initially inherits from the field to which it's bound. However, the formatting information can be modified on the control's property sheet.

The `Format` Property

The main formatting property is the `Format` property, initially inherited from the field to which it's bound. There are a variety of other built-in formats that you can select by using the drop-down list of the `Format` property's text box. The list shows valid built-in formats for the data type of the field to which a control is bound (all formats for an unbound control). The built-in formats are as follows:

- General Number—Displays a number as entered.
- Currency—Displays a number using the currency symbol, the thousands separator, and parentheses for negative numbers. The `DecimalPlaces` property value is set to 2.
- Fixed—Displays at least one digit. The `DecimalPlaces` property value is set to 2.
- Standard—Uses the thousands separator. The `DecimalPlaces` property value is set to 2.
- Percent—Displays the value multiplied by 100. Displays a percent sign. The `DecimalPlaces` property value is set to 2.
- Scientific—Displays a number using standard scientific notation.
- General Date—This setting is a combination of the Short Date and the Long Time settings.
- Long Date—Same as the Long Date setting in the Regional Settings section of the Windows Control Panel.
- Medium Date—Displays as *dd-mmm-yy,* where *dd* is the day of the month, *mmm* is a three-letter abbreviation for the month, and *yy* is the year (without the century).
- Short Date—Same as the Short Date setting in the Regional Settings section of the Windows Control Panel.
- Long Time—Same as the Time setting in the Regional Settings section of the Windows Control Panel.
- Medium Time—Displays the time as *hh:mm AM/PM.*
- Short Time—Displays the time in 24-hour format.
- Yes/No data types—Can be displayed as Yes/No, True/False, or On/Off.

TIP

Use the currency format sparingly. Because the currency format uses a currency symbol, such as the dollar sign ($), every place it is used, a form with a lot of financial information gets quite cluttered. Try using the fixed 2-decimal place format for all but the totals on a page.

In addition to these built-in formats, you also can specify a custom format using a variety of formatting characters. The `Format` property value for text and memo fields can contain three sections, separated by a semicolon. The first section is used for fields with text, the second for fields with a zero-length string, and the third for strings with null values. This third section is useful if you want to have some default text when nothing is entered in the field. Likewise, for numeric data, the `Format` property value can have four sections: the first for positive numbers, the second for negative numbers, the third for fields with a value of zero, and the fourth for fields with null values.

As an example, modify the format for a text box that is tied to the Freight field of the (Northwind) Orders table. Use the following for the `Format` property: `$#,##0.00;;"(n/c)";"(n/c)"`. The first section is for the values that are greater than zero, in this case a standard currency format with three optional places (#) and three required places (0). The second section isn't specified, but assumes that there is no possibility for a negative freight charge. The last two sections specify that if the value is zero or if no data is entered, `(n/c)` should be displayed in the text box. If you also add a calculated control that uses the Freight control as part of its expression, the text displayed doesn't affect the outcome of the expression: the value of 0 or null is still used in the calculation.

> **TIP**
>
> Null values play havoc when used in calculated fields. Use the built-in function `Nz(value)` to prevent this. `Nz` returns a zero if the value is null. (It also has some alternate forms for special situations; see the Access help file.)

The `Decimal Places` Property

The `Decimal Places` property specifies the number of digits that appear to the right of the decimal point for numeric fields in fixed format numbers only. The default setting is Auto, which means that the number appears as specified in the `Format` property. You also can set the property value to an integer value from 0 to 15. Also, if the `Format` property value is blank, Access uses the General Number format.

The `InputMask` Property

The `InputMask` property enables you to specify how data is input into a control. Use the `InputMask` property to display literal characters in the field with blanks to fill in. For example, you could create an input mask for a Phone Number field that specifies exactly how to enter a new number: *(000) 000-0000*. This example specifies that digits 0 through 9 must be entered at the places indicated by the *0*. The *(,)*, and - characters are literals placed in the field to aid in entry.

If you define both a display format and an input mask for a field, Access uses the input mask when you're adding or editing data, and the Format setting determines how the data is displayed when the record is saved. When you're using both the Format and InputMask properties, be careful that their results don't conflict with each other.

The InputMask property has a wizard to assist in creating an input mask. The wizard enables you to test out the mask before applying the mask to the control. Unfortunately, this wizard does not offer a 4-digit year code (we are approaching the year 2000, after all), but you can manually construct a 4-digit year mask using the wizard.

> **WARNING**
>
> Access internally stores a full year value, so in that sense, it's prepared for year 2000 issues. But you must be aware that if your user enters a two-digit year and they enter 00 to 29, it will be interpreted as 2000 to 2029. If you are cataloging World War I battles, for example, your dates would be quite wrong. Whenever there is any question, it is advisable to require four-digit dates from your users.

> **NOTE**
>
> The Input Mask property is visible on all the field properties, but it's usable only on text fields or date fields.

Aligning and Sizing: Controls and Control Placement

Access provides a treasure chest of tools to align and size controls in form design view. After controls are added to a form, you need to align and size them to present a readable, usable form for both data display and entry. Access provides several tools to help you lay out the controls in such a manner.

Control Alignment and Placement

The most obvious tool to use in laying out forms is the alignment grid. This grid is displayed as dots when the form is in design view. You can turn the grid on and off by choosing View|Grid. To change the grid spacing, change the form's `GridX` and `GridY` properties on the property sheet by double-clicking the form selector in the upper-left corner of the form.

One way the grid is useful when you're adding controls to a form is evident when you use the Snap To Grid feature. It causes Access to place controls on the nearest grid point. Also, when you're moving or sizing controls, Access snaps to the nearest grid point. You turn this feature on or off by choosing Format|Snap To Grid in design view.

If some controls aren't aligned to the grid, you can place them at the nearest grid point. To accomplish this, select a control and then choose Format|Align|To Grid.

In addition to using the grid for alignment, Access also enables you to align a group of controls using a common side. For example, a group of controls can have their left sides all on the same vertical line. To align them, select a group of controls by lassoing them or by Shift+clicking each control to be included in the group and then choose Format| Align|Left, Right, Top, or Bottom, depending on which side you want to be aligned. The position to which they are aligned depends on the direction of alignment. For example, Left Align would align all selected controls with the control already at the farthest left.

> **NOTE**
>
> If any of the selected controls are going to overlap after being aligned, Access doesn't overlap them. Instead, it places the controls with their edges next to each other.

You can change the horizontal or vertical spacing between a group of controls by choosing Format|Horizontal Spacing or Format|Vertical Spacing. These menu items are available only when a group of controls is selected. Select at least three controls. To make the distance between the tops and bottoms of these controls evenly spaced, choose Format| Vertical Spacing|Make Equal. The middle controls then move to make the spacing even. The top and bottom controls stay in their original positions. To increase or decrease the vertical distance between each of the controls, choose Format|Vertical Spacing|Increase or Format | Vertical Spacing | Decrease. The Horizontal Spacing menu options work in the same way, but affect the distances between the left and right edges of controls.

Moving and Sizing Controls

> **TIP**
>
> The shape of the mouse cursor as it passes over a control indicates which control movement will occur if the operator clicks and drags at that point. A flat hand means the entire control (including the control's label, if it has one) will be moved. A double-headed arrow (horizontal, vertical, or diagonal) means the edge(s) will be moved, changing the overall size. A hand with a single finger pointing is for moving a control without moving its label, or a label without its control.

The Format menu also contains a Size submenu, which aids in sizing controls. The first item on the Size submenu, To Fit, sizes a control or group of controls so that all the data in the control is visible. This control is mainly useful for labels. The second item, To Grid, is similar to the Align To Grid menu discussed earlier. This menu item causes Access to size the selected control or group of controls with the nearest grid points.

> **TIP**
>
> To quickly resize a label to fit text, slide the cursor over the control until a double-headed arrow appears, then double-click.

The next four items on the Size submenu are active only when multiple controls are selected. The first item, To Tallest, sizes all the controls to be as tall as the tallest selected control. The next item, To Shortest, sizes all the controls to be as short as the shortest selected control. To Widest sizes all the controls to be as wide as the widest selected control. Finally, To Narrowest makes the controls as narrow as the narrowest selected control.

Text Alignment

The `TextAlign` property of a control affects how the text (whether it is characters or numbers) is aligned in the control. Although there is no real guideline stating that all form labels must be left-aligned and all text boxes must be right-aligned, it's important to keep all the forms within a database consistent.

You have four choices for the `TextAlign` property:

- General—Text is aligned left. Numeric data and dates align to the right.
- Left—Everything aligns to the left.
- Center—Everything is centered.
- Right—Everything aligns to the right.

To change the `TextAlign` property, select the control(s) to be modified and double-click to open the property sheet. The `TextAlign` property is on the Format tab. You also can use the alignment buttons on the Formatting toolbar (discussed later) to change the `TextAlign` property value quickly. The default setting is General (unless the default has been modified).

Colors

Colors make forms easier to read and understand. One good use of color on a data entry form is to distinguish fields that require values to be entered before a record can be saved. Typically, either the data entry control itself has its `Back Color` property modified, or the label attached to the control has a different `Fore Color` property value than the rest of the labels on the form. The default colors match those of the system colors (unless the default control style has been modified).

Access provides a Color Builder dialog box that you can use when you're modifying the color properties. In this dialog box, shown in Figure 6.11, you can choose the value by selecting from colored boxes. (If you were to use the text box for a color property on the property sheet, on the other hand, you would need to know the long integer representation of the color you wanted.) To use this dialog box, click the builder button to the right of a color property's text box on a control's property sheet. In the Color Builder dialog box, select the color to be used and click OK. You can also create custom colors by using the Define Custom Colors button.

The following properties are provided to control how color is used on a form:

- `BackColor`—Specifies the color of the interior of a control or form section.
- `ForeColor`—Specifies the color of the text of a control.
- `Border Color`—Specifies the color of a control's border.

FIGURE 6.11.

The Color Builder dialog box.

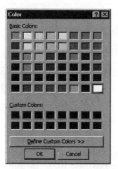

Borders

Several properties affect the borders of controls and forms. They are `Border Style`, `Border Width`, and `Border Color` (discussed earlier).

The `Border Style` property sets the type of border to be used for a control. For a form, this property sets the type of border and border elements to use for the form (title bar, Control menu, Minimize and Maximize buttons). The `Border Style` property, as it relates to forms, is discussed later.

The `Border Width` property is an integer property that specifies the width of a control's border. The settings range from 0 to 6. A setting of 0 specifies the narrowest possible border. The `Special Effect` property (discussed next) must be set to Flat or Shadowed, and the `Border Style` must be set to something other than Transparent for this property to have any effect.

Effects

The `Special Effect` property for a control or form section enables you to specify how the control or section appears. Setting this property affects the `Border Style`, `Border Color`, and `Border Width` properties. (For instance, if the property value is set to Raised, the settings of the `Border Style`, `Border Color`, and `Border Width` properties are ignored.)

Changing Text Fonts and Sizes

Other properties that should remain consistent throughout the application are the font properties. Special fields or labels can be denoted by different font sizes, for example, or by the use of italic. Typically, form headers have larger font sizes than the data fields.

The font properties are `Font Name`, `Font Size`, `Font Weight`, `Font Italic`, and `Font Underline`. You set these properties either by using a control's property sheet or the Formatting toolbar.

The `Font Name` property lets you set the font used to display text to any font installed on your system. If the `Font Name` property value is set to a font that isn't on the system, Windows substitutes a similar font. If you choose a TrueType font, the text appears the same onscreen and when printed.

The `Font Size` property specifies the point size of the font. For all controls except command buttons, the default font size is 8. Command buttons have a default font size of 10. The `Font Size` property text box has a drop-down list from which you can choose values, and you can also type into the text box to set `Font Size` to a value not on the list. Be careful when setting `Font Size` to make sure that the text will display properly on all possible screen resolutions. If you're using a font that isn't a TrueType font and you modify the value to be less than the minimum size for the font, it still appears using the minimum size. Also, using such a font might not produce the easiest-to-read output on all possible devices, especially if you modify the `Font Size` property.

The `Font Weight` property enables you to specify the thickness of the characters that Windows uses to display the text. The text may appear different between the screen and its printed version, depending on the display and printer being used.

The last two properties, `Font Italic` and `Font Underline`, are Boolean properties (that is, they have values of Yes or No). If you change any of the font properties and want to resize the control to fit the new settings, choose Format | Size | To Fit.

About the Formatting Toolbar

In addition to letting you set control properties with the property sheet, Access provides a useful Formatting toolbar. The Formatting toolbar gives you easy point-and-click access to most of the format properties for a control. Figure 6.12 shows the standard Formatting toolbar and its various components. You can modify the buttons appearing on the toolbar by using the Customize Toolbars feature. You can remove a button from the toolbar by simply dragging it off the toolbar onto the Access main window.

FIGURE 6.12.

The standard Formatting toolbar.

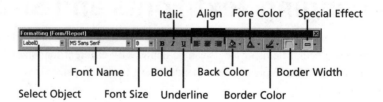

Copying Formatting Properties Between Controls

Access provides a handy feature called the Format Painter, which enables you to copy formatting properties from one control to another. The Format Painter button is on the standard toolbar between the Paste and Undo buttons. Its icon is a paintbrush.

To copy the formatting information from a selected control to another control, click the Format Painter button. Then click the control to which you want to copy the information. If you want to copy the same formatting information to many controls, double-click the Format Painter icon. It stays clicked, and Access continues to copy formatting information to any control clicked until you click the button again or press the Esc key.

The following properties are copied if they're valid for both the source and destination controls:

Back Color	Font Name	Label X
Back Style	Font Size	Label Y
Border Color	Font Underline	Line Slant
Border Style	Font Weight	Special Effect
Border Width	Fore Color	Text Align
Display When	Label Align	Visible
Font Italic		

Changing a Control to Another Type

As you're designing forms, you may sometimes need to change a control to another type. For instance, suppose a text box appears on a form, but you realize a combo box would better serve the users. The drop-down list would contain commonly used values, for instance. You could delete the text box, add a combo box, and then go to all the trouble of setting the new control's properties to match the look of the form. However, Access provides a more efficient method.

If you need to change a control to another type, you don't need to delete the control and start over. Simply select the control you want to change and then choose Format | Change To. Then select the type of control you want to change it to. Access copies the appropriate properties from one control to the other. You can also right-click over the selected control, select the Change To flyout menu, and select the control type you want to change it to.

Unbound Controls

Most of the controls discussed so far have been *bound* controls; that is, they are automatically tied into a field in a data set. Changing the control changes the data. An *unbound* control is used to convey information to the users or to receive it from them, but is not linked to a field in the database. Most controls that are considered bound controls can be used unbound for specialized purposes. Here are some examples of unbound controls:

- A label for a text box that's used to describe what the text box represents.
- Text boxes or drop-down list boxes that can be used to select different scenarios on a what-if form.
- A line placed on a form to separate different sections of the form.
- A company logo that can be placed on the form to add graphical effects.
- A command button.

Command Buttons

Command buttons are among the most-used unbound controls. Fortunately, when you insert a command button into a form, the wizard sets it up to do many of the most popular actions. None of these are integral to the button itself; all a button can do is respond to events (clicks, focus, and so on). To perform the different actions, the Button Wizard creates a short Visual Basic routine that is executed when the button is clicked. It is quite informative to create a form with several different kinds of buttons and then look at the associated Visual Basic code to see how it was done. The following is an example of wizard-generated code for a button that opens another form:

```
Private Sub open_Click()
On Error GoTo Err_open_Click

    Dim stDocName As String
    Dim stLinkCriteria As String

    stDocName = "Job List"
    DoCmd.OpenForm stDocName, , , stLinkCriteria

Exit_open_Click:
    Exit Sub

Err_open_Click:
    MsgBox Err.Description
    Resume Exit_open_Click

End Sub
```

Creating Interactive Forms

CHAPTER 6

177

6

CREATING
INTERACTIVE
FORMS

(For more information on Visual Basic, see Chapter 10, "Visual Basic for Applications.")

The preceding function is tied to the event On Click. This is the most common event to which the command button responds, but there are a range of others as well, such as On Got Focus, On Lost Focus, and On Key Press.

The wizard automatically creates an error trap (On Error), which is good policy for any VBA function. It next sets arguments and then calls the new form with the Docmd.Openform method.

Calculated Controls

Calculated controls use expressions to derive their data, rather than direct user or database field input.

Expressions are combinations of operators, fields, control names, functions, and constants. Although text boxes are the most common form of calculated control, any control having the Control Source property can be a calculated control.

All expressions must begin with an equals sign. A sample expression is

```
=[OrderForm]![SalesTaxRate]*[OrderForm]![OrderTotal]
```

The [OrderForm]![SalesTaxRate] part refers to a control named SalesTaxRate on the form named OrderForm. [OrderForm]![OrderTotal] refers to the control named OrderTotal on the same form. A control with this expression in its Control Source property value displays the value of the order total multiplied by the applicable sales tax rate.

The expression can also be a Visual Basic function (either built-in or user-written). For example:

```
=Date + 30   'yields 30 days from now

=myfunction() 'custom user function
```

User-written functions are similar to the direct expressions, but can be internally as complex as required. For example, you could write a function that calculates shipping rates by looking up the ZIP code in a table, multiplies the weight times the rate, and returns the calculated value.

To create a calculated control while in design view, follow these steps:

1. Select the type of control to be used from the Toolbox and position the control on the form. (See the section "Adding Controls to a Form" earlier in this chapter.)

2. Enter the expression using one of the following methods:

- If the control is a text box, you can enter the expression directly into the control. Click inside the text box portion until the blinking edit cursor is visible. Type the expression into the edit box.

- If the control isn't a text box or if you don't want to enter the expression directly, double-click the control to open its property sheet. Move to the ControlSource property. Here you can enter the expression as text or use the Expression Builder. (Click the Build button to the right of the ControlSource text box.) The Expression Builder, shown in Figure 6.13, is a useful tool for creating expressions because it enables you to browse all the objects in the database, including controls from other forms, fields from queries, and built-in functions.

FIGURE 6.13.

The Expression Builder in action.

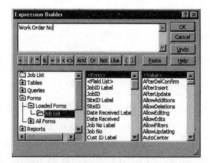

> **TIP**
>
> If you're typing in the Control Source property and need a larger text box, Access provides a Zoom box that you can activate by pressing Shift+F2.

Adding Shapes and Lines to Forms

Forms don't have to contain only data and labels. You can make forms more readable by breaking up sections using shapes and lines. To add a shape or line to a form, select the desired control on the Toolbox and draw it onto the form.

The Line control has the following format properties that affect its display, which were discussed earlier: Special Effect, Border Style, Border Color, and Border Width.

The Rectangle control has the same formatting properties as the Line control. It also has the Back Color property, which specifies the color with which the rectangle is filled.

Adding Graphics to a Form

Using graphics is another means of creating an impact or drawing attention to a form. Access supports two methods for adding graphics to a form. For an overall graphic background, add a background picture to the form:

1. In form design view, open the form's property sheet.

2. Select the `Picture` property and use the Picture Builder to open a picture file. (You access the Picture Builder by clicking the button to the right of the `Picture` property's text box.) Picture Builder is basically a file selector dialog—to preview a picture, right-click on the file in question and select Quick View.

3. Use the `Picture Alignment` property to specify the location of the picture on the form.

4. Set the `Picture Tiling` property to determine whether the picture is repeated across the form.

5. Set the `Size Mode` property according to how you want the picture to be proportioned. The possible settings are as follow:

   - Clip—The picture is actual size. If the picture is larger than the form, the image is cut off.

   - Stretch—The picture is sized to fit within the form and may be distorted.

   - Zoom—The whole picture is displayed after it's sized to fit either the height or width of the form. The picture isn't distorted.

The other method of adding a graphic to a form is to use the image control. With this method, you can place many graphics on the form and position them wherever you want. Add the image control from the Toolbox or choose Insert | Picture, and Access opens the Picture Builder dialog box. The other picture properties are identical to those described earlier.

To remove the picture from either the form background or an image control, select the `Picture` property on the appropriate property sheet, highlight the text in the edit box, and press the Delete key. The text should change to (none), and the picture should be blank.

TIP

Image and picture controls can be either `Linked` or `Embedded`, as set in the property sheet. Embedded images, as their name implies, actually place a copy of the image in the form itself. Because images can be quite large, if you have the

continues

same image appearing in many forms in the application, a lot of space can be wasted. With linked images, only a reference to the image file is included in the form. The disadvantage here is that the image files must be available in the appropriate directory every time (and place) the application is run.

Modifying Default Control Properties

Every control has a default control style, which specifies the default properties for new controls added to a form. For instance, the `Text Align` property has a default value of General. Default control styles can be changed, saving work when you're designing forms.

Follow these steps to modify the default control style for a control:

1. Make sure the property sheet is open.
2. In the form design view, click the button on the Toolbox for the control you want to modify.
3. Without placing the control anywhere, move the mouse directly to the property sheet. The title of the property sheet should read "Default xxx," where "xxx" is the control type.
4. Modify the properties to match your desired set of defaults.

These changes affect only new controls added to the form, not existing controls.

Properties of Forms

Like controls, forms have a wide range of properties. Some, like `Record Source`, have already been discussed. Many more are available to the form developer.

Although this chapter gives a brief description of each topic, the definitive source remains the Help file and the manuals. Each of the properties described in the following sections has its own entry in the Microsoft Access Help file.

To set the properties of a form, you must display the property sheet. To do so, right-click the form selector in the upper-left corner of the form, or click on the background of the form view, anywhere off the form.

> **NOTE**
>
> Property names, when used in Visual Basic, are slightly different and have no embedded spaces.

Setting the Format Properties

Each of the items in the Format tab of the property sheet changes an aspect of the form that is visible to the users. Because it's important to use a consistent format when presenting data, most designers select one form style or format to use for most of their data. The Format properties are located on the first tab on the property sheet.

Controlling Views

You can adjust two aspects of a form's view from the Format tab:

- `Default View`
- `Views Allowed`

The `Default View` property determines which of the three types of form views is the default view. The default view is automatically displayed when the form is opened in view mode. The `Views Allowed` property determines which of the available views can be selected by the user.

Three different views are allowed to be the default view:

- Single form
- Continuous forms
- Datasheet

Single forms are those that display only one record at a time. *Continuous forms* allow multiple records to be displayed at one time within the same window. This is accomplished by appending copies of the detail section of the form one after another, which then display a different record in each copy of the detail section. *Datasheet* view consists of rows and columns like a grid. It's the same type of view that is used by the Access QBE tool or an Excel spreadsheet. The default view is single form view.

The `Views Allowed` property allows three values:

- Form
- Datasheet
- Both

The `Default View` and `Views Allowed` properties also interact to produce *transition effects*. You can use these effects to restrict how the users view the data at certain points in a process or transaction. For example, if the form's `Default View` is set to Form and `Views Allowed` is set to Datasheet, the transition is set to switch from form view to datasheet view but not back to form view. A complete list of the different conditions that the combinations of these controls create is given in the Access Help file under the heading "Default View, Views Allowed Properties."

The `Record Selectors` and `Dividing Lines` Properties

The `Record Selectors` and `Dividing Lines` properties are most useful when used on continuous forms. Together they help make continuous forms easier to view.

The `Record Selectors` property enables and disables a bar on the left side of the form in form view. (This bar always appears in datasheet view.) Record selectors indicate the status of the current recordset record. Four states are displayed: Current, Editing, Locked, and New. Current simply indicates the current record. Editing indicates that the current record has been edited but not saved. Locked indicates that the record is locked by another user. New indicates the new record row on the form. This row doesn't actually exist in the database until it's edited and saved. The Record selectors are enabled by default.

The `Dividing Lines` property enables and disables horizontal lines that separate each record detail section from the others in Continuous Form view. Dividing lines are enabled by default.

The `Navigation Buttons` and `Scroll Bars` Properties

Access provides two methods by which users can traverse the records in a recordset: navigation controls and scroll bars. They are enabled and disabled by setting the `Navigation Buttons` and `Scroll Bars` properties, respectively.

The `Navigation Buttons` property toggles the display of the recordset navigation controls in the bottom-left corner of the form for both Form and Datasheet views. These controls give the users an easy method of traversing the records in the recordset. Buttons that move to the first, last, previous, next, and new records in the recordset are included. The record number box indicates the number of the currently selected record, and a record count is provided as well. By default, the navigation controls are enabled.

The `Scroll Bars` property enables you to display the standard horizontal and vertical scroll bars on the right side and bottom of the form window. These scroll bars may be enabled separately or one at a time. The default setting enables both scroll bars.

Creating Interactive Forms

CHAPTER 6

183

6

CREATING
INTERACTIVE
FORMS

The `Auto Resize` and `Auto Center` Properties

The `Auto Resize` and `Auto Center` properties provide a means by which you can adjust the overall size and position of the form. The `Auto Resize` property, when enabled, ensures that the form will always display at least one entire record on the form. If this property is disabled, you can size the form in design view and save it so that, when the form is opened, it defaults to the set size. The `Auto Center` property ensures that the form is automatically centered in the application window when the form is opened. The defaults are `Auto Resize` on and `Auto Center` off.

Title Bar Buttons

The following four properties, each turning on a different control, enable the buttons on the form's title bar (see Figure 6.14). (The appearance of each of these controls is modified by the `Border Style` property.)

- `Control Box` enables the Control menu in the upper-left corner of the form. The Control menu contains the usual entries: Restore, Move, Size, Minimize, Maximize, Close, and Next. Setting the `Control Box` property value to No disables not only the Control menu but also the Minimize, Maximize, and Close buttons.

> **TIP**
>
> Unless the `Min Max Buttons` property is also disabled, you can maximize the form by double-clicking the form's title bar.

- `Close Button` enables the Close button in the upper-right corner of the form. Clicking this button closes the form. The Control menu entry is also disabled.
- `Min Max Buttons` enables the Minimize and Maximize buttons in the upper-right corner of the form. As you might expect, the Minimize button reduces the form to an icon at the bottom of Access's parent window. The Maximize button expands the form so that it fills Access's parent window. The Control menu entry is also disabled.
- `Whats This Button` enables the What's This button in the upper-right corner of the form. Clicking the What's This button changes the mouse pointer to the Help-select pointer (question mark is displayed), which you can use to access the Help topic referenced by a control's `Help Context ID` property.

FIGURE 6.14.

Anatomy of a title bar.

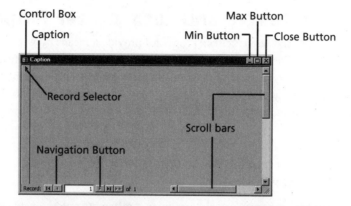

> **NOTE**
>
> You cannot enable the Minimize and Maximize buttons if the What's This button is enabled, and vice versa. Furthermore, if the Minimize and Maximize buttons are enabled, you cannot disable the Close button.

The `Border Style` Property

The `Border Style` property enables you to set or change the style of the form's border. Each of these styles is generally used to border a particular type of form:

- `None`—No border or related border elements. This style is most often used for start-up splash screens.
- `Thin`—A thin border with most border elements, except that sizing is disabled. This style is most often used for pop-up forms.
- `Sizable`—The default border for Access forms. It can include any of the border elements. This style is used for standard Access forms.
- `Dialog`—A thick border with only a title bar and a Control menu. You can't maximize, minimize, or resize the form. (The related items are disabled on the Control menu.) It is most often used for custom dialog boxes.

Setting the Data Properties

Each of the items in the Data tab, the second tab of the property sheet, changes the way data is used on the form.

The `Record Source` Property

The `Record Source` property specifies either the name of the table or query from which data for the form should originate, or a SQL statement used to create a recordset of data. You can use the SQL Builder by clicking the button to the right of the property's text box on the property sheet. The drop-down list for this property contains the names of all named tables and queries available in the current database.

The `Filter`, `Order By`, and `Allow Filters` Properties

The `Filter`, `Order By`, and `Allow Filters` properties give you more control over the data that is displayed on a form. These properties, used individually or in combination, enable you to limit and/or sort the data that is displayed to the users.

- `Filter` contains the SQL `where` clause that defines the subset of records to be displayed when a filter is applied to the recordset associated with a form.
- `Order By` contains the names of the field(s) by which the recordset is to be sorted.
- `Allow Filters` determines whether the `Filter` property is applied to the recordset to limit the data that is visible to the users.

Filters are most commonly used to view a subset of the records in a recordset. When a filter is applied, only the records that meet specific criteria are displayed. With these filters, limit the records displayed to those that are currently significant.

The `Allow Edits`, `Allow Deletions`, `Allow Additions`, and `Data Entry` Properties

These properties control the users' ability to change the data displayed on a form. They can be used in combination to give you a wide range of control over the users' manipulation of the data.

- `Allow Edits` enables changes to the saved records that are displayed by a form.
- `Allow Additions` enables the addition of records to a form.
- `Allow Deletions` enables the deletion of records that are displayed by a form.
- `Data Entry` enables the entry of new records onto the form.

To set the recordset to read-only status, all these `Allow` properties must be set to False.

The Recordset Type Property

The `Recordset Type` property lets you determine which type of recordset to use for the bound controls on the form. You can choose from three types of recordsets. Each of these types has a different effect on the users' ability to edit and view the data in the recordset.

- `Dynaset` allows the editing of a table or tables in a one-to-one relationship. (The join field on the "one" side of a one-to-many relationship can't be edited unless Cascade Update is enabled between the tables.)

- `Dynaset (Inconsistent Updates)` enables fields in all tables to be edited.

- `Snapshot` prevents the fields in any table from being edited.

Dynasets and Snapshots

The result set returned from the execution of a query is either a dynaset or a snapshot. One of the main differences between a dynaset and a snapshot is the ability to update. Dynasets generally can be edited, but snapshots cannot. Additionally, the result sets for dynasets and snapshots are populated in different ways. The overall effect is that snapshots are better suited for small, uneditable queries, and dynasets are better suited for queries in which the result set is large or in which editing is required.

Populating Result Sets

Initially, dynasets and snapshots are populated with the same data, enough for the first screen or two. After the initial records in the result set are retrieved, the snapshot continues to populate the recordset with the rows from the query, whereas the dynaset fetches and caches only the primary key values. The remaining values in the result set are retrieved as follows:

- As a result of user actions—Snapshots fetch the data in all the columns up to the current record; dynasets fetch only primary keys up to that point and then fetch a small amount of data surrounding the current record.

- During Access idle time—Snapshots fetch and store all queried columns; dynasets fetch and store primary keys, as well as a 100-row data window, during this idle time.

In either case, the dynaset has to perform a second query, which employs the cached primary keys, to retrieve the remaining columns in the records surrounding the current record. Snapshots, in contrast, continue to fetch the entire result set, row by row.

Part of the reason for the dynaset caching only the primary keys is to ensure that the data that is fetched is always the most current, thus giving dynasets a greater "liveliness" of data. A snapshot, in contrast, caches the entire result set, and it is not refreshed except by complete reexecution of the query. This is one reason why snapshots are not updateable.

Performance Issues

Because of their differences in retrieving and caching data, snapshots and dynasets provide different performance characteristics and thus are better suited to distinct tasks:

- For small result sets, snapshots are faster to open and scroll through. Also, if you don't need to update data or see changes made by other users, use a snapshot.

- For larger result sets, dynasets are faster and more efficient. Moving to the end of a snapshot requires the entire result set to be downloaded to the client. In contrast, a dynaset downloads only the primary key columns and then retrieves the last screen of data that is referenced by those keys.

- Dynaset open time and scrolling speed are affected most negatively by the number of columns you select and the number of the query's tables that are output. Select only the columns you need; outputting all columns using `Table.*` is more convenient but slower. Sometimes joins are used simply as restrictions and don't need to be output at all.

The `RecordsetClone`

You cannot get direct programmatic access to a form's underlying recordset. However, Access provides a DAO (Data Access Object) twin of the underlying recordset in the `RecordsetClone` property. This object shares an identical recordset with the form's underlying recordset. At the same time, it supports the methods supported by a dynaset DAO, such as `FindFirst`, `FindNext`, and so on. The form recordset and its clone have separate record pointers and can be accessing separate records, but because they share compatible bookmarks, they can be synchronized at any time desired. More information is presented in Chapter 16, "Data Access Objects."

For a brief preview of the potential usefulness of this feature, the following is code for a combo box that allows a user to select a record to move to, using the Northwinds Employee table for the example. Unlike a typical combo box application, this box is not bound to any data field. Rather, the data from the box controls the form itself. This is the basic routine that is produced if you select the combo box wizard item "Find a record on my form based on the value I selected in my combo box." This is the combo box `After Update` event function:

```
Sub CmbSrch_AfterUpdate()
    ' Find the record that matches the control.
    Me.RecordsetClone.FindFirst "[EmployeeID] = " & Me![CmbSrch]
    Me.Bookmark = Me.RecordsetClone.Bookmark
End Sub
```

The first line calls the `FindFirst` method of the recordset clone. Because the bookmarks are directly compatible (they would not have been if you had merely created a recordset on an identical query), you can pass the value directly to the form's `Bookmark` property to effect the move.

Setting the Other Properties

The remaining properties are used to control aspects of the form that aren't covered by the property sets described earlier. These properties touch on both the data and the format of the form, as well as some of the events associated with the form.

The `PopUp` and `Modal` Properties

The `PopUp` and `Modal` properties combine to help create different types of form behavior. They are used in conjunction with the `Border Style` property to create common dialog boxes.

- The `PopUp` property determines if the form is to remain on top of all other forms in the Access window. This property is useful for creating floating toolbars and menu bars. The default is non-pop-up (No).

- The `Modal` property determines whether the form opens in modal form. This means that the users must finish with this form before doing anything else in the application, such as setting focus to a control on another form. The default is non-modal (no).

> **TIP**
>
> While working in Visual Basic, leave the `Popup` and `Modal` properties off during development and debugging. They can interfere with access to the source code and debug windows. Once all code is working correctly, you can set these properties.

The `Cycle` Property

The `Cycle` property specifies how the cursor behaves if the Tab key is pressed when the last control on a bound form has the focus. You can choose from the following three settings:

- All Records moves the focus to the first field in the next record in the underlying source of data.

Creating Interactive Forms

CHAPTER 6

189

6

CREATING
INTERACTIVE
FORMS

- Current Record moves the focus to the first control in the tab order on the form in the same record.
- Current Page moves the focus back to the first control in the tab order on the same form page.

The `Cycle` property is affected by the tab order. To determine which control is first in the tab order, you must set the `Tab Index` property for the control that is to be first to 0. (See the section "Setting the Tab Order" later in this chapter for a complete discussion of tab order.)

The `Has Module` Property

The `Has Module` property specifies whether the form has an associated class module. By setting this property value to No, you can decrease both the time it takes Access to load the form and the amount of space the form takes up in the database. However, forms having this property set to No do not appear in the object browser, and you cannot create new instances of the form by using the `New` keyword. You can still use the form as a subform, and it will appear in the `Forms` collection. Also, any public procedures can still be called using the property sheet.

If your form doesn't require a code module, setting this property value to No can increase the performance of the form. As soon as you attempt to view the form's code, however, Access sets this property value back to Yes. The applications of this feature are somewhat limited. Any form with command buttons, or one that uses a combo box to jump to records, will have code (provided by the wizard), so only simple forms that just have fields and the built-in navigation controls are likely to fall into this category.

Forms and Visual Basic

Any form can have Visual Basic (VBA) code behind it. It has already been pointed out that command buttons, as well as many other controls created by wizards, automatically generate VBA code. User functions and subroutines defined in a form's code page are normally invisible outside the form.

Certain properties are really most useful when they are accessed through code. For example, what point would there be in creating a command button with the `Visible` property value set to False?

However, you can create controls that are only `Enabled` or `Visible` under certain conditions. Here's is a snippet of code from an order entry form:

```
Private Sub Form_Current()
'tied to the On Current event
```

```
      if Me![isDealer] then
          Me![WholesalePrice].Visible = True
      Else
          Me![WholesalePrice].Visible = False
      End If

End Sub
```

The On Current event is triggered when a new customer record is selected. The field displaying the wholesale price is dependent on the customer type.

The reference Me refers to the underlying form. Any control on the form can be referenced by this syntax:

```
Me![control name].property
Me![control name].method   arguments
```

(Note that many controls have their Value property as the default property, so it need not always be explicitly referenced.)

Forms also have methods and properties of their own. You can reference form properties and methods as follows:

```
Me.property
Me.method arguments
```

The Access help file extensively lists methods and properties available for each object type.

> **NOTE**
>
> Note that a "." (pronounced "dot") separates the form name from *properties* and *methods,* but the "!" ("bang") separates the form name from control names. Earlier versions of Access accepted these interchangeably. Now the syntax is strictly enforced.

Bound forms work quite well for straightforward data entry. In the real world, though, you will encounter situations where binding a control to a field simply will not accomplish what is desired. Here are some real-world examples:

- A production control program where the user enters a production order for a product. The application then deducts from inventory the appropriate quantities of all parts needed to assemble the product and prints a pick list.
- An order form where the order total must also be added to the salesperson's month-to-date record.

Creating Interactive Forms

CHAPTER 6

191

6

CREATING
INTERACTIVE
FORMS

- Very strictly controlled handling of multi-user conflicts, requiring the use of the `BeginTrans`, `CommitTrans`, and `Rollback` methods to assure data integrity.

- A requirement that keystroke behavior match as closely as possible existing software to which the users are accustomed, rather than Access conventions.

An entire form can be built with unbound controls, using VBA and DAO to handle the actual storage. The standard menu operations (filter, save record, and so on) and keystroke significance (Esc cancels record changes) can be bypassed for other behaviors specific to the job requirements. This is more work, but it greatly extends the power of Access forms if used appropriately.

Forms and Subforms

Subforms provide an additional view for data in forms. Figure 6.15 provides an example from the Northwinds database.

FIGURE 6.15.

A simple form/subform generated by the Form Wizard.

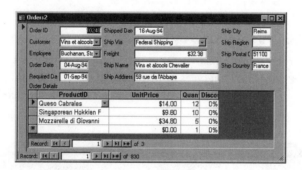

To create a form/subform outside of the Form Wizard, or to convert an existing form, proceed as follows:

Design the subform. Most often subforms are datasheet-style forms to best display one-to-many relationships; other small forms are sometimes used. Set the `Default View` and `Views Allowed` properties to reflect how you want this subform displayed. Save the form as a named form.

Make sure a relationship exists between one of the fields on the subform `Record Source` and the main form `Record Source`. It is possible to have a form/subform without an established relationship, but editing of data may not be possible depending on the details of the link.

Design the main form. Reduce the size of the form design view so that the database con-tainer view (at the form page) is also visible. Click and drag the subform and drop it on the main form.

Access will typically link the child field in the subform to the master field in the main form if the relationship is unambiguous. Otherwise it will be necessary to set these val-ues yourself. See Figure 6.16.

FIGURE 6.16.

Master and child link fields in the subform property sheet.

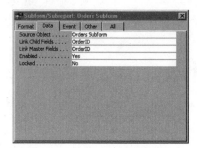

Multipage Wizard-Style Forms

The multipage form is useful when your users need to be led through a sequence of events. One of the most common types of multipage form is the wizard-style form. This type of form can also be useful for step-by-step instructions, questionnaires, or simple messages.

> **TIP**
>
> Although still useful for certain applications, many of the uses for multipage forms can be better served with the newly improved Tabbed control.

To make a multipage form, start with a simple form. Enlarge it vertically so that it is large enough to hold the different pages to be displayed.

The pages are placed in the Detail section of the form. On this sample, each page has a single-line message contained in a label control. A page can contain as many controls and subforms as can be displayed onscreen.

Each page is separated by a `PageBreak` control. The page breaks are represented by the little dots next to the 1 and 2 marks along the left ruler.

The footer contains the control buttons for moving through the pages. These could just as easily be placed in the header. Both the header and the footer can contain any instructions or controls that need to remain for the entire form.

The following code is required in this form.

In the General Declarations section:

```
Dim curpage As Integer
```

In the Form Open event:

```
Private Sub Form_Open(Cancel As Integer)
curpage = 1
End Sub
```

In the Prev Page button:

```
Private Sub PrevPage_Click()
    curpage = curpage - 1
    If curpage < 1 Then curpage = 1
    DoCmd.GoToPage curpage
End Sub
```

In the Next Page button:

```
Private Sub NextPage_Click()
    curpage = curpage + 1
    If curpage > 6 Then curpage = 6
    DoCmd.GoToPage curpage
End Sub
```

Other Form Settings

The topics discussed in the following sections have an overall effect on the way a form behaves. They are included here because of their importance in form design and because they don't really belong under any other heading.

Form Headers and Footers

One of the useful features of the Access form is its ability to display headers and footers. These areas on the form are most useful for displaying the column names and column sums on continuous forms.

Both the header and footer remain stationary during the scrolling of continuous forms, and thus are the most useful places to display command buttons or other input or selection controls that need to remain fixed in place.

Setting the Tab Order

Tab order refers to the sequence in which the cursor traverses the fields and controls on a form. The cursor follows the sequence of the Tab Index property of the controls that have their tab stop enabled. Setting the tab order of the controls is simply a matter of changing the number in the Tab Index property of each control. This task can be tedious at best. Fortunately, Access provides a handy tool that enables you to set the order in which the cursor traverses the fields on a form: the Tab Order dialog box, as shown in Figure 6.17. To display it, right-click the Form Selector and choose Tab Order from the pop-up menu.

FIGURE 6.17.

The Tab Order dialog box.

The list of control names is displayed in the Tab Order dialog box. To move a control or controls, click the left pane by the named control (it will be highlighted). If you are moving a group at a time, hold down the Shift key and select the additional controls. Release the Shift key, left-click on one of the highlighted choices, and drag to the desired location.

In case the form contains many controls, the Auto Order button is provided to align the controls on the form automatically, from left to right and from top to bottom. Even after you use the Auto Order button, you can make changes to the order of the controls on the form so that you can customize the tab order to your users' needs.

Printing Forms

Although it's true that reports are most often used for printing information contained in Access databases, now and then you may need to print what is displayed on a form. You must consider a number of points when designing forms that are to be printed. Access gives you a great deal of control over many aspects of a form's format.

You can control what appears on certain parts of forms when printing and other parts when displaying onscreen. The Display When property of controls and subforms determines this.

Creating Interactive Forms

CHAPTER 6

195

6

CREATING
INTERACTIVE
FORMS

`Layout For Print` enables you to choose which type of font to use when printing to the printer or screen. If the form is to be printed, the printer fonts are the best choice because they leave a crisp, clear image.

> **TIP**
>
> Even though forms can be printed, they often don't show up well. Access reports are very easy to design, and they provide far more satisfactory results. Because a report and a form can use the same named query, the data will be identical.

Forms for Multiple Users

Perhaps more so than with most other types of applications, databases are most effective when shared among a number of simultaneous users. This introduces tricky problems which do not exist in a single user environment. Access includes a number of features to help manage multiple users, but selection of the best approach requires careful consideration of the advantages and disadvantages of each method.

Problems Caused by Multiple Users

When more than one person can edit the same record (typically in a networked environment), complications occur. For example, suppose user Andrew is editing a customer's address, while user Betty is assigning the customer's new account representative. Andrew then saves the updated record, but Betty still has the record open. Then Betty saves. The result is that the older address in Betty's record overwrites the newly updated address from Andrew.

It can get messier. Suppose Andrew and Betty have a joint bank account with $5,000 in it. The bank (whose programmer did not read this book) has not paid a lot of attention to multiuser matters. Andrew goes to one branch with a deposit of $500. The teller brings up the information, but while the information is on the screen, Betty goes to another branch to withdraw $250. Her teller also brings up the $5,000 figure (remember that the other transaction has not yet been completed). Andrew's teller adds the $500 and saves the new account balance of $5,500. Betty's teller then subtracts her withdrawal and saves the new account balance of $4,750, which overwrites the $5,500. Oops.

Unfortunately, there is no single good solution to multiple user problems. Different approaches trade off advantages and disadvantages. Access does provide the tools to construct reasonable solutions to the issues faced by the form designer.

Handling Edit Collisions

Even the simple form generated by the AutoForm Wizard has basic multiuser awareness. The default form (unless the defaults have been modified) is created with the Record Locks property value set to No Locks (optimistic locking).

Access divides the form-based record edit process into three phases:

While a user is looking at a record, no lock of any kind is placed on it. If someone else on the network changes the data, the record will eventually be updated in any bound form (subject to the Refresh Interval set in Tools | Options | Advanced).

Once the user starts typing in any field of the record, it is in edit mode. With optimistic locking (Record Locks=No Locks), changes made in the underlying data by other users are permitted, but these changes will no longer update the display. With pessimistic locking (Records Locks=Edited Record), all other users are immediately blocked from editing that record.

Once the record is saved (by going to another record, closing the form, or selecting Save Record from the menu), Access goes back to the underlying record and checks to see if anyone has changed it during the editing period. If it has been changed, a warning appears (see Figure 6.18). Note that this step is only necessary with optimistic locking. Pessimistic locking would have maintained full control of the record during the transaction.

FIGURE 6.18.

A write conflict has occurred with optimistic locking.

Optimistic Locking

Although optimistic locking alerts the user to the conflict problem, it does not do much to help resolve it other than letting the user choose to overwrite or throw away the changes. For simple forms without complex data, probably the best way to handle the problem is to click the Drop Changes button, and then load a fresh copy and reenter. The second button, Copy to Clipboard, is enough to send some users into a panic. The first button, Save Record, is probably an invitation to trouble.

Pessimistic Locking

With pessimistic locking, these questions will not arise because the first person editing the record owns it for the duration. There are a few snags, however.

If any of your forms use pessimistic locking, you should be sure that all your forms have those seemingly unnecessary record selectors activated. With record locking, anyone who attempts to edit a record that is already in edit will be blocked, and the only indication of this is that the small triangle pointer in the record selector changes to a "No access" symbol (see Figure 6.19). Without that clue, users will have no idea why they cannot type into the fields. (The user doing the editing will see the selector turn into a pencil.) This is safe and secure, but what happens when Andrew absentmindedly starts entering data (a single keystroke does it) and gets called into a three-hour meeting? No one on the system can get access to that record, or even find out who is holding it. Worse, Access locks not on the record level but on the block level (2KB), which can include a fair number of records. During Andrew's absence, all records in that 2KB will be locked.

FIGURE 6.19.

A small "No access" symbol is the only clue as to why this record cannot be edited.

The third choice for form-based locking, `All Records`, is a great way to frustrate other users. It has few uses in a multiuser system except, perhaps, administrative maintenance.

Programmatic Approaches to Record Locking

Access provides two methods for more sophisticated record locking control. The most powerful is to handle the data programmatically in VBA and DAO rather than binding fields directly to controls. This is the level of control that would be necessary to handle the bank problem described previously. The `BeginTrans`, `CommitTrans`, and `Rollback` methods permit precise control of the granularity of the transaction. They are discussed in Chapter 16.

A simpler approach would be to use optimistic locking but to protect the user from the unfriendly default error handling. Access 97 generates a trappable error that can allow your error handling in place of the standard warning. This example goes for the simplest approach—presenting the user with the revised record and telling him that someone has changed the record, and that it is necessary to make his changes on the newest version. While this could be a little annoying to the user, the alternatives are more troublesome. Presenting old and new data and asking the user to reconcile them can be confusing. Overwriting another user's data without looking could cause the loss of valuable information.

When a write conflict occurs, Access returns error 7787. It can also return error 7878 if, upon entering edit mode, another user has updated the record and the refresh has not yet occurred. These are Jet Database errors, not VBA errors, so an On Error...Resume statement is not used. Also, because they are not VBA errors, these errors are not referenced in Basic's Err Object.

When a form error occurs, the Form_Error event is called (Figures 6.20 and 6.21) with two arguments: the error number passed into the routine, and a response passed back to tell Access whether to proceed with standard error handling or not.

FIGURE 6.20.

Enable the form error event.

```
Private Sub Form_Error(DataErr As Integer, Response As Integer)
'DataErr is the value passed to us from Access
'Response is value we return to Access
 'depends on what we want to happen next
 On Error GoTo handler 'trap any unexpected VBA errors
    '(unlikely in this simple routine)
    If DataErr = 7787 Or DataErr = 7878 Then 'write conflict
    Response = acDataErrContinue
        'tell Access not to post warning
        MsgBox "Someone else changed this record. The new data_
           will be displayed, please make your entries again",_
           vbExclamation + vbOKOnly
    Else
        Response = acDataErrDisplay 'we're not handling this
                    'one, tell Access to handle it normally
    End If
leave:
Exit Sub

handler:
    MsgBox "Unexpected Basic error: " & Err
    Resume leave
End Sub
```

FIGURE 6.21.

A less threatening error message.

TIP

Chapter 16 gives an example of creating an audit trail for form changes. Implementing such a feature will enable reconstruction of write conflicts for review, making real-time record resolution less critical.

Making Forms Legible

The wide range of properties available for form design gives you an excellent opportunity to create user-friendly forms. Unfortunately, there is also an excellent opportunity to get carried away. To make your forms as friendly as possible, observe the following guidelines:

- Use decorative graphics sparingly. A granite-textured form might look really nice as a title splash, but it can get old fast to someone who is entering 200 form pages of data a day.

- Don't mix type styles. Use different weights, colors, and sizes of one or two compatible styles to emphasize and identify text. Use Arial or Times Roman rather than Old English or Script.

- Group controls by function. Highlight the groups with rectangles or by gentle coloring. Use tabbed controls to keep the form uncluttered.

- Keep most lettering in the 10-14 point range. Avoid very small or very large type (except, possibly, for form titles).

- Design your form while working at the lowest resolution your users are likely to have. In many cases, that may mean working at 640×480, with 256 or even 16 colors.

- Test your tab order. Users entering a great deal of data don't normally use a mouse, so make sure keyboard entry proceeds in a logical sequence.

- Don't overdo special effects like sunken text boxes. On a simple form, the effect is very attractive. A complex form that's full of sunken text boxes looks excessively busy. A simple flat control is often best.

- Use selections from combo boxes, list boxes, or option groups in situations where a user selects from predetermined values. The less the user needs to remember, the better.

Summary

Forms are the main feature your users will see. Careful attention to form design can make the difference between a smooth, reliable application and an error-prone, frustrating one. Use the wizards to create a basic form, and then modify the properties of the form and its controls for an efficient design. Don't forget to pay attention to multiuser problems, readability, performance, and other user-centered issues.

Using ActiveX
Controls for
Interactivity

CHAPTER 7

ActiveX Controls Explained

One of the most powerful aspects of Access 97 is that it is extensible. In addition to the controls that are available as part of the product, you can incorporate ActiveX controls on your forms. This means that you are not limited to the controls that Access 97 provides, but only by the imagination of third-party developers who design ActiveX controls. You can also design your own ActiveX controls to use in your Access 97 database applications by using either Visual Basic 5 or the freely downloadable Visual Basic 5 Control Creation Edition. The VB5 CCE can be downloaded by simply joining the Site Builder Network and then downloading the software from the following URL:

`http://www.microsoft.com/sbnmember/download/default.htm`

The system requirements for using the Visual Basic Custom Control Edition are as follows:

- A system processor that is at least a 486.
- Windows 95 or Windows NT 4.0 or later.
- 10MB of free disk space.
- Mouse or similar pointing device.

Make sure you download the sample applications and tutorials that are available from the same Web page at the URL given previously.

ActiveX controls were known as custom controls or OLE controls in previous versions of Access. ActiveX controls have an `.OCX` filename extension. You use ActiveX controls to enhance the user's experience in your Access 97 database applications. ActiveX controls can add a great deal of additional functionality to your Access 97 applications.

ActiveX controls support the OLE 2.0 custom control architecture and provide support for 32-bit operating systems. They contain their own code, methods, events, and properties. An ActiveX control's functionality is stored in a file with the `.OCX` extension. This is why ActiveX controls are often referred to as OCXs. A Calendar OCX ships as part of Microsoft Access 97. Additional OCX controls are included in the Microsoft Office Developer Edition Tools for Windows 95 and are also available from third-party vendors. These vendors include Crescent, Sheridan, Far Point, and many others.

Two types of ActiveX controls are available. The first type is visible at both design time and runtime. After being placed on a form, this type of control provides a front-end interface that allows the user to directly manipulate the object in some way. This type of control also provides a visible interface at design-time for the application designer to work with. One example is the Calendar control that ships with Access 97. The second type of

ActiveX control is visible at design time, but not at runtime. An example of such a control is one that gives you access to all the Windows common dialog boxes, such as Open and Print. The control itself is not visible to the user, but its functionality is available to the user at runtime. Another example is a timer control. This control operates within the application, triggering event code to run, but it is not actually visible to the user.

ActiveX controls enable you to easily incorporate additional functionality in your applications. For example, if you need to include a calendar on your form, you don't need re-invent the wheel. Instead, you can include a custom calendar control on the form. You can modify the calendar's behavior by changing its properties and executing its methods.

Incorporating ActiveX Controls in Access 97

Before you can incorporate an ActiveX control in your Access 97 database application, you must perform three steps:

1. Install the ActiveX control.
2. Register the control.
3. Add the control to a form.

When you purchase an ActiveX control, it generally ships with an installation program. Usually, the installation program copies the OCX file to your Windows system directory. The name of this directory can vary depending on whether you are running Windows 95 or Windows NT and what you named your Windows directory during your operating system installation.

You should note that ActiveX controls are COM objects that can have interfaces not supported by Access 97. If you are purchasing an ActiveX control specifically for your Access 97 application, make sure that Access 97 supports the interface implemented by the ActiveX control.

Registering an ActiveX Control

After you have properly installed the control, you are ready to register it with Access. Often a control is automatically registered during the installation process. This is true with the Calendar OCX that ships with Access, as well as all the OCX controls that are included as part of the Microsoft Office Developer Edition Tools for Windows 95. OCX controls are registered within the HKEY_LOCAL_MACHINE key under the SOFTWARE/Classes class in the Windows Registry (see Figure 7.1). In the figure, the ImageList control, registered as COMCTL.ImagelistCtrl, is selected.

FIGURE 7.1.
OCX controls in the Windows Registry.

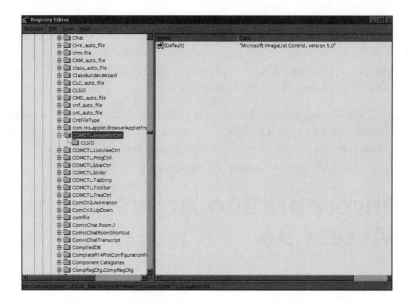

If an ActiveX control is not registered, you can register it using the ActiveX Controls dialog box. To open this dialog box, select Tools | ActiveX Controls from your Access 97 menu bar. The ActiveX Controls dialog box is shown in Figure 7.2.

FIGURE 7.2.
The ActiveX Controls dialog box allows you to register ActiveX controls.

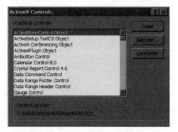

This dialog box lists all the ActiveX controls that are currently registered within Access. To add an ActiveX control to the list, click Register. The Add ActiveX Control dialog box appears, as shown in Figure 7.3.

Make sure you're pointing to the directory containing the OCX you want to register. The control you are registering must already be installed. If it has not been installed, it will not appear on the list. Select the OCX you want to register, and click OK. You are returned to the ActiveX Controls dialog box, and the ActiveX control you selected appears on the list of registered controls and is automatically entered in the Registry. You are now ready to include the control on a form.

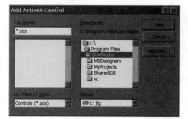

FIGURE 7.3.

The Add ActiveX Control dialog box allows you to locate the ActiveX control you want to register.

If you no longer plan to use an ActiveX control, you will want to use the `Unregister` function. This function removes the Registry entries for controls you no longer plan to use.

Adding ActiveX Controls to Forms

After you have registered an ActiveX control, you are ready to include the control on your forms. ActiveX controls can be added to forms in one of two ways:

- Select the ActiveX control from the toolbox by clicking the More Controls icon in the toolbox.

- Select ActiveX Control from the Insert menu when in Form or Report Design view.

The More Controls tool in the toolbox shows you all ActiveX controls registered by your system. This includes ActiveX controls that are part of Excel, Visual Basic, and any other application that utilizes ActiveX controls. Some of these controls will not work properly with Access. To determine which controls you can safely include in your application, you can read the readme file that ships with Access or contact the vendor of the ActiveX control. The More Controls menu is shown in Figure 7.4.

You can also select an ActiveX control from the Insert menu. The Insert ActiveX Control dialog box appears, as shown in Figure 7.5. After you select a control from the Select an ActiveX Control list box, the control is placed on the form. You can move the control around the form and size it as needed.

After you have placed an ActiveX control on a form, the control is ready to operate in its default format. If you insert the Calendar OCX in a form and run the form, it will look as shown in Figure 7.6.

The Calendar control knows how to display all the months of the year, along with the corresponding days for each month. So far, you have not set any properties for the calendar, nor have you written code to respond to any events of the calendar. Setting an ActiveX control's properties, executing an ActiveX control's methods, and responding to an ActiveX control's events are all covered in the sections that follow.

FIGURE 7.4.

The More Controls menu shows all ActiveX controls installed on the system.

FIGURE 7.5.

The Insert ActiveX Control dialog box allows you to add an ActiveX control to a form.

FIGURE 7.6.

A Calendar OCX with no properties explicitly set.

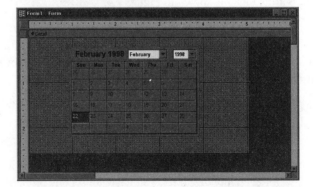

Understanding and Managing the Control Reference Within Your Access Application

When you insert an ActiveX control on a form, Access automatically creates a reference to the control's Type Library. This reference appears in the References dialog box, as shown in Figure 7.7. To invoke the References dialog box, select Tools | References with any module in your database application open in Design view. Note that the full path to the control is stored within the References dialog box. For example, Figure 7.7 shows that the Calendar OCX is stored within C:\WINDOWS\SYSTEM. If the OCX is moved, VBA might not be able to resolve the reference. If this occurs, you must open the References dialog box and manually remove the check mark from the reference marked as missing and set a reference to the ActiveX control in its new location.

FIGURE 7.7.

The References dialog box allows you to add and remove library references.

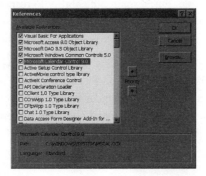

If you are distributing an application containing ActiveX controls, the application might work without problems or then again it might not. Access does its best to attempt to resolve references to ActiveX controls. If the controls reside in the Windows\System directory or in the directory within which Access is installed, Access can automatically resolve the references, even if the application is installed in a different directory on the user's machine than it was on your machine.

Remember, not only do ActiveX controls need to be referenced, they also need to be registered in the Windows Registry. If you use the Setup Wizard included with the Microsoft Office Developer Edition Tools for Windows 95 to distribute your application, the OCXs are automatically registered when the user installs your application. If you do not use the Microsoft Office Developer Edition Tools for Windows 95 setup program to distribute your application, either you need to write code to register the .OCX, or the user must manually register the ActiveX control. You can manually register a control by using the REGSVR32.EXE utility that is included with VB 5.

Setting Properties of an ActiveX Control at Design Time

The methods, events, and properties associated with each ActiveX control differ. They are specific to that control and are determined by the author of the control. They are used to manipulate the control's appearance and behavior. Each control's methods, events, and properties are contained in a separate .OCX file.

If you do not modify a control's properties, it functions with its default appearance and behavior. Much of the richness of third-party controls comes from the ability to customize the controls by changing their properties at both design time and runtime. Some controls support data binding. Data binding enables you to store or display data in a control from an underlying field in a table. Furthermore, the ability to respond to an ActiveX control's events allows you to respond to the user's interaction with the control. Finally, the ability to execute the control's methods enables you to manipulate the control.

Figure 7.8 shows some of the Calendar control's many properties. As with any control, most of the properties of the Calendar control can be set at design time and modified or read at runtime. To access the properties of the Calendar control, right-click the control icon that is embedded in a form in your application and click the Properties option in the dialog box that appears.

FIGURE 7.8.

The Calendar control property sheet.

Another way to set custom properties for an ActiveX control is to set them graphically using a custom dialog box. Not all ActiveX controls give you a custom dialog box to adjust the properties of the control. If the properties dialog box for the control shows a

Custom property, the ActiveX control provides a custom properties dialog box to adjust the properties of the control. For some ActiveX controls, the only way that you can set some properties of the control in Design view is by utilizing this custom properties dialog box. You can access this custom properties dialog box by selecting the Custom property from the ActiveX control's property sheet and then clicking the Build button that appears. For example, if you select the Custom property from the Calendar control's property sheet and click Build, the Calendar control Properties dialog box appears, as shown in Figure 7.9. Another way to access this custom properties sheet is by right-clicking the control, selecting the object name, and then selecting Properties, as shown in Figure 7.10. The Calendar control Properties dialog box allows you to modify many important attributes of the calendar, including the first day of the week, whether you want the days of the week to show, and the colors and fonts for the calendar. The properties shown in this dialog box will vary for each control.

7

USING ACTIVEX CONTROLS FOR INTERACTIVITY

FIGURE 7.9.

The Calendar control Custom Properties dialog box.

FIGURE 7.10.

Selecting the Calendar control's Custom Properties dialog box graphically.

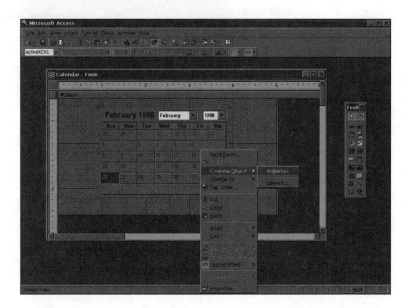

Coding Events of an ActiveX Control

Just as the properties of the control can be set or evaluated at runtime, the events of the control can be coded. To obtain a list of all the events associated with an ActiveX control, right-click the Calendar control that is embedded into your form when it is in Design view and select the Build Event option from the dialog box that pops up to open the Procedure box in the Module window. Make sure that the control name for your ActiveX control is listed in the Object box. Figure 7.11 shows all the events for the Calendar control.

FIGURE 7.11.

Viewing the events of the Calendar control.

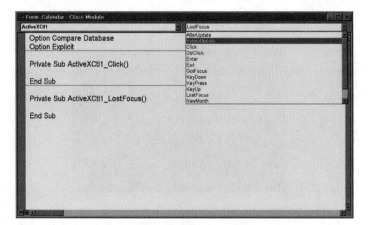

The `AfterUpdate` event of the Calendar control is triggered when the user selects a date from the calendar. The following code changes the value of a text box named `txtDateSelected` to the `Value` property of the `calPickADay` Calendar control. This text box is located on the same form as the Calendar control. The code is placed in the `AfterUpdate` event of the Calendar control so it executes any time the user selects a date on the calendar.

```
Private Sub calPickADay_AfterUpdate()
    txtDateSelected.Value = calPickADay.Value
End Sub
```

This sample code and most of the code in this chapter are contained in a file called `cha07.MDB` located on the Web site for this book. This example is found in the form called `frmPickADay`.

The Calendar Control

The Calendar control ships as part of the standard Access 97 package. Understanding the properties and methods associated with the Calendar control makes it a lot easier with which to work. The properties and methods specific to the Calendar control are covered in the sections that follow.

Properties of a Calendar Control

The Day, Month, and Year properties are used to designate the day, month, and year displayed on the calendar. These properties are automatically changed at runtime as the user selects different dates on the calendar. You can modify the values programmatically, thereby changing the day, month, or year that is selected.

The Value property is one of the most important properties of the Calendar control. It is used to retrieve the selected calendar date or to move the date highlight to a specific day. The following code uses the Value property to display the selected day in a message box:

```
Private Sub cmdDisplayDate_Click()
    MsgBox calPickADay.Value
End Sub
```

The ValueIsNull property allows you to indicate that no date is selected on the calendar. This property is used when you want to ensure that the user explicitly selects a date.

The DayFont and DayFontColor properties are used to specify the font and color for the display of the day titles. The DayFont property is further broken down into the properties Name, Size, Bold, Italic, Underline, and Strikethrough. An individual property can be modified like this:

```
calPickADay.DayFont.Italic = True
```

You can use the With...End With construct to change several font properties at once:

```
With calPickADay.DayFont
      .Bold = True
      .Italic = True
      .Name = "Arial"
End With
```

You can use the DayFontColor property to easily modify the color of the day titles:

```
calPickADay.DayFontColor = 16711680
```

The GridFont and GridFontColor properties are similar to the DayFont and DayFontColor properties. GridFont is used to determine the font attributes for the text within the calendar, and GridFontColor is used to indicate the color of the text within the calendar. For example, the following routine modifies the Bold, Italic, and Name properties of the GridFont property and changes the color of the days that are displayed on the calendar:

```
Private Sub cmdChangeGridFont_Click()
    With calPickADay.GridFont
        .Bold = True
        .Italic = True
        .Name = "Arial"
    End With
    calPickADay.GridFontColor = 8388736
End Sub
```

The DayLength and MonthLength properties are used to designate how you want the day and month titles to display. The available choices for DayLength are Short (0), Medium (1), and Long (2). The Short option displays the day as one character. Medium displays the day as a three-character abbreviation, and Long displays the full day (for example, Monday). The available choices for MonthLength are Short (0) and Long (2). Short displays the month as a three-character abbreviation, and Long displays the full month name. The following code is used to display the DayLength as Short and the MonthLength as Short:

```
Private Sub cmdChangeLength_Click()
    calPickADay.DayLength = 0
    calPickADay.MonthLength = 0
End Sub
```

The ShowDateSelectors property is used to indicate whether combo boxes appear at the top of the calendar, allowing the user to select a month and year. This property can be set to True or False.

The ShowTitle property is used to indicate whether the month and year are displayed at the top of the calendar.

The GridCellEffect and GridLinesColor properties are used to specify whether the gridlines are Raised, Sunken, or Flat and to specify the color of the gridlines.

The BackColor property is used to specify the background color for the Calendar control. The FirstDay property indicates the first day of the week that is shown in the control. The ShowDays property determines whether to show the days of the week. The ShowHorizontalGrid and ShowVerticalGrid properties determine if the gridlines of the Calendar control are visible, and the TitleFont and TitleFontColor properties determine how the control's title is displayed.

Methods of a Calendar Control

Just as the Calendar control has numerous properties, it has several methods. These methods are actions you can take on the `Calendar` object.

The `NextDay`, `PreviousDay`, `NextWeek`, `PreviousWeek`, `NextMonth`, `PreviousMonth`, `NextYear`, and `PreviousYear` methods are all used to move the `Value` property of the control forward or backward by the specified time period.

The `Refresh` method is used to repaint the Calendar control.

The `Today` method is used to set the `Value` property to the current date as indicated by the system time on the machine your application is running on.

The `AboutBox` method is used to display the About box associated with the Calendar control.

> **NOTE**
>
> The following examples require controls provided with the Microsoft Office Developer Edition Tools for Windows 95 (ODE). You must have the ODE for the following code samples to run. If you have the ODE, you can distribute these tools royalty-free to your users.
>
> If you have the ODE properly installed and are still unable to run some of the examples, you might want to check the References dialog box to ensure that the controls are properly referenced.

Events of a Calendar Control

The Calendar control that is distributed with Access 97 also includes several events you can use programmatically in your application.

The `AfterUpdate` event occurs when the user moves to a new date in the control and the calendar has been refreshed. The `BeforeUpdate` event also occurs after the user has moved to a new event in the control but the `BeforeUpdate` event occurs before the calendar has been refreshed.

The `Click` and `DblClick` events occur when the user has either clicked or double-clicked a date in the Calendar control. The `KeyDown`, `KeyUp`, and `KeyPress` events occur as the user presses and releases keys on the keyboard while the Calendar control is in focus.

The `NewMonth` and `NewYear` events both occur when the Calendar control date is changed to either a new month or a new year.

The UpDown Control

The UpDown ActiveX control is a replacement for the Spin Button control that was used with Visual Basic 4.0. The UpDown control is a part of the group of controls that make up the COMCT232.OCX file. You must be sure that this file is added to your application as a reference to be able to use the UpDown control in your Access 97 application. This file is listed as Microsoft Windows Common Controls-2 5.0 in the Available References list box of the References dialog box in Access 97. If you are creating an application to distribute to users you must make sure that the COMCT232.OCX file is installed into the user's Windows System directory. The UpDown control has a pair of arrow buttons that can be used to increment and decrement values. The UpDown control can also be used to set values in an associated control known as a *Buddy control*. In fact, the Buddy control and the UpDown control often appear to the user as a single control. The Buddy control can be set to any control available that has some property that can be updated by the UpDown control. An exception to this is some windowless controls, such as the label control, because they have no properties that can be updated by the UpDown control. The UpDown control has a property known as the BuddyControl property that can be used to set the identity of the Buddy control for the UpDown control.

The UpDown control has a property called AutoBuddy that, if set, uses the previous control in the form's tab order automatically as its Buddy control. If there is no compatible control in the tab order before the UpDown control, the AutoBuddy property will use the next control that is compatible in the tab order as its Buddy control. When the AutoBuddy or the BuddyControl properties are set, the UpDown control will position itself next to the indicated Buddy control.

To be able to use the UpDown control in your Access 97 application, you must insert the UpDown control on a form in your application by using either the More Controls icon in the Toolbox or by choosing Insert | ActiveX Control from the Access 97 menu bar. You must then set the BuddyControl property of the UpDown control to another control and set the BuddyProperty property of the UpDown control to an updateable property on the other control. Figure 7.12 shows an example of setting the BuddyControl property of an UpDown control to Buddy with a Calendar control called calPickADay along with setting the BuddyProperty property of the UpDown control to the Value property of the calPickADay Calendar control.

The StatusBar Control

The StatusBar control allows you to quickly and easily add professional-looking status bars to your forms. A status bar provides a window through which to display system information to the user of your application. The status bar is made up of a maximum of 16 panels that are stored in a Panels collection. The StatusBar control is part of the group of ActiveX controls that make up the COMCTL32.OCX file. You must be sure that this file is added to your application as a reference to be able to use the StatusBar control in your Access 97 application. This file is listed as Microsoft Windows Common Controls 5.0 in the Available References list box of the References dialog box in Access 97.

FIGURE 7.12.

Setting the custom properties of an UpDown control.

If you are creating an application to distribute to users you must make sure the COMCTL32.OCX file is installed into the user's Windows System directory. You have the option of placing the StatusBar control at the top, bottom, or sides of your Access 97 application, or you can set the StatusBar control to "float" within the application window by setting the properties of the StatusBar control. An example of the use of the StatusBar control is illustrated in the frmCalendar form that is part of the sample database cha07.mdb included on the Web site for this book that comes with this book. This form is shown in Figure 7.13.

The status bar displayed in the figure has six panels. The first two panels have been configured to display the current date and time. The last three panels have been configured to display the status of the Caps Lock, Num Lock, and Insert keys. The items to display in the panels are configured through the use of the Custom Properties box of the StatusBar control that is available by double-clicking the StatusBar control when the form is in Design view and selecting the Panels tab of the custom properties dialog box that appears. You can easily set up a StatusBar control to the configuration shown in Figure 7.13 without writing any code. The Panel object of the StatusBar control can be set to one of the following constants which display the listed attributes.

- sbrText   Displays text
- sbrCaps   Displays CAPS if Caps Lock is on
- sbrNum   Displays NUM if the Number Lock is on
- sbrIns   Displays INS if the insert key is enabled

- sbrScrl   Displays SCRL if the Scroll Lock is on
- sbrTime   Displays current time
- sbrDate   Displays current date

FIGURE 7.13.

A form with the StatusBar control inserted.

Properties can be set for the StatusBar control as a whole or for each of the individual panels that make up the StatusBar control. The properties for the StatusBar control are shown in Figure 7.14. The Style property of the StatusBar control is used to specify whether you want the status bar to include multiple panels or only a single panel. The SimpleText property is used only for single-panel status bars. It is used to specify the text contained within the panel. Finally, the MousePointer property allows you to select the type of mouse pointer that will appear when the mouse is located over the StatusBar control.

FIGURE 7.14.

The general properties of the StatusBar control.

Each panel of the StatusBar control has properties that can be used to affect the look and behavior of that panel. The panel properties are shown in Figure 7.15. The Style property is an important one. It is used to specify what information will be displayed within the panel. It can be set to Text, Caps, Num Lock, Ins, Scroll, Time, Date, or Kana Lock. These properties are described in detail in the previous section. When set, the control can automatically sense whether the Caps Lock or other keys are active. The Text property is used to indicate the text displayed within the panel when the `Style` property is set to Text. The value of this property is often modified at runtime to display a specific message to the user. The `Alignment` property is used to specify whether the information is left-aligned, right-aligned, or centered within the panel. The `Bevel` property of the panel can be set to None, Insert, or Raised.

FIGURE 7.15.

The StatusBar panel properties.

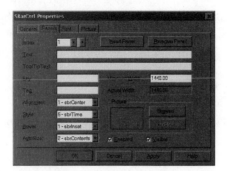

As you insert and remove panels, each panel is assigned an index. The `Index` property is used to refer to a specific panel at runtime. Here's an example:

```
Private Sub calPickADay_AfterUpdate()
    If calPickADay.Value = Date Then
        sbrStatus.Panels(3).Text = "TODAY!!!"
    Else
        sbrStatus.Panels(3).Text = ""
    End If
End Sub
```

This code evaluates the `calPickADay Value` property to see whether it is equal to the current date. If so, the text of the third panel is set to `"TODAY!!!"`. Otherwise, the text of the third panel is set to a zero-length string.

WARNING

Access is a world where almost everything is zero-based. Of course, there are exceptions to every rule. The StatusBar control is one of those exceptions—it is one-based. The code in the preceding example really does modify the text within the third panel.

The Common Dialog Control

The Common Dialog control is actually like many controls in one. It is used to display the standard Windows File Open, File Save As, Font, Color, and File Print common dialog boxes. The Common Dialog control can also run the Windows Help engine, enabling you to use Windows Style Help files within your Access 97 application. The Common Dialog control is an interface to the routines that are contained in the Microsoft Windows dynamic link library (DLL) Commdlg.dll. If you plan on using this control within your Access 97 application, the file Commdlg.dll must be installed in your Windows System directory. The Common Dialog control uses the file COMDLG32.OCA. You must be sure that this file is added to your application as a reference to be able to use the Common Dialog control in your Access 97 application. This file is listed as Microsoft Common Dialog Control 5.0 in the Available References list box of the References dialog box in Access 97.

The Common Dialog control is a hidden control that does not appear at runtime but whose properties and methods can be manipulated with Visual Basic for Applications (VBA) code. The form called frmCommonAndRich is shown in Figure 7.16. This form illustrates the use of several of the common dialog boxes as well as the Rich Textbox control, covered in the next section.

FIGURE 7.16.

The form used to illustrate common dialog and rich text boxes.

The Button Font and Screen Color command buttons illustrate the use of the Common Dialog control. They invoke the Color and Font common dialog boxes, respectively. The code under the Click event of the cmdColor command button looks like the following:

```
Private Sub cmdColor_Click()
    dlgCommon.Flags = cdlCCFullOpen
    dlgCommon.ShowColor
    Me.Detail.BackColor = dlgCommon.Color
End Sub
```

The code begins by setting the Flags property of the Common Dialog control. The Flags property is used to specify attributes of the common dialog box. The value of cdlCCFullOpen for the Color common dialog box indicates that the entire Color dialog box, including the portion that enables the user to create custom colors, will be displayed. The ShowColor method, when applied to the Common Dialog control, invokes the Color common dialog box, shown in Figure 7.17. The color that the user selects is put into the Color property of the Common Dialog control. This color is used to modify the BackColor property of the detail section of the form.

7

USING ACTIVEX
CONTROLS FOR
INTERACTIVITY

FIGURE 7.17.
The Color common dialog box.

The code under the Click event of the cmdFont command button looks like this:

```
Private Sub cmdFont_Click()
    Dim ctl As Control
    dlgCommon.Flags = cdlCFScreenFonts
    dlgCommon.ShowFont
    For Each ctl In Controls
        If TypeOf ctl Is CommandButton Then
            With ctl
                .FontName = dlgCommon.FontName
                .FontBold = dlgCommon.FontBold
                .FontItalic = dlgCommon.FontItalic
                .FontSize = dlgCommon.FontSize
            End With
        End If
    Next ctl
End Sub
```

The Click event of cmdFont first sets the Flags property of the Common Dialog control to cdlCFScreenFonts. For the Font common dialog, the value of cdlCDFScreenFonts causes the dialog box to list only the screen fonts supported by the user's system. The ShowFont method is used to invoke the actual dialog box (see Figure 7.18). Using a With...End With construct, the code takes each property set in the common dialog box and uses it to loop through the Controls collection of the form, modifying the font attributes of each command button.

FIGURE 7.18.

The Font common dialog box.

The File Open, File Save, and File Print common dialog boxes are covered as you work through the Rich Textbox control in the next section.

The Rich Textbox Control

The Rich Textbox ActiveX control allows the user to enter and edit text just as a normal Textbox control, but allows the application user much more control over the formatting of that text than is allowed by the normal Textbox control. The Rich Textbox does not have the capacity limitations of the normal Textbox control, and you can use the Rich Textbox as a data-bound control by binding it to a memo field in your Access 97 database application or a similar field in an attached SQL Server table. The Rich Textbox ActiveX control also supports the OLE drag-and-drop method of pasting objects into the control. Dragging and OLE object into a Rich Textbox will result in the insertion of the object into the Rich Textbox control. The Rich Textbox control uses the file RICHTX32.OCX. You must be sure that this file is added to your application as a reference to be able to use the Rich Textbox control in your Access 97 application. This file is listed as Microsoft Rich Textbox Control 5.0 in the Available References list box of the References dialog box in Access 97.

When you distribute an Access 97 application that uses the Rich Textbox AxtiveX control, you must install the RICHTX32.OCX file into the user's Windows System directory. The Rich Textbox control allows you to design a text box that gives you the opportunity to write code affecting the selected text. Properties that can be specified for the selected text include the Font, Font Size, Bold, and Italic properties. You can even add bullet points to the selected text. Furthermore, you can save the contents of the Rich Textbox control in a rich text format (RTF) file and later retrieve those contents into the control.

```
Private Sub cmdTextColor_Click()
    dlgCommon.ShowColor
    rtfDocument.SelColor = dlgCommon.Color
End Sub
```

This sample code uses the Color common dialog box, discussed in the preceding section, to set the `SelColor` property of the Rich Textbox control. The selected text will appear in whatever color the user selects from the common dialog box.

The Rich Textbox control contains a method called `SaveFile`. This method allows you to save the contents of the Rich Textbox control to an RTF file. The code looks like the following:

```
Private Sub cmdSave_Click()
    dlgCommon.Filter = "RTF Files (*.rtf)¦*.rtf"
    dlgCommon.ShowSave
    If dlgCommon.FileName = "" Then
        MsgBox "You Must Specify a File Name", vbExclamation, "File NOT
➥Saved!"
    Else
        rtfDocument.SaveFile dlgCommon.FileName
    End If
End Sub
```

The code begins by setting the `Filter` property of the Common Dialog control. This filters the filenames that are displayed in the File Save As common dialog box. The `ShowSave` method is used to invoke the Save As common dialog box, shown in Figure 7.19. After the user types or selects a filename, the `FileName` property of the Common Dialog control is filled in with the name of the file that the user specified. If the user clicks Cancel, the `FileName` property contains a zero-length string, and the user is warned that the file was not saved.

FIGURE 7.19.

The Save As common dialog box.

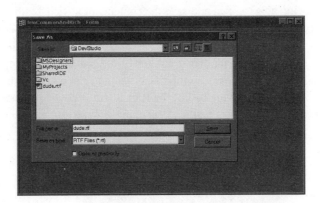

As mentioned, just as you can save the contents of a Rich Textbox control, you can retrieve the contents of an RTF file into the control. The code looks like the following:

```
Private Sub cmdOpen_Click()
    dlgCommon.FileName = ""
    dlgCommon.Filter = "RTF Files (*.rtf)¦*.rtf"
```

```
    dlgCommon.InitDir = CurDir
    dlgCommon.ShowOpen
    If dlgCommon.FileName = "" Then
        MsgBox "You Must Specify a File Name", vbExclamation, "File Cannot
Be Opened!"
    Else
        rtfDocument.LoadFile dlgCommon.FileName
    End If
End Sub
```

The Click event of the cmdOpen command button uses the ShowOpen method to invoke
the Open common dialog box, shown in Figure 7.20. If the user selects a file, the
LoadFile method of the Rich Textbox control uses the FileName property of the
Common Dialog control as the name of the file to open. If the user does not select a file
to open, he or she will be warned that he or she must specify a filename.

FIGURE 7.20.

*The Open com-
mon dialog box.*

In addition to being able to open and save the contents of a Rich Textbox control, you
can print the contents of the control. The Click event of the cmdPrint command button
sets the Flags property of the Common Dialog control to cdlPDAllPages. This selects
the All option button in the Print dialog box (and deselects the Pages and Selection
option buttons). The ShowPrinter method displays the Print common dialog box, shown
in Figure 7.21. The SelPrint method of the Rich Textbox control is then used to print
the selected text with the printer that is selected in the Print common dialog box.

FIGURE 7.21.

*The Print com-
mon dialog box.*

```
Private Sub cmdPrint_Click()
   dlgCommon.Flags = cdlPDAllPages
   dlgCommon.ShowPrinter
   rtfDocument.SelPrint dlgCommon.hDC
End Sub
```

The ImageList Control

The ImageList control is used to store images you will be using within a form in your Access 97 application. The ImageList ActiveX control is found in the COMCTL32.OCX file. To use the ImageList control within your Access 97 application you must make sure you have a reference to the COMCTL32.OCX file in your application project. When you distribute your application to users you must ensure that the COMCTL32.OCX file is installed into the user's Windows System directory.

The ImageList control is populated at design time with the images you will be using. It is hidden at runtime, but any of the images it contains can be used within your form. The ImageList control is not meant to be used by itself, but it is intended instead to serve as a convenient storage place for images used by other controls in your application's form. The ImageList control can also perform modifications on the images it contains before it delivers them to other controls.

The form called frmImageList, shown in Figure 7.22, is similar to a typical tabbed form. The difference is that each tab contains an image. The images come from the ImageList control called imgPictures. The properties of the imgPictures ImageList control appear in Figure 7.23. Notice that three pictures have been inserted. The size on the General tab has been set to Custom. The tabSelect TabStrip control has been modified to include imgPictures as its ImageList under the General properties tab. The index of each picture in the imgPictures ImageList control has been added as the Image property for each tab in the TabStrip control. The Image property is used to specify which image in the bound ImageList should be displayed within the particular tab.

FIGURE 7.22.

The frmImageList *form, with pictures for tabs.*

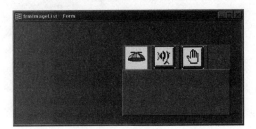

FIGURE 7.23.

The properties of the ImageList control.

The MAPI Controls

Two MAPI (Messaging Application Program Interface) controls ship with Visual Basic 5.0. They can be utilized from within your Access 97 applications. One is called the MAPI Session control, and the other is called the MAPI Message control. Together, they allow you to send a mail message from within your Access 97 application.

The MAPI controls use the `MSMAPI32.OCX` file. To use these controls within your Access 97 application, you must be sure that you have a reference to this file in your application project. The MAPI controls also require that the Microsoft Mail or the Microsoft Exchange service be installed on the machine that the MAPI controls are to be run on. The MAPI controls are not visible at runtime and there are no events for the controls. The MAPI Session control handles logging on to the email client located on the user's machine. The MAPI Message control handles the tasks of resolving the recipient's name, composing the mail message, and accessing the messages currently in the inbox of the user's email service among other tasks. Figure 7.24 shows a simple form, `frmSendMail`, that allows the user to supply a recipient and a message. When the user clicks the Send Message command button, the message is sent to the recipient.

FIGURE 7.24.

Using the MAPI controls.

Here's what the code looks like:

```
Private Sub cmdSendMessage_Click()
    mpiSession.LogonUI = True
    mpiSession.DownloadMail = False
    mpiSession.SignOn
    With mpiMessage
        .MsgIndex = -1
        .MsgNoteText = txtMessage
        .RecipDisplayName = txtRecipient
        .AddressResolveUI = True
        .SessionID = mpiSession.SessionID
    End With
    On Error Resume Next
    mpiMessage.ResolveName
    Select Case Err.Number
        Case 0
            mpiMessage.Send False
        Case Else
            MsgBox "Error # " & Err.Number & ": " & Err.Description
    End Select
End Sub
```

This routine begins by setting the `LogonUI` property to `True`. When set to `True`, the `LogonUI` property indicates that a dialog box is provided for sign-on. Next, the `DownloadMail` property is set to `False`. This means that no mail will be downloaded during the process. Then, the `SignOn` method is issued on the mpiSession control. The `SignOn` method logs the user into the account specified by the `UserName` and `Password` properties and provides a session handle to the underlying message subsystem. The session handle is a memory handle to whatever mail system is being used.

Now the routine is ready to interact with the mpiMessage control. Several properties of the mpiMessage control are set. The `MsgIndex` property is set to –1. This is the index that is always used for the current outgoing message. Next, the `MsgNoteText` property is set. This property is used to indicate the text for the message. The `RecipDisplayName` property is used to reference the currently indexed recipient. The `AddressResolveUI` is set to `True`. This means that the recipient name dialog box will be displayed if Access is unable to resolve the recipient. Finally, the `SessionID` property is set to the messaging handle from the mpiSession control.

After all the properties have been set, you are ready to send the message. The `ResolveName` method of the mpiMessage control resolves the name of the currently indexed recipient. This means that the recipient is validated to see whether it actually exists. If the name is resolved, the `Send` method of the mpiMessage control is used to send the message.

Licensing and Distribution Issues

Some OCX controls can be distributed freely, and others contain various levels of restrictions. The licensing policies for a particular OCX control are determined by its vendor.

The licensing rules that are in effect for an OCX are enforceable by law. This means that improper distribution of the control is a crime. Distributing an OCX control without proper licensing is just like copying a software product illegally.

If you have any questions about the licensing of a third-party control, consult the vendor who authored the control. Sometimes a one-time fee is required so that you can freely distribute the OCX. In other cases, a royalty might be required for each copy of the control that is distributed. If you aren't sure whether you want to purchase a third-party control, you might want to contact the vendor of the control. Many vendors allow potential customers to try out their products for a limited time. In fact, many of the demo versions are available online.

A Practical Example–Implementing ActiveX Controls

ActiveX controls can be utilized in many ways. Your imagination determines where controls will enhance the usability of the application. The following example illustrates a potential practical use of an ActiveX control.

The example is shown in the `frmReportDateRange` (see Figure 7.25). The Calendar control can be used to populate the Beginning Date and Ending Date text boxes.

FIGURE 7.25.

Adding the Calendar control to the Report Criteria form.

The code for this example looks like this:

```
Private Sub cmdSetDates_Click()
    On Error GoTo cmdSetDates_Error

    If cmdSetDates.Caption = "Set Beginning Date" Then
        BeginDate = calSetDates.Value
        cmdSetDates.Caption = "Set Ending Date"
    Else
        EndDate = calSetDates.Value
        cmdSetDates.Caption = "Set Beginning Date"
    End If

    Exit Sub

cmdSetDates_Error:
    MsgBox "Error # " & Err.Number & ": " & Err.Description
    Exit Sub

End Sub
```

Because the same calendar is used to populate the beginning date and ending date text boxes, the form contains a command button with a caption that toggles. The user can select a date and then click Set Beginning Date. The BeginDate text box is populated with the value selected on the calendar, and the caption of the command button is set to display "Set Ending Date." If the caption of the command button says "Set Ending Date" and the user clicks the command button, the EndDate text box is populated with the value selected on the calendar, and the caption of the command button is changed to say "Set Beginning Date."

Summary

ActiveX controls greatly extend the capabilities of Access 97. They allow you to incorporate additional functionality into your applications. ActiveX controls are easy to use and extremely powerful. Each control contains its own properties, events, and methods.

By modifying properties, reacting to events, and executing methods, you can take advantage of the rich features contained within each ActiveX control. The licensing of ActiveX controls varies, so you need to investigate the licensing aspects of each control you want to use to know whether and under what conditions you can distribute it to your users.

Working with Command Bars

IN THIS CHAPTER

CHAPTER 8

What Are Command Bars?

The term *command bars* in Microsoft Access 97 refers to menu bars, toolbars, and short-cut menus. All of these tools are used to organize Access 97 commands so you can find and use the ones you need quickly and easily. Although toolbars in earlier versions of Access only contained buttons, the creation of a command bar object in Access 97 means that you can include both buttons and menus on the same command bar object. The command bars that you build as a part of your Access application can include both built-in and custom commands.

Command bars are represented in Visual Basic as the `CommandBar` object. The entire collection of `CommandBar` objects that exist in your application is known as the `CommandBars` collection object.

> **NOTE**
>
> If you have an Access 95 application that you want to convert to Access 97, all toolbars that are in the Access 95 application will be automatically converted to command bars, except those custom menu bars that have been created with the Access 95 Menu Builder or with a macro. You can use the Create Menu from Macro and Create Shortcut Menu from Macro subcommands (on the Macro command under Tools on the Access 97 menu bar) to manually convert these menu bars to command bars.

Creating and Editing Menu Bars

When you have developed an application in Access 97 and are ready to deploy it to your users, you generally do not want to use the default built-in menu bars that appear at the top of your screen in the Access 97 desktop. Prior to Access 97, if you wanted to create a custom menu bar or shortcut menu, you needed to use a macro to build it. With Access 97, you can customize the existing command bars or create your own without using a macro. You can code your custom command bar in Visual Basic, create it using the user interface in Access 97, or use the Command Bar Wizard that is available for download from the Microsoft Web site at the following URL:

```
http://www.microsoft.com/access/enhancements/wzcmbr80.asp
```

> **WARNING**
>
> Although the Command Bar Wizard was written by Microsoft and is available for download from its Web site, it is not supported by Microsoft Technical Support. Microsoft will let you know that you use the Command Bar Wizard at your own risk.

Once you have downloaded the `wzcmbr80.exe` file to your desktop, double-click the file. The Command Bar Wizard self-extracts and installs itself into Access 97 as an add-in tool. If you decide to uninstall the Command Bar Wizard, simply go to your Control Panel and click the Add/Remove Programs icon. When the Add/Remove Programs dialog box appears, click the Command Bar Builder selection in the select box, click the Add/Remove button, and click Remove All.

Developing a Menu Bar with the Command Bar Wizard

To create a custom menu bar with the Command Bar Wizard, follow these steps:

1. With the database active that you want the menu bar to be created in, choose Tools | Add-Ins and click the Command Bar Wizard option. The dialog box shown in Figure 8.1 appears.

FIGURE 8.1.

The Command Bar Wizard for Access 97.

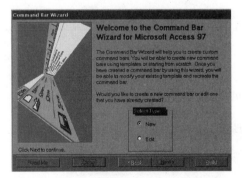

2. Choose New in the Select Type box and click the Next button. The dialog box shown in Figure 8.2 appears. You can select an existing template on which to base your menu bar, or you can choose to create a new blank command bar. The second option displayed on this dialog box enables you to create either a menu bar or a toolbar. For the purposes of this example, choose New Blank Command Bar and Menu Bar before clicking the Next button.

FIGURE 8.2.

Selecting the template to use in creating the menu bar.

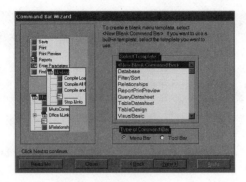

3. The dialog box that is shown in Figure 8.3 is the next step in the process of creating a menu bar with the Command Bar Wizard. This dialog box allows you to build the menu bar component by component, and is divided into two sections named Location and Detail. Under Location, you choose where on the new menu bar the controls you build will be placed. You can create an entry on your menu bar, insert a new entry, and delete an entry. The Detail section contains seven controls that enable you to create virtually any component for your menu bar that is allowed by Access 97. You can use these controls to do the following:

- Select the type of command bar you create.
- Select an icon to represent a component on your menu bar.
- Create a Caption for your command bar.
- Create a Tool Tip for a component of your menu bar.
- Select an action to be run when a component of your menu bar is clicked.
- Insert arguments to the actions that will run for the components of your menu bar.
- Insert options into a combo box displayed on your menu bar.

FIGURE 8.3.

Adding controls to the new menu bar.

Once you have added all the components to your menu bar that you need, click the Next button. The Command Bar Wizard prompts you to name the command bar that you have just created. Once you have done so, click the Build button to have the Command Bar Wizard automatically generate your custom menu bar. The default menu bar for your application disappears and your new menu bar appears. A Show System Menu button appears on the Command Bar Wizard dialog box. You may click this button to restore the default menu bar.

If you are finished with the Command Bar Wizard, click the Close button to exit.

> **TIP**
>
> One very good reason to use the Command Bar Wizard to create command bars for Access 97 applications is that it creates its menus from a blank slate using custom templates. If you create a custom command bar using the Access 97 user interface and that command bar contains commands from the built-in menus category, any changes that you make to your custom command bar are shown in the built-in Access 97 menu bars. Because the Command Bar Wizard does not utilize the built-in menus, you bypass this problem if you use it to create custom command bars for your Access 97 application.

Creating a Menu Bar with the Access 97 User Interface

To create your own menu bar from the Access 97 user interface, follow these steps:

1. With the Database window active, choose View | Toolbars and then click the Customize option. The Customize dialog box shown in Figure 8.4 opens. This dialog box has three tabbed sections titled Toolbars, Commands, and Options. The Toolbar tab is the default view of the dialog box and shows you a list of all the default toolbars, along with the custom toolbars that you have created. You have the option of renaming or deleting the custom toolbars that you have created. You can also edit any of the default toolbars and reset a default toolbar to its original settings.

> **NOTE**
>
> You can't restore a toolbar to its default settings until Access 97 detects that the toolbar has been modified from its original settings. You cannot restore a custom toolbar.

FIGURE 8.4.

The Customize dialog box.

2. Click the New button. The New Toolbar dialog box shown in Figure 8.5 appears. This dialog box prompts you to name the toolbar that you are about to create.

FIGURE 8.5.

The New Toolbar dialog box.

3. You can accept the default name for the new toolbar or give it a name that is more appropriate for your application. After you have done this, click the OK button.

4. The Customize dialog box shown in Figure 8.4 reappears, with the new menu bar that you just added highlighted. To make it a menu bar, click the Properties button. The Toolbar Properties dialog box shown in Figure 8.6 appears.

FIGURE 8.6.

The Toolbar Properties dialog box.

5. To change the new menu bar from a toolbar into a menu bar, click the Type list box and select Menu Bar from the list. You may set several other options for your new menu bar in this dialog box, including its docking attributes, its name, and what actions to allow the user to perform with it. Once you have customized the new menu bar to your satisfaction, click the Close button. You are returned to the

Customize dialog box that was shown in Figure 8.4. To exit, click the Close button.

Creating a Menu Bar Programmatically

The final method of creating a menu bar in Access 97 is to use the programming tool included with Office 97, Visual Basic for Applications (VBA). This is a subset of Microsoft's Visual Basic programming language that allows you to add quite a bit of programmed functionality to your Access 97 application. To create a menu bar using VBA, you must set a reference to the Microsoft Office 8.0 Object Library. You can do this by following these steps:

1. Open the database to which you are adding the new menu bar, and then click the Modules tab of the Database window. Open an existing module in Design view. Or, if you have not created a module in this application yet, click the New button to create a new module. You should have the module opened to a view like that shown in Figure 8.7.

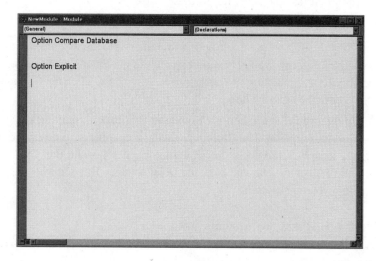

FIGURE 8.7.

A new menu module in Access 97.

8

WORKING WITH
COMMAND BARS

2. While the module is open in Design view, choose Tools | References. The dialog box shown in Figure 8.8 appears. This dialog box lists all the reference libraries that are available to Access 97 and your application. You can select reference libraries and adjust their relative priority from this dialog box.

3. Click in the check box next to Microsoft Office 8.0 Object Library to set a reference to that library. If you do not see this reference library in the list, click the Browse button to search your hard drive for the `Mso97.dll` file. This is usually

installed by default into the `C:\Program Files\Microsoft Office\Office\` folder on your hard drive.

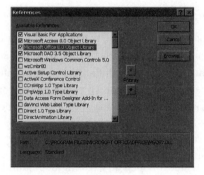

The following sample code in Listing 8.1 creates a new menu bar for your Access 97 application and adds a simple button to the menu bar that pops up a message box for the user. To run this sample code, follow these steps:

1. Open an existing module in the Database window or create a new module.

2. Copy the following sample code and paste it into the module window. Open the Debug window, type in `NewMenuBar`, and hit the Enter key. The new menu bar appears at the bottom of your application window. Click the Click Me! button and observe the message box.

3. To remove the new menu bar from your application, right-click it and select the Customize option. The Customize dialog box appears, as described in the preceding section. Scroll down the list until you see My Menu Bar. Click the box to the left of this menu bar and click the Delete button. This removes the new menu bar from your application.

LISTING 8.1. SUBROUTINE TO ADD A MENU BAR.

```
'****************************************************************
'This sub creates a new menu bar for your application.
'This sub uses the Add Method of the CommandBars
'Collection Object in Access 97.
'****************************************************************

Sub NewMenuBar()

    Dim strMenuBarName As String
    Dim NewMenuBar As CommandBar
    Dim NewMenuBarCtl As CommandBarControl
    Dim NewMenuBarPopup As CommandBarPopup
```

```
Dim NewMenuBarSubCtl As CommandBarControl

strMenuBarName = "My Menu Bar"

'***************************************************************
'Create a new menu bar and dock it on the bottom of the
'application window. The Add Method uses the following syntax:
'
' expression.Add(Name, Position, MenuBar, Temporary)
'
'Where expression is a required expression that returns a
'CommandBars object. Name and Position are optional variants that
'can be used to name the menu bar and indicate where to dock the
'menu bar when it is created. If the Name argument is not given,
'Access 97 will assign a default name to the menu bar. The
'Position argument can be any of the following constants:
'
'msoBarLeft           - docks the menu bar to the left
'msoBarRight          - docks the menu bar to the right
'msoBarTop            - docks the menu bar to the top
'msoBarBottom         - docks the menu bar to the bottom
'msoBarFloating       - creates a floating menu bar
'msoBarPopup          - creates a shortcut menu
'
'The MenuBar argument is optional and if it is set to True causes
'the new menu bar to replace the active menu bar. If this argument is
'not given it is set to the default  of False. The Temporary argument
➥is
'optional and if set to True will cause the new menu bar to be a
➥temporary
'menu bar, that is it will be deleted when the container application
➥is closed.
'The default value for this argument is False.

    Set NewMenuBar = CommandBars.Add(strMenuBarName, msoBarBottom, False,
➥False)

'Set CommandBar protection so that users cannot move it. The value
'that you set for the .Protection property of the CommandBar can be
➥any
'of the following constants:
'
'msoBarNoProtection
'msoBarNoCustomize
'msoBarNoResize
'msoBarNoMove
'msoBarNoChangeVisible
'msoBarNoChangeDock
'msoBarNoVerticalDock
'msoBarNoHorizontalDock
```

8

WORKING WITH
COMMAND BARS

continues

LISTING 8.1. CONTINUED

```
'
'Set the new menu bar as visible.

With NewMenuBar
    .Protection = msoBarNoMove
    .Visible = True
End With

'Create a control on the popup and set some properties.
Set NewMenuBarSubCtl = NewMenuBar.Controls.Add(msoControlButton)
With NewMenuBarSubCtl
    .Caption = "&ClickMe!"
    .Style = msoButtonCaption
    .OnAction = "=MsgBox(""You clicked ClickMe"")"
End With

Exit Sub
End Sub
```

Editing a Menu Bar

Now that you have created a new menu bar using one of these three methods, you will want to populate it with some components. This section will walk you through building a first-level menu with the following items: File, Edit, Window, and Help. The File menu item will have these options: Open Table, Open Form, and Exit. The Edit, Window, and Help menu items are copies of the Edit, Window, and Help items that are presented in the default Access 97 menu bar.

The first step is to add the File, Edit, Window, and Help menu items. To do so, you need to repeat the following steps for each of the menu items:

1. If the Customize dialog box is not still open, choose View | Toolbars | Customize or right-click your new menu bar and click Customize. This opens the Customize dialog box shown in Figure 8.4.

2. Click the Commands tab of the dialog box. Here you have many command options, including All Tables, All Queries, and New Menu. On the left side of the dialog box are the categories, and on the right side are the commands available for the currently selected category.

3. In this case, select the New Menu category. Doing so puts New Menu in the Commands window.

4. To add New Menu to your custom menu bar, left-click it, hold down the mouse button, and drag it to the new menu bar. Once you have New Menu over the new

menu bar, a symbol that looks like an I-beam appears on the new menu bar. This symbol tells you where the new menu will be placed. When you have the I-beam in the place you want the new menu to appear, release the mouse button.

5. On the menu bar, you now see New Menu. To rename this menu item, right-click the new New Menu button. In the pop-up menu that appears, choose Properties. The dialog box shown in Figure 8.9 appears.

FIGURE 8.9.

The My Menu Bar Control Properties dialog box.

6. To change the name of the menu item to File, click in the Caption box and type `File`. You also can set the Shortcut Text, ToolTip, Help File, Help ContextID, Parameter, On Action, and Tag fields here. After you set the options for the new menu item, click Close.

7. Repeat this step for the Edit, Window, and Help menu items.

After you set up the first level of the menu items for the new menu bar, you can add the second level. In the following steps, you add the items Open Table, Open Form, and Exit:

1. If you are not at the Customize dialog box shown in Figure 8.4, choose View | Toolbars and select the Customize option. Once the dialog box is open, select the Commands tab.

2. From the Category window, select New Menu.

3. From the Commands window, select New Menu and drag it on top of the File menu item on the menu bar. Notice that the File menu opens and the I-beam symbol appears above the File menu item. When you see the I-beam, drop New Menu to place it under the File menu.

4. Right-click New Menu and choose Name from the pop-up menu. Then change the name to Open Table and press Enter. The Open Table menu item is now set up under the File menu.

8

WORKING WITH COMMAND BARS

Repeat the preceding steps to add an item called Open Form to the File menu. After you are done, you can add the Exit option. Before you can do so, you first need to program a macro to close the Database window:

1. Select the Macro tab in the Database window and click the New button. The macro dialog box opens up.

2. In the first action line, select Quit from the list of available actions. Leave all the other options at their defaults.

3. Choose File | Save. Name the macro `MainClose` and click OK.

Now that you have built the macro, you need to go back to the Customize dialog box for the menu bar. Then you can add the Exit Menu option, as follows:

1. From the Category window on the Commands tab, select All Macros.

2. From the Commands window, select `MainClose` and drag it on top of File on the menu bar. Notice that the File menu opens and the I-beam symbol appears below File. Now move all the way to the bottom of the list of menu options and drop the new menu item. Doing so places `MainClose` on the File menu.

3. Right-click `MainClose`, and in the pop-up menu that appears, choose Name. Then change the name to `Exit`, and at the bottom of the pop-up menu, choose Begin a Group. Press Enter. You then see that the Exit menu option is set up under File, and it has a gray separator line above it.

At this point, you have a new menu bar with File, Edit, Window, and Help menu items. Under the File menu, you have Open Table, Open Form, and Exit. The last step is to add menu options to Open Table. To do so, you need to open the Customize dialog box again:

1. From the Category window on the Commands tab, select All Tables.

2. From the Commands window, select a table. For this example, a table called MyTable is used. Drag the table on top of File on the menu bar. Notice that the File menu opens and the I-beam symbol appears below File. Now move it on top of Open Table. Again, notice that this item opens and the I-beam symbol appears beside Open Table. Now drop the new menu item. Doing so places your table (MyTable, in this example) on the Open Table menu option.

3. Right-click MyTable, and in the pop-up menu that appears, choose Text Only (in Menus). By choosing this option, you make sure that it displays only Text as the name instead of a symbol and Text. Press Enter. You then see that the MyTable table appears under the Open Table menu option without the table symbol beside it.

You can now repeat these steps to add all the menu options that you need for your application. Figure 8.10 shows the completed menu bar.

FIGURE 8.10.

The new menu bar.

Using the New Menu Bar

You can use your new menu bar in your Access 97 applications in two ways: either as the default menu for your database application, or as a custom menu bar for a form or report.

Using the New Menu Bar as the Default for the Database

To set the new menu bar that you created in the preceding section as the default menu for your Access 97 application, you need to open the Startup dialog box by choosing Tools|Startup. This dialog box is shown in Figure 8.11.

FIGURE 8.11.

The Startup dialog box.

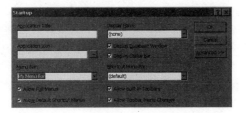

To make the new menu bar that you just built the default for the database application, click the Menu Bar list box. In this list box, you see (default) and all the other menu bars that are available in the current database application. Select My Menu Bar from the list and click OK. This way, you can make your new menu bar the default for this database application each time it opens.

If your new menu does not appear in the list box, the properties for that menu have not been set to Menu Bar. To set the properties, close the Startup dialog box by clicking Cancel. Then right-click the new menu bar and choose Customize. Find the New Menu Bar name in the Toolbars list and click the name once. Then click the Properties button. In the Type list box, change Toolbar to Menu Bar and then click the Close button.

Using the New Menu Bar for a Form or Report

When you're using a form or report, you can assign it one toolbar and one menu bar to use when you open it. To do so, you need to open the report or form in Design view and then open the Properties window by choosing View | Properties. Scroll down the list until you see Menu Bar. Click the Menu Bar list box to see all the available menu bars. Select My Menu Bar, the one you just built.

Creating and Editing Toolbars

Building or editing a toolbar using the Access 97 user interface is exactly the same as building or editing a menu bar, except that you leave the Type property set to Toolbar. You will find another difference when you add your new toolbar to a form or a report. The toolbar does not appear in the Menu Bar list box; it appears in the Toolbar list box.

Creating and Editing Pop-Up Menu Bars

Creating or editing a pop-up menu bar is the same as creating or editing a toolbar or a menu bar, except that you need to set the type to Popup. Additionally, when you want to change a pop-up menu to a toolbar or a menu bar, you need to go to Properties and select Popup Menu from the list at the top of the screen. A pop-up menu does not appear in the list of available toolbars.

Another thing to remember is that when you're setting the properties for a form or report, you need to look for Shortcut Menu Bar and make sure that Shortcut Menu is set to Yes. Otherwise, the shortcut menu does not appear when you right-click the open form.

Using More Than One Command Bar on a Form

To use more than one menu bar or toolbar on a form, you need to write some VBA code, as follows in Listing 8.2. If you look at the multiple Menu bars.mdb file included on the Web site for this book, you will see that the Customers form uses two menu bars and two toolbars. Also notice that the Menu Bar list box is set to nothing, and the Toolbar list box is also set to nothing. If you open the Customers form, you see that New Menu Bar, New Toolbar, and New Menu Bar 3 are open, and all other menu bars and toolbars are hidden.

LISTING 8.2. USING MORE THAN ONE MENU BAR.

```
Public Function startup_Application(pMenus As Variant)
    Dim iFor As Integer
    Dim objCommandBar As Object

    Set objCommandBar = CommandBars

    On Error Resume Next
    For iFor = 0 To objCommandBar.Count - 1
        If objCommandBar(iFor).Visible = True Then
            objCommandBar(iFor).Visible = False
        End If
    Next iFor

    For iFor = 0 To UBound(pMenus)
        objCommandBar(pMenus(iFor)).Visible = True
    Next iFor
End Function
```

Troubleshooting Command Bars

8

WORKING WITH
COMMAND BARS

This section contains hints and tips that will help you troubleshoot the command bars in your Access 97 application. Here are the hints that make up this section:

- How do I add separator bars to menus or toolbars?

- How do I show or hide the CommandBar objects in my application?

- All the built-in toolbars and menus have disappeared from my application. Can I get them back?

- Users of my application cannot reopen my custom CommandBar objects once they are closed.

- I receive runtime error 5 when I try to create a new menu bar in my application.

- I get an error message saying "Microsoft Access can't find the macro [name of command bar]" when I try to use a shortcut menu on a form in my application.

- When I try to reference a Shortcut menu with the CommandBars object in VBA, I get a runtime error 5 message.

- I want to enable or disable a command bar using VBA.

- I can only get one menu bar to be visible at a time when I use the .Visible property of a menu bar in my VBA code.

How Do I Add Separator Bars to Menus or Toolbars?

Access 97 uses separator bars to group related buttons, commands, and menu items on its CommandBar objects. You can add separator bars to your custom command bar objects to accomplish the same task. To add a separator bar to a new menu bar, follow these steps:

1. Choose View | Toolbars and click the Customize option.

2. Select the CommandBar object that you want to add the separator bar to, and then right-click the CommandBar object to bring up the shortcut menu.

3. click the Begin a Group check box to enable a separator bar. You can click the separator bar a second time to remove it.

How Do I Show or Hide the CommandBar Objects in My Application?

There are several ways to accomplish this. If the CommandBar object that you want to hide is a floating toolbar, you can simply click its Close button to hide it. If you want to hide a menu bar or toolbar including your custom CommandBar objects, you can right-click it and then click the name of the CommandBar object that you want to hide from the shortcut menu that pops up.

One way to close several CommandBar objects at once is to choose View | Toolbars and select the Customize option. Make sure that you have selected the Toolbars tab of the Customize dialog box, and clear the check box that is to the left of each CommandBar object that you want to hide.

All the Built-In Toolbars and Menus Have Disappeared from My Application. Can I Get Them Back?

If you have lost some or all of the built-in toolbars or menus from your Access 97 database application, you can get them back by changing some of the Startup settings of your application:

1. Choose Tools | Startup and click next to Allow Built-in Toolbars and Allow Full Menus.

2. Close the database and then reopen it.

This should restore any missing built-in toolbars and/or built-in menus. If this does not work, you can temporarily bypass the Startup parameters of your Access 97 database application by pressing the Shift key while you open the database. Once your database application is open, you can open the Startup configuration dialog box by following the preceding steps and reset the options to allow display of the built-in toolbars.

Users of My Application Cannot Reopen My Custom `CommandBar` Objects Once They Are Closed

If you have created an Access 97 application that uses custom `CommandBar` objects, such as menu bars or toolbars, and you do not have the docking status set correctly, the users of your application will not be able to reopen the menu bars or toolbars if they are accidentally closed. This is because you cannot change the `CommandBar` object settings in the Access 97 runtime environment, which is typically used for Access 97 applications.

To prevent this from happening in your applications, make sure that you set the docking status for your toolbars and menu bars to Can't Move so that the users of your application will not be able to close or undock the menu bars and toolbars that make up your Access 97 application.

I Receive Runtime Error 5 When I Try to Create a New Menu Bar in My Application

This error usually occurs because you are trying to create a menu bar with the same name as an existing menu bar. This error generally only occurs if you are using VBA. If you are using the Access 97 user interface, you will get an error message that tells you the menu bar name is already in use.

You cannot create two menu bars that use the same name.

I Get an Error Message Saying "Microsoft Access Can't Find the Macro [Name of Command Bar]" When I Try to Use a Shortcut Menu on a Form in My Application

If the shortcut menu or form that you are trying to use does not exist, Access 97 will generate this error message. Microsoft admits that this message is misleading because the error is that the macro is missing, not that the command bar is missing. The reason that this error message refers to macros is that in earlier versions of Access, menu bars were created from macros.

When I Try to Reference a Shortcut Menu with the `CommandBars` Object in VBA, I Get a Runtime Error 5 Message

You cannot reference the Shortcut menu by using VBA. However, this is the only toolbar that you cannot reference by using VBA. You can reference a custom shortcut menu through code with VBA.

I Want to Enable or Disable a Command Bar Using VBA

The following section of sample code in Listing 8.3 will allow you to disable all the menu items on your command bar using VBA. To test this sample code, copy and paste it into a new module in the Access 97 database in which you want to disable the command bar. The function in this sample code takes two arguments. The Name argument is the name of the command bar that you want to disable or enable, and the Switch argument is a Boolean value that you set to either `True` or `False` to tell the function whether to disable or enable the command bar. Once you have pasted or entered the sample code into a module in your Access 97 database application, open the Debug window and type in the following line:

```
?MenuOnOff("My Menu Bar", False)
```

Then press Enter to test the function.

You can substitute any command bar name for `"My Menu Bar"`. Remember that a value of `True` will enable the command bar, and a value of `False` will disable the command bar.

LISTING 8.3. DISABLE/ENABLE MENU BAR.

```
Function MenuOnOff(Name As String, Switch As Boolean)

    Dim MyCmdBar As CommandBar
    Dim MyCmdBarCtl As CommandBarControl

    Set MyCmdBar = CommandBars(Name)

    If MyCmdBar.Visible = False Then MyCmdBar.Visible = True

    For Each MyCmdBarCtl In MyCmdBar.Controls
        MyCmdBarCtl.Enabled = MyCmdBar.Enabled
    Next MyCmdBarCtl

Exit Function

End Function
```

I Can Only Get One Menu Bar to Be Visible at a Time When I Use the `.Visible` Property of a Menu Bar in My VBA Code

When you use the `.Visible` property to make a menu bar visible, you can only make one menu bar visible at a time. For example, if you set a menu bar's `.Visible` property to `True`, the application's current menu bar disappears. This is because when you set a menu bar to be visible in VBA code, Access 97 automatically sets the `.Visible` property of all other menu bars to `False`.

If you want to show more than one menu bar at a time, you must set the `.Visible` properties of the menu bars through the Access 97 user interface by choosing View | Toolbars and clicking the Customize option. When the Customize dialog box appears, click next to the menu bars that you want to make visible in your Access 97 database application.

If you create a database with two menu bars, such as MenuBar1 and MenuBar2, you can test this with the following line of code:

```
CommandBars("MenuBar2").Visible = True
```

This line of code sets the `.Visible` property of the other menu bar, MenuBar1, to `False`. And if you replace MenuBar2 in this line of code with MenuBar1, the reverse effect will be `True`.

Summary

In this chapter you have created several different command bars. You have seen how to create command bars with the Access 97 user interface, with the Command Bar Wizard that you can download from Microsoft's WWW site, and with VBA code. You can use custom command bars to enhance the experience of your application's users and extend the Access 97 interface to achieve your application's purpose. You can also use custom command bars to attach tables, forms, reports, queries, or macros to menu bars or toolbars. With the information you have learned in this chapter, you should now be able to build any command bar object that you need for your Access 97 database application.

Reacting to Events
in the Interface

CHAPTER

9

Understanding Events in Access

Events lie at the heart of Windows programming, and nowhere more so than in Access. In Access application programming, both with macros and VBA, application code sits dormant until an event occurs that wakes it up to perform its function. From a programming perspective, this is really easier to code, but it must be approached properly.

Almost everything of significance that happens in Access has a corresponding event. If you choose the appropriate event, the actual code to be written can be quite simple. Controls generate events when they are selected, unselected, before they are changed, after they are changed, when keys are pressed, when the mouse is moved, and so on. Similarly, forms have events when they open, close, are loaded, are unloaded, and so on.

An *event* is a recognized action (such as a mouse click, the opening of a form or report, or the pressing of a key) that occurs within an Access application and returns some type of response. That response can be the execution of a macro, the running of some VBA code (a *subprocedure*), or a user-built expression that returns a value. You can determine what the response will be through the Event properties of the specified control, form, or report.

Macros, subprocedures, and expressions are initiated in the Event property of an object. You create and edit them through the properties sheet of a control, form, or report. Within the properties sheet, click the Events tab and then click the Build button of the event for which you want a response to be returned. The Choose Builder dialog box appears, giving you the option of creating an expression, writing a macro, or writing a subprocedure using Visual Basic code.

Unlike applications in procedural programming languages, which are written using top-down methodology, Access applications are designed to respond to events from users. The order in which the code is executed depends on which event is invoked by a user action. This is the essence of event-driven programming; it puts the user in charge, and your code responds accordingly. Considering this factor is important when you're designing your own applications. You cannot make many assumptions about the order in which actions may occur, or the state of controls. For example, you cannot simply assume that a text box will be filled in before a command button is clicked. To code for a situation in which it isn't, disable the command button until something has been entered in the text box, or provide a warning message box to the user if the button is clicked prematurely.

Types of Access Events

Access offers many different events to give the application developer several options in responding to an action taken by a user. The different types of events are summarized in the following sections.

Data Events

Data events occur whenever data is added, updated, or deleted from a form or control—for example, when text changes in a text or combo box, or when updates happen to data in a control (in form view) or a record (in datasheet view). Another example is when the focus moves from one record to another.

Current

The Current event occurs when you open a form or when you move from one record to another. This event also occurs when you refresh or requery a form's underlying table or query.

> **NOTE**
>
> Many form and control level events are passed Response and/or Cancel arguments by Access. These allow you to determine what Access does after you are done handling your event. Both values default to False (zero).
>
> With events where there is further action yet to be done by Access, setting the Cancel argument to True will tell Access to terminate the activity that triggered the event, such as *not* to delete selected records, *not* to update the changed records, and so on.
>
> Similarly, the Response argument, when present, gives the programmer some control over the error or confirmation messages the user sees. The precise significance of the Response argument varies according to the specific event.

Delete

The Delete event occurs when the user performs a record delete action, such as pressing the Delete key or clicking a command button that performs the delete operation. This event occurs before the record is actually deleted by Access. The event procedure for a delete takes one parameter, Cancel, which can be modified. If Cancel is set to

True within this procedure, the delete action isn't performed and the `BeforeDelConfirm`, `AfterDelConfirm`, and `Current` events don't occur. If `Cancel` isn't set to True any time during the delete, the following events occur in order:

1. `Delete`
2. `Current` (accesses the next available record)
3. `BeforeDelConfirm`
4. A system message box confirming the deletion
5. `AfterDelConfirm`

> **WARNING**
>
> If you have Confirm Record Changes set to Off under Tools | Options | Edit/Find, the `Delete` event will occur, but the `BeforeDelConfirm` event, the system confirmation, and the `AfterDelConfirm` event won't occur.

BeforeDelConfirm

The `BeforeDelConfirm` event occurs after the user deletes one or more records and before a dialog box appears to confirm the deletion. This procedure takes two arguments: `Cancel` and `Response`. Setting `Cancel` to True (any nonzero value) cancels this event and restores the record, and the confirm dialog box doesn't appear. If you set `Cancel` to False, the `Response` parameter determines whether the confirm dialog box appears. `Response` can have one of two values: 0 or 1. A setting of 0 tells Access to continue deleting without displaying the confirm dialog box. A setting of 1 tells Access to display the confirm dialog box.

Constant Name	Value	Meaning
`acDataErrContinue`	0	Resume without confirmation dialog
`acDataErrDisplay`	1	Display confirmation dialog

AfterDelConfirm

The `AfterDelConfirm` event occurs after the confirmation and/or deletion of the record(s) or when the deletion is canceled. Even if the `BeforeDelConfirm` event is canceled, this event still occurs. This event procedure carries one argument, `Status`, which determines whether a record has been deleted. `Status` can have one of three values: 0, 1, or 2.

Constant Name	Value	Meaning
acDeleteOK	0	Successful deletion
acDeleteCancel	1	Canceled within Access
acDeleteUserCancel	2	Canceled by user

BeforeInsert

The BeforeInsert event occurs when the user types the first character of a new record but before the record is actually inserted into the table. This event enables you to determine whether an insert should be allowed. This event procedure has one argument, Cancel. Setting Cancel to True cancels this event; however, you can't cancel the AfterInsert event.

AfterInsert

The AfterInsert event occurs after a new record is added to a table. This event enables you to requery a recordset each time a record is added to keep your users up to date.

BeforeUpdate

The BeforeUpdate event occurs before any data in a control or record is updated in the record. This event procedure has one argument, Cancel. Setting Cancel to True cancels this event and the update action; however, you can't cancel the AfterUpdate event.

AfterUpdate

The AfterUpdate event occurs after data in a record or control has been updated. For bound controls, you can use this event along with the OldValue property to cancel an update. The OldValue property keeps the value of the control before it was updated until after this event has occurred. Therefore, you can set the control equal to its OldValue. The following syntax is an example of restoring a control to its previously updated value (your own undo command):

FORMS!formname!controlname = FORMS!formname!controlname.OldValue

9

> **TIP**
>
> Changing any data in a control or record using a macro or Visual Basic doesn't trigger the control's BeforeUpdate or AfterUpdate events, but it will trigger the form's BeforeUpdate and AfterUpdate events when you move to another record or save the record.

Change

The Change event occurs when the contents of a text box or the text portion of a combo box changes. A change can be any character directly inserted or deleted.

> **WARNING**
>
> You must be very careful with the Change event because if you have two text boxes that affect each other when one is changed, it can cause an infinite loop of Change events (known as *cascading events*).

NotInList

The NotInList event occurs only within combo boxes and when the user enters a value in the text portion of the combo box that isn't in the list. For this event to occur, you must set the LimitToList property, which allows only values that are in the list, to Yes. This event procedure carries two arguments: NewData, the data entered by the user, and Response, which indicates how the event is handled. Response can have one of three values: 0, 1, or 2. A setting of 0 tells Access not to display the default message and not to add the new data to the list. This value gives you the opportunity to display a custom-built message. A setting of 1 tells Access to display the default message to the users, telling them that they have entered a value not in the list. A setting of 2 tells Access not to display a message. You must add the new data to the combo box list before exiting the event handler, and Access then requeries and refreshes the combo box. These three values are stored in predefined constant variables.

Constant Name	Value	Meaning
acDataErrContinue	0	Resume without dialog
acDataErrDisplay	1	Show dialog (default)
acDataErrAdded	2	Data was added in NotInList, and Access will recheck the list

> **NOTE**
>
> When Response is set to acDataErrAdded, you must still add the new data to your control source of the combo box, programmatically. You don't need to refresh the combo box.

Updated

The Updated event occurs when an OLE object's data has been modified. This event applies only to bound and unbound object frames. The event procedure has one argument, Code. This argument indicates how the OLE object was updated. Code can have one of four values: 0, 1, 2, or 3. A setting of 0 tells Access that the object's data has been changed. A setting of 1 tells Access that the object's data was saved by the application that created the object. A setting of 2 tells Access that the OLE object file was closed by the application that created it. A setting of 3 tells Access that the OLE object file has been renamed by the application that created it.

Constant Name	Value	Meaning
acOLEChanged	0	Object was changed
acOLESaved	1	Object saved by application
acOLEClosed	2	Object closed by application
acOLERenamed	3	Object renamed by application

> **NOTE**
>
> This Updated event isn't related to the BeforeUpdate and the AfterUpdate events for bound and unbound object frames. This event happens when the object's data changes. BeforeUpdate and AfterUpdate occur when the object is updated and after the Updated event.

Error Events

Error events occur when an error is encountered.

Error

The Error event occurs whenever a runtime error occurs within your Access application. This event applies to forms and reports and includes errors that occur using the Microsoft Jet database engine. However, this event doesn't happen when an error occurs in Visual Basic code within a function or procedure; these errors are handled by VBA error handling routines. The OnError event enables you to trap any Access error messages and display your own custom error message to your users. This event procedure has two arguments: DataErr, which is the error code returned by the Err function that is executed each time an error occurs, and Response, which determines if a system-default error message should be displayed. You can use the DataErr argument with the Error$ function to map the error code to its appropriate message. Response can have one of two values: 0 or 1. A setting of 0 tells Access to continue without displaying the default error message. This way, you can display your own message. A setting of 1 tells Access to display the default error message.

Constant Name	Value	Meaning
acDataErrContinue	0	Resume without dialog
acDataErrDisplay	1	Display confirmation dialog

To interactively view the text description of an Access and Jet error in the debug window, use the Accesserror(errno) syntax. Error(errno) does not work with non-VBA errors.

Timing Events

Timing events occur when you're setting the TimerInterval property on a form.

Timer

The Timer event occurs at regular intervals when specified by the TimerInterval property within a form. When the TimerInterval property is set to 0, this event doesn't occur; however, when the property is set to any value greater than 0 and less than 65,536, the Timer event does occur as scheduled. This event can be used to keep data synchronized in a multiuser environment.

NOTE

The time setting in the TimerInterval property is expressed in milliseconds.

Timer Example: Events in a Multiuser Environment

This is a demonstration module that illustrates use of the Timer event, and a technique to keep screens up-to-date across a multiuser system.

Timer events on forms are typically used for splash screens or to wake up inattentive users. The following example demonstrates a different use of Timer events to solve a somewhat difficult problem. When multiple users are sharing common Access tables, updates to existing records in recordsets happen automatically, subject to the Refresh Interval (set in Tools | Options | Advanced). If one user updates a record and this record is currently displayed on other users' computers as a form, datasheet form, list, or combo box, the changes will "ripple" through the system, keeping everyone up-to-date.

However, this does not happen automatically when records are added or deleted, because the recordsets are refreshed but not requeried. First, queries are expensive in CPU time and especially network traffic. Second, Jet has no way to know what a user/application is currently doing with a recordset. A change that unexpectedly modified the composition of the set could play havoc with algorithms in process. Third, a requery invalidates all outstanding bookmarks, which could cause some surprising results. (Requerying a form or recordset on your own machine will have no effect on other machines on the network.)

Many times, however, there is a need to keep recordsets fully synchronized, but without unnecessary requeries. The following is an example of a general-purpose, event-driven signaling system that lets the programmer control when and if requeries take place.

It requires only two public functions, `Timestamp(label as String)` and `Checkstamp(stamp as Double, label as String)`, and a small table called `timestamp`. A sample module and table are included in this chapter's database on the Web site.

`Timestamp()` is called from any function that modifies information in a table in such a way as to change the size of the recordsets (remember that it is not necessary to worry about propagating data changes within individual records). The string argument is simply an arbitrary label to designate the particular data being updated (such as "addresses"). This way, forms need only respond to changes that are likely to affect them. `Timestamp` changes an entry in the table keyed to this value (if there is no entry for the label, one is created).

The `Checkstamp()` function is called by objects (typically forms) that need to know if underlying data has changed. Each such form maintains a local `Double` variable, which serves as a token when checking the status of the data source. At regular intervals, the form calls `Checkstamp`, passing this token, as well as the label for the data source being checked. If there is no change since last call, `Checkstamp()` returns 0 and that is all. Otherwise `Checkstamp()` returns −1 and also updates the token for the next check. (The precise value of the token is unimportant to the calling form. Those details are exclusively handled by the `Checkstamp()` function.)

All forms have an `On Timer` event that occurs every so many milliseconds, as specified in `Timer Interval`. (A value of 0 turns off the timer event.) Simply select an appropriate interval (30000=30 seconds) at which to call `Checkstamp()` to see if an update is in order. The requery can then be performed as appropriate. The following is the skeleton for a form utilizing this update method:

```
Option Compare Database
Option Explicit
Dim stamp As Double    'timestamp token
```

```
Private Sub Form_Open(Cancel As Integer)
    Call Checkstamp(stamp, "this label")
'call when first open to initialize stamp
End Sub

Private Sub Form_Timer()
    Dim rval As Integer
    rval = Checkstamp(stamp, "this label")
    If rval Then
        Me.Requery
        'put whatever code here to update as  needed
    End If
End Sub

Function changedata()
'skeleton function for a routine that changes table information
    'make changes here, then...
    Timestamp ("this label")
    'tell all interested forms about it
End Function
```

The calling form keeps a copy of the timestamp token, but never evaluates it directly. It merely passes it periodically to Checkstamp, which manages all the determination of whether the table (or other object) has changed or not.

The Timestamp module uses DAO functions (see Chapter 16, "Data Access Objects"), but knowledge of DAO is not required to use these functions. Just include the module and the Timestamp table in your Access application. Here's the code for the Timestamp module:

```
Option Explicit

Dim rec As Recordset, db As Database

Public Function Checkstamp(tstamp As Double, lbl As String) As Double
    On Error GoTo handler
    rec.Seek "=", lbl
    If rec.NoMatch Then
        tstamp = addlabel(lbl)
        Checkstamp = -1
    Else
        If tstamp <> rec!stamp Then 'stamp has changed
            tstamp = rec!stamp
            Checkstamp = -1
        Else
            Checkstamp = 0   'has not changed
        End If
    End If
```

```
leave:
Exit Function

handler:
    If Err = 91 Then 'DAO object not yet open
        opentable
        Resume
    Else
        MsgBox "Error : " & Err & " in Checkstamp"
        Resume leave
    End If
End Function

Private Function addlabel(lbl As String)
    Dim tm As Double
    rec.addnew
    rec!Label = lbl
    tm = Time
    rec!stamp = tm
    rec.update
    addlabel = tm
End Function
Private Sub opentable()
    Set db = CurrentDb
    Set rec = db.OpenRecordset("Timestamp")
    rec.Index = "Label"
End Sub
Public Sub Timestamp(lbl As String)
    On Error GoTo handler
    rec.Seek "=", lbl
    If rec.NoMatch Then
        Call addlabel(lbl)
    Else
        rec.Edit
        rec!stamp = Time
        rec.update
    End If
leave:
Exit Sub

handler:
    If Err = 91 Then
        opentable
        Resume
    Else
        MsgBox "Error: " & Err & " in Timestamp"
        Resume leave
    End If
End Sub
```

It is necessary for the db and rec object variables to be initialized the first time they are used. Notice that the code uses the error handler to accomplish this in the background. The calling programs do not need to worry about whether they need to call an initialization routine. Furthermore, the calling forms do not need to know if the particular label is new or not; if it is new, it is quietly added to the table.

Focus Events

Focus events occur when any control, form, or report receives or loses focus (or becomes active or inactive).

Enter

The Enter event occurs before a control receives the focus from another control on the same form. Or when a form is first opened, the Enter event occurs on the first control. This event occurs before the GotFocus event and after the Current event.

Exit

The Exit event occurs just before a control loses the focus to another control on the same form. This event occurs before the LostFocus event.

> **NOTE**
>
> Unlike the GotFocus and LostFocus events, the Enter and Exit events don't occur if the focus leaves a control and goes to another form or report. These events are best used to display messages or instructions before allowing an update of controls, or to change the tab order of the controls on a form.

GotFocus

The GotFocus event occurs when a form or a control on a form receives the focus. This event doesn't occur for a form unless all the controls on the form have been disabled. Also, a control can receive the focus only when it is enabled and visible. This event occurs after the Enter event.

LostFocus

The LostFocus event occurs anytime that the focus leaves a form or a control on a form. This event occurs after the Exit event unless the Exit event doesn't happen, which would be the case if the focus goes from a control on one form to a control on another form.

Activate

The Activate event occurs when a form or report receives the focus to become the active form. A form or report receives the focus when it is opened, when a control on it is clicked, or when you use the SetFocus method within Visual Basic code. A form or report must be visible for this event to occur.

Deactivate

The Deactivate event occurs when a form or report loses the focus to another window, such as the table, query, form, report, macro, module, or database. However, this event doesn't occur when the focus goes to a dialog box or another application.

Keyboard Events

Keyboard events occur when a key is pressed or as the result of the SendKeys action or statement.

KeyDown and KeyUp

The KeyDown event occurs anytime a key is pressed within a control or within a form that has the focus. The KeyUp event occurs anytime a key is released within a control or in a form that has the focus.

The KeyDown and KeyUp events are best used to distinguish when a user presses a function key, a navigation key (the arrow keys, Home, End, Page Up, and so on), or a combination of keys with Shift, Ctrl, or Alt. However, these events don't occur when you press the Enter or Esc key if a command button appears on the form or report with its Default or Cancel property set to Yes.

These two event procedures have two arguments: KeyCode and Shift. KeyCode is an integer representing the key that was pressed. To prevent a control from receiving a keystroke, you just set KeyCode to 0. Shift is an integer that determines if Shift, Ctrl, or Alt was pressed in combination with another key. The value of Shift is 0 if none of the keys were held down, 1 if the Shift key was down, 2 if the Ctrl key was down, and 4 if the Alt key was down. If any combination of these keys is held down together, the value of Shift is the sum of the keys' individual values.

KeyPress

The KeyPress event occurs when the user presses and releases any combination of keys within a control or a form that corresponds to a printable character. This event doesn't occur when the user presses the function keys, navigation keys, or any of the mask keys (Shift, Alt, and Ctrl). Unlike the KeyDown and KeyUp events, this event distinguishes

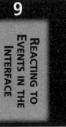

9

REACTING TO
EVENTS IN THE
INTERFACE

between uppercase and lowercase. This event procedure has one argument, `KeyAscii`, which is an integer representing the character pressed. To determine the character pressed, you can use the `Chr` function.

`KeyAscii` can also send information back to Access. If you set `KeyAscii` to zero in the `KeyPress` event handler, the keystroke will subsequently be ignored and no further action will occur. You can also modify the keystroke so that Access will process a different key than was pressed.

> **WARNING**
>
> Although these keyboard events are a good way of determining what a user is doing, be careful where and when you use these events. If a key is held down, the `KeyDown` and `KeyPress` events occur repeatedly, which greatly increases the chances of an application locking up (running out of system resources). You may want to consider using the data events that are available, such as `Change` and `Updated`.

Mouse Events

Mouse events occur when the mouse performs some action on a form or control.

Click

The `Click` event occurs when the mouse is clicked over a control on a form, a section of a form, or the form itself. This event doesn't occur on controls within an option group, but it does occur on the option group. This event also occurs in the following situations when the mouse button isn't clicked:

- An item is selected from a combo box by using the arrow keys and pressing the Enter key to place it in the text property of the combo box.
- The spacebar is pressed when a check box, command button, or option button has the focus.
- The Enter key or Esc key is pressed on a form that has a button with the `Default` property of Yes or the `Cancel` property of Yes, respectively.
- A command button is accessed using its shortcut key (Alt plus the underlined letter in the caption of the command button).

To determine which mouse button was clicked, refer to the `MouseDown` and `MouseUp` events.

DblClick

The DblClick event occurs when the mouse is double-clicked over a control on a form, a section of a form, or the form itself. This event doesn't occur on controls within an option group, but it does occur on the option group itself.

The DblClick event procedure takes one argument, Cancel, which cancels this event when set to True.

For some controls, double-clicking has other responses after the DblClick event. For example, clicking an object that contains an OLE object causes the object to be opened in the application that created it. However, by using this event effectively, you can change what happens when you double-click an object. For example, when double-clicking an OLE object, you can first send the object to a printer to print and then set the Cancel argument to True, which then cancels the event and does not start up the application that created the object.

> **TIP**
>
> The Click event occurs when you enter a value and then leave a combo box, even if you don't use your mouse—for example, pressing Tab to move to the control, entering a value, and then pressing Tab to move to the next control.

MouseMove

The MouseMove event occurs when the user moves the mouse over a control, a form, or a section of a form. This event is repeated continuously as the mouse is moved over a control. Even if a form or control is moved using Visual Basic code within a procedure and it passes underneath the mouse pointer, this event occurs. It's best used when you want to display a small form whenever a user moves the mouse over a certain control.

This event procedure has four arguments: Button, which specifies which mouse button was clicked; Shift, which tells you if the Shift, Ctrl, or Alt key is being held down while clicking; and X and Y, which give you the coordinates of the current mouse pointer. X and Y are always measured in twips (1/1440 of an inch) rather than pixels.

The Button argument has the following values: a setting of 0 indicates that no mouse button is pressed; a setting of 1 indicates that the left mouse button is pressed and is defined as constant value acLeftButton; a setting of 2 indicates that the right mouse button is pressed and is defined as constant value acRightButton; and a setting of 4 indicates that the middle mouse button is pressed and is defined as constant value acMiddleButton. Combination presses are the sums (actually the OR'd values) of these constants.

Constant Name	Value	Meaning
acLeftButton	1	Left button pressed
acRightButton	2	Right button pressed
acMiddleButton	4	Middle button pressed

The Shift argument tells Access if the Shift, Ctrl, and/or Alt keys are pressed while the event occurs. The value of Shift is 0 if none of the keys are held down. The value is 1, defined as constant value acShiftMask, if the Shift key is down. The value is 2, defined as constant value acCtrlMask, if the Ctrl key is down. The value is 4, defined as constant value acAltMask, if the Alt key is down. If any combination of these keys is held down together, the value of Shift is the sum of the keys' individual values.

Constant Name	Value	Meaning
acShiftMask	1	Shift key pressed
acCtrlMask	2	Ctrl key pressed
acAltMask	4	Alt key pressed

> **TIP**
>
> The constant values for the Shift and Button arguments represent bit positions in these values (1, 2, 4, 8, and so on) If you are interested in a specific value, you can test for it in VBA with the And operator. For example, to test for the right button:
>
> ```
> If (button And acRightButton) then
>     'code for right button response
> End If
> ```

MouseDown and MouseUp

The MouseDown and MouseUp events occur when a mouse button is clicked while over a control, a form, or a section of a form. These events enable you to determine which button (or combination of buttons) was used, which you can't determine in the Click and DblClick events. You can also find out if the user held down any combination of the Shift, Ctrl, and Alt keys.

This event procedure has four arguments: Button, which specifies which mouse button was clicked; Shift, which tells you if the Shift, Ctrl, or Alt key was held down while clicking; and X and Y, which give you the coordinates of the current mouse pointer. X and Y are always measured in twips rather than pixels.

The Button argument has the following values: a setting of 1 indicates that the left mouse button is pressed and is defined as constant value acLeftButton; a setting of 2 indicates that the right mouse button is pressed and is defined as constant value acRightButton; and a setting of 4 indicates that the middle mouse button is pressed and is defined as constant value acMiddleButton.

Constant Name	Value	Meaning
acLeftButton	1	Left button pressed
acRightButton	2	Right button pressed
acMiddleButton	4	Middle button pressed

The Shift argument tells Access if the Shift, Ctrl, and/or Alt keys are pressed while the event occurs. The value of Shift is 0 if none of the keys are held down. The value is 1, defined as constant value acShiftMask, if the Shift key is down. The value is 2, defined as constant value acCtrlMask, if the Ctrl key is down. The value is 4, defined as constant value acAltMask, if the Alt key is down. If any combination of these keys is held down together, the value of Shift is the sum of the keys' individual values.

Constant Name	Value	Meaning
acShiftMask	1	Shift key pressed
acCtrlMask	2	Ctrl key pressed
acAltMask	4	Alt key pressed

> **NOTE**
>
> The Button argument for the MouseDown and MouseUp events is somewhat different from the MouseMove event. For MouseDown and MouseUp, this argument indicates only one button per event. Therefore, two buttons being clicked would result in two events for both MouseDown and MouseUp. On the other hand, MouseMove would have only one event and would indicate only the current state of all the mouse buttons—in this case, adding up the values of the mouse buttons.

9

REACTING TO EVENTS IN THE INTERFACE

Print Events

Print events occur when a report is being formatted for printing or is actually printed. These events occur for each section of a report. Properly attaching event procedures to print events allows creative enhancement of reports, changing them on-the-fly according to the status of printed information.

Format

The Format event occurs before Access actually formats each section of a report but after data has been selected. For the detail section of a report, this event occurs for each record, enabling you to format each record differently if you want. In the group headers of a report, this event occurs each time a group by field changes value.

This event procedure has two arguments: Cancel and FormatCount. Cancel, if set to True, cancels the formatting for the current section and moves on to the next section. FormatCount is the number of times the Format event has occurred for the current section. You use this argument so that you know if a section spans more than one page.

Retreat

The Retreat event occurs when Access must return to a previous section of a report while formatting. This event occurs after the Format event but before the Print event. This way, you can change any formatting you may have already done. This capability can be useful if you want to change any headers when a section spans more than one page, or if you want to change the font size of a section to fit on a single page.

Print

The Print event occurs after the data has been formatted but before anything is displayed or printed. Separate Print events happen for headers, footers, groupings, and each item in the detail section. This event procedure has two arguments: Cancel and PrintCount. Setting Cancel to True doesn't print the section or the current record on the report, but instead leaves a blank space. The PrintCount argument keeps track of the number of times this event has occurred for the current record. This way, you can tell if a record spans more than one page and can cancel it if you want.

This is your last chance to modify labels on the page, insert photos into Image controls, change text colors per user preference, and so on.

NoData

The NoData event happens after Access has formatted the report but before the report is printed. This event enables you to detect if the report is based on an empty recordset, so you can cancel the printing if the recordset is empty.

Page

The Page event, which is called before the page is printed but after the NoData event. It is the recommended time to draw any graphics on the page (using Line, Pset, and so on).

Window Events

Window events occur when any window (form or report) is sized, opened, or closed.

Open

The Open event occurs whenever a form or report is opened but before the first record is displayed, or before a report is previewed or printed. This event occurs before the Load event. The Open event has one argument, Cancel. When Cancel is set to True, the form or report isn't opened. This event is best used to prompt a user for some criteria that will affect the data shown when the form is displayed. For example, if you're displaying a generic form, you can prompt the user to enter a table name and then code that name in the record source of a control on the form (after first validating the name, of course). The Open event is also the best place to set the focus to a particular control on the form.

Close

The Close event occurs whenever a form or report is closed and no longer visible on the screen. This event occurs after the Unload event. The Close event is usually the place where you open another form or display an existing message if the user is leaving the application.

Load

The Load event occurs whenever a form is opened and records are displayed. This event occurs before the Current event for the first record or control but after the Open event. You can't cancel this event; however, if the Open event is canceled, this event does not occur.

Unload

The Unload event occurs whenever a form is closed but before it's removed from the screen. This event is triggered by the closing action and occurs before the Close event. This event procedure has one argument, Cancel. When Cancel is set to True, the form doesn't close or unload from the screen.

WARNING

Be careful when setting Cancel to True in the Unload event. If you do so, you cannot close the form or remove it. Therefore, if you don't set Cancel back to False programmatically, you can never close this form unless you end the application. Also, if the form is modal, you might not have access to any other applications, which could be cause for a reboot.

Resize

The Resize event occurs whenever a form is opened or the size of the form changes in any way. This event enables you to change the size of any controls on the form when it is resized. Also, this event is the best place to use the Repaint method, which updates all controls on the form.

The Ordering of Access Events

Each control and form has several events, and understanding the order in which they're executed is important because it affects how and when your macros and procedures run. For example, if you have more than one procedure that must run in order, you must make sure that the events occur in the correct order, assuming that the events trigger a subprocedure.

> **WARNING**
>
> The event orders described in the following section are general, but all events are affected by user activity. Some events do not occur if an earlier event is canceled, and control event sequences may terminate slightly differently if a user clicks away with the mouse or tabs away.

Documentation notwithstanding, there is sometimes no substitute for testing to be sure a control or form behaves as you might expect. There is an easy way to experiment with event sequences for a control: Make an extra copy of your form. Simply create an event procedure for each event of interest. In each procedure, place a single line:

```
Sub eventProcedure()
Debug.print "Event Name", [arguments, if any]
End Sub
```

Execute different anticipated sequences of mouse clicks and keystrokes on the control or form, then examine the event trail in the Debug window to see the order in which they were (or sometimes, were not) executed.

Don't forget to remove these if you decide to keep the control. Even invisible Debug.Print statements take overhead and slow response.

Event Order for Controls on a Form

When a control receives the focus by the user's clicking it or pressing Tab to move to it, the order of events is as follows:

- Enter
- GotFocus

When you enter or change data in a control and then move the focus to another control, the following events are performed in basically this order:

- KeyDown
- KeyPress
- Change
- KeyUp
- BeforeUpdate
- AfterUpdate
- Exit
- LostFocus

However, the keystroke order is a bit more complex for some controls, particularly text boxes and combo boxes. See the event maps in Figures 9.1 and 9.2.

9

REACTING TO EVENTS IN THE INTERFACE

FIGURE 9.1.

Event map for a text box.

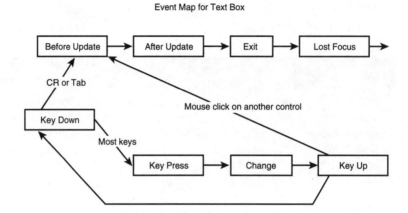

FIGURE 9.2.

Event map for a combo box.

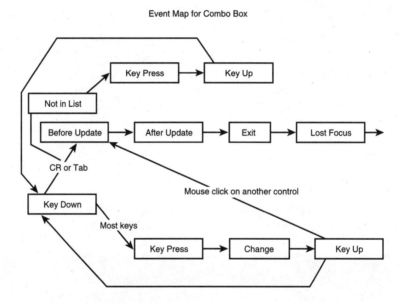

Event Order for Records on a Form

Separate events occur for records when they're displayed on a form. These events are different from those that occur for the controls that hold the data of the fields that make up a record. Record events in the form reflect the activity to the record as a whole—updating, deleting, and so on, that is performed after the individual events of the controls on the form.

When you change a record by moving within the controls on a form and then move to the next record, the following events occur in order:

- Current (form)
- Enter (control)
- GotFocus (control)
- BeforeUpdate (control)
- AfterUpdate (control)
- BeforeUpdate (form)
- AfterUpdate (form)
- Exit (control)
- LostFocus (control)
- Current (form)

> **NOTE**
>
> This example assumes that the focus is on the last control on a form. For controls other than the last one, you would have an Enter event and a GotFocus event before the AfterUpdate event for the form would occur.

When you delete a record on a form, the following events occur in order:

- Delete
- BeforeDelConfirm
- AfterDelConfirm

> **NOTE**
>
> In the Delete event subprocedure, you can test to determine if you really want to allow the user to delete the current record. If not, you can set Cancel to True; the deletion doesn't happen, and the BeforeDelConfirm and AfterDelConfirm events aren't executed. The confirm dialog box doesn't appear either.

When you move the focus to a new (blank) record, the following events occur in order:

- Current (form)
- Enter (form)
- GotFocus(control)
- BeforeInsert (form)
- AfterInsert (form)

> **NOTE**
>
> The BeforeUpdate and the AfterUpdate events for the controls and records on a form occur after the BeforeInsert event and before the AfterInsert event.

Event Order for Forms

Events that occur within forms include opening, closing, moving between forms, and working with the data on a form.

The following list illustrates the form event occurrences (in order) when you open form1, click a button to open form2, and then move back to form1:

- Open (form1)
- Load (form1)
- Resize (form1)
- Activate (form1)
- Current (form1)
- Open (form2)
- Load (form2)
- Resize (form2)
- Deactivate (form1)
- Activate (form2)
- Current (form2)
- Deactivate (form2)
- Activate (form1)

Each time a form receives the focus, the Activate event occurs. However, if the form is already open, the Open and Load events don't occur. This is true even if a form is called by the OpenForm action.

As you can see from the preceding example, when you open a second form, the Deactivate event from the first form doesn't occur until the second form executes its Open, Load, and Resize events. This way, you can check that the second form opens without any errors. If it does have errors, you can just close the form and the focus returns to the calling form. (Don't forget about displaying the appropriate error message.)

When you're working with forms and subforms, the order of events is as follows:

- Events for the subform's controls
- Events for the form's controls
- Events for the form
- Events for the subform

> **NOTE**
>
> Remember, the only events on a subform control are Enter and Exit. Any events tied to controls within the subform happen when the subform receives the focus or is updated by the result of the Link Master Fields changing.

Event Order for Keystrokes and Mouse Clicks

Keyboard and mouse events occur for forms and controls when they receive the focus.

The order of events for keystrokes is as follows:

- KeyDown
- KeyPress
- KeyUp

The MouseMove event occurs when you move the mouse over a control or form. The other mouse events occur in the following order when you click a mouse button while pointing at a control on a form:

- MouseDown
- MouseUp
- Click

A DblClick event occurs after the Click event.

Event Order for Reports

Events occur for reports and all the sections of a report when you print, print preview, or close a report.

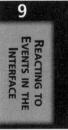

When you open a report to print or print preview and then close it, the following events occur in this order:

- Open (report)
- Activate (report)

Section events repeat as many times as necessary.

- Format (report section)
- Print (report section)
- Page (report level, each page)
- Close (report)
- Deactivate (report)

The Open event occurs before any underlying query is executed, enabling you to update or add SQL as needed.

The Format and Print events enable you to run macros or execute procedures. This capability gives you the opportunity to perform calculations (such as running totals) or change the layout of a report before printing it.

The NoData event occurs if the report doesn't generate any records to print.

The Retreat event occurs if Access has to go back to a previous section because all the data doesn't fit in a current section. This capability enables you to run a macro or sub-procedure to reformat your report in some way.

Assigning Code to Events

After you decide the events in which you want some action to take place, you need to assign a macro or Visual Basic code to the event procedure. By clicking the down arrow to the right of any event in the properties sheet, you can choose any currently defined macro or the event procedure.

> **TIP**
>
> When is it appropriate to use macros, and when is it better to use Visual Basic (VBA)? Think of macros as very consistent but stupid robots that are operating your program. If you can define an action as "Click the mouse here, then here, then press this key" and this action never varies, with little chance of an error, consider using a macro. Otherwise VBA is preferable (you can always call specific macros from VBA if necessary.)

Creating an Event Macro

If the activity desired already exists as a named macro, it can be selected from the pull-down list. If you select Macro Builder, the builder will open and macros can be constructed from the menu selections. By and large, macros simply replicate the kinds of activities you normally do with your mouse and keyboard. Table 9.1 is a summary of common macro commands and their options.

TABLE 9.1. MACRO ACTIONS.

Action	Arguments	Function
AddMenu	Menu Name Menu Macro Name Status Bar Text	Creates a menu bar containing drop-down menus. The menu bar appears when the form to which AddMenu has been assigned is active.
ApplyFilter	Filter Name Where Condition	Restricts or sorts the data available to a form or report using a filter, query, or SQL WHERE clause on the underlying table.
Beep	(no arguments)	Produces a beep tone for use in warnings or alerts.
CancelEvent	(no arguments)	Cancels the Access event that caused the macro with this action to run. If a validation macro failed, the update of the database could be canceled.
Close	Object Type Object Name Save	Closes the active window (the default) or a specified window. Lets you specify whether the object should be saved before being closed.
CopyObject	Destination Database New Name Source Object Type Source Object Name	Duplicates the specified database object in another database or in the original database using a different name.
DeleteObject	Object Type Object Name	Deletes the specified object.
Echo	Echo On Status Bar Text	Turns the screen refresh on or off during macro operation. Hides results until they are complete, and speeds macro operation.

continues

TABLE 9.1. CONTINUED

Action	Arguments	Function
FindNext	(no arguments)	Finds the next record specified by the FindRecord action or the Find command.
FindRecord	Find What Match Match Case Search Search As Formatted Only Current Field Find First	Finds the next record after the current record meeting the specified criteria. Searches through a table, form, or datasheet object.
GoToControl	Control Name	Selects the control named in the argument. Is used to select a control or field when a form opens.
GoToPage	Page Number Right Down	Selects the first field on the designated page in a multipage form. The first field is the first field as designated by tab order.
GoToRecord	Object Type Object Name Record Offset	Displays the specified record in a table, form, or datasheet object.
Hourglass	Hourglass On	Displays an hourglass in place of the mouse pointer while the macro runs. Use it for long macros.
Maximize	(no arguments)	Maximizes the active window.
Minimize	(no arguments)	Minimizes the active window to an icon within the Access window.
MoveSize	Right Down Width Height	Moves or changes the size of the active window.
MsgBox	Message Beep Type Title	Displays a warning or informational message box.

Action	*Arguments*	*Function*
OpenForm	Form Name View Filter Name Where Condition Data Mode Window Mode	Opens or activates a form in one of its views. The form can be restricted to data-matching criteria, different modes of editing, and whether the form acts as a modal or pop-up dialog box.
OpenModule	Module Name Procedure Name	Opens the specified module and displays the specified procedure.
OpenQuery	Query Name View Data Mode	Opens or activates a datasheet or crosstab query. You can specify the view and data entry mode.
OpenReport	Report Name View Filter Name Where Condition	Opens a report in the view you specify and filters the records before printing.
OpenTable	Table Name View Data Mode	Opens or activates a table in the view you specify. You can specify the data entry or edit mode for tables in datasheet view.
OutputTo	Object Type Object Name Output Format Output File Auto Start	Copies the data in the specified object to a Microsoft Excel (.XLS), rich text format (.RTF), or DOS text (.TXT) file. Autostart = Yes starts the application with the association to the extension.
PrintOut	Print Range Page From Page To Print Quality Copies Collate Copies	Prints the active datasheet, report, or form.
Quit	Options	Exits from Access and saves unsaved objects according to the command you specify.
Rename	New Name Object Type Old Name	Renames the specified database object.
RepaintObject	Object Type Object Name	Completes recalculations for controls and updates specified or active database objects and/or screens.

9

REACTING TO EVENTS IN THE INTERFACE

continues

TABLE 9.1. CONTINUED

Action	Arguments	Function
Requery	Control Name	Updates the specified control by repeating the query of the control's source.
Restore	(no arguments)	Restores a maximized or minimized window to its previous window.
RunApp	Command Line	Runs a Windows or MS-DOS application.
RunCode	Function Name	Runs a user-defined function written in Access Basic.
RunCommand	Command	Runs an Access command.
RunMacro	Macro Name Repeat Count Repeat Expression	Runs the specified macro.
RunSQL	SQL Statement	Runs an action query as specified by the SQL statement or a data-definition query.
Save	Object Type Object Name	Saves the specified database object, or the active object if a specific object is not named.
SelectObject	Object Type Object Name In Database Window	Selects a specified database object.
SendKeys	Keystrokes Wait	Sends keystrokes to any active Windows application.
SendObject	Object Type Object Name Output Format To Cc Bcc Subject Message Text Edit Message	Sends the specified object as an attachment to a Microsoft Mail 3.*x* or Microsoft Exchange or Outlook message. You enter the recipients of the message with the values of the To, Cc, and Bcc arguments. You can specify the subject header for the message, add text to the message, and edit the message in Microsoft Mail.
SetMenuItem	Menu Index Command Index Subcommand Index Flag	Sets the state of menu items on custom menus (including shortcut and global menus) for the active window. Items can be enabled or disabled and checked or unchecked.
SetValue	Item Expression	Changes the value of a field, control, or property.

Action	Arguments	Function
SetWarnings	Warnings On	Turns warning messages on or off.
ShowAllRecords	(no arguments)	Removes any filters or queries and displays all records in the current table or query.
ShowToolbar	Toolbar Name Show	Displays or hides a built-in toolbar or a custom toolbar. You can display a built-in toolbar in all Access windows or just the view in which the toolbar is normally displayed.
StopAllMacros	(no arguments)	Stops all macros.
StopMacro	(no arguments)	Stops the current macro.
Transfer Database	Transfer Type Database Type Database Name Object Type Source Destination Structure Only	Imports, exports, or attaches to Access and non-Access databases.
Transfer Spreadsheet	Transfer Type Spreadsheet Type Table Name File Name Has Field Names Range	Imports or exports Access data to a worksheet or spreadsheet file.
TransferText	Transfer Type Specification Name Table Name File Name Has Field Names	Imports or exports Access data to a text file.

Creating an Event Procedure

When you assign VBA code to an event, Access automatically sets up the following skeleton subprocedure for you:

```
Sub procedure name ()

End Sub
```

Using this skeleton event procedure, you can customize any process within your Access application—for example, formatting reports, creating and running queries, setting properties to controls, or adding, updating, and deleting database records using recordsets.

Subprocedures and functions both execute code, but subprocedures are executed from event procedures, not functions. However, you can call a function from a subprocedure. Also, subprocedures can't return a value, but functions do return a single value from where they were called.

> ## WARNING
>
> Having a *recursive* (calling itself) subprocedure or function is possible, but you run the risk of a stack overflow. Also, you can't nest subprocedure definitions or function definitions, but you can call other subprocedures from within a subprocedure.

Wizards for command buttons, combo and list boxes, option groups, and other controls actually do much of their work by creating event procedures for the appropriate events. Looking at the code created by these wizards can be quite educational. Once the wizard creates the code, feel free to make additions to it to accomplish any additional actions you desire.

This chapter concentrates on using the event procedure with VBA code rather than using macros, because procedures are much faster, more flexible, and easier to maintain. VBA also enables you to easily trap any errors that might occur in your application. You can supply your own error messages and prevent the application from crashing (utilizing the Error event and the OnError function), which macros can't do. A few macro actions do not have corresponding VBA functions, but these can always be called from VBA code using DoCmd if needed. The Autoexec action must be a macro, but you can overcome this limitation by making the Autoexec macro action a one-line Runcode macro that calls your VBA code.

To create an event procedure, which is invoked automatically in response to an event, follow these steps:

1. Select the object (form or control) whose event you wish to handle. Be sure the property sheet is open to the Events page.
2. Select the event that will trigger the event procedure.
3. Select [Event Procedure] from the list.

4. Click the Build button to display the Module window.

5. Type the event procedure code between the Sub line and the End Sub line.

6. Click the Compile button or Debug | Compile Loaded Modules to force an immediate compile as a first check for syntax errors.

TIP

There is nothing privileged about event procedures. It is legal to call an event procedure from any other procedure in the module. For example, if you have more than one Close button, they can all actually execute the same code.

WARNING

If an error message appears during a compile, you need to correct the source of the error and then recompile.

When the form or report is open, each occurrence of the event will cause the event procedure to be called. To debug an event procedure, it is helpful to set a breakpoint on its first line and step through it (using the F8 key) for the first few times until you are comfortable that the event handler is performing as you expected.

WARNING

Be careful when you're deleting controls that have code written behind them. Remember that the code isn't deleted with the control—it is just placed in the general object of the form or report. This is also the case when you rename a control, so make sure that you cut and paste the code back to the appropriate control. If you forget to do so, the code will stay out there and never execute, but it won't cause any runtime errors. On the other hand, don't forget that when you're pasting a control on a form or report, any code that's behind the control that was cut or copied doesn't get pasted with the new control.

Class Modules

Class modules extend the programming flexibility of VBA. They permit the programmer to create unique objects, much like intrinsic VBA and DAO objects, with their own methods and properties. Multiple copies of these objects can be created, stored, and manipulated in object variables. To create a class module in Access, select Insert | Class module.

Difference Between Class Modules and Standard Modules

The difference between standard modules and class modules is both subtle and profound. A standard module is global. Its functions, unless declared `Private`, can be called from anywhere in Access, and there is only one copy of each of the global and static variables within the module. It always represents a single instance.

It is possible to (mis)use a class module in the same way. But the importance of the class module is as a foundation for complete, user-defined objects. The internal variables in each instance are unique to that instance. Every object created on a class module has the same original characteristics, but each instance of a class module can itself be stored in a single object variable and can be created, used, and deleted independently of any other copies.

Since the advent of Windows 95, form modules have also been a special type of class module. From VBA, you can create as many copies of a form as desired, each one with its own internal variable values and life span. Non-form class modules are similar, without the accompanying forms or form events, but they have their own two specialized events: `Initialize` and `Terminate`.

Class Modules as Objects

To demonstrate the use of class modules as objects, the database for this chapter (see the Web site for this book) contains a simplified example using object properties to communicate between different forms on the screen. Just as people exchange phone numbers to remain in contact at a distance, forms and classes can exchange object references with each other and remain in continuous contact.

To illustrate this technique, the sub-procedure `wintest` (you can call this function from the debug window) opens two forms of class `Parent`. Each `Parent` form, in turn, opens a child form of class `User Response`. These pairs of forms maintain two-way communications throughout their lifetimes. Any entry put into the field in the user response form is immediately relayed back and displayed on its parent as soon as it is completed. (A keystroke-by-keystroke response could have been constructed using the `KeyPress` event.)

First, the code for the Parent forms:

```
Option Compare Database
Option Explicit

Dim ufrm As Form_User Response
'ufrm remains in scope during life of this form

Sub update_display(s As String)
    Me!remote = s
End Sub

Private Sub Form_Close()
On Error Resume Next      'if no child to close, skip it
    ufrm.SetFocus
    DoCmd.close
End Sub

Private Sub Form_Open(Cancel As Integer)
    Me.Visible = True 'make ourselves visible
    Randomize
    DoCmd.MoveSize 1500 * Rnd(), 1500 * Rnd()
    'so windows are not exactly on top of each other
    Set ufrm = New Form_User Response
    Set ufrm.callback = Me
    ufrm.Visible = True
    ufrm.SetFocus
    DoCmd.MoveSize 1500 * Rnd(), 1500 * Rnd()
    'same for child windows

End Sub

Private Sub see_child_Click()
    'sets the child back to focus
    On Error GoTo handler
    ufrm.SetFocus
Exit Sub

handler:
    If Err = 2467 Then
        MsgBox "Sorry, that form has been deleted"
        Resume Next
    End If
End Sub
```

First, notice the declaration of the object variable ufrm. It is declared in scope module level to this instance of Parent because if it went out of scope, the child window would go out of scope as well. Also important is the special syntax to create a reference to a form: preface the form name with Form_ (if the child form has already been saved, this construct will be available from the pull-down selection list). Note that this is not the same as the more conventional DoCmd.OpenForm "User Response". The DoCmd syntax simply opens the named instance of the form, a single global instance.

In the Open_Form event handler, a new instance of form User Response is created and assigned to ufrm. Then the child form is notified by setting its callback property to this window, so the child window knows who to notify when the time comes.

Here is the code for the child window:

```
Option Compare Database
Option Explicit
Dim parentfrm As Form_Parent


Property Set callback(frm As Form_Parent)
    Set parentfrm = frm
End Property

Private Sub close_Click()
    Me.Visible = False
End Sub

Private Sub ctlresponse_AfterUpdate()
'contents have changed, tell parent immediately
    parentfrm.update_display Nz(Me!ctlresponse)
    parentfrm.SetFocus
End Sub
```

In the child window, the first thing to do is establish the identity of the parent. This is done through the Property Set callback method, which in this case simply sets an object variable. (Property Let is similar, except it handles normal variables instead of object references.)

The interesting code is in the sub ctlresponse_AfterUpdate. This subroutine calls the update_display method of the parent form, passing the value needed to update. To keep the child alive the Hide button simply makes it invisible rather than actually closing it. It can be restored from its parent form, with contents intact.

> **NOTE**
>
> Traditionally, object-oriented programming makes a strong distinction between a class (the abstract pattern for an object) and its instantiations (the objects themselves). Partly for the purpose of maintaining compatibility with more traditional Access programming, the boundaries here are more blurred. `Classname` is always a valid instance of a class even if it's never instantiated with the `New` keyword. That way, references like `Formname.Requery` are legitimate references to the `Requery` method of the global instance of (form) class `Formname`.
>
> Be careful if you're using both generic named classes and object instantiations in the same program.

Surprisingly, in Access 97 there is no close or delete method on an object variable. An object instance form or class object will terminate after the last reference to it has gone out of scope, has been set to some other value, or has been set to the special value `Nothing`. Terminating a class by emptying its variable may be trickier than it appears. In this demonstration, each `Parent` form is referenced both in the `win()` array and by the `parentfrm` variable in the user response form, so clearing just one variable may not produce the expected result. With forms, an alternate approach to force a close is to first make sure the form is active, and then use the `Close` method of `DoCmd`:

```
Objectname.SetFocus    'force form active
DoCmd.Close
```

This is less than graceful because it sends the form to the front of the screen before closing it, potentially distracting the user.

> **WARNING**
>
> In the preceding technique, be sure to user proper error trapping! If `Objectname.SetFocus` fails (for example, if `Objectname` was already closed) and you resume on `DoCmd.Close`, whatever view is currently in the front of the screen will be closed.

Summary

Understanding how events work is an important step in developing Access applications. Using event procedures enables you to customize any type of application easily. Event procedures also give you the flexibility to develop an open system that can be modified quickly and easily to meet the changing needs of any business environment.

Visual Basic for Applications

CHAPTER 10

Visual Basic for Applications (VBA) is the programming language used by Access. VBA code is used when you need to go beyond the scope of macros to tie your application together. In this version of Access, VBA replaces the Access Basic language. VBA is a superset of the language that was used in the previous version of Access and includes new commands, functions, enhancements, and object-oriented capabilities. VBA is a language that is common to other Microsoft products and allows these products to interact and share data easily.

An Introduction to VBA Code

VBA enables you to develop more complex and robust applications. Typical uses are controlling the user interface, field and record validations, and trapping errors.

When to Use Visual Basic

Without using VBA, you can still write many applications by incorporating macros into your Access application. However, macros lack some of the more complex features that can be found only in VBA.

Here's a partial list of the advantages of using VBA in your Access applications:

- You can make use of Data Access Objects (DAO).
- You can add your own error handling routines, giving you more control of applications.
- You can incorporate Object Linking and Embedding (OLE).
- You can incorporate Dynamic Data Exchange (DDE).
- You can make use of transactions.
- You can make use of the Windows APIs.
- You can make use of decision looping (`If...Then...Else, Do...While, Select Case`).
- You can create reusable and generic code.

The Module Window

The Module window, shown in Figure 10.1, is where you add and maintain all the code in your application. This is the same window that is used by both standard modules and class modules.

Figure 10.1.

The Module window.

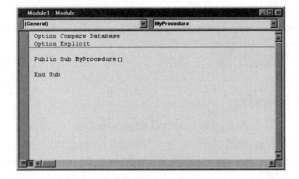

All the procedures you write can be stored in one module or kept in separate modules. It's best to use separate modules and group similar procedures together in their own module. For example, all the code that is needed to import an ASCII file of daily sales should be kept in one module.

When you're in the Module window, the module toolbar is displayed. This toolbar provides you with shortcuts when you're working on procedures.

As with all Access toolbars, the buttons change depending on where you are and what you're doing. Figure 10.2 shows the basic toolbar for the Module window. You can modify this toolbar by adding, removing, and changing the faces of the toolbar buttons. For more on how to work with toolbars, refer to Chapter 8, "Working with Command Bars."

Figure 10.2.

The Module toolbar.

Several related new features of the Module window have been introduced with Access 97. All of them are enabled by default. You can turn them off by selecting Tools | Options and using the Module tab.

Automatic Statement Builder

The first new feature is Automatic Statement Builder (see Figure 10.3). This feature is activated when you press the spacebar after a keyword, like *as*. A list is presented, showing you all available keywords and pointing to the closest match to what you have typed. If the highlighted selection is what you want, press Tab, Enter, or the spacebar and Access completes the keyword for you.

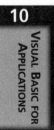

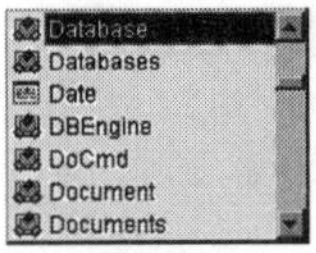

FIGURE 10.3.

FIGURE 10.3.

The Auto Statement Builder window.

Auto Quick Info

Another aspect of the code helper is activated when you type a function name. The function name can be intrinsic, part of VBA, or a function or subroutine you have written. The code helper presents you with the list of parameters the function will accept. This feature can save you from spending a lot of time hunting for how to fill in the parameter list.

For intrinsic functions and object methods, Auto Quick Info also provides a list of acceptable values for certain parameters. For example, the `OpenRecordset` DAO method takes two parameters, the query or table name and the type of recordset to return. After you have typed the query or table name and the comma parameter separator, Access shows you a list of constants identifying the possible choices for the recordset type parameter.

If you have dimensioned an object variable (for example, `rs` is dimensioned as a `Recordset` object), Auto Quick Info presents a list of possible object methods (see Figure 10.4).

FIGURE 10.4.

The Auto Quick Info window listing object methods.

Auto Quick Info also shows you the defined parameter list for the function, subprocedure, or object method you are trying to use. When you type the left parenthesis to begin entering parameters, a tip window appears with the parameters for the function, as shown in Figure 10.5. The parameter you are currently ready to enter is highlighted in this tip window. When you have finished with the first parameter and type the comma separator, the next parameter is highlighted.

These new Module window features are there to help you become more comfortable and productive in writing VBA code for Access. They can help you, whether you're a beginner or an advanced user, by showing you what is possible and legal without your having to search through books or online Help. After a while, you can turn off these features if they become more annoying than helpful.

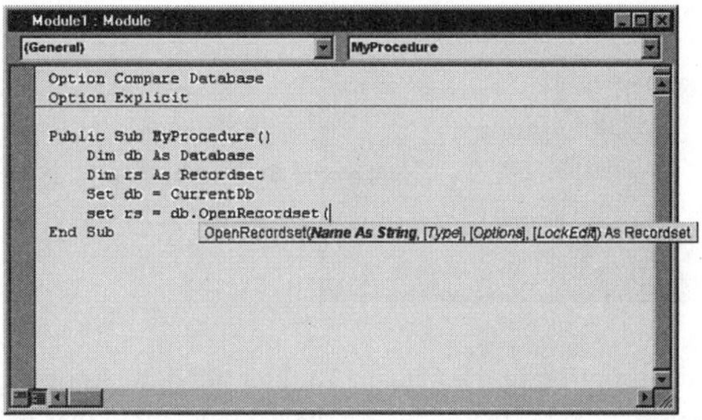

FIGURE 10.5.

The Auto Quick Info window showing method parameters.

Code Modules

Code modules are database objects that contain VBA code. There are three fundamental kinds of code modules: the standard module, the forms module, and a new kind, the class module.

Each kind of module has a distinct purpose. A standard module contains functions and subprocedures that are available to other modules and code behind forms. A module associated with a form has code that is available to the form only. Subprocedures in such a module can be associated with events on the form, such as a button click or database record change. A class module provides a way for the programmer to create new objects that resemble standard objects, such as data access objects, form objects, and so on. The programmer has control over which properties and methods are exposed to the rest of the application.

Standard Module

As stated earlier, standard modules are the procedures you create in the Module window of the database container. These functions and subprocedures are available to the application at all times. They can be called from other procedures, forms, reports, queries, and macros. They're loaded into memory when the application is loaded and stay there until the application terminates.

Code Behind Forms Module

Code behind forms (CBF) is a term to describe where the procedures for forms and reports are located. In the CBF method, you place the event code procedures inside the form or report. You do this by clicking the Builder button (...), shown in Figure 10.6, to invoke the Choose Builder.

FIGURE 10.6.

The Property window, including the Builder button.

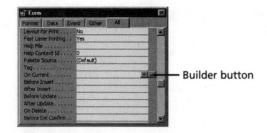

Builder button

Select the Code Builder option in the Choose Builder window. Another window appears. This window is where you enter the code. It's the same window that modules use, and it has all the same functionality as well. When you're finished writing the code, close the window. You'll return to the form or report.

The CBF modules are composed of three sections: the object events section, the form or report events section, and the general section. The object events section is made up of all the events for that object. The number and type of events differ from object to object. The form or report events are those events that relate only to the form or report itself. The general section is where you place the procedures that are common to all objects in the form or report. To move to this section, select the General option from the Object box on the toolbar.

An example of a general procedure is an audit trailing routine. When the user adds, edits, or deletes a record, an audit trail record is written. Because this same code is used in different places, you should have to write the procedure only once. If you place the code in the general section, all the procedures in the form have access to it.

The scope of the CBF modules is limited to the form or report. If a form opens another form, the modules in the first form aren't available in the second form.

Any procedure in the form can call any other procedure. For example, the form contains a command button named cmdSave. Its OnClick event code can call a procedure in the general section. The code for the cmdSave button would look like this:

```
Function cmdSave_Click ( )
    '--    See if all required entries are there.
    If OkToSave() Then
        Me.Refresh
    Else
        Msgbox "Missing Information.", 16, "Data Entry"
        DoCmd.CancelEvent
    End If
End Function
```

You can also have one command button call the `OnClick` procedure of another command button. The code to do this is as follows:

```
Function cmdExit_Click  ( )
    '--     See if there were any changes to the current record.
    If Me.Dirty Then
        '--    Save the changes to the record.
        cmdSave_Click()
    End If
    DoCmd.Close
End Function
```

Class Module

A new feature of Access 97 is the capability to create new classes similar to the form or report classes. The code in a class module of this type is very similar to that in a standard code module. The difference is in how the code is used and referenced by other portions of your application.

Simply put, a class module provides a way to create nonvisual objects with properties and methods in your application. Listing 10.1 shows a simple class that encapsulates the `GetSetting` and `SaveSetting` VBA functions that are used to manage options for your application. The code is in a class module called `CSetting`. The `C` prefix to the class name indicates that an instance of the class represents a single object.

LISTING 10.1. A SIMPLE CLASS.

```
Option Compare Database
Option Explicit

'/// define public properties
Public Section As String
Public Key As String

'/// declare internal housekeeping variables
Private mvValue As Variant

Public Sub Save()
    '/// save setting
    SaveSetting appname:="MyApp", _
        Section:=Section, _
        Key:=Key, _
        Setting:=mvValue
End Sub

Public Sub Read()
    '/// get setting
```

continues

10

LISTING 10.1. CONTINUED

```
    mvValue = GetSetting(appname:="MyApp", _
        Section:=Section, _
        Key:=Key, _
        Default:=mvValue)
End Sub

Property Get Value()
    Value = mvValue
End Property

Property Let Value(vValue As Variant)
    mvValue = vValue
End Property

Property Get ValueType()
    ValueType = VarType(mvValue)
End Property
```

The functions are quite useful by themselves, and you might not actually want or need to hide them in a class module. The main purpose of these examples is to show the techniques used to create and use a class.

Listing 10.2 shows how you can use this `CSetting` class. First, a new instance of the class is created. The three properties are then set inside a `With...End With` block. Finally, the `Save` method is called to make the new setting permanent.

LISTING 10.2. USING THE `CSetting` CLASS.

```
Private Sub cmdSave_Click()
    Dim oCSetting As New CSetting

    On Error GoTo Err_cmdSave_Click
    With oCSetting
        .Section = "Settings"
        .Key = txtKey
        .Value = txtValue
    End With
    oCSetting.Save
    DoCmd.Close

Exit_cmdSave_Click:
    Exit Sub

Err_cmdSave_Click:
    MsgBox Err.Description
    Resume Exit_cmdSave_Click

End Sub
```

It is also possible, and often desirable, to create a collection class. This is a kind of class that allows you to refer to a collection of objects as a single entity. Expanding on the CSetting class, the code for a collection of CSetting objects might look like the code given in Listing 10.3. This is in a class module called NSettings. The N prefix indicates that it is a collection class.

LISTING 10.3. USING THE CSetting CLASS IN A COLLECTION.

```
Option Compare Database
Option Explicit

Private clsSettings As New Collection

Private Sub Class_Initialize()
    Dim rCSetting As CSetting
    Dim vSettings As Variant
    Dim iSettings As Long
    Dim sAppName As String

    sAppName = CurrentDb.Name
    vSettings = GetAllSettings(appname:="MyApp", Section:="Settings")
    If Not IsEmpty(vSettings) Then
        For iSettings = LBound(vSettings, 1) To UBound(vSettings, 1)
            Set rCSetting = New CSetting
            With rCSetting
                .Section = "Settings"
                .Key = vSettings(iSettings, 0)
                .Value = vSettings(iSettings, 1)
            End With
            clsSettings.Add rCSetting
        Next iSettings
    End If
End Sub

Public Property Get Items() As Collection
    Set Items = clsSettings
End Property

Public Property Get Count()
    Count = clsSettings.Count
End Property

Public Function Item(vItem As Variant)
    On Error Resume Next
    Set Item = clsSettings(vItem)
    If Err <> 0 Then
        Set Item = Nothing
    End If
```

continues

LISTING 10.3. CONTINUED

```
End Function

Public Sub Refresh()
    Set clsSettings = Nothing
    Class_Initialize
End Sub
```

Classes are an excellent way to provide an object-oriented interface around your application code.

However, take care to use the right kind of module for the purpose at hand. You will find cases in which creating a class module is not the best way to do things in Access. This is particularly true of specialized data processing tasks that are highly sequential in nature.

The Purpose of Reusable and Generic Code

The purpose of reusable and generic code is to minimize the amount of code written for an application. The less code there is, the faster it runs and the easier it is to maintain.

It's easier to maintain generic code because you have to make the modifications in only one place. For example, let's say you use a common function to exit all forms. If the client requests that the user be prompted before exiting all forms, you need to make the change in only one place. If your application has 50 forms, think of the time this technique will save.

The drawback to using generic code is that when you make a change, you need to think about the effect it will have throughout the application.

Design Considerations

Before you write your own reusable and generic code, you should be aware of a few design considerations. Following these guidelines should help you write better routines.

The Scope of the Routine

What is the scope of the routine? Will it be used throughout the application or just for a few forms, reports, queries, macros, or modules? Will it be used only in this application, or will other applications use it as well?

Avoid Direct References to Objects

Avoid making references to objects that are on a form or report. What happens if the form or report that called this routine doesn't have that control? It's better to pass the control's value to the routine as a parameter.

The following is an example of changing the `Visible` property for a `Save` command button. This is the calling procedure:

```
Sub Button0_Click ()
     SetVisible Me!cmdSave
End Sub
```

This the generic code that changes the `Visible` property:

```
Sub SetVisible (pControl As Control)
     pControl.Visible = Not pControl.Visible
End Sub
```

In the preceding sample code, you can pass in the name of any control and change its `Visible` property. Another way to do this is to have a `cmdSave` command button on all the forms that call it.

Documentation and Comments

It's a well-known fact that programmers hate doing documentation of any type. Documenting and commenting your generic routines is extremely important, however. If you don't do this, it will be next to impossible for anyone else to use and fix your routines later.

When it comes time to document your routines, here are some places you should pay particular attention to:

- Procedure header—Include one or two sentences about what the procedure does, just enough to explain its purpose.

- Parameter list—Include a list of the parameters that are passed in, with a description for each and information as to whether they're required or optional parameters. If you're using the parsing method to pass in a parameter that contains several options, you need to show how to pass each option and its default value.

- Calls to other procedures—Include one line about what that procedure will do. It should look something like this:

  ```
  '--    Get the list order number for this customer.
  LastOrder = LastCustOrder(tblCustomer!CustomerId)
  ```

- Common blocks of code—Include a comment about what that block of code does. Because this is a common block of code, you might want to spend more time documenting it.

Datatypes

When you're writing VBA code, you often need to store values temporarily. Variables are similar to fields in a table—they both have a datatype. The datatype states the type of value and the size that can be stored in it.

Defining the Variables

Before you can use a variable, you must declare it. To guarantee this, you will need to set Require Variable Declaration. To set this option, you need to select Tools | Options. At the Module tab, you will see Require Variable Declaration. To declare a variable, you use the Dim statement. The Dim statement declares a variable and allocates storage space for it. You then can store a value in it.

The syntax for the Dim statement is as follows:

```
Dim varname[([subscripts])][As [New] type][, varname[([subscripts])]][As
[New] type]] ...
```

The arguments for the Dim statement are shown in Table 10.1.

TABLE 10.1. THE Dim STATEMENT ARGUMENTS.

Argument	Description
varname	The name of the variable to be created.
subscripts	The dimensions of an array variable. You can declare a multidimensional array.
New	A keyword used to indicate that a declared object variable is a new instance of an object.
As type	A reserved word that is used to declare the datatype of the variable.

The datatype value can be one of several types, as shown in Table 10.2.

TABLE 10.2. THE DATATYPE VALUES.

Datatype	Description
Integer	A numeric value within the range of –32,768 to 32,767.
Long	A numeric value within the range of –2,147,483,648 to 2,147,483,647.

Datatype	Description
Single	A numeric value within the ranges of –3.402823E38 to –1.401298E-45 for negative numbers, and 1.401298E-45 to 3.402823E38 for positive numbers and 0.
Double	A numeric value within the ranges of –1.79769313486232E308 to –4.94065645841247E-324 for negative numbers, and 4.94065645841247E-324 to 1.79769313486232E308 for positive numbers and 0.
Currency	A numeric value within the range of –922,337,203,685,477.5808 to 922,337,203,685,477.5807.
String	0 to around 65,535 bytes of text.
Variant	Any numeric value up to the length of a Double datatype or any character text.

Arrays

Arrays are created in the same way you would create any other variable. When defining an array, you not only give it a name, you also set the upper and lower subscripts.

To define an array, you can use one of the following lines of code:

```
Dim aNames(4)
```

or

```
ReDim aNames(4)
```

or

```
Static aNames(4)
```

All three lines of code declare an array called aNames that contains five elements. The first element number is 0, and the last is 4. If you want the first element number to be 1, you can use one of the following lines of code:

```
Dim aNames(1 to 5)
```

or

```
ReDim aNames(1 to 5)
```

or

```
Static aNames(1 to 5)
```

Now the starting element number is 1 and the ending element is 5. For some developers, this makes it a little easier to read because you don't have to add or subtract 1 from the element number to know its real location in the array.

You can also use negative numbers as the starting and ending element numbers. Here is how you do it:

```
Dim aNames(-5 to -1)
```

or

```
ReDim aNames(-5 to -1)
```

or

```
Static aNames(-5 to -1)
```

The ReDim statement does one other thing. It enables you to resize a dynamic array that has already been declared. The array must have been created using either the ReDim command or the Dim command without specifying any of the elements of the array. For example, say that you have an array defined as having six elements and you need to add one more element to it. To do this, you use the ReDim statement like this:

```
ReDim aItems(1 To 7)
```

This statement erases all the data that was stored in the six elements of the aItems array. To save the data that was in the array when you resize it, add the key word Preserve. Now when you resize the array, all its original data is left intact:

```
ReDim Preserve aItems(1 to 7)
```

If you don't want to declare the number of elements in your array initially and later want to store six elements, you could code this in your Declarations section:

```
dim aItems()
```

Then in a procedure, this would be the code:

```
ReDim aItems(1 To 7)
```

If you need to determine the starting and ending elements in your array, you use the lBound and uBound functions. For example, if you use the preceding ReDim statement, lBound(aItems) would return 1 and uBound(aItems) would return 7.

Variable Scope

When you create variables in VBA, they have a set scope or lifetime. *Scope* refers to where and when you can make references to a variable.

Local Scope

Variables declared within a procedure are private to that procedure and can't be made public. Local variables can be referenced only within the procedure that declares them. If a local variable is declared as `Static`, the variable exists whenever its module is a part of the running program, and it retains its value throughout the life of the application. Nonstatic local variables are created each time the procedure runs and are destroyed when the procedure ends. This means that a nonstatic local variable is reinitialized each time that particular procedure runs.

If you call another procedure, the variable declared in the calling procedure can't be referenced by the called procedure. You can use the `Dim` statement to declare a variable of the same name in the new procedure and even assign a different datatype to it. When you leave that procedure and return to the first procedure, the variable still contains its original value. Try these two procedures to see how it works:

```
Sub mvar_Local ()
    Dim txtName As String
    txtName = "Alan McConnell"

    '--   Call another procedure.
    mvar_Local2

    MsgBox txtName, 0, "Back in the main procedure."
End Sub


Sub mvar_Local2 ()
    Dim txtName As Double
    txtName = 100
    MsgBox Str(txtName), 0, "In the called procedure."
End Sub
```

To see how this works, run `mvar_Local` in the Scope module of `Acc10.mdb` on the book's Web site.

Module Scope

Variables declared at the module level are, by default, private to the module. This means that the variable can be referenced by any procedures within the module but not by any procedures outside it. To create a module scope variable, you define it in the Declarations section of a module, form, or report.

You can't assign a value to the variable in the Declarations section—you have to do it within a procedure. From that point on, any other procedure in the module has access to it and can also change its value. Module-level variables are essentially static variables and retain their value throughout the life of the application.

10

VISUAL BASIC FOR
APPLICATIONS

Here's an example of how this works:

```
Dim mCompany As String

Sub module_Test ()
    mCompany = "Big Ben's Tire Barn"

    '--    Call the other procedure.
    module_Test2

    MsgBox mCompany, 0, "Back in the main procedure."
End Sub


Sub module_Test2 ()
    MsgBox mCompany, 0, "In the called procedure."
    mCompany = "Brian's Auto Shop"
End Sub
```

To see how this works, run `module_Test` in the Scope module of `Acc10.mdb` on the book's Web site. If you call a procedure that resides within another module, the variables don't have any values. You can declare the variables again in the new module, give them new values, and manipulate them with code. When you return to the calling procedure, they once again have their original values.

Application-Wide Scope

The `Public` statement is used to declare a variable that can be referenced by all the procedures in the application. The `Public` syntax is the same as the `Dim` statement. The only difference is that it must be declared in the Declarations section of the module. The correct syntax is as follows:

```
Public varname[([subscripts])][As [New] type][, varname[([subscripts])]
➥[As [New] type]]...
```

Before you can have access to the `Public` variable and its value, you need to call a procedure in the module that sets a value to it. For this reason, it's best to create one module that defines and stores an initial value for all the `Public` variables that are used in an application. This way, you don't have to search all over your application for where each one was created. To see how this works, run `public_Test` in the Scope module of `Acc10.mdb` on the book's Web site.

Access Scope

Although `Public` module-level variables can't be viewed through the Object Browser, they're still available to referencing databases. This provides an access-wide scope to the variable. For example, pCompany is declared in the Scope module. This module is part of database Acc10.mdb. The value of pCompany is then set in the procedure public_Test. See Listing 10.4.

LISTING 10.4. Public VARIABLES.

```
Option Compare Database
Option Explicit
Public pCompany As String

Sub public_gTest()
    pCompany = "Big Ben's Tire Barn"

    MsgBox pCompany
End Sub
```

You can now close the Access database Acc10.mdb and open Acc10_Scope.mdb. In Acc10_Scope.mdb, you can establish a reference to Acc10.mdb. To establish a reference to another database, you need to open a module or class module and select Tools | References, as shown in Figure 10.7.

FIGURE 10.7.

References.

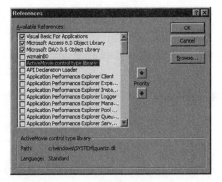

Here you can select an already registered type library, executable file, ActiveX control, or Access database, or you can browse and find your own file. If this is the first time you have referenced Acc10.mdb, you will need to select the Browse button. Here you will need to change the File type to Microsoft Access Database (*.mdb). Access is a little different than most programs because it will allow you to reference other Access databases and not just the normal type libraries, executable files, and ActiveX controls. Now locate the Acc10.mdb file on this book's Web site. Once you have the datbase referenced, you can add the code to call public_gTest. Assuming that you have a command button named cmdMsg on a form, you can execute the code that appears in Listing 10.5.

10

VISUAL BASIC FOR APPLICATIONS

LISTING 10.5. USING Public VARIABLES FROM ANOTHER DATABASE.

```
Private Sub cmdMsg_Click()
    Call public_gTest
End Sub
```

To see how this works, open the form Public_Test in Acc10_Scope.mdb on the Web site for this book and click the Test Scope button.

> **NOTE**
>
> Since Acc10.mdb was located and referenced on my machine in one directory, it is possible that you will need to re-reference Acc10.mdb on your machine for the preceding example to work.

Static Variables

A static variable is one that doesn't lose its value when you exit the procedure, as local variables do. When you return to the procedure, the variable still contains the value it had before, just like a module-level variable. The difference is that only this procedure has access to the value. No other procedures have access to the variable or its value.

Here's how you declare a static variable. You can declare it only from within a procedure:

```
Static  variablename[([subscripts])] [As type] [, variablename
➥[([subscripts])] [As type] ]...
```

Constants

Constants are variables that are assigned a value and can't be changed. After they're assigned a value, you can refer to them by name. Access uses constants to store values in, so you don't have to remember the value—just the name of it. The use of constants makes your code easier to read and more maintainable because you can avoid the use of hard-coded literals.

The syntax for the Const statement is as follows:

```
[Public ¦ Private] Const constname [As type] = expression
```

Constants follow the same scope rules as variables.

Functions and Subprocedures

Code routines that are written in VBA are in the form of either functions or subprocedures. The code contained in each of them is the same. The only difference is that a function can return a value. The term *procedure* is used to refer to both functions and subprocedures.

Functions

A function is a VBA routine that is written to perform a specific task and return a value. You can have it return a customer's average order dollar amount or update an employee record with a new address. You can make the function as complex or simple as you like.

To have a function return a value, you simply assign the return value to the name of the function. For example, if the function is called `GetSalesRepId()`, to return a value you store the value to `GetSalesRepId (GetSalesRepId = tblReps("RepId"))`.

The syntax for the `Function` statement is as follows:

```
[Public ¦ Private] [Static] Function functionname [(arglist)] [As type]
```

Here's an example of a typical function:

```
Function TotalSales (pCustomerId As String) As Double
    '--- code block

    '-- return a value
    TotalSales = 100
End Function
```

Let's break down the components of the `Function` statement to make it easier to understand. The `Function` statement has six parts: `Public`, `Private`, `Static`, *functionname*, *arglist,* and `As type`. They are described here:

- `Public`—Makes the function available to all other procedures in all modules.

- `Private`—Makes the function available only to the procedures within the same module. No other procedures can access it.

- `Static`—Indicates that all the function's local variables have their values preserved between calls. Any variables that are declared outside the function aren't affected by it.

- *functionname*—Is the name the function is called by. This name must be unique within the form, report, or module. If a procedure with the same name appears in more than one module in an Access application, you can execute the correct procedure by qualifying the procedure name with the module name. For example, to designate the procedure myFunction in module myModule, you would specify Sub [myModule].myFunction().

- *arglist*—Is a list of the parameters that are passed to the function. Each argument contains the name of the variable and its datatype.

- As type—Is used to denote the datatype that is returned by the function.

To exit a function at any time, use the Exit Function statement. This exits the function and returns control to where it was called from.

> **NOTE**
>
> When you're writing a Private procedure, it's a good idea to add some comments at the top explaining where the procedure is called from. This reminds you and other programmers why this procedure needs to be private.

Subprocedures

A subprocedure works the same way as a function. The only difference is that it can't return a value. This difference doesn't limit what you can do with a subprocedure in any way. It simply means that you can't have it return a value.

Here is the syntax for the Sub statement:

```
[Private ¦ Public] [Static] Sub subname [(arglist)]
```

Here's an example of a subprocedure:

```
Private Sub TotalSales (pCustomerId As String)
    '--- code block

End Sub
```

The following list breaks down the components of the Sub statement to make it easier to understand:

- Static—Indicates that all the Sub's local variables have their values preserved between calls. Any variables that are declared outside the subprocedure aren't affected by it.

- Private—Makes the function available only to the procedures within the module. No other procedures have access to it.

- `Public`—Makes the subprocedure available to all other procedures in all modules.

- *subname*—Is the name the subprocedure is called by. This name must be unique within the form, report, or module. If a procedure with the same name appears in more than one module in an Access application, you can execute the correct procedure by qualifying the procedure name with the module name. For example, to designate the procedure `mySub` in module `myModule`, you would specify `Sub [myModule].mySub`.

- *arglist*—Is a list of the parameters that are passed to the subprocedure. Each argument contains the name of the variable and its datatype.

To exit a subprocedure at any time, use the `Exit Sub` statement. This exits the subprocedure and returns control to the calling procedure.

Passing Parameters

The way you pass parameters or arguments to a subprocedure is a little different from passing them to a function. Let's look at how to pass parameters to a subprocedure first.

You can pass a parameter to a subprocedure in two ways. How you send the parameter depends on how the subprocedure is called. Here is one example:

```
Dim nCustId as Integer
nCustId = tblCustomer.SalesRepId
GetCustomerSalesRep nCustid
```

Here is another example:

```
Dim nCustId as Integer
nCustId = tblCustomer.SalesRepId
Call GetCustomerSalesRep(nCustid)
```

What makes the second example different is the `Call` statement. The `Call` statement is a reserved word and isn't required when a subprocedure is being called. If you do use it, you need to enclose all the parameters in parentheses. If you don't use the reserved word, you must omit the parentheses around the parameter list.

Passing parameters to a function is similar to using the `Call` statement with a subprocedure. The parameters are enclosed in parentheses. The main difference between subprocedures and functions is that a function returns a value. Therefore, you must do something with the value that is returned.

You can store the returned value in a variable or a field in a table, display it in a message, use it as an object's property, or do whatever you want with it.

The syntax for passing parameters to a function looks like this:

```
Dim txtSalesRep As String
Dim RepId As Integer
RepId = 1234
txtSalesRep = GetSalesRepName(RepId)
```

If for some reason you want to ignore the value being returned by the function, you can use the Call statement just like you did with the subprocedure. But if you do this and it is not an intrinsic function, then I would wonder if this function should actually be a sub-procedure instead.

Receiving Parameters

After you send the parameters to a procedure, you must receive them. Receiving parameters works the same way for both subprocedures and functions. In both cases, you assign a name to the parameter and declare its datatype. Here's an example of how subprocedures receive parameters:

```
Sub GetRepName (pRepId As Integer)
```

And here's an example of how functions receive parameters:

```
Function GetRepName (pRepId As Integer) As String
```

By default, when you pass a parameter to a procedure, you're passing it by reference. "By reference" means that you're passing the actual variable to the procedure. When you return to where the procedure was called from, the variable that was passed contains any changes that were made to it. For example, let's say you pass a procedure a variable that contains the name of a company. The procedure converts the company name into uppercase. When you return to the main procedure, the variable that contains the company name is now in uppercase.

Here are two procedures to show how this works:

```
Sub Parameter_Reference ()
   Dim txtMsg As String
   txtMsg = "Test Value"
   '--   Call the procedure.
   Parameter_Reference2 txtMsg

   MsgBox txtMsg, 0, "Back in the main procedure."
End Sub


Sub Parameter_Reference2 (pMsg As String)
   MsgBox pMsg, 0, "Passes by Reference"
   pMsg = "MS Access"
End Sub
```

To see how this sample works, open the module procedures in `Acc10.mdb` and run `Parameter_Reference`. There is a way to pass parameters to a procedure without changing the variable's data. To do this, pass the parameter `ByVal` (by value). When you pass a parameter by value, just the contents of the variable are passed, not the actual variable. Any changes that are made to the variable or value aren't reflected in the variable back in the calling procedure.

Here's some code that shows how do carry out this task:

```
Sub Parameter_ByVal ()
    Dim txtMsg As String
    txtMsg = "Test Value"

    '--   Call the procedure.
    Parameter_ByVal2 txtMsg

    MsgBox txtMsg, 0, "Back in the main procedure."
End Sub

Sub Parameter_ByVal2 (ByVal pMsg As String)
    pMsg = "MS Access"
    MsgBox pMsg, 0, "Passed by Value"
End Sub
```

To see how this sample works, open the module procedures in `Acc10.mdb` and run `Parameter_ByVal`.

Required and Optional Parameters

The passing of parameters to a procedure determines whether a routine is developer-friendly. The number of parameters that need to be passed to a routine also determines how easy it is to use. The more parameters that can be passed, however, the more flexible the routine is. So where do you draw the line on parameters?

Parameters are divided into two groups: required and optional. Required parameters are the ones that must be provided in order for the routine to work. Optional parameters are the ones the routine can work with or without. If they aren't passed, the routine uses default values in their place.

To make a parameter optional, you must include the keyword `Optional` in the subprocedure or function declaration line. The datatype for the parameter must be `Variant`. If you use the `Optional` keyword for one parameter, all parameters that follow must also be declared as `Optional`. In addition, you can't use the `Optional` keyword if `ParamArray` is used. You can use the `IsMissing` function to check for missing parameters. Listing 10.6 provides an example of how to write a function that has an optional parameter.

10

VISUAL BASIC FOR APPLICATIONS

LISTING 10.6. USING OPTIONAL PARAMETERS.

```
Function optional_Parameter (pCode As String, Optional pRegion As Variant,
Optional pId As Variant)
dim myRegion as Variant
if ismissing(pRegion) then
    myRegion = "US"
else
    myRegion = pRegion
end if
End Function
```

Calling this function is performed the same as before. If you want to omit all the optional parameters, you would call the function like this:

```
mvar = MyFunction("ABC123")
```

To omit only the second parameter, you would need to use a comma as a placeholder. In this case, you would call the function like this:

```
mvar = MyFunction("ABC123", , 1)
```

When you have several optional parameters, passing and receiving parameters can become complicated. You must get all the comma placeholders correct or your procedure will fail to function properly. One solution to this problem is to group all the optional parameters into one argument and pass it to the routine. The routine then parses out the optional parameters and assigns a default value to any that are missing. The advantage to this method is that you can choose the parameters to pass in and put them in any order you want. You can do this by using the `ParamArray` keyword.

The `ParamArray` keyword can be used only as the last argument in the parameter list. It's an optional array of `Variant` elements. The `ParamArray` keyword can't be used with the `Optional`, `ByVal`, or `ByRef` keywords. Here's an example:

```
Sub ParameterPassing2(ParamArray pNameAddress() As Variant)

    Dim Var As Variant

    Debug.Print "Name and Address"
    For Each Var In pNameAddress
        Debug.Print Var
    Next Var

End Sub
Sub ParameterPassing()
    Call ParameterPassing2("First", "Second", "Third", 4)
End Sub
```

To see how this example works, run `ParameterPassing` in the Procedures module of `Acc10.mdb` on the Web site for this book. As you can see from the preceding code example, it's possible to pass just one parameter or four parameters and parse out the individual components.

Naming Requirements for Modules, Functions, and Subprocedures

When it comes time to save a module, Access prompts you for a name. Typically, you enter a meaningful and descriptive name that informs you which types of procedures are stored in the module. Access has some rules about the names that you can use for modules:

- The name can't start with a space. If you type one or more spaces before the module name, Access removes them.
- The name can contain only characters and numbers.
- The name can't contain either exclamation points (!) or periods (.). These characters are reserved by Access and are used in referencing objects on forms and reports.
- The name is limited to 64 characters.
- The name can contain spaces for readability.
- The name can use mixed-case letters to aid readability.
- The name must be unique within the current database (`.MDB`).
- The name can't be a VBA keyword.

> **NOTE**
>
> Even though you can use spaces in module names, it is suggested to use underscore characters instead.

Just as with modules, there are rules for naming subprocedures and functions:

- The name must start with a character.
- The name can contain numbers.
- The name can't contain spaces.
- The name can't contain any exclamation points (!) or periods (.). These characters are reserved by Access and are used in referring to objects on forms and reports.

- Names must be unique within the module, form, or report.
- The name can't exceed 200 characters.

> **NOTE**
>
> Even though you can use 200 characters for the name of a function or subprocedure, it is wise to keep the name short and to the point. This way there is less chance of making a spelling mistake.

Objects and Collections

Access enables you to manipulate objects without any need for programming, and VBA greatly expands this capability. With VBA, you can create, delete, and modify objects at runtime.

In Access, objects of a specific type are grouped together in collections. For example, the Forms collection consists of all the open forms in the application, and the Controls collection consists of all the controls on a specific form. The objects that are part of the Microsoft Jet engine are called the Data Access Objects (DAOs). These objects are also accessible from your VBA code. For more information about DAOs, see Chapter 16, "Data Access Objects."

Referring to Objects

You can refer to an object that is part of a collection by following one of the ways presented in Table 10.3.

TABLE 10.3. REFERRING TO OBJECTS.

Syntax	Use
`identifier![ObjectName]`	Directly names an object as a member of a collection. This syntax is required for referring to an object whose name contains a space or is a restricted VBA identifier.
`identifier("ObjectName")`	Directly names an object as a member of a collection or uses a string variable to contain the object name.
`identifier(index)`	Refers to an object by its position in the collection. You can use this syntax to loop through all the members of a collection.

For example, the following code shows the three ways of referring to the form
`frmCustomers`. The last method assumes that `frmCustomers` is the first form in the Forms
collection:

```
Forms![frmCustomers]
Forms("frmCustomers")
Forms(0)
```

In VBA, you can refer to properties of an object by using the syntax *Object.property*.
For example, you can set the `Caption` property of the form `frmCustomers` as shown here:

```
Forms![frmCustomers].Caption = "Customers"
```

If you wanted to set the `Caption` property for all the forms in the Forms collection, you
could use the `Count` property. The `Count` property reflects the total number of objects in a
collection. Because it's zero-based, the last or highest object is always one less than the
actual `Count` property. An example of this is shown in Listing 10.7.

LISTING 10.7. SETTING PROPERTIES FOR ALL MEMBERS OF THE FORMS COLLECTION.

```
Sub SetCaption()
    Dim  intCounter as Integer
    For intCounter = 0 to Forms.count -1
        Forms(intCounter).Caption = "Customers"
    Next intCounter
End Sub
```

Declaring and Assigning Object Variables

An object variable is a variable that refers to a specific type of object, such as a form or
report. You can declare an object variable using the same syntax as you'd use for any
other type of variable. Table 10.4 shows the Access objects and which of those objects
can be represented by a variable.

TABLE 10.4. ACCESS OBJECTS.

Object	Description	Variable Permitted?
Application	Access	Yes
Control	Control on a form or report	Yes
DoCmd	Macro actions used in VBA	No
Debug	Immediate window	No
Form	Forms and subforms	Yes

continues

TABLE 10.4. CONTINUED

Object	Description	Variable Permitted?
Report	Reports and subreports	Yes
Module	Form, report, and standard	Yes
Screen	Screen display	No
Section	Form or report section	No

Before you can use an object variable, you must associate it with an existing object by using the Set statement. This is the syntax for the Set statement:

```
Set variablename = objectexpression
```

If you use the Set statement to associate more than one variable with a specific object, you're always referring to the same object. This means that changing the properties of one variable also changes the properties of all variables that refer to that object. For example, Listing 10.8 shows how to associate a variable name with an object.

LISTING 10.8. ASSOCIATING A VARIABLE NAME WITH A SPECIFIC OBJECT.

```
Dim myform1 as form
Dim myform2 as form
set myform1 = Forms![frmCustomers]
set myform2 = Forms![frmCustomers]
myForm1.caption = "Customers"
```

After this code has been run, myForm2.Caption is also set to Customers.

Using the New Keyword

The New keyword enables you to create a new instance or version of an existing object. When a new instance is created, it has its own set of properties. Setting the Caption property of a new instance of frmCustomers doesn't affect the Caption property of another instance. For example, Listing 10.9 creates a new instance of frmCustomers.

LISTING 10.9. CREATING A NEW INSTANCE.

```
Sub NewForm()
Dim myForm As New Form_frmCustomers
myForm.Caption = "Customers -2"
myForm.Visible = True

End Sub
```

Determining the Type of Control

In Access, all variables that represent controls on a form or report are declared generically using the `Control` keyword; a specific control type isn't specified. As a result, you need to use a variation of the `If...Then...Else` statement (covered later in this chapter) to determine which type of control your variable is referring to. For example, Listing 10.10 shows how to set the `ForeColor` property of all the text boxes on a form to red.

LISTING 10.10. USING THE `TypeOf` CONTROL.

```
Sub SetColor(myForm As Form)
    Dim myControl As Control
    Dim intCounter As Integer
    Dim intRed As Integer

    intRed = RGB(255, 0, 0)
    For intCounter = 0 To myForm.Count - 1
        Set myControl = myForm(intCounter)
        If TypeOf myControl Is TextBox Then
            myControl.ForeColor = intRed
        End If
    Next intCounter
End Sub
```

The capability to have multiple instances of an object allows for great flexibility in your application. For example, each of the `frmCustomers` instances could represent a different customer from the Customers table. This would enable the users of your application to work with more than one customer at a time.

> **NOTE**
>
> You can't use the `Not` keyword with the `TypeOf` syntax. Instead, code an empty statement block combined with the `Else` clause.

Properties and Methods

Properties describe an object's characteristics. When you change a property setting, you change that particular characteristic. Methods enable you to control how an object behaves. For example, the `SetFocus` method can be used in VBA code to move the focus to a specific control on a form.

10

VISUAL BASIC FOR
APPLICATIONS

Setting and Retrieving Properties

Assigning a property to a variable in VBA enables you to retrieve its value. You can change a property value by setting it to something else. In Listing 10.11, the ForeColor property of txtText1 is obtained via the variable lngColor. Then lngColor is used to set the ForeColor property of txtText2.

LISTING 10.11. SETTING AND RETRIEVING PROPERTIES.

```
Dim lngColor As Long

    lngColor = txtText1.ForeColor
    txtText2.ForeColor = lngColor
```

Setting Multiple Properties

The With statement provides a way to set multiple properties without specifying the object each time a new property is set. For example, Listing 10.12 shows how several text box properties can be set using With...End With.

LISTING 10.12. SETTING PROPERTIES USING THE With...End With CONSTRUCT.

```
Private Sub Form_Load()
    With Text1
        .Text = "Text"
        .ForeColor = RGB(255, 0, 0) 'Red
        .BackColor = 0
    End With
End Sub
```

> **WARNING**
>
> Errors or unpredictable behavior can occur if your code jumps out of a With block and either the With or the End...With statement isn't executed.

Using Methods

Methods are similar to other VBA functions and statements. For example, if a method returns a value, it's like a function and you enclose its arguments in parentheses. However, there is one major difference between methods and other functions and statements: a method acts directly on an object or reflects a predetermined object behavior. In Listing 10.13, you can examine the use of the ItemData method. The ItemData method returns the data in the bound column for the specified row in a list box or combo box. In this case, the `ItemData` method is used to retrieve the customer ID when the combo box `cboCust` is clicked.

LISTING 10.13. USING THE `ItemData` METHOD.

```
Private Sub cboCust_Click()
    Dim lngCustid As Long

    lngCustid = cboCust.ItemData(cboCust.ListIndex)

End Sub
```

Properties That Represent Objects

With VBA you can refer to whatever object is in a particular state without referring explicitly to that object by using properties. For example, you might want to refer to the form, report, or control that is currently active. Properties that represent objects enable you to work with the properties, methods, and controls of that object. Table 10.5 shows the properties that can be used to represent objects.

TABLE 10.5. PROPERTIES THAT REPRESENT OBJECTS.

Property	*Applies To*	*Refers To*
`ActiveControl`	Screen object, form, or report	Control with the focus.
`ActiveForm`	Screen object	Form with the focus or the form that contains the control with the focus.
`ActiveReport`	Screen object	Report with the focus or the report that contains the control with the focus.
`Form`	Subform control or form	Subform: Form associated with the subform control. Form: The form.
`Me`	Form or report	Form or report.
`Module`	Form or report	Module of a form or report.
`Parent`	Control	Form or report that contains the control.
`PreviousControl`	Screen object	The control that previously had the focus.
`RecordSetClone`	Form	Clone of a form's recordset.
`Report`	Subreport or report	Subreport: Report associated with the subreport control. Report: The report.
`Section`	Control	Section of a form or report where a control is located.

Screen Properties

The `PreviousControl`, `ActiveControl`, `ActiveForm`, and `ActiveReport` properties refer to the screen object. You can use these properties when your code depends on which form, report, or control has the focus. For example, you might have a `Save` routine that calls different routines depending on which form is active. Listing 10.14 shows how to use `ActiveForm` for this purpose.

LISTING 10.14. USING THE `ActiveForm` PROPERTY.

```
Sub SaveData()
    Dim sMyForm As String

    sMyForm = Screen.ActiveForm.Name
    Select Case sMyForm
        Case "frmCustomers"
            SaveCustomers
        Case "frmEmployees"
            SaveEmployees
        Case Else
            MsgBox "Invalid Form"
    End Select
End Sub
```

Form and Report Properties

The `Me`, `Module`, and `RecordSetClone` properties apply to forms or reports. The `RecordSetClone` property is covered further in Chapter 16, "Data Access Objects." The `Module` property can be used to insert a procedure into a module at runtime. You can use the `Me` property to indicate the form or report where code is currently running. For example, Listing 10.15 shows how to use `Me` to pass the form as a parameter to a procedure.

LISTING 10.15. USING THE `Me` PROPERTY.

```
Private Sub cmdSave_Click()
    SaveData Me
End Sub
Sub SaveData(myForm As Form)
    Dim sMyForm As String

    sMyForm = myForm.Name
    Select Case sMyForm
        Case "frmCustomers"
            SaveCustomers
        Case "frmEmployees"
            SaveEmployees
```

```
        Case Else
            MsgBox "Invalid Form"
    End Select
End Sub
```

Control Properties

The `Form` and `Report` properties refer to subforms and subreports. For example, in the expression

```
Forms![frmCustomers].Form![frmSubCusts]
```

the term `Form` refers to the subform currently displayed by the subform control. The form that is displayed is controlled by setting the `SourceObject` property of the subform control on the form `frmCustomers`.

The `Parent` property represents the container for the control. For example, the parent of a text box is the form it's on. The parent of an option button is the option group it's in. The `Parent` property is frequently used with subforms and subreports. For example, Listing 10.16 shows how the `Parent` property is used with a subform.

LISTING 10.16. USING THE `Parent` PROPERTY.

```
Private Sub Form_Load()
    Dim sFormName As String
    sFormName = Form![frmSubCusts].Parent.Name
End Sub
```

The `Section` property refers to the section of a form or report on which a control is located. For example, a control might be located in a form, header, detail, or footer section. The following example shows how to display a message based on whether the detail section of a form (referred to as `section(0)`) is visible:

```
If Forms![Cust].Section(0).Visible = False Then
        MsgBox "no detail"
    Else
        MsgBox "detail"
    End If
```

User-Defined Objects

User-defined objects are custom objects developed in a class module. In the class module, you can create procedures that are the methods for the custom object. To create properties, you would make use of the `Property Let`, `Property Set`, and `Property Get` statements.

Property Let

The `Property Let` statement assigns a value to a property. The syntax for the `Property Let` statement is as follows:

```
[Public | Private][Static] Property Let name [(arglist)]
```

The components of the `Property Let` statement are shown here:

- `Public`—Indicates that the `Property Let` procedure is accessible to all other procedures in all modules.

- `Private`—Indicates that the `Property Let` procedure is accessible only to other procedures in the module where it's declared.

- `Static`—Indicates that the `Property Let` procedure's local variables are preserved between calls.

- *name*—Is the name of the `Property Let` procedure. It follows standard variable naming conventions, except that the name can be the same as a `Property Get` or `Property Set` procedure in the same module.

- *arglist*—Is a list of variables representing arguments that are passed to the `Property Let` procedure when it's called. The name and datatype of each argument in a `Property Let` procedure (except the last one) must be the same as the corresponding arguments in a `Property Get` procedure. The last argument is the value assigned to the property on the right side of an expression. The datatype of the last (or sometimes the only) argument must be the same as the return type of the corresponding `Property Get` procedure.

Property Set

The `Property Set` statement sets a reference to an object. The syntax for the `Property Set` statement is as follows:

```
[Public | Private][Static] Property Set name [(arglist)]
```

The components of the `Property Set` statement are shown here:

- `Public`—Indicates that the `Property Set` procedure is accessible to all other procedures in all modules.

- `Private`—Indicates that the `Property Set` procedure is accessible only to other procedures in the module where it's declared.

- `Static`—Indicates that the `Property Set` procedure's local variables are preserved between calls.

- *name*—Is the name of the Property Set procedure. It follows standard variable naming conventions, except that the name can be the same as a Property Get or Property Let procedure in the same module.

- *arglist*—Is a list of variables representing arguments that are passed to the Property Set procedure when it's called.

Property Get

The Property Get statement gets the value of a property. The syntax for the Property Get statement is as follows:

```
[Public ¦ Private][Static] Property Get name [(arglist)]
```

The components of the Property Get statement are as follows:

- Public—Indicates that the Property Get procedure is accessible to all other procedures in all modules.

- Private—Indicates that the Property Get procedure is accessible only to other procedures in the module where it's declared.

- Static—Indicates that the Property Get procedure's local variables are preserved between calls.

- *name*—Is the name of the Property Get procedure. It follows standard variable naming conventions, except that the name can be the same as a Property Let or Property Set procedure in the same module.

- *arglist*—Is a list of variables representing arguments that are passed to the Property Let procedure when it's called. The name and datatype of each argument in a Property Get procedure must be the same as the corresponding arguments in a Property Let procedure.

Using Property Procedures

If you wanted to open the form frmCustomers to add new customers or edit existing customers, you could use a combination of the Property Get and Property Let procedures. In the Property Let procedure, you would set the AllowEdits and AllowAdditions properties of the form. In the Property Get procedure, you would retrieve the values that had been set. Listing 10.17 shows an example of how to do this. Notice that you can refer to the custom object EditType just as you would any other property on the form.

LISTING 10.17. DESIGNING CUSTOM OBJECTS WITH Property Let AND Property Get.

```
Option Compare Database
Option Explicit
Private intFormType As Integer
Const TYPE_INSERT = 0
Const TYPE_EDIT = 1

Property Let EditType(NewValue As Integer)


    Select Case newValue
        Case TYPE_INSERT
            AllowEdits = False
            AllowAdditions = True

        Case TYPE_EDIT
            AllowEdits = True
            AllowAdditions = False
    End Select
    intFormType = NewValue
    text1 = AllowEdits
End Property

Property Get EditType() As Integer
    EditType = intFormType
End Property
```

If you wanted to use these custom objects from the click events on the buttons in the form shown in Figure 10.8, you would follow the code in Listing 10.18.

FIGURE 10.8.

*Setting properties
of custom objects.*

LISTING 10.18. SETTING PROPERTIES OF CUSTOM OBJECTS.

```
Option Compare Database
Option Explicit
Const TYPE_INSERT = 0
Const TYPE_EDIT = 1
Private Sub cmdEdit_Click()
    DoCmd.OpenForm ("frmCustomers")
    Forms![frmCustomers].EditType = TYPE_EDIT
End Sub

Private Sub cmdInsert_Click()
    DoCmd.OpenForm ("frmCustomers")
    Forms![frmCustomers].EditType = TYPE_INSERT
End Sub
```

To see how this works, open `frmMain` in `Acc10.mdb` and click the buttons to see how the `frmCustomers` form is opened.

The Object Browser

You can use the Object Browser to display the types of objects available in Access and other applications. This way you can find and use objects as well as move through the procedures in your application.

You can open the Object Browser, shown in Figure 10.9, by selecting Object Browser toolbar button when a VBA module is open.

FIGURE 10.9.
The Object Browser.

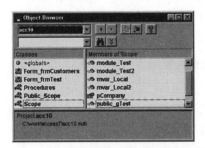

The Object Browser has several parts. At the top is the Libraries/Databases box. This is where you select the libraries or databases to browse. The Modules/Classes box displays the types of objects available, and the Methods/Properties box shows the related properties and methods. After selecting the property or method, you can use the Paste Text button to add code from the Object Browser into your application. You can add additional databases and libraries to the Object Browser by establishing references to them.

Debugging and Error Handling

The next sections discuss debugging and error handling through the use of such things as the Debug window, setting breakpoints, pausing code execution, error trapping, and more.

The Debug Window

The Debug window is used to test VBA subprocedures, functions, and expressions. To test a function or expression, you must preface it with the keyword `Print` or the `?` sign. The returning value is displayed.

To test a subprocedure, enter its name in the Immediate window. Because a subprocedure can't return a value like a function, `Print` and `?` aren't needed.

To see the value of a variable, enter the name of the variable and preface it with the keyword `Print` or the `?` sign. Its value is displayed on the line below it.

Setting Breakpoints

A breakpoint is a place in a procedure where you want it to stop running. Setting breakpoints enables you to stop and watch the execution of the procedure.

You set the breakpoints by first selecting the line where you want to stop. You can either click the hand icon on the toolbar or press the F9 key. The line where the breakpoint occurs is now highlighted, as shown in Figure 10.10. This line isn't executed until you press the F8 key to step through the line or Shift+F8 to step over the line.

FIGURE 10.10.

A block of code with a breakpoint.

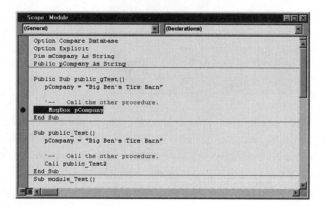

Pressing F8 causes Access to execute the current line of code. If the line contains a call to a function or subroutine, Access jumps to the first executable line of that routine. If you're sure you don't want to debug the function or subroutine, you can press Shift+F8.

You can have as many breakpoints as you like in a procedure. To remove the breakpoint, select the line of code with the breakpoint and click the hand icon on the toolbar or press the F9 key.

When the procedure has stopped running, you have several options. You can run the rest of the code line-by-line or resume execution of it. To step through it line-by-line, you can use either the Step Into or Step Over toolbar icon.

The Step Into icon executes the current line of code. If the line of code is a call to another procedure, it displays that code onscreen. You can now walk through each line of this code as well.

The Step Over icon executes the current line of code. If the line of code is a call to another VBA procedure, the other procedure is executed without interruption—unless, of course, a breakpoint is set in the other procedure. After the other procedure is done, the line following the call to the other procedure is set as the next line to be executed.

When the procedure has stopped running, you can use the Watch window to query the values of variables. You can also change the values of these variables.

To continue executing the procedure, press the F5 key. After you resume the procedure, you don't see the lines of code that are being executed.

Pausing Code Execution

Another way to pause the code is to use the Stop command. The Stop command halts execution of a procedure the same way a breakpoint does.

The difference between the breakpoint and the Stop command is that when you close a module with a breakpoint, it disappears. The breakpoint isn't saved. However, the Stop command is part of the code and remains there. This is helpful when you're debugging a module in a form or report.

Resuming execution of a procedure with a Stop command is done the same way as with a breakpoint.

> **TIP**
>
> When you're using the Stop command or any other code for debugging, it's a good idea not to indent the command with the rest of the code. If it's placed at the far left, it stands out and is easier to remove later.

> **WARNING**
>
> Be sure to remove all the Stop commands from your application before delivering it.

Debugging with Auto Value Tips

Auto Value Tips is helpful when you are debugging your VBA code. It allows you to examine the current value of a variable while your code execution is paused by placing the mouse pointer over the variable. After a moment, a ToolTip-style window appears, showing the variable and its current value.

By default, this new feature of Access 97 is disabled. To enable it, select Tools | Options and use the Module tab.

The Need for Error Trapping

As with all good VBA procedures, there is the need for some sort of error-trapping routine. This need is based on the two types of errors: syntax and runtime. Your code should be written so that it can handle these errors without always terminating the application.

Syntax errors are caused by not using a VBA function or keyword correctly. For example, if you enter the line of code If age = 5 in your procedure, an error occurs. The correct syntax for this statement is If age = 5 Then. Most syntax errors are caught by the syntax checker in Access, but not all of them are.

You can turn the syntax checking on and off by selecting Tools | Options. Select the Module tab, shown in Figure 10.11, and select or deselect Auto Syntax Check.

FIGURE 10.11.

The Module tab of the Options dialog box, with syntax checking enabled.

Runtime errors are the hardest to catch because you don't know they exist until you run the code. Not only do you have to run the code, but special conditions might have to be in place before the error shows up. These errors can be caught only by testing the procedure.

Runtime errors are divided into two types: recoverable and nonrecoverable. Recoverable errors are those that can be corrected with or without the user's involvement. Here's an example of a recoverable error: Before creating a new QueryDef, you should delete it if it already exists. If you try to delete it and it doesn't exist, Access gives you an error. This error should be ignored and the code should continue.

Here's another example of a recoverable error: A report is based on selections that were made on a form. The report's record source is a SQL statement that is made based on these selections. One of the required entries on the form is missing, causing the SQL statement to fail because one of its required parameters is now missing. You can handle the error by displaying a message informing the user to enter the information before proceeding.

Nonrecoverable errors, sometimes called fatal errors, are the dangerous ones, from which there is no escape. When these occur, the application should be terminated and corrective action should be taken to fix them.

Fatal runtime errors can include incorrect Windows API declarations or incorrect calls to a correctly declared API. An error of this kind can be as simple as a complaint about a bad DLL calling convention or as severe as a general protection fault.

How a runtime error is handled depends on where it occurred. If the error occurred in the Access interface or Jet engine, you should add code to the `Error` event procedure of the form or report where it occurred. Otherwise, you should add an `OnError` statement and error handling code to your procedures.

The `Err` Object

Access provides you with several ways to determine which error has occurred. The `Err` object displays information about runtime errors via its properties. It also provides two methods, `Raise` and `Clear`, that enable you to set and clear errors. By using the `Err` object, you can decide how to handle the errors and what to do next. When you use the `Err` object, you don't need to create a new instance of it in your code because it already has global scope.

`Err.Number`

The `Err.Number` property returns a `Long Integer` value of the runtime error code that occurred. The error numbers start at 3. Unused error numbers in the range of 1 to 1000 are reserved for future use by VBA.

The vast majority of these error codes fall into the category of reserved errors. As a general rule, these are the errors that occur right before the project deadline.

`Err.Description`

The `Err.Description` property returns a string that contains the message for the error code.

Some of the error messages use internal variables to help provide specific information about the error. When the error occurs, Access adds the appropriate text to the error message. If Access can't provide the appropriate text, it displays `Application-defined or object-defined error`. For example, the following procedure tries to open a form that doesn't exist:

```
Sub OpenCustomerForm ()
    On Error GoTo ErrorTrap
    DoCmd.OpenForm "Customer"
    Exit Sub

ErrorTrap:
    MsgBox err.number
    MsgBox err.description
    Resume Next

End Sub
```

Two different error messages are displayed to the user. The first message box displays the error number, and the second displays the message.

Err.Source

This property is the name of the VBA procedure or application where the error was raised.

Err.HelpFile

This is the name of the help file associated with the VBA project.

Err.HelpContext

This property is the help file context ID.

Err.LastDLLError

This property is the system error code for the last DLL call made. For more information on calling DLLs, see Chapter 17, "Working with the Windows API."

Err.Raise

This method generates a runtime error. Here is the syntax for `Err.Raise`:

```
Err.Raise(Number, Source, Description, HelpFile, HelpContext)
```

The arguments for `Err.Raise` are shown in Table 10.6.

TABLE 10.6. `Err.Raise` ARGUMENTS.

Argument	Description
Number	A Long integer that identifies the error. This argument is required.
Source	A string expression naming the object or application that originally generated the error.
Description	A string expression describing the error.
HelpFile	The fully qualified path to the Microsoft Windows Help file in which help for this error can be found.
HelpContext	The context ID identifying a topic within the Help file that provides help for the error.

Err.Clear

The `Err.Clear` method is used to clear the `Err` object after an error has been handled. This method provides the same functionality that was included in previous versions of Access by `Err = 0`. Listing 10.19 provides an example of using `Err` object methods. This case simulates the `Out of memory` error. When the code is run, a message is displayed as though an actual out-of-memory condition occurred. Figure 10.12 shows how this error message is displayed.

FIGURE 10.12.

Generating an error condition.

LISTING 10.19. USING `Err` OBJECT METHODS.

```
ErrorTrap:
    Err.Clear
    Err.Raise (7)
Resume Next
```

> **NOTE**
>
> The `Err` object and the `Error` statements are still retained for compatibility with prior versions of Access. Mixing the use of the `Err` object and the `Error` statement, however, can lead to unexpected results. For example, even if you fill in the `Err` object's properties, they're reset to their default values when an `Error`
>
> *continues*

statement is run. Although you can use the Error statement to generate VBA runtime errors, it's retained mainly for compatibility with existing code. You should use the Err object and the Raise and Clear methods for system errors and in new code, especially for OLE Automation objects.

On Error Statements

The On Error statement enables you to direct Access where to go when it encounters an error. It's also used to disable an error-trapping routine. The On Error statement can be used several different ways.

On Error GoTo LabelName/LineNumber

This statement enables the error-handling routine that starts at that line number or line label. From that point on, if any error is encountered, the program control branches to that line or label. If you use the line number, it must reside in the same procedure as the On Error statement. If it does not, a compile-time error results.

On Error Resume Next

If you use this statement, the program control goes to the next line of code following an error. Using this statement as the only error trapping isn't a good idea. It could cause a snowball effect, resulting in lost or damaged data. It's best used inside an error-trapping routine after the error has been dealt with. Then the program can continue working.

On Error GoTo 0

This statement is used to disable any error-trapping routine in the current procedure. If there is no On Error routine, Access displays its own error message. If the application is running in runtime mode, the application terminates.

Error-Trapping Routines

Before you begin writing error-trapping routines, you need a naming convention. Access doesn't let you have two error routines with the same name in the same module, form, or report.

One possible naming convention is to use the name of the procedure and add _Error to it. For example, if the procedure is called cmdAdd_Click, its error-trapping routine is called cmdAdd_Click_Error. This way, all your error routines have unique names.

Most error-trapping routines are made up of two parts. The first part is for responding to the error, and the other is the action taken as a result of the error.

Responding to the error might involve informing the user or prompting him for a response. For example, if a file can't be opened for import, you might want to inform the user about it and allow him to try to open it again.

The action that is taken as a result of the error largely depends on the type of error. If a table's index is missing, you might want to exit the procedure. If information is missing on a form, you might want to put the cursor back in that control. If a form, report, or table is missing, exiting the application would be a good idea.

Error-trapping routines normally end with one of these statements:

- `Resume Next`—This returns program control to the next line of code after the one that caused the error.

- `Resume`—This returns program control to the line of code that caused the error. Access then reexecutes the line of code that caused the error. Be sure that the error has been fixed; otherwise, you might be trapped in an endless loop.

- `Exit Sub` or `Exit Function`—This exits the current procedure and returns program control to where the procedure was called from.

> **WARNING**
>
> If you use error trapping in a procedure, be sure to add the statement `Exit Sub` or `Exit Function` before the error routine. If you don't, the error routine will be executed even if there was no error.

Form and Report Error Trapping

Both forms and reports have a built-in error-trapping event, `OnError`. It's triggered when an error caused by either the Access interface or the Microsoft Jet engine occurs on a form or report that is open. You can use a macro or write a procedure for each form and report. You can also write a generic error-handling function for all your forms and reports.

The basic design of an error routine for a form or report is the same as one that is used in a module. In the code for the `Error` event, the type of error and response are passed into the procedure. The example in Listing 10.20 specifically checks for the duplicate index error number 3022. If it finds this error, it displays a message box and sets `Response` to `acDataErrContinue`, which tells the application to continue processing after receiving a data access error.

An easy way to handle these types of errors is to write an `OnError` routine that looks like the one in Listing 10.20.

LISTING 10.20. HANDLING DATA ACCESS ERRORS.

```
Private Sub Form_Error(DataErr As Integer, Response As Integer)
Const DUPLICATE_INDEX = 3022

    If DataErr = DUPLICATE_INDEX Then
        MsgBox "This is a duplicate customer ID"
        Response = acDataErrContinue
    End If
End Sub
```

You need to expand the `Select Case` code to handle any other type of error that might occur.

In the procedure `Form_Error`, two parameters are passed. `DataErr` and `Response` both have the datatype of `Integer`. The `DataErr` parameter contains the code for the error that has just happened. You can use this error number to trap for any recoverable errors.

The `Response` parameter contains the value 1. If you assign any value to the parameter, it prevents the Access error message from being displayed. In other words, if you don't give the parameter a value, you see your error message followed by an Access error message.

> **NOTE**
>
> You can use the `Debug.Print` command to display values in the Immediate window while the procedure is running.

Looping Constructs

The looping construct is one of the fundamentals of VBA code. Looping constructs are used throughout most of the procedures that are written. They enable you to navigate through records in a table and execute blocks of code. The following sections cover basic syntax and how to use each of these looping constructs.

If...Then...Else

The `If...Then...Else` statement is one of the most basic looping constructs in many programming languages. It is made up of two possible situations—true and false. If the condition is true, certain code is executed. If it's false, another set of code is executed.

In VBA code, this statement can take on several different appearances. The basic syntax for the statement looks like this:

```
If <condition> Then
    ' A block of code for the condition being true.
ElseIf <condition n> Then
    ' A block of code for the condition n being true.
Else
    ' A block of code for the condition n being false.
End If
```

The reserved word `Then` is required and must follow every line that contains an `If` or `ElseIf`, such as `If...Then` or `ElseIf...Then`.

As you can see from the preceding example, the `If` statement can have several levels of conditions. Only one block of code can ever be executed in the `If` statement. When a true condition has been found, VBA executes that block of code and exits the `If` statement when it encounters an `ElseIf`, `Else`, or `End If`.

Now let's take a look at the different ways to use this statement. Here's a simple example. If a condition is true, a value is stored in a variable:

```
If x = 1 Then
    answer = "Yes"
End If
```

In this example, if x is equal to 1, the string `"Yes"` is stored in the variable `answer`. You can also write the example like this:

```
If x = 1 Then answer = "Yes"
```

Both of these examples carry out the same action. The only problem is that if x isn't equal to 1, the variable doesn't have a value stored in it. To correct this situation, add an `Else` condition to the `If` statement. The `Else` condition is optional:

```
If x = 1 Then
    answer = "Yes"
Else
    answer = "No"
End If
```

You can also rewrite this line to use the one-line `If` statement version. If you decide to use this method, it's a good idea to first store a default value in the variable. Here's how it would look:

```
answer = "No"
If x = 1 Then answer = "Yes"
```

Select Case

The `Select Case` statement is another type of looping construct. It looks somewhat like the `If...Then...Else` statement. The basic syntax for the `Select Case` statement looks like this:

```
Select Case <testexpression>
Case expressionslist
    'Statement block

Case expressionslistn
    'Statement block n

Case expressionslistn
    'Statement block n

Case Else
    'None of the other cases was true
End Select
```

To understand how this command works, let's break it down. The first line is where the variable used for the testing is named. For example:

```
Select Case tblCustomers!State
```

Here the state ID field in the Customer table is used for the comparison testing.

The `Case` *expressionslist* lines are where the variable is compared to a value. For example, you might want to see whether the state ID field is equal to `"FL"`. To do this, you need this line of code:

```
Case "FL"
```

If the condition is true (`state ID = "FL"`), the next block of code is executed. After executing the code in the block, VBA exits the `Select Case` statement and executes the first line of code following the statement.

If none of the conditions are true, none of the blocks of code are executed. However, you can add the `Case Else` condition to trap for this condition. This condition is run if none of the other conditions are true.

Here's an example of how to use the `Case Else` condition when no match is made:

```
Select Case txtGrade
Case "A"
    grade = "Excellent"

Case "B"
    grade = "Good"
```

```
Case "C"
   grade = "Fair"

Case "D"
   grade = "Poor"

Case Else
   grade = "None"
End Select
```

As you can see, the `If...Then...Else` and `Select Case` statements look and act somewhat alike. There are advantages to using one or the other in different situations. It's often simpler and clearer to use `Select Case` when there are many conditions for which the same variable will be tested. The preceding code provides a good example of this situation. On the other hand, `If...Then...Else` is a good choice when the branching decision is based on varying criteria requiring different variables.

IIf() (Immediate If)

The Immediate If (`IIf()`) is another very powerful programming construct. It's like the one-line `If...Then...Else` statement, but it returns a value. The syntax for the `IIf()` is as follows:

```
lvar = IIf(<expression>, <true return value>, <false return value>)
```

`IIf()` can be used in places that `If...Then...Else` can't. For example, you can use it as part of the control source for an object on a report. If the value of the object is 0, you might not want to print a 0 on the report. To do this, you use the `IIf()` statement in its place:

```
=IIf(DiscountRate = 0), " ",DiscountRate)
```

You can also use `IIf()` to trap for the dreaded divide by zero error that always seems to show up on reports. Here's how you use it to trap for this error:

```
=IIf(DiscountRate = 0, 0, (TotalSales / DiscountRate))
```

Now if the value of [DiscountRate] is 0, a 0 value is returned.

Do...Loop

The `Do...Loop` statement is used to repeat a block of code until a condition occurs or a condition is no longer valid. This statement can be written in two ways:

```
Do While¦Until [condition]
   <block of code to execute>
   Exit Do
Loop
```

or

```
Do
    <block of code to execute>
    Exit Do
Loop While¦Until [condition]
```

Both sets of code look as though they should perform the same way. The condition is tested at entirely different points, however. Consider the following example: The first message box will be displayed, even though iFoo is already greater than the constant BAR, because iFoo is not tested until the end of the loop. The second message box will not be displayed because iFoo = BAR as soon as the loop is entered. Both constructs are useful, but you must take care to ensure that you get the results you expect.

```
Function FooOne()

    Const BAR = 1
    Dim iFoo As Integer

    iFoo = 1
    Do
        iFoo = iFoo + 1
        MsgBox "Late do = " & iFoo
    Loop Until iFoo >= BAR

    ·iFoo = 1
    Do Until iFoo >= BAR
        iFoo = iFoo + 1
        MsgBox "Early do = " & iFoo
    Loop

End Function
```

You can easily lose track of what the Do...Loop statement is doing in a large procedure. It gets even more complicated when you have several nested Do...Loop statements.

To exit a Do...Loop statement at any point, you need to issue the Exit Do command. This terminates the loop and executes the next line of code following the Loop statement.

Here's an example of how to use the Do...Loop statement to skip through the records in a recordset. The Do...Loop statement ends when the first customer whose name starts with a *B* is encountered:

```
Dim dbName As Database
Dim tblName As Recordset
Set dbName = CurrentDb()
Set tblName = dbName.OpenRecordset("Customers")

Do While Left$(tblName!CompanyName, 1) <> "B"
    tblName.MoveNext
Loop
```

You can replace `While` with `Until` in the preceding example. However, this change has a major effect on the outcome and how the procedure executes:

```
Dim dbName As Database
Dim tblName As Recordset
Set dbName = CurrentDb()
Set tblName = dbName.OpenRecordset("Customers")

Do Until Left$(tblName!CompanyName, 1) <> "B"
    tblName.MoveNext
Loop
```

The two blocks of code are very similar, except that the `Until` clause was used in this code. Changing the code to use the `Until` clause causes different results. The `While` clause causes a loop to be executed while the condition is true. On the other hand, the `Until` clause causes a code segment to be executed until the condition is true. If the first record in the table starts with an *A*, the rest of the records aren't processed in the `Until` loop. To make this code act the same way as the `While` clause did, you would have to change the condition to the following:

```
Do Until Left$(tblName!CompanyName, 1) = "B"
```

While...Wend

The `While...Wend` statement is very similar to the `Do...Loop` statement. Both are used to loop through a block of code, executing it until a condition is met. The difference between the two is that the `While...Wend` statement doesn't have an exit point. Access continues to execute the block of code until the condition is no longer true. Here's the syntax for this statement:

```
While <condition is true>
    <code to be executed>
Wend
```

You can nest this statement as many deep as you want. Try not to have too many levels, however, because you might not be able to debug the code later.

Here's an example of how you might use this statement in your code:

```
Dim dbName As Database
Dim tblName As Recordset
Set dbName = CurrentDb()
Set tblName = dbName.OpenRecordset("Customers")

tblName.MoveFirst
While Left$(tblName!CompanyName, 1) <> "B"
    MsgBox tblName!CompanyName, 0, "First Test"
    tblName.MoveNext
Wend
```

For...Next

The `For...Next` statement is used to repeat a block of code for a set number of times. The syntax for this statement is as follows:

```
For <counter?> = start To end [Step increment]
    <code to be executed>

    Exit For

Next [counter, counter2]
```

Just as with the `Do...Loop` statement, you can exit the statement from within the loop. The `Exit For` command exits the loop at any point, and Access executes the next line of code after the `Next` command.

Next is an example of how to use the `For...Next` statement. In this example, the value of x is displayed until it reaches 10:

```
For x = 1 To 10
    <block of code to be executed each time>

    MsgBox Str(x), 0, "For...Next"
Next
```

The following example displays the value of x 19 times (1, 1.5, 2, 2.5, and so forth):

```
dim x as single
For x = 1 To 10 Step .5
    MsgBox Str(x), 0, "For...Next"
Next
```

You can modify the `Step` value so that it never reaches the end. The ending value in this example is 10, so Access terminates the looping whenever the value of x is greater than 10. For example, the maximum value displayed by the following code segment is 9:

```
Dim x As Single
For x = 1 To 10 Step 4
    MsgBox Str(x), 0, "For...Next"
Next
```

Summary

Using VBA code in your application enables you to go beyond the scope of macros and to tie an application together. Without this code, many of today's applications would be impossible or severely limited in what they could do. Learning to write code is a slow and steady process that begins with mastering the fundamentals outlined in this chapter.

Creating Sophisticated Output

PART IV

IN THIS PART

Designing and Customizing Reports

IN THIS CHAPTER

CHAPTER 11

Printing a report from Access is often the final result of the database effort. No matter how great a user interface is, printed output is more comprehensible to most people. Even though reports can be simply rows and columns of text displayed in the Courier font, people have high expectations for how a report will look. In the days of DOS, people didn't question a report that resembled a teletype printout, but now reports have to be not only functionally correct but cleverly formatted as well. This chapter focuses on creating the backend data structures that make up a good report, along with the powerful formatting tools included in Access 97.

Access is an excellent tool for data publishing, which is the database equivalent of desktop publishing. Many people use Access just as a publishing tool, publishing data that has been downloaded from their company mainframe or an existing database. Reports in Access are now created much like newsletters are laid out in PageMaker or Quark. The tools in Access, known as *controls*, are used to draw lines, words, fields, and pictures. You can use knowledge gained from creating the company newsletter to create company reports. Microsoft has included functional similarities between desktop publishing applications and Access. For instance, holding down the Shift key while drawing with the Line tool lets you draw a straight line.

The major improvement made in Access 97 reports was the support for hyperlinks. When a hyperlink is embedded in a report and that report's output is sent to Word 97, that link becomes active, meaning that the hyperlink can be clicked and followed to its target.

Customizing Reports

Forms and reports are very similar in how they manipulate controls, sections, and properties. The tricks and techniques in form and report design could fill an entire book themselves. This section covers the foundations of customizing, which should be the base needed to drive creativity.

Many developers who rush into report creation and assume that customizing is just as intuitive as the wizards are often left frustrated. They feel tricked when 90 percent of the report is built in a few minutes and the last 10 percent takes several hours. By studying the techniques covered next, you can cut that last 10 percent of the building process drastically. The techniques discussed here are best learned through hands-on experimentation.

Toggling Between Design View and Print Preview

Reports have only two views: Design view and Print Preview. Previewing is split into the actual Print Preview or a formatted sample of records, the Layout Preview. The View menu shows all views; it appears in both Print Preview and Design view.

These are the shortcuts for toggling the view: In Print Preview, you can click the Close button to enter Design view; in Design view, the toolbar choices are Layout Preview and Print Preview.

> **TIP**
>
> In the Database window, hold down Ctrl and double-click a report to enter Design view, or right-click a report and choose Design from the shortcut menu.

The Layout Preview displays a quick formatted sample of records, giving an instant example of the formatting. Print Preview shows the actual formatting of all the records.

Moving and Sizing Controls

Move a control and its label together by placing the cursor on the border of a selected control, as shown in Figure 11.1. You can also press Ctrl+arrow keys to move the control.

FIGURE 11.1.
Moving the control and label together with the flat hand.

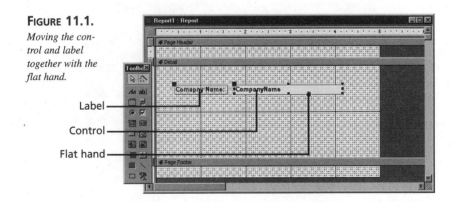

Label

Control

Flat hand

Move a control independently of its label by placing the cursor on the large black square of a selected control. The "index finger" will be visible only over the large black square in the upper-left corner of a selected control, as shown in Figure 11.2.

FIGURE 11.2.
Moving the control independently of its label with the index finger.

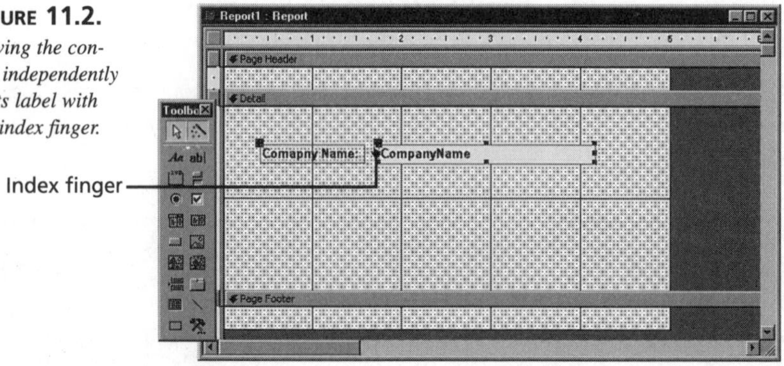

Index finger —

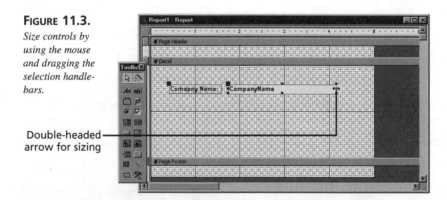

> **TIP**
>
> To have the control not snap to grid, hold down the Ctrl key while moving it.

You can size a control by placing the cursor on one of its handlebars and dragging, as shown in Figure 11.3. You can also press Shift+arrow keys to size the control.

FIGURE 11.3.
Size controls by using the mouse and dragging the selection handlebars.

Double-headed arrow for sizing —

> **TIP**
>
> To size a control automatically, hold the cursor over a sizing handle until the double-headed arrow appears, and then double-click.

The Four Methods of Selecting Controls

When more than one control is selected, the controls can be manipulated as a group and moved, sized, or deleted. Here are the four methods of selecting controls:

- Hold down the Shift key while clicking separate controls.
- Select View I Select All.
- Click the report's background and drag a square around one or more controls to capture a group, as shown in Figure 11.4.

FIGURE 11.4.

Dragging around a group to select controls.

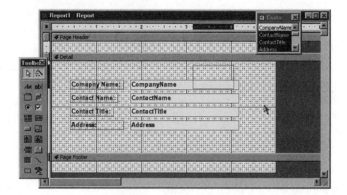

- Click in one of the rulers at the top or left edges of the report to "shoot" across the report's design, which selects every control in its path, as shown in Figure 11.5.

FIGURE 11.5.

Shooting the controls by clicking in the ruler.

Deleting and Re-establishing Controls

To delete a control, simply select it and press the Delete key. To re-establish a control, display the report's field list by selecting View | Field List. Then drag the fields off the list and onto the report. (Hold down Ctrl to select more than one field.)

> **NOTE**
>
> The field list displays the fields in the underlying table or query.

Changing Control Properties

Changing control properties is the final step in manipulating the report. Everything in Access has properties: the report has properties, each control has properties, and each report section has properties. Changing a property to Yes or No can change the entire structure of the report.

Here are four methods of displaying the Property Sheet:

- Select View | Properties.
- Click the Properties tool on the toolbar.
- Right-click a control and choose Properties.
- Double-click any control or section.

If you select multiple controls, only the common properties are available in the properties window. If a property is then modified, the changed is rippled down through all selected controls.

The most crucial report property is the Record Source property. If the developer deletes the contents of this property, the report no longer has data to display. If you activate the drop-down list box of the Record Source property, as shown in Figure 11.6, you can redirect the data source to another table or query.

FIGURE 11.6.

The Record
Source *property
defines the
report's underly-
ing record set.*

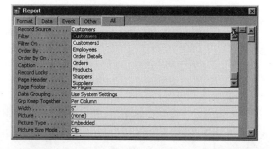

> **TIP**
>
> To see the Help screen for any property, press F1 while the cursor is inside the property.

> **TIP**
>
> While the Property Sheet is open, click any element of the report to show its properties. To see the overall report properties, click the square in the upper-left corner of the Report window where the two rulers meet.

Report Controls Explained

A control is Microsoft's term for objects that the developer places in the sections of a report (or form). Controls are placed on reports (and forms) by clicking icons in the Toolbox. Examples of tools include the Label, Image, and Line. Because forms and reports are so similar in their development, Microsoft decided to include the same control toolbox for both. However, many of the tools in the Toolbox are rarely if ever used in reports. An example is the Combo Box tool. The purpose of a combo box is to choose items from a list; because reports are designed to be printed, there is no reason to use a combo box. Figure 11.7 illustrates all the tools in the Toolbox.

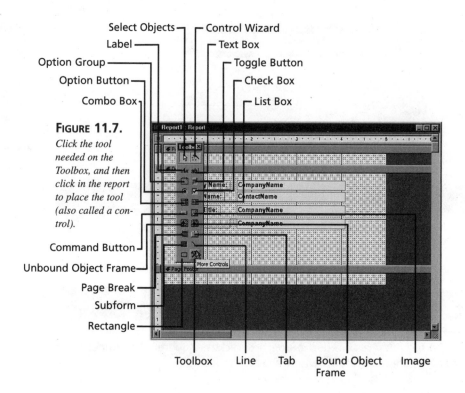

FIGURE 11.7.

Click the tool needed on the Toolbox, and then click in the report to place the tool (also called a control).

The following list describes each of the tools on the Toolbox:

- *Select Objects*. Returns the cursor to the selecting pointer.

- *Control Wizard*. When turned on (pushed in), invokes a helpful wizard when you're placing certain controls like the Subreport tool.

- *Label*. Used for placing text on reports, such as a label for a field or the title of a report in the header. The Label tool is one of the ways to embed a hyperlink.

- *Text Box*. Used for "live" data fields that are tied to the table or query that underlies this report.

- *Option Group*. Utilized mainly in forms for placing option buttons such as check boxes, toggle buttons, or option buttons.

- *Toggle Button*. Used mainly in forms inside option groups.

- *Option Button*. Used mainly in forms inside option groups.

- *Check Box*. Used mainly in forms inside option groups.

- *Combo Box*. Used mainly in forms.

- *List Box*. Used mainly in forms.

- *Command Button*. Used mainly in forms.
- *Image Control*. One of two controls used for placing static graphics on a report. A graphic placed with this tool, as opposed to the Unbound Object Frame tool, does not carry the extra baggage of OLE and therefore loads faster.
- *Unbound Object Frame*. Used to place OLE objects on a report. Examples could include graphics, Excel objects, and Visio objects. A benefit of the Unbound Object Frame over the Image Control is that the developer can double-click the object in Design view and edit that object through OLE.
- *Bound Object Frame*. Used to place "live" data fields that are bound to an OLE datatype field in the underlying recordset. An example would be a photo of a contact in the database.
- *Page Break*. Used to force a page break in reports.
- *Tab Control*. Used mainly in forms.
- *Subform\Subreport*. Used to embed one report into another reports. The embedded report is called a subreport.
- *Line*. Used to draw lines on reports.
- *Rectangle*. Used to draw boxes on reports.
- *More Controls*. Used to gain access to the registered ActiveX controls on your system. Although these controls are used mostly in forms, you will surely see some clever report ActiveX's appear on the market as this technology advances.

Placing Controls with the Toolbox

You can display the Toolbox by selecting View | Toolbox or clicking the wrench and hammer icon on the toolbar. The Toolbox is just what it sounds like—a construction kit for controls.

Making Massive Changes with the Format Menu

The new features that show up under the Format menu in this version of Access are AutoFormat, Control Morphing, and some new sizing tools.

Formatting with AutoFormat

Identical in functionality to AutoFormat in Word and Excel, the Access AutoFormat can be very useful. If a report has been built from scratch or modified and needs a new look, AutoFormat reformats every control, as shown in Figure 11.8.

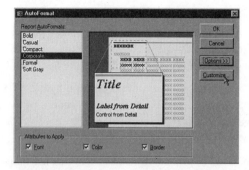

FIGURE 11.8.
AutoFormatting a report quickly changes the format of the entire report.

NOTE

AutoFormats can be customized and you can create new ones. Use the Help screens to learn more about this amazing feature.

Aligning and Sizing Multiple Controls

The Format menu changes depending on the report element chosen. If several controls are selected, you have the option of aligning or sizing them.

TIP

Right-clicking a selected control brings up the option to align. This is very useful if many controls are selected.

NOTE

Because labels and controls are linked to each other, aligning columns can be frustrating. Try selecting only the labels, aligning them in the opposite direction. Then move one label to where the group should align. Finally, realign them to desired position.

Redefining the Default for Controls

When controls are created from the tools in the Toolbox or dragged off the field list, they assume the default size and fonts. The developer can change these defaults. With this technique, report development time can be radically decreased.

11

To redefine a text box control's default properties, set the size, font, and other properties to those desired, and then Select Format | Change Default. All new text boxes for this report now assume the new default set.

Building a Report from Scratch and Modifying Its Controls

Creating a report from scratch is an excellent way to learn what the Report Wizards do and how to harness that power. An example of when not to use the Report Wizards is when a report should look the same as an existing business report, such as an insurance policy, for example, which has many lines and boxes with lots of fine print. In this case, creating the report from scratch is the only choice.

The next few sections are tasks that build on themselves to create the Categories report that shows the categories and products of Northwind Traders. Included on this report will be a graphic, a hyperlink, page numbering, timestamp, lines, and a subreport.

Creating a Tabular Report from the Categories Table

1. Open up the Northwind sample database that ships with Access 97. In the Database window, choose the Report tab. Click New and then click OK. A blank report is generated, and at this point it is not bound to any recordset.

> **TIP**
>
> To change the Normal template for blank reports, choose Tools | Options | Forms/Reports. In the Report Template dialog box, type the name of a report in the current database.

2. Set the record source. Choose View | Properties to display the properties box if it's not already displayed. Click in the square box to the left of the horizontal ruler to display the report properties. Set the Record Source property, which is the first choice, to the table called Categories. Click inside the Record Source property, and then choose the table from the drop-down list.

3. Create a Report Header by choosing View | Report Header/Footer.

4. In the Report Header, carry out the following actions:

- Add a report title. Display the Toolbox. Select the Label tool. Click in the left side of the Report Header and type `Categories and Products`. Click outside the label to set its text. Click again on the label to select it. This activates the formatting toolbar. Set the format to 14 points and Bold. Choose Format | Size | To fit.

- Add a timestamp. Choose Insert | Date and Time to display the Date and Time dialog box. Choose the format desired and press Enter. This action places the text box with an expression to display the date and time. Click and hold on the new text box, and move to the right side of the Report Header.

- Increase the width and height to accommodate the logo and hyperlink. Begin by placing the cursor on the right edge of the "paper" until the cursor changes to a double-headed arrow. At this point, drag to the right to increase the width. Then increase the height of the header by putting the cursor on the top of the Page Header divider (gray) and dragging down.

- Insert a hyperlink. Choose Insert | Hyperlink. Type the fictitious Web address `www.northtrade.com` and press Enter. A new box appears with a blue Web address. Move this link into position in the header. This link is not active until it is exported to any Office 97 product, such as Word.

- Insert a graphic. Select the Image Control on the Toolbox. Draw a square in the right side of the header. The Insert Picture dialog box appears. Point to and select a graphic. It might be necessary to set the size mode property to stretch.

- Insert a line. Select the Line Control on the Toolbox. Hold down the Shift key while clicking and dragging a line. By using the Shift key, you get straight lines.

- Save the report as `CategoryRPT`.

5. In the Report Detail section, carry out the following actions:

- Place the data fields. Choose View | Field List to display the field list if it's not already shown. Drag the CategoryName and Description fields from the field list, and drop them into the Detail section. Delete the labels by selecting them individually and pressing the Delete key. (To drag more than one field at a time, hold down Ctrl and drag the fields.)

- Arrange the fields. Using the customizing techniques discussed earlier in this chapter, move, size, and change the fields inside the Detail section. Refer to Figure 11.9.

Designing and Customizing Reports

CHAPTER 11

353

11

DESIGNING AND
CUSTOMIZING
REPORTS

FIGURE 11.9.

*The Design view
of the report for
these exercises.*

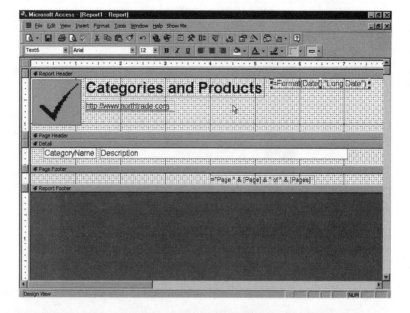

TIP

Pressing Ctrl+arrow key moves controls in fine increments; pressing Shift+arrow key sizes them. The Format menu also contains useful design tools.

- Decrease the height of the Detail section to match that shown in Figure 11.9.
- Double-click the Description field to display the property sheet. Change the CanGrow property to Yes. This allows long Description fields to wrap.

6. In the Report Footer section, carry out the following actions:

- Choose Insert | Page Numbers. Set the options to show the page numbers in the preferred format.

7. Use Print Preview to see the new masterpiece. Figure 11.10 shows the report in Print Preview.

FIGURE 11.10.
The final result of the report.

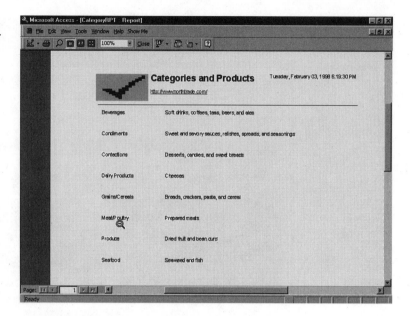

Inserting a Subreport

A subreport is literally one report inserted into another. Subreports are a very useful way of showing information from two or more tables that have a relationship, although a relationship isn't required in certain circumstances. One example of a main report/subreport is the same as for a main form/subform. In the database are two tables with a one-to-many relationship, also known as a parent-child relationship. A subreport displays the children of the parent report, as shown in Figure 11.11. Although this can be accomplished with a grouping report, some situations require the use of a subreport. Subreports are particularly useful for displaying the parent record and multiple child records from unrelated tables. Note that a relationship isn't required to use subreports. Figure 11.11 shows the underlying one-to-many relationship for the proposed subreport.

Figure 11.12 shows the use of a subreport in a report. Using a subreport is similar to having a groups and totals report. The advantage of using a subreport is that more than one grouping can be displayed for a single group.

Designing and Customizing Reports

CHAPTER 11

355

11

DESIGNING AND
CUSTOMIZING
REPORTS

FIGURE 11.11.
Main reports and subreports are based on one-to-many relationships.

Relationship

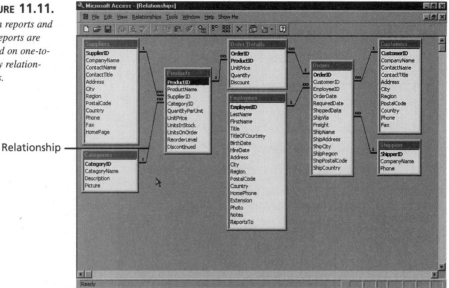

FIGURE 11.12.
Subreports can show related data. Shown here are the many products for the category Beverages.

Parent record

Child records

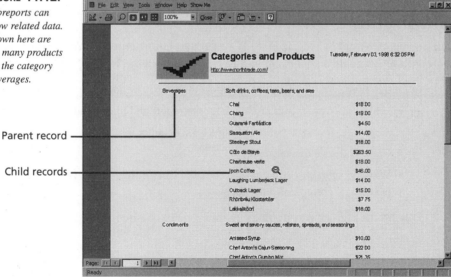

Subreporting can be accomplished through the Subreport Wizard or by manual construction. Use of the wizard is recommended for beginners because the concept of subreports is often confusing. The following task is a continuation of the preceding one. This subreport will display each of the products by category.

1. Click the Control Wizard tool in the report Toolbox.
2. Click the Subreport tool.
3. Click below the Description field in the Detail section.
4. Answer the wizard's questions:
   - Question 1: Choose the table\Query option.
   - Question 2: Choose the Products table. Then double-click `ProductName` and `UnitPrice`.
   - Question 3: Choose the default. The wizard found a linking field in the `CategoryID`.
   - Question 4: Title your report and choose Finish.
5. Delete the unneeded label for the subreport, adjust its width and height, and preview your new subreport.

Modifying a Subreport

The Subreport Wizard builds and embeds a subreport into your report. You can edit the embedded report by double-clicking it in Design view. Refer to Figure 11.13.

1. In Design view, double-click the subreport and make needed changes as followed.
   - Under the View menu, remove both the report and page header and footer.
   - Adjust the font to 8 point and adjust the detail height.
   - Close and save the subreport.
   - With the subreport still chosen, click the Line/Border Color tool on the toolbar. Set its border color to transparent.
2. Preview the finished report. Make modifications as desired.

FIGURE 11.13.

The Design view of the subreport. Notice that all unneeded elements have been removed to allow the least amount of white space.

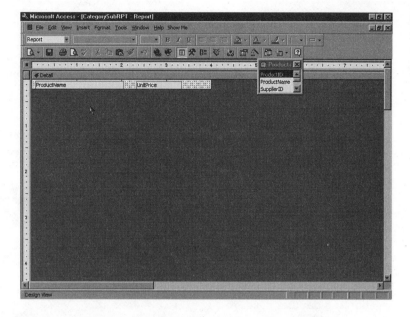

Creating a Subreport Without the Wizard

Usually, when a report needs a subreport, the task is very specialized and requires manual intervention. The wizards can be useful, but they are limited. This will show you the steps to create a subreport and embed it into a report. The process of building a main report or subreport has several steps:

1. Ensure that the two tables have a one-to-many relationship. Take note of the field that links the two tables.

2. Compose and save a report based on the parent table. This will be the main report.

3. Create and save a report based on the child table. This will be the subreport. Be sure to include the linking field in the soon-to-be subreport. Subreports are usually of the tabular style.

4. Open the Main report in Design view. Using the Subreport tool in the toolbox, with the Control Wizard tool off, draw a rectangle where the subreport will go.

5. Display the subreport's properties and set the `Source Object` property to the name of the saved subreport.

6. Examine the subreport properties `Link Child Fields` and `Link Master Fields`. If the linking fields have the same field name, Access fills in this property automatically. If Access doesn't populate these properties, the field names need to be typed in manually.

If all goes well, you should have created a working main report\subreport. To edit the subreport, double-click the subreport in Design view. Some common problems with subreports occur with the sizing of controls and having proper linking.

CAUTION

The architecture of subreports that display related tables hinges on the properties `Link Child Fields` and `Link Master Fields`. If these properties are left blank, the subreport will not work. Keep in mind that subreports do not need to be linked in order to be useful. For example, a subreport could display an address block that needs to be next to every record.

NOTE

The main report doesn't have to be based on records. For example, the parent record could come from a reference to a form, a global variable, a parameter query, or a field in another section of the report. The creative use of subreports can greatly extend reporting in Access.

Advanced Report Customization with Properties

Numerous properties must be set when a report is created. The report has properties, each section has properties, and each control has properties. New developers can easily become overwhelmed and confused by the number of properties. This section walks you through some of the most useful new properties in Access 97. The tasks here are a continuation of the previous ones.

Designing and Customizing Reports

CHAPTER 11

359

11

DESIGNING AND
CUSTOMIZING
REPORTS

To begin, display the CategoryRPT created in the preceding task in Design view. Display the Property Sheet. Click the square to the left of the ruler to display the report properties (as opposed to properties of a section).

Using the OrderBy Property

As indicated by its name, this property orders the report in the manner specified. Type CategoryName in the OrderBy property, and set the OrderByOn property to yes. This action will sort the report in alphabetical order by CategoryName.

Using the Caption Property

Type Category and Products Report into this properties box. This entry will be displayed in the report's title bar. Additionally, the text typed into the Caption property is used for establishing a hyperlink to this report.

Using the Picture Properties

There are five picture properties that when manipulated can create various creative effects. For instance, by setting the PictureTiling property to Yes, you can give the report a Web-page background look. The watermark effect, such as the word *CONFI-DENTIAL* lightly appearing on paper, can be achieved with a light gray graphic. In this task, you will put a decorative graphic down the left edge of the paper.

1. Click the Picture property. Then click the builder button. In this example, point to the graphic \\msoffice\clipart\backgrounds\ and choose the .bmp called leaves on the side.
2. Set the Picture Alignment property to Top Left.
3. Set the Picture Tiling property to Yes.

Using the HasModule Properties

Use the HasModule property to tell Access whether the report has a module page (code behind the report). Setting this property to No can decrease the size of your database and improve the performance of the report.

Great Ways to Customize Reports with Expressions

The key role of a good report is displaying data in an understandable fashion. When table data is simply placed on a form, it can be confusing for the user. For example, it's easier to understand the combination of the first and last names than it is to display them separately (*Jill Smith* as compared to *Jill   Smith*). You can do much of this fine-tuning through clever expressions written in a text box control. This section covers 8 examples of common report expressions:

- Concatenating fields for a text box
- Turning a Yes/No field into text
- Using If...Then statements with the IIF function
- Turning the display off for a field if the value is Null
- Retrieving records through Dlookup statements
- Combining text fields for an address block
- Referencing an open form on the report
- Adding up report data using the Sum function

Concatenating Fields for a Text Box

The text box shown in Figure 11.14 combines the values of the following three elements: FirstName, a space, and LastName. This is known as a calculated control. This control was created with the Text Box tool. Inside the control or in the Control Source property, write the calculated expression. Calculated fields always start with an equal sign (=). Here are some rules to observe:

- Field names must have square brackets around them if they have spaces: [Order ID]
- Text values must have quotation marks around them: "Title"
- Date values must have pound signs on both sides: #12/22/65#
- Remember that, when naming your controls and using concatenation, don't name the control with the same name as the field name. If you do you will get a #Error instead of the value of the field.

Designing and Customizing Reports

CHAPTER 11

361

11

DESIGNING AND
CUSTOMIZING
REPORTS

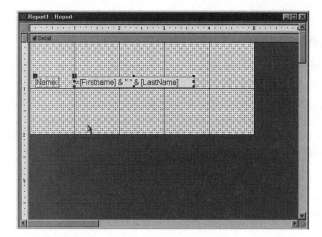

FIGURE 11.14.
*The concatenation
of text fields.*

Turning a Yes/No Field into Text

The properties of Yes/No fields are divided into three parts. The first part is not used, the
second part is for `True` values (–1), and the third part is for `False` values (0). These are
separated by semicolons. The example shown in Figure 11.15 was created by placing an
unbound text box on the report, setting its `Control Source` property to the field
`Discount`, and typing the expression in the `Format` property. See Figure 11.15 for an
example. This expression changes a –1 value to read "Discount" and a 0 value to "No
Discount." Refer to the online Help for more details.

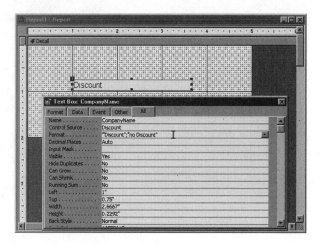

FIGURE 11.15.
Exploit the `Format`
*property to
change the display
of a Yes/No field.*

Using If...Then Statements with the IIF Function

The IIF, or immediate if, function performs a simple If...Then test. The arguments for this function have three parts: the Test, True value, and False value. In the Test portion, write a test against a field value. If that test passes, it displays the contents of True; otherwise, it displays the contents of False. These True and False values can be text values surrounded by quotation marks, such as "PAID"; field values enclosed in brackets, such as [Order Amount]; or calculations, such as Date()-30.

Figure 11.16 shows an IIF statement in action. This simple expression displays No Discount if there was a value in the field Discount = 0. If the value of Discount was not equal to zero, it displays the actual value. To re-create this example, follow these steps:

1. Create a blank report in Northwind based on the OrdersDetails table.

2. Using the toolbox, choose the Text Box tool, and draw an unbound control on the report.

3. Type the Name property CheckDiscount. If the actual field named Discount is placed in the Name property, it is likely to produce an #Error value.

4. Type the expression into the Control Source property, as shown in Figure 11.16.

FIGURE 11.16.

The IIF function is a simple If...Then test.

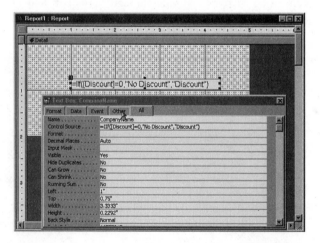

Turning the Display Off a Field If the Value Is Null

If a customer on an invoice report doesn't get a discount, you don't display the control for `Discount` or its label. The `IsNull` function, like the `IIF` function, is a built-in Access function. In the preceding example, the `IIF` function performs a test. The `IsNull` function tests whether a field is `null`. If the field is `null`, it displays `""`. (Two quotation marks print as nothing.) If it isn't `null`, it prints the value of the field. In the example above you knew that the field was going to either be `null` or have a value. If you did not know this for sure, it would be best to use the `Nz` function instead of `IsNull`. The `Nz` function can return either a zero length string or a 0. Optionally, it could return what ever you wanted by using the optional parameter. The syntax for `Nz` is

```
Nz(variant[, valueifnull])
```

Note that the example in Figure 11.17 is identical in structure to the one shown in Figure 11.16. The only difference is in the `Control Source` expression. To re-create this example, follow the steps outlined in the preceding example, but change the expression.

FIGURE 11.17.

Combining the IsNull *and* IIF *functions.*

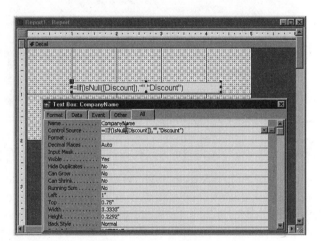

Retrieving Records Through Dlookup Statements

When the report requires a record from a foreign table, and a subreport is not justified, the `Dlookup` statement is a solution. The `Dlookup` function is syntactically identical to the other domain functions: `Dcount`, `Dmax`, `Dfirst`, and so on. The example in Figure 11.18

looks up the value of the field named `Discount` in the table named `Orders`, where the `OrderID` is equal to the `OrderID` on the open form called `MyForm`. (The online Help provides additional information.) The `Dlookup` syntax can be dissected as Look up what?, Where?, and When?, each enclosed in quotation marks and separated by commas.

FIGURE 11.18.

Using the `Dlookup` *function.*

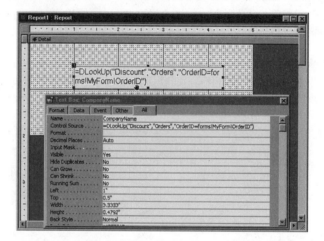

Combining Text Fields for an Address Block

Address blocks are common in reports and can be frustrating. For an address block, use regular text concatenation in a text box with the ASCII character codes `CHR$(13)` and `CHR$(10)`. These ASCII codes are the line feed and carriage return codes that drop down a line. To have the address block confirm the existence of a second address, insert the following code:

```
=IIf(IsNull([Address2]),[Address],[Address] & Chr$(13) & Chr$(10) &
[Address2])
```

Figure 11.19 delivers the address with each part concatenated and placed on its proper line.

Designing and Customizing Reports

CHAPTER 11

365

11

DESIGNING AND
CUSTOMIZING
REPORTS

FIGURE 11.19.
*Combining fields
for an address
block.*

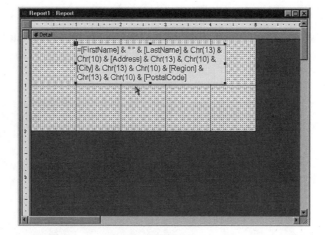

Referencing an Open Form on the Report

Sometimes a report is run from a button the user presses on a form. The data on that
form can be used in the report without queries or Dlookups. The expression can be typed
into the Control Source property of a text box; however, it's much easier to use the
Expression Builder. To invoke the Expression Builder, display the Property Sheet for a
new text box control, and click the Control Source property (see Figure 11.20). Click
the Builder button on its right, which invokes the Expression Builder. Begin drilling
down into the form's objects to find the field in question. Danger: When referencing
open forms, do not name the control with a name already used in the underlying table or
query. Note that the text box name property is TitleRef instead of Title.

FIGURE 11.20.
*Referencing a
form from the
report.*

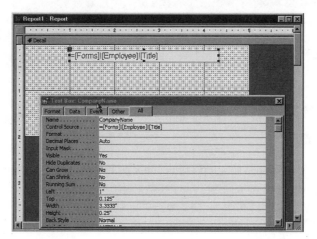

Adding Up Report Data with the Sum Function

You can use a wizard to insert the Sum function into the Report Footer automatically, as shown in Figure 11.21. The Sum function sums up the field specified in the Detail section.

FIGURE 11.21.

Using the Sum function in a Report Footer.

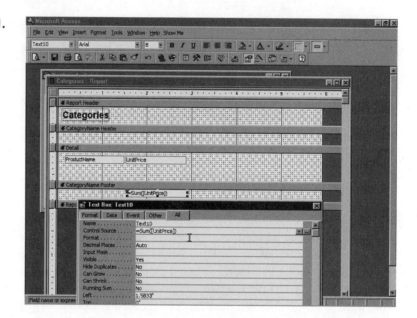

Embedding Hyperlinks into Access Reports

When a hyperlink is added to a report, it cannot be used directly as a clickable item, but the hyperlink will print on a sheet of paper as underlined text. It will also be displayed in a different color in Print Preview, but you cannot click it to follow its link. In Access reporting, hyperlinks are used for exports to other office products such as Word or Excel.

After the report is exported, it becomes live when viewed with an Office 97 product. That Office product can be Access.

Hyperlinks can be used in tables, queries, forms, and reports. In reports only, labels, command buttons, and graphics can be made "hot" when output. Hyperlink fields in the underlying query are not hot when output, but they will show up in the report as underlined and in a different color. To make hyperlink fields hot in an external output, output a table or query directly.

> **NOTE**
>
> The behavior of hyperlinks differs based on where and how they are inserted in Access. For example, creating a report with the Report Wizard does not make a hyperlink field underlined and blue, but dragging that field onto a report in Design view will make it underlined and blue.

One of the shortcomings of hyperlinks and reports is in the outputting of hyperlink data fields. An unusual limitation in this release is that only labels, command buttons, and graphics with hyperlinks are hot when output to other formats, but not hyperlink data fields. To add to this confusion, depending on which format was chosen for output, different elements are turned into hyperlinks.

An example of this behavior is to output the `Suppliers` table as an `.rtf` file (open the table and use File | Save As\Export). Open this file in Word, and notice the Homepage field (a hyperlink field) is an active hyperlink. Now, create a report based on the `Suppliers` table using the Report Wizard, and then output the report as an `.rtf` file and open it in Word. The Homepage field that was active in the table output is no longer active. Create another report in Access based on the `Suppliers` table without the wizard, output it to a `.rtf` file, open it in Word, and notice that the hyperlinks *are* active, and underlined, and blue. What this means to the developer is that when he is using exporting as tool, experimenting with different techniques and formats will be necessary.

Adding Internet and Document Hyperlinks to a Report

The following exercise will guide you through adding hyperlinks in reports. The fictitious purpose of this report is that it will be a link page that will be output to HTML and put on the company's intranet.

1. Open the Northwind Traders sample database.

2. Create a table with a hyperlink field. This table will have three fields: LinkID (Autonumber), LinkName (Text), and LinkAddress (Hyperlink). See Figure 11.22 for an example. Save the table with the name LinkTBL.

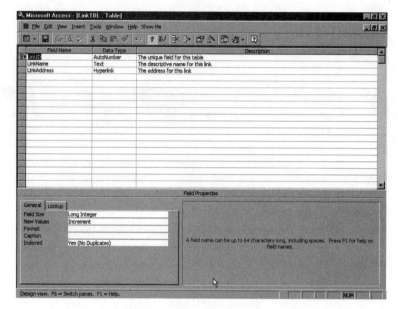

3. Populate the table with hyperlinks. Create some dummy documents on your system that you can link to. Then in Table Datasheet view, insert the hyperlinks either by typing them or by using the hyperlink tool on the toolbar. See Figure 11.23 for an example. Create Web links using the same method of document links.

4. Create a tabular report based on the LinkTBL. In the Database window, click the Reports tab. Click the New button and then double-click Report Wizard. In step 1 of the wizard, choose the LinkTBL, and add the fields LinkName and LinkAddress to the list of selected fields. Click Finish.

5. Modify the new report. Choose View|Design View to make the following modifications.

   - Change the report name label to Northwind HotLinks.

   - Add a Command Button Hyperlink. Display the toolbar. Make sure that the wizard is turned off. Place a Command button in the Report Header. Display the property sheet for the Command button. In the Caption property, type Northwind Traders. In the HyperlinkAddress property, type www.northtrade.com.

Designing and Customizing Reports

CHAPTER 11

369

11

DESIGNING AND
CUSTOMIZING
REPORTS

FIGURE 11.23.

*Datasheet view of
the LinkTBL.*

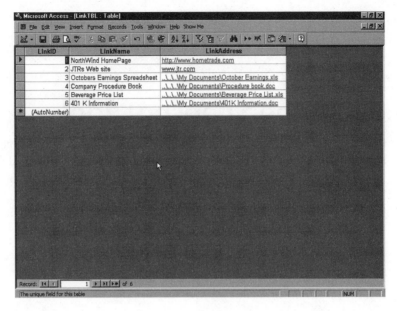

- Add a Label Hyperlink. Click the Label tool on the toolbar and create a label
  in the header. Type Northwind Traders. In the Hyperlink Address property, type www.northtrade.com. Change the text format to bold, blue, and
  underlined.

- Add a Graphic Hyperlink. Click the Image tool on the toolbar and embed a
  picture in the header. In the Hyperlink Address, type www.northtrade.com.
  Place a label underneath the image that reads Click graphic to jump to
  Northwind homepage.

6. Save the report and display it in Print Preview. Notice that the report links look
   clickable, but they will not be active until they are output to another format. Saving
   is an essential step. Outputting to another format is not possible unless the report
   has been saved.

7. Output the report by choosing File|Save As\Export. Choose the option of out-
   putting To an External File or Database, and click OK. In the Save As dialog box,
   activate the Save As Type drop-down list. Note the many choices:

   - Export to HTML. A dialog box prompts for an HTML template. This tem-
     plate is an existing Web document that will govern the style of the upcoming
     HTML document. Use of different templates delivers different looks to your
     Web page, such as background colors.

- Export to Excel. The datafields are active but the heading information is not.
- Export to Word. The datafields are not active but the heading information is—just the opposite of Excel. To make datafields active in .rtf files, export a table or query directly.

Using the Snapshot Tool

One of Access's downfalls was the inability to view reports without having it. Microsoft has fixed this problem with SnapShot Viewer, a tool that can be installed from the ValuPack in Microsoft Office 97 Service Release 1, the ValuPack in Microsoft Access 97 Service Release 1, or if you have access to the Web and you do not have the ValuPack, you can go to http://www.microsoft.com/accessdev/prodinfo/ snapshot.htm to download the application.

This application allows you to export and view reports that are from Access. To be able to view the report you must first export the report to Snapshot Format (*.snp). To do this you will need to follow these 7 easy steps.

1. Select the report you wish to have created as a Snapshot.
2. Select File | Save As/Export.
3. In the Save As dialog select External File or Database.
4. In the Save As Type box, select Snapshot Format (*.snp).
5. Select the location where you would like the file to be saved.
6. The default name for the file is Reportname.snp. You can change this by clicking the File Name box, removing the current name, and adding a new name.
7. Click Export.

> **NOTE**
>
> If the report is based on a parameter query, you will be prompted for the parameters before the report is extracted.

You can also send a report by electronic mail if your email application supports Messaging Application Programming Interface (MAPI). To do this select Send on the file menu and, when prompted, select Snapshot Format. At this point a new mail message is opened with the report embedded in the subject.

> **NOTE**
>
> For users to view a Snapshot files, they will need Snapshot viewer installed to their machines. It is not as easy as copying snapview.exe to their machines. They must run snpvw80.exe, which will install the application for them.

Summary

The report creation process can be a simple five-second task or a challenging week-long effort. You'll find that during report building, flaws in the underlying database design emerge. This redesign time results in extra project hours. To avoid this common pitfall, begin the project with a sketch of all the reports, and test the database design by working backward.

Studying the techniques and examples in this chapter will greatly decrease your report creation time. The tools available in Access 97 offer an incredible amount of creativity. With the new freedom found in reporting, you'll also find new frustrations. Because you can do so much, things can become even more confusing. Complex reporting will be easier after you study the literature, read the Help screens, investigate examples, and get plenty of practical experience. As with most elements of Access 97, nothing is more beneficial than hands-on experience.

Programming in Reports

The Application Object

The Application object represents the Microsoft Access application that is currently executing. The Application object owns a set of collections including the Forms, Reports, and Modules collections. The Reports collection represents all the open Access reports, whether the report is opened through Print Preview or Design view (see Figure 12.1). This chapter examines the events, methods, and properties of the Report object, which comprises the Reports collection.

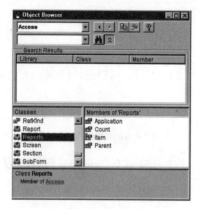

The Report Object

The Northwind Traders database contains several examples of reports used in this chapter, including Sales by Category, Products by Category, and Summary of Sales by Year. The Report object refers to an open Access report (see Tables 12.1 and 12.2). Open reports within the Reports collection can be referenced several ways in macros or VBA code.

TABLE 12.1. REFERRING TO A Report OBJECT IN CODE.

Syntax	Comments
Reports(0)	Refers to the first open report in the collection
Reports![Sales by Category]	Explicitly refers to the Sales by Category report
Reports!("Sales by Category")	Explicitly refers to the Sales by Category report
Reports!("rptReportName")	Refers to the report name, which is stored in a variable called rptReportName

Each `Report` object contains a Controls collection that is comprised of controls defined for that report. The Sales by Category report includes several controls such as text boxes, labels, and charts. To refer to a control and its properties on this report, write the following code:

```
Reports![Sales by Category].Controls![CategoryID].Visible = False
Reports![Sales by Category].Controls![DateLabel].FontSize = 12
Reports![Sales by Category].Controls![SalesChart].BorderColor =
➥RGB(255,255,0)  'Yellow
```

As Controls is the default collection of the Reports collections, you can shorten each of these lines of code:

```
Reports![Sales by Category]![CategoryID].Visible = False
Reports![Sales by Category]![DateLabel].FontSize = 12
Reports![Sales by Category]![SalesChart].BorderColor = RGB(255,255,0)
➥'Yellow
```

THE ME OBJECT

The `Me` keyword acts as an implicitly declared variable. `Me` is a way to refer to the specific instance of an object when code is executing. The first example from the preceding code can be written `Me![CategoryID].Visible = False`.

Events of the `Report` Object

TABLE 12.2. THE EVENTS OF THE `Report` OBJECT.

Event	Event Property	Triggered
Open	OnOpen	Occurs when the report is opened but before the report is previewed or printed
Activate	OnActivate	When the report receives focus and becomes the active window
Deactivate	OnDeactivate	When the report loses focus, which means that you have selected another form, query, or report
NoData	OnNoData	Occurs after Access has formatted a report for printing but with an empty recordset
Page	OnPage	Occurs after Access formats a page of a report for printing but before the page is printed

continues

TABLE 12.2. CONTINUED

Event	Event Property	Triggered
Error	OnError	Occurs when a run-time error is produced in Access
Close	OnClose	Occurs when the report is closed and removed from the screen

The Sales by Category Report Example

The Northwind Traders database, which accompanies Access 97, includes a report called Sales by Category, whose RecordSource is the Sales by Category query. If you look at the query in design mode, you will find that the OrderDate field contains Between #1/1/95# and #12/31/95#. This example adds some flexibility to this report, as well as illustrate the use of events of the Report object.

Open Event

The Open event occurs when the report is opened but before the report is printed or previewed. Below is VBA code in the OnOpen event property of the Sales by Category report (see Figure 12.2), which opens frmSalesCategory, requesting from the user a range of dates to be used when generating the report.

FIGURE 12.2.

Dialog form for the Sales by Category report.

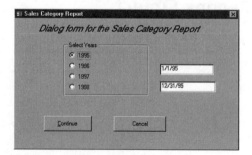

frmSalesCategory consists of option buttons for each year, two command buttons, and two text boxes. The text boxes, txtFromDate and txtToDate, contain the dates after an option button is selected. Normally, these two text boxes are hidden on the form; they pass data to frmSalesCategory.

The Sales by Category query needs to be modified. The criteria for OrderDate should read

```
Between [Forms]![frmSalesCategoryDialog]![txtFromDate] And
➥[Forms]![frmSalesCategoryDialog]![txtToDate].
```

Also, the datatype for these two values needs to be set to Date/Time (Query | Parameter). Listing 12.1 is the VBA code for the OnOpen event for this report.

LISTING 12.1. THE Open EVENT FOR THE SALES BY CATEGORY REPORT.

```
Private Sub Report_Open(Cancel As Integer)
'Variable used to determine the status of the form
Dim intObjectState As Integer

DoCmd.OpenForm "frmSalesCategoryDialog", , , , , acDialog
intObjectState = SysCmd(acSysCmdGetObjectState, acForm,
"frmSalesCategoryDialog")

'If frmSalesCategoryDialog has been closed, cancel the report
If intObjectState = 0 Then   'frmSalesCategoryDialog has been cancelled
MsgBox "Report cancelled"
Cancel = True
End If
End Sub
```

The DoCmd object is used to open frmSalesCategoryDialog. After it's opened, the user can cancel the action, which would mean he did not intend to run the report. The SysCmd function interrogates the state of frmSalesCategoryDialog. If it is not opened, then the report is cancelled. If the user selected Continue on frmSalesCategoryDialog, the form is hidden. Later, the dates selected are printed in a text box in the Report Header section of the report.

> **THE SysCmd FUNCTION**
>
> The SysCmd function can be used to determine whether an object is open, new, or has been changed but not saved. If the object referred to by the SysCmd function is not opened, it returns a value of zero.

The NoData Event

The NoData event occurs after Access has formatted a report for printing but with an empty recordset. If you select the year 1997 or 1998 from frmSalesCategoryDialog,

12

PROGRAMMING
IN REPORTS

this event triggers. The detail section of the Sales by Category report was modified to include a text box, which contains a printed message that there was no data selected (see Figure 12.3). Listing 12.2 is the VBA code for the NoData event.

LISTING 12.2. THE NoData EVENT FOR THE SALES BY CATEGORY REPORT.

```
Private Sub Report_NoData(Cancel As Integer)
Me.Section(acGroupLevel1Header).Visible = False
Me.Section(acDetail).Visible = True
Me![txtMessage] = "No Data To Report"
End Sub
```

Note that the first group level is hidden, whereas the detail section is made visible. This is just the opposite of the report in design mode.

FIGURE 12.3.

Sales by Category report with the No Data to Report message.

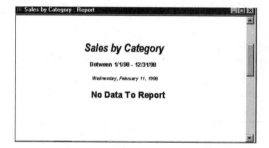

The Page Event

The Page event occurs after Access formats a page of a report for printing but before the page is printed. This can be used to add some finishing touches to the page. For example, the VBA code in Listing 12.3 prints a blue horizontal line 1/4-inch above the page footer using the RGB function.

LISTING 12.3. THE Page EVENT FOR THE SALES CATEGORY REPORT.

```
Private Sub Report_Page()
Dim plngLineColor As Long
plngLineColor = RGB(0, 0, 255)
Me.Line (0, Me.ScaleHeight - 360)-(Me.ScaleWidth, Me.ScaleHeight - 360),
➥plngLineColor
End Sub
```

The Error Event

The Error event can trigger for situations such as no permissions to the query, table/query not available, or the table/query is held exclusively by another user. Listing 12.4 is a generic VBA routine that displays an error code and description. After the message box is acknowledged, the report is cancelled. The Close event closes frmSalesCategoryDialog.

LISTING 12.4. THE Error EVENT FOR THE SALES BY CATEGORY REPORT.

```
Private Sub Report_Error(DataErr As Integer, Response As Integer)
 Dim pstrErrMessage As String
 pstrErrMessage = "Error: " & CStr(DataErr) & " - "
 pstrErrMessage = pstrErrMessage & Application.AccessError(DataErr)
 MsgBox pstrErrMessage
 Response = acDataErrContinue
End Sub
```

The Close Event

The Close event occurs when the report is closed and removed from the screen. The following VBA code in Listing 12.5 illustrates that frmSalesCategoryDialog is closed.

LISTING 12.5. THE Close EVENT FOR THE SALES BY CATEGORY REPORT.

```
Private Sub Report_Close()
DoCmd.Close acForm, "frmSalesCategoryDialog"
End Sub
```

Methods of the Report Object

Table 12.3 lists the methods of the Report object. Earlier, the Page event illustrated the Line method used in the Sales by Category report.

TABLE 12.3. METHODS OF THE Report OBJECT.

Method	Description
Circle	Draws a circle, an ellipse, or an arc when the Print event occurs
DefaultControl	Returns a Control object for which you can set default properties
Line	Draws a line or rectangle when the Print event occurs
Print	Prints text on a Report object

continues

TABLE 12.3. CONTINUED

Method	Description
Pset	Sets a point on a Report object to a specified color when the Print event occurs
Scale	Defines the coordinate system for a Report object
TextHeight	Returns the height of a text string as printed in the current font of a Report object
TextWidth	Returns the width of a text string as printed in the current font of a Report object

Report Section Property

The Section property of the Report object is used to identify a section and provide access to its properties. The Section property uses a read-only integer data type to reference a particular section. Simply, the Section property is an array of all its existing sections in the report specified by this integer value. Table 12.4 describes each section and its integer value, constant, and description.

TABLE 12.4. SECTIONS OF THE Report OBJECT.

Integer Value	Constant	Section Description
0	acDetail	Detail Section of the report
1	acHeader	Report Header Section
2	acFooter	Report Footer Section
3	acPageHeader	Report Page Header Section
4	acPageFooter	Report Page Footer Section
5	acGroupLevel1Header	Group1 Header Section
6	acGroupLevel1Footer	Group1 Footer Section
7	acGroupLevel2Header	Group2 Header Section
8	acGroupLevel2Footer	Group2 Footer Section

If a report has additional group-level sections, the header/footer pairs are numbered consecutively beginning with 9. In the earlier example when producing the Sales by Category report, the NoData event used VBA code to hide the Grouping by Category header and make the detail section of the report visible using these statements.

```
Me.Section(acGroupLevel1Header).Visible = False
Me.Section(acDetail).Visible = True
```

Report Section Events

All sections of a report, Report Header/Footer, Group Header/Footer, and Detail can be programmed to react to the Format event, Print event, and Retreat event. The Page Header/Footer sections can be programmed to react only to the Format event and Print event. Each Section event is described next.

The Format Event

The Format event executes code attached to a section's OnFormat event property when Microsoft Access determines what data should be in that section but before it formats the section for previewing or printing.

For group headers, the Format event triggers at each group change. At this point, the data in the group header along with the data in the first record of the detail section is available. For group footers, the Format event triggers at each group change, with the data in the group footer along with the last record in the detail section being available.

For the detail section, this event triggers for each new record in the section, just prior to Access formatting the data in the record. Again, at this point, the data in the current record is made available.

Typically, the Format event is used to provide additional formatting based on conditions provided by the data. The Yellow Highlighter listed in the next section provides an example.

The Print Event

The Print event executes code that has been attached to a section's OnPrint event property after the data in that report section has been formatted for printing but before the section has been printed.

For group headers, the Print event triggers at each group change. At this point, the data in the group header along with the data in the first record of the detail section is available. For group footers, the Format event triggers at each group change, with the data in the group footer along with the last record in the detail section being available.

Typically, the Print event for a section is used to determine a count. The Yellow Highlighter listed in the next section provides an example.

The Retreat Event

If a group level's KeepTogether property is set to Whole Group or With Detail Row, Microsoft Access formats the group header and then checks to ensure that both the group header and the first row or group fit on the page. If both sections cannot be printed on the same page, Microsoft Access backs up to a necessary location so that succeeding sections print on the next page. In this case, the Retreat event occurs for each section.

Code that you place in the Format event for each report section might be needed in the Retreat event to reverse an action. For example, a calculation incrementing a value in the Format event might need to decrease that value in the Retreat event.

THE FORMATCOUNT AND PRINTCOUNT PROPERTIES

The FormatCount property determines the number of times the OnFormat property has been evaluated for the current section on a report. Microsoft Access increments a section's FormatCount property each time it executes the Format event for that section. When formatting the next section, the FormatCount property is reset to one.

The PrintCount property is used to determine the number of times the OnPrint property has been evaluated for the current section of a report. Microsoft Access increments a section's PrintCount property each time the Print event has triggered. This can be useful to determine a running total in a group.

The Yellow Highlighter Example for the Products by Category Report

The Northwind Traders database includes the Products by Category report. This report is a three-column report that lists the units in stock for each product name within a category. This report illustrates section events for the Report Footer, Category Name Header/Footer, and Detail sections.

Assume that each product name with a quantity of zero for units in stock needs to be yellow highlighted. Additionally, the group footer for each category displays a count of the total number of products highlighted, whereas the report footer indicates the page numbers where product names with a quantity of zero units in stock appear. Figure 12.4 shows page two of the modified Products by Category report.

THE RGB AND QBCOLOR FUNCTIONS

You can use the RGB (0–255,0–255,0–255) function to set the color of an object such as the background color of the detail section. Its three arguments represent the intensity of red, green, and blue respectively. RGB(255,255,0) represents the color yellow.

You can also use the QBColor (color) function to set the color of an object. The color argument is a whole number in the range of 0–15, which means the function is limited to sixteen colors. QBColor(6) represents the color yellow.

FIGURE 12.4.

Products by Category report with yellow highlighting.

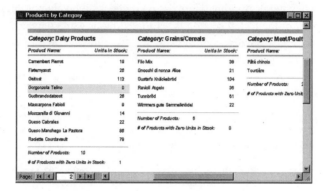

To incorporate this functionality into the report, open the Products by Category report in design mode and then complete the following steps.

1. Change the Backstyle property of the ProductName and UnitsInStock controls to Transparent. This allows for the background color of the section to appear through the controls.

2. Add a text box with a name of txtTotalHighlighted to the CategoryName footer. Change the Caption property on its associated label to *# of Products with Zero Units in Stock.*

3. In the Report Footer, create a text box with a name of txtPageNos. Change the name of the associated label to lblRptPageNos. This text box will be used to refer to pages in the report that report units in stock of zero.

4. In the Declarations section of the report, declare two variables as shown next. MintUnitsInStock will be used to store a count of product names with units in stock of zero, whereas mstrReportPageNos will store the page numbers for product names with units in stock of zero. See Listing 12.6.

LISTING 12.6. THE DECLARATION SECTION FOR THE PRODUCTS BY CATEGORY REPORT.

```
Option Compare Database
Option Explicit
Private mintUnitsInStock As Integer
Private mblReportFooterMessage As Boolean
Private mstrReportPageNos As String
```

The On Format event for the Detail section triggers before Microsoft Access formats the section for previewing or printing. Here the code checks the value of UnitsInStock. The background color of the Detail section is set to yellow or white depending on the value contained in the UnitsInStock control using the RGB function. See Listing 12.7.

LISTING 12.7. THE OnFormat EVENT FOR THE DETAIL SECTION OF THE PRODUCTS BY CATEGORY REPORT.

```
Private Sub Detail_Format(Cancel As Integer, FormatCount As Integer)
If Me![UnitsInStock] = 0 Then
Me.Section(acDetail).BackColor = RGB(255, 255, 0) 'Yellow
Else
Me.Section(acDetail).BackColor = RGB(255, 255, 255) 'White
End If
```

The OnPrint event for the Detail section triggers for each new record in the section. Here is where mintUnitsInstock is incremented. Placing the code here instead of the OnFormat event is more predicatable, as this represents a line ready to print. See Listing 12.8.

LISTING 12.8. THE OnPrint EVENT FOR THE DETAIL SECTION OF THE PRODUCTS BY CATEGORY REPORT.

```
Private Sub Detail_Print(Cancel As Integer, PrintCount As Integer)
If Me![UnitsInStock] = 0 Then
mintUnitsInStock = mintUnitsInStock + 1
End If
End Sub
```

A group header is created with the change of a category in the report. When this happens, VBA code resets the value of the counter back to zero. See Listing 12.9.

LISTING 12.9. THE OnFormat EVENT FOR THE GROUP HEADER SECTION OF THE PRODUCTS BY CATEGORY REPORT.

```
Private Sub GroupHeader0_Format(Cancel As Integer, FormatCount As Integer)
'Reset the counter for Units in Stock
'at each Group level
```

```
mintUnitsInStock = 0
End Sub
```

When a change has occurred within a category, the `CategoryName` footer is printed. The following code moves the value of `mintUnitsInStock` to `txtTotalHighlighted` to be printed. Additionally, if indeed there were units in stock with a quantity of zero, the value of `mblReportFooterMessage` is set to True. Initially, the value of `mblReportFooterMessage` had been set to False in the `Open` event of the report. Also note the use of the `Page` property (`Me.Page`). This property, which has the current page number, is stored in the variable `mstrReportPageNos`. See Listing 12.10.

LISTING 12.10. THE `OnPrint` EVENT FOR THE GROUP FOOTER SECTION OF THE PRODUCTS BY CATEGORY REPORT.

```
Private Sub GroupFooter1_Print(Cancel As Integer, PrintCount As Integer)
Me![txtTotalHighlighted].Value = mintUnitsInStock
If Me![txtTotalHighlighted].Value > 0 Then
mblReportFooterMessage = True
mstrReportPageNos = mstrReportPageNos & Me.Page & ", "
End If
End Sub
```

The `OnFormat` event of the Report Footer contains VBA code, which determines whether or not to display the two controls in the Report Footer based on the value of `mblReportFooterMessage`. If `mblReportFooter` message has been set to True, the value of `txtPageNos` is formatted to list the page numbers where units in stock of zero can be found in the report. See Listing 12.11.

LISTING 12.11. THE `OnFormat` EVENT FOR THE REPORT FOOTER SECTION OF THE PRODUCTS BY CATEGORY REPORT.

```
Private Sub ReportFooter_Format(Cancel As Integer, FormatCount As Integer)
If Not mblReportFooterMessage Then
Me![lblRptPageNos].Visible = False
Me![txtPageNos].Visible = False
Else
Me![txtPageNos] = Left$(mstrReportPageNos, Len(mstrReportPageNos) - 2)
End If
End Sub
```

Next is a listing of the last page of the Products by Category report displaying the Report Footer section (see Figure 12.5). Although the report highlights only units in stock with a quantity of zero, it could have been enhanced in similar fashion as the Sales Category report displaying a form to the user requesting the level of units in stock that should be highlighted, if any.

FIGURE 12.5.
Report Footer for the Products by Category report.

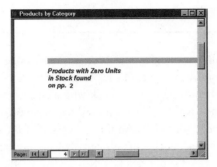

Sorting and Grouping

You can design Microsoft Access reports to have up to 25 sections:

- Five standard sections including the Report Header/Footer, Page Header/Footer, and the Detail
- Up to ten groups with both a Header and Footer

Figure 12.6 is the Summary of Sales by Year report that is included in the Northwind Traders database, which illustrates a report containing seven sections. Although seven sections are visible, only the Report Header, Page Header, ShippedDate Header, ShippedDate Footer, and the Page Footer will print data. The Detail and Report Footer sections have no height, which means nothing will print in these sections.

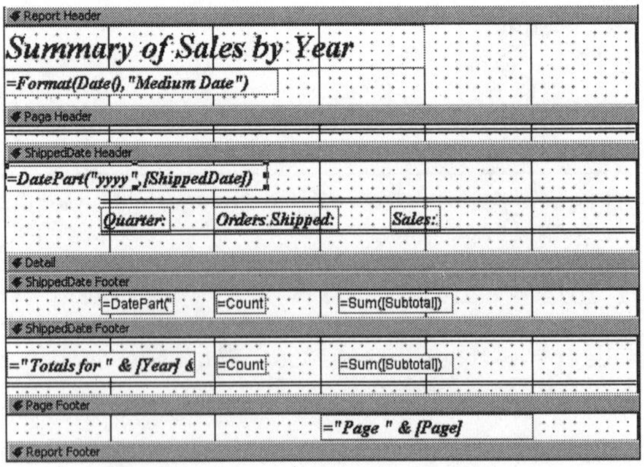

FIGURE 12.6.
Design mode of the Summary of Sales by Year report.

When this report is executed, order counts are generated by quarter within year. Figure 12.7's Sorting and Grouping dialog form defines how the report is to be grouped and sorted.

FIGURE 12.7.

Sorting and Grouping dialog box for the Summary of Sales by Year report.

Setting the group header/footer properties for each grouping expression creates group headers/footers. If you examine the Sorting and Grouping dialog box for this report, you will find the information displayed in Table 12.5.

TABLE 12.5. SORTING AND GROUPING OPTIONS.

Field/ Expression	Group Header	Group Footer	Group On	Group Interval	Keep Together
ShippedDate	Yes	Yes	Year	1	Whole Group
ShippedDate	No	Yes	Qtr	1	No

Referring to Group Levels

Microsoft Access treats group levels similar to sections, that is, group levels are treated as an array. The following code executed in the debug window displays the current property for the first group level.

```
?  Reports![Summary of Sales by Year].GroupLevel(0).GroupOn
'Will return a value of  5
?  Reports![Summary of Sales by Year].GroupLevel(0).GroupInterval
'Will return a value of  2
?  Reports![Summary of Sales by Year].GroupLevel(0).KeepTogether
'Will return a value of  1
```

GroupLevel Properties

Group levels alone cannot be accessed, but the properties they expose are available through code. They can be set in design mode or the Open event of the report only. Here are the properties exposed by the GroupLevel:

- GroupHeader/Footer
- GroupOn
- GroupInterval

- KeepTogether
- SortOrder
- ControlSource

GroupHeader/Footer Property

This property indicates whether or not a specific group level displays a Header or Footer section. The property is read-only and returns True (–1), the section exists or False (0), the section does not exist. Using the Summary of Sales by Year report and the Debugger, the following line of code returns a value of True.

```
? Reports![Summary of Sales by Year].GroupLevel(1).GroupFooter
```

GroupOn Property

This property specifies how the data is to be grouped in a report. Table 12.6 indicates possible values.

TABLE 12.6. GroupOn PROPERTY SETTINGS.

Setting	Value
Each Value	0
Prefix Characters	1
Year	2
Qtr	3
Month	4
Week	5
Day	6
Hour	7
Minute	8
Interval	9

Using the Summary of Sales by Year report and the Debugger, the following line of code returns a value of 3, meaning the grouping was by quarter.

```
? Reports![Summary of Sales by Year].GroupLevel(1).GroupOn
```

GroupInterval Property

This property is used in conjunction with the GroupOn property to specify a further grouping of data. The interval is dependent upon the GroupOn setting. For example, if the

GroupOn value is 6 (Day) and the GroupInterval is set to 2, the data returned will be biweekly.

KeepTogether Property

This property indicates whether the data in the group level is kept together when printed. Possible values are listed in Table 12.7.

TABLE 12.7. KeepTogether SETTINGS.

Setting	Value	Comments
No	0	No attempt is made to keep header, footer, and detail on same page.
Whole Group	1	Access attempts to print header, detail, and footer on the same page.
With First Detail	2	Access attempts to print the header and its first detail line on the same page.

Using the Summary of Sales by Year ereport and the Debugger, the following line of code returns a value of 1, meaning a desire to keep the header, detail, and footer on the same page.

```
? Reports![Summary of Sales by Year].GroupLevel(0).KeepTogether
```

ControlSource Property

This property indicates the field or expression on which the group is grouped/sorted. Using the Summary of Sales by Year report and the Debugger, the following line of code returns a value of ShippedDate.

```
?  Reports![Summary of Sales by Year].GroupLevel(0).ControlSource
```

SortOrder Property

This property is used to set the sorting order of rows in the detail section of a group level. Used in conjunction with the ControlSource property, it defines a sort sequence. Possible values are 0 (ascending) and –1 (descending). Using the Summary of Sales by Year report and the Debugger, the following line of code returns a value of False, meaning the data was sorted by ShippedDate in ascending order.

```
?  Reports![Summary of Sales by Year].GroupLevel(0).SortOrder
```

An Example Using the Summary of Sales by Year Report

The VBA code in Listing 12.12 was placed in the Open event of the Summary of Sales by Year report. It illustrates overriding some of the properties of GroupLevel(1), which was the grouping by quarter. Instead of grouping by quarter, the grouping is done by month.

LISTING 12.12. THE Open EVENT OF THE SUMMARY OF SALES BY YEAR REPORT.

```
Private Sub Report_Open(Cancel As Integer)
Dim pstrFilter As String
Const dblQuote As String = """"
pstrFilter = "=DatePart(" & dblQuote & "m" & dblQuote & ",[ShippedDate])"
Me![QuarterLabel].Caption = "Month"
Me![Quarter].ControlSource = pstrFilter
Me.GroupLevel(1).GroupOn = 4 'Group by month
Me.GroupLevel(1).GroupInterval = 1
Me.GroupLevel(1).SortOrder = False 'Ascending order
End Sub
```

Figure 12.8 shows the results of the modified report.

FIGURE 12.8.

Summary of Sales by Year Report grouping by month.

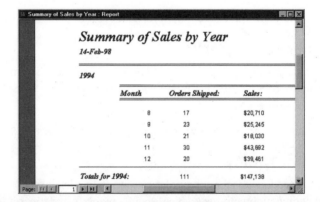

THE CREATEREPORT AND CREATEGROUPLEVEL FUNCTIONS

Up to this point, all examples have illustrated reports opened in design mode from the Interactive Development Environment (IDE). VBA code can be used to create reports on-the-fly, such as building a custom report wizard requesting from the user a choice of fields on which to group data. Microsoft Access provides two functions for doing this: the `CreateReport` and `CreateGroupLevel` functions.

The `CreateReport` function enables you to create a report using VBA code. When this function is executed, it creates a report in design mode containing a Page Header, Detail, and Page Footer section. The syntax of the function is `CreateReport([database],[reporttemplate])` where the first argument indicates the database containing the report template, and the second argument identifies the template for creating the report. If the latter is left blank, this function uses the report template found in the Forms/Report tab of Tools/Options.

The `CreateGroupLevel` function can be used in conjunction with the `CreateReport` function to include grouping/sorting in the report. The syntax of the function is `CreateGroupLevel(report,expression,header,footer)`. The `report` argument indicates the name of the report, which will contain the new group level, the `expression` is the field/expression on which to group, whereas the `header` and `footer` arguments indicate whether or not to create each of these. A value of True for both arguments creates both a group header and a group footer, whereas a value of False will not create a group header or group footer.

Using a Form to Select Reports and Conditions

This next section illustrates how to create a Microsoft Access dialog form, which will list all reports in the database for previewing or printing. It ties together the entire application nicely.

Creating a Report Dialog Form

This example illustrates using a dialog form to create a report menu. The form, `frmReportDialog`, contains a list box and a frame with two option buttons (see Figure 12.9). When a report name is double-clicked in the list box, the `DoCmd` object generates the report using the Print Preview or Print option.

The VBA code that populates the list box is found in the `Load` event of `frmReportDialog`. To list all the reports in the database, the code enumerates the Documents collection of the `Reports Container` object using the `Name` property. As each report name is made available, it is added to the `RowSource` property. When complete, the list box contains a list of all reports in the database. See Listing 12.13.

FIGURE 12.9.

*Report dialog
form for the
Northwind
Traders database.*

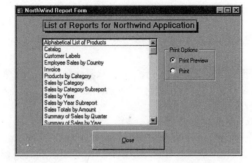

LISTING 12.13. THE Load EVENT FOR FORM frmReportDialog.

```
Private Sub Form_Load()
Dim db As Database
Dim docDef As Document
Set db = CurrentDb()
With db.Containers![Reports]
For Each docDef In .Documents
lstReportNames.RowSource = lstReportNames.RowSource & docDef.Name & ";"
Next docDef
End With
End Sub
```

The VBA code for the double-click event of lstReportNames sets the Print option of the
DoCmd object and then opens the report (see Listing 12.14). Opening the Sales by
Category report discussed earlier opens a form dialog box that will request information
from the user.

LISTING 12.14. THE DblClick EVENT FOR LIST BOX lstReportNames.

```
Private Sub lstReportNames_DblClick(Cancel As Integer)
Dim intViewType As Integer
Select Case Me![fraPrintOptions].Value
Case 1   'Print preview
intViewType = acViewPreview
Case Else    'Print the report
intViewType = acViewNormal
End Select
DoCmd.OpenReport ReportName:=lstReportNames.Value, View:=intViewType
End Sub
```

Summary

The `Application` object includes a Reports collection, which contains open Microsoft Access reports, or the `Report` object. The `Report` object can be manipulated programmatically through the use of VBA code. The events of the `Report` object are `Open` event, `Activate` event, `Deactivate` event, `NoData` event, `Page` event, `Error` event, and the `Close` event.

Reports are divided into sections. The five standard sections of a report are the Report Header/Footer, Page Header/Footer, and the Detail. Additionally, a report can be designed for up to ten group-level sections. Properties of each section in a report can be reference in code and respond to events. The section events are the `OnFormat` event, `OnPrint` event, and the `OnRetreat` event.

Finally, to list all the designed reports in a database, enumerate the Documents collection of the `Reports Container` object using the `Name` property. By creating a report dialog form, you will do an excellent job of tying the application together.

12

PROGRAMMING IN REPORTS

CHAPTER 13

Producing Mailings

IN THIS CHAPTER

Many times, the data contained in databases needs to be available to other people—people who might not have access to the database. When considering the mailing process, one has to decide exactly what is going to be mailed and to whom it is going to be mailed. A user might need to mail a letter to all employees in a database. A developer might need to email an object to a project manager for approval. This chapter covers both aspects—regular mail (snail-mail) and email. It also covers customization of labels as well as label wizards and mail merge. On the email side, the chapter covers how to email an object from Access 97 via the office network.

A Mailing Process

Many things need to be considered before the process of a mailing task can begin. Printing labels is a little trickier than simply clicking the Print button from the Print Preview of a report. You need to address the following issues:

- What kind of labels are being used—sheet or continuous?
- What kind of printer will be printing the labels?
- Will the same printer be used every time for these particular labels?
- How many labels are being printed at one time?
- Which font is being used?
- Will this database be used by people other than the developer?
- What is the default printer?

Start with the first question—What kind of labels are being used? If the labels have small holes on the edges of the paper and one sheet is connected to another sheet, they are probably continuous labels. The small holes on the edges indicate that they are tractor-feed labels usually meant for a dot-matrix printer. If the labels are on a single sheet, they are probably meant for a laser, inkjet, or deskjet printer.

> **NOTE**
>
> Tractor-feed laser printers do exist. Big government offices, like the IRS, use them. They are priced on the high end, and most companies use regular lasers or dot-matrix printers instead.

What printer are the labels being printed on? If they are tractor-feed labels, they should go through a dot-matrix printer. Sheet labels, however, can go through a dot-matrix, laser, inkjet, or deskjet printer.

How many labels are being printed at one time, and what font is being used for those labels? Some developers like to make their labels artistic. They use larger pitches and TrueType fonts, and sometimes have logos. The more artistic the label, the slower the print job. Having very artistic labels is fine for a few labels, but if the number of labels is large, the printer could be tied up for hours. One way to increase the speed of a large print job is to change the font being used.

Using the Label Wizard

A large percentage of databases contain some kind of table that tracks people information—Name, Address, City, State, Zip Code. With this information, mailings can be created. Access offers several report wizards that create sophisticated reports by having the developer answer a few questions. This section shows how to create mailings with the Access Label Wizard.

To create mailing labels, whether with a wizard or without, it is highly recommended that there be an existing source of records that contain the information found on mailing labels. In fact, if a wizard is used to create anything other than a table, a record source must be stated before the wizard will execute. The following examples are based on a table called `Employees`. This table contains the following fields:

```
LastName

FirstName

Title

TitleofCourtesy

BirthDate

HireDate

Address

City

Region

PostalCode

Country
```

HomePhone

Extension

Photo

Notes

ReportsTo

To create a mailing label using the wizard, it is necessary to click the Reports tab in the database container and click the New button. In Figure 13.1, the Label Wizard is selected. The Employees table is selected to be the source for the wizard.

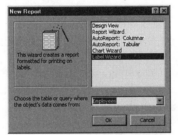

FIGURE 13.1.

The Employees
*table is selected
for the Label
Wizard.*

NOTE

Some wizards, whether form or report wizards, cannot be executed without a data source. The data source for each can be found in the drop-down box on the New Form or New Report dialog box.

After selecting a data source for the wizard, click OK to continue. The great thing about wizards is that they do the bulk of work concerning the operation being performed. In this case, the Label Wizard is doing the sizing and centering of a label and entering in all the measurements concerning the labels being used. Figure 13.2 shows the next step in the Label Wizard process.

Users can select an Avery label by choosing the corresponding Unit of Measure and Label Type from the option boxes that appear in the middle of the form shown in Figure 13.2. The different types of label formats are discussed later in this chapter, in the section "Custom Label Formats." The next dialog box of the Label Wizard deals with the font and color of the text on the labels. This screen is shown in Figure 13.3. On this screen, a developer can choose from 31 different fonts. Depending on the font chosen, the developer can also choose the font size, more commonly referred to as the pitch.

FIGURE 13.2.

Selecting the label format is the next step in the Label Wizard.

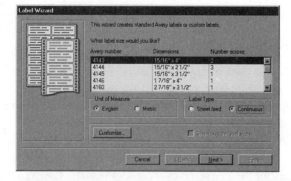

CAUTION

Even though a font size can run up to 72 points (there are 72 points to 1 inch), it is recommended that the smaller font sizes be used. Common sense dictates that a mailing label that is 2 inches tall cannot have 3 lines of text that are 1 inch tall each.

FIGURE 13.3.

Selecting the text format for the label is the next step.

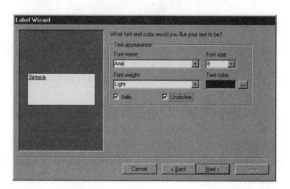

Font weight and text color can also be selected. The Access Label Wizard gives the developer the options to make the text appear italicized and underlined. To select these options, click the box that appears next to the desired option. These options are toggles, meaning that a subsequent click removes the check mark. Toggles are switches that are either on or off, like a light switch.

The left side of the screen contains a simulated label. As changes are made to the text options, these changes are reflected on the simulated label on the left of the screen. In Figure 13.3, the Italic and Underline options are on, and the word "Sample" on the label to the left appears italicized and underlined. Remember, this simulation contains only one line. When choosing font and size, it is important to remember that more than one line will need to appear on the label.

Click Next > to get to the third screen in the Label Wizard. On this screen, Access is asking how the label is to be filled out. In Figure 13.4, different fields appear on the label. You can add these fields to the prototype label by highlighting the desired field and pressing > or by double-clicking the field. You can also choose the punctuation that is to appear on every label. For example, it is grammatically correct to have a comma appear after the name of a city and before the name of a state on a mailing label, but it is an unnecessary character for the postal optical character readers. Carriage returns, spaces, punctuation, and literal words are entered onto the prototype. As they appear on the prototype, so will they appear on every label.

FIGURE 13.4.

The prototype represents how each label will appear.

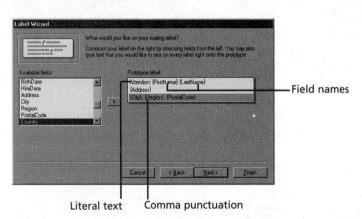

Field names

Literal text   Comma punctuation

In Figure 13.4, three carriage returns are included on the prototype (pressing Enter brings the focus to the next line down). Using the mouse to click the next line down works too. The City field is immediately followed by a comma and a space. These might be hard to see but they are present. The label is slightly different from the basic name, address, city, state, zip label in that there is an attention line. To get the word *Attention* to appear, it was typed directly onto the label prototype. The word *Attention* will appear on every label.

Press Next > to move to the fourth screen in the Label Wizard. This is where the developer can specify the Sort Order of the mailing labels. In Figure 13.5, the PostalCode was selected as the only sort order. This is an excellent feature for companies that utilize the bulk mailing rates offered by the postal service. A developer can choose one field or multiple fields for the sort order. All the fields that are selected here will appear on the Sort Order of the report's Design view.

Figure 13.5.

Select the fields for the sort order of the mailing labels.

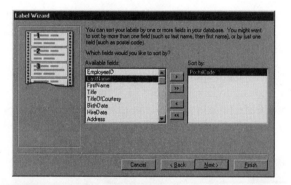

13

PRODUCING MAILINGS

The last of the five screens in the Label Wizard is shown in Figure 13.6. On this screen, you can opt to keep the name of the report as it is assigned by the Access Wizard or remove the current name and type a new one. Reports have only two views: Design and Preview. In this screen, you can choose the view to go into when the Finish button is clicked. A small box appears near the bottom of the screen. When this box is checked,

Access displays additional Help at the time of creation of the new report. This Help file demonstrates how to customize the label report.

Figure 13.6.

The final screen in the Label Wizard gives the developer the chance to rename the report and choose the view to go into.

Click Finish to create the label report. If you need to go back to previous screens to change labels, fields, or options, you can do so by clicking < Back. The < Back button allows you to go all the way back to the first screen in the wizard if so desired.

Because the Modify the Label Design option was checked on the last wizard screen, the report is brought up in Design view. In Figure 13.7, the Sorting and Grouping dialog box is onscreen. The PostalCode field is already placed in the cell. This act was performed by the Access Label Wizard based on the information entered on the Sorting screen.

Figure 13.7.

The Sorting and Grouping information is already in place based on the answers given in the Sorting screen in the Access Label Wizard.

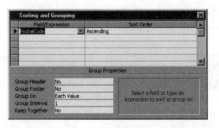

Looking at the fields on the screen, the first few fields have the word TRIM before the name of the field. This was added by the wizard; if the same field were pulled down to the report, TRIM would not appear on the field. In Figure 13.8, the properties box for the Address field is shown. On the Control Source for the field, this expression appears as follows:

```
=Trim([Address])
```

When users enter data into tables and forms, invariably some records have some fields that have extra spaces. If one of the fields on the label has additional spaces, the label looks uneven. That is why the word TRIM appears in the Control Source of the fields on the label. The word TRIM refers to the TRIM function. The TRIM function removes the leading and trailing spaces found in a field, ensuring that the label is left-aligned.

> ### TIP
>
> Three TRIM functions are available: LTRIM, RTRIM, and TRIM. LTRIM removes all the spaces to the left of an expression. RTRIM removes all the spaces following an expression. TRIM removes all the spaces before and after an expression.

FIGURE 13.8.

The fields created by the Label Wizard have the TRIM *function associated with them.*

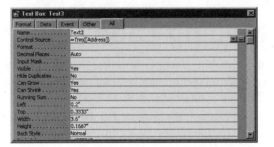

13

PRODUCING
MAILINGS

Several things are going on in Figure 13.8. The TRIM function is being performed on some of the fields in the label. The FirstName and LastName fields were automatically concatenated by the wizard. A question was raised earlier about records that have two lines of address in the Address field. Notice that the fields have the Can Shrink and Can Grow properties turned on. Having these properties turned on compensates for fields in which the address might be longer than the field drawn for it. Because the Can Grow property is set to Yes, the entire address prints. Conversely, the City field also has the Can Shrink property set to Yes. This means that if the city is only a couple of letters long, the entire field size is not used. The result is shown in Figure 13.9.

The Access Label Wizard helps developers turn out advanced labels in a short amount of time. Certain functions, properties, and expressions are created based on the answers to a few simple questions. The next section covers the printing of the labels and some examples.

FIGURE 13.9.

The Can Shrink *and* Can Grow *properties make the labels look better.*

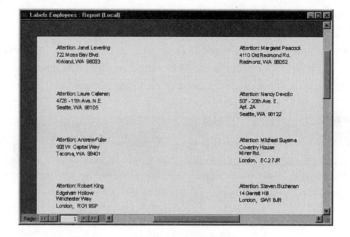

Printing Mailing Labels

You cannot discuss printing mailing labels without touching on the printer fonts. Three types of fonts are available: TrueType, system, and printer. TrueType fonts are the fancy fonts that have a small TT icon associated with them. System fonts are those that come with Windows. Printer fonts are the fonts contained in the printer itself. System fonts and printer fonts are faster than TrueType fonts. How can you tell which font is which? There are a few ways. The first is to refer to the documentation that comes with the software, computer, and printer being used. That can be a hassle at times. An easier way is to go to the properties of a field on the label. Go to the Font property and click the drop-down box, as shown in Figure 13.10.

FIGURE 13.10.

Printer and system fonts are faster than TrueType fonts.

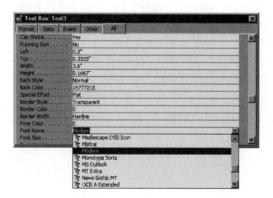

The TrueType fonts have the small TT icon to the left of the name. The system fonts and printer fonts have the "small sheet of paper leaving a printer" icon to the left. Printer fonts are the fastest fonts and have the word "Printer" following the name of the font. The drawback to using printer fonts is that they are not as attractive as the TrueType fonts. A good rule of thumb to follow: The more labels to be printed, the less attractive they need to be.

> ### CAUTION
>
> With TrueType fonts, the pitch can actually be as small as 1 point (4 points is the smallest legible font). When the font is changed to a printer font, the pitch is usually 8 or 10 points. This change in size affects the output. Fewer lines per label fit. Make sure that when the font is changed, the label is viewed in Print Preview mode first.

If the database is used on a network or is developed for mass distribution, complications with reports can arise. Every report, whether it be a label report or a regular report, can have the printer settings saved with it. For example, the Labels Employees report is used by the developer only. The developer can save the printer settings with the report. Every time that report is executed, the developer can set the report to go to a specific printer, the HP LaserJet 4. The developer does this by selecting File|Page Setup and clicking the Page tab. As shown in Figure 13.11, the report can be saved to the default printer or a specific printer.

13

PRODUCING
MAILINGS

FIGURE 13.11.

Reports can be saved to specific printers.

If the Use Specific Printer option is selected, the Printer button is activated. Clicking this button brings up the Page Setup dialog box. Here, the report can be saved to a specific printer, such as the HP LaserJet 4, as shown in Figure 13.12. If this report is used by other people, however, they might not have access to the HP LaserJet 4. In this case, every time the Labels Employees report is executed, an error will result. The developer needs to save the report to the default printer—whether the default printer is the HP LaserJet 4. This way, every person who uses the Labels Employees report can execute the report without errors from Access, because everyone has a default printer. Each person needs to specify his own label printer and save the report.

FIGURE 13.12.

Setting the specific printer for a report.

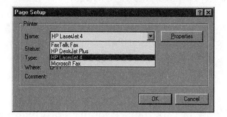

From machine to machine, the default printer can vary. If there are multiple printers, how can you tell which printer is your default printer? Pull up Printers from the Settings icon in the Start menu of Windows 95, or pull up the Control Panel for the machine and select Printers. In Figure 13.13, three printers are associated with this machine.

FIGURE 13.13.

The properties of the printer show that it is the default printer for this machine.

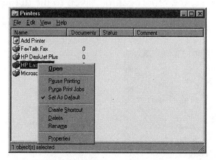

Right-clicking the printer brings up the shortcut list. The default printer line has a check to the left indicating that the HP LaserJet 4 is the default printer for this machine. Even though initially a report is saved to the default printer, the labels still need to come out of another printer that is not the default. On a machine-by-machine basis, each report should be resaved to the printer that produces the labels.

Custom Label Formats

Designing labels manually is not as difficult as some might think. One of the reasons developers design labels manually is that the labels being used are not one of the 197 predefined Avery labels. An Access Label Wizard can help here too. The Customize feature of the Label Wizard was touched on earlier. With this feature, Access can help you create a template for a box of labels that can be used again and again.

> **NOTE**
>
> Before the manual design of labels can begin, it is necessary to cover a few constants about printers. These constants pertain only to the printer fonts. Printer fonts are printer-specific, meaning that a printer font found on an Epson might not be exactly like the one found on a Panasonic. Printer fonts are usually available in a 10-point pitch. The pitch is important in determining how many lines there are per page. Sheet printers (like laser printers) can hold up to 60 lines per page. Continuous printers (like tractor-feed printers) can hold as many as 66 lines per page.

For this example, the label that needs to be manually created is for a dot-matrix printer. To create a label manually, you need to have a sheet of the labels within arm's reach and a good ruler. Go to the Reports tab of the database container. After the printer has been selected, you must change the default printer of the computer to match the printer for the labels. You can do this by selecting Printers from the Windows Control Panel, which you can bring up by clicking Start. Highlight the desired printer and choose File|Set As Default. Again from the File pull-down menu, select the Properties for the desired printer, and click the Paper tab. From the Paper Size box, double-click the Custom icon. This action brings up the User-Defined Size dialog box, shown in Figure 13.14. This is where you enter the label size.

FIGURE 13.14.

Custom dot-matrix labels are partially defined in the Printer Properties.

13

PRODUCING
MAILINGS

Select the unit of measure from the Unit option box. The paper size is determined by a measurement of a sheet of the labels. Measure from the left edge of the top-left label to the right edge of the top-right label. Include the gutter width (the area that is between the labels). This determines the Width of the labels. Determine the Length by measuring from the top of the first label to the top of the second label. This also includes any gutter that appears between the labels. Enter the numbers into their respective fields, click OK to save the Unit option box, and click OK to save the Properties box for the printer. Now that the properties for the desired printer have been set, the labels can be designed with the help of a wizard or via Design view. You can check the information you just entered into the Printer Properties by selecting File|Page Setup in Access. Click the Page tab.

After making all the changes via the Windows Control Panel, you can create the label report for a dot-matrix printer with or without the guidance of a Label Wizard. Return to Access to begin the creation of the labels. Select the Reports module and click New. Select the Data Source for the label by choosing an object from the drop-down list of existing tables and queries and then clicking the Design View option. This example covers creating a label without the help of a wizard.

NOTE

If the label being created is a label for a diskette or a shipping label, a data source does not need to be selected.

The report will automatically display the page header and footer. Select View|Page Header/Footer to remove the header and footer from the label, as shown in Figure 13.15. They are not needed for this type of report.

FIGURE 13.15.

The page header and footer are not needed for label reports.

Measure the label and change the detail section of the label to match the measurements of one label. To do so, click and drag the bottom edge or the right edge of the detail section. You can enter the exact measurement of the width into the Properties of the report and the exact measurement of the height into the Properties of the Detail section. The information that will appear on the labels can be added from the Field List or labels can be selected from the Toolbox, as shown in Figure 13.16.

FIGURE 13.16.

Items that appear on labels either come from the Field List or are created with labels from the Toolbox.

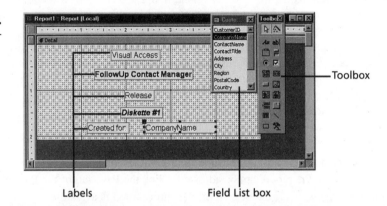

Labels

Field List box

Toolbox

> **TIP**
>
> You can create margins for the labels by making sure that all the objects that appear in the label—fields, labels, text boxes, and so on—are at least .02 inches from every edge of the detail section.

Multiple text fields can be added to any label. These fields can be concatenated to make the report look better. Usually, first-name and last-name fields are concatenated to make the flow of the entire name look more pleasing. Also, you should change all the fields' `Can Shrink` and `Can Grow` properties to Yes. You can complete this task in one stroke by highlighting all the fields on the label and pulling up the Properties sheet. This represents the properties for all the fields highlighted. Change the `Can Shrink` and `Can Grow` properties to Yes. For the `Can Grow` property to take effect, the fields below it cannot be touching it. For example, an address field might have two text lines in it; for the `Can Grow` property to take effect, the top of the City, State, Zip field cannot be touching the bottom of the Address field.

> **CAUTION**
>
> For the Can Grow property to be active, the field below it cannot *mathematically* be touching the Can Grow field. To check the mathematics of each field, pull up the properties of the Can Grow field. Add the value that appears in the Top field to the value that appears in the Height field. Here's an example: An Address field can be set to Can Grow. If the Top value of the Address field is .375" and the Height value is .1667", the two are added together to be .5417. The next text box should show the city, state, and zip. Usually, they are concatenated together. If the Top value of the concatenated text box is .5417, the Can Grow property of the address field is nullified. This means that if a record has an address field that contains more than one text line (like a suite number), the address field will not grow to accommodate the second text line. The Top value of the concatenated field should be something below .5417.

The label is almost ready for printing. Select File|Page Setup. Here is where the page information for the report can be adjusted. Click the Page tab of the Page Setup box. As shown in Figure 13.17, the default printer information is available.

FIGURE 13.17.

The default printer information can be seen here.

The paper size should already be set to User-defined size, and the Source should be set to Tractor. If not, you can make the changes here. Click the Margins tab and set all the margins to zero, as shown in Figure 13.18.

FIGURE 13.18.

The margins need to be changed.

Move to the Columns tab, shown in Figure 13.19. If there are multiple labels across the label page, the information is entered here. Row Spacing is the amount of space that is between the bottom of the first label and the top of the label below it. Column Spacing is the amount of space that appears between the right edge of the first label and the left edge of the label next to it. Make sure that the Same as Detail box in the Column Size area is checked.

FIGURE 13.19.

Multiple columns of labels can have their specifications entered here.

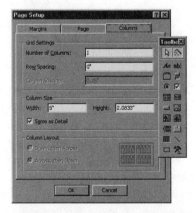

NOTE

If the default printer is not the dot-matrix printer, click the Specific Printer button and select the dot-matrix printer from the list.

The method for creating custom labels works well if the only person using the database is the one who created it, and if that person is going to use that database only on the machine on which it was developed. But what if a developer needs to create a database to be used by multiple people on various machines? A number of variables come into play; the user's default printer might be different from the developer's, for example. These issues will be addressed along with another option for creating a custom label—the Label Wizard.

In the Reports module of the database container, click New. Choose the desired table or query on which the new labels will be based. It is possible to create a new report without selecting a data source. Select the Label Wizard and click OK.

The first Label Wizard screen is where all the predefined labels are displayed. A button in the center of the form is labeled "Customize." Click that button to bring up the New Label Size screen, shown in Figure 13.20.

FIGURE 13.20.

New labels can be customized in the Label Wizard provided by Access 97.

Choose the Unit of Measure and Label Type before clicking the New button. The heart of the custom label process can be seen in Figure 13.21. Type the desired name of the new label being created. Press the Tab key once and confirm the Unit of Measure being used—an English measure (inches) ruler or a Metric ruler (centimeters). Press the Tab key to confirm the type of labels being used. If there are small tractor holes on the edges of the label paper, click the Continuous button. Press the Tab key again and enter the number of labels that go across the top of the label paper.

NOTE

The number entered for the Number Across field must be an integer from 1 to 20.

This is where the ruler comes into play. As shown in Figure 13.21, measurements need to be entered in eight stations to complete the new custom label. To move from station to station for this example, press the Tab key. Following is an explanation of the information to be entered in each station:

Station 1: Enter the height of the label itself in inches or centimeters.

Station 2: Enter the width of the label itself in inches or centimeters.

Station 3: Enter the number of inches or centimeters from the left edge of the label to the left edge of the label paper.

Station 4: Enter the number of inches or centimeters that should appear as the upper margin of the label itself.

Station 5: Enter the number of inches or centimeters that should appear as the left margin of the label itself.

Station 6: Enter the number of inches or centimeters from the right edge of the top-right label to the right edge of the label paper.

Station 7: Enter the number of inches or centimeters from the bottom edge of one label to the top edge of the next label (horizontal gutter).

Station 8: Enter the number of inches or centimeters from the left edge of one label to the right edge of the next label (vertical gutter).

FIGURE 13.21.

The heart of the custom label process.

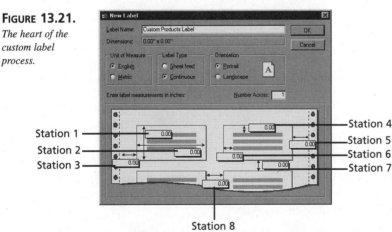

Station 1
Station 2
Station 3
Station 4
Station 5
Station 6
Station 7
Station 8

> **NOTE**
>
> A label must have a horizontal and vertical dimension set before the wizard can proceed. It is not possible to print on a label if station 2 and station 3 are not positive numbers.

After the new label is finished, click OK. The new custom label now appears in the New Label Size dialog box, as shown in Figure 13.22. The custom labels can be edited, duplicated, or deleted at any time.

FIGURE 13.22.

New custom labels appear here.

The custom label appears as a selection from the Label Wizard dialog box as the appropriate label type (either Sheet feed or Continuous). That is, it appears if the Show custom label sizes box is checked, as shown in Figure 13.23. The rest of the Label Wizard dialog boxes pertaining to the prototypes and naming will be the same as for pre-existing labels.

FIGURE 13.23.

New custom labels appear here also.

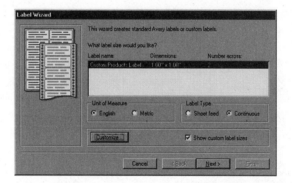

Each report can have a different printer saved to it. This usually is not recommended if the database will be used by multiple people or on different machines. To save a particular report to a particular printer, select File|Page Setup and select the printer from the Specific Printer button found on the Page tab.

Remember, the printer saved with this report is the one that will be used when the report is executed again. If this report will be used by other people, it is suggested that the default printer be saved with the report. Each user of the custom report can resave the report to coincide with his or her specific printer.

The custom label is now ready for print preview. After the print preview of the custom label report is satisfactory, the report is ready to be printed. If it is not satisfactory, return to Design view and make corrections.

Here is a quick review of the custom label process:

1. Set the desired printer for the custom label as the default printer through the Windows Printer settings.
2. Customize the paper size of the label through the Windows Printer settings.
3. Return to Access and create a new, blank report.
4. Turn off the Header and Footer groupings.
5. Bring the desired fields onto the detail section of the report.
6. Concatenate any fields that will appear on the same text line on the label.
7. Turn on the Can Shrink and Can Grow properties for all the fields on the label.
8. Make sure that any text fields are not mathematically touching each other.
9. Change the margins of the report to zero in the File|Page Setup menu item.
10. Change the layout in the File|Page Setup menu item.

Using the Mail Merge Wizard

You can access the Mail Merge Wizard by highlighting an object in the Table or Query module of the database container and clicking Office Links, shown in Figure 13.24. This option is available only for table and query objects, not forms, reports, macros, or modules. Clicking this button brings the records from the datasheet into a Microsoft Word document.

When this option is exercised, Word is automatically loaded. You are prompted for a document from Word. A new document or an existing document can be selected. If an existing document is selected, you can navigate to the desired document through the Select dialog box, which can be set to view any extension or only Word file extensions. Click Open to proceed through the Mail Merge Wizard.

The Word document, whether it is an existing document or a new document, is loaded. Across the top, an additional toolbar has been activated, the Mail Merge toolbar, as shown in Figure 13.25.

13

PRODUCING
MAILINGS

Office Links button

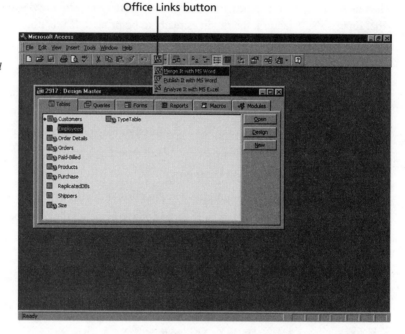

FIGURE **13.24.**
*The Mail Merge
Wizard is executed
through the Office
Links button.*

Mail Merge Helper ─┐   ┌─Check for Errors

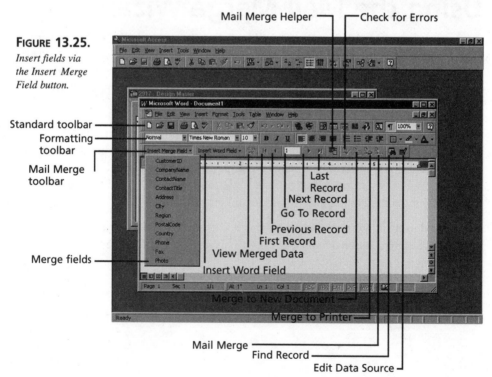

FIGURE **13.25.**
*Insert fields via
the Insert Merge
Field button.*

Standard toolbar ─

Formatting
toolbar ─

Mail Merge
toolbar ─

Merge fields ─

The following pages describe the buttons on the toolbar and how each is used.

- Insert Merge Field—Lists all the fields from the Access database data source. These fields are from either a table or a query.

- Insert Word field—Allows parameters to be set on the incoming data. This gives more control to the developer on the records being exported by Access. All the different options are shown in Figure 13.26.

FIGURE 13.26.

The different ways parameters and conditions can be set on the incoming records.

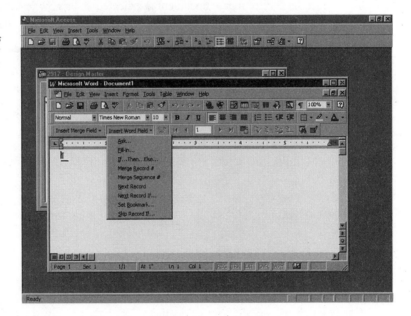

13

PRODUCING MAILINGS

Nine different fields can be inserted. By inserting different fields into the main document, you can control how the data merges. The nine fields are described here:

- Ask field—Displays a prompt so that the user can add personal notes to individual records.

- Fill-in field—Displays the response to the Ask field when the document prints.

- If...Then...Else... field—Performs an action depending on the condition specified.

- Merge Record # field—Displays the record number after it has been successfully merged.

- Merge Sequence # field—Displays the sequential order of the data record selected.

- Next Record field—Displays the next record in the data source that meets any criteria placed on the merge.

- Next Record If field—Compares two expressions; if the true part is valid, the next record is merged.

- Set Bookmark field—Assigns a value to a bookmark or placeholder.

- Skip Record If field—Compares two expressions; if the comparison is true, the current merge document is canceled and a new one is started.

- Mail Merge Helper—Produces form letters and other documents for merging. In Figure 13.27, the Mail Merge Helper shows the database and the data source and allows the user to make changes to the merging process.

FIGURE 13.27.

The Mail Merge Helper.

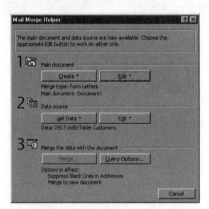

- Check for Errors—Checks for errors that might have prevented the merge. The Checking and Reporting Errors dialog box is shown in Figure 13.28. It allows the user to view any errors before the document has been merged, during the merge, or after the merge.

FIGURE 13.28.

The Checking and Reporting Errors dialog box.

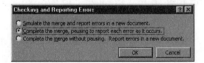

- Merge to New Document—Takes existing results and moves them to a new document. In Figure 13.29, a second document is actually created called Form Letters1. This document takes each merged record, creates a second page of the original document, and places the merge record information in each additional page of the document. Hence, if there were 55 records to be merged, the document would be 55 pages long.

FIGURE 13.29.

Merging the records to a new document.

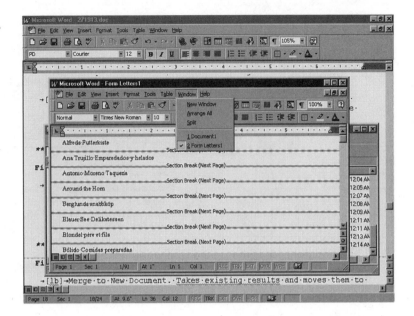

- Merge to Printer—Opens the Print dialog box. Using this button is different from selecting File | Print. That option prints only the currently active document. The Merge to Printer option allows the user to print all the documents that have been merged. Merge to Printer does not allow for the Print Current Page option.

- Mail Merge—Displays a dialog box that allows you to merge the records to a new document, merge the documents to the printer, or merge the documents via email.

- Find Record—Helps find a record depending on the criteria in the Find What field and the field selected. The Find in Field dialog box, shown in Figure 13.30, works much like any other find function.

- Edit Data Source—Returns the user to the data source by giving the Access data source—whether a table or query—the focus. The datasheet is shown in Figure 13.31.

13

TIP

Access uses the field names from a table or query in its mail merge, in what is called the Header row. Field names that are longer than 20 characters are truncated. If any characters in the field names are not letters, numbers, or underscores, those characters are converted to underscores.

FIGURE 13.30.

The Find Record button's dialog box.

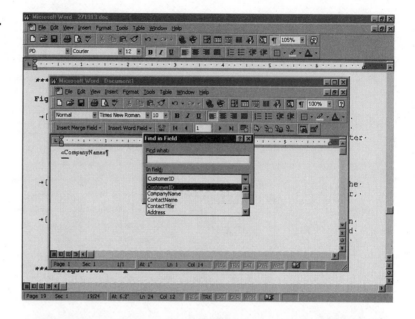

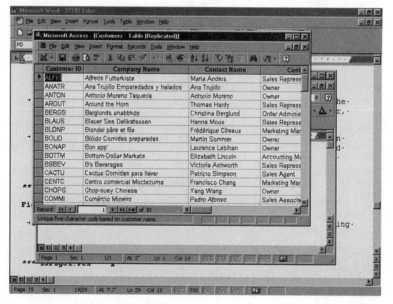

When the merge finishes, simply close the document. You are asked whether to save any changes to the document. Answering Yes to this question saves every record as an individual page to the document. So if there are 55 records in the merge, saving this document changes it from a 1- or 2-page document to a 55- or 110-page document. This could take up valuable disk space unnecessarily.

Summary

This chapter covered information pertaining to the production of mailings. The mailing process can be broken down into two halves. The first half concerns the mailing labels. The second half deals with the merging of records with Microsoft Word (or any word processor) documents. The operation of creating custom labels from a set of predefined Avery labels was covered, along with the process of creating custom labels (labels that are not one of the 197 predefined Avery labels) from scratch. After the labels were printed, the documents needed to be produced. The act of merging records into word processing documents was detailed, as was the process of merging records into spreadsheets.

Using Graphs for Visual Output

CHAPTER 14

Graphs Explained

Graphs can enhance an Access application by representing data as graphic information. Graphs provide more flexibility for your application by offering a rich set of powerful tools not built into Microsoft Access forms or reports.

Graphs are OLE objects that become embedded as part of your application. After a graph object or any other OLE object has been embedded, you can size it, move it, and edit it. You can edit a graph by using Microsoft Graph 97 Chart, its parent application, or VBA code. Each of these methods is explored further in this chapter.

Creating a Graph

The first step in working with graphs is to create a graph object on a form or report. In Form Design or Report Design view, choose Insert | Object or select Unbound Object Frame from the Toolbox. Select Microsoft Graph 97 Chart from the list. See Figure 14.1 to see how to select a Microsoft Graph 97 Chart object for the form or report using the Insert Object dialog box.

FIGURE 14.1.

In the Insert Object dialog box, you can choose what object type you want to insert.

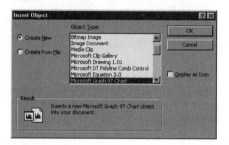

Microsoft Graph 97 Chart then appears. At this point, you can choose from a number of configuration items. See the section called "Customizing the Graph" later in this chapter to see the customizing choices and how to change these options at runtime. For now, choose File | Exit & Return to *formname*: form from the Microsoft Graph 97 Chart Editor.

The graph is then inserted into the form or report in Design view. Select the graph using the mouse, and right-click to select the properties or choose View | Properties. Place your cursor on the Row Source property. Then select a table or query using the drop-down box.

Preparing the Data Source for the Graph

Before a graph can be displayed, you must create a data source. The information you want displayed on your graph dictates how your data source should be organized.

Data

Decide which table or query will supply the data for the chart. If you want to use a query, create the query and include these fields:

- The fields containing the data to be graphed. At least one of these fields must have a number field (Number, Currency, or AutoNumberfield datatype).
- The fields containing the labels you want to display in the chart.
- The linking fields. If you want the chart to change from record to record, the value in the graph's linking field must match the value in a field in the underlying table or query of the form or report. If the form's underlying query includes the ProjectName field, include the ProjectName field in your graph's underlying query so that you can link that graph's child field to the form's master field.

Titles and Legends

Titles are not required but are a valuable component of describing graphs. Pay attention to titles to get the most out of your graphs. The legend entries are a reflection of whatever column headings are in your table or query. The query name likewise appears in the graph's title section.

> **NOTE**
>
> To ensure valuable legend entries, use an expression in your graph's underlying query for each column heading, such as `Billed: SumOfAmountBilled` (instead of just selecting `SumOfAmountBilled`) or `Paid: SumOfPaymentAmount` (instead of just `SumOfPaymentAmount`). The word `Billed` replaces `SumOfAmountBilled`, and the word `Paid` replaces `SumOfPaymentAmount` in your graph's legend.

14

About the Graph Types

Fourteen main graph types are available in Microsoft Graph 97 Chart, and each has one or more subtypes. Twenty graph type and subtype combinations are available through the Chart Wizard. The following sections briefly describe graph types available through the Chart Wizard.

Area Chart

An area chart shows the amount of change over a period of time. The area chart emphasizes the sum of plotted values and the association of individual values to the total rather than to a time and rate of change.

3D Area Chart

A 3D area chart shows a 3D view of an area chart, which emphasizes the sum of plotted values and separates chart-data series into distinct rows to show differences between the data series.

Line Chart

A line chart compares values to other values and often compares values over time. It's similar to an area chart but shows only the relationship between values.

3D Line Chart

A 3D line chart shows a three-dimensional view of a line chart, which emphasizes not only compared values but also emphasizes a particular data series.

Pie Chart

A pie chart shows the relationship or proportions of parts to the whole. It always contains only one data series, which makes it useful for emphasizing a significant element.

3D Pie Chart

The 3D pie chart not only shows the relationship or proportions of parts to the whole but also emphasizes a particular set of data within that graph.

Doughnut Chart

A doughnut chart shows the relationship or proportions of parts to the whole and can contain more than one data series. The doughnut chart, like the pie chart, shows the proportions of parts to a whole. The main difference is that a doughnut chart can show more than one data series.

XY (Scatter) Chart

An xy (scatter) chart shows either the relationship among the numeric values in several data series or plots two groups of numbers as one series of x-y coordinates. It can show clusters of data and is commonly used for scientific data. The points can be open, connected by straight lines, or connected by curved lines.

Bubble Chart

A bubble chart is a type of x-y (scatter) chart with bubbles as data markers. The size of the bubble data marker indicates the value of the third variable.

3D Bubble Chart

A 3D bubble chart is a type of x-y (scatter) chart with 3D bubbles as data markers. The size of the 3D bubble data marker indicates the value of the third variable.

Column Chart

A column chart shows variation compared to other data, often over a period of time, or illustrates comparisons among items. Categories are organized horizontally, and values are organized vertically, placing emphasis on variation over time.

3D Column Chart

A 3D column chart not only shows variation compared to other data, often over a period of time, but also emphasizes a particular data series, much like the 3D bar chart.

Cylinder Column Chart

A cylinder column chart is just like the column chart, except it makes use of the cylinder data markers.

Cone Column Chart

A cone column chart is just like the column chart, except it makes use of the cone data markers.

Pyramid Column Chart

A pyramid column chart is just like the column chart, except it makes use of the pyramid data markers.

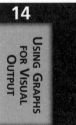

Bar Chart

A bar chart shows individual figures at a specific time or illustrates comparisons among items. A bar chart is much like a column chart, except that the data appears horizontally instead of vertically.

3D Bar Chart

The 3D bar chart is much like the bar chart, except that it can emphasize a particular data series as well.

3D Cylinder Bar Chart

A 3D cylinder bar chart is just like the 3D bar chart, except it makes use of the cylinder data markers.

3D Cone Bar Chart

A 3D cone bar chart is just like the 3D bar chart, except it makes use of the cone data markers.

3D Pyramid Bar Chart

A 3D pyramid bar chart is just like the 3D bar chart, except it makes use of the pyramid data markers.

Customizing the Graph

Customizing the graph is necessary for showing data in a format that is acceptable for the data presented. Seldom does a graph look perfect when it's first created. You can customize the graph by using the Microsoft Access internal Chart Wizard, the Microsoft Graph editor, or through VBA code.

Using the Chart Wizard

The Chart Wizard is the internal Microsoft Access tool for creating and customizing a graph.

To create a form with a new graph, first create a new form by selecting the Form object type from the Database window. Then select the New Button from the Database window. Select Chart Wizard from the list box and choose a table or query for a record source. See Figure 14.2 for an example of the New Form dialog box, which can be a starting point for the Chart Wizard.

FIGURE 14.2.

Selecting Chart Wizard in the New Form dialog box.

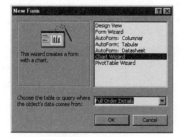

Click OK to start the Chart Wizard. In the Chart Wizard dialog box, shown in Figure 14.3, select the fields you want to use in your graph from the record source. In this example, select all the fields from the query.

FIGURE 14.3.

In the first step, you can choose fields for the graph.

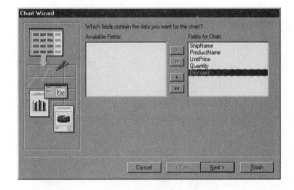

Click the Next button to continue. The next dialog box of the Chart Wizard then appears. Select the graph type you want to use. The options are illustrated in Figure 14.4.

FIGURE 14.4.

In the second step, you can choose a graph type.

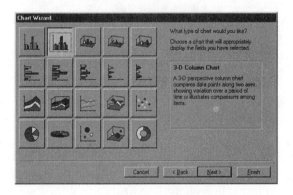

For this example, choose 3D column chart for your graph type and click the Next button to continue. You can choose from several options at this level of the Chart Wizard. To see the options, refer to Figure 14.5.

The Chart Wizard makes some assumptions about how the data should be displayed. UnitPrice, for example, is made into SumOfUnitPrice. To correct this (it has already been summed at the query level), modify the field as follows: Double-click the SumOfUnitPrice section just above the graph. A summarize screen appears, wherein the choices of summarizing a field include None, Sum, Average, Min, Max, and Count.

Choose None for this example and click OK. Click the Quantity button on the right side of the Chart Wizard and drag the Quantity field to the Chart area. This way, you add the Quantity field to the same section as the Billed field. You also need to change the summary from Sum to None within the summarize screen, shown in Figure 14.6.

FIGURE 14.5.

In the third step, you can modify the presentation.

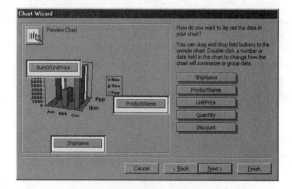

FIGURE 14.6.

This fourth step modifies the data field.

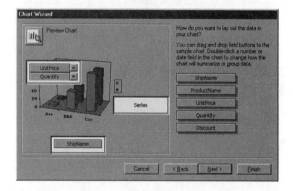

To finish this type of Graph, you must also remove the ProductName grouping. To do this click on the word ProductName and drag it to the list of fields on the right of Wizard. Click the Next button to continue. The final Chart Wizard screen then appears. In this final screen, you can change the chart title, choose whether a legend will appear, choose to open the form in Design or Form view, and choose whether to show help on graphs.

Click the Finish button to continue. The form is then created and displayed on the screen with a graph object already inserted. Right-click the graph object and choose Properties from the list. Look at the Row Source property. The row source is changed to a SELECT statement. A SELECT statement is the Microsoft Access Structured Query Language in written form. It might or might not be what you want. If your query was already formatted correctly to display the data in an appropriate manner, select your query as the Row Source property instead. If you had initially selected a table, the SELECT statement created will most likely satisfy your graphing needs. Open the form in Form view to see how the graph appears.

Customizing the Graph Through Microsoft Graph 97 Chart

Microsoft Graph 97 Chart provides full options for changing an existing graph. To invoke the Microsoft Graph 97 Chart editor, open your form in Design view and then double-click the graph object.

At this level, you have a host of options from which to choose. The format options provide flexibility and customization possibilities. Select any part of the graph object you want to customize and choose the first option from the Format menu. The formatting options you can select are Axis, Plot Area, Chart Title, Data Series, Walls, Legend, and Chart Area. Each option also has one or more subsections.

Format Axis

In the Format Axis dialog box, you can choose Axis options, Tick-Mark Label options, and Tick-Mark Type options. Figure 14.7 shows the choices from which you can select.

FIGURE 14.7.

In the Microsoft Graph 97 Chart Format Axis dialog box, you can customize axis options.

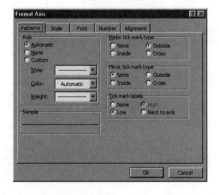

14

USING GRAPHS FOR VISUAL OUTPUT

You can change the scale to reflect a different minimum or maximum, and so on. If the minimum value is increased, graphs appear to have less change. However, if the maximum is decreased, the change appears greater. Figure 14.8 shows a formatting figure for scale changes.

FIGURE 14.8.

On the Scale tab of the Microsoft Graph 97 Chart Format Axis dialog box, you can change the data scale.

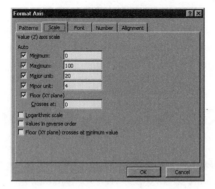

You can change fonts on the axis as well as anywhere on the graph that text appears. Refer to Figure 14.11 for a view of how font styles and sizes can be changed.

You also can adjust the way the axis numbers appear by using the Number tab on the Format Axis dialog box, as shown in Figure 14.9. If the Linked to Source check box is checked, the data on the axis reflects the way that the data is formatted at the data level. (Refer to Figure 14.12 for text-alignment options.)

FIGURE 14.9.

You can use the Number options to modify the numbers on the graph's axis.

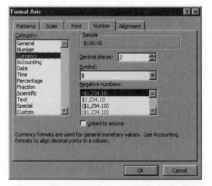

NOTE

Use a currency format with no decimal places to have the axis reflect a currency value instead of raw numbers.

Plot Area

The plot area is the graph only. To format the plot area, select the chart only and choose Format | Selected Plot Area. You can format the entire plot area's pattern, color, and borders in the pattern section. For an example, see Figure 14.10.

FIGURE 14.10.

In this dialog box, you can change pattern options, including the border, color, and pattern of the section you're formatting.

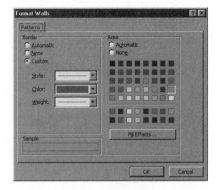

Chart Title

To format the graph's chart title, click the chart title and choose Format | Selected Chart Title. You can change the font in the dialog box shown in Figure 14.11. You can also change the pattern of the chart title; Figure 14.10 shows the customization options of the pattern section. Figure 14.12 shows text-alignment options.

FIGURE 14.11.

The Font subsection of the formatting options.

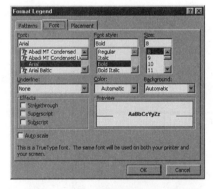

FIGURE 14.12.

The choices available for text alignment.

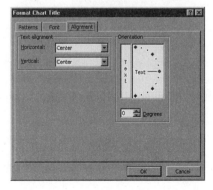

Data Series

The data series is the chart's graph section (a single column in a column chart or a single slice of a pie in a pie chart). Select a data series and choose Format | Selected Data Series. Within this option, you can customize patterns (refer to Figure 14.10), the axis (see Figure 14.13), and data labels (see Figure 14.14).

FIGURE 14.13.

Using the Axis options, you can change on what axis you want your data

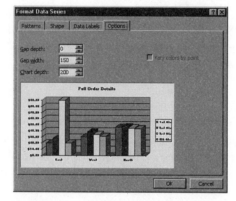

FIGURE 14.14.

Using the Data Labels options, you can customize how your data labels appear.

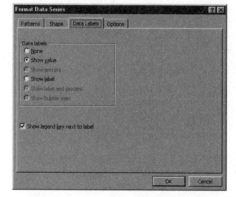

Walls

By using the Pattern options, you can change the walls. These changes affect the borders and the graph's background. To adjust the walls, select the border area, choose Format | Selected Walls, and make changes as necessary. Refer to Figure 14.10 for a sample of pattern choices.

Legend

You can customize the legend to your liking by selecting the legend and choosing Format | Selected Legend. Options include changes to legend patterns (refer to Figure 14.10), fonts (refer to Figure 14.11), and placement (see Figure 14.15).

FIGURE 14.15.

The Placement choices.

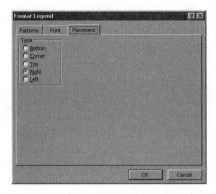

Chart Area

The chart area refers to the chart only, not including the title, legend, and so on. To customize the chart area, select the chart and choose Format | Selected Chart Area. You can change patterns (refer to Figure 14.10) and fonts (refer to Figure 14.11).

Explore these options through Microsoft Graph 97 Chart to get a better understanding of everything that you can customize.

Customizing the Graph Through VBA Code

This section provides a programmatic reference on how to customize graphs. Although the following information provides a starting point and valuable reference guide, the material is by no means a complete programming reference for Microsoft Graph 97 Chart. Refer to the Microsoft Office Developer's Kit for more detailed information.

To refer to a graph object, you must refer to the following:

`[Form]![Control].Object.[object section or property]`

You can do so by creating pointers to the object in some early stages of a form's creation. To begin, include the following code in the general declarations section of your form's code:

```
Option Compare Database
Option Explicit
'used to refer to graph OLE Object
Dim oGraph as Object
```

In the form load event, set the `oGraph` object to the graph control name and to the `Object` property, as follows. This initialization of an object pointer makes referencing the graph object easier and faster.

```
Private Sub Form_Load
    Set oGraph = Me!OgMain.Object
End Sub
```

Changing Graph Types

You can change graph types at runtime by referring to the object's `Type` property.

WARNING

Don't change the graph type unless necessary. Changing a type forces a graph redraw, which is memory-intensive.

You can use the following subroutine as a test to examine each one of the possible graph types:

```
Private Sub SetGraphType (iGraphType as Integer)

    'Set OLE graph type to user-selected graph type, if necessary
    If oGraph.Type <> iGraphType Then
        oGraph.Type = iGraphType
    End If
End Sub
```

You can create this subroutine at the module or form level and test it through the Debug window. Here's another method:

1. Create a form similar to the one shown in Figure 14.16 to change graph types.

2. Create an option group named `GraphTypes`.

3. Create a series of toggle buttons inside this option group with the option values for each button set to the corresponding values from Table 14.1. (Some of the buttons have been omitted from the example.)

TABLE 14.1. GRAPH TYPES AND THE VALUES USED TO CHANGE TO THE GRAPH TYPES WITH THEIR CODE VALUES.

Chart	*Type*	*SubType*	*ChartType*
Column – Clustered Column	3	1	51

Chart	Type	SubType	ChartType
Stacked Column	3	2	52
100% Stacked Column	3	3	53
Clustered Column with 3D Visual Effect	-4100	1	54
Stacked Column with 3D Visual Effect	-4100	2	55
100 % Stacked Column with 3D Visual Effect	-4100	3	56
Clustered Bar	2	1	57
Stacked Bar	2	2	58
100% Stacked Bar Chart	2	3	59
Clustered Bar with a 3D Visual Effect	-4099	1	60
3D Stacked Bar Chart	-4099	2	61
3D 100% Stacked Bar Chart	-4099	3	62
3D Column	-4100	4	-4100
Line	4	1	4
Stacked Line	4	2	63
100% Stacked Line	4	3	64
Line with markers displayed at each data value	4	1	65
Stacked line with markers displayed at each data value	4	2	66
100% Stacked Line with markers displayed at each data value	4	3	67
3D Line	-4101	4	-4101
Pie	5	1	5

continues

TABLE 14.1. CONTINUED

Chart	Type	SubType	ChartType
Pie with a 3D visual effect	-4102	1	-4102
Pie of Pie. Pie with user-defined values extracted and combined into a second pie	5	2	68
Exploded Pie	5	1	69
Exploded Pie with a 3D visual effect	-4102	1	70
Bar of Pie	5	3	71
XY Scatter	-4169	1	-4169
XY Scatter with data points connected by smoothed lines	-4169	1	72
XY Scatter with data points connected by smoothed lines without markers	-4169	1	73
XY Scatter with data points connected by lines	-4169	1	74
XY Scatter with data points connected by lines without markers	-4169	1	75
Area	1	1	1
Stacked Area	1	2	76
100% Stacked Area	1	3	77
Area with a 3D visual effect	-4098	3	-4098
Stacked Area with a 3D visual effect	-4098	1	78

Chart	Type	SubType	ChartType
100% Stacked Area with a 3D visual effect	-4098	2	79
Doughnut	-4120	1	-4120
Exploded Doughnut	-4120	1	80
Radar	-4151	1	-4151
Radar with markers at each data point	-4151	1	81
Filled Radar	-4151	2	82
3D Surface	-4103	1	83
Wireframe 3D Surface	-4103	1	84
Contour	-4103	1	85
Wireframe Contour	-4103	1	86
Bubble	-4169	2	15
Bubble with a 3D visual effect	-4169	2	87
Stock – High-Low-Close	4	1	-4111
Stock – Open-High-Low-C	4	1	89
Stock –Volume-High-Low-Close	3		90
Stock – Volume-Open-High-Low-Close	3		90
Column with a cylindrical shape	-4100	1	92
Stacked column with a cylindrical shape	-4100	2	93
100% Stacked column with a cylindrical shape	-4100	3	94
Bar with a cylindrical shape	-4099	1	95
Stacked bar with a cylindrical shape	-4099	2	96
100% Stacked bar with a cylindrical shape	-4099	3	97

continues

TABLE 14.1. CONTINUED

Chart	Type	SubType	ChartType
3D Column with a cylindrical shape	-4100	4	98
Column with a conical shape	-4100	1	99
Stacked column with a conical shape	-4100	2	100
100% Stacked column with a conical shape	-4100	3	101
Bar with a conical shape	-4099	1	102
Stacked bar with a conical shape	-4099	2	103
100% Stacked bar with a conical shape	-4099	3	104
3D Column with a conical shape	-4100	4	105
Column with a pyramid shape	-4100	1	106
Stacked column with a pyramid shape	-4100	2	107
100% Stacked column with a pyramid shape	-4100	3	108
Bar with a pyramid shape	-4099	1	109
Stacked bar with a pyramid shape	-4099	2	110
100% Stacked bar with a pyramid shape	-4099	3	111
3D Column with a pyramid shape	-4100	4	112

Now insert a graph object. Then invoke the Microsoft Graph 97 Chart editor by double-clicking the graph object and choose Data | Series in Columns. This action renders the data applicable for most of the graphs used in this example.

Create the following code in the option group's After Update event. This code sets the graph's chart type at runtime:

```
Private Sub GraphTypes_AfterUpdate( )
    'Set OLE graph type to user-selected graph type, if necessary
    If oGraph.Type <> Int(Me!GraphTypes) Then
        oGraph.Type = Int(Me!GraphTypes)
    End If
End Sub
```

FIGURE 14.16.

An example of how to change graph types at runtime.

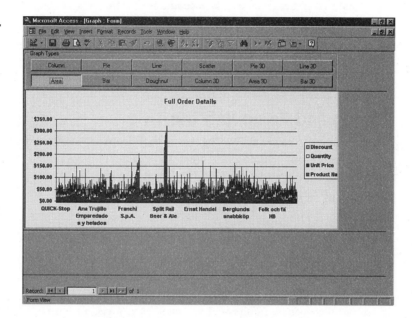

Changing the Underlying Data

You can completely change the underlying data by changing the graph's Row Source property. As you know, you can make this change at design time, but it offers more possibilities at runtime.

To change the underlying data, you can use the previous example with some extra code and more objects added to the form. You can change the row source to different queries or different select statements in a number of ways, so explore this example.

Create a list box filled with a list of queries that you want to use. You can create a table to house the queries that can be used. When a different query is chosen, change the row source with the following code:

```
Me!OgMain.RowSource = Me!lstQueries
```

The underlying data set is changed, and the graph is automatically redrawn to reflect the new changes. This example might change the way the graph ultimately looks, and the formatting for the previous graph might not be adequate for the new set of data.

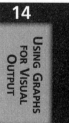

14

USING GRAPHS FOR VISUAL OUTPUT

Adding and Removing the Legend

Using code to add or remove a legend is a simple process. To begin, create a control on the form that you want to use as your legend changer.

This example uses a command button with the caption Add/Remove Legend and with the name ChgLegend. Create an event procedure for the button's `OnClick` event with the following code. This code makes the legend visible if it wasn't visible originally and makes it not visible if it was visible.

```
Sub ChgLegend_Click( )
    oGraph.HasLegend = Not oGraph.HasLegend
End Sub
```

Adding and Removing the Title

Create a command button called ChgTitle with the caption Add/Remove Title and a text box called txtTitle to be used as the graph's title. Then create an event procedure for the button's `OnClick` event with the following code:

```
Private Sub ChgTitle_Click( )
    oGraph.HasTitle = Not oGraph.HasTitle
    oGraph.Title = Me!txtTitle
End Sub
```

Exploding Pie Slices: Rotating and Elevating a 3D Graph

At runtime, data can be emphasized in a number of ways. You can emphasize a set of data by exploding or pulling out one or more of its slices. You can also rotate the set of data around its vertical or horizontal axis.

Create a list box named `lstPieSlices` and set the `Row Source` property to `Payment Method`. `Payment Method` is a query that gives all the possible payment methods of the time and billing database along with the sum of the amounts paid on each method. You can create the `Payment Method` query with the following SQL:

```
SELECT DISTINCTROW [Payment Methods].PaymentMethod,
Sum(Payments.PaymentAmount)

AS SumOfPaymentAmount

FROM [PaymentMethods]

RIGHT JOIN Payments ON [PaymentMethods].PaymentMethodID =
➥ Payments.PaymentMethodID

GROUP BY [PaymentMethods].PaymentMethod;
```

Create a graph object named `ogMain` with the Row Source set to `Payment Method`. Now you have a list of payment methods in the list box and a graph with the slices equal to those payment methods.

Create command buttons for rotating up, down, left, and right. Create a command button for exploding a pie slice and create a command button for setting the graph back to its default. The command button names should match the subroutine names. Figure 14.17 shows the form with exploding and rotating options.

FIGURE 14.17.

This form can explode and rotate a pie graph.

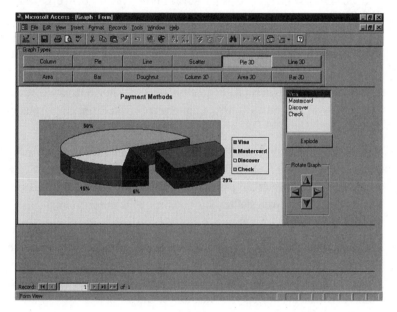

Create the following code on your form to implement exploding and rotating options:

```
Option Compare Database
Option Explicit
Dim OGraph As Object
Const GRAPH_ROTATE_CHANGE = 10
Const GRAPH_EXPLODE_CHANGE = 20
Private Sub Form_Load( )
    Set OGraph = Me!OgMain.Object
End Sub
Private Sub Explode_Click( )
    Dim iSlice As Integer
    iSlice = Me!lstPieSlices.ListIndex + 1
    OGraph.SeriesCollection(1).Points(iSlice).Explosion =
    ➥OGraph.SeriesCollection(1).Points(iSlice).Explosion + GRAPH_EXPLODE
    ➥CHANGE
End Sub
```

```
Private Sub RotateDown_Click( )
On Error Resume Next
    OGraph.Elevation = OGraph.Elevation + GRAPH_ROTATE_CHANGE
End Sub
Private Sub RotateLeft_Click( )
On Error Resume Next
    OGraph.Rotation = OGraph.Rotation - GRAPH_ROTATE_CHANGE
End Sub
Private Sub RotateRight_Click( )
On Error Resume Next
    OGraph.Rotation = OGraph.Rotation + GRAPH_ROTATE_CHANGE
End Sub
Private Sub RotateUp_Click( )
On Error Resume Next
    OGraph.Elevation = OGraph.Elevation - GRAPH_ROTATE_CHANGE
End Sub
```

When the left and right rotate buttons are clicked, the graph rotates around its vertical axis. When the up and down rotate buttons are clicked, the graph rotates around its horizontal axis.

When a slice name is clicked in the slice list, the pie slice is pulled away from the center of the pie by 10 points. As the list item is clicked more times, the slice moves further away from the center of the pie. To see the preceding VBA code working, refer to 291714.mdb on the Web site for this book and look at form Graph.

You can customize all these options to your satisfaction by adjusting the amount of change and the method in which the form is changed. You can adjust the amount of change by setting new values for the constants, or you can create a flexible environment by building a configuration form. In such a form, the user can adjust by how many points he wants his objects to rotate, move, and so on.

Sizing the Chart and the Legend

Sizing the chart (plot area) and sizing the legend can be valuable in rounding out the charting capabilities of your application. In the following example, you create a form to size the different sections of the graph and to allow the legend and title to be toggled visible and invisible. Figure 14.18 shows the form that can size objects and can turn the legend and title on or off.

Use the following code to create the form in Figure 14.18:

```
Option Compare Database
Option Explicit
Dim oGraph As Object
Dim objSection As Object
Const GRAPH_SIZE_CHANGE = 5
Private Sub Form_Load( )
    Set oGraph = Me!OgMain.Object
```

```
        Call lstObject_AfterUpdate
End Sub
Private Sub HeightLarger_Click( )
    objSection.Height = objSection.Height + GRAPH_SIZE_CHANGE
End Sub
Private Sub HeightSmaller_Click( )
    objSection.Height = objSection.Height - GRAPH_SIZE_CHANGE
End Sub
Private Sub LegendVisible_Click( )
    oGraph.HasLegend = Not oGraph.HasLegend
End Sub
Private Sub lstObject_AfterUpdate( )
    Select Case Me!lstObject
        Case "Chart"
            Set objSection = oGraph.PlotArea
        Case "Legend"
            Set objSection = oGraph.Legend
    End Select
End Sub
Private Sub TitleVisible_Click( )
    oGraph.HasTitle = Not oGraph.HasTitle
End Sub
Private Sub WidthLarger_Click( )
    objSection.Width = objSection.Width + GRAPH_SIZE_CHANGE
End Sub
Private Sub WidthSmaller_Click( )
    objSection.Width = objSection.Width - GRAPH_SIZE_CHANGE
End Sub
```

FIGURE 14.18.

This form, which can manipulate a 3D pie chart, provides sizing and titling options.

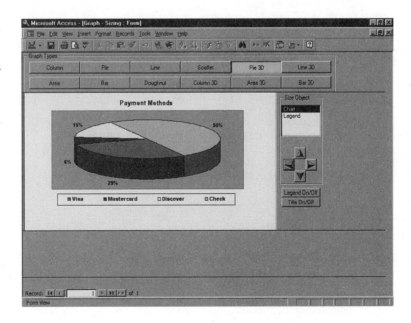

To see this VBA code working, refer to 291714.mdb on the Web site for this book and look at form Graph - Sizing.

Sizing the Title

Sizing the title is somewhat different than sizing other elements. The chart title doesn't have Width or Height properties. You can adjust the size of the title only by referencing the ChartTitle.Font.Size property of the graphing object using the following code:

```
oGraph.ChartTitle.Font.Size = 12
```

You can also change the font by referring to the ChartTitle.Font.Name property using the following code:

```
oGraph.ChartTitle.Font.Name = "Arial"
```

Moving the Chart, Legend, and Title

Using code to move objects is also an easy task. The plot area, the chart title, and the legend can all be moved with routines similar to those that are used for sizing. Here movement is made by referring to the object's Top and Left properties.

Use the following code for a form that manipulates object movement:

```
Option Compare Database
Option Explicit
Dim oGraph As Object
Dim objSection As Object
Const GRAPH_MOVE_CHANGE = 5
Private Sub Form_Load( )
    Set oGraph = Me!OgMain.Object
    Call lstObject_AfterUpdate
End Sub
Private Sub MoveUp_Click( )
    objSection.Top = objSection.Top - GRAPH_MOVE_CHANGE
End Sub
Private Sub MoveDown_Click( )
    objSection.Top = objSection.Top + GRAPH_MOVE_CHANGE
End Sub
Private Sub lstObject_AfterUpdate( )
    Select Case Me!lstObject
        Case "Title"
            Set objSection = oGraph.Title
        Case "Chart"
            Set objSection = oGraph.PlotArea
        Case "Legend"
            Set objSection = oGraph.Legend
    End Select
End Sub
Private Sub MoveRight_Click( )
```

```
     objSection.Left = objSection.Left + GRAPH_MOVE_CHANGE
End Sub
Private Sub MoveLeft_Click( )
     objSection.Left = objSection.Left - GRAPH_MOVE_CHANGE
End Sub
```

Bound Versus Unbound Graphical Objects

Deciding whether to use a bound or an unbound graphical object takes some consideration. First, you must know what you want your graph to accomplish. The following sections provide you with information helpful in choosing bound or unbound graphs.

Bound Graphical Objects

Bound graphs are stable; you know what the data should look like. For an application in which seeing the data the same way every time is important, using a bound graph is the best answer. Of course, you can customize the graph, but a bound graph doesn't provide the flexibility of an unbound graph.

Unbound Graphical Objects

Unbound graphs provide flexibility in changing what the user can see. If your application has a large amount of data to graph and will be changing in the future, utilizing unbound graphs might be best. With unbound graphs, you don't need to know exactly what the graph must look like; all you need to know is a relative framework. If you simply change the Row Source property, the graph can be redrawn with a new set of data.

With both bound and unbound graph types, the graph type can be changed. If the graph type is changed at runtime, the set of data will most likely not be formatted correctly. To fix this possible problem, you might need to institute a system of defaults.

For more complex scenarios, you can create a system with both flexibility and structure. You can have a list of graphs to choose from in a list box or combo box. Each graph can relate to a record in a table that has information on the row source, the graph type, the sizing of each object, where each section (title, plot area, and legend) is located, and so on.

When the user selects a graph, the graph is redrawn with the new set of data, and all the sections can be moved and sized to their optimum settings; thus, the user doesn't need to move or size any of the objects. However, you can give the user the option of making modifications as needed and the option of resetting the default values for that graph. Of course, adding these capabilities takes much more code and quite a bit of time.

Changing the Graph While Navigating Through Records

Another powerful feature of a graphed object is the ability to show a new graph with each new record. This is done by linking master and child fields. The Master Field property refers to the parent form field to link on. The Child Field property refers to the graph field to link on. In Figure 14.19, the graph is linked on the field called ProjectName for both child and master fields.

FIGURE 14.19.

The graph on this form changes as you go to new records using the navigation buttons.

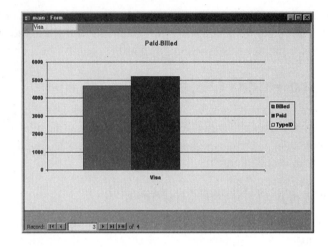

When the navigation button is clicked, not only is information regarding that record displayed on the form, but significant data is also automatically shown on the graph for the linked objects.

The form is bound to the query Paid-Billed/Type, which includes fields called Type Name, Billed, Paid and TypeID. You can create the query by using the following SQL information:

```
SELECT TypeTable.TypeName, Sum([Paid-Billed].Billed) AS Billed, Sum([Paid-
➥Billed].Paid) AS Paid

FROM [Paid-Billed] INNER JOIN TypeTable ON [Paid-Billed].TypeID =
TypeTable.TypeID

GROUP BY TypeTable.TypeName, TypeTable.TypeID

HAVING (((TypeTable.TypeID)=[forms]![main].[typeid]));
```

The graph needs to have a Row Source property that has TypeID in it. The graph can show anything significant that can be linked by TypeID. In this example, the graph's Row Source property is set to table TypeTable. This example shows a graphical representation of the information that is shown as text on the form. To see this form working, refer to 291714.mdb on the Web site for this book and look at form main.

This use of the graphing possibilities is powerful. Graphs can be redrawn to show specific information about a particular record. This capability is also simple because it doesn't require any special coding.

Summary

Experiment with Microsoft Graph 97 Chart and with Microsoft Access 97. Their functionality can be intermixed to create powerful decision-support systems and to add polish to any application. Spending time with the graphing functions will pay off in the long run.

Advanced Programming in Access

PART V

IN THIS PART

Integrating Objects and Other Microsoft Office Products

CHAPTER 15

You are probably familiar with the Windows concept of sharing objects between applications. An example of this would be pasting a bitmap picture from Paintbrush into a Word document that you are editing. This chapter is about the technology called *Object Linking and Embedding (OLE)* that enables you to "share" objects from one Windows program with other Windows programs. OLE is a protocol for sharing an object with another application by linking or embedding that object within an *OLE container*, which is any application that can contain a linked or embedded OLE object from another application. OLE is so convenient that you don't even have to open the OLE server to be able to edit a shared object. An OLE server is an application that can supply a linked or embedded OLE object to another application. The process of using OLE from within Access 97 is known as *automation* and is covered in depth in this chapter.

> **NOTE**
>
> In previous versions of Access, OLE containers were known as *container applications* and OLE servers were known as *object applications*.

This chapter begins with some necessary definitions and an explanation of some of the concepts that automation relies on. You will create an Access 97 application that allows you to experiment with several aspects of OLE and Access 97.

Prior to the release of Access 97, Microsoft Access used custom controls and OLE controls. Those controls have been encapsulated into one control type, the ActiveX control for Access 97. An ActiveX control functions much like a built-in control in Access 97, in that you insert an ActiveX control into a form or report to enhance your user's experience with your application. You can even use ActiveX controls that are not included with Access 97.

Activating ActiveX in Access 97

To use your custom ActiveX controls within Access 97, you must register the control with Access 97. You can do this by following these steps:

1. Make sure that the files for the ActiveX control are saved on your hard drive.
2. Choose Tools | ActiveX Controls.
3. An ActiveX Controls dialog box appears, with a listing of all the ActiveX controls that are currently registered with your copy of Access 97. To register a new ActiveX control, click on the Register button.

4. An Add ActiveX dialog box appears. Point to the ActiveX control that is stored on your hard drive and click on the Open button.

5. The Add ActiveX dialog box disappears and you are sent back to the ActiveX Controls dialog box. Click on the Close button to exit back to your Access 97 application.

A Few Definitions

Before you go any further, you need a few definitions to increase your understanding of OLE. The most important definition, that of an *object*, is covered first.

Objects

Anything that your users can interact with is probably viewed as an object by Access 97. Some examples of objects within Access 97 are forms, fields, controls, tables, reports, and queries. In fact, you could consider any part of your Access application that you can control, either directly through mouse or keyboard input or programmatically through macros or VBA, to be an object.

Objects have both *properties* and *methods*. The properties of an object are simply aspects of that object. For example, if you have a Command button on a form in your application, some of the properties of that object are button height, caption, font name, and name. You can also use properties to describe an object's behavior. *Methods* are a way of interacting with an object through its properties.

Objects in Office 97 share many similarities. A dialog box in Microsoft Word looks and acts much the same as a dialog box in Access 97. The similarities between these objects are what enables OLE technology to exist. If you import a Word document into your Access 97 application, you know that you can manipulate the document in much the same way that you can in Word. For example, you can adjust the font color and size using the same types of commands and controls in Access 97 that you would use from within Word.

Exposed Objects

For an application to be considered an OLE application, it must be able to expose its objects for automation. That is, the application must expose a programmability interface that another application can use to share its objects and the methods and properties associated with those objects. Generally, the application that is sharing the object runs hidden in the background. This background application is really controlling its exposed objects, even though all your application sees are the objects that are being used by your application.

15

INTEGRATING
OBJECTS

Access as Client or Server

Access 97 can be either an OLE server or an OLE client. If Access 97 is serving an Access table or report to another application that supports OLE, such as Microsoft Excel, Access 97 is playing the role of an OLE server. However, if your Access 97 application is making use of another application's object, such as a spreadsheet from Excel or a document from Word, Access 97 is playing the role of an OLE or automation client.

OLE is the protocol by which applications share objects. These objects can either be linked from the client application to the server application, or the objects can be embedded (inserted) into the client application from the server application. The link between an OLE server and an OLE client is known as the *OLE link*. For the purposes of this chapter, we cover the use of OLE as a way to introduce objects into your Access 97 applications. For this reason, throughout this chapter Access 97 is considered an OLE client or an automation client.

Automation

Automation is a feature of the industry-standard *Component Object Model* (*COM*) that Microsoft is actively promoting as the software model of the future. COM is the architecture that lies underneath Microsoft's higher-level software services like OLE. Automation was called *OLE automation* in previous versions of Access, and it provides a way to work with another application's objects from within your application using your application's tools.

An example of this would be a word processor that exposes some of its objects, such as documents, bookmarks, or even a selection of text in a document. If the word processor supports automation, the objects that the word processor exposes can be accessed by another application that supports automation, even by an application such as Visual Basic. In fact, you can use Visual Basic to set the object's properties and call its methods.

Most of the time, the definitions of an application's objects and the properties and methods that apply to those objects can be found in the application's *object library*. An object library is a file with an .olb extension that automation controllers use to discover information about the objects that are available within the application. If you are going to work with a component through automation in your Access 97 application, you can improve your application's performance by setting a reference to the component's *type library*. A type library can usually be found within an application's object library. (You can use the Object Browser included within Access 97 to examine the contents of an object library.) Type libraries can also be standalone, in which case they will have .tlb as a file extension. The following steps illustrate using the Object Browser to view the ComboBox class within the Access object library:

1. Open up any module in your application's database window.

2. While the module is open, press the F2 key.

3. The Object Browser dialog box will appear, as shown in Figure 15.1.

FIGURE 15.1.

Viewing the Access object library through the Object Browser.

Embedded Objects

An embedded OLE object in Access 97 is a copy of an object that is sent to the Access 97 OLE client from an OLE server application. Once an object is embedded into the OLE client application, any changes that are made to that object are not saved back to the original object that is still in the OLE server application. In the same way, any changes that are made to the original object are not reflected in the copy of the object that is now embedded into the OLE client application.

For example, if you embed a picture into one of the forms in your Access 97 application that was created in Paintbrush, that picture can no longer be modified with the Paintbrush application. Instead, you must open your Access 97 application to be able to modify the Paintbrush picture. You can still manipulate the picture in the same way that you could in Paintbrush, but you can no longer modify the picture outside of the application that it is embedded into.

You can embed an object as either a bound object or an unbound object. The information about a bound object is stored in a table, and when you move to a new record within that table, the object that is displayed within the OLE client application changes. An example of a bound object would be an inventory table for a store's inventory control application. The table contains a picture of each piece of merchandise as an embedded OLE object. As the user of the application pages through a form connected to the table containing the embedded object, the picture on the form changes to reflect the merchandise that is being viewed.

15

INTEGRATING OBJECTS

An unbound object, on the other hand, is stored as a part of the form or report that is in the application. An example of an unbound object would be the company's logo that is displayed in the corner of the form in the inventory control application.

Linked Objects

In contrast to an embedded object, a *linked object* is an object that is connected to your application, but not inserted into it. The object still comes from an OLE server application, but the OLE server sends a link to the original object, not a copy of that object, to the OLE client. This means that a linked object can be changed outside of the application that it is linked to. For example, if you have a Paintbrush picture linked into a form in your Access 97 application, someone could load the picture into Paintbrush and edit it without your knowledge. If this happens, the linked object within your application changes as soon as the miscreant saves his changes to your picture.

You can still change the picture using the controls within your application, but other users can change the picture themselves at will if they can get to the original file's location. Other users can also link the same picture to their OLE client applications.

> **TIP**
>
> You can use OLE automation to link a file stored anywhere you have access to it. This location could be on your own hard disk, as in the preceding example, or it could be on another computer networked to yours.

> **NOTE**
>
> Clearly, the trade-offs between linking and embedding objects have to do with how the access to the objects needs to be controlled. If it's okay—and more efficient—for everyone to be able to manipulate the object, link it. However, the object is more secure if it is embedded.

Pictures are not the only objects that can be linked to or embedded within an Access 97 application. You can also link to external tables, reports, graphs, documents, and many other OLE objects. An external table that is linked to an Access 97 application is known as a *linked table*. In previous versions of Access, linked tables were known as *attached tables*. When you link to an external table, you can manipulate the data stored in the table in any way that you are allowed. That is, you can add, edit, and delete records just as if the table were stored locally in your Access 97 application. You cannot change the structure of a linked table in Access 97, however.

A Comparison of Linking and Embedding

As you decide whether you want to link to a file or embed a file into your OLE client application, you should keep a couple of points in mind. The first is the difference in the potential size of your OLE client application data file; the second is the performance differences between embedding and linking.

When you link a file, it mostly remains separate from the OLE client application. The only things the OLE client application needs to keep track of internally are pointers to the linked file's location, what kind of file it is, and so on. Obviously, you don't have a big size hit here. On the other hand, if you embed an object into your OLE client application, all of the object is incorporated into your application. This includes not only the data involved, but also all the information the client application needs to find the object's server application so that the object can be edited in place. Embedding usually represents a significant size hit. A simple image record, for example, can add hundreds of kilobytes of data to your database.

The performance differences are less easy to qualify. Usually, dealing with an embedded object is faster. Because everything necessary to edit it is already there in your client application, you don't have to worry about the executable seek/load/run constraints of the network or your own system. On the other hand, because of the potentially extreme size (and therefore practical performance) hit, quite often you should link data objects instead.

A Project: Clever Ideas and a Way to Remember Them

The project that this chapter is designed around is an Access 97 database application that enables you to store and access your clever ideas easily. This application stores a description of your idea and a picture of the idea's concept in an Access 97 database, and uses the concepts of OLE and automation to bolster Access 97's limited picture-drawing and word-processing capabilities. The application is presented as a way to demonstrate all the OLE topics that have been covered in this chapter so far. You can build upon the ideas presented in this Access 97 application to build more sophisticated applications.

The application consists of a table to store your data in and a form to make data entry to that table easier. It uses controls placed on that form to automate your use of OLE and automation.

15

INTEGRATING OBJECTS

Creating the Database

There are two ways to create a database application within Access 97. You can manually create a blank database application and add the tables, forms, reports, and other objects when you need them, or you can use the Database Wizard that is supplied with Access 97. In either case, you can add to or delete from your database application at any time after it has been created. For the purposes of this chapter, you will create your database application manually. Follow these steps to create the Clever Ideas database application:

1. If you do not have Access 97 running already, start it up. You're presented with the dialog box shown in Figure 15.2. Choose the Blank Database option and click on the OK button.

FIGURE 15.2.

Choosing the Blank Database option.

2. Name the database "Clever Ideas" and save it in the folder of your choice. If Access 97 is already open, select File | New Database and double-click on the Blank Database icon. In the next dialog box, name the database `Clever Ideas` and save it in the folder of your choice. Click on the Create button to save the database.

> **TIP**
>
> With Access 97's control-naming syntax, you can include spaces in your database names.

3. With the Tables tab selected, click New in the Database window to create a new table. Access 97 opens its New Table dialog box. Select Design View and click the OK button.

4. Create a table composed of the following four data fields. (The result is shown in Figure 15.3.)

Field Name	Datatype	Description
Name*	Text	A name for my idea
Category	Text	A category for my idea
Picture	OLE Object	A place to sketch my idea
Comments	OLE Object	A place to describe my idea

*Make the Name field the primary key by selecting the row and clicking the Key button if the Table Design toolbar is visible. You can also choose Edit|Primary Key.

FIGURE 15.3.

Clever Ideas table design.

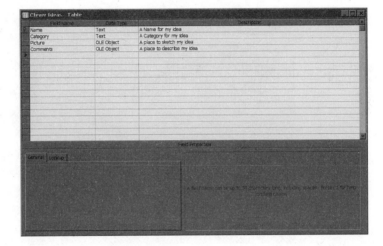

5. Save your table and name it Clever Ideas.

NOTE

The OLE datatype is a bit different from the "normal" datatypes, such as integer, that represent some actual data in your table and that can be used as a sorting index. Instead, it's more like the memo type in that it is a pointer—in this case, a pointer to the OLE object that will be embedded or linked to the OLE object field in your table. It is stored in your database field as a 4-byte address.

15

INTEGRATING
OBJECTS

A Quick OLE

You can use this table right away to enter OLE objects into your Access 97 application. These OLE objects will be stored in the table you have just created. Enter the OLE objects by following these steps:

1. Click the Table View button on the far left of the Table Design toolbar. If the toolbar is not visible, double-click the table or choose View I Datasheet View. Access 97 opens your table in Datasheet view, as shown in Figure 15.4.

2. Because the Name field is the primary key in the sample table, you always need to enter data into the Name field. Also, because it's a text field, all you need to do is move to the field and start typing a name for your idea. Enter a name there now. Remember that all names in this field must be unique because this field is the primary key for your table.

3. Move to the Category field and enter a category that your idea would fit into.

4. Move the mouse cursor to the Picture column and right-click. (Alternatively, you can choose Insert I Object.) As shown in Figure 15.5, Access 97 displays a pop-up menu containing the Insert Object option, which you should then select. The Insert Object dialog box will appear, as shown in Figure 15.6.

FIGURE 15.5.

Select Insert Object from the pop-up menu.

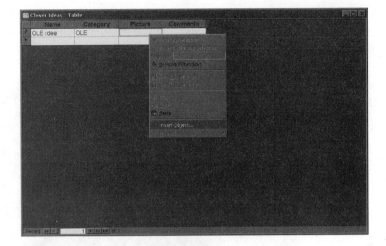

FIGURE 15.6.

Insert a graphic object into the OLE object field.

5. Pick one of the graphical objects to insert into your picture field by moving down the Object Type list box. If you want to use clip art, Microsoft includes a ClipArt Gallery with Word for Windows. If, on the other hand, you want to draw something yourself, choose Paintbrush Picture or Microsoft Draw. For the purposes of this example, work with Paintbrush. Make sure that the Create New option to the left of the Object Type list box is selected, and click the OK button after you make your decision.

> **NOTE**
>
> Microsoft Word Picture is a term that can fool you. It's not a drawing program in the sense that you use lines and circles to create pictures. Instead, it's an application that enables you to manipulate text objects graphically. For example, you can use it to create a fancy word logo.

15

INTEGRATING OBJECTS

6. In this case, you're using Paintbrush to sketch an idea (see Figure 15.7). After you're done with your sketch, open the File menu. Its Exit option should read something like `Exit & Return to Clever Ideas Table`, as shown in Figure 15.8.

FIGURE 15.7.

A sketch in the making.

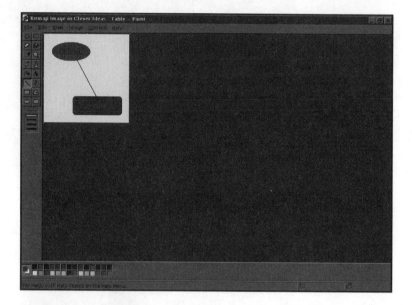

FIGURE 15.8.

Exiting this application puts its output right into your table.

7. You are then prompted with the message, `The command you have chosen will close the connection between this open embedded object and Table. Do you want to update the open embedded object before proceeding?`. This message tells you that while you're using another application, its product becomes part of your database's table. Click Yes.

That's about all there is to creating an OLE object and putting it into your table. As shown in Figure 15.9, Access 97 notes the existence of the object within your file with the words `Bitmap Image`.

FIGURE 15.9.

OLE objects become part of your table.

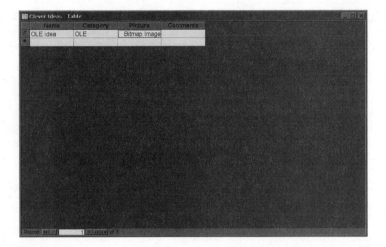

Activating Your Object In-Place

One of the features of OLE objects is that of in-place activation of the object's OLE server from within the control or field that the object is contained in. If an object supports in-place activation, when you double-click the control or field that contains the object, the Access 97 menus and toolbars are replaced with the menus and toolbars of the OLE server for the object. You can treat an OLE object in a table just as any other kind of data. That is, you can delete it, copy it, move it, or edit it. To see an example of in-place activation or visual editing, follow these steps:

1. Display your Clever Ideas table in datasheet form.
2. Right-click the OLE object field that contains the Paintbrush picture it. Access 97 displays a pop-up menu that includes an option regarding the kind of object in that field, as shown in Figure 15.10.
3. Select the Bitmap Image Object option. Access 97 displays a submenu that gives you the option of editing or converting the object.
4. Select the Edit option on the submenu. Access 97 calls up its server application, loads the object into that server application, and then lets Windows display it for you to edit.

After you're done with your edits, save the newly edited object back to your database by choosing the appropriate Exit option from the object's File menu and clicking Yes when prompted, as before.

15

INTEGRATING OBJECTS

FIGURE 15.10.

Access 97 knows what kind of object is pointed to by the OLE object field and what kind of manipulations you can perform on it.

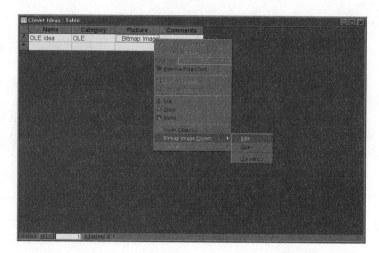

Creating a Form for Your Project

Now that you have created a database, set up a table for your project, and started populating the table, it is time to create a form to make it easy to enter and view data in your application. Because this is a very simple example database to illustrate the use of OLE, a simple form is all that you need to create the front end to your database application. To create the form that you will use for this purpose, follow these steps:

1. If it's not already running, start Access 97 and open up the Clever Ideas database.

2. In Access 97's database container, click the Forms tab to make it active.

3. Click the New button to call up the New Form dialog box.

4. In the New Form dialog box, make sure that the name of the Clever Ideas table appears in the drop-down list box in the lower-right portion of the dialog box. That indicates to Access 97 that the Clever Ideas table is the source of the form object's data. Also make sure that Design View is selected in the large list box at the right side of the dialog box. The form should appear like the one shown in Figure 15.11.

FIGURE 15.11.

Building a form from the Clever Ideas table in your database.

5. Click OK and Access 97 creates a blank form, ready for you to put in the fields from the Clever Ideas table.

6. Save the form under the name `Clever Ideas`.

Placing the Fields on the Form

Now that you have a form in your database, you are ready to add some fields to the form that are linked to your Clever Ideas table. To add fields to your form, follow these steps:

1. If it isn't already displayed, open the field list by choosing View | Field List, as shown in Figure 15.12. Drag field names down from the field list onto the form itself, as shown in Figure 15.13.

FIGURE 15.12.

Choosing the field list.

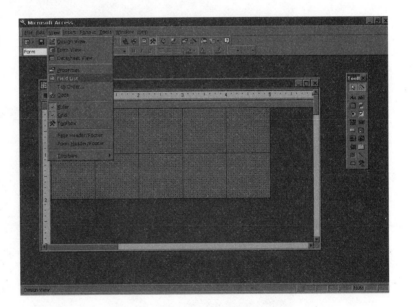

2. Add a Command button just below the Comments field. (Later, you'll attach code to it that will enable you to use OLE automation.) The Command Button Wizard appears. This is a shortcut for basic Access 97 button functions. Click Cancel. Right-click on the Command button and select the Properties option. In the dialog box that pops up, select the All tab. Under the `Name` property, enter `cmdAddText`. Then select the `Caption` property and give the new Command button the caption of `&Add Text`. The dialog box should appear as that shown in Figure 15.14. Close the dialog box and save the form.

FIGURE 15.13.

Adding fields to the form from the field list.

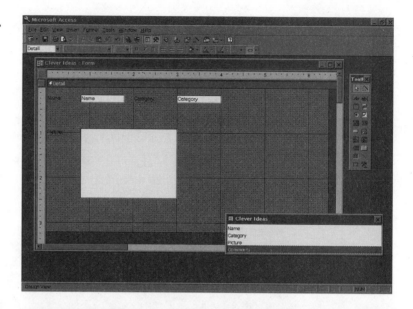

FIGURE 15.14.

Editing the properties of the Add Text Command button.

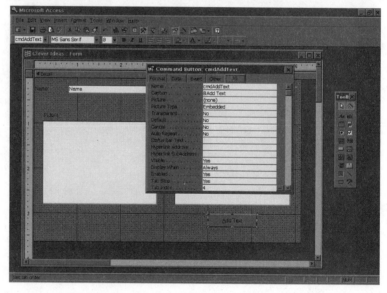

3. On the form, right-click on the field underneath the Picture label, which is the Picture OLE object field.

4. Select the Properties option from the pop-up list that appears and select the Format tab on the Properties dialog box. For the Size Mode property at the top of the list, choose Zoom from the drop-down list, as shown in Figure 15.15. With that done, you can see the entire picture object regardless of its size when it is manipulated in its server application.

FIGURE 15.15.
Zooming provides just the right objective view.

5. Be sure to save your form once again.

15

INTEGRATING OBJECTS

You should now change the background color of the form, set up the labels so that they stand out on your form, and adjust the label text font size and color. To configure your form so that it looks like the one shown in Figure 15.16, complete the following adjustments to the properties of the form.

1. Set the Back Color property of the Detail section to the value of 4227200.

2. Hold down the Shift key while you click on all the labels to select them. On the Format tab of the Properties dialog box, set the Fore Color property to the value of 16384, set the Font Size property to the value of 14, set the Special Effect property to Raised, and set the Back color property to the value of 12632256.

3. Make sure that you save the changes to your form.

FIGURE 15.16.

Viewing the completed form.

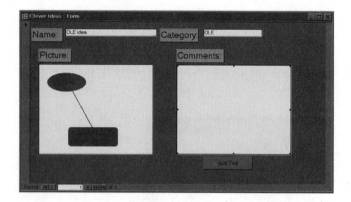

Displaying OLE Images

Well, you've got a form to serve as the front end to your Clever Ideas database application now. If you want to insert an object into the Picture or Comments fields, you can do so as easily as following these steps:

1. Display the form in form mode by choosing View | Form View. Select either the Picture field or the Comments field.

2. Choose Insert | Object or right-click the field. Access 97 displays the Insert Object dialog box (refer to Figure 15.6).

3. Choose an object type from the list in the dialog box and click OK. Access 97 calls up its server application, activates it, and then stores the data in the appropriate OLE object field in your Clever Ideas table.

Automatically Inserting an OLE Object

Earlier in this chapter, you learned that you could double-click an OLE object field with the table in Datasheet view and that Access 97 would automatically call up the Insert Object dialog box. Unfortunately, that's not true with OLE object forms. As a matter of fact, if you were to do so, Access 97 would display an error dialog box prompting you to link or embed an object.

One solution is to create an Access 97 macro that is invoked whenever you double-click an empty OLE object field. To try that for the Picture field in your Clever Ideas database, carry out the following steps:

1. With the Database Container window active, click the Macros tab.

2. Click the New button. Access 97 displays a blank macro sheet.

3. Display the Macro Name column by choosing View | Macro Names or clicking the Macro Names button if the toolbar is displayed. Type the name "AutoInsertObject" in the Macro Name field. This becomes the name by which this macro will be known.

4. In the Action field, select RunCommand from the drop-down list. (Note: Access 97 has replaced DoMenuItem with RunCommand.) Access 97 places it in the Action field.

5. In the Command window below the macro list, select InsertObject, as shown in Figure 15.17.

FIGURE 15.17.

A macro can comprise a single line.

6. Save the macro sheet under the name MyMacros.

Adding the Macro to an Event

With the macro created, all you need to do is add its name to the On Dbl Click event in the Clever Ideas form property sheet. To do so, perform the following steps:

1. Open the Clever Ideas form in Design view.

2. Select the Picture OLE object frame. Access 97 indicates that it is active by displaying a border and sizing handles around it.

3. With the Properties sheet active, click the Event tab. Access 97 displays the contents of the Event tab.

4. Sliding the mouse cursor down to the On Dbl Click event, select MyMacros.AutoInsertObject from the drop-down list box, as shown in Figure 15.18.

FIGURE 15.18.

The On Dbl Click *event is called when a control is double-clicked.*

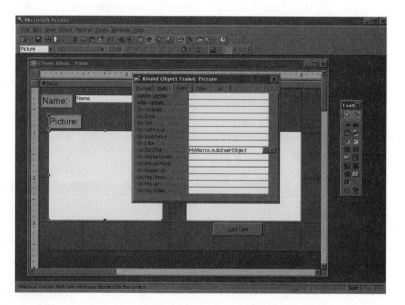

5. Repeat the preceding steps for the Comments OLE object frame and save the form.

When you double-click the Picture OLE object field, Access 97 automatically displays its Insert Object dialog box. And as you can do with the table in Datasheet view, you can select an object type to insert into your field. If an object is already in the field and you click Cancel, Access 97 calls up the object's server application so that you can edit the object. You now have a complete Access 97 sample application that illustrates OLE and automation. The concepts shown in this sample application can be extended to work in more advanced applications.

Bound and Unbound Fields

Fields on an Access 97 form can be *bound* or *unbound*. Bound fields are connected to a field in the underlying table. Fields or controls on a form can also be bound to an underlying query or SQL statement. Bound fields automatically display the contents of the underlying field. Unbound fields, on the other hand, don't derive their content from an underlying table, query or SQL statement. They display whatever you programmatically tell them to—the results of a calculation, for example. They can also be used to accept user input.

Because you dragged the field names down to the form from the Field List, they are automatically bound fields. They display the text or OLE object contained in the corresponding field in the Clever Ideas table.

Excel, Access, and OLE

As part of the overall philosophy of more tightly integrating the various Office 97 elements, a package called AccessLinks comes with Excel as an add-in (to Excel) to make working directly with Access forms and reports easier. To use AccessLinks, you must have both Access 97 and Excel 97 installed. If the Access Form, Access Report, and Convert To Access commands don't appear on Excel's Data menu, you need to install AccessLinks. From Excel, choose Tools | Add-ins. In the Add-ins Available box, select the check box next to the add-in you want to load. Be sure to have the Office 97 CD handy, or rights to the network where Office 97 is located.

If the add-in you want to load doesn't appear, click Browse and then locate it. If the add-in isn't installed on your computer, check the Excel User Manual for instructions on how to load the add-in from your original disks or CD-ROM.

Using Access Forms in Excel

The first step in using Access forms in Excel is to create a new Access form from Excel that is built specifically to take into account the link with the spreadsheet. To do so, follow these steps:

1. From Excel, choose Data | Access Forms.
2. The dialog box shown in Figure 15.19 appears. It specifies information about the worksheet and how to link it to Access.
3. Choose to either create a new database or associate this form with an existing database, and then click OK.
4. Access is loaded with a defined link to the spreadsheet.

15

INTEGRATING
OBJECTS

FIGURE **15.19.**

*A dialog box for
specifying which
database to put
the link and
form in.*

5. The Access Form Wizard is then loaded, using the linked table with data from the
   spreadsheet. It guides you through building a data entry form for the Excel list.
   You can enter additional data into the list by clicking the View Access Form button, which is placed in the worksheet by the Access Form Wizard.

Be aware that a significant amount of time can pass between steps 3 and 4, and again
between steps 4 and 5. If it seems that nothing is going on, wait a couple of minutes and
see what happens before killing the process. Fortunately, Windows 95 is a multitasking
operating system that lets you work on other tasks while these steps are taking place.

After you've created a form, you might want to use the existing form again. To do so,
simply click one of the cells and then click the Forms button on your worksheet. If Excel
can't find the form, the Locate Microsoft Access Form dialog box enables you to browse
your folders for the .MDB file that is linked with your worksheet.

Using Access Reports in Excel

Using Access Reports is similar to using Access Forms. The procedure looks like this:

1. Choose Data | Access Reports.

2. A dialog box like the one shown in Figure 15.19 comes up to prompt you for the
   database to put the link and report in.

3. Choose to either create a new database or associate this report and linked table
   with an existing database, and then click OK.

4. Access is loaded with a defined link to the spreadsheet.

5. The Access Report Wizard is then loaded, using the linked table with data from the
   worksheet. It guides you through building a report for the Excel data.

Just as when adding an Access Form to Excel, a significant amount of time can pass
between steps 3 and 4, and again between steps 4 and 5. If it seems that nothing is going
on, remember to wait a couple of minutes and see what happens before killing the
process.

After you've created a report, you might want to use it again. To do so, simply click one of the cells and then click the Report button that was placed on your worksheet. If Excel can't find the report, the Locate Microsoft Access Report dialog box enables you to browse your folders for the .MDB file that is linked with your worksheet.

Working with PivotTable Dynamic Views

Sometimes being able to use the cross-tabulation features of a pivot table on a form is nice—for example, to analyze sales patterns. Cross-tabulation involves summarizing data across different fields. For example, you might want to view total sales by month and product category. A PivotTable is perfect for such a function. With Access 97, you can now create a form that has a PivotTable embedded in it but uses the data from your Access table or query. The process is run through the PivotTable Wizard. To get to it, follow these steps:

1. Open the database that has the table or query from which your data comes. This sample uses the Northwind database that comes installed with Access 97.

2. Go to the Forms tab and click the New button. You then see a number of choices in a list on the right side; the one you want for this process is the PivotTable Wizard.

3. Choose the Orders table from the pull-down box and then click OK.

4. Click Next to bypass the initial dialog box. You then see the second dialog box of the PivotTable Wizard, as shown in Figure 15.20.

FIGURE 15.20.

The second dialog box of the PivotTable Wizard in Access 97.

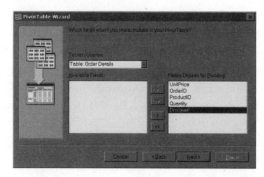

5. Notice that the Order table is being used and that the CustomerID and ShipRegion fields from that table have been selected. Any query or table in Access can supply one or more fields to this form.

6. Click Next to open the layout window, shown in Figure 15.21. It contains a diagram of the PivotTable along with the fields that can be used to build it.

FIGURE 15.21.

The PivotTable layout window in the PivotTable Wizard.

7. Drag the fields to the proper places to provide the answers you're looking for. Press Alt+D to add to the Summary field in the DATA area. In this case, a comparison of Customers to Regions is created, so the fields are arranged as shown in Figure 15.22, where Customer ID has been defined as the Row, ShipRegion as the column, and Count of Customer ID as the result.

FIGURE 15.22.

The layout window with the fields arranged for the form.

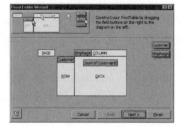

8. Select Next to open the final dialog box in the PivotTable Wizard, where you can make some final changes to your form before actually creating it. The default name is changed (as you can see in Figure 15.23) to better represent what is actually displayed in the form. Using "(Pivot)" to indicate that this is a PivotTable form is a good way to help differentiate this form from others in the database, and to let other users know that this form might be a bit slow to load.

9. Click Finish.

FIGURE 15.23.

The final dialog box in the PivotTable Wizard, with the recommended changes.

Once you have completed the PivotTable, take a minute to see if this is really what you want. Because you used Customer ID and Region, the PivotTable has as many rows as it has customers. What you really want to do is summarize some of this data before comparing it (by dollar amount or type of customer, for example). You can do the summarization in a table (if the base table is large) or through a query (for smaller tables). After walking through this example, you should feel comfortable enough to try this feature for yourself. Think of some business questions you're interested in examining and then try creating a PivotTable form.

Embedding and Linking Excel Worksheets in Access

The next section contains a full walkthrough of the process of embedding and linking Excel worksheets in Access, but the basic steps are as follows:

1. Create a field in the table that holds your data with a type of OLE object.

2. Create a form that includes that field. If you use one of the Access Form Wizards, a Bound Object Frame is automatically created for you. Otherwise, you need to create it yourself.

3. When you're ready to enter data into the OLE field, choose Insert | Object.

4. Select the type of object you're interested in (in this case, most likely an Excel worksheet) and the icon for representing it, if you choose to use an icon rather than always showing all the contents.

5. Either create a new worksheet or specify an old one to be embedded or linked.

6. When you're done with the Excel object, be sure to choose File | Close and return to the current application.

Word, Access, and OLE

When it comes to Word and Access, the main forms of sharing data are through exports between the two products and through embedding and linking. Before you choose whether you want to do one or the other with Word, consider the following:

Link	You have an employee table for a group of computer consultants, and you want to be able to search through your database for the ones who have Access experience. After you find them, you want to be able to print their resumes. The resumes should be linked Word documents so that changes to the resumes are picked up automatically.

15

INTEGRATING OBJECTS

Embed   You are an author and have to track changes to chapters that
                     are being written. You want to be able to call up various ver-
                     sions of a chapter to track changes. The chapters should be
                     embedded so that you can lock them from further changes.

So, if you have a document that must always be available and is fairly static, you should
embed it. If you have a document that changes often, you should probably link it. The
one point to keep in mind if you choose to link, however, is that if the base file is moved
or renamed, the link is broken.

Summary

In this chapter you built a simple Access 97 database application that gave you an
overview of the uses of OLE objects and automation. This chapter's intention was to
show you how to add graphics and other objects to your forms and reports in your
Access 97 application. You have seen that it is a very simple process to link Excel worksheets and Word documents into your applications. This greatly broadens the possibilities
that you have available for creating diverse and useful Access 97 applications. And
remember, although this chapter focused on Access 97 as an OLE client, you can also
use Access 97 as an OLE server and share your database application objects with other
OLE-compliant applications.

Data Access Objects

CHAPTER 16

Information in Access can be controlled in several ways. At the most ad hoc end of the spectrum are direct manipulation tables and query-by-example. Forms and stored queries provide a more structured approach, often desirable when a variety of users will need to input or read data. As powerful as bound forms are, however, there are many situations that they just cannot accommodate by themselves. Access provides a third, and extremely powerful, level of data manipulation called Data Access Objects, or DAO.

This chapter covers DAO, the DAO hierarchical model, the differences between the Microsoft Jet hierarchy and the new ODBC Direct hierarchy, and the different types of objects and collections that compose the hierarchy. You'll learn about the power of DAO, how to programmatically use the same capabilities of the user interface, and many more topics.

What Is DAO?

To understand the underlying core of DAO, you need to understand several interrelated components. Some of this information is covered in more detail elsewhere in this book, but reviewing it here will give you some perspective on the DAO and its uses.

> **NOTE**
>
> DAO must be installed on your machine to be available. To see if it is installed on your machine, open any module in design mode and select Tools|References. If you can see DAO Libraries 3.5, 3.0, and 2.5/3.5, DAO is installed.
>
> If it is not, rerun setup from your install CD-ROM and select Add/Remove. Select the Data Access installation options.

Microsoft Jet Engine

The Microsoft Jet (Joint Engine Technologies) Engine is the underlying database management component. Jet is not Access-specific—it is also used by Excel, Visual Basic (VBA), Visual C++, and other Microsoft products. It controls how all the data in .mdb files (Jet's native file format) is stored, read, found, and interpreted. Additionally, Jet can communicate with other kinds of data generated by other data systems. The two main categories of outside data are ISAM data sources and ODBC data sources.

ISAM (Indexed Sequential Access Method) data sources are conceptually similar to Jet's own .mdb. They vary in power and features, but basically they are file structures on a PC or a network file server, with indexing, often relational capabilities, and often some degree of data type enforcement. Popular ISAM packages include dBASE III and IV,

FoxPro, and Paradox. Jet is ideally suited as a form of "Rosetta stone" in that it can freely communicate with these disparate formats.

ODBC sources, on the other hand, are a different type of system: a client/server. In the client/server model, a highly optimized data engine runs on a database server. Front-end user programs (clients) never have direct access to the actual data files. They only pass requests or information to the server, and the server itself actually locates the information or makes the changes to the files. Client/server applications provide greater data security (there is no way a client program can crash and corrupt the database file) and, most importantly, network efficiency for larger systems.

The ODBC interface was developed to provide a (more or less) standard communication between client programs and client/server systems. A Jet .mdb is not a client/server system, but Access can be a client in a client/server installation.

Data Access Objects

DAO is an interface layer that sits between Jet and the VBA code of an application. DAO encapsulates functionality from the various database types into a coherent set of objects and methods. Almost every aspect of data organization, tables, fields, queries, indexes, data types, record sets, and so on, are represented by specific objects, each with appropriate properties and methods that can be created, modified, and executed.

A key feature of this object-based layer is that the objects can be used with native .mdb databases as well as (to a significant degree) non-native ISAM and ODBC databases. When there is no corresponding functionality, the objects simply will not respond. But for all appropriate actions, your interaction with DAO is essentially the same regardless of the data source.

> **NOTE**
>
> In addition to DAO, Access supports object-based programmatic control of forms and reports. The syntax and organization are similar to DAO, but these forms and reports are part of Access itself and are not directly available to other DAO-using applications such as VBA.

ODBC Direct

A new part of DAO, ODBC Direct provides a method to more directly interact with a database client in its native ODBC dialect. This can provide opportunities for increased performance, and Jet is bypassed, but it requires complete familiarity with the data source, and the code is not likely to be portable.

DAO Today

Access 97 includes a new version of DAO called DAO 3.5. It is an incremental but significant update to DAO 3.0, which was introduced with Access 95. DAO 3.5 is a fully host-independent set of OLE objects that any OLE-compatible client can use. New properties, methods, and objects have been added, and some have been changed. Probably the biggest addition is ODBC Direct.

DAO 3.5 is a shared resource (usually installed in the `\Program Files\Common Files\` `Microsoft Shared\DAO` directory). Any OLE-compatible client can use DAO 3.5, including C developers (using dbDAO and its SDK).

> **NOTE**
>
> DAO is 32-bit in Microsoft Access 97. That is, you can create only 32-bit applications with Access and thus can use only DAO 3.5. New development with DAO 2.5 is not supported in Access 97.

What's Different in DAO 3.5

Some major changes have been made to DAO. If you're converting or porting your application to Access 97, you'll probably want to take full advantage of this new functionality. Following are some of the changes made to DAO. (For more information, see the section "DAO Compatibility" later in this chapter, or the online help for DAO.)

- `DBEngine.IniPath` property—Windows 95 and Windows NT no longer support the use of INI files, but instead store INI-type information in the system registry. `IniPath` now returns the path in the system registry. Here's an example:
  ```
  DBEngine.IniPath = "HKEY_CURRENT_USER\Software\VB and VBA Program
  ➡Settings\MYDBApp"
  ```
- `Recordset` object—Rows from a `Recordset` object can now be retrieved into an array with the `GetRow` method, eliminating the need to iterate through the recordset.
- `Container` and `Document` objects' `AllPermissions` property—This property returns the permissions pertaining to each object (either a `Document` or `Container` object) that the user or the user's group has access to. `AllPermissions` differs from `Permissions` in that it includes the permissions for the group as well as permissions for the user. If the `UserName` property is set to a group, `AllPermissions` and `Permissions` function the same.

- ODBC Direct—DAO 3.5 now supports a new workspace type, ODBC Direct, which exposes ODBC functionality through an extension to the fundamental DAO object model. This allows the developer to create high-performance client/server applications using familiar objects. Whenever you need to write an application that uses a remote database such as SQL Server or Oracle, use ODBC Direct. You use ODBC Direct by creating an ODBC Direct workspace.

- Backward compatibility—Access 97 supports both DAO 3.0 and DAO 2.5 and includes a compatibility layer for older applications. If you're porting your application to Access 97, the DAO 2.5/3.5 Compatibility Library is automatically selected. You can either use the DAO 2.5/3.5 Compatibility Library for compatibility with older versions of DAO or deselect this reference to use the DAO 3.5 library only. The latter choice removes support for the older objects, properties, and methods.

DAO Tutorial by Example

In the following section, several examples of DAO use are presented with explanations. This is intended to provide a practical introduction to the power of DAO, but it only scratches the surface. There is much more additional information; most DAO methods have a range of options. Many of these are discussed in the "DAO Reference" section later in this chapter. Also, the Access help system has considerable reference material on the details of DAO objects, properties, and methods.

The fundamental organizing principles of DAO are containers and membership. Objects are multi-layered—databases contain tables and queries, tables contain fields and indexes, and so on. In a way the structure is fairly complex, but just think of those Russian babushka dolls—each doll you open up holds another doll inside it.

> **NOTE**
>
> C++ programmers who are new to DAO should notice that the relationship between objects is based on embedding rather than inheritance. The key words in a DAO relationship are "contains" rather than "is a...".

Almost every component of the Access user interface can be programmatically controlled with the matching DAO components. As an example, the following code creates a table like the Products table in the Northwind (nwind.mdb) database. Of course, it is probably easier to use the Access user interface for this fixed example, but the beauty of this system is that you can generate new tables on-the-fly without knowing the structure ahead of time. Also, you can generate "throwaway" tables that are used for a specific purpose and then discarded.

> **TIP**
>
> Many DAO collections can be addressed in alternate ways. For example, you can reference a specific field in a table with one of the following forms of syntax:
>
> ```
> Set Fld = Tabledef.fields("Product ID")
> ```
>
> or
>
> ```
> Set Fld = Tabledef.fields(3) 'if you know the index value
> ```
>
> The first approach is more convenient when you're addressing a specific field, while the second might be more convenient when you're looping through all the fields in a table.

Constructing a Table in DAO

The following simple example duplicates the creation of the Products table of the Northwinds database entirely in code (without the display and formatting details):

```
Function maketable()
Dim db As Database, tbl As TableDef, fld As Field, idx As Index
Dim rel As Relation

    Set db = CurrentDb
    Set tbl = db.CreateTableDef("products2")
    With tbl
        .Fields.Append .CreateField("ProductID", dbLong)
        .Fields.Append .CreateField("ProductName", dbText, 40)
        .Fields.Append .CreateField("SupplierID", dbLong)
        .Fields.Append .CreateField("CategoryID", dbLong)
        .Fields.Append .CreateField("QuantityPerUnit", dbText, 20)
        .Fields.Append .CreateField("UnitPrice", dbCurrency)
        .Fields.Append .CreateField("UnitsInStock", dbInteger)
        .Fields.Append .CreateField("UnitsOnOrder", dbInteger)
        .Fields.Append .CreateField("ReorderLevel", dbInteger)
        .Fields.Append .CreateField("Discontinued", dbBoolean)
    End With
    tbl.Fields("ProductID").Attributes = dbAutoIncrField + dbFixedField
    Set idx = tbl.CreateIndex("PrimaryKey")
    idx.Fields.Append idx.CreateField("ProductID")
    idx.Primary = True
    tbl.Indexes.Append idx
    Set idx = tbl.CreateIndex("CategoryID")
    idx.Fields.Append idx.CreateField("CategoryID")
    tbl.Indexes.Append idx
```

```
        Set idx = tbl.CreateIndex("ProductName")
        idx.Fields.Append idx.CreateField("ProductName")
        tbl.Indexes.Append idx
        Set idx = tbl.CreateIndex("SupplierID")
        idx.Fields.Append idx.CreateField("SupplierID")
        tbl.Indexes.Append idx
        tbl.Fields("Discontinued").DefaultValue = False
        db.TableDefs.Append tbl

        'now build a relation to the suppliers table
        Set rel = db.CreateRelation("relation1", "Suppliers", "Products2")
        Set fld = rel.CreateField("SupplierID")
        fld.ForeignName = "SupplierID"
        rel.Fields.Append fld
        db.Relations.Append rel 'relations are appended to database,
➥not to TableDefs

End Function
```

First, db is set to the current database using the special `CurrentDb` function. (Despite the fact that it looks like a simple assignment, `CurrentDb` is a true function and has a fair amount of overhead associated with it. If you will need it multiple times, assign it once to an object variable with sufficient scope and use that variable in all references.)

Next, the new, empty table is created. It will remain invisible to DAO and Access until it is appended to the `TableDefs` collection. Because some changes to `TableDef` components, such as fields, cannot be done once the `TableDef` is appended to the database, it is advisable to do all construction first.

The block of code that builds the fields uses some convenient shortcuts, which may be a little confusing until you realize what is happening. The `With` statement simply means that until the matching `End With`, all the dotted statements are assumed to refer to tblNew. The line

```
.Fields.Append .CreateField("ProductID", dbLong)
```

is basically shorthand for

```
Set fldNew = tblNew.CreateField("ProductID", dbLong)
tblNew.Fields.Append fldNew
```

The compiler first executes the `CreateField` function and then uses the returned value directly in the `Append` statement. After all the fields are created and inserted into the `TableDef`, the `ProductID` field is modified into an `AutoIncrement` type. The indices are now created, one at a time, with fields created and attached to each index. Then the indexes are attached to the table. The table is next attached to the database, and the `TableDefs` collection is refreshed to make sure it is visible to other users on the system. Finally, the relation to `"Suppliers"` is created and appended to the database (*not* to either of the related tables).

> **NOTE**
>
> In the table example, field objects are used in three different ways: table fields, index fields, and relation fields. Even though these are different functions internally, because of the object structure of DAO, the same `Field` type object variable can be used to hold all three versions.

If you are looking at the Database window table view, you won't see the new table added. You'll see it only after flipping to another view page and back. If you try to run this example more than once, you will get an error because Products2 will already exist. Delete the Products2 table before trying the example a second time.

> **TIP**
>
> With most of the object creation functions, some of the arguments are optional. They can be set at the initial object creation, or they can be set subsequently as properties. Once the object is attached to its larger collection, however, not all of these properties are still changeable.

Manipulating Data in DAO

Now that the table is created and populated (you can append directly from the Northwind Products table to get some sample data), it is time to demonstrate how DAO can be used to find and edit information.

Records are manipulated through DAO recordset objects. There are several types of recordsets, but this first example will illustrate the table type recordset. Table type recordsets, which can only be used in `.mdb` databases, have a very efficient search method (`Seek`) for indexed fields. If your application does not have table type recordsets available, the dynaset and snapshot types are also available.

The following demonstration code is run from the Access debug window to demonstrate how lookup is accomplished:

```
Sub showrecord(id As Long)
    Dim db As Database, rec As Recordset
    Set db = CurrentDb
    Set rec = db.OpenRecordset("products2", dbOpenTable)
```

```
        rec.Index = "PrimaryKey"
        rec.Seek "=", id
        If rec.NoMatch Then
            Debug.Print "ID Not Found"
        Else
            Debug.Print rec![ProductName]
            Debug.Print rec![UnitPrice]
        End If
End Sub
```

This simple function is called from the debug window as follows:

```
Showrec 55
```

First, the database reference and the recordset reference are created and the index is set to `"PrimaryKey"` (normally, of course, you would avoid reconstructing these structures for every function call).

The `Seek` method takes a variable number of arguments depending on the number of fields in the referenced index. The first specifies the comparison type, `"="` obviously refers to an equal match, and other options such as `">"`, `">="`, `"<"`, `"<="` are also possible. For example, `">"` will return the first pointer to a record with a value greater than specified, moving front-to-back in the current index sequence. The arguments `"<"` and `"<="` start from the back of the recordset and report the first match coming in that direction.

After each search operation, the recordset's `.nomatch` property is set to true if the search was unsuccessful. Always check this property before trying to do anything with data; if a search is unsuccessful, the position of the current record pointer is unspecified.

Any of the fields can be read using the `recordset![field name]` notation. They cannot be written to, however, until the recordset is placed into edit mode:

```
rec.Edit
rec![UnitPrice] = 1.98
rec.Update
```

It's necessary to use the `Edit` method before setting the value, and the `Update` method after setting the value, for the operation to succeed. If you move to another record, close the recordset, or permit the recordset variable to go out of scope before the update, the changes will be cancelled. If you want to add a record, use the `AddNew` method instead of `Edit`. The locking method determined when the recordset was opened is engaged upon entering the edit mode. See the "Recordsets" section later in this chapter for more information on locking options.

> **NOTE**
>
> After you add a record with AddNew, the current record is *not* changed. It still points to whichever record was current (if any) before the addition. If you want to go to the new record, use the LastModified property, which is actually a bookmark on the most recently modified record. (See "Bookmarks" later in this chapter.)

The Seek method is not always appropriate. First, it only works on table-type recordsets (which are only available in native .mdb databases). Additionally, it requires an indexed field and will only find the first record matching the condition. The FindFirst and FindNext methods are a bit more flexible in operation on a dynaset or snapshot record-set.

The following is a similar example, as used for the Seek demo. In this case, the user inputs a supplier number and the function prints a list of all products from that supplier, utilizing the FindFirst and FindNext methods.

```
Sub FindDemo(id As Long)
    Dim db As Database, rec As Recordset
    Set db = CurrentDb
    Set rec = db.OpenRecordset("products2", dbOpenDynaset)
    rec.FindFirst "[SupplierID]=" & Str$(id)
    If rec.NoMatch Then
        Debug.Print "No matches..."
        Exit Sub
    End If
    Do
        Debug.Print rec![ProductName]
        Debug.Print rec![UnitPrice]
        rec.FindNext "[SupplierID]=" & Str$(id)
    Loop Until rec.NoMatch
    Debug.Print "That's all folks.."
End Sub
```

Unlike Seek, where the appropriate values were simply passed as arguments, FindFirst and FindNext require construction of an SQL Where clause (without the "where"). The clause can be compound and does not require indexed fields, although constructing the clause to utilize indexed fields where possible will substantially improve performance. The sequence in which records are returned with the Find* methods is indeterminate.

Queries

Queries, too, can be addressed in DAO. The QueryDef object can refer to both selection and action queries. QueryDefs based on selection queries (those that return a recordset) can be used as the object on which a recordset object is opened:

```
Dim qy as QueryDef, rec as RecordSet
Set db = CurrentDb
Set qy = db.CreateQueryDef("", "SELECT Orders.OrderID, Orders.OrderDate
➡FROM Orders WHERE (((Orders.OrderDate)>#12/31/96#));")
Set rec = qy.OpenRecordSet()
```

Action queries do not return a recordset, however, so they must be executed to perform their function. Only action queries have an `Execute` method:

```
Sub QueryDemo()
    Dim qy As QueryDef, db As Database
    Set db = CurrentDb
    Set qy = db.CreateQueryDef("", "INSERT INTO products2
➡SELECT Products.* FROM Products;")
    qy.Execute
End Sub
```

This function can be used to copy all the records from the Products table to the Products2 table. `CreateQueryDef` is a bit different from `CreateTableDef` in that there is no need to append it to the `QueryDefs` collection. The first argument in a call to `CreateQueryDef` is normally the name of the query being created, but in this example it was left as an empty string.

> **NOTE**
>
> If an empty string (" ") is passed as the name argument to `CreateQueryDef`, the query is created but is *not* appended to the `QueryDefs` collection. The object variable can be executed, but the `QueryDef` itself will disappear as soon as the object variable goes out of scope or is assigned to another object. This makes it convenient to create, execute, and delete one-shot queries.

Bookmarks

Frequently there is a need to reference specific records to return to later. If there is a unique key the search can be repeated, but that is not always possible or convenient. If you've arrived at the record after a `FindFirst` and a series of `FindNexts`, traversing that route again is impractical. Bookmarks provide a convenient way of handling record navigation.

A bookmark is like the serial number on a coat check ticket. The numeric value has no special meaning to you, except to match to your coat when you return. To bookmark a record, declare a variable of type `Variant` or `String`. To mark a location, simply set this variable equal to the property `recordset.Bookmark`. To return to that location, set `recordset.Bookmark` to the previous value. There is no limit to the number of bookmark variables you can use.

To demonstrate bookmarks, the Sub `BookMarkDemo` is a rehash of `FindDemo`, except that after listing all the products, the current record is returned to the first entry found:

```
Sub BookMarkDemo(id As Long)
    Dim db As Database, rec As Recordset, bk As Variant
    Set db = CurrentDb
    Set rec = db.OpenRecordset("products2", dbOpenDynaset)
    rec.FindFirst "[SupplierID]=" & Str$(id)
    If rec.NoMatch Then
        Debug.Print "No matches..."
        Exit Sub
    End If
    bk = rec.Bookmark 'bookmark first record
    Do
        Debug.Print rec![ProductName]
        Debug.Print rec![UnitPrice]
        rec.FindNext "[SupplierID]=" & Str$(id)
    Loop Until rec.NoMatch
    Debug.Print "Now to return to start"
    Rec.Bookmark = bk
    Debug.Print rec![ProductName]
    Debug.Print rec![UnitPrice]
End Sub
```

There a few more important details regarding bookmarks. Just as when you return to the same restaurant with the same coat, you get a different ticket number, you can run the same query on the same data and get different bookmarks. Requerying a recordset will also invalidate all bookmarks.

There is one way to have bookmarks refer to more than one recordset object: by cloning.

Cloning Recordsets

Unlike creating a new recordset on an identical query, the `Clone` method creates a new object that points to the existing recordset, behaving in most ways as if it were a new recordset. Each clone has its own current record, and so on. Obviously, the overhead is much reduced in creating a clone compared to creating a new recordset, so it can be helpful if you need a lot of copies of a single recordset. The other significant advantage is that bookmarks can be shared between all clones of a single recordset. Syntax to create a clone is as follows:

```
Dim rec as Recordset, rec2 as Recordset, db as Database
Set db = Currentdb
Set rec = db.OpenRecordset("Products")
Set rec2 = rec.Clone
```

Closing Recordsets

VBA and DAO attempt to automatically close recordsets (as well as databases and work-spaces) when the last referencing object variable goes out of scope. However, it is a good practice (and often downright useful) to precisely control this behavior. When a recordset is closed, all pending actions (such as edits) are terminated and no further activities can be performed.

Setting an object variable to the special value Nothing, which terminates all association between the variable and the object, will also generally close the object. But there are important differences. These are most significant when multiple variables refer to the *same* object:

```
Dim db as Database
Dim rec1 as Recordset, rec2 as Recordset, rec3 as Recordset
Set db = CurrentDb
Set rec1 = db.OpenRecordset("Employees")
Set rec2 = rec1
Set rec3 = rec1
'rec 3, rec2 and rec1 now reference the exact same recordset
Set rec2 = Nothing
'rec2 is now inactive, it cannot be used unless reassigned
'however rec3 and rec1 are still active, the recordset is still open
rec3.Close
'now the underlying recordset is closed, neither rec1 nor rec3 can be
used.
```

In general, you should close objects when you are done with them and set object variables to Nothing when they're no longer needed.

A Working Example

To bring some of these points together, we will demonstrate how DAO can enable a form to accomplish functions that are difficult or impossible in simple bound forms.

The form Products, supplied as part of Northwind, is impractical for most real-world businesses because changes can easily, even accidentally, be made to product details, prices, and so on, without any record. Included in the sample database for this chapter is an improved form titled Product Changes. This form maintains an automatically updated audit trail of all changes made to records, with the date, user, old, and new values. For convenience, this trail is displayed at the bottom of the Product Changes form.

Import the table Product Changes as well as the forms Product Changes and Product Changes Sub if you want to follow along.

Product Changes has code tied to three events: On Open, On Close, and Before Update. The On Open event is as follows:

```
Private Sub Form_Open(Cancel As Integer)
    'initialize the DAO objects for change tracking
    Set db = CurrentDb
    Set rec = db.OpenRecordset("Product Changes")
End Sub
```

This sub simply assigns the object variable rec for use later. Similarly, the On Close event simply closes rec. Although an object normally closes when it goes out of scope, good programming practice calls for explicit closing of objects and helps avoid any unexpected behavior.

Finally, the Before Update event does all the real work:

```
Private Sub Form_BeforeUpdate(Cancel As Integer)
'this is called when a record is about to be saved
    Dim ctl As Control
    If IsNull(Me![ProductID].OldValue) Then   'this is a new record
        AddChange "New Record", Null, Null
        Exit Sub
    End If
    For Each ctl In Me
    With ctl
        If .ControlType = acTextBox Or .ControlType = acCheckBox Or
➥ .ControlType = acComboBox Then
            If .OldValue <> .Value Then 'this was changed
                AddChange .Name, .OldValue, .Value
            End If
        End If
    End With
    Next
End Sub
```

The Before Update event is called when a field has been changed and the user is about to move to another record or otherwise induce the saving of changed information. At this moment, bound controls have both a Value and an OldValue property. If they are different, the control has been changed during this session. The event handler first checks to see if the ProductID field has changed from Null to a value. If so, this is a new record and is handled a little differently. Otherwise, the loop checks through all the controls (ignoring the non-data-carrying controls) and looks for changes. If it finds any, it calls AddChange to append them to the audit trail. (Note how convenient it is to use the For Each notation when dealing with collections.)

AddChange is where the actual DAO manipulation occurs:

```
Private Sub AddChange(fld As String, old As Variant, newval As Variant)
    'this routine creates a detailed record of any change and saves it to
    'Product Changes table
```

```
        rec.AddNew
        rec![ProductID] = Me![ProductID].Value  'tie it to this product
        rec![User] = CurrentUser 'needed in multiuser system
        rec![Date] = Date
        rec![Field] = fld
        rec![Old Value] = old
        rec![New Value] = newval
        rec.Update
End Sub
```

DAO Reference

DAO in Access 97 is a set of OLE objects that represent the functionality of the Jet engine. This layer of objects sits between your application and the database you're trying to manipulate. This insulates you, the developer, from the complexities of database programming while providing a high level of flexibility and control.

You dimension a DAO object as a type class just as you dimension a variable as a datatype. Here's an example:

```
Dim MyWorkSpace As Workspace
Dim iCount As Integer
```

Each of the data access objects has its own properties that help define it and methods that manipulate it, and almost every object is part of a collection. Collections are simply a way to refer to groups of like objects. In other words, an object can have a collection that contains other objects with collections that contain other objects, and so forth. This is how the hierarchy is implemented—through collections. For more on objects, properties, methods, and collections, see Chapter 10, "Visual Basic for Applications."

The DAO hierarchy can be confusing at times, but when you get the big picture, you can begin to see the ease of use and power of DAO. Figure 16.1 shows the DAO hierarchy when a Microsoft Jet workspace is used (each object/collection is represented by one object).

Figure 16.2 shows the DAO hierarchy when an ODBC Direct workspace is used.

Throughout the remainder of this chapter, object hierarchies will represent objects unique to one workspace type with the name of that workspace type.

DBEngine

The DBEngine object, shown in Figure 16.3, is the top object in the DAO hierarchy. It is a predefined object and can't be created. The DBEngine object represents and directly manipulates the Jet Database Engine. There is only one instance of the DBEngine object per application. Therefore, it isn't an element of a collection; it is the object that contains everything else.

Figure 16.1.

The Jet DAO hierarchy.

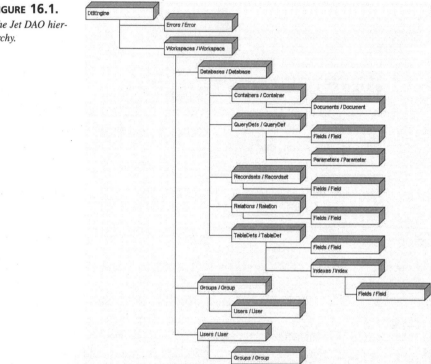

The DBEngine object can be used to compact or repair databases, register ODBC databases, get the Jet version number, and set the login timeout. Errors that occur due to DAO actions will be placed into the DBEngine object's Errors collection. Table 16.1 shows the methods, properties, and collections of the DBEngine object.

FIGURE 16.2.

*The ODBC Direct
DAO hierarchy.*

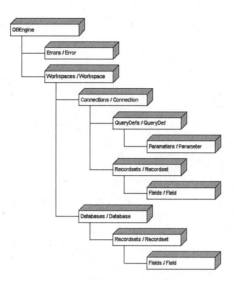

FIGURE 16.3.

The DBEngine
object.

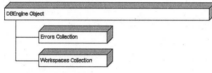

TABLE 16.1. THE METHODS, PROPERTIES, AND COLLECTIONS OF THE DBENGINE OBJECT.

Methods	Properties	Collections
CompactDatabase	DefaultPassword	Errors
CreateWorkSpace	DefaultUser	Workspaces (default)
Idle	IniPath	Properties
RepairDatabase	Version	
RegisterDatabase	LoginTimeOut	SystemDB

Error

The Error object, shown in Figure 16.4, receives all errors when an action or activity
performed by DAO fails. The collection is cleared and all errors are placed into the collection. This action is taken because multiple errors might occur during a given activity
or action by DAO. Errors in the Errors collection are ordered by number; that is, the
error with the lowest number is the first element, the next highest error is the next element, and so forth. Error handling for this collection is discussed later in this chapter.
Table 16.2 shows the properties and collections of the Error object.

FIGURE 16.4.
The Errors collection and the Error *object.*

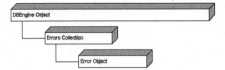

TABLE 16.2. THE PROPERTIES AND COLLECTIONS OF THE ERROR OBJECT.

Properties	Collection
Description	Properties
HelpContext	
HelpFile	
Number	
Source	

If an error occurs in your Access application, you'll need to find out what went wrong and gracefully handle the error. I'll show you more about this later in this chapter in the section titled, imaginatively enough, "Handling Errors."

Workspace

To define a session for the user, use the Workspace object, shown in Figure 16.5. This object contains all open databases and a transaction scope for that user. A Workspace also defines how Access will communicate with the database, whether it is with Jet or ODBC Direct. Transactions within a Workspace object are global across all databases for that Workspace object. Access creates a Workspaces(0) object by default. If there is no security set up for the current database, the Name property is set to #Default Workspace# and the UserName property is set to Admin. This is commonly referred to as the default Workspace.

FIGURE 16.5.
The Workspaces collection and the Workspace *object.*

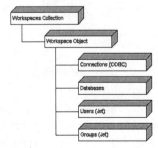

> **NOTE**
>
> Unlike with other collections, you *cannot* remove the default Workspace object. It can never be closed or removed from its collection, and it is always available.

The Workspaces collection is a collection of all Workspace objects. Table 16.3 shows the methods, properties, and collections of the Workspace object.

TABLE 16.3. THE METHODS, PROPERTIES, AND COLLECTIONS OF THE WORKSPACE OBJECT.

Methods	*Properties*	*Collections*
BeginTrans	DefaultCursorDriver	Connections
Close	(ODBC Direct)	ODBC Direct
CommitTrans	IsolateODBCTrans	Databases (default)
CreateDatabase	LoginTimeout	Groups
CreateGroup	(ODBC Direct)	Properties
CreateUser	Name	Users
OpenDatabase	Type	
(Jet)	UserName	
OpenConnection		
(ODBC Direct)		
Rollback		

Database

The Database object, shown in Figure 16.6, represents a database that has been opened by or created with DAO. You use the Database object to connect to the current database or an ISAM database, such as an external Access database, FoxPro, or Paradox. You can also use it to connect to any ODBC datasource, such as SQL Server or Oracle, although it is recommended that you use the Connection object of an ODBC Direct workspace instead. If you use the CreateDatabase method of the Workspace object, the database is automatically appended to the Databases collection. Closing the Database object (using the Close method) removes it from the Databases collection.

FIGURE 16.6.

The Databases collection and the Database *object.*

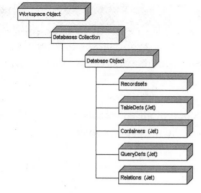

Connection

The Connection object, shown in Figure 16.7, represents a connection to a remote database through an ODBC Direct workspace. You use the Connection object in much the same way as the Database object discussed in the preceding section, except that the databases you can connect to are remote databases such as SQL Server or Oracle.

FIGURE 16.7.

The Connections collection and the Connection *object.*

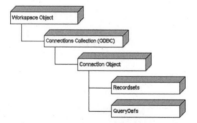

NOTE

If you use the Close method to close a Workspace, Database, or Connection object, all open Recordset objects close and any pending transactions (updates or changes you have made) are rolled back. Also, it's important to note that if your Workspace, Database, or Connection object falls out of scope, any pending updates or changes are also rolled back. With this in mind, it is a good practice to explicitly close currently open Recordset objects before closing a Workspace, Database, or Connection object. (For more information on the scoping of variables, see Chapter 10.)

The Databases collection is a collection of all the `Database` objects opened by DAO, including the current database that was opened by Access. Note that the internal or hidden databases used by Access (wizards, `system.mda`, and so on) aren't in this collection and aren't accessible through this collection.

> **NOTE**
>
> `Databases(0)` is the current database opened by Access every time. You can normally use the `CurrentDB` object, which is the approximate equivalent of `DBEngine.Workspaces(0).Databases(0)`. See "Using the Current Database" later in this chapter.

Table 16.4 shows the methods, properties, and collections of the `Database` object. Note that some of the methods and properties are specific to the kind of `Workspace` object the database is opened under.

TABLE 16.4. THE METHODS, PROPERTIES, AND COLLECTIONS OF THE DATABASE OBJECT.

Methods	Properties	Collections
Close	CollatingOrder	Containers
CreateProperty	Connect (Jet)	Properties
CreateQueryDef	Connection	QueryDefs
CreateRelation	(ODBC Direct)	Recordsets
CreateTableDef	DesignMasterID (Jet)	(Default for ODBC Direct)
Execute	KeepLocal	Relations
MakeReplica (Jet)	Name	TableDefs (default)
NewPassword (Jet)	QueryTimeout	
OpenRecordset	RecordsAffected	
PopulatePartial (Jet)	Replicable (Jet)	
Synchronize	ReplicaID (Jet)	
	ReplicationConflictFunction	
	(Jet)	

continues

Table 16.4. CONTINUED

Methods	Properties	Collections
	Transactions	
	Updatable	
	V1xNullBehavior	
	Version	

User

In a Microsoft Jet workspace, each User object represents users that exist in the work-group database (see Figure 16.8). Note that this object is not valid for an ODBC Direct workspace. The User object represents a user account as defined in the workgroup database. For more information on security, see Chapter 23, "Security." Table 16.5 shows the methods, properties, and collections of the User object.

Figure 16.8.

The Users collection and the User object.

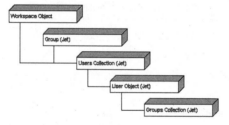

Table 16.5. The methods, properties, and collections of the User object.

Methods	Properties	Collections
CreateGroup	Name	Groups (default)
NewPassword	Password	Properties
	PID	

Group

Like the User object, the Group object in a Microsoft Jet workspace (shown in Figure 16.9) represents groups that have been defined in the workgroup database. The Group object also is not valid for an ODBC Direct workspace. A Group object usually represents groups of users and their appropriate security. Each user in a group is represented by a User object in the Users collection of the Group. For more information on security, see Chapter 23. Table 16.6 shows the methods, properties, and collections of the Group object.

FIGURE 16.9.
The Groups collection and the Group *object.*

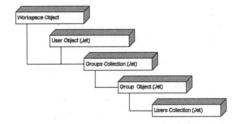

TABLE 16.6. THE METHODS, PROPERTIES, AND COLLECTIONS OF THE GROUP OBJECT.

Methods	*Properties*	*Collections*
CreateUser	Name	Users (default)
	PID	Properties

QueryDef

Each query that has been defined in Access or created using CreateQueryDef is represented by a QueryDef object in the QueryDefs collection (see Figure 16.10). With the QueryDef object, you can create Recordset objects, add your own properties (more on this topic later), look at the underlying SQL code, tell whether it returns records, or just execute it. Because QueryDefs are precompiled SQL statements, they generally run faster than dynamic SQL (Jet doesn't have to compile it on-the-fly). You can create queries with the CreateQueryDef method.

Similarly, a SQL Server database can have precompiled SQL statements called *stored procedures* that are represented by a QueryDef object when an ODBC Direct workspace is being used.

Table 16.7 shows the methods, properties, and collections of the QueryDef object.

TABLE 16.7. THE METHODS, PROPERTIES, AND COLLECTIONS OF THE QUERYDEF OBJECT.

Methods	*Properties*	*Collections*
Cancel	CacheSize	Fields
(ODBC Direct)	(ODBC Direct)	Parameters (default)

continues

TABLE 16.7. CONTINUED

Methods	Properties	Collections
CreateProperty	Connect	Properties
(Jet)	Connection	
Execute	(ODBC Direct)	
OpenRecordset	Date Created (Jet)	
	KeepLocal (Jet)	
	LastUpdated (Jet)	
	LogMessages (Jet)	
	MaxRecords	
	Name	
	ODBCTimeout	
	Prepare	
	(ODBC Direct)	
	RecordsAffected	
	Replicable (Jet)	
	ReturnsRecords (Jet)	
	SQL	
	StillExecuting	
	(ODBC Direct)	
	Type	
	Updatable	

TableDef (Jet Only)

In a Microsoft Jet workspace, TableDef objects represent tables or stored table definitions in a given database (see Figure 16.11). The table can be in the current database or in an attached table from an external database. With the TableDef object, you can tell whether the table is attached and find out its validation rules, whether it is updateable, or the number of records in it. Table 16.8 shows the methods, properties, and collections of the TableDef object.

FIGURE 16.10.
*The QueryDefs
collection and the*
`QueryDef` *object.*

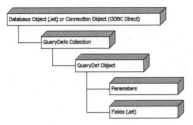

FIGURE 16.11.
*The TableDefs col-
lection and the*
`TableDef` *object.*

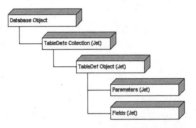

> **NOTE**
>
> When a table is attached, the properties that define its definition are read-only. You must go back to the source database (where the table physically resides) and make changes there.

TABLE 16.8. THE METHODS, PROPERTIES, AND COLLECTIONS OF THE TABLEDEF OBJECT.

Methods	Properties	Collections
CreateField	Attributes	Fields (default)
CreateIndex	ConflictTable	Indexes
CreateProperty	Connect	Properties
OpenRecordset	DateCreated	
RefreshLink	KeepLocal	
	LastUpdated	
	Name	
	RecordCount	

continues

TABLE 16.8. CONTINUED

Methods	Properties	Collections
	Replicable	
	ReplicaFilter	
	SourceTableName	
	Updatable	
	ValidationRule	
	ValidationText	

Index (Jet Only)

Indexes of a recordset or TableDef are represented by the Index object, shown in Figure 16.12. The developer can set the index for a table, for instance, just by referring to an index in the Indexes collection. Table 16.9 shows the methods, properties, and collections of the Index object.

FIGURE 16.12.

The Indexes collection and the Index object.

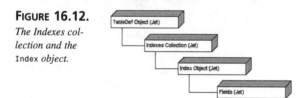

TABLE 16.9. THE METHODS, PROPERTIES, AND COLLECTIONS OF THE INDEX OBJECT.

Methods	Properties	Collections
CreateField	Clustered	Properties
CreateProperty	DistinctCount	Fields (default)
	Foreign	
	IgnoreNulls	
	Name	
	Primary	
	Required	
	Unique	

Field

`Field` objects represent common columns of data sharing similar properties and a common datatype (see Figure 16.13). `Relation`, `Recordset`, `TableDef`, `QueryDef`, and `Index` objects all have a Fields collection. For instance, if you're looking at a table using Access, each column of information is a field and is represented by a `Field` object. The attributes of a field are represented by the different properties (and can be modified), as well as the value of the field. Table 16.10 shows the methods, properties, and collections of the `Field` object.

FIGURE 16.13.

The Fields collection and the `Field` *object.*

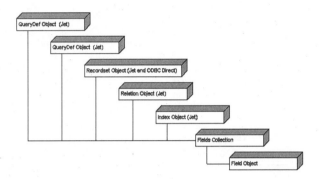

TABLE 16.10. THE METHODS, PROPERTIES, AND COLLECTIONS OF THE FIELD OBJECT.

Methods	Properties	Collection
AppendChunk	AllowZeroLength (Jet)	Properties
CreateProperty	Attributes	
GetChunk	CollatingOrder (Jet)	
	DataUpdatable	
	DefaultValue (Jet)	
	FieldSize	
	ForeignName	
	Name	
	OrdinalPosition	
	OriginalValue (ODBC Direct)	
	Required	

continues

TABLE 16.10. CONTINUED

Methods	Properties	Collection
	Size	
	SourceField	
	SourceTable	
	Status (ODBC Direct)	
	Type	
	ValidateOnSet (Jet)	
	ValidationRule (Jet)	
	ValidationText (Jet)	
	Value	
	VisibleValue (ODBC Direct)	

Recordset

The Recordset object, shown in Figure 16.14, is probably the most-used object DAO provides. With this object, you can programmatically access tables in the connected database. This type of object is somewhat different from the other objects in that it is created each time your application runs and you create recordsets. These objects are not stored on disk—or anywhere, for that matter. They're just temporary.

FIGURE 16.14.

The Recordsets collection and the Recordset *object.*

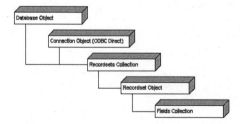

> **NOTE**
>
> The properties, methods, and collections of a `Recordset` object vary depending on the type of the recordset and the type of the current workspace. See the DAO online Help for a complete listing of properties, methods, and collections for this object.

Recordset objects are created with the `OpenRecordSet` method. Recordsets can be based on a connection or database, or on other recordsets or selection type queries.

- Table type recordsets—These can only be opened on Jet `.mdb` databases. They are efficient for locating unique records on indexed fields using the `Seek` method. Table type recordsets can generally be edited.

- Dynasets are the more general recordset type. Dynasets can be opened (with some restrictions) on Jet, ISAM, or ODBC data sources. Dynasets can generally be edited.

- Snapshots also can be opened on a variety of sources. They can be more efficient under some circumstances, particularly if the data to be transferred is a relatively small amount. (See "Dynasets and Snapshots" in Chapter 6, "Creating Interactive Forms.") Snapshots cannot be edited.

Recordsets can be opened optionally as Forward Only, which provides some performance efficiency gains, particularly in ODBC environments.

Record Locking

The record locking choices, optimistic and pessimistic, are discussed in Chapter 6 in the section "Forms for Multiple Users." These can be selected by setting the `recordset.LockEdits` property. Under DAO, the sequence is as follows:

- Optimistic locking—Set `LockEdits` property to false. When the `Edit` method is executed, DAO checks the value of the field but does not lock it. When the `Update` method is executed, DAO checks to see if anyone else has altered the field in the meantime. If so, VBA runtime error 3197 or 3260 is generated, which can be trapped and handled appropriately.

- Pessimistic locking—Set `LockEdits` property to True. As soon as the Edit method is executed, all other users are locked out of editing the record. (Because Access uses page locking rather than record locking, they are actually locked out of the entire 2KB block surrounding the record.) After `Update` is executed, the record is released.

> **TIP**
>
> In the debug window, use the function AccessError(errno) to display the text of a non-VBA error (such as 3197 or 3260 above), rather than VBA's Error(errno).

> **TIP**
>
> The Access help documentation describes arguments for setting LockEdits from the OpenRecordSet method. Attempting to do so generates a runtime error. Set LockEdits to True or False as you would any other property.

Transaction Locking

There are times when saving a single record is not sufficient, such as when a number of records need to be saved to different tables, and it is essential that the whole process go as a single entity—all or nothing. DAO offers transaction processing to handle these situations:

```
'skeleton Transaction Processing code
On Error GoTo Errorhandler
Dim wrk as Workspace
Set wrk = DBEngine.Workspaces(0)
'Transaction locking requires reference to current workspace
Wrk.BeginTrans
    'place data activity in here
wrk.CommitTrans 'at this point attempt the whole process
… more code

Errorhandler:
'if any error occurs, execution will wind up here.
If transaction_error then
    wrk.Rollback 'depending on what happened we can choose to
        'roll the transaction back to the BeginTrans point
    … more processing…
```

Basically, Rollback undoes everything processed since the corresponding BeginTrans. Transactions are workspace-scoped and can be nested, like For…Next loops. If you need to keep several non-overlapping transactions pending, you can create additional workspaces.

Transaction processing is available with Jet databases and many ODBC databases, but currently not in non-Jet ISAM.

GetRow Method

A new feature of DAO in Access 97, `GetRow` permits populating a VBA array with a recordset in a single operation:

```
Public Sub GetRowsSample()
    Dim dbsDatabase As Database, rstSampleRecordSet As Recordset
    Dim varMyRecords As Variant, iCount As Integer

    Set dbsDatabase = CurrentDb()
    ' Place this all on one line
    Set rstSampleRecordSet = dbsDatabase.OpenRecordset("SELECT FirstName,
" &
    ➥"LastName, Title FROM Employees", dbOpenSnapshot)

    varMyRecords = rstSampleRecordSet.GetRows(3)

    Debug.Print "First Name", "Last Name", "Title"

    ' The first subscript of the array identifies the Fields
    ' collection (moves horizontally across the record)
    ' Print the first field in the first record
    Debug.Print varMyRecords(0, 0),

    ' Print the second field in the first record
    Debug.Print varMyRecords(1, 0),

    ' Print the third field in the first record
    Debug.Print varMyRecords(2, 0)

    ' The second subscript of the array identifies the record number
    ' (moves vertically through records)
    ' Print the first field in the second record
    Debug.Print varMyRecords(0, 1),

    ' Print the second field in the second record
    Debug.Print varMyRecords(1, 1),

    ' Print the third field in the second record
    Debug.Print varMyRecords(2, 1)

End Sub
```

Bookmarks

Bookmarks provide a means of identifying and returning to individual records. To bookmark a record, first declare a variable of type `Variant` or `String`. Then, to mark a location, simply set this variable equal to the property `recordset.Bookmark`. To return to that location, set `recordset.Bookmark` to the previously saved value. There is no limit to the number of bookmark variables you can use.

A bookmark is not a true data type, but is instead a special form of string. Most Access recordsets and some other attached recordsets support bookmarks. You can be sure at runtime because all recordset objects have a property `Bookmarkable` that is true if the object supports bookmarks.

> **NOTE**
>
> Normally, all you do with bookmarks is save them and set them. If for any reason you do a comparison of bookmarks in VBA, be sure to do it in a module compiled under `Option Compare Binary`. String comparisons under `Option Compare Text` or `Option Compare Database` are unreliable for bookmarks.

Bookmarks are not compatible between recordsets, even if they're created on the same table or query. Only cloned recordsets can share bookmarks.

Clone

Unlike creating a new recordset on an identical query, the `Clone` method creates a new object that points to the existing recordset, behaving in most ways as if it were a new recordset. Each clone has its own current record, and so on. There's much less overhead in creating a clone, so it can be helpful if you need a lot of copies of a single recordset. If a clone closes or goes out of scope (even the original clone), the others are not affected. The other significant advantage is that bookmarks can be shared between all clones of a single recordset.

Relation (Jet Only)

All relations of an Access database are represented by a `Relation` object, shown in Figure 16.15. A *relation* is defined as a relationship between fields in two or more tables. The Relations collection contains all the defined relationships for that `Database` object. For more information on creating and manipulating relationships from Access 97, see the "Relationships" section in Chapter 3, "Creating Sophisticated Queries." Table 16.11 shows the methods, properties, and collections of the `Relation` object.

TABLE 16.11. THE METHODS, PROPERTIES, AND COLLECTIONS OF THE RELATION OBJECT.

Methods	Properties	Collection
CreateField	Attributes	Fields (default)
	ForeignTable	Properties
	Name	

Methods	*Properties*	*Collection*
	PartialReplica	
	Table	

FIGURE 16.15.

The Relations collection and the Relation *object.*

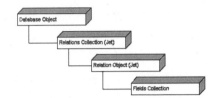

Parameter

In Access, you can define queries that require formal parameters and supply these parameters at runtime. Formal or *explicit* parameters are those that have been defined in a query's SQL using the Parameters keyword.

Similarly, a QueryDef object that represents a stored procedure in a remote SQL Server database can have parameters. A parameter in such a QueryDef can be either an input parameter (you pass the parameter to the QueryDef), an output parameter (the QueryDef returns information to you through the parameter), or a return value. The type of parameter is determined by the Direction property, which is specific to ODBC Direct.

These formal parameters are represented in the Parameters collection by the Parameter object, shown in Figure 16.16. It's important to note that *explicit,* not *implicit,* parameters are represented. The Parameter object only provides information on existing parameters. You cannot append or delete objects from the Parameters collection. Table 16.12 shows the properties and collections of the Parameter object.

FIGURE 16.16.

The Parameters collection and the Parameter *object.*

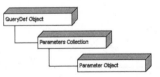

TABLE 16.12. THE PROPERTIES AND COLLECTIONS OF THE PARAMETER OBJECT.

Properties	*Collection*
Direction	Properties
(ODBC Direct)	

continues

TABLE 16.12. CONTINUED

Properties	Collection
Name	
Type	
Value	

Container (Jet Only)

Using `Container` objects is one way DAO achieves its application independence (see the "Using DAO" section later in this chapter). The `Container` object, shown in Figure 16.17, stores such items as Access forms, databases, and modules. This object is generic enough to store these types of objects, yet flexible enough to maintain independence from any one application. Table 16.13 shows the properties and collections of the `Container` object.

FIGURE 16.17.

The Containers collection and the `Container` *object.*

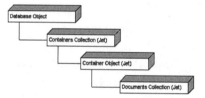

TABLE 16.13. THE PROPERTIES AND COLLECTIONS OF THE CONTAINER OBJECT.

Properties	Collections
AllPermissions	Documents (default)
Inherit	Properties
Name	
Owner	
Permissions	
UserName	

Document (Jet Only)

The `Document` object, shown in Figure 16.18, represents each *individual* application object (such as forms, modules, or tables). For instance, when you create your database, DAO creates a Forms container that contains a `Document` object for each form in the database. Table 16.14 shows the properties and collections of the `Document` object.

FIGURE 16.18.

The Documents collection and the Document *object.*

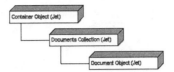

TABLE 16.14. THE PROPERTIES AND COLLECTIONS OF THE DOCUMENT OBJECT.

Method	Properties	Collection
CreateProperty	AllPermissions	Properties
	Container	
	DateCreated	
	KeepLocal	
	LastUpdated	
	Name	
	Owner	
	Permissions	
	Replicable	
	UserName	

Property

A Property object represents the characteristics of an object (see Figure 16.19). Every object in DAO has a Properties collection, and each Property object can be a built-in or user-defined characteristic. The developer can manipulate these properties at runtime and can even add new properties using the CreateProperty method.

FIGURE 16.19.

The Properties collection and the Property *object.*

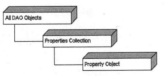

User-defined properties are those added at runtime to a specific instance of an object. It's important to note that properties added to an object type are for just that instance of that object type and will disappear when the object is closed. The developer is responsible for setting and changing values in user-defined properties. This is the only type of property that can be deleted from the Properties collection; built-in properties cannot be deleted. Table 16.15 shows the properties and collections of the Property object.

TABLE 16.15. THE PROPERTIES AND COLLECTIONS OF THE PROPERTY OBJECT.

Properties	Collection
Inherited	Properties
Name	
Type	
Value	

Using DAO

Now that you understand the hierarchy, you can get down to the basics of using DAO. By now you're comfortable with accessing data through Access 97's user interface or by using the built-in data control of a form. When you use the user interface to manipulate the database (creating queries, adding or creating tables, and so on), Access 97 calls Jet directly. That is, it doesn't hand off the request to DAO. The only time Access 97 uses DAO is in a code module. Refer to Figure 16.20 to see where DAO sits in relation to your application or database.

FIGURE 16.20.

The application object model.

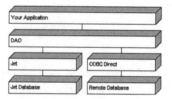

DAO can now be accessed from any OLE-compatible client (Microsoft Visual Basic 4.0 and 5.0 32-bit, Microsoft Excel 95, or Microsoft Access 97). All the objects, properties, and methods are exposed to the developer as an OLE in-process server.

In-process servers are OLE Automation servers that are compiled as DLLs and that share the same process space as the calling application (your application). What is the difference between a DLL and an OLE server? An OLE server exposes all its objects, properties, and methods to the developer (just like a DLL), but an OLE server also exposes descriptions and explanations of each object, property, and method in an associated *type library.*

You can browse the type libraries of all the OLE servers in your application during design time by using the Object Browser, shown in Figure 16.21. You can activate the Object Browser from the Access 97 Toolbar, by pressing F2, or by selecting

View | Object Browser. For more help with using the Object Browser, see Chapter 20, "Using Access in the Client/Server Model."

FIGURE 16.21.

*The Object
Browser.*

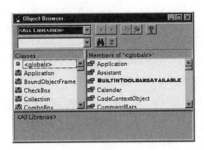

With the Object Browser, you can navigate through the DAO hierarchy and see each property and method for each object in the hierarchy. This feature is useful because it offers Help, an example, and a paste function that enables you to paste the method or property (or collection) into your code.

Objects and Collections

The concept of objects and collections is very important in DAO. In the hierarchy most objects have collections that contain that object type's members. For instance, the `DBEngine` object has a collection of workspaces that contain individual `Workspace` objects. Most objects are part of a collection that has objects, which in turn can have collections.

Usually in the object-oriented world, a collection is the plural of the object type that the collection contains. For example, the Workspaces collection contains `Workspace` objects.

Declaring DAO

To use DAO, first declare an object variable of whichever object type you want to use. As mentioned earlier, although DAO is actually a hierarchy of classes, this chapter refers to the classes as objects to avoid confusion. Classes are usually a type of object that you declare something as, and that you can't use directly. For example, I don't have an object called `Workspace`, but instead have a variable `wksMyWorkspace` of the Workspace type or class:

```
Dim wksMyWorkspace as Workspace
```

Object Variables

Due to the nature of DAO's hierarchical structure, it could become cumbersome to keep referring to objects through the DAO hierarchy. This is where object variables come in. An object variable is simply a pointer or reference to another object. Using an object variable instead of using the hierarchy directly will make your code more readable and easier to type (no more typing those long references!). Overall, you should always use object variables if you're referencing a property more than once. Here's an example:

```
Dim rstMyRecordset As Recordset, strName As String, strConnect As String
Dim iCount As Integer, strUpdatable As String, dbsMyDatabase As Database
Set dbsMyDatabase = CurrentDb
' This is the SLOW method (DON'T DO THIS)
' References get resolved through each iteration
For iCount = 1 To 10
    Debug.Print dbsMyDatabase.Name
Next

' This is the FAST method
' References get resolved just once
strName = dbsMyDatabase.Name
For iCount = 1 To 10
    Debug.Print strName
Next

' Use the With when referring to the same object a bunch of times
With dbsMyDatabase
    strUpdatable = .Updatable
    strName = .Name
    strConnect = .Connect
End With
```

> **NOTE**
>
> You can declare a variable of type `Object`, and this variable can hold any type of object: `Recordset`, `Field`, and so on. There are times when this can be useful, but in general it's advisable to avoid it. Declaring objects by their specific type (such as `Field`) helps prevent you from accidentally misusing it. Perhaps more importantly, generic `Object` variables are resolved at runtime—that is, when the code is executed, VBA figures out which kind of variable it is and then determines which method code is appropriate for that class. This takes a lot of CPU cycles. If you explicitly type the variable, VBA can resolve the step at compile time into a straightforward call. In tests, it took nearly 40 times as long to call a method on a user-defined class using `Object` as the exact same call with the variable declared by class name.

DAO Unleashed

DAO is broken down into two parts: Data Definition Language, or DDL, and Data Manipulation Language, or DML. DDL is the part of DAO that *defines* the database, its objects, and its data, whereas DML *manipulates* the database, its objects, and its data. The following discussion covers how to create a database and then manipulate it using DAO.

Creating Databases

Creating databases with DAO is a fairly easy and straightforward process from a mechanical point of view. The hard part is designing the data model for your database. If you have a good data model driving this process, things will flow much more smoothly. Too many developers design their data model on-the-fly. Although this technique might help you beat a deadline, it will probably come back to bite you! The saying "A house is only as good as the foundation" also rings true for databases. A database is only as good as the data model it is designed from (database meaning a physical database, not a database application). That being said, let the process begin!

> **NOTE**
>
> Access can create only Access databases (.MDB), and to a lesser extent other ISAM databases such as FoxPro and dBASE, by exporting tables. ODBC client/server databases, however, must be created in their native environments. Access has the capability only to manipulate these databases, not to create them. Once connected to a running client/server database, however, new tables can often be created by Access, depending on the specific application.

Follow these steps to create an Access database using DAO:

1. Declare a `Database` object for the database you want to create:

   ```
   Dim MyNewDatabase as Database
   ```

2. Use the `CreateDatabase` method of the `Workspace` object to create an empty database and database file:

   ```
   Set MyNewDatabase = WorkSpaces(0).CreateDatabase("MyNewDB")
   ```

3. Define each table in your new database. You should already know which fields and indexes should go into this table (from your data model).

4. Use the `CreateTableDef` method to create each table in the database:

```
Dim tdfNewTable as TableDef

Set tdfNewTable = MyNewDatabase.CreateTableDef("Employees")
```

5. Use the new `TableDef` object to create fields in the new table by using the `CreateField` method of the `Field` object. This example creates a few different fields:

```
Dim fldNewField As Field
Set fldNewField = tdfNewTable.CreateField("Employee_ID", dbLong)
fldNewField.Attributes = dbAutoIncrField
tdfNewTable.Append fldNewField

Set fldNewField = tdfNewTable.CreateField("First_Name", dbText, 25)
fldNewField.Attributes = dbAutoIncrField
tdfNewTable.Append fldNewField

Set fldNewField = tdfNewTable.CreateField("Last_Name", dbText, 25)
fldNewField.Attributes = dbAutoIncrField
tdfNewTable.Append fldNewField
```

6. Now that the table is defined, append it to the database. This step actually creates the table in your database and appends it to the Databases collection. After this step is done, though, you can't make any changes to the appended fields (you can, however, add and delete new ones):

```
MyNewDatabase.Append tdfNewTable
```

7. At this point, you can create one or more indexes using the `TableDef` object's `CreateIndex` method. Use `CreateIndex` to create an `Index` object:

```
Dim idxNewIndex As Index

Set idxNewIndex = tdfNewTable.CreateIndex("Employee")
```

8. Use the `CreateField` method of the `Index` object to create a `Field` object for every indexed field in the `Index` object, and then append it to the `Index` object:

```
Set fldNewField = idxNewIndex.CreateField("Employee_ID")
fldNewField.Primary = True
idxNewIndex.Fields.Append fldNewField
```

9. Now append each `Index` object to the Indexes collection of the `TableDef` object using the `Append` method. Your table can have several indexes or no indexes:

```
TdfNewTable.Indexes.Append idxNewIndex
```

You have just created your first database. Using the Access user interface is a much easier way of accomplishing this task, but it's always good to know how to do it the hard way. For example, if you need to have your end users create a new database, such as a local lookup database, you can include a utility in your application to do this for them.

Using the Current Database

Normally, when you're developing Access applications, you are using the database that was opened from the design environment. DAO has a function called `CurrentDB` that is a pointer to the currently open database.

`CurrentDB` references the database almost the same way `DBEngine.Workspaces(0).Databases(0)` does. You can't close `Databases(0)` or `CurrentDB`. (`CurrentDB.Close` has no effect and is ignored.) Although the second method is supported in Access 97 and probably will be supported in future versions, it is recommended that you use the `CurrentDB` function instead. The `CurrentDB` function is a lot friendlier in multiuser environments than the older method. `CurrentDB` creates another instance of the open database (similar to using `OpenDatabase` on the current database) instead of referring to the open instance.

What are the practical differences between `CurrentDB` and `DBEngine.Workspaces(0).Databases(0)`? First, `CurrentDB` actually creates a new database reference. This is slower than the full syntax, but on the other hand, the copy is always fully refreshed. `CurrentDB` presents problems if used as part of a longer expression, such as `CurrentDB.Containers.Tables.Documents(0)`. The `CurrentDB` reference will go out of scope as soon as the line is complete, so any objects set by this expression will also go out of scope. Finally, `CurrentDB` cannot be used if you are calling Access as an automation object from outside.

Handling Errors

Error handling is done with the DBEngine's Errors collection of Error objects. Whenever an error occurs, you can examine the Errors collection for all errors. The Errors collection holds all errors that occur during an action or transaction, and each error is represented by an Error object. If you're writing a generic error handler, you can examine the Errors collection and report errors (based on an Error table or a basic Select Case statement). Here's an example to run from the debug window:

```
Sub testerr()
'demonstrates using error object to report errors.
On Error GoTo ErrorBlock_Err:
Dim dbsMyDatabase As Database, errErrorObject As Error
Set dbsMyDatabase = OpenDatabase("BogusDB.MDB")
dbsMyDatabase.Close
Exit Sub
ErrorBlock_Err:
    For Each errErrorObject In DBEngine.Errors
        Debug.Print errErrorObject.Description
        Debug.Print errErrorObject.Source
        Debug.Print errErrorObject.Number
    Next
Resume Next

End Sub
```

In applications that use DAO, the most interesting error—the most specific error—is often the last error in the collection. You could choose to log all errors but display only the one error you felt was most useful to your end users.

DAO Compatibility

With the new, improved object model, some of the following DAO 2.5 objects, methods, and properties are no longer supported in DAO 3.5. Table 16.16 shows the object, method, or property and its corresponding replacement.

TABLE 16.16. DAO COMPATIBILITY.

DAO 2.5 Functionality Not Present in DAO 3.5	Recommended DAO 3.5 Replacement
FreeLocks	Not needed in Access 97
SetDefaultWorkSpace	DBEngine.DefaultUser/DBEngine.DefaultPassword
SetDataAccessOption	DBEngine.IniPath
BeginTrans (Database object)	BeginTrans method of the Workspace object

DAO 2.5 Functionality Not Present in DAO 3.5	Recommended DAO 3.5 Replacement
CommitTrans (Database object)	CommitTrans method of the Workspace object
RollBack (Database object)	RollBack method of the Workspace object
CreateDynaset (Database object)	(Database.)OpenRecordSet of type Dynaset
CreateSnapshot (Database object)	(Database.)OpenRecordSet of type Snapshot
DeleteQueryDef (Database object)	QueryDefs collection's Delete method
ExecuteSQL (Database object)	Execute method and RecordsAffected property of the Database object
ListTables (Database object)	TableDefs collection of the Database object
OpenQueryDef (Database object)	QueryDefs collection of the Database object
OpenTable (Database object)	(Database.)OpenRecordSet of type Table
Table ListIndexes	Indexes collection of the TableDef object
CreateDynaset (QueryDef object)	OpenRecordset method of the QueryDef object
CreateSnapshot (QueryDef object)	OpenRecordset method of the QueryDef object
ListParameters (QueryDef object)	Parameters collection of the QueryDef object
Dynaset object	Recordset object of type Dynaset
Snapshot object	Recordset object of type Snapshot
Table object	Recordset object of type Table
ListFields method (Table, Dynaset, and Snapshot)	Fields collection of the Recordset object
CreateDynaset (QueryDef and Dynaset object)	OpenRecordset method of the object with type Dynaset
CreateSnapshot (QueryDef and Dynaset object)	OpenRecordset method of the object with type Snapshot

If you have an Access 95 project, you should have no compatibility issues when you convert it to Access 97. However, if you have an Access 2.0 project that contains some of the older objects, properties, or methods and you just want to convert to Access 97, you can use the Microsoft DAO 2.5/3.5 Compatibility Library. This library provides backward-compatibility with older versions of DAO and Jet. To check whether you're using this type library, select Tools | References from a Module window, and look in the References dialog box for the Microsoft DAO 2.5/3.5 Compatibility Library option (see Figure 16.22).

FIGURE 16.22.

The References dialog box.

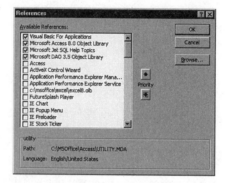

It's important to note that applications or databases converted to Access 97 automatically reference this type library. Likewise, applications and databases created in Access 97 don't have this reference. If you have an older application and you're not sure whether you're using any of the older objects, deselect the Microsoft DAO 2.5/3.5 Compatibility Library option, and select Run | Compile All Modules while in a Module window. If your application recompiles without errors, you don't have to use the Compatibility Library.

To ensure proper compatibility with future versions of DAO, it is recommended that you convert to DAO 3.5. Your application won't have the additional overhead of another layer, and you won't have to distribute the Compatibility Library with your application.

> **NOTE**
>
> A note on version 2.5 of DAO and Jet: Access 97 won't use DAO 2.5 directly because it's a fully 32-bit environment and DAO 2.5 is 16-bit. Databases created as 2.5 can be converted to 3.5, or the developer can use the Compatibility Library.

NOTE

At one time, the dot (.) and bang (!) could be used interchangeably. Current usage is more rigorously enforced, however, with ! separating members of collections and . separating properties and methods.

OPTIMIZING DAO

The following items cover some of the actions you can take to improve the performance of your application (strictly related to DAO). It's important to note that although some optimizations might provide a significant performance increase, some or all of the suggestions discussed here might not do anything for your application. Some external factors affect how much you can gain from each suggestion. Identifying key areas of functionality would be a good place to start optimizations—usually, only 10 percent of the code in an application provides 90 percent of the functionality. Start by concentrating on the 10 percent.

- Start with a Good Database Design

  First and foremost, make sure that the database is designed properly for its intended purpose. No amount of code optimization will completely overcome a deficient database design.

- Use Object Variables

  As stated earlier, whenever your application needs to reference a DAO property, store its value in an explicitly typed variable. Here's a simple rule of thumb: If the same object or property is used more than once, use an object variable.

- Refreshing

  Avoid refreshing unless you absolutely can't avoid it. Refreshing a collection gives you an up-to-date view of that collection's objects and properties or data, but in a multiuser environment or a speed-critical application, this is a very "expensive" method to use (in other words, it takes a lot of processor time or system resources).

- Using Queries for Access Databases

  Queries are precompiled SQL statements stored in your Access database. When your application uses dynamic SQL (SQL created in your code

continues

on-the-fly), Jet still needs to optimize and compile the SQL statement during runtime. If you use queries whenever possible, the optimization and compilation are done beforehand (when the query is created in Access), and you don't suffer the degradation in speed at runtime.

- Using Stored Procedures for Remote Databases

  If you are using a remote database such as SQL Server, use ODBC Direct and write your queries as stored procedures. Stored procedures are precompiled SQL statements in your remote database. When the stored procedure is compiled on your database, the server optimizes the query similarly to how Access optimizes its own queries. The big difference here is that when you run the stored procedure, all the processing occurs on the remote server and only the data you asked for comes back to your workstation. If you use the Access query engine, much more data is returned to your workstation, so the searching can occur there.

- Recordset Snapshots

  If your application doesn't need to update data in a recordset, use a snapshot rather than a dynaset. A snapshot's data is brought locally into your system's memory (except MEMO and OLE fields) and doesn't need the additional overhead a dynaset requires to update data. Additionally, if you're ever populating list boxes or combo boxes manually, use the dbForwardOnly option when creating the snapshot. This technique keeps links to only the next record (and realizes more memory savings), and can only go forward through the recordset.

Summary

This chapter has discussed the use of Data Access Objects (DAO) and Access 97, including the new ODBC Direct capabilities. With DAO, you have the tools to build feature-rich, robust database applications. Adding ODBC Direct puts Access 97 in a good position to be a solid client/server development platform.

Working with the Windows API

CHAPTER 17

Microsoft Access gives you a great deal of flexibility and control over your Access applications. Using macros and Visual Basic for Applications (VBA), you can develop sophisticated applications that can satisfy even the most demanding users. Sometimes, however, you might want more control of your application or want to do something that isn't directly supported by Access. You can make a whole new set of functionality available to you by calling procedures contained in dynamic link libraries (DLLs).

This chapter has an overview of the Windows Applications Programming Interface (API), shows you how to use it and gives you reasons you might want to, and offers you some examples of how easily you can include this functionality in your database application.

An Overview of the Windows API

DLLs are files that contain a function or set of functions that can be called from your Access database application (or other Windows programs). They're libraries of procedures that are dynamically linked to your application and loaded into memory when the application uses them, and then unloaded when the application is closed. Because these DLLs are executable lines of code, many applications can use them simultaneously.

Microsoft Windows's operating system contains several DLLs that make up what is called the *Windows API*. In fact, all Windows applications use the Windows API to perform tasks such as creating windows, changing window size, reading and writing files, and so on. DLLs have several advantages:

- Functions can be reused and shared between many applications.
- You need only one copy of the DLL (not one for each of your applications).
- You can modify the DLL without modifying your application (assuming that you don't change the `Declare` statement).
- DLLs are usually written in the C/C++ programming language. These DLLs tend to be faster because they're linked and compiled into a standalone executable, unlike VBA code, which must first be translated.

The WIN32 API consists mainly of three DLLs: GDI32.DLL, KERNEL32.DLL, and USER32.DLL. If you have an earlier version that contains API calls, refer to the section "Converting Code That Calls a DLL" in the Access 97 help file for information on converting your API calls. In addition to these DLLs, several other DLLs make up the core functionality of Windows 95 and Windows NT API. These 32-bit DLLs contain system-related procedures that include functions, data structures, datatypes, messages, and statements that you can use while developing applications to run under Windows 95 and Windows NT.

Making Access Aware of Your API Routines

To use the Windows API or other DLLs, you must first *declare* the function you want to use. By declaring the function, you give Access VBA the information it needs to make the appropriate call to the external procedure. Once you use the `Declare` statement, you can call the function just like any other procedure. The declaration of the function contains the following information:

- The name of the function you want to call
- The name of the DLL you're calling
- The number of arguments and their datatypes to be passed to the DLL
- The datatype of the returning value if the procedure is a function

The following are the two basic steps to making a call to an external procedure:

1. Use the `Declare` statement to tell VBA which procedure to call and the arguments it expects.
2. Make the call to the procedure.

The Structure of API Routines

The `Declare` statement is used to declare a reference to an external procedure. You can declare the external procedure at the module level of a standard module, which is public by default. You can also declare an external procedure at the form or report module level by placing the `Private` keyword before `Declare`. The syntax for the `Declare` statement is

```
[Public ¦ Private ] Declare Sub name [CDecl] Lib "libname" [Alias
➥"aliasname" ]
➥[([arglist])]
```

or

```
[Public ¦ Private ] Declare Function name [CDecl] Lib "libname" [Alias
➥"aliasname" ] [([arglist])][As type]
```

If the external procedure doesn't return a value, it is declared as a `Sub` procedure. For example:

```
Declare Sub FreeSid Lib "advapi32.dll" Alias "FreeSid" (pSid As Any)
```

If the external procedure does return a value, it is declared as a Function procedure. (Sub procedures simply perform a task and then end.) For example:

```
Declare Function GetDriveType Lib "kernel32" Alias "GetDriveTypeA" (ByVal
nDrive
➥As String) As Long
```

> **NOTE**
>
> Declaring the procedure correctly is very important. The best way to do it is to copy and paste the declaration from a source such as the Windows API view that is included in the Office Developer's Edition. Also note that functions in the 32-bit Windows API are case-sensitive.

The Lib clause in the Declare statement specifies the name of the DLL you're calling and can also specify the exact location of the file. The following example specifies KERNEL32.DLL in the \WINDOWS\SYSTEM directory:

```
Declare Function GetDriveType Lib "c:\windows\system\kernel32.dll" Alias
➥"GetDriveTypeA" (ByVal nDrive As String) As Long
```

Most external procedure API calls should not contain the fully qualified path of the DLL. Instead, the name of the DLL is given without the path and the .DLL extension. If the path and extension aren't included in the Lib section, VBA assumes a .DLL extension and looks for the DLL in the following order:

1. The application's directory
2. The current directory
3. The Windows 32-bit system directory (in Windows NT)
4. The Windows system directory
5. The Windows directory
6. The PATH environment

The Alias section and passing arguments to the external procedure are discussed in the following sections.

Aliasing API Calls

The optional keyword Alias is often used in the declaration of an external procedure. On several occasions, you need to use the Alias clause when declaring a procedure:

- When the external procedure name is the same as a keyword in Access.
- When the external procedure has the same name as a public variable, constant, or any other procedure within the same scope.
- When the external procedure name isn't allowed by the DLL naming convention in Access.
- When the external procedure doesn't contain the name of the procedure and you must specify the *ordinal number* of the procedure.

If you find that an external procedure name is the same as a keyword in Access, or the procedure name is already a public variable, constant, or other procedure within the same scope, you must alias the procedure. You might find this approach useful if, for example, you write a great deal of code, and you later add external procedure calls and find that the name of the procedure has already been used as a variable. Instead of going back and replacing all occurrences of the variable, you can simply alias the procedure to give VBA the unique name it needs to make the appropriate procedure call.

You need to alias any external procedure that contains characters that aren't allowed by VBA. The procedure name must contain alphanumeric characters or the underscore (_) character, and the first character of the procedure must be a letter. The following is an example of a function call that uses the `Alias` clause because the function contains an underscore as the first character:

```
Declare Function lclose Lib "kernel32" Alias "_lclose" (ByVal hFile As
Long)
➥As Long
```

Each procedure in a DLL is assigned a number called the *ordinal number*. You can call the procedure by its name (if it exists) or by its ordinal number. The ordinal number is another way of referencing the procedure you're calling. In fact, some DLLs don't even contain the name of the procedure—only the ordinal number.

TIP

Although calling the procedure by the ordinal number is slightly faster than calling it by its name, I don't recommend it. The name of the procedure is usually much more descriptive than the ordinal number, it's easier to read, and you're less likely to call the wrong procedure by mistake.

If you call a procedure by ordinal, you must first find out the number that you want to call by referring to the documentation for the DLL you're calling. You then alias the procedure by inserting the number sign (#) and the ordinal number you're calling. The following is an example of a fictitious external procedure call using the ordinal number instead of the name:

```
Declare Function MyRemoveSpaces Lib "MyDLL" Alias "#100" (ByVal
lpszMyArgument As
➥String) As Long
```

Here is the same procedure call using the name:

```
Declare Function MyRemoveSpaces Lib "MyDLL" Alias "RemoveSpaces" (ByVal
➥lpszMyArgument As String) As Long
```

Passing Parameters

When you pass parameters to a DLL, you must be sure to pass arguments that the DLL expects, both in terms of the order in which they're passed and their datatype. Additionally, you must specify how each argument is passed. Making sure that you pass the right argument(s) is the most difficult part of making DLL calls. If you pass the wrong datatype to an external procedure, for example, you can cause Access to crash, which will result in a General Protection Fault (GPF).

> **TIP**
>
> Be sure to save your work before running your application if you use external procedure calls. If you do cause a GPF while testing your application, you will likely lose your work up to the point you last saved.

By default, VBA passes all arguments `ByRef` (by reference). Passing an argument `ByRef` means that you're passing a memory address, not the actual value, to the procedure of the variable. When passing `ByRef`, you give the calling procedure the ability to change the actual value of the variable, rather than simply changing a copy of the variable as with passing the variable `ByVal` (by value). Most DLLs expect arguments `ByVal`, which means that a copy of the actual value is passed to the procedure.

Of course, there is an exception to every rule. The exception to this rule occurs when you use `ByVal` with the string datatype. VBA handles string datatypes a little differently. To compensate for the differences and to be able to pass the string in a format that the external procedure can use, passing a string `ByVal` is slightly different than passing other datatypes. Passing a string `ByVal` actually means that you're passing the memory address of the first data byte in the string (kind of like what `ByRef` does). The first data byte in the string gives the calling procedure the information it needs to access the variable. Passing a string `ByRef` actually means that you're passing the memory address where another address is located, in which that address points to the first data byte of the string.

The Registry and INI Files

Under Windows 3.*x*, the standard way of storing configuration information, such as the hardware configuration, installed software applications, user preferences, and other settings, is in the form of initialization (INI) files. These INI files normally reside in the Windows directory, and most PCs have dozens of them. To organize and consolidate these settings, Microsoft released the Registry in Windows 95 and Windows NT. The Registry is a system-defined database that contains all system settings. To view entries in the Registry, simply run the `regedit` application in Windows 95 and the `regedit32` application in Windows NT. For additional information on the Windows Registry, refer to the documentation provided by Microsoft Windows.

Access 97 uses the Registry to save its settings. As you can see from Figure 17.1, settings are contained in the Registry database in `HKEY_LOCAL_MACHINE\SOFTWARE\Microsoft\Office\8.0\Access`.

FIGURE 17.1.

The Registry for Access 97.

Interacting with the Registry and INI Files

You might want to save configuration information or store user preferences for your Access application. The Windows Registry is a good place to save these settings. The following examples of saving user preferences include saving settings to INI files as well as saving to the Windows Registry. The preferred method, and the one sanctioned by Microsoft, is to use the Registry for these values. Using the Registry rather than INI files is one of the requirements of the "Designed for Windows 95" logo programs. To find out more about the logo program for Windows 95, go to `http://www.microsoft.com/windows/thirdparty/winlogo/logo`.

The following examples show you how to read and write to INI files and also how to read and write to the Windows Registry. They are intended to show you the differences between the two methods and give you some real examples of API calls.

> **TIP**
>
> Although writing to INI files is still supported, the preferred method of saving settings is saving them to the Windows Registry.

Writing to INI Files

As I mentioned earlier, when you're using the Windows API, you must first declare the function you're calling. The `WriteProfileString` API function call opens the `WIN.INI` file, writes the section, key name, and setting provided in the argument list, and closes the file. The following is an example of writing a user preference in the `Myapp` application, which saves the default location for exporting data:

```
Declare Function WriteProfileString Lib "kernel32" Alias
"WriteProfileStringA"
➥(ByVal lpszSection As String, ByVal lpszKeyName As String, ByVal
➥lpszString As String) As Long
Sub WriteSettings
    Dim vReturnValue as Long
    vReturnValue& = WriteProfileString("MyApp", "Default Export",
"c:\data\")
End Sub
```

Reading from INI Files

Now that you've saved the user preference to `WIN.INI`, you need to be able to read that setting. You can do so by using the `GetProfileString` API call. The following is an example of how to read the setting that was written in the preceding example:

```
Declare Function GetProfileString Lib "kernel32" Alias "GetProfileStringA"
(ByVal
➥lpAppName As String, ByVal lpKeyName As String, ByVal lpDefault As
➥String, ByVal lpReturnedString As String, ByVal nSize As Long) As Long
Sub ReadSettings()
    Dim vReturnValue As Long, vReturnString As String * 255
    vReturnValue& = GetProfileString("MyApp", "Default Export", "c:\",
➥vReturnString$, 255)
    vReturnString$ = Left$(vReturnString$, vReturnValue&)
End Sub
```

Writing to the Registry

Because the SaveSetting statement is already a part of the functionality of Access VBA,
you don't need to declare it as you would with the API call to WriteProfileString. The
following is the syntax for the SaveSetting statement:

SaveSetting(*appname*, *section*, *key*, *setting*)

Writing to the Registry then becomes quite easy. The following is an example that writes
to the Windows Registry:

```
Call SaveSetting("MyApp", "User Preference", "Default Export", "c:\data\")
```

As you can see from Figure 17.2, using the SaveSetting statement in VBA writes to the
Registry database in HKEY_CURRENT_USER\Software\VB and VBA Program Settings.

FIGURE 17.2.

*A display of the
Registry.*

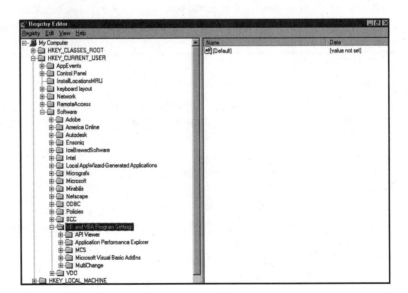

Reading from the Registry

Similar to the SaveSetting statement, the GetSetting function is also a part of Access VBA and doesn't need to be declared as an API call. Note that because SaveSetting returns a value, it is a function. The following is the syntax for the GetSetting function:

```
GetSetting(appname, section, key[, default])
```

The following example returns the setting written in the preceding example into the variable vReturnValue:

```
Dim vReturnValue As Variant
vReturnValue = GetSetting("MyApp", "User Preference", "Default Export")
```

APIs Useful to Access 97

There are many APIs that are useful to the Access developer, with only a few demonstrated in this section. These API calls provide capabilities not directly available otherwise.

Centering a Form on the Screen

This example uses the API calls GetWindowRect and SetWindowPos to center a form on the Access screen. For example, this is useful when you are presenting information to different levels of audiences. No doubt you have seen a dialog box that has an Advanced button on the bottom, and when you click it the dialog box expands and shows you advanced options. Using the following methods, you could resize and then center the form in the middle of the screen.

In Access 97, it is now a simple task to resize the form programmatically by using the Form's properties InsideWidth and InsideHeight. Try the following: Create a new form in Access and add a command button named btnResize. In the button's OnClick event, place the following code:

```
Private Sub btnResize_OnClick()
  Me.InsideWidth = me.InsideWidth + 100
End Sub
```

Notice that when you click on the button, the form resizes itself. But notice also that the form is now off-center. Using the APIs GetWindowRect and SetWindowPos, we can recenter the form.

Declares and Constants and Types

```
Public Const SWP_SHOWWINDOW = &H40

Declare Function GetClientRect Lib "user32" Alias "GetClientRect" (ByVal
➥hwnd As Long, lpRect As RECT) As Long

Declare Function GetWindowRect Lib "user32" Alias "GetwindowRect" (ByVal
➥hwnd As Long, lpRect As RECT) As Long

Declare Function FindWindowEx Lib "user32" Alias "FindWindowExA" (ByVal
➥hWnd1 As Long,
➥ByVal hWnd2 As Long, ByVal lpsz1 As String, ByVal lpsz2 As String) As
Long


Declare Function SetWindowPos Lib "user32" Alias "SetWindowPos" (ByVal
hwnd As Long,
➥ByVal hWndInsertAfter As Long, ByVal x As Long, ByVal y As Long, ByVal
cx As Long,
➥ByVal cy As Long, ByVal wFlags As Long) As Long


Type RECT
        Left As Long
        Top As Long
        Right As Long
        Bottom As Long
End Type
```

Code

Place this code in a code module:

```
Public Sub CenterForm(frmToCentr As Form)
  Dim lreturn As Long, rectClient As RECT, rectForm As RECT, rectNew As
RECT
  lreturn = GetClientRect(Application.hWndAccessApp, rectClient)
  lreturn = GetWindowRect(frmToCentr.hwnd, rectForm)
  rectNew.Left = ((rectClient.Right - rectClient.Left) / 2) -
➥((rectForm.Right - rectForm.Left) / 2)
  rectNew.Top = ((rectClient.Bottom - rectClient.Top) / 2) -
➥((rectForm.Bottom - rectForm.Top) / 2)
  rectNew.Right = rectForm.Right - rectForm.Left
  rectNew.Bottom = rectForm.Bottom - rectForm.Top
  lreturn = SetWindowPos(frmToCentr.hwnd, 0, rectNew.Left, rectNew.Top,
    ➥rectNew.Right, rectNew.Bottom, SWP_SHOWWINDOW)
End Sub
```

Create a new form and place a command button on it (or add the code to the form you just created). In the OnClick event for the button, place the following code:

```
Me.InsideWidth = Me.InsideWidth + 100
Call CenterForm(Me)
```

When you click on the button in form view, the form will resize itself and then recenter itself, using the CenterForm function.

Since we wanted to center the form within the client area of the main window, we used the GetClientRect API. (The client area is the inside portion of the window, which does not include the area taken up by scroll bars and docked toolbars.) Given the handle to a window, this API call put the window's position and size in the rectClient variable. Since the property, Application.hWndAccessApp, is the handle to the Access main window, we passed it to GetClientRect.

The new position and size are calculated and placed in the RECT, rectNew. The SetWindowPos API call can size, position, and change the z-order and visibility of a window.

Creating a Unique Splash Screen

This example uses the API call CreateEllipticRgn and the SetWindowRgn to create an elliptical form, as opposed to a rectangular form. We will use this example to create a truly unique splash screen. Because Access uses rectangular forms only, we have to create our own region and make the form use that for its region. There are several API calls that can create regions: CreateEllipticRgn, CreateEllipticRgnIndirect, CreatePolygonRgn, CreatePolyPolygonRgn, CreateRectRgn, CreateRectRgnIndirect, and CreateRoundRectRgn. These can be used to create any shape that can be defined by points. We will only use CreateEllipticRgn in this example.

Declares

Place the following declares in a separate code module:

```
Declare Function CreateEllipticRgn Lib "gdi32" (ByVal X1 As Long, ByVal
➥Y1 As Long,
➥ByVal X2 As Long, ByVal Y2 As Long) As Long


Declare Function SetWindowRgn Lib "user32" (ByVal hWnd As Long, ByVal
➥hRgn As Long,
➥ByVal bRedraw As Boolean) As Long
```

Code

Place the following code in the form module:

```
Private Sub Form_Load()
  Dim rectForm As RECT
  Dim lreturn As Long
  Dim rgnHwnd as Long
  lreturn = GetClientRect(Me.hWnd, rectForm)
  rgnHwnd = CreateEllipticRgn(rectForm.Left, rectForm.Top, rectForm.Right,
rectForm.Bottom)
  lreturn = SetWindowRgn(Me.hWnd, rgnHwnd, True)
End Sub

Private Sub Form_Timer
  ' open another form here; like your switchboard form
  Docmd.CloseForm acform, Me.Name
End Sub
```

On the form, set the following properties as indicated:

```
Scrollbars = None
Record selectors = No
Navigation buttons = No
Dividing lines = No
AutoCenter = Yes
AutoResize = Yes
Borderstyle = None
Timer interval = 1100
```

Then set your startup properties to use this form.

Flashing the Title Bar of a Form

This example uses the API call `FlashWindow` to get the user's attention. This is good to use for processes that will take some time, to signal to the user that you are done.

Declares

Place the following `declare` in a code module:

```
Declare Function FlashWindow Lib "user32" Alias "FlashWindow" (ByVal hwnd
➥As Long, ByVal bInvert As Long) As Long
```

Code

Place the following in the form module:

```
Dim bLastFlash As Boolean
Dim iCount As Integer
```

17

WORKING WITH THE WINDOWS API

```
Private Sub Form_Timer()
  Dim lreturn As Long
  If IsEmpty(iCount) Then iCount = 0
  If iCount > 5 Then
    Me.TimerInterval = 0
  Else
    iCount = iCount + 1
  End If
  lreturn = FlashWindow(Me.hwnd, bLastFlash)
  bLastFlash = Not bLastFlash
End Sub
```

Set your `Me.TimerInterval` to a value from 300 to 500 when you are done with the long process. You can also set `iCount` to a larger value than 5 to get the form to flash more times.

Getting the Logged-On Username

This example uses the API call `GetUserName` to get the name of the user logged into the computer. For example, this is useful when you're using a centralized error handler that logs the name of the user logged in when the error occurred.

Declares and Constants

```
Declare Function GetUserName Lib "advapi32.dll" Alias "GetUserNameA"
➥(ByVal lpBuffer As String,
➥nSize As Long) As Long
```

Code

```
Public Function TheUserName() as String
  Dim szUName as string, lCnt as Long, lreturn as Long
  szUname = String$(255, 0)
  lCnt = 255 'the size must be set initially
  lreturn = GetUserName(szUname, lCnt)
  If (lCnt > 0) or (lreturn <> 0) Then
    TheUserName = Left(szUname, lCnt)
  Else
    TheUserName = ""
End Function
```

Notice that `lCnt` and `szUname` have to be initialized before the call to the API, `GetUserName`. Also note that after the call to `GetUserName`, `lCnt`'s value is now the number of characters that are in the username. That allows us to use the `Left` function to return the username from the string variable `szUname`.

Summary

This chapter gave you a foundation for understanding and using the Windows API. Calls to DLL and API routines were covered, aliasing was detailed, and you were shown methods for passing parameters. Programming techniques were presented for reading and writing to the Registry and INI files, and several examples of using API calls in Access were demonstrated.

17

**WORKING WITH
THE WINDOWS
API**

Developing Online Help

No matter how skillfully you design an Access application or how intuitively the application functions, your users will still have questions from time to time. At such moments, nothing will please them more than the availability of clear, concise, and thoughtfully organized online Help. Providing Help for your Access applications takes a little extra time, but in the long run it will not only endear you to your users but also greatly reduce the number of technical support calls you receive.

Like most Windows 95 programs, Access 97 has been designed to support the Windows 95 Help system. Using word-processing software such as Microsoft Word for Windows or a Help authoring tool (see "Help Authoring Tools" later in this chapter), Access developers can create their own Windows 95 Help files, complete with hypertext hotspots and colorful graphics. What's more, Access enables you to equip a database with several kinds of *context-sensitive* Help, enabling users to get Help immediately for the form, report, or control they are using.

In this chapter you'll learn how to plan, design, and create a Windows 95 Help file, as well as how to provide context-sensitive Help for the objects and controls in an Access database. You'll also learn more about some of the Help authoring tools currently available.

Understanding Windows 95 Help

The following sections introduce you to the basic elements of Windows 95 Help. For Windows 95, Microsoft has added new features to Help and modified previously existing ones, so reading these sections is a good idea even if you're familiar with prior versions of Windows Help.

Elements of Windows 95 Help

At its most basic, the Windows 95 Help system (commonly referred to as WinHelp) consists of a program named WINHLP32.EXE that serves as a standard Help interface for Windows software. The text and graphics that WinHelp displays are stored in a Help file. When you view Help for a Windows program, WINHLP32.EXE loads and displays the Help file for that program.

By convention, Help files have the extension .HLP. The main Access 97 Help file, for example, is named MSACCESS.HLP. Material within a Help file is divided into Help topics. Using WinHelp, you view one Help topic at a time.

Under Windows 3.*x*, users could usually get Help by opening a Help menu and then choosing either the Contents command or the Search command. In most Windows 95 programs, these commands have been replaced with a single new command called Help Topics. When you choose the Help Topics command, WinHelp displays the Help

Topics dialog box, shown in Figure 18.1, which you can use to find Help about a particular subject. By choosing tabs in the Help Topics dialog box, you can view its various pages.

The Contents tab displays a Help file's table of contents in an expandable/collapsible format. The Find tab enables you to search the text in a Help file for a particular word or phrase. The Index tab (which replaces the Search dialog box that came with the Windows 3.*x* version of WinHelp) enables you to search for Help topics using keywords. In the text box at the top of the Index tab, you type the subject for which you are searching. As you type, WinHelp displays the most similar keywords in the keyword list. When you double-click a keyword, WinHelp displays the Help topic associated with that keyword. If more than one Help topic is associated with the keyword you've double-clicked, WinHelp lists the topics in the Topics Found dialog box, shown in Figure 18.2. You can move to the Help topic you want by double-clicking it.

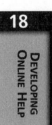

FIGURE 18.2.

The Topics Found dialog box lists Help topics that match the keyword you chose on the Index tab.

The Help Topics dialog box can integrate several Help files and present them to you as a single Help system. For example, the Contents tab can send you to topics in multiple Help files, and the Index tab can include keywords from multiple Help files.

WinHelp displays most Help topics in two kinds of windows: the main Help window and secondary windows. In a typical Windows 95 Help file, you view overview information about an application in the main Help window and step-by-step instructions for specific tasks in a secondary window. A typical secondary window is shown in Figure 18.3.

FIGURE 18.3.

Secondary windows often display instructions for carrying out a task.

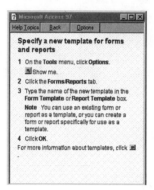

Unlike secondary windows, the main Help window features a menu bar with commands you can use to open other Help files, print Help, bookmark particular topics for future reference, and perform other tasks.

Both the main Help window and secondary windows usually come with button bars you can use to navigate Help and carry out other essential tasks. These button bars can be customized. For example, some button bars come with browse buttons (labeled << and >>) that enable you to move to the next or previous Help topic. (For information about customizing a button bar, see "Creating and Customizing Help Windows" later in this chapter.)

In many Help topics, portions of the text are underlined and printed in green. These underlined words, phrases, and sentences are called *hotspots*. When you point the mouse at a hotspot, the pointer turns into a small hand. If you then click the mouse, WinHelp performs an action. When you click a hotspot underlined with a solid line, WinHelp either moves you to a different topic or runs a macro, depending on how the hotspot has been configured. When you click a hotspot underlined with a dotted line, WinHelp displays a topic in a special pop-up window that appears above the current Help window. The pop-up window disappears when you click your mouse again.

Some Help files include pictures that have been set up to function like hotspots. Such pictures are called *hypergraphics*. They can be formatted to perform one hotspot action or can contain multiple hotspot regions, each of which performs a different action.

Within the text of some Help topics are *authorable buttons* that execute commands when you click them. Figure 18.4 shows sample authorable buttons.

FIGURE 18.4.

Authorable buttons enable you to carry out actions.

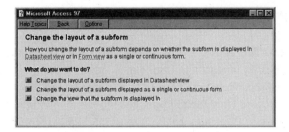

When you view a Help topic in the main Help window, a line usually appears under the topic title. As you scroll through the topic, the text above the line doesn't scroll out of view. The portion of a Help topic that always stays visible is called the topic's *nonscrolling region*. The nonscrolling region usually contains just the topic title, but sometimes it contains hotspots or buttons that display examples or a list of related topics.

The Help Project

Every Help file is based on a series of source files. Collectively, these source files are referred to as a *Help project*. To create a Help file, you compile the Help project using the Microsoft Help Workshop. When you compile a Help project, Help Workshop combines and compresses the source files into a new file with an .HLP extension that WinHelp can load and display.

Unlike previous versions of the Windows Help compiler, Help Workshop does more than just compile Help files. It comes with a graphical user interface that enables you create and edit important source files. It also comes with a detailed online Help file called the Help Author's Guide. To use Help Workshop, you need three files: HCW.EXE, HCRTF.EXE, and HWDLL.DLL. To use the Help Author's Guide, you need two additional files: HCW.HLP and HCW.CNT. These files are available on the Office Developer's Edition (ODE), the Windows System Development Kit (SDK), and the Microsoft Developer Network level-2 CD-ROM.

Every Help project must include the following source files:

- A Help Project file—This ASCII text file defines the Help project. It specifies the other source files that belong to the Help project, the windows you use to display Help topics, and various option settings. Help Project files usually have an .HPJ extension. For more information, see "Creating the Help Project File" later in this chapter.

- One or more Topic files—These rich text format (RTF) documents contain the Help file's text and formatting codes. Every Help project must include at least one Topic file, but can include more. Topic files generally have an .RTF extension. For more information, see "Creating a Topic File" later in this chapter.

In addition to the files already listed, a Help project can also include the following source files:

- A Contents file—This ASCII text file defines the table of contents in the Help Topics dialog box's Contents tab. Unlike most other source files, the Contents file must be shipped separately with your Help file. In other words, whenever you distribute a copy of your Help file to users, you must also distribute a copy of the Contents file. Use of Contents files is optional but highly recommended. Contents files generally have a `.CNT` extension. For more information, see "Creating a Contents File" later in this chapter.

- One or more Map files—These ASCII text files associate each Help topic in the Topic files with a unique number. You use these numbers in your Access database to provide context-sensitive Help for objects and controls. For more information about Map files, see "Creating Map Files" later in this chapter.

- Any number of graphics files—These bitmaps, metafiles, and other graphics appear as illustrations in the Help file. For more information, see "Adding Graphics" later in this chapter.

- A full-text search file—WinHelp uses this file when you conduct full-text searches with the Find tab in the Help Topics dialog box. You can instruct Help Workshop to create this file automatically during the compile process. If you do, you must distribute a separate copy of the full-text search file with each copy of your Help file that you ship to users. If you don't ship a full-text search file, WinHelp creates one automatically when needed. Full-text search files usually have an `.FTS` extension. For more information, see "Creating a Full-Text Search File During the Compile" later in this chapter.

Planning a Help File

A well-designed Help file is not only more effective at getting users the Help they need, but it is easier to write as well. Before you begin creating your Help file, spend some time thinking about the kind of information you want it to include and how you want to present that information. The following sections discuss strategies for planning and organizing a Help file.

Deciding What Information to Include

Help files are divided into Help topics, which users view one at a time. Topic files must be divided into Help topics as well. Before you begin writing your Help file, you must decide which topics you want it to cover. If you will be providing context-sensitive Help, you will want to include topics that describe the forms, reports, and possibly controls in your application. However, you might also want to include overview topics that describe your application in general terms and reference topics that define key terms and concepts.

Depending on the nature of your application and the types of people who will be using it, consider including some combination of the following topics in your Help file:

- An introductory or "About" topic that describes what the application does.

- Topics that describe forms and reports. Devoting one topic to each form and report in your application is generally best. You can use these topics to provide context-sensitive Help. If you will also be including topics about the controls on forms (see the following bulleted entry), the topics about the forms themselves can be quite brief.

- Topics that describe the function of a control on a form. These topics also should be used as context-sensitive Help. Creating a separate topic for every control on every form takes time, but is the most complete way to document an application online. If you do create a topic for every control on the form, you can use the "What's This" Help style that is used in Windows 95.

- Topics that provide step-by-step instructions for carrying out a task. Unlike topics that discuss an individual form or control, these topics describe how to use forms and controls in sequence to accomplish a particular task. Keep these topics as short as possible. If users can perform a task in more than one way, describe only the quickest method.

- Topics that define important terms and concepts, especially those most likely to be unfamiliar to users.

- Topics that provide general information about using your application, such as how to open and close it and how to log in. In a user manual, this kind of information is often included in a "Getting Started" chapter.

- Topics that describe custom menus and toolbars. You can create one Help topic per custom menu and toolbar, or you can give each menu command and toolbar button a Help topic of its own.

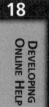

18

DEVELOPING ONLINE HELP

TIP

Using hypergraphics is a nice way to provide Help for a custom toolbar. Create a bitmap of the toolbar, and then define a separate hotspot region for each button. When a user who's viewing your Help file points at a button and clicks his or her mouse, Help for the button is displayed. For information about creating hypergraphics with multiple hotspot regions, see "Creating Shed Graphics" later in this chapter.

- Topics that describe basic Windows 95 and Access skills. These topics are especially helpful if some of your users will be new to either system.

> **NOTE**
>
> As you plan the contents of your Help file, remember that the size of your Help file can have a variety of implications. You will, of course, want the information in your Help file to be complete. However, if you include too much information, your Help file might become so large that maintaining it is difficult. Large Help files take longer and require more memory to compile. In addition, large Help files consume more space on distribution disks and user hard drives, and operate more slowly. One common reason that Help files get too big is the inclusion of too many graphics, especially large bitmaps. If you feel your Help file has become unwieldy, consider removing a graphic or two instead of eliminating text or whole Help topics.

Presenting Help Topics to Users

You can use the main Help window, a secondary window, or a pop-up window to display Help topics to users. Microsoft has developed a set of conventions regarding the use of windows in Windows 95 Help files. If you want your Help file to resemble other Windows 95 Help files, try to follow these conventions:

- Topics that provide overview information about an application or one of its features should be displayed in the main Help window. In general, use the main window to display longer topics that describe a subject at length and are likely to require scrolling.

- Topics that provide step-by-step instructions should be displayed in a secondary window. When you're designing the secondary window you will use to display such topics, set its initial position to a corner of the user's screen so that the user can use the application and read your instructions at the same time.

- Topics that provide reference information about terms and concepts should be displayed in a pop-up window that appears when the user clicks a hotspot. Users can't scroll through pop-up windows, so they are a poor means of displaying lengthy topics. However, they are a great way to give users a quick look at information related to the topic being viewed without exiting that topic altogether.

Tips for Writing Help

As you write Help, keep these guidelines in mind:

- Write for your most likely audience. If most of your readers will be Access novices, don't assume they're familiar with even the most elemental terms and techniques. For instance, most readers new to relational databases won't know what a record is or what it means to sort records. On the other hand, if your audience is largely composed of system administrators or other developers, you can employ a more complex vocabulary and without defining common terms and concepts.

- Express yourself clearly and directly. Fewer words are always better than more, and small words are always better than long ones.

- Be as brief as you can without leaving out vital information. In a step-by-step procedure, describe the simplest and shortest way to accomplish the task. In an overview, don't waste space on information that won't benefit the user (such as which procedures or macros run behind the scenes when a form is loaded). Consider breaking longer topics into shorter ones.

- Be consistent, especially in your terminology. If you use the expression "click the button" in one place, don't use "press the button" elsewhere. Similarly, don't call a form a "form" in one place and a "window" or "dialog box" in another.

- Refer to a form or report by the name that appears in the title bar (as specified in the `Caption` property), not by its Access name. The name in the title bar is the one users see when they use your application. For example, say that your application includes a form whose Access name is `Sales_Order_Form`, and whose `Caption` property is set to `Sales Order Entry`. In your Help file, you should refer to the form as "the Sales Order Entry form," not "the Sales_Order_Form."

- Put an extra space between every third or fourth sentence to break up the monotony for users that are reading the Help file onscreen. The use of whitespace between the sentences keeps users from skimming over important information.

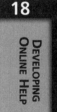

Creating a Help File

In the following sections, you'll learn how to create a Windows 95 Help file without the assistance of a Help authoring tool. Spending some time with the material in this section is worthwhile even if you intend to use a Help authoring tool, because a solid grounding in the structure of the Help project source files will help you get the most from such products.

NOTE

The examples in the following sections show you how to perform various tasks using Microsoft Word 97. You can use a different editor, however, as long as it can save files in rich text format (RTF), with the curious exception of WordPad.

Creating a Topic File

A Topic file is a rich text format document that contains the text users read when they view your Help file. You must use a text editor or word processing program that can save files in rich text format to write a Topic file.

To create a new Topic file, simply start a new document and save it in rich text format.

TIP

You can base a Topic file on any existing template in Word or another word processing program. To standardize the look and feel of your Help files, consider creating a Help template and using it as the basis for all your Topic files.

Creating and Saving a Sample Topic File

Follow these steps to create a sample Topic file and save it in rich text format:

1. Open Word 97 and choose File | New.
2. In the New dialog box, select a template and then click OK or press Enter.
3. Choose File | Save.
4. In the Save dialog box, type a filename and select a drive and directory.
5. In the list for the Save File As Type box, select Rich Text Format.
6. Click OK or press Enter.

Adding Help Topics

To start a new Help topic, perform the following steps:

1. Insert a hard page break.

NOTE

The first Help topic in a Topic file need not be preceded by a hard page break.

2. Immediately after the hard page break (that is, in the same paragraph), insert a special series of footnotes (as described in the following sections). Each footnote defines a different attribute of the Help topic, and each must be marked with a particular character.

3. Immediately after the footnotes (still in the same paragraph), type the Help topic title as you want it to appear onscreen.

Figure 18.5 shows a typical completed Help topic.

FIGURE 18.5.

A typical completed Help topic with footnote codes.

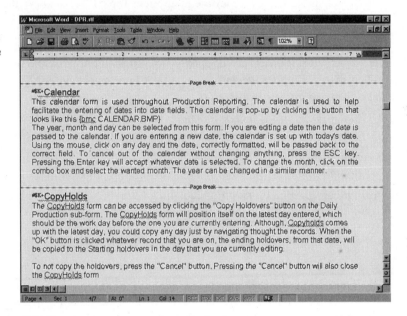

The Asterisk (*) Footnote

The Asterisk footnote specifies the *build tags* with which the Help topic is associated. Build tags enable you to create several versions of a Help file from the same set of Topic files. Each version of the Help file can contain a different combination of Help topics, based on their build tags. For more information, see "Specifying the Build Tags to Include in the Help File" later in this chapter.

The Asterisk footnote is optional and is often omitted. If you choose to include it, it must precede all other footnotes in the Help topic. Use the asterisk (*) as the footnote mark. In the footnote text, type one or more build tag names, separated by semicolons.

18

DEVELOPING
ONLINE HELP

The following are some examples:

```
* USER
* WORKSTATION;SERVER
* SHAREWARE;COMPLETE;ADMIN
```

The Pound Sign (#) Footnote

The Pound Sign footnote specifies the Help topic's unique topic ID. The *topic ID* is the name by which WinHelp identifies the topic internally. No two Help topics anywhere in a given Help project, even if they are in different Topic files, can have the same topic ID. This footnote is required for every Help topic.

Use the pound sign (#) as the footnote mark. In the footnote text, type a name for the Help topic. Topic IDs can include spaces, but you should try to avoid using leading and trailing spaces. The topic ID and title of a Help topic can be different, but it's helpful to make them as similar as possible.

The following are some examples:

```
# Reference
# Saving Purchase Orders
# Using_the_Main_Switchboard
```

The Dollar Sign ($) Footnote

The Dollar Sign footnote specifies the Help topic's title as it appears in the Topics Found dialog box, the Bookmark dialog box, and the History window.

Use the dollar sign ($) as the footnote mark, and type the title in the footnote text. Like topic IDs, titles can include spaces.

> **TIP**
>
> To avoid confusing your users, be sure that the title you type in the Dollar Sign footnote matches the title that appears onscreen when the topic is displayed. If a user selects Entering Employee Data in the Topics Found dialog box, for example, he or she might be disoriented if the title of the Help topic he or she moves to is something other than Entering Employee Data.

The following are some examples:

```
$ Glossary
$ Exiting the Application
$ Printing a Report
```

The K Footnote

The K footnote specifies the *search keywords* for the Help topic. Search keywords appear in the Index tab of the Help Topics dialog box and are also used in KLink() macros (for more information about KLink() macros, see "The ALink() and KLink() Macros" later in this chapter). Use of the K footnote is optional, but users cannot find a Help topic with the Index tab if it lacks a K footnote.

Use a capital K as the mark for this footnote. In the footnote text, type the Help topic's search keywords, separated by semicolons.

Unlike Windows 3.x Help, Windows 95 Help enables you to create second-level keywords. Second-level keywords are like subcategories of a first-level keyword. In the Index tab, they are indented directly under the first-level keyword with which they are associated. Figure 18.6 shows typical second-level keywords.

FIGURE 18.6.

Second-level keywords are indented for easier viewing.

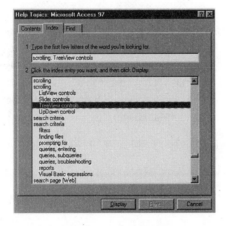

To create a second-level keyword, type a first-level keyword followed by a semicolon. Then type the first-level keyword again, followed by a comma or colon, and the desired second-level keyword. You can include a space after the comma or colon, if you want. For example, to associate a Help topic about invoices with the second-level keywords Creating and Deleting, you include the following entry in the text for the topic's K footnote:

```
Invoices;Invoices, Creating;Invoices, Deleting
```

The following are some examples:

```
K Users Form;Adding a User;Deleting a User;Users;Users, Adding;Users,
Deleting
K Sales Orders;Sales Orders,Editing;Editing;Editing, Sales Orders
K Main Switchboard;Switchboards;Switchboards, Main;Reports Button;Exit Button
```

> **TIP**
>
> Consistency is important when you assign keywords to Help topics. If you use the keyword `invoice` with some Help topics but `invoices` with others, it will look awkward in your Help file's Index tab. To ensure consistent use of keywords, you might want to assign keywords to topics when you plan your Help file, before you actually begin writing.
>
> Also, when you're assigning keywords to a Help topic, try to cover as many of the synonyms for the topic as possible. For instance, a user who needs Help about closing an application might search for Help about "closing," "exiting," or "logging out." The topic in your Help file that describes exiting the application should include all three of these terms as keywords in its K footnote.

The A Footnote

Use the optional A footnote to specify the keywords searched by `ALink()` macros (for more information about `ALink()` macros, see "The `ALink()` and `KLink()` Macros" later in this chapter). Whereas keywords in the K footnote are visible to the user (in the Index tab), keywords in the A footnote never are. This means that you can use any desired code or notational scheme in the A footnote, and A footnote keywords need not be changed if you translate your Help file into a foreign language.

The footnote mark must be a capital A. Keywords, separated by semicolons, should appear in the footnote text.

The following are some examples:

```
A Backend;maintenance;admin
A Chap. 1;Appendix A
A Controls;text boxes;buttons
```

The Plus Sign (+) Footnote

The Plus Sign footnote identifies the name of the *browse sequence* to which the Help topic belongs. Browse sequences enable you to control the order in which users move through the topics in your Help file when they click the browse buttons. If you will be equipping any of your Help windows with browse buttons, you must include this footnote in every Help topic you want the user to be able to browse to. If you won't be using browse buttons, or if you're creating a Help topic you don't want users to browse to, you can leave out this footnote.

> **NOTE**
>
> For information about adding browse buttons to the main window or a secondary Help window, see "Creating and Customizing Help Windows" later in this chapter.

You can create a single browse sequence for an entire Help file, or create multiple browse sequences that correspond to the different components of your Access application or the different sections of your Help file. If your Help file has multiple browse sequences, users cannot move from one to another with the browse buttons.

The footnote mark must be a plus sign (+). In the footnote text, type a browse sequence code in this format:

```
browse-sequence[:sequence-number]
```

browse-sequence is the browse sequence name (which can't include spaces). Type a colon and the *sequence-number* after the *browse-sequence* only if you want to assign the Help topic a specific, numbered position in the browse sequence. Use of *sequence-numbers* is generally worth avoiding. If you don't include *sequence-numbers* in your Plus Sign footnotes, the browse buttons automatically send users to the next or previous sequential topic in the same browse sequence. The simplest way to determine the sequence in which users browse through topics, then, is to arrange the topics in the desired sequence in your Topic files.

18

DEVELOPING ONLINE HELP

> **TIP**
>
> If you plan to create only one browse sequence, use auto as the footnote text in all Plus Sign footnotes. When you compile the Help file, Help Workshop automatically creates a browse sequence that mimics the order in which topics appear in your Topic files.

The following are some examples:

```
+ Browse_String
+ GettingStarted
+ INTRO_STRING:005
```

> **CAUTION**
>
> When you're assigning browse sequence numbers to Help topics, be sure to include leading zeros. Use 050 or 0050 instead of 50, for example. Help Workshop sorts sequence numbers in ANSI order rather than numerical order.

The Greater Than (>) Footnote

The optional Greater Than footnote enables you to specify the window in which the Help topic is displayed when a user reaches it from the Index tab, the Find tab, or a macro. The Greater Than footnote can be useful if you've specially formatted a topic to be displayed in a particular secondary window.

Use the greater than symbol (>) as the footnote mark, and type a window name in the footnote text. The name of the main Help window is always "main"; the names of secondary windows are up to you. (For more information, see "Creating and Customizing Help Windows" later in this chapter.)

The following are some examples:

```
> Main
> Task
> Wnd2
```

The Exclamation Point (!) Footnote

The optional Exclamation Point footnote indicates the names of the *entry macros* you want WinHelp to run whenever this Help topic is displayed. Entry macros can be used to open a secondary window, add a button to a button bar, or perform other tasks. For more information, see "Using Macros" later in this chapter.

Use an exclamation point (!) as the footnote mark, and type one or more macro names, separated by semicolons, as the footnote text.

The following are some examples:

```
! FocusWindow(main)
! CloseSecondarys();CreateButton("HelpOnHelp","&Help on Help","HelpOn()")
```

The At Sign (@) Footnote

You can use the optional At Sign footnote to record comments about the Help topic for reference purposes.

Use the at sign (@) as the footnote mark, and type the comments in the footnote text.

> **TIP**
>
> Using At Sign footnotes is a good way to document a Help project that other people will be supporting.

The following are some examples:

```
@ Context-sensitive Help topic for the View Invoice form.
@ Do not use this topic with pop-up hotspots.
@ The entry macro for this topic adds an Index button to the button bar.
```

Adding a Sample Help Topic to a Topic File

The following steps show how to add a typical Help topic to a Topic file. To simplify the example, you can exclude the Asterisk, A, Plus Sign, Greater Than, Exclamation Point, and At Sign footnotes (which are all optional).

1. Open a Topic file and then insert a hard page break by pressing Ctrl+Enter.

2. Choose Insert | Footnote.

3. In the Footnote dialog box, select the Footnote option and the Custom Mark option.

4. In the box next to the Custom Mark option, type # and then click OK or press Enter.

5. In the lower window pane, type a topic ID (such as `Printing_a_Sales_Order`).

6. Click the end of the paragraph in the upper window pane (or press F6) and then repeat steps 2 and 3.

7. In the box next to the Custom Mark option, type $ and then click OK or press Enter.

8. In the lower window pane, type a title (such as `Printing a Sales Order`).

9. Click the end of the paragraph in the upper window pane (or press F6) and then repeat steps 2 and 3.

10. In the box next to the Custom Mark option, type K and then click OK or press Enter.

11. In the lower window pane, type search keywords, separated by semicolons. For example, you might type `Printing;Printing, Sales Orders;Sales Orders;Sales Orders, Printing`.

12. Click the end of the paragraph in the upper window pane (or press F6) and then type the Help topic's title as you want it to appear onscreen.

18

DEVELOPING
ONLINE HELP

13. Type the Help topic's content.

14. To begin the next Help topic, repeat steps 1 through 13.

> **TIP**
>
> Windows 95 Help can display up to 255 different fonts, so you can use any combination of fonts in your Help file. However, when you write Help topics, try to use the same fonts that appear in your Access application. Using the same fonts integrates your Help file with your application, providing a consistent look and feel.

Adding Nonscrolling Regions to Help Topics

The nonscrolling region is the portion of a Help topic that remains visible when a user scrolls through the topic. Use of nonscrolling regions is optional and is recommended only for Help topics that will be displayed in the main Help window.

Typically, you use nonscrolling regions to keep topic titles in view at all times, but you can include other information in a nonscrolling region as well. For example, you could include a hotspot that reads "See Also" in every nonscrolling region; when the user clicks the hotspot, a list of related topics is displayed.

Two basic rules apply to nonscrolling regions:

- You can have only one nonscrolling region per Help topic.

- A nonscrolling region must include the first paragraph of a Help topic (the one with the footnotes). You can include any number of additional paragraphs as well, but nonscrolling regions generally look and work best when kept as small as possible.

> **CAUTION**
>
> Don't add a nonscrolling region to Help topics you intend to display in a pop-up window. When a topic that has a nonscrolling region is displayed in a pop-up window, only the text in the nonscrolling region is visible; any other text in the topic isn't displayed.

To create a nonscrolling region for a Help topic, simply mark the paragraphs you want to include in the region as Keep With Next. To conduct this process with Word 97, perform the following steps:

1. Select the paragraphs you want to include in the nonscrolling region.
2. Choose Format | Paragraph.
3. In the Paragraph dialog box, choose the Line and Pagebreaks tab.
4. Select the Keep With Next check box.
5. Click OK or press Enter.

> **NOTE**
>
> The default background color of the nonscrolling region is gray. You can, however, change the background color as it appears in the main Help window or any secondary window. For more information, see "Creating and Customizing Help Windows" later in this chapter.

Adding Hotspots

You can create three kinds of hotspots:

- Jumps send the user from the current Help topic to a different one.
- Pop-ups display a Help topic in a pop-up window that appears over the current Help window.
- Macro hotspots run a WinHelp macro. Macros are routines that enable you to carry out tasks such as printing a Help topic, adding a button to a button bar, or closing a Help window. For more information about macros, see "Using Macros" later in this chapter.

The topic that a jump or pop-up displays can be either part of the same Help project as the hotspot itself or a topic from another Help file altogether.

Wherever possible, follow these guidelines regarding hotspots:

- Use jumps to help users navigate your Help file. If your Help file includes an overview topic about creating reports, for example, you might want to include a jump that sends the user to a topic that provides step-by-step instructions.
- Use pop-ups to display definitions of important terms and names. For example, using pop-ups is a great way to let novice users take a quick look at Help topics that explain basic Access concepts and terminology.

- Use hotspots sparingly. Too many hotspots in a Help topic can overwhelm a user. You can reduce the number of pop-ups in a Help topic by creating one only for the first occurrence of each unfamiliar term in the topic text.

> **NOTE**
>
> You will find it easier to follow along with the next procedures if you configure your word processing software to display hidden text. In Word 97, you can do so by choosing Tools | Options | View and then selecting the Hidden Text check box.

To create a jump hotspot, perform the following steps:

1. Type the hotspot text, followed immediately by the topic ID of the Help topic you want the jump to display. Don't insert a space between the hotspot text and the topic ID. Here's an example:

   ```
   Jump TextTopic_ID
   ```

2. If the Help topic that the jump displays is in another Help file, append @ and the relevant Help file's name. Here's an example:

   ```
   Jump TextTopic_ID@OTHER.HLP
   ```

3. To display the topic in a specific window, append > and a window name. Here's an example:

   ```
   Jump TextTopic_ID>second
   ```

4. Select the hotspot text and then *double*-underline it by selecting the text and then choosing Format | Font and selecting Double from the Underline drop-down box, or by pressing Ctrl+Shift+H. Here's an example:

   ```
   Jump TextTopic ID
   ```

5. Select the topic ID (and the Help file's name and window's name, if relevant) and then mark it as hidden text. Here's an example:

   ```
   Jump Text
   ```

To create a macro hotspot, follow the steps in the preceding procedure, substituting an exclamation point and a macro name for the topic ID. For example, the following hotspot runs the `CloseWindow()` macro when clicked:

```
Close Help!CloseWindow(main)
```

To create a pop-up hotspot, perform the following steps:

1. Type the hotspot text, followed immediately by the topic ID of the Help topic you want the hotspot to display in a pop-up window. Don't insert a space between the hotspot text and the topic ID. Here's an example:

```
Popup TextTopic_ID
```

2. If the Help topic that the pop-up hotspot displays is in another Help file, append @ and the relevant Help file's name. Here's an example:

```
Popup TextTopic_ID@OTHER.HLP
```

3. Select the hotspot text and then *single*-underline it. Here's an example:

```
Popup TextTopic ID
```

4. Select the topic ID (and the Help file's name, if relevant) and then mark it as hidden text. Here's an example:

```
Popup Text
```

> **NOTE**
>
> By default, WinHelp displays hotspot text underlined and in green, regardless of how the text is colored or formatted in the underlying Topic file. To display hotspot text as underlined but in a color other than green, you must insert an asterisk (*) character before the topic ID. The following is an example:
>
> ```
> Hotspot Text
> ```
>
> To display hotspot text in a color other than green and *not* underlined, insert a percent-sign character (%) before the topic ID. The following is an example:
>
> ```
> Hotspot Text
> ```

18

Creating a Sample Jump

For the next example, carry out the following steps to create a jump hotspot that reads "Using the Main Switchboard." When a user clicks this hotspot, a Help topic of the same name is displayed in a secondary window.

1. Open a Topic file and then insert a new paragraph into a Help topic.

2. Type `Using the Main Switchboard`.

3. Type `Using_the_Main_Switchboard` (the topic ID of the topic that the jump will display).

4. Type `>task`. (`task` is the name of a secondary window.)

5. Select the hotspot text ("Using the Main Switchboard") and then double-underline it by pressing Ctrl+Shift+D.

6. Select the topic ID (`Using_the_Main_Switchboard`) and secondary window name (`>task`) and then mark them as hidden text by pressing Ctrl+Shift+H. The jump is now finished and should look like this:

<u>Using the Main Switchboard</u>`Using the Main Switchboard>task`

Adding Graphics

WinHelp supports four kinds of graphics files:

- Device-independent bitmaps. These files usually have either `.BMP` or `.DIB` extensions.

- Windows metafiles. These files usually have `.WMF` extensions.

- Shed graphics. These bitmaps contain multiple hotspot regions. They usually have `.SHG` extensions.

- Multiresolution bitmaps. These special bitmaps are formatted to support multiple screen resolutions, and they usually have `.MRB` extensions. You use the Microsoft Multi-Resolution Bitmap Compiler to create multiresolution bitmaps (for more information, see the Help file for the Microsoft Help Workshop).

If you want to use a graphic saved in another format (such as a `.GIF` file) in your Help file, you first must convert the graphic into one of the previously listed formats. A number of commercial and shareware products can convert graphics from other formats into bitmaps or metafiles. (For more information, see "Graphics Conversion Utilities" later in this chapter.)

Graphics can be embedded directly in a Topic file, but generally should not be. Bitmaps are often quite large, and a Topic file that contains even a few embedded images might become so big that your computer won't have enough memory to compile it. Instead of embedding a graphic directly, you should use the preferred technique of inserting a graphic by reference. The reference indicates the name of a graphics file stored separately. During the compile process, Help Workshop locates the file you referenced and includes it in the Help file.

To insert a graphic by reference, you insert the following statement where you want the graphic to appear in a Help topic:

`{bmx[t] filename}`

filename is the name of the graphics file you're inserting. You can set the *x* parameter to any of three letters: c, l, or r. If you use c, WinHelp treats the graphic as if it were a character, so it flows with any text that shares the same paragraph. If you use l, WinHelp displays the graphic as if it were in a left-justified frame. If you use r, WinHelp displays the graphic as if it were in a right-justified frame. In either of the last two cases, text that's in the same paragraph as the graphic flows around the picture. Adding the optional t parameter causes WinHelp to replace the background color in the graphic with the background color of the Help topic that contains the graphic.

The following are some examples:

```
{bmc BITMAP.BMP}
{bmrt SHED.SHG}
{bml METAFILE.WMF}
```

Figure 18.7 shows how graphics inserted with the various reference statements look in a finished Help file.

FIGURE 18.7.

A graphic inserted with the {bmc} statement flows with the surrounding text; text flows around a graphic inserted with the {bml} or {bmr} statement.

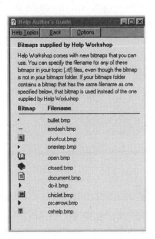

Help Workshop comes with several built-in bitmaps, as shown in Figure 18.8. If you insert a reference to one of these bitmaps into a Topic file, Help Workshop includes it in your Help file even if no corresponding graphics file appears in your Help project.

NOTE

If one of the graphics files in your Help project has the same name as a built-in bitmap, Help Workshop uses your bitmap rather than the built-in one.

18

DEVELOPING ONLINE HELP

WinHelp provides some built-in bitmaps, as shown in Figure 18.8.

Figure 18.8.

Built-in WinHelp bitmaps.

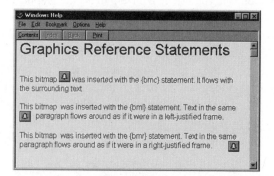

Tip

WinHelp doesn't support many symbol characters, such as the bullet points used by most word processing programs. To include bulleted lists in your Topic files, insert a reference to the built-in BULLET.BMP bitmap at every position where you want a bullet mark to appear. Here's an example:

```
{bmc BULLET.BMP}        First line of the bulleted list
{bmc BULLET.BMP}        Second line of the bulleted list
{bmc BULLET.BMP}        Third line of the bulleted list
```

Adding Hypergraphics

A *hypergraphic* is a picture that functions like a hotspot. In fact, to add a hypergraphic to a Help topic, you create a hotspot in which one of the graphic reference statements described previously is substituted for the hotspot text. For example, the following pop-up hotspot displays the Using_the_Print_Button topic when the user clicks a bitmap of the Print button:

{bmc Print.bmp}Using_the_Print_Button

You can also create hypergraphics called *Shed graphics* that contain multiple hotspot regions. For more information, see "Creating Shed Graphics" later in this chapter.

Graphics Conversion Utilities

As mentioned earlier, WinHelp supports a limited number of graphics formats. However, many commercial and shareware products can convert graphics into a format that WinHelp supports. The following are some of these products:

HiJaak:

> IMSI Corporate Headquarters
>
> 1895 Francisco Blvd. East
>
> San Rafael, CA 94901-5506
>
> Phone: (800) 833-8082
>
> Fax: (415) 257-3565
>
> WWW: `http://www.imsisoft.com/hijaak/hijaak.html`

Collage Complete:

> Inner Media, Inc.
>
> 60 Plain Road
>
> Hollis, NH 03049
>
> Phone: (603) 465-3216
>
> Fax: (603) 465-7197
>
> WWW: `http://www.innermedia.com`

Paint Shop Pro:

> JASC Software, Inc.
>
> P.O. Box 44997
>
> Eden Prairie, MN 55344
>
> Phone: (800) 622-2793
>
> Fax: (612) 930-9172
>
> WWW: `http://www.jasc.com`

18

DEVELOPING
ONLINE HELP

For additional information about graphics conversion utilities, consult CompuServe's Graphics Vendor forums (GO GRAPHAVEN, GO GRAPHBVEN, and GO GRAPHCVEN) or the Desktop Publishing forum (GO DTPFORUM).

Creating Map Files

In a Map file, you associate Help topics with *context numbers*. As you will see later, you use these context numbers to provide context-sensitive Help for the forms, reports, and controls in an Access database. Use of Map files is optional, but is recommended for all but the smallest Help projects. If you prefer, however, you can map Help topics to context numbers directly in the Help Project file. For more information, see "Specifying the Map Files in Your Help Project" later in this chapter.

Map files are written in ASCII text, so you can use Notepad or any other ASCII text editor to create them. If you use a word processing program to edit a Map file, be sure to save the file as type MS-DOS Text. For convenience, give Map files a `.MAP` extension.

Each paragraph of a Map file should employ this syntax:

```
#define topic-ID context-number
```

`topic-ID` is the topic ID of a Help topic, and `context-number` is the unique context number with which you want to associate the topic.

The following are some examples:

```
#define Using_the_Main_Switchboard 100
#define Creating_a_Sales_Order 150
#define Printing_a_Sales_Order 200
#define Deleting_a_Sales_Order 250
```

You will find working with Map files easier if you follow these guidelines:

- Create a corresponding Map file for each Topic file in your Help project. For instance, if your Help project includes Topic files named `USER.RTF` and `ADMIN.RTF`, create Map files named `USER.MAP` and `ADMIN.MAP`.

- Leave room between context numbers for new topics. For example, if the first two topics in a Topic file are `Getting_Started` and `Logging_In`, assign them context numbers such as 100 and 200, rather than 1 and 2. That way, if you later add a new topic between the first two topics, you can keep your Map file in sequence.

- Avoid changing context numbers after you've used them in your Access database. Tracking down and updating every occurrence in an Access application of a context number that has changed is a time-consuming and difficult process. You can avoid it altogether by "freezing" the context numbers in your Map files after you have linked objects and controls to them.

> **TIP**
>
> During the compile process, Help Workshop confirms that every topic whose topic ID begins with `IDH_` has been mapped to a context number. To take advantage of this feature, be sure to start the topic ID of every context-sensitive Help topic in your Help file with `IDH_`.

Creating a Contents File

The table of contents that appears in the Contents tab of the Help Topics dialog box is defined in a Contents file. Contents files should be given `.CNT` extensions. You must distribute a copy of your Contents file with each copy of your Help file that you ship to users. In other words, whenever you ship an `.HLP` file, you must also ship the corresponding .CNT file. Like Map files, Contents files are saved as ASCII text, so you can use Notepad or another ASCII text editor to create them.

> **NOTE**
>
> You can also use Help Workshop to create and edit Contents files. For more information, see the Help file for Help Workshop.

The first paragraph of a Contents file should always contain the :Base statement, which specifies the name of the compiled Help file with which the Contents file is associated. For example, if you're creating a Contents file for a Help file named SAMPLE.HLP, the following would be the first line of your Contents file:

```
:Base SAMPLE.HLP
```

You can also specify a default window for your Help file in the :Base statement by appending > and a window name. Help topics displayed via the Index and Find tabs, an ALink() or KLink() macro, or the Contents tab appear by default in the window you specify, unless a different window is specified in the topic's Greater Than footnote. If you don't specify a default window, WinHelp simply treats the main Help window as the default window.

In addition to the :Base statement, a Contents file can also include any combination of these optional statements:

- The :Title statement specifies the name that appears in the title bar of the Help Topics dialog box (as well as the default name that appears in the title bar of Help windows). For example, to have the title "Help for My Application" appear in the title bar of the Help Topics dialog box, you include the following paragraph in your Contents file:

  ```
  :Title Help for My Application
  ```

- The :Index statement identifies a Help file whose keywords you want to include in the Index tab. First, you type a name by which the Index tab can identify the Help file to the user, and then an equal sign and the name of the relevant Help file itself. Including other Help files' keywords in your Index tab gives users access to the topics in those external Help files. For example, you could let users search for Help in the Access Help file as well as your own by including the following paragraph in your Contents file:

  ```
  :Index Access 97 Help=MSACCESS.HLP
  ```

  To include multiple Help files in your Help file's keyword list, simply insert multiple :Index statements into your Contents file.

18

DEVELOPING ONLINE HELP

- The :Link statement identifies a Help file whose keywords you want to include in ALink() and KLink() macros. To have ALink() and KLink() macros search the keywords in NOTEPAD.HLP, for example, you insert the following paragraph into your Contents file:

```
:Link NOTEPAD.HLP
```

To include multiple Help files in ALink() and KLink() macros, insert multiple :Link statements into your Contents file.

After the :Base and other opening statements, you define the table of contents itself. Figure 18.9 shows a typical Contents tab. As you can see, it's divided into headings (marked with a book icon) and topics (marked with a page icon). A *heading* is a category of Help topics; when you double-click a heading, WinHelp displays an indented list of subheadings and topics. A *topic* corresponds to a specific Help topic; when you double-click a topic, Help displays the corresponding Help topic in your Help file.

FIGURE 18.9.

The Contents tab breaks a Help file's contents into headings and topics.

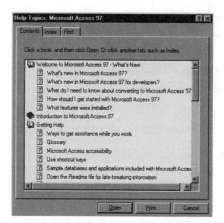

In your Contents file, each heading and topic must have its own paragraph. Each heading paragraph must be followed by paragraphs for the topics and subheadings that belong to the heading (the topics and headings that the Contents tab displays when a user expands the heading). If you plan to nest headings (that is, display subheadings under headings), you must precede each heading and topic paragraph with a number that indicates its indentation level. Use 1 for first-level headings and topics, use 2 for second-level headings and topics, and so on.

To create a heading paragraph, type a number (if necessary) and then the heading name as you want it to appear in the Contents tab. Here's an example:

```
1 Getting Started
```

To create a topic paragraph, type a number (if necessary) and the topic name as it should appear in the Contents tab, followed by an equal sign and the topic ID of the Help topic to display. Here's an example:

```
2 Logging In=logging_in
```

When you're creating topic paragraphs, keep the following points in mind:

- If the topic you want to display is in another Help file, append @ and the other Help file's name to the topic ID.
- If you want to display the topic in a window other than the default window (as specified in the :Base statement), append > and a window name.
- To have a topic in the Contents tab run a macro rather than display a Help topic, type ! and a macro (or multiple macros, separated by colons) after the equal sign.

A sample Contents file appears in Figure 18.10.

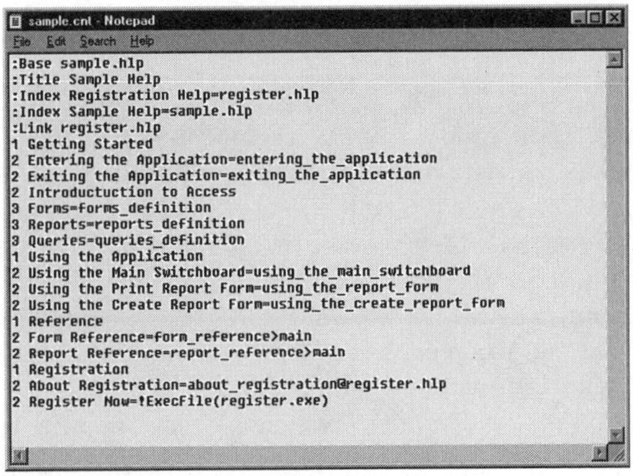

FIGURE 18.10.

A sample Contents file, with opening statements, headings, and topics.

```
:Base sample.hlp
:Title Sample Help
:Index Registration Help=register.hlp
:Index Sample Help=sample.hlp
:Link register.hlp
1 Getting Started
2 Entering the Application=entering_the_application
2 Exiting the Application=exiting_the_application
2 Introductuction to Access
3 Forms=forms_definition
3 Reports=reports_definition
3 Queries=queries_definition
1 Using the Application
2 Using the Main Switchboard=using_the_main_switchboard
2 Using the Print Report Form=using_the_report_form
2 Using the Create Report Form=using_the_create_report_form
1 Reference
2 Form Reference=form_reference>main
2 Report Reference=report_reference>main
1 Registration
2 About Registration=about_registration@register.hlp
2 Register Now=!ExecFile(register.exe)
```

18

DEVELOPING ONLINE HELP

In the finished Help file, the Contents file in Figure 18.10 produces the Contents tab shown in Figure 18.11.

Using the :include statement, you can include another Contents file within your own. The syntax for this statement is as follows:

```
:include contents-file
```

contents-file is the name of the Contents file you are including. Type the :include statement, in its own paragraph, at the position in your table of contents where you want the external table of contents to appear. For example, to include the Access table of contents as the last heading in your Help file's table of contents, add a paragraph to the end of your Contents file and type the following:

```
:include msaccess.cnt
```

FIGURE 18.11.

This Contents tab includes three levels of indentation.

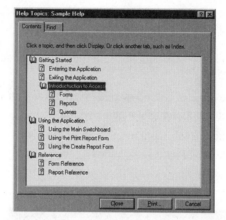

> **NOTE**
>
> If, when you open your Help file, WinHelp can't find the Contents file mentioned in an :include statement or the Help file mentioned in a topic paragraph, it omits the included file or topic paragraph without displaying an error message. Similarly, if WinHelp can't find the Help file mentioned in an :Index or :Link statement, it leaves the keywords out of the Help file but doesn't display an error message. This means that in a Contents file, you can safely refer to other Contents files and Help files even if you don't know for sure that all users have those files on their computers. For example, you can refer to a Help file that belongs to a modular component of your Access application that the user might not have installed.

Creating the Help Project File

The Help Project file contains essential reference information about a Help project. When you compile a Help project, Help Workshop looks in the Help Project file for the following information:

- A list of the Topic files in the project
- A list of the Map files in the project
- The name of the Contents file for the project

- The path to the folder (or folders) in which graphics files can be found, or a list of the graphics files themselves

- Definitions of the main and secondary windows in the project

- The title of the Help file, as you want it to appear in the title bar of Help windows

In addition, you can set various options in the Help Project file. These options determine how stringently Help Workshop reports errors during compiling, what level of compression it uses when compiling, and other details of operation.

Use Help Workshop, shown in Figure 18.12, to create the Help Project file:

1. Open Help Workshop (HCW.EXE).

2. Choose File | New.

3. In the New dialog box, select Help Project and then click OK.

4. In the Project File Name dialog box, select the folder in which you want to store the Help Project file, and then type a name (with an .HPJ extension) in the File Name box.

5. Click the Save button.

FIGURE 18.12.

Use the Microsoft Help Workshop to create and edit Help Project files.

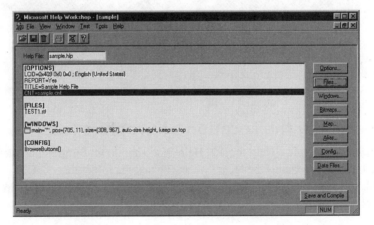

Specifying the Topic Files in Your Help Project

To specify the Topic files in your Help project, follow these steps:

1. In Help Workshop, open the Help Project file.

2. Click the Files button.

3. In the Topic Files dialog box, click the Add button.

4. In the Open dialog box, click the first (or only) Topic file in the Help project and then click the Open button.

5. To add more Topic files, repeat steps 3 and 4.

6. After you finish adding Topic files, click OK in the Topic Files dialog box.

Specifying the Map Files in Your Help Project

To specify the Map files in your Help project, follow these steps:

1. In Help Workshop, open the Help Project file.

2. Click the Map button.

3. In the Map dialog box, click the Include button.

4. In the Include File dialog box, type the name of the first (or only) Map file in the Help project and then click OK.

5. To add more Map files, repeat steps 3 and 4.

6. After you finish adding Map files, click OK in the Map dialog box.

> **NOTE**
>
> To map Help topics to context numbers in the Help Project file itself, rather than in Map files, click the Add button in the Map dialog box and specify a topic ID and context number in the Add Map Entry dialog box. Repeat this procedure for each topic you want to map.

Specifying the Location of Graphics Files

When you compile a Help project, Help Workshop looks for graphics files by default in the folder that contains the Help Project file and the folder that contains the Topic file in which a graphic appears. However, you can instruct Help Workshop to look in additional folders for graphics files as well. To do so, follow these steps:

1. In Help Workshop, open the Help Project file.

2. Click the Bitmaps button.

3. In the Bitmap Folders dialog box, click the Add button.

4. In the Browse For Folder dialog box, select a folder and then click OK.

5. To add more folders, repeat steps 3 and 4.

6. After you finish adding folders, click OK in the Bitmap Folders dialog box.

Creating and Customizing Help Windows

Every Help file comes with a main Help window by default; you must create secondary windows yourself. A Help project can contain up to 255 secondary windows. In actual practice, you will probably need only a few. At the very least, following the Windows 95 convention requires that you create a secondary window in which to display step-by-step procedures. To create a secondary window, follow these steps:

1. In Help Workshop, open the Help Project file.
2. Click the Windows button.
3. In the Window Properties dialog box, choose the General tab.
4. Click the Add button.
5. In the Add A New Window Type dialog box, type a name for the window and then click OK.

NOTE

You can't name a secondary window "main" because WinHelp reserves this name for the main Help window.

6. In the Title Bar text box, type the text you want to be displayed in the new window's title bar.
7. To have WinHelp automatically size the height of this window to fit the Help topic it's displaying, select the Auto-Size Height check box.
8. To have WinHelp keep this window visible even when users switch to another window or application, select the Keep Help Window On Top check box.
9. Click OK.

NOTE

If you want to customize the main Help window in any of the ways described in the following text, you must first follow the steps in the preceding procedure, typing the name main in step 5.

Using Help Workshop, you can specify where you want WinHelp to position a window when it opens. To specify the position of a window, follow these steps:

1. In Help Workshop, open the Help Project file and then click the Windows button.

2. In the Window Properties dialog box, select the window you want to position from the list for the Window Type box.

3. Choose the Position tab and then click the Auto-Sizer button.

4. Position and size the Help Window Auto-Sizer window, shown in Figure 18.13, and then click OK in that window.

FIGURE 18.13.

To set the initial position of a window, position the Help Window Auto-Sizer on your screen.

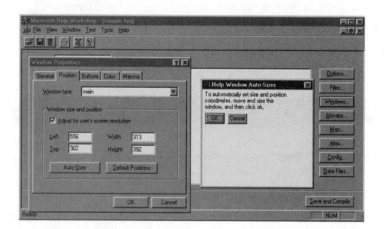

5. To have WinHelp automatically proportion the new window so that it retains its size relative to the screen regardless of the user's screen resolution, select the Adjust for User's Screen Resolution check box.

6. Click OK.

By default, Help Workshop sets the background color of a window to yellow and sets the background color of the nonscrolling region to gray. You can change either or both of these settings by following these steps:

1. In Help Workshop, open the Help Project file and then click the Windows button.

2. In the Window Properties dialog box, select the window whose background colors you want to change from the list for the Window Type box.

3. Choose the Color tab.

4. To change the background color of the nonscrolling region, click the Change button next to the sample nonscrolling region and then select a color in the Color dialog box.

5. To change the background color of the topic text area, click the Change button next to the sample topic text area and then select a color in the Color dialog box.

6. Click OK.

You can customize a window's button bar. When you create a new secondary window, Help Workshop automatically places the Help Topics, Back, and Options buttons on the button bar. These buttons are the recommended minimum set of buttons that every secondary window's button bar should include. However, you can remove any of these buttons or add more buttons by following these steps:

1. In Help Workshop, open the Help Project file and then click the Windows button.

2. In the Window Properties dialog box, select the window whose button bar you want to customize from the list for the Window Type box.

3. Choose the Buttons tab.

4. Select the check box of each button you want to include on this window's button bar. To include browse buttons on the button bar, for example, select the Browse check box.

5. Click OK.

For each window you create, you can define entry macros for WinHelp to run whenever the window opens. If you want to add a button not included among the choices in the Buttons tab (such as a "See Also" button) to a window's button bar, you can define an entry macro that creates the desired button. You can also use entry macros to perform other functions. For more information about WinHelp macros, see "Using Macros" later in this chapter. To define entry macros for a window, follow these steps:

1. In Help Workshop, open the Help Project file and then click the Windows button.

2. In the Window Properties dialog box, select the window for which you want to define entry macros from the list for the Window Type box.

3. Choose the Macros tab.

4. Click the Add button.

5. In the Add Macro dialog box, type the first (or only) entry macro for this window and then click OK.

6. To add more entry macros, repeat steps 4 and 5. When this window opens, WinHelp runs entry macros in the order in which they are listed in the Macros tab.

7. Click OK.

18

DEVELOPING ONLINE HELP

Specifying Help Project Options

Among the options you can specify for a Help project are the title that appears in the main Help window's title bar, the name of the Contents file that belongs to the Help project, and the level of compression you want to use when compiling the Help project. To specify options for your Help project, follow these steps:

1. In Help Workshop, open the Help Project file.

2. Click the Options button.

3. In the Options dialog box, choose the General tab.

4. To specify the title of the Help file as you want it displayed in the main Help window's title bar, type a title in the Help Title box.

5. Choose the Compression tab and then select a compression option. The greater the compression level selected, the longer it takes to compile the Help file, but the smaller the Help file will be. Smaller Help files take up less space on distribution disks and user hard drives, and they also load more quickly and operate somewhat faster. Before you compile the final version of your Help file, select the Maximum compression option so that your Help file will be as small as possible.

6. Choose the Files tab and then type the name of the Contents file for the Help project in the Contents File box.

7. Click OK.

> **NOTE**
>
> The preceding procedure tells you how to specify all the most important options, but you can specify many other options as well. For more information about Help project options, see the Help file for Help Workshop.

Creating a Full-Text Search File During the Compile

When you conduct a full-text search using the Find tab in the Help Topics dialog box, WinHelp draws on the contents of an index stored in a full-text search (.FTS) file. WinHelp creates the .FTS file itself automatically if none exists when it's needed, so you need not deliver one with your Help files. The process of building an .FTS file can take awhile, however, especially if the Help file being indexed is large. To save your users time, you can build an .FTS file in advance when you compile your Help file, and then ship the .FTS file with your Access application. Because .FTS files can be quite large, including one with an application you intend to distribute on floppy disks might affect the number of disks required. If you plan to distribute your application on CD-ROM, however, including an .FTS file is highly recommended.

To create an .FTS file automatically during the compile process, perform the following steps. The .FTS file you create will have the same name as your Help file, but with an .FTS extension.

1. In Help Workshop, open the Help Project file.
2. Click the Options button.
3. Choose the FTS tab.
4. Select the Generate Full Text Search Index check box.
5. Select other options as desired.
6. Click OK.

Creating an Alias for a Help Topic

Using Help Workshop, you can create an alias for a topic ID. During the compile, Help Workshop substitutes the alias for the original topic ID whenever it encounters the original topic ID in a hotspot definition or Map file.

This feature can be useful when you replace a topic with a new one or change a topic ID. For example, say that you delete the Opening_Forms and Closing_Forms topics and replace them with a new topic called Using_Forms. Rather than search your Topic files for every reference to the invalid Opening_Forms and Closing_Forms topic IDs, you can make Using_Forms an alias for both Opening_Forms and Closing_Forms. Whenever the user clicks a hotspot linked to either of the deleted topics, WinHelp displays the Using_Forms topic instead. Similarly, if you change a topic ID from Printing_a_Report to Printing_Reports, you can avoid searching for the old topic ID by making Printing_Reports an alias for Printing_a_Report.

To create an alias for a Help topic, follow these steps:

1. In Help Workshop, open the Help Project file.
2. Click the Alias button.
3. In the Topic ID Alias dialog box, click the Add button.
4. In the Add Alias dialog box, fill in the text boxes as appropriate and then click OK.
5. To add more aliases, repeat steps 3 and 4.
6. In the Topic ID Alias dialog box, click OK.

Specifying the Build Tags to Include in the Help File

Using the Asterisk footnote (see "The Asterisk (*) Footnote" earlier in this chapter), you can assign one or more build tags to a Help topic. In the Help Project file, you can then specify which build tags to include in the compiled Help file. The Help file will contain only Help topics that include the build tags you specified and Help topics that haven't been assigned any build tags.

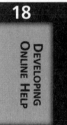

WinHelp's build tag feature enables you to create several versions of a Help file based on the same set of Topic files. For example, in addition to the standard version of your Help file, you could create a smaller version to ship with the demo build of your application, and a larger version for system administrators that contains information you don't want to make available to ordinary users. Creating this version would entail assigning footnotes such as DEMO, USER, and ADMIN to Help topics using the Asterisk footnote. Before compiling the demo version of the Help file, you would specify in the Help Project file that you want to include only topics that have been assigned the DEMO build tag (or no tag). Then you could modify this setting before producing the administrator's version of the Help file, and finally recompile.

To specify the build tags to include in your Help file, follow these steps:

1. In Help Workshop, open the Help Project file.
2. Click the Options button.
3. Choose the Build Tags tab.
4. To include topics with a particular build tag, click the Add button below the upper text box.
5. In the Add Build Tag dialog box, type the build tag name to include in the Build Footnote Text box and then click OK.
6. To include additional build tags, repeat steps 4 and 5.
7. To exclude topics with a particular build tag, click the Add button below the lower text box.
8. In the Add Build Tag dialog box, type the build tag name to exclude in the Build Footnote Text box and then click OK.
9. To exclude additional build tags, repeat steps 7 and 8.
10. In the Options dialog box, click OK.

Compiling the Help Project

To compile a Help project, follow these steps:

1. Open Help Workshop (HCW.EXE).
2. Choose File | Compile.
3. In the Project File box, type or select the name of the Help Project file for the project you want to compile.
4. Click the Compile button.

TIP

If you want to compile the Help project whose Help Project file you're currently editing in Help Workshop, click the Save And Compile button at the bottom of the Help Workshop window.

When the compile is complete, you will find a Help file in the same folder as the Help Project file. The Help file will have the same name as the Help Project file, but with an .HLP extension.

Tips for Designing Help Topics

You can display a Help topic in the main Help window, in a secondary window, or in a pop-up window. Generally speaking, you should design each Help topic to appear in only one of these window types. When you're creating Help topics, try to follow these guidelines:

- Help topics that will appear in the main Help window should be given a non-scrolling region, and should always include a K footnote so that the topic is accessible from the Index tab and KLink() macros. If you intend to include browse buttons with your Help file, be sure to also include the Plus Sign footnote with these Help topics.

- Help topics that will appear in a secondary window can be given a nonscrolling region, but shouldn't be if you want to follow Microsoft's design conventions. Most topics displayed in secondary windows are short enough to not require scrolling. As with topics that appear in the main Help window, always include a K footnote with these topics.

- Help topics that will appear in a pop-up window should never be given a non-scrolling region, nor should they include a Dollar Sign footnote, a K footnote, an A footnote, or a Plus Sign footnote. This rule is especially true of context-sensitive topics that describe Access controls. Topics displayed in pop-up windows are generally most helpful when read in context. By excluding the footnotes previously mentioned, you prevent users from accessing the topic out of context via the Index or Find tabs, a KLink() or ALink() macro, or the browse buttons.

Adding Advanced Help Features

So far, you've learned how to create a fully equipped Windows 95 Help file, utilizing the most essential components of WinHelp. In the following sections, you'll learn how to use advanced features—such as macros, Shed graphics, and authorable buttons—to create even more useful and powerful Help files.

Using Macros

WinHelp comes with various built-in macros you can call from your Help files. You can use macros to add new buttons to a window's button bar, display a Help topic, open or close a Help window, or even run an external program or application.

You can run a macro from a Help file in one of five ways:

- Create a macro hotspot that runs the macro. For more information about macro hotspots, see "Adding Hotspots" earlier in this chapter.

- Create a hotspot region on a Shed graphic that runs the macro. For more information about Shed graphics, see "Creating Shed Graphics" later in this chapter.

- Create an authorable button that runs the macro. For more information about authorable buttons, see "Creating Authorable Buttons" later in this chapter.

- Add a topic to a Contents file that runs the macro. For more information, see "Creating a Contents File" earlier in this chapter.

- Specify the macro as an entry macro for a Help topic, a Help window, or the Help file itself. You specify entry macros for a Help topic in the Exclamation Point footnote (for more information, see "The Exclamation Point (!) Footnote" earlier in this chapter). You specify entry macros for a Help window in the Help Project file (for more information, see "Creating and Customizing Help Windows" earlier in this chapter). To specify entry macros for a Help file, open the Help Project file in Help Workshop and then click the Config button. For more information, see the Help file for Help Workshop.

Several dozen macros are available. A few of the most useful are described next. For more complete information about macros, see the Help file for Help Workshop.

The `ALink()` and `KLink()` Macros

The `ALink()` and `KLink()` macros search your Help file's A and K footnotes, respectively, for one or more specified keywords, and then display a list of the Help topics that include any of the keywords in the Topics Found dialog box. For example, say that you create a `KLink()` macro that searches for the "Printing Reports" and "Reports, Printing" keywords. When the macro runs, WinHelp lists in the Topics Found dialog box every topic whose K footnote includes either (or both) of these keywords. (For information about A and K footnotes, see "The A Footnote" and "The K Footnote" earlier in this chapter.)

The ALink() and KLink() macros simplify the inclusion of "See Also" or "Related Topics" hotspots in your Help file, provided that you are thorough and consistent in assigning A and K footnote keywords. To return to the given example, say that you want to include a "See Also" hotspot in your Help file's "Printing Reports" topic. You can configure the "See Also" hotspot to run an ALink()or KLink() macro that searches A or K footnotes for the keywords "Printing Reports" and "Reports, Printing" (or other similar keywords). Such a hotspot might look like this:

<u>See Also</u>!Klink("Printing Reports;Reports, Printing")

When a user clicks the hotspot, WinHelp automatically finds related topics and displays them in the Topics Found dialog box. Thanks to ALink() and KLink() macros, you need not create or maintain a separate "See Also" topic for every "See Also" hotspot in your Help file.

The syntax for ALink() and KLink() macros is

```
ALink("keyword[;keyword]"[,type[,"topic-ID"[,window]]])
KLink("keyword[;keyword]"[,type[,"topic-ID"[,window]]])
```

in which the parameters have the following meanings:

- *keyword* denotes the keyword you want to search for. Separate multiple keywords with semicolons. If a keyword includes a comma, you must enclose this parameter in quotation marks.

- *type* specifies how you want WinHelp to respond when it finds topics that contain a keyword. By default, WinHelp displays the topics in the Topics Found dialog box and doesn't indicate the Help file from which each topic came. If you set this parameter to JUMP, however, WinHelp jumps directly to a topic if it finds only one with a matching keyword. If you set this parameter to TITLE, WinHelp displays in the Topics Found dialog box the name (as indicated in the Contents file) of the Help file in which it found each topic. The TITLE setting is relevant only if you have included other Help files in the keyword list using the :Link statement (for more information about the :Link statement, see "Creating a Contents File" earlier in this chapter). You can set the *type* parameter to either or both of these values; if you use both, you must separate them with a space (as in JUMP TITLE).

- *topic-ID* denotes the topic ID of the topic to display (in a pop-up window) if no topics with matching keywords are found. This topic should contain a custom message explaining that no matches were found and perhaps telling the user how to proceed. If the topic is in a different Help file, append @ and the Help file's name to the topic ID (as in `no_match_msg@OTHER.HLP`). If you don't specify a topic in this parameter, WinHelp displays a standard message box to inform users that no matches were found.

- *window* denotes the name of the window in which you want WinHelp to display the topic that the user chooses in the Topics Found dialog box. If you don't specify a window, WinHelp uses the window in the topic's Greater Than (>) footnote (if any), the default window for the Help file (again, if any), or the current window.

The following example shows an `ALink()` macro that searches A footnotes for the keywords "Getting Started" and "Reference":

```
ALink(Getting Started;Reference)
```

In the next example, the `KLink()` macro searches K footnotes for the "Invoices" and "Deleting Invoices" keywords. If only one matching topic is found, WinHelp jumps to that topic directly. If no matching topics are found, WinHelp displays the standard Windows message box. Topics that the user views via this macro are displayed in the win2 window:

```
KLink(Invoices;Deleting Invoices,JUMP,"",win2)
```

The `CloseSecondarys()` Macro

The `CloseSecondarys()` macro closes all secondary windows but the current one. This macro has no parameters.

The `CloseWindow()` Macro

The `CloseWindow()` macro closes a Help window. The syntax for this macro is

```
CloseWindow(window)
```

in which *window* is the name of the window to be closed. The following example closes a window named howto:

```
CloseWindow(howto)
```

The `CreateButton()` Macro

You use the `CreateButton()` macro to add a button to a Help window button bar. The syntax for this macro is

```
CreateButton(button-ID,name,macro)
```

in which *button-ID* is the name by which WinHelp identifies the button internally, *name* is the text that appears on the button, and *macro* is the macro that WinHelp runs when a user clicks the button.

> **TIP**
>
> To specify a keyboard shortcut for a button you create with the `CreateButton()` macro, insert an ampersand character (&) before a letter in the *name* parameter. For example, if you set the *name* parameter to `Close &Window`, the user can choose the Close Window button by pressing Alt+W.

The following example creates a button labeled Print that prints the current topic. Because an ampersand appears before the "P" in "Print," the user can press Alt+P to choose the Print button.

```
CreateButton(PrintButton,&Print,Print())
```

The `ExecFile()` Macro

You use the `ExecFile()` macro to run a program or to open a file. You can use this macro to display a file (such as a `README.TXT` file) in Notepad, execute a batch file, or even open an Access database. This is the syntax for the `ExecFile()` macro:

```
ExecFile(program[,arguments[,display-state[,topic-ID]]])
```

program is the name of the program to run or file to open (if you specify a file, WinHelp opens the file that has the program with which the file is associated). *arguments* specifies any command-line arguments for the program. *display-state* is a value indicating how the program's window should be displayed. *topic-ID* is the ID of the Help topic you want WinHelp to display if the specified program or file can't be opened. (If this topic is in another Help file, append @ and the Help file's name, as in `not_found@OTHER.HLP`.)

The *display-state* parameter has 10 values, including `SW_SHOW` (activate the window in its default size and position), `SW_SHOWMAXIMIZED` (activate the window maximized), and `SW_SHOWMINIMIZED` (activate the window minimized). For a complete list of *display-state* values, see the Help file for Help Workshop.

The following example opens Notepad, maximized:

```
ExecFile(NOTEPAD.EXE,,SW_SHOWMAXIMIZED)
```

The `Exit()` Macro

The `Exit()` macro closes the Help file. This macro has no parameters.

The `Print()` Macro

The `Print()` macro prints the current Help topic. This macro has no parameters.

The `Search()` Macro

The `Search()` macro displays the Index tab in the Help Topics dialog box. This macro has no parameters.

Creating Shed Graphics

A Shed graphic is a hypergraphic that has multiple hotspot regions, which can be configured to function like a jump or pop-up or to run a macro. Using Shed graphics, you can add interactive illustrations to a Help file. For example, you can define pop-up hotspot regions on a bitmap of an Access form. Whenever a user points at a control on the bitmap and clicks his or her mouse, Help for the control appears in a pop-up window. Similarly, you can create a Shed graphic that shows a menu from your Access application, and enables users to get Help for a menu command by pointing to the command and clicking.

To create Shed graphics, you use the Microsoft Hotspot Editor (`SHED.EXE`). You can acquire a copy of the Hotspot Editor from the same place as the Help Workshop (see "The Help Project" earlier in this chapter for more information). The Hotspot Editor enables you to open an existing bitmap or Windows metafile, define hotspot regions, and then save the graphic in Shed format. Shed graphics are usually given an `.SHG` extension.

> **CAUTION**
>
> Always save a Shed graphic under a different name than the original bitmap or metafile on which it is based. Otherwise, the Hotspot Editor simply converts the original graphic into a Shed graphic, which you can't open or modify as you would a standard bitmap or metafile.

To create a Shed graphic, perform the following steps:

1. Open the Hotspot Editor (`SHED.EXE`).
2. Choose File | Open. Choose and then open an existing bitmap or Windows metafile.

3. Drag the mouse pointer over the portion of the graphic you want to define as a hotspot region. A rectangular border surrounds the area you specify.

4. Choose Edit | Attributes (or double-click anywhere inside the hotspot region).

5. In the Attributes dialog box, select the type of hotspot you want to define from the list for the Type box.

6. If you selected Jump or Popup in the Type box, type the topic ID of the Help topic you want the hotspot region to display in the Context String box. If you selected Macro in the Type box, type the name of the macro you want the hotspot region to run in the Macro box.

7. If you want the borders of the hotspot region to be visible to the user, select Visible from the list for the Attribute box. If you want the borders of the hotspot region to be invisible, select Invisible instead.

8. Click OK or press Enter. The hotspot region is now defined.

9. To define additional hotspot regions, repeat steps 3 through 8. You can include any combination of jump, pop-up, and macro regions on a Shed graphic.

10. After you finish defining hotspot regions, choose File | Save As and then save the graphic as a new file with an `.SHG` extension.

Creating Authorable Buttons

WinHelp enables you to add *authorable buttons* to a Help file. Authorable buttons run macros, so you can use one to do anything a macro can. For example, you might create a "See Also" authorable button that runs an `ALink()` or `KLink()` macro.

To insert an authorable button into a Help topic, you use the `{button}` statement. The syntax for this statement is

```
{button [label],macro1[:macro2:macro3...]}
```

in which `label` is the text you want printed on the button, and the `macro` values denote the macros you want Help to run when the user chooses the button. You can specify one macro or a series of macros separated by colons. If you don't specify a label for the button, Help displays it as a small blank square.

The following two sample `{button}` statements create two authorable buttons in a topic. The first statement creates a See Also button that displays a list of topics about reports; the second statement creates a blank button that closes all secondary windows and then jumps to the Registration topic:

```
{button See Also,KLink(Reports)}
{button ,CloseSecondarys():JumpId(Registration)}
```

Providing Help for an Access Database

You can give users Help for an Access database in several ways. You can write tips that Access displays in a pop-up window whenever a user points at a control with the mouse. To assist users in searching for Help, you can create a custom Help menu from which users can open the Help Topics dialog box. You can also provide context-sensitive Help, which users can get either by pressing F1 or by clicking the What's This button (marked with a question mark) on the title bar of a form and then clicking a control.

In the following sections, you learn how to provide each of these kinds of Help.

> **NOTE**
>
> For information about creating a custom Help Menu, see Chapter 8, "Working with Command Bars."

Creating Control Tips

Access 97 lets you add control tips to your databases. They are much like the tooltips that come with most Windows programs. A *control tip* is a description of a control that appears in a pop-up window when the user points at the control with the mouse. You can provide control tips only for the controls on a form.

To create a control tip, perform the following steps:

1. Open a form in Design view.
2. To display a control's property sheet, double-click the control.
3. Choose the Other tab and then type the text of the control tip in the ControlTipText box. This text can be up to 255 characters long.

Providing Context-Sensitive Help

You can provide context-sensitive Help for reports, forms, and controls on forms. Providing context-sensitive Help involves establishing a link between a form, report, or control and a specific Help topic in a Help file.

Before you can establish these links, you must assign a unique context number to each Help topic in your Help file. For more information, see "Creating Map Files" earlier in this chapter.

To link a form or report to a Help topic, you set its `HelpFile` property to the name of a Help file and its `HelpContextID` property to the context number of a topic within that Help file. To link a control on a form to a Help topic, you set its `HelpContextID` property to the context number of a Help topic in the Help file you specified in the form's `HelpFile` property.

For example, say that you want to display a Help topic named `Using_the_Main_Switchboard` whenever a user requests Help for your application's Main Switchboard form. This topic is in a Help file named `DATABASE.HLP`, and you mapped it to context number 550. You would set the `HelpFile` property for the Main Switchboard form to `DATABASE.HLP`, and the `HelpContextID` property to `550`. You can then link the controls on the Main Switchboard form to different Help topics in the `DATABASE.HLP` Help file by setting each control's `HelpContextID` property to another context number.

> **TIP**
>
> If you don't specify a path in the `HelpFile` property, Access looks for the Help file in the folder that contains your application. It's a good idea to place your Help file in the same folder as your application and omit a path in the `HelpFile` property. This way, your `HelpFile` properties are always correctly set regardless of where your users install your application.

18

DEVELOPING
ONLINE HELP

If a user requests Help for a control you didn't link to a Help topic, Access opens the Help file to the topic for the form that contains the control. If the form hasn't been linked to a Help topic, Access displays the Microsoft Access Help Topics dialog box.

> **TIP**
>
> If your Help file contains one Help topic that describes every control on a form, as opposed to separate Help topics for each control, you can provide context-sensitive Help for the form and all its controls simply by setting the form's `HelpFile` and `HelpContextID` properties.

You can display context-sensitive Help to users in two ways:

- Open the Help file for your application, and display the context-sensitive Help topic in the main or a secondary Help window.

- Display the context-sensitive Help topic in a pop-up window. Figure 18.14 shows how Help looks when it's displayed this way.

FIGURE 18.14.

You can display context-sensitive Help topics to users in pop-up windows.

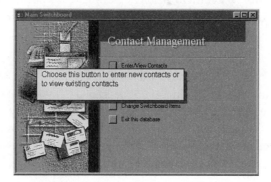

The procedure for linking forms, reports, and controls to Help topics varies depending on which way you want to display context-sensitive Help. Both procedures are discussed in the following sections.

Displaying Context-Sensitive Help in a Help Window

To have Access open your Help file and display context-sensitive Help in a Help window, perform the following steps:

1. Open a form or report in Design view.
2. To display the property sheet for the form or report, choose View | Properties.
3. Choose the Other tab and then type the name of your Help file in the HelpFile box.
4. In the HelpContextID box, type the context number of a Help topic. Access displays the topic you specified if the control that has the focus when the user pressed F1 hasn't been linked to a Help topic, or if the control to which the user pointed with the What's This button hasn't been linked to a Help topic.
5. To provide Help for a control on a form, click the control.
6. In the HelpContextID box, type a context number.

Displaying Context-Sensitive Help in a Pop-Up Window

To have Access display context-sensitive Help in a pop-up window, perform the following steps:

1. Open a form or report in Design view.
2. To display the property sheet for the form or report, choose View | Properties.

3. Choose the Other tab and then type the name of your Help file in the HelpFile box.

4. In the HelpContextID box, type a minus sign (–) and then the context number of a Help topic. Access displays the topic you specified if the control that has the focus when the user pressed F1 hasn't been linked to a Help topic, or if the control to which the user pointed with the What's This button hasn't been linked to a Help topic.

5. To provide Help for a control on a form, click the control.

6. In the HelpContextID box for the control, type a minus sign and then a context number.

Displaying a Contents and Search Menu in Your Applications Through Code

If you want your application to have the standard Windows look and feel, you need a Contents and Search item in the Help menu. The Contents section is usually the home page for the Help application. This screen outlines all the sections contained in the Help file. This section is not as important for Help files in Windows 95 because the newer Help uses a .CNT file. This new Contents screen is a series of books that are arranged in a tree structure. The books can be opened, and the topics are then expanded. The topics are depicted as a series of pages. You can double-click and browse them, just like a standard Windows topic. The Search screen remains the same for Windows 3.*x* and Windows 95.

Now you're ready to see how to invoke both of these functions.

Contents Menu

An easy way to invoke a Contents menu is to use the SendKeys method. Insert the following code into the Click event of your Contents menu:

```
SendKeys "{F1}"
```

Search Menu

Invoking the Search menu is a little more difficult than invoking the Contents menu. You have to call the WinHelp API to open the help's Search window. The Search window is invoked by passing the constant HELP_PARTIALKEY to WinHelp. If you're using an API, you need a declare.

You should include the following code in the declarations section of your projects module:

```
Public Const HELP_PARTIALKEY = &H105    " Call the search engine in
                                          WinHelp
```

18

DEVELOPING ONLINE HELP

```
Declare Function WinHelp Lib "user32" Alias "WinHelpA" _
    (ByVal hwnd As Long, ByVal lpHelpFile As String, _
    ByVal wCommand As Long, ByVal dwData As Long) As Long
```

Then place this code in your Search menu Click event:

```
Private Sub mnuSearch Click()

    Dim lDummVal As Long, Temp As Long

    Forms!form1.HelpFile = "d:\data.hlp"
    lDummVal = 0

    'Call API to invoke search window
    Temp = WinHelp(Forms!form1.hwnd, Forms!form1.HelpFile,
➥HELP_PARTIALKEY, lDummVal)

End Sub
```

When the Search Click event is fired, the API locates your Help file and opens the Search window.

Adding the What's This Button to Forms

For users to get Help for a control on a form by clicking the What's This button and then clicking the control, you must add the What's This button to the title bar of your forms by following these steps:

1. Open the form in Design view.

2. Choose View | Properties.

3. Choose the Format tab and then select Yes in the list for the WhatsThisButton box.

> **NOTE**
>
> The WhatsThisButton cannot be displayed unless the Minimize and Maximize buttons are set to None.

How Can Error-Handling Routines Reference the Help File?

Associating your Help file topics is easy with Access 97. All it requires is the path to your Help file and the correct Context ID mappings. *Correct mappings* means that your Help file must have a Context ID topic that matches the error in Access. This means that if you receive an error, such as 91 Access, your Help file should have a topic 91 for the error. The error number is not important; it's the ability to trap many errors that is significant. You can get around this exact mapping, but this method is the most straightforward. First, you'll see an example that uses the mapping technique, and then we'll discuss an alternative approach.

> **NOTE**
>
> The Help file is not automatically invoked. The user has to press the F1 key when the message box is presented on the screen.

The following example raises an error number 290. The Help file also has an error 290:

```
Private Sub Command2_Click()

    Dim msg As String

    On Error GoTo ErrTrap:
    Err.Clear
    Err.Raise 290    ' Generate a user-defined error, that is associated
                     ' with a help Context ID.
    Exit Sub
ErrTrap:
    If Err.Number <> 0 Then
        msg = "Error # " & Str(Err.Number) & " was generated by " _
        & Err.Source & Chr(13) & Err.Description

        MsgBox msg, , "Error", "d:\help\data.HLP", Err.Number
    End If
End Sub
```

The last two parameters in the message box are the Help file path and Context ID. Notice that the path to the Help file is specified, and the Err.Number value is used for the Context ID. This approach works fine if you have a topic for each error the user will encounter, but what if you want only certain error messages to go to the Help file? A simple solution is to trap for a certain error number and then pass the Context ID parameter a predefined value.

Here's how to take this approach in code:

```
Private Sub Command3_Click()

    Dim msg As String, y As Integer

    On Error GoTo ErrTrap:
    Err.Clear
    y = 1 / 0        ' Generate an error
```

```
        Exit Sub

ErrTrap:
    Select Case Err.Number
    Case 6, 7, 9, 11, 28
        msg = "Error # " & Str(Err.Number) & " was generated by " _
        & Err.Source & Chr(13) & Err.Description
        MsgBox msg, , "Error", "d:\help\data.HLP", 290
    Case Else
        msg = "Error # " & Str(Err.Number) & " was generated by " _
        & Err.Source & Chr(13) & Err.Description
        MsgBox msg, , "Error", "d:\help\data.HLP", Err.Number
    End Select
End Sub
```

In this code, you trap for errors 6, 7, 9, 11, and 28. An appropriate help topic (#290) that covers the five different error possibilities is constructed. All other messages are mapped according to the Err.Number. Obviously, in the real world this would be very difficult to accomplish. You would probably construct a catch-all topic in your Help and use that Context ID as the value. This example is by no means the only way to map to your Help file; I have presented these examples only as ideas. Ultimately, your job is to implement the right solution for your needs.

Using Help Authoring Tools

Inserting Help topic footnotes and formatting hotspots are repetitive and time-consuming tasks. Fortunately, there are various Help authoring tools that simplify these and other processes. Help authoring tools make creating Help topics, adding hotspots, and inserting graphics faster and easier. They also create and maintain Help Project files and Map files for you automatically. The more sophisticated authoring tools can even convert user manuals into Help files, enabling you to develop both printed and online documentation in less time than it would take you to create each separately.

Currently, none of the major Help authoring tools provides complete support for the Windows 95 version of WinHelp, so if you want to make use of new features (such as the A and Greater Than footnotes, authorable buttons, and ALink() and KLink() macros), sometimes you still have to edit source files manually. However, if you expect to be developing Help files on a regular basis, a Help authoring tool still makes an excellent investment.

Help Authoring Tools

The following are a few WinHelp Help authoring tools that are available:

Doc-To-Help:

> WexTech Systems, Inc.
> 310 Madison Ave., Suite 905
> New York, NY 10017
> Phone: (212) 949-9797
> Fax: (212) 949-4007

ForeHelp:

> ForeFront, Inc.
> 4710 Table Mesa Dr. Suite B
> Boulder, CO 80303
> Phone: (800) 357-8507
> Fax: (303) 494-5446
> Email: 74777.2132@compuserve.com

HelpBreeze:

> SolutionSoft
> 370 Altair Way, Suite 200
> Sunnyvale, CA 94086
> Phone: (408) 736-1431
> Fax: (408) 736-4013
> Email: 75210.2214@compuserve.com

RoboHELP:

> Blue Sky Software Corporation
> 7486 La Jolla Blvd., Suite 3
> La Jolla, CA 92037
> Phone: (619) 459-6365
> Fax: (619) 459-6366

18

DEVELOPING
ONLINE HELP

Summary

In this chapter, you learned how to create Windows 95 Help files and how to provide context-sensitive Help for an Access database. Thorough planning is the key to developing Help files that will get your users the help they need. If you will be creating Help files regularly, consider investing in a Help authoring tool. Help authoring tools greatly reduce the time you spend performing chores such as inserting footnotes, formatting hotspots, and maintaining Map files, thus enabling you to focus on your writing.

For more information on creating Help files, you can get a copy of the Microsoft Windows 95 Help Authoring Kit or read the Help authoring information that ships with the Office Developer's Edition.

Multiuser and Client/Server Issues

PART VI

IN THIS PART

CHAPTER 19

Access in a Network Environment: File Server

IN THIS CHAPTER

With the rapidly increasing popularity of shared information systems and groupware-enabled applications, providing methods for ensuring secure, stable, centrally accessible databases is a high priority in any Relational Database Management System (RDBMS). Without these methods, the usability of your database, data integrity, and performance will begin to degrade the moment the database is used by more than one person. Fortunately, Access has provided various means of controlling the availability of records, objects, and even the entire database that give the developer tools for creating a sensible approach to designing and maintaining a multiuser application.

Controlling Access in a Network

Some Access developers think that to make the change from single-user to multiuser applications, all they have to do is move the .MDB file and have everyone access it via a shared network drive. When dealing with an Access database on the network, as the administrator, you may find that your job becomes more difficult because you must worry about many more issues:

- You must make sure that all users have read/write access to the common database's shared folder.
- You need to add the user to the workgroup file. For more information on how to add a user or new groups to the database, refer to Chapter 23, "Security."
- You should run Setup to give the user an Access installation.
- You should set up Access so that it runs against the correct workgroup.
- You should make sure that the application opens and runs correctly for the user.
- When you need to make changes to the database, all users must close the database. This way, you can make the necessary changes. If the users don't close the database, some of the users may run the incorrect version of an object, which could cause data corruption. More information on updating a database appears in the next section.

Splitting the Database

In a multiuser situation, you need to have the data in one place and all the code in another place. You cannot place your application on a LAN shared drive and let everyone access it. This will drastically affect performance because all those forms, reports, and code modules have to be downloaded from the LAN to the users' workstation over the wire. On top of that, several people will be sharing the *same* forms, reports, and so on.

Access offers you two ways to split the data from the main application. The first is to use the Database Splitter Wizard, and the second is to manually link the table objects from the table database back into the current database.

The Database Splitter Wizard

Most of the time, you should back up the data being added by the users. One of the ways to do so is to use the Database Splitter and split the table objects away from all the other objects of a database. You then have the table object database located on a network share and all of the database's other objects located on the user's local machine. The Database Splitter Wizard helps you make the move from local tables in the current database to linked tables in a new database. After the splitter exports the tables to the new database, it links the table objects from the new database back into the original database. To start the Database Splitter, choose Tools | Add-ins | Database Splitter.

1. In the Database Splitter Wizard, you are first asked to verify that you want to split the database. If you are sure you want the database split, click the Split Database button.

2. The Create Back-End Database dialog box, shown in Figure 19.1, asks where you want the new database to be located.

FIGURE 19.1.

The location find-er for a new data-base.

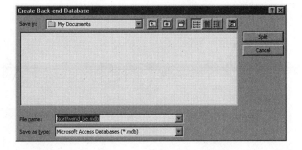

3. After you locate the folder and add the name to the File Name list box, click the Split button.

4. The status bar displays the current tables being exported and then which table is being linked. On completion of the export and link, a Database Splitter Success or Failure dialog box appears. Click OK to return to the Database window.

Notice that the tables now have a black arrow beside them. This arrow tells you at a glance which tables are linked and which are not.

19

ACCESS IN A NETWORK ENVIRONMENT

Issues with Splitting the Database

When you start to split a database, you need to be aware of some possible pitfalls:

- Linked tables can run slower than nonlinked tables since the linked tables are now shared with other network users. Design your multiuser applications to make less use of the linked data if possible.

- If you write VBA code to work against the linked tables, don't use any open-table calls, the "Seek" command for example. Open-table calls do not work against linked tables. You will have to use an OpenDatabase method first to Seek on a linked table. (See Chapter 16, "Data Access Objects," for more information.)

- With everything but the data residing in another database, you need to have a plan to update any changes that will be made to the nondata database. As any fixes are made to database objects, you need a way to roll these changes out to the users' databases that are residing on local machines. You can tackle this issue by using replication. For more information on replication, refer to Chapter 21, "Replication."

Linking Tables Manually

To link tables manually, follow these steps:

1. Choose File | Get External Data | Link Tables. The Link dialog box, shown in Figure 19.2, appears.

FIGURE 19.2.

Creating a database link.

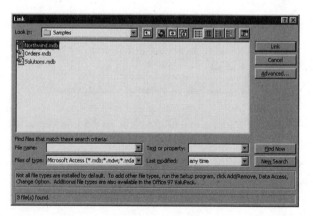

2. Locate the database file from which you want to link the tables.

3. After you select the database, click the Link button.

4. The Link Tables dialog box, shown in Figure 19.3, appears and lists the tables that are available for linking.

FIGURE 19.3.
Tables to be linked.

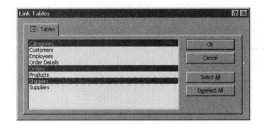

5. In this dialog box, select the tables that you want to link to your current database. You can select the tables in two possible ways. The first is to click the Select All button, which causes all tables to be marked to be linked. The second is to click the table name, which marks it to be linked. If at any time you want to deselect a table, click the table name again. If at any time you want to start the selection process over, click the Deselect button.

6. After you mark the table(s) to be linked, click OK.

7. Upon completion of the linking, you are returned to the database.

> **NOTE**
>
> If an error occurs while you're trying to link a table, an error message appears, letting you acknowledge the error. Then you can continue linking the other tables.

Maintaining Linked Tables

After you link tables, you need to manage these links. Sometimes you may need to move databases from one folder to another. If so, you need to refresh the link, letting the database know where the tables are now located. To carry out this task, open the add-in called the Linked Table Manager by choosing Tools | Add-ins | Linked Table Manager. The dialog box shown in Figure 19.4 appears, listing the tables that are currently linked.

To the right of the table name is the path and database name in parentheses. You can update one table or all the tables in the list. You can select tables from the list in the following two ways:

- To select one table at a time, click the box that is located to the left of the table name.

- To select all the tables simultaneously, click the Select All button.

19

ACCESS IN A NETWORK ENVIRONMENT

FIGURE 19.4.

The Linked Table Manager.

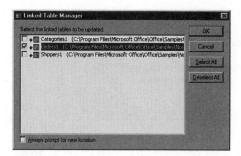

You can deselect tables that have been selected in the following two ways:

- To deselect one table, click the box that is located to the left of the table name.
- To deselect all currently selected tables, click the Deselect All button.

After you select the tables that you want to refresh, click OK. If any tables can't be refreshed or you've clicked the Always Prompt for New Location check box, the Link dialog box appears, prompting you for the location and name of the database to refresh the tables with. After you select the database, click Find Now. If the Linked Table Manager is successful in locating the table objects you have selected, a Microsoft Access dialog box acknowledgment appears, telling you that the selected tables were successfully refreshed. Then you are returned to the Linked Table Manager dialog box. Otherwise, if the table objects couldn't be located, you receive a Linked Table Manager error. If you click OK, you're placed back in the Linked Table Manager dialog box, and the tables that could not be refreshed are still selected.

If you want to view where the database is getting its data from, you can go into design mode of the table and choose View | Properties. Under Description, you will see something like DATABASE=D:\test.mdb;TABLE=Ship. You can't make any changes to the Description field, but at least you can view it without going into the Linked Table Manager.

Multiuser Workgroup Issues

Normally, when you're running Access in a network environment, multiple users can use the database. To make sure that Access is set up for this situation, you must do the following:

- First, if it's a secured database, you will need to set up the local copy of Access to use the correct workgroup file.
- Second, you need to set some options in Access to ensure that it behaves correctly when users try to save a record to the database.

Database Security

When you're dealing with multiple users, most of the time you will want to implement database security. While security is covered in Chapter 23, you must be aware that the workgroup information file takes on a new role in a networked environment. Although some of this material is covered from a different viewpoint in that chapter, I've mentioned enough here to help you understand how to manipulate the workgroups.

Locating Your Workgroup

To locate your workgroup, go into the Access program group and locate the Workgroup Administrator icon. If it isn't present, choose Start | Run. Then type `c:\msoffice\access\wrkgadm.exe`, assuming that Access is installed in the default directory. If it's installed in a different directory, replace `c:\msoffice\access` with the location where you installed Access. After you click OK, the dialog box shown in Figure 19.5 appears.

FIGURE 19.5.

The Workgroup Administrator dialog box.

Two choices are available: Join an existing workgroup or create a new workgroup.

Joining an Existing Workgroup

To join an existing workgroup, click the Join button at the bottom of the Workgroup Administrator dialog box. You then are prompted for the location and the filename of the new workgroup. If you know the drive, the folder name, and the name of the file, type them into the new dialog box. Otherwise, click the Browse button, which opens the File Locator dialog box. Here you can navigate to the workgroup you want to join. After you locate the file and select it, click Open. Notice that the file you have selected now appears in the Database Name text box. If you are satisfied with your selection, click OK. If you can join this workgroup, a Success dialog box appears. Confirm the Success dialog box by clicking OK.

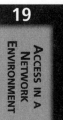

> **NOTE**
>
> Location can be a drive and a folder, or it can be a network share, as long as the workgroup is located when you click OK (for example, d:\data\newworkgroup.mdw or \\mymachine\data\newworkgroup.mdw).

Creating a New Workgroup

To create a new workgroup, click the Create button at the bottom of the Workgroup Administrator dialog box. The dialog box shown in Figure 19.6 appears, requiring you to fill in three text boxes.

FIGURE 19.6.

The Workgroup Owner Information dialog box.

The Name text box, which is first, defaults to the registered owner of Access. Next is the Organization text box, which defaults to the registered organization name. Third is the Workgroup ID text box, which requires a unique ID number. By entering the ID number, you guarantee that the new workgroup will be unique. The minimum information required is the registered owner, but I strongly recommend that you fill in all three options.

> **WARNING**
>
> Make sure that you keep a copy of the name, organization, and workgroup ID. Always confirm that you have it in the same syntax that it was typed in. If you ever need to re-create the workgroup file, you must supply the same information exactly as you entered it the first time. If you can't do so, you might not be able to regain access to your applications that have been secured based on this workgroup file.

After you fill in the information in the Workgroup Owner Information dialog box and click OK, you're prompted for the location and the name to be used for the new workgroup. You can type the new name and folder, or you can simply click the Browse button and change the folder using the File Locator dialog box. To create the new workgroup, click OK. To stop the creation of the workgroup, click Cancel. If you click Cancel, you're placed back at the Workgroup Owner Information dialog box (shown in Figure 19.6); otherwise, a Please Confirm Information dialog box appears. This dialog box shows you the information you have filled in. If the information is correct, click OK. If it isn't, click the Change button. When you click the Change button, you're placed back at the Workgroup Owner Information dialog box with the same information filled in. Otherwise, a Success dialog box appears, letting you know that the workgroup was created. After you click OK, a Success or Failure dialog box appears. By accepting the dialog box, you are placed back at the Workgroup Administrator dialog box.

Command-Line Options

Access has a wide selection of command-line options that enable you to start an Access session with specific parameters you supply. You can create a shortcut on your desktop (search Windows Help for shortcuts) or add them to your Windows Start menu. In a multiuser situation, using the following techniques may be helpful, since you can implement security from a desktop shortcut icon or perform user logons from the command line.

One good use for these shortcuts is in developing and testing an Access application. You can have several shortcuts on your desktop—each with a different user or workgroup, for example—for testing database concurrency and locking issues. Table 19.1 shows some of the command-line options that can be useful in a multiuser database.

TABLE 19.1. ACCESS STARTUP COMMAND-LINE OPTIONS.

Option	*Description*
/Excl	Opens a database exclusively. If the database is currently open by another user, this generates an error dialog box.
/User *username*	Starts Access using the specified username.
/Pwd *password*	Is used with the /User switch. It's useful only if your database is using Access security.
/Wrkgrp *Information File*	Starts Access with the specified Workgroup Information File. See Chapter 23 to learn how to set up workgroups.

An Overview of Locking

Relational databases are open systems by nature. In a properly designed system, where the data applies to one or more of the "normal forms" as defined in the relational model, a particular entity (a customer, for example) might be combined from several different data sources. Because of this openness, the RDBMS must enforce rules on when and how the data needs to be protected to ensure its integrity. Locking areas of the data when certain actions are requested ensures this.

Locking Methods Used by Access

Unlike other desktop RDBMSs that implement a fixed-length record structure and use true single record locking, Access, because of its variable-length record structure, employs the page-locking method to provide multiuser access to an Access database. This locked page is a *static* (it can't be changed) 2KB (2,048-byte) chunk of data that contains your record and any other surrounding records that Access needs to fill the 2KB page. So, for example, if you have a record that is 1,200 bytes long, to fill the 2KB page buffer, Access locks the surrounding records when a lock is activated.

Because of this type of locking, it's important to know how and when to enforce the various methods of locking and when to be aware of certain actions that cause Access to enforce its own locks. There is nothing worse than an arcane record-locking violation message abruptly interrupting your application or preventing another user from getting to needed data. (See the section "Handling Multiuser Locking Errors," later in this chapter.)

Access uses the following types of locking in a multiuser setting (see the later section titled "Optimistic Locking Versus Pessimistic Locking" for more information on locking):

- Optimistic—This method locks the record only while the record is being updated. This is the default-locking method used by Access.

- Pessimistic—This method locks the record when editing begins and releases it when the record is updated.

- Full or Exclusive—This method locks the entire recordset. This is a very restrictive lock and is generally used only when batch updates are being performed or when changes are being made to database objects where exclusive control over the data or object is required.

> **NOTE**
>
> When you edit data in a linked SQL database table using ODBC, Microsoft Access doesn't lock records; instead, the rules of that SQL database govern the locking.

Differences in Locking Behavior Between Jet 2.*x* and Jet 3.0

With Access 97, several changes were made to the locking behavior used in version 3.*x* of the Jet database engine. These changes, which include support for multithreading and implicit transactions, were added to improve performance in a multiuser application mainly by reducing the number of read/write and locking operations performed on the database. In Jet Version 2.*x*, data was written immediately after each `Recordset.Update` method. With Jet Version 3.*x*, the locks remain and edits are cached and written when the cache is full or until two seconds pass.

> **NOTE**
>
> The Jet database engine for Access 97 is Jet 3.5. There were some bugs in Jet 3.5 that corrupted your database in locking situations of long value (LV) or memo type fields. To obtain a fix, download the latest version of Jet (as of this writing Jet 3.51 from the Microsoft Web site). Search for Jet 3.51.

In most situations, this would be a desired improvement, but this new locking behavior has a side effect. Because locks can be in place for longer periods, the number of concurrent users who have access to the locked records can be reduced. In some situations, you might want to mimic the locking behavior in Jet 2.*x* by modifying your code to use explicit transactions. (See the section titled "Transactions," later in this chapter.) You can also use queries that employ Data Manipulation Language (DML) commands such as UPDATE, INSERT, and DELETE (which aren't affected by the new locking behavior).

The `RecordLocks` Property

The `RecordLocks` property is used to determine how records are locked when Access queries, forms, or report objects are being used. You can set this property individually for each object by using the object's property sheet, a macro, or VBA.

19

ACCESS IN A NETWORK ENVIRONMENT

> **NOTE**
>
> You can set the default RecordLocks setting by selecting Tools I Options I Advanced. This setting affects the RecordLocks setting for most Access objects that have this property.

The .LDB File

The .LDB file is a special file used by Access to maintain control of the locking for shared databases. Access automatically creates the file for every database whenever you open the database in a shared environment. The .LDB file is named with the same name as the database file but with the .LDB extension. For example, MyDatabase.mdb would have a file called MyDatabase.ldb. This file is kept in the same folder (directory) as the parent .MDB file.

In previous versions of the Jet engine, after Access created the .LDB file, the file was permanent (unless deleted by the user). With Jet 3.*x*, this file is now temporary. Access automatically deletes the .LDB file when the last user closes the database, and re-creates it when the database is reopened. This is done primarily to handle database replication and improve performance-managing locks on the database.

> **WARNING**
>
> If you intend to use an Access database on a NetWare 3.11 file server, you need to be aware of a bug that limits the amount of data that Access can lock to 1MB (later versions of NetWare have solved this problem). The problem lies with the default in NetWare that limits the number of locks on a single workstation to 500; when this limit is reached, it can bring down the entire server. If you're using NetWare 3.11, you can use a patch to resolve this error. The file 311PTD.ZIP is located in the libraries of the NOVFILES forum on CompuServe. The patch is in the form of a NetWare Loadable Module that needs to be loaded on your server.
>
> In addition to the patch, you can also increase the server's maximum record locks parameters to their maximum limits. In the file server's AUTOEXEC.NCF file, enter the following commands:
>
> ```
> set maximum record locks per connection = 10000
> set maximum record locks = 20000
> ```

Optimistic Locking Versus Pessimistic Locking

In any well-designed multiuser application, it's critical to have a good, solid understanding of record locking. This section looks at two methods of record locking, optimistic and pessimistic, to help you decide which strategy might work best for your application.

Optimistic Locking

Optimistic locking is the default locking method used by Access. It's easy to implement and is the preferable method when many users will be editing or adding records. With this type of lock, the edited record is locked only for an instant when the record is being updated, such as when Access is moving to the previous or next record, closing the recordset, or specifically updating the recordset. This locking method significantly reduces the problems and locking conflicts that result from concurrent editing of the same record. An optimistic lock is also less likely to prevent other users from editing the same record or even adding a new record than is a pessimistic lock.

When Access is using optimistic locking, a good error handler is needed to handle any conflicts that might arise when the recordset is being updated. For example, the Write Conflict dialog box, which can be confusing to the user, can be replaced by a custom dialog box and a procedure created to save the data temporarily and reattempt the update later.

Pessimistic Locking

When *pessimistic locking* is enforced, the record (or page) is locked when the user begins to edit it. This type of locking is similar to the record locking used by other RDBMSs; consequently, your users might be more accustomed to having this type of control while editing. And with this type of locking, you can avoid having to deal with the Write Conflict dialog box. You should be aware of some problems with using pessimistic locking in Access, however.

As explained previously, when Access locks a record, it grabs any records near the one you're editing, up to the 2KB limit. Thus, it usually locks multiple records and can even prevent the user from adding new records if the locked record is at or near the bottom of the recordset. Another problem is that if the user begins to edit a record and is delayed from updating it for some reason, a record (or multiple records) can be locked for a long time. For these reasons, pessimistic locking should generally be avoided, particularly if you have many concurrent users, because there will likely be a large number of locking conflicts.

19

ACCESS IN A NETWORK ENVIRONMENT

Handling Multiuser Locking Errors

Record-locking conflicts are the inevitable consequence of having users concurrently editing the same set of records in a multiuser application. Fortunately, Access has provided some options for preventing and handling these conflicts when they arise. These options should be used in combination to give your application the best chance to prevent locking errors. And when the inevitable happens, you can deal with the error in a manner that is the least confusing to your users and that minimizes the disruption to your application. The following sections discuss a couple of ways to handle errors after they appear, but first look at some ways to help prevent locking errors.

Access's Data-Locking Settings

Access enables you to specify certain default settings to help you avoid record-locking conflicts between users in a multiuser environment. These settings are located under Tools | Options | Advanced, as shown in Figure 19.7. These are the available settings:

- OLE/DDE Timeout—This property sets the number of seconds Access will attempt OLE/DDE communications after an error occurs. The range is 0–300.

- Number of Update Retries—This setting controls the number of times Access attempts to save a changed record when it encounters a lock. Valid settings are 0–10.

- ODBC Refresh Interval—This setting specifies the interval for automatically refreshing records in an ODBC database. Valid settings are 1–3,600.

- Refresh Interval—This setting specifies the number of seconds for refreshing records in Datasheet or Form view. Valid settings are 1–32,766.

- Update Retry Interval—This setting specifies the number of milliseconds for Access to attempt to save a changed record that is locked by another user. Valid settings are 0–1,000.

> **NOTE**
>
> With Access 2.0 and earlier, the default method for opening a database was in exclusive mode. Now Access sets the default open mode to shared, which subtly conveys the shift in importance of developing in a shared database environment.

FIGURE 19.7.

Access data-locking settings.

These settings are useful in preventing certain errors. It's important that you experiment with them in your particular LAN environment to achieve the optimal setting for each property. Although these settings can be used to prevent or at least delay some of the locking conflicts you will encounter, your application still needs to be able to handle the errors in a graceful manner that will prevent confusion and create a stable multiuser environment. (See the section "A Generic Form Error Handler," later in this chapter for sample code to handle these errors.)

The Form_Error Event

Microsoft added the OnError event to forms in Access 2.0. This event, triggered by the Error event, was added to help the developer trap for standard data errors. For some reason, however, the Error event didn't pass locking or Write Conflict errors to the OnError event. This situation created difficulties for Access developers when they were deciding whether to use bound forms in a multiuser application because of the lack of programmatic control of locking errors.

With Access 97, this oversight has finally been fixed. The developer now has an extra measure of control when designing an application using bound forms and reports. Using this event, you can replace an often-confusing default error message with an error message of your own.

19

ACCESS IN A
NETWORK
ENVIRONMENT

> **NOTE**
>
> When using bound forms, you're still limited in dealing with certain errors—in particular, the Write Conflict error. Although you can trap for this error, your only options are to allow Access to display its normal Write Conflict dialog box or to just ignore the error, in which case the user loses his changes. For this reason, using unbound forms might still be the better option in some cases.

The structure of the `Form_Error` procedure looks like this:

```
Private Sub Form_Error(DataErr As Integer, Response As Integer)
```

The `Error` event procedure uses the following arguments:

- `DataErr`—The error code returned by the `Err` object when an error occurs.
- `Response`—A constant value used to specify whether an error message is displayed. These are the response choices:

    `acDataErrContinue`—Ignore the error and continue code execution. This allows you to display a custom error message.

    `acDataErrDisplay`—Display the default error message.

A Generic Form Error Handler

This section shows you some ways to handle record-locking errors that can be called by all your data access forms. By taking advantage of these techniques, you can give your users an application capable of handling most of the common data-locking conflicts gracefully. Some of the common multiuser errors are shown in Table 19.2.

TABLE 19.2. SOME COMMON MULTIUSER ERRORS.

Error Number	Error Message
3006	Database *<Item>* is exclusively locked.
3186	Couldn't save; currently locked by *username* on *machine name*.
3188	Couldn't update; currently locked by another session on this machine.
3197	Data has changed; operation stopped.
3260	Couldn't update; currently locked by *username* on *machine name*.

Two of the more common locking errors your application will need to be capable of handling are the Write Conflict error and the Locked Record error.

The Write Conflict Error

The Write Conflict error appears when optimistic locking is used and the user attempts to update changes to a record that has been changed by another user. This error dialog box, shown in Figure 19.8, can be confusing to your users, particularly if they've had experience using other RDBMSs that use individual record locking or if they are new to an Access multiuser application.

FIGURE 19.8.

The Write Conflict dialog box.

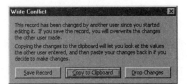

The Locked Record Error (Error 3260)

The Locked Record error happens when you try to update data located on a page that is currently locked. For example, if one user is using pessimistic locking on a set of records, and another user edits the same records using optimistic locking and attempts to update the records, this error occurs.

> **TIP**
>
> Access 97 includes two new Data Access Objects (DAOs) for handling errors. The Error and Err objects contain details about data access errors, each of which pertains to a single operation involving data access objects. (See Chapter 10, "Visual Basic for Applications," for more information.)

A Generic Error Procedure for Use with Bound Forms

The following code example shows some of the techniques you can employ for handling errors when using bound forms in Access. Although the more common errors are trapped in this procedure, it could be enhanced to include specific error trapping for many different situations:

```
Private Sub Form_Error(DataErr As Integer, Response As Integer)

' a generic form level error handler
' traps for the common record locking errors and displays
' a custom error message
```

19

ACCESS IN A NETWORK ENVIRONMENT

```
' use constants for error codes because they can change between versions
Const conDatabaseLocked = 3006
Const conFileInUse = 3045
Const conLockedByAnotherSession = 3188
Const conDataHasChanged = 3197
Const conTooManyUsers = 3239
Const conLockedByUser = 3260


Dim strMsg As String

Select Case DataErr

    Case conDatabaseLocked   ' 3006 Database <Item> is exclusively locked.
        Response = acDataErrContinue
        strMsg = "The database is currently locked by another user" &
➥Chr(13)
        strMsg = strMsg & "and is unavailable at this time. Please try
➥running application later"
        MsgBox strMsg, vbExclamation
        End

    Case conFileInUse   ' 3045 Couldn't use <Item>; file already in use.
        Response = acDataErrContinue
        strMsg = "The database is currently locked by another user" &
➥Chr(13)
        strMsg = strMsg & "Please try running application later"
        MsgBox strMsg, vbExclamation
        End


    Case conLockedByAnotherSession ' 3188 Couldn't update; currently
➥locked by
                                        ' another session on this machine.
        Response = acDataErrContinue
        strMsg = "This record is currently locked by another user" &
➥Chr(13)
        strMsg = strMsg & "Please try updating it later"
        MsgBox strMsg, vbExclamation

    Case conDataHasChanged   ' 3197 Data has changed; operation stopped.
        Response = acDataErrDisplay

    Case conTooManyUsers   ' 3239 Too many active users.
        strMsg = "The database is opened by the maximum number of users
➥(255)" & Chr(13)
        strMsg = strMsg & "Please try running application later"
        MsgBox strMsg, vbExclamation
        End

    Case conLockedByUser   ' 3260 Couldn't update; currently locked by
```

```
                              ' user 'Item2' on machine 'Item1'.
        Response = acDataErrContinue
        strMsg = "This record is currently locked by another user" &
➡Chr(13)
        strMsg = strMsg & "Please try updating it later"
        MsgBox strMsg, vbExclamation

    Case Else
        Response = acDataErrDisplay

End Select

End Sub
```

Figures 19.9 and 19.10 illustrate how you can use your own custom messages to reduce confusion and control what the user sees. (You wouldn't want him or her to "debug" your code, would you?)

FIGURE 19.9.

Error 3260: Access's standard error dialog box.

FIGURE 19.10.

Error 3260: A custom error dialog box.

Transactions

Transaction processing is a method of performing batch updates and modifications to a database in a single operation. It's an excellent choice for use in a multiuser database application and should be used in your applications whenever possible. By using transactions, you have greater control over when locks are placed on the data and, to an extent, greater control when dealing with locking conflicts. Transactions can also improve performance in your application because it saves computing resources when you update data in batches rather than using code or bound forms.

Data integrity is better maintained using transactions as well. Because you can abort, or roll back, your transaction if one or more updates fail, you can ensure referential integrity rules more easily when using transaction processing. For example, if you've started a transaction session and an error occurs or some data validation rules fail, you can cancel any records created that might be incomplete by simply issuing a Rollback statement without violating any entity relationships that are in place. This would very difficult or impossible to duplicate using implicit transaction methods.

The following is the transaction syntax:

workspace.BeginTrans ¦ CommitTrans ¦ Rollback

Table 19.3 describes the three transaction methods.

TABLE 19.3. TRANSACTION METHODS.

Method	Description
BeginTrans	Begins a new transaction.
CommitTrans	Ends or commits the current transaction and saves the changes.
Rollback	Cancels the current transaction and restores the data to the condition it was in when the current transaction began.

The basic form of a transaction session looks like this:

```
Sub SomeProcedure()
On Error GoTo Err_SomeProcedure

    Dim wspTrans As Workspace
    Set wspTrans = DBEngine.Workspaces(0)

    wspTrans.BeginTrans    ' Start of transaction.
    'Code to edit dynaset

    wspTrans.CommitTrans    ' Commit changes.

Err_SomeProcedure:
    wspTrans.Rollback    ' In case of error, cancel changes.

End Sub
```

The BeginTrans Method

The BeginTrans method is used to start a new transaction. After the transaction process begins, all the additions, changes, and deletions are retained by Access until you issue the CommitTrans method or the operation is canceled with the Rollback method.

The CommitTrans Method

The CommitTrans method commits the current transaction and saves the changes to the database. When you issue CommitTrans, appropriate record locks are implemented, and all updates are made (unless errors are encountered). You must issue a `CommitTrans` for each level of `BeginTrans` that was started.

The `Rollback` Method

The `Rollback` method is used to cancel the changes made during the editing session and return the data to the state it was in before the `BeginTrans` was issued. The `Rollback` method is usually called when errors have occurred during the `CommitTrans` method.

Here are some things you should be aware of when using transaction processing:

- You can nest transactions up to five levels deep. You must resolve your transactions from the lowest level back to the highest level.

- If you close a `Workspace` object without using the `CommitTrans` or `Rollback` methods, the transactions are automatically rolled back, releasing any changes to the data.

- Using the `CommitTrans` or `Rollback` methods without first using the `BeginTrans` method creates an error. Remember to always resolve each level of transactions just as you would with nested `If...End If` or `Select Case...End Select` constructs.

- Some databases don't support transactions (Paradox, for example). To make sure that the database you're using supports transactions, you should check whether the value of the `Transactions` property of the `Database` object is set to True before using the `BeginTrans` method.

- When using external ODBC SQL databases, you can issue only one transaction at a time. You can't nest transactions.

Summary

Many issues can arise when you're dealing with a network, and you should look at them from the start of application development. Always remember that you will face performance problems when running databases from the network because you have added a new piece to the application, and it must get the data from your machine to the database on the network.

19

ACCESS IN A NETWORK ENVIRONMENT

Using Access in
the Client/Server
Model

IN THIS CHAPTER

In this chapter you learn about the client/server model for database applications and how to use Access as part of a client/server database solution. This chapter contains hints on designing the application and optimizing its performance, as well as special considerations for working with particular database servers.

Client/Server Defined

Client/server architecture, illustrated in Figure 20.1, is a form of distributed processing in which one process (the *client*) initiates a transaction by sending a message to another process (the *server*). Client/server architecture is the basis of many modern operating systems and software applications. In operating systems such as Windows 95, Windows NT, and UNIX, separate processes are assigned to system services. When a program needs a service, such as when it's printing a document, a message is sent from one program to another. This architecture isolates services from one another and simplifies application development by sharing common services among programs. For this reason, you need not concern yourself with setting up Access 97 when a new printer is installed. When the printer is installed in Windows, it's automatically available to Access (and to all other Windows programs).

FIGURE 20.1.
Client/server architecture.

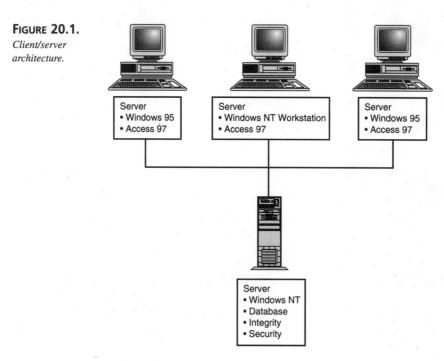

Microsoft Exchange is an example of a client/server application for electronic mail and group communications. The client portion is the exchange inbox that resides on each workstation. It enables users to read their mail, compose new messages, and move their messages among folders even if they aren't connected to other users on a network. The server portion is the exchange server or another mail server (for example, Microsoft Mail). When a workstation connects to the network (through either a local area network connection or dial-up networking), the client communicates with the server and transmits and receives new messages. Schedule+ works in a similar fashion as a client/server application.

In a client/server database, the client (also called the *front end*) is the program that runs on a user's workstation. The server (sometimes called the *database engine* or *back end*), which might be running on another computer on the network, stores data and processes requests for information sent by clients. For instance, Access might be used as a front end to corporate data in a Microsoft SQL Server database running on a DEC Alpha or other computer.

Using Access as a client/server front end is different from running Access on a file server. The file server merely makes a database file available to several workstations so that they can share data. When a user needs the data, the file is read from the file server hard disk and is sent to the workstation across the network. The workstation must perform all the processing to select rows from the table or join multiple tables. The file server doesn't really help with the processing. In a client/server database, however, the workstation submits a request for information in the form of an SQL query. The database server processes the query and returns only the rows and columns that the user requested. The database server assists with processing and greatly reduces the network traffic and the work that the workstation must do. After the data reaches the workstation, Access simply formats the data and displays it for the user.

You can even argue that Access is inherently client/server, in that front-end functions are separated from data-management functions handled by the Jet engine. The Jet engine is essentially the native database server for Access. Fortunately, Access can also connect to other database engines. This chapter addresses only the use of Access as a front end to a database engine.

If this is your first client/server project, you might want additional sources for general information on client/server architecture. You can find much more information on client/server concepts in *Client/Server Computing, Second Edition* (Sams Publishing, 1994) or *Client/Server Unleashed* (Sams Publishing, 1996). Also, many magazines cover client/server databases, including *DBMS*, *Data Based Advisor*, *Database Programming and Design*, *Software Magazine*, and *Client-Server*.

20

USING ACCESS IN
CLIENT/SERVER
MODEL

When to Use a Client/Server Database

Why would you want to use Access as a front end? When would you need to go to client/server architecture for a database application? Several requirements might force you to go client/server.

The most common situation for switching from Access standalone or on a LAN to client/server is a time when you have large data requirements or large numbers of con-current users. Although Access performs well with a few hundred or a few thousand records in a table, it tends to bog down with hundreds of thousands or millions of records. Imagine, if you will, a database containing the income-tax returns of all U.S. residents for the past 10 years. This database wouldn't fit well on the laptop computer I'm using to write this chapter, or even on a high-performance file server. Client/server solves this problem because I can run the database server on any computer, not just on a PC; I could have terabytes of storage and dozens of processors on a mainframe or even a supercomputer. Client/server architecture allows enterprise-wide access to your database.

A related reason to switch to client/server architecture is to improve the speed of search-es and other database transactions. Database server software is highly optimized and can provide much faster processing than the Jet engine, which is suitable for small and medium-sized databases.

Database engines such as Microsoft SQL Server, Sybase SQL Server, Informix, Oracle, CA-Ingres, and DB/2 provide better security and reliability than Access alone can offer. Some of these products have special support for multiprocessor servers, whereas others have highly efficient optimization algorithms, and often they offer special functions Access is lacking.

Client/server architecture is useful in a heterogeneous computing environment. Imagine that your organization has 500 people with PCs, 75 with UNIX workstations, and 25 with Macintoshes. Access isn't available for UNIX or the Mac, but client/server offers you a way out of this problem. Other UNIX and Mac packages can access data on the database server. You therefore can have all the computer users in the company sharing the same corporate data, reducing redundant data entry.

A final reason to switch to client/server is to provide more friendly, more responsive tools to look at data in mainframe systems. The increased productivity of Windows applications compared to their terminal-based predecessors, combined with the prospect of cost savings, is driving the trend toward downsizing mainframe applications (legacy systems). A *legacy system* is a system that was built long ago, and the people who built it might not even be at your organization any longer. Still, the data in the system is valuable, and you can't give up the old system overnight. With Access, you can allow users to read and write legacy data, and potentially move the application to a larger or smaller database server as needed.

Access as a Front End

Access 97 works as a front end in a client/server database by means of linked tables. They were called "attached" tables in Access 1.0 and 2.0. Data in a linked table isn't actually stored in the Access database. Instead, the Access table contains a pointer to the location where the information is physically stored, such as a dBASE file or an Oracle database table. See Table 20.1.

TABLE 20.1. LAYERS IN AN ACCESS CLIENT/SERVER APPLICATION.

Layer	*Function*
Access User Interface (Database windows)	Displays on user workstation; interacts with user
Jet Engine	Fetches data requested by Access; enforces referential integrity and validation rules
ODBC Driver Manager	Links from Access to all ODBC data sources
ODBC Driver (SQL Server, Oracle, other)	Links from ODBC Driver Manager to a particular data source; might be provided by a third party
Network Library (NetLib, SQL*Net)	Network communications software that allows data to be exchanged between client and server
Database Server (SQL Server, Oracle, Informix)	Software that processes requests for data and sends resulting rows or messages to client

Built-In and ODBC Drivers

Access can link to other database formats through either built-in drivers or Open Database Connectivity (ODBC). Built-in drivers are provided for other Microsoft Access databases; FoxPro files (versions 2.0, 2.5, 2.6, and 3.0); Paradox files (3.*x*, 4.*x*, and 5.0); dBASE III, IV, and 5 files; Microsoft Excel files; Lotus 1-2-3 files; fixed-length text; and variable-length text. Access can also export to Word for Windows mail merge, although Access does not have a driver to read Word files directly. The built-in drivers enable you to import, export, and link to these foreign data files.

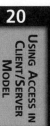

The typical Access installation doesn't include all the drivers for linking data, not even the ODBC drivers. To include the drivers, run the Setup utility and choose Add/Remove. (Or when you first install Access, choose Custom installation and select all the drivers.) The dialog box shown in Figure 20.2 appears. Select Data Access in the Options list and then click the Change Option button. The Data Access options appear, as shown in Figure 20.3.

FIGURE 20.2.

Selecting the Data Access option.

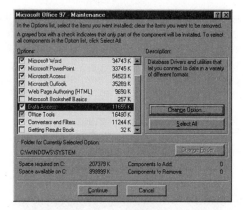

FIGURE 20.3.

The Data Access options.

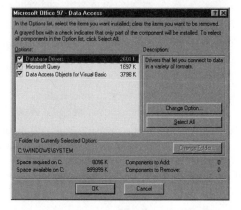

Choose Database Drivers from the new Options list and click on the Change Option button. You can now select from the available drivers, including the Microsoft SQL Server Driver option, as shown in Figure 20.4, and click OK to continue installing other new components.

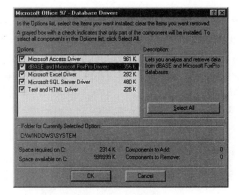

FIGURE 20.4.

The Database Drivers options.

ODBC as a Translator

In addition to the built-in drivers, the standard that makes it easy to link Access to SQL and other data sources is Open Database Connectivity (ODBC). It is the most popular standard for sharing data files in Windows. ODBC can connect an ODBC client to both relational and nonrelational data sources.

Access can act as an ODBC client or an ODBC server. The focus in this chapter is on Access as an ODBC client, but other applications (such as Excel and Crystal Reports) can serve as front ends to Access databases.

ODBC needs a driver for each data source. ODBC drivers are usually provided by the vendor of the server. The driver must be 32 bit and compliant with ODBC 1.0.

ODBC doesn't include its own networking capability, so you need a network library in addition to the ODBC driver for your server. For instance, you might use the Oracle SQL*Net, Named Pipe Net-Libraries, DECNET, or FTP 2.2 with Net-Library. If you encounter problems with your Net library, search Microsoft TechNet for your Net library. You might need patches or upgrades to the Net library to work with Access 97. Microsoft TechNet is a great source of technical information on all Microsoft products, especially for advanced topics. TechNet members receive a monthly CD-ROM with the latest information and several other benefits. To enroll, call Microsoft at (800) 344-2121, extension 115.

Working with ODBC Connections

In most cases, Access hides the complexity of the ODBC connection from the user and the developer. This section explains how to create and manipulate ODBC connections through the Access user interface and with Access Basic code.

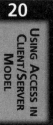

ODBC Connection String

Access databases can connect to ODBC data sources through tables or queries. When linked, the tables and queries behave just as a native Access table behaves, and they can serve as the row source for a query, report, or form. The ODBC connection string is stored in the Description property of a table. It's created automatically by Access if you link a table from the Access menu. It can also be created or modified programmatically in Access Basic.

Here is an ODBC connection string for a linked Access table:

```
DATABASE=D:\msoffice\access95\Samples\Northwind.mdb;TABLE=Customers
```

This connection string is simple in that it needs to identify only the Access database filename and the table name.

Here is an ODBC connection string to attach to an SQL Server table:

```
ODBC;DSN=Pubs;APP=Microsoft Access;WSID=D5;DATABASE=pubs;TABLE=dbo.titles
```

If the connection string reads "ODBC;" or is blank, Access prompts you for the connection information at runtime. Managing your ODBC connections this way usually isn't convenient.

You also can create and update ODBC connections with Visual Basic for Applications. The following lines show the syntax for creating a linked table:

```
Dim sDatabase As String
Dim sUser As String
Dim sPassword As String
'/// prompt user for id and password
sUser = InputBox("Enter valid user ID", Get User ID")
sPassword = InputBox("Enter valid password", "Get Passwprd")
'/// create the ODBC connect string
sDatabase = "ODBC;DSN=Pubs;"
sDatabase = sDatabase & "UID=" & sUser & ";"
sDatabase = sDatabase & "PWD=" & sPassword & ";"
sDatabase = sDatabase & "LANGUAGE=us_english;DATABASE=Pubs;"
'/// create the link
DoCmd.TransferDatabase acLink, "ODBC Database", sDatabase, acTable,
"Authors",
➥ "dboAuthors"
```

Creating SQL Pass-Through Queries

Pass-through queries are a powerful feature introduced in Access 2.0. They enable you to send SQL statements to the server just as you enter them, without being parsed or generated by Access. With pass-through SQL, you can take advantage of server-specific features such as SQL extensions or stored procedures.

Access Pass-through queries don't use the graphical design features of the Query window. This means that you receive no help from Access in formulating the query or checking its syntax. You therefore might save time and reduce errors by following these generalized steps instead:

1. Write the query in whatever interactive query tool your server provides. The query tool checks the query syntax and perhaps assists with table and field names.

2. Fully test the query in its native environment.

3. Copy the query into an Access Pass-through query or an Access module using cut and paste.

Creating an SQL Pass-Through Query

Here are the basic steps to perform in Access to create a Pass-through query:

1. Click the Queries tab in the Database window, and then click New.

2. Click New Query. No Query Wizard is available for SQL Pass-through queries, so choose Design View.

3. Close the Show Table dialog box without choosing a table or query.

4. Choose Query | SQL Specific | Pass-Through.

5. The Query Properties sheet, as shown in Figure 20.5, normally appears at this point. If you don't see the Query Properties sheet, open it by choosing View | Properties or clicking the View Properties tool on the toolbar.

6. Enter the ODBC connection string in the ODBC Connect Str property.

Be careful not to switch the query type of a Pass-through query because you will lose the SQL you have been typing.

FIGURE 20.5.

*The Query
Properties sheet
in an SQL Pass-
through query.*

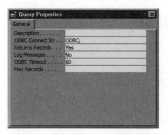

Pass-Through Query Properties

The properties of Pass-through queries are different from those of Access Select queries:

Property	Description
Returns Records	Set to Yes if the query will return rows; set to no for other queries.
Log Messages	Set to Yes to create a table to store messages returned by the server.
ODBC Timeout	Set the time in seconds before the query times out.
Max Records	Limit the number of records returned by the query.

ODBC Connection String Builder

In SQL Pass-through queries, Access provides help for constructing an ODBC connection string so that you don't have to write it from scratch.

The ODBC connection string builder is available only in Pass-through queries; it's not available in the `Source Connect Str` property in the Query Properties sheet. Note that the ODBC connection string builder isn't installed as a standard option. You must run Setup, choose Add/Remove, and then check the Developer Tools option.

Click the button with the three dots next to the `ODBC Connect Str` property. You can now choose to connect to a file data source using the first tab, as shown in Figure 20.6, or a machine data source using the second tab, as shown in Figure 20.7. Access then assists you with building a connection string. For this example, use the Pubs database that comes with Microsoft SQL Server and choose the second tab.

The second tab shows a list of all ODBC machine data sources available to you. If you do not see an entry called Pubs, you can create it by clicking the New button, which brings up the Data Source Wizard shown in Figure 20.8.

FIGURE 20.6.

The ODBC File Data Source tab of the Select Data Source dialog box.

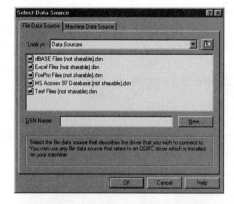

FIGURE 20.7.

The ODBC Machine Data Source tab of the Select Data Source dialog box.

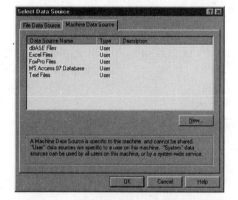

FIGURE 20.8.

The Data Source Wizard.

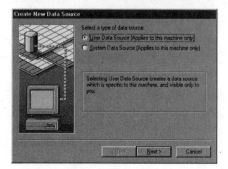

To begin setting up your new data source, select the type of data source you want to create. A User data source is one that will be available on the local machine for the current user only. A System data source is one that will be available on the local machine for all users that logon to the machine.

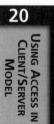

20

USING ACCESS IN
CLIENT/SERVER
MODEL

The Data Source Wizard next requests the database driver to use for the new data source, as shown in Figure 20.9. Because the database is Pubs on SQL Server, SQL Server is the correct choice. The drivers listed in this dialog box will vary with each installation.

FIGURE 20.9.

Select the ODBC driver for the new data source.

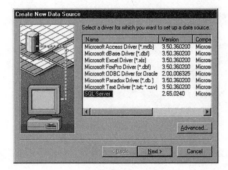

After you make these selections, the Data Source Wizard displays the settings it has collected so far, similar to Figure 20.10, giving you a chance to go back to make adjustments.

FIGURE 20.10.

Completing the Data Source Wizard.

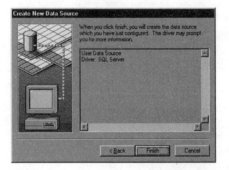

Because SQL Server is the selected database driver, the dialog box shown in Figure 20.11 then appears. For the purposes of this chapter, be sure to enter Pubs in the Data Source Name field. Replace the server name with the appropriate name for your installation of SQL Server.

After you specify the data source, you might be prompted for a username and password, as shown in Figure 20.12. If you want, you can store the password in the connection string so that you aren't prompted for it again when you run the query (see Figure 20.13).

FIGURE 20.11.

ODBC SQL Server Setup dialog box.

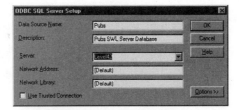

FIGURE 20.12.

The username and password dialog box for the ODBC connection string builder.

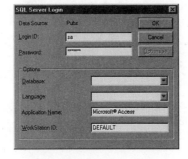

FIGURE 20.13.

Choosing whether to store the password in the connection string.

Now that you have answered all the questions posed by the ODBC connection string builder, a finished ODBC connection string is entered in the connection string property, as you can see in Figure 20.14.

FIGURE 20.14.

The completed ODBC connection string.

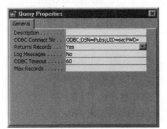

To see whether your connection is working, write a simple query in SQL. For instance, a query of SELECT * FROM PRODUCTS yields the result shown in Figure 20.15. This result proves that the ODBC connection is working and that you are retrieving rows from the server.

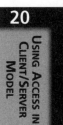

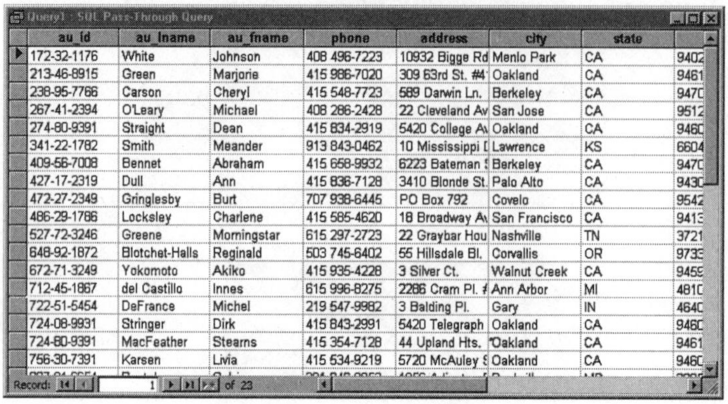

au_id	au_lname	au_fname	phone	address	city	state	
172-32-1176	White	Johnson	408 496-7223	10932 Bigge Rd	Menlo Park	CA	9402
213-46-8915	Green	Marjorie	415 986-7020	309 63rd St. #4	Oakland	CA	9461
238-95-7766	Carson	Cheryl	415 548-7723	589 Darwin Ln.	Berkeley	CA	9470
267-41-2394	O'Leary	Michael	408 286-2428	22 Cleveland Av	San Jose	CA	9512
274-80-9391	Straight	Dean	415 834-2919	5420 College Av	Oakland	CA	9460
341-22-1782	Smith	Meander	913 843-0462	10 Mississippi D	Lawrence	KS	6604
409-56-7008	Bennet	Abraham	415 658-9932	6223 Bateman S	Berkeley	CA	9470
427-17-2319	Dull	Ann	415 836-7128	3410 Blonde St.	Palo Alto	CA	9430
472-27-2349	Gringlesby	Burt	707 938-6445	PO Box 792	Covelo	CA	9542
486-29-1786	Locksley	Charlene	415 585-4620	18 Broadway Av	San Francisco	CA	9413
527-72-3246	Greene	Morningstar	615 297-2723	22 Graybar Hou	Nashville	TN	3721
648-92-1872	Blotchet-Halls	Reginald	503 745-6402	55 Hillsdale Bl.	Corvallis	OR	9733
672-71-3249	Yokomoto	Akiko	415 935-4228	3 Silver Ct.	Walnut Creek	CA	9459
712-45-1867	del Castillo	Innes	615 996-8275	2286 Cram Pl. #	Ann Arbor	MI	4810
722-51-5454	DeFrance	Michel	219 547-9982	3 Balding Pl.	Gary	IN	4640
724-08-9931	Stringer	Dirk	415 843-2991	5420 Telegraph	Oakland	CA	9460
724-80-9391	MacFeather	Stearns	415 354-7128	44 Upland Hts.	Oakland	CA	9461
756-30-7391	Karsen	Livia	415 534-9219	5720 McAuley S	Oakland	CA	9460

FIGURE 20.15.
The result of the query SELECT * FROM PRODUCTS.

If you don't enter an ODBC connection string when you write the query and you don't use the ODBC connection string builder, you will be prompted to choose a data source each time you run the query.

Saving the Results of a Pass-Through Query

You might want to store the results of a Pass-through query in an Access table for later use. A simple way to accomplish this task is to create a Make Table query based on the Pass-through query, including all the fields you want to store in the local table. Each time you run the Make Table query, it will create a new table that stores the results of the Pass-through query. If you don't want to continue duplicating this data in new tables, you can use an Update query instead or delete the table before the Make Table query is run.

For this example, you run a stored procedure called `SP_HELP` included with SQL Server. This procedure returns a list of objects contained in the database.

1. Start by defining a Pass-through query, as described earlier. In the SQL window, type `SP_HELP`.
2. Run the query to see which rows are returned. The result should look something like Figure 20.16. You are prompted to choose the data source and enter your name and password.
3. Close the query and save it as `qrySP_HELP`.
4. Create a new query and choose `qrySP_HELP` as the input for the query in the Show Table dialog box.
5. Change the query type to make it a Make Table query.
6. In the Make Table dialog box, enter `tblSP_HELP` as the table name and click OK.

FIGURE 20.16.

The results of running the SP_HELP *stored procedure.*

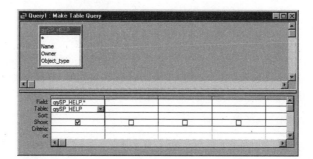

7. Double-click the asterisk (*) in the qrySP_HELP data model to select all the fields from the query. Your query should now look like Figure 20.17.

FIGURE 20.17.

A Make Table query based on the SP_HELP *stored procedure.*

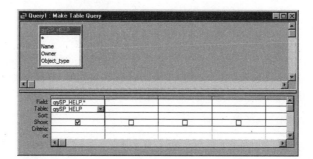

8. Run the query.
9. Go to the Database window. Access has created two new tables—tblSP_HELP and tblSP_HELP1—as shown in Figure 20.18. The first table contains the rows produced by the stored procedure, and the second contains an entry for each field definition in that table.

You can create a Pass-through query in Access Basic as well. To do so, follow these steps:

1. In the Database window, choose Modules and then New.
2. Create a new subprocedure by clicking the Insert Procedure button on the toolbar.
3. Make the procedure a sub rather than a function and enter CreatePassThroughSQL as the subprocedure name. Click on OK.
4. Enter the following in this procedure:

```
Public Sub CreatePassThroughSQL()
    Dim dbs As Database, qdf As QueryDef, strSQL As String
    Set dbs = CurrentDb
    strSQL = "SELECT au_lname , au_fname FROM Authors ORDER BY
➥au_lname"
    Set qdf = dbs.CreateQueryDef("qrySelectAuthors", strSQL)
    DoCmd.OpenQuery qdf.Name
End Sub
```

5. Be sure to save the module.

FIGURE 20.18.

Tables produced based on the SP_HELP *stored procedure.*

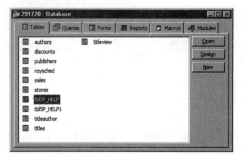

Next, test the procedure by going to the Debug window. Click the Debug Window tool on the toolbar, press Ctrl+G, or choose View|Debug Window. Type the following in the lower portion of the Debug window:

```
call CreatePassthroughSQL
```

When you press Enter, the code is executed. If it works, you see a datasheet view of the list of author names.

Using the SQL IN Clause

Another way to retrieve data from outside the Access database is to use an IN clause in an SQL query. You can use an outside table as either the source or the destination for a query. The IN clause specifies the database where the foreign table is stored. In xBASE products, the filename and table name are identical, as in the following instance:

```
SELECT CompID FROM Companies
IN "C:\DBASE\DATA\COMP" "dBASE IV;"
WHERE City = "New York";
```

An alternative syntax is also supported. This syntax combines the database type and path in the second argument for IN:

```
SELECT CompID FROM Companies
IN "" "dBASE IV; [DATABASE=C:\DBASE\DATA\COMP;]
WHERE City = "New York";
```

The same syntax is used with INSERT INTO and SELECT INTO statements.

Optimizing the Performance of a Client/Server Application

It isn't enough to build your client/server application as you would build any other Access database except for linking tables from a server database to your Access database. Although this technique might work, it would be unlikely to perform well.

Client/server architecture provides you with many options for improving the performance of an application. Unfortunately, the sheer number of parameters you can tune might make client/server development confusing at first. Many optimization techniques are also trade-offs between different types of performance, or between performance and some other factor, such as the portability of the application. The following sections give you general guidelines for getting the most out of your client/server application.

Make the Server Do the Work

In general, the goal of client/server database design is to divide the work between the workstation and the server to take advantage of the strengths of each and avoid their respective weaknesses.

The workstation is best suited for these activities:

- Presenting an attractive and useful user interface
- Formulating queries based on user input and submitting them to the server
- Formatting data on the screen
- Formatting data in a report
- Performing calculations based on retrieved data

The server is best suited for these activities:

- Storing large data sets
- Retrieving, sorting, and manipulating shared data
- Optimizing queries
- Enforcing data integrity rules that apply to all applications

Therefore, it follows that the server should do as much as possible to sift through all the data and return only the rows that the user wants to view or process on the workstation.

Avoid Local Joins and Selects

When you join tables in a query, a database evaluates rows from each table to find which records in one table are related to which records in the other. In client/server architecture,

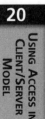

20

USING ACCESS IN
CLIENT/SERVER
MODEL

this join operation can be performed on the server or on the client. If a join is performed on the server, only the selected rows (the final result of the join) are transmitted across the network to the workstation. To perform a join locally, rows from both tables to be joined must be sent to the workstation before the join can be carried out. In most cases, particularly when large numbers of records are involved, performing the join on the server is more efficient than performing it on the client.

In addition to avoiding local joins, you should steer clear of functions that aren't supported by the server and therefore must be performed by the client.

Joins from Tables from Different Servers

Access enables users to join tables from different servers, even servers that are different types (such as Sybase and Oracle). Unfortunately, the join can be performed on neither of the servers because they don't have distributed join support for each other. The join is therefore performed on the workstation.

Operations That Can't Be Processed on the Server

Like many other database products, Access adds special features that go beyond the ANSI and ISO standards. The extensions listed next force local query processing because they can't be handled by the server.

The following are the extensions to SQL that are offered by Access but aren't available in most database servers:

- Top *n* or Top *n* Percent
- TRANSFORM (crosstab)
- IN (remote database connection)
- DISTINCTROW (allows duplicates)
- WITH OWNERACCESS (allows query without table rights)

Similarly, user-defined functions can't be processed on the server, forcing the rows to be processed on the workstation. If a user-defined function is frequently used in a client/server application, converting it into a stored procedure on the server will pay off.

You should also avoid the following items:

- Joining queries that contain aggregation or the DISTINCT SQL keyword: Joins that require calculations for each row of the sets to be joined force your server to do a significant amount of hard work. If you frequently need to perform these types of queries, you might want to store the results of the aggregation for this purpose.

- ORDER BY expressions not supported by the server: Performance suffers if the workstation must sort a large data set. All the rows would have to be sent to the workstation for processing.

- Multiple levels of GROUP BY: Consider the impact of grouping and sorting operations. You might find that sorting beyond one or two levels has no benefit for presenting data and hurts performance. If you sort customers by last name and first name, you probably don't also need to sort them by postal code and phone number in that query.

- Crosstab queries with more than one aggregate: Most servers can't handle crosstab-style aggregation and therefore end up sending all the detail rows to the workstation.

- Operations with more than one SQL statement, such as nested SELECT: Retrieving with criteria expressed as constants is nearly always faster than using the result of a subquery.

- Access extensions to SQL: All these special Access functions force rows to be returned to the workstation rather than processed on the server:

  Special Access operators and functions (for example, financial functions)

  User-defined functions in VBA code that use remote fields

  Mixing datatypes without explicit type conversion

  Heterogeneous joins between local and remote tables or multiple ODBC sources

  Functions supported by some but not all servers

  Outer joins

  Numeric, string, and date functions

  Data conversion functions

Make the Criteria Match the Server Data Structure as Much as Possible

Assume that shipping methods are stored as integers but entered by the user as a full name in the combo box of a data entry form. The following is an example of a bad query:

```
SELECT * FROM Orders WHERE [What Shipping Method?] = IIF (Shipping Method
= 1 ,
"Federal Express" , IIF (Shipping Method = 2 , "UPS" , "US Mail" ))
```

The following example selects based on the value in the field instead of evaluating the value and determining whether the immediate IF applies. This query yields better performance:

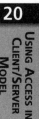

20

USING ACCESS IN
CLIENT/SERVER
MODEL

```
SELECT * FROM Orders WHERE [Shipping Method] = IIF (What Shipping Method?
➥=
"Federal Express" , 1 , IIF ([What Shipping Method?] = "UPS" , 2 , 3 ))
```

Use Stored Procedures If They Are Supported by Your Server

Stored procedures are precompiled SQL programs that can be invoked from the workstation. They run much faster than ad hoc SQL statements that must be compiled every time they are invoked. Many servers, such as Microsoft SQL Server, Sybase SQL Server, and Oracle, offer this feature.

Minimize Unnecessary Calls for Server Data

The less often you have to fetch data from the server, the faster your application will run. The suggestions in the following sections will reduce the frequency at which you go to the server.

Open Forms Without Retrieving Data

By default, when opening a form, Access opens the recordset underlying the form, retrieves all rows, and displays the first record from the recordset. This method would be inefficient at best in a client/server environment. For instance, if you open a Customer form that contains millions of records, opening the recordset and sending a page of records to the workstation consume significant server and network resources. Moreover, the likelihood that the user would even need to edit that particular record becomes increasingly small as the number of records grows larger.

Place a button on the form to allow the user to search for records based on criteria furnished by the user. In a Customer form, the user might enter a Customer ID or a last name. When the button is clicked, the workstation sends the query to the server, and a small number of rows is returned to the workstation and displayed.

Ask Only for What You Need

As your parents might have taught you, there is virtue in taking only what you can use right now. This lesson is as true in client/server database implementation as it was in kindergarten.

Only fetch rows and columns that you need. When you use the asterisk (*) rather than listing the fields from a table by name, the database retrieves all the fields from the table. Don't select fields with * unless you really need all the fields.

Download Reference Tables

You can significantly improve response time by storing reference tables on the workstation rather than on the server. The more frequently these tables are consulted, the more they should be located on the server. If the tables are static, they will be easy to update. Otherwise, you should consider a provision for synchronizing workstation copies with a master copy on the network.

The following code updates a local department reference table from a server-based reference table. You can allow users to run the procedure by clicking a button or include the code in an Autoexec function that runs each time the application is opened.

```
Sub UpdateDeptRecords()
    Dim dbs As DATABASE

    ' Return Database variable pointing to current database.
    Set dbs = CurrentDb
    dbs.Execute "delete * from tbldepts"
    dbs.Execute "INSERT INTO tbldepts SELECT * FROM tblRemoteDepts"

End Sub
```

Create Temporary Local Tables for Users to Manipulate Server Data

In some applications, users need to retrieve data from the server and then perform analysis on this data, such as what-if calculations, statistics, or graphs. If a user performs a number of queries on the same data, creating a temporary local (or file server) table where this data can reside might be worthwhile. This technique reduces the server workload and network traffic and provides better response time for the user. For instance, a business analyst might request sales totals by product type and location for a specified period. Without a local table, if graphs are generated showing this data broken down in several dimensions, the database is required for each form or report as it is run.

Create Views on the Server and Link Them

Views are a powerful feature for controlling access to specified rows and columns and joining tables on the server. If your server supports the technique, you can link the view instead of linking the tables and creating the view in Access.

Avoid Operations That Move the Cursor Through Recordsets

Moving the cursor to the last of 100,000 records is time consuming because the server must handle all the records between the record 1 and record 100,000. Relational databases aren't optimized for navigational operations, and in most cases simply moving to a

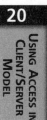

20

USING ACCESS IN
CLIENT/SERVER
MODEL

record based on its location in a recordset isn't necessary for a business function. Relational databases are designed to find records based on the values in their fields rather than their relative locations.

Transactions on Linked Tables

Using transactions, you can group several actions together and ensure that they aren't left partially completed. Remember that attached tables must be opened as dynasets rather than tables.

Also, create and close the dynaset on the attached SQL Server table outside the transaction itself, as shown in the following examples:

Incorrect:

```
Dim MyDyna As Dynaset
BeginTrans
    MyDyna = CreateDynaset("Table1")
    'Inserts/Updates/Deletes here
    MyDyna.Close
    CommitTrans/Rollback
```

Correct:

```
Dim MyDyna As Dynaset
MyDyna = CreateDynaset("Table1")
BeginTrans
    'Inserts/Updates/Deletes here
CommitTrans/Rollback
MyDyna.close
```

Use Linked Tables Whenever Possible

Although you can open tables directly in code, linked tables are faster, more convenient, and more powerful. Linked tables are visible as objects in the Database window, and users can access them for queries, forms, and reports.

Use ForwardOnly Snapshots If You Do Not Need to Update or Scroll Backward

By default, Access lets you scroll both forward and backward in snapshot recordsets. If you don't need this capability, use the dbForwardOnly flag to specify a recordset that allows only forward scrolling. The recordset is placed in a buffer area and can perform faster than a default snapshot.

Use Remote Data Caching

Access automatically handles caches for remote data behind datasheets and forms, but you can improve the performance of dynasets by explicitly managing the CacheStart and CacheSize properties to set the number of records that will be cached. You can force the cache to be filled with the FillCache method, as shown in Listing 20.1.

LISTING 20.1. USING THE FILLCACHE METHOD TO FILL A RANGE OF DATA.

```
Dim MyRecordset As Recordset, MyDatabase As Database
Set MyDatabase = CurrentDB.OpenDatabase("",0,0,_
"ODBC;DATABASE=MySqlDb;DSN=
 orpSQL;UID=Guest;PWD=")
' Open ODBC database.
Set MyRecordset = MyDatabase.OpenRecordset("OrderDetail",DB_OPEN_DYNASET)
    ' Open local recordset.
MyRecordset.FindFirst "CustID = 1001"
MyRecordset.CacheStart = MyRecordset.Bookmark
  ' Start caching records at Customer ID 1001.
MyRecordset.CacheSize = 12       ' Set cache size to 12 records.
MyRecordset.FillCache      ' Fill cache.
...' Display rows.
```

Do Not Use Combo Boxes Based on Large Numbers of Records

Although having a combo box that enables the user to choose a state when entering an address might make sense, having a combo box to choose a customer in an Orders form if you have millions of customers makes less sense. In a case like this, replace the combo box with a dialog box. The user can enter criteria in the top of the dialog box and click a button to see matching records. The user then can select the desired record and click a Done button to return to the main form.

Use Snapshot Recordset Objects to Populate Combo Boxes

Because the content of combo boxes is often static and the recordsets for combo boxes are often small, you can get extra speed from using snapshots rather than dynasets to populate combo boxes. However, you should use dynasets if the user is allowed to add new values to the combo box list.

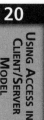

20

USING ACCESS IN CLIENT/SERVER MODEL

Use Background Population to Take Advantage of Idle Time

During idle time, Access retrieves rows from the server by creating a server table called MSysConf. You can change the settings for background population to reduce the network traffic by increasing the interval between each retrieval or reducing the number of rows that are retrieved at a time.

First, you must create a table called MSysConf on the server. It should have the following columns:

Column Name	Datatype	Allows Null?
Config	A datatype that corresponds to a 2-byte integer	No
chValue	VARCHAR(255)	Yes
nValue	A datatype that corresponds to a 4-byte integer	Yes
Comments	VARCHAR(255)	Yes

Next, add up to three records to the MSysConf table as follows:

Config	nValue	Meaning
101	0	Doesn't allow local storage of the login ID and password in attachments.
101	1	(Default) Allows local storage of the login ID and password in attachments.
102	D	D is the delay, in seconds, between each retrieval (default: 10 seconds).
103	N	N is the number of rows retrieved (default: 100 rows).

Using Access with Specific Products

To get the best results with Access as a front end, you should understand the behavior of the particular database server product you're using. You must be aware of special features the engine offers (or lacks) and of how to tune it for optimum performance. Although most of the popular database engines conform to the SQL-92 standard, they also offer their own, proprietary extensions to SQL.

Field types aren't the same for all database products. You therefore must consider how your Access field types will map to the database server or vice versa. For instance, some databases don't have counter fields, OLE fields, or even time fields.

Field and table names have different formats in Access and server databases. For instance, Access allows spaces in field names, but spaces are prohibited in SQL Server. Many server products allow periods in table names, but periods aren't permitted in Access. Access automatically allows for this restriction and renames tables as it attaches them, substituting an underscore for the period. Another interesting naming convention is that Access appends the table name to the owner name of an attached table. If you attach to a table called Customers on Watcom SQL, for instance, your Access table name will be `admin_Customers` if you use the default user account. This means that SQL using the original table name of Customers will no longer work with the attached table. You can rename the attached table and remove the username portion to solve this problem.

Access 97 offers declarative referential integrity, a feature that isn't yet supported by all server vendors. *Declarative referential integrity* means that the developer need only define the relationship and specify the rules for enforcing referential integrity for them to be universally enforced. Microsoft SQL Server 6.0 offers declarative referential integrity as well. In some products, such as SQL Server 4.*x*, triggers are in place of declarative referential integrity. A *trigger* is an SQL procedure that is run automatically when a certain event occurs (in this case, an `INSERT`, `UPDATE`, or `DELETE`).

Access fields have the `Required` property to make a value in a field mandatory before the record can be saved. Some servers lack this feature. You can work around this difficulty by using `NOT NULL` as the default value for a required field.

In general, you should reoptimize your queries after they have been migrated to the server. The optimization schemes used by servers are quite different and might even differ from one server version to the next.

Security schemes on the server are likely to differ from the Access security model. You can opt to redefine all your security rules on the server or to enforce them both at the application level and on the server. Ultimately, server security is more important than application security because it's the last line of defense for your data. If you have security at both levels, maintaining usernames, passwords, and privileges is more complicated.

Microsoft SQL Server 6.*x*

Of all the servers, Access is best integrated with Microsoft SQL Server. This should be no surprise because Microsoft produces both products. Their features therefore are coordinated, and special interoperability is provided.

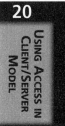

20

USING ACCESS IN CLIENT/SERVER MODEL

The Upsizing Wizard has been written for Microsoft SQL Server to automate moving from Access to SQL Server.

Sybase SQL Server

Access is also compatible with Sybase because Microsoft SQL Server is a descendant of Sybase SQL Server. Migrating from Microsoft SQL Server to Sybase SQL Server is therefore relatively painless. The field types are the same, and both products use the same SQL extensions in Transact-SQL.

In the future, this interoperability is not guaranteed to continue as the feature sets of Microsoft SQL Server and Sybase SQL Server diverge.

Oracle 7.*x*

Although Oracle offers many of the same features as SQL Server, these features are implemented differently. For instance, Oracle uses a different language (PL/SQL) for stored procedures than SQL Server (Transact-SQL) uses.

Oracle enables the developer to choose whether a trigger is executed before or after the action on the table takes place. In SQL Server, the trigger always runs after the action.

Oracle field types are different from Access or SQL Server field types. For instance, Oracle uses a special field type ROWID in place of the timestamp used by SQL Server. Oracle indexes also include two options, hash and sequence indexes, not found in SQL Server.

Some extensions of SQL that aren't supported in SQL Server exist in Oracle, and vice versa. For instance, there is no SQL Server equivalent for the ON CASCADE of Oracle; you must write a trigger to provide the same functionality.

If you're migrating an Oracle application to SQL Server, you can import the tables into Access, create the relationships in Access, and then use the Upsizing Wizard to transfer the data model to the SQL Server.

Exporting Tables to a Client/Server Database

After you choose a server, you need to figure out how to move your data in the server but your application in Access.

It's often easier to develop the application in Access and then move the data to the server because the developer can work standalone or on a file server without being concerned about server features or performance.

You can even use Access as an intermediary when transferring tables from one server to another. If you have sufficient disk space on your workstation or the file server, you can import tables from the old server into Access and then export them to the new server. You can also attach tables from both servers and use Append queries to move the data from one server to the other.

Exporting tables to a server database is nearly as easy as exporting them to another format such as dBASE or Lotus. It also uses the same menu options. Follow these steps to export a table to a client/server database:

1. Select the table to be exported in the Database window. Choose File | Save As | Export.
2. Choose To An External File Or Database in the Save As dialog box and then click OK.
3. Choose ODBC Databases for the Save As Type (it's the last item on the list) and then click Export.
4. Choose the ODBC data destination or click New to define a new data source.
5. If prompted, enter the username and password for the destination database.

You can also create tables with DLL Pass-through queries. For instance, the following are examples of queries that create tables.

This query creates a new table called `This Table` with two Text fields:

```
CREATE TABLE [This Table] ([First Name] TEXT, [Last Name] TEXT);
```

This query creates a new table called `MyTable` with two Text fields, a Date/Time field, and a unique index composed of all three fields:

```
CREATE TABLE MyTable ([First Name] TEXT, [Last Name] TEXT,
[Date of Birth] DATETIME, CONSTRAINT
MyTableConstraint UNIQUE ([First Name], [Last Name], [Date of Birth]));
```

This query creates a new table with two Text fields and an Integer field. The SSN field is the primary key:

```
CREATE TABLE People ([First_Name] TEXT, [Last_Name] TEXT,
SSN INTEGER CONSTRAINT MyFieldConstraint
 PRIMARY KEY)
```

Creating Indexes on New Tables

After you create the table, you should define the indexes. Servers such as the SQL server don't automatically create indexes on tables you export from Access. You can use the

20

USING ACCESS IN
CLIENT/SERVER
MODEL

tools provided by your server vendor, or you can write a Pass-through query in Access, such as the following one. This query creates an index consisting of the fields Home Phone and Extension in the Employees table:

```
CREATE INDEX NewIndex ON Employees ([Home Phone], Extension);
```

This query creates an index on the Employees table using the Social Security Number field. No two records can have the same data in the SSN field, and no Null values are allowed:

```
CREATE UNIQUE INDEX MyIndex ON Employees (SSN) WITH DISALLOW NULL;
```

This query creates an index on an attached table. The table's remote database is unaware of and unaffected by the new index:

```
CREATE UNIQUE INDEX MailID ON MailList ([Client No.])
```

Using the Upsizing Wizard

Microsoft provides a special tool to simplify migrating a standalone Access application to a client/server application with Microsoft SQL Server as the database engine. You can order this software, called the Upsizing Tool, from Microsoft. This version of the Upsizing Tool works with Access 97 and SQL Server 6.5.

Here's how the Upsizing Wizard works:

1. Starting from an Access database with native Access tables, the wizard creates a table on the server for each Access table. The fields are mapped from Access field types to the corresponding SQL Server field types. If necessary, fields are renamed to remove internal spaces and to conform with SQL Server field-naming rules.

2. Primary keys in Access become primary keys in the SQL Server. For compound primary keys, clustered indexes are automatically created.

3. Indexes are created for all fields indexed in Access.

4. Referential integrity rules in Access are translated into declarative referential integrity (SQL Server 6.*x*) or triggers (SQL Server 4.*x*).

5. Data is transferred from Access to the server.

6. The Access table is renamed.

7. A query is created in Access for each table on the server. It is called an *aliasing query* because it renames any fields to their original Access names. The query has the same name as the original Access table. Because Access queries are updatable, this query can serve as the row source for all the other Access objects that originally used the table, such as forms, other queries, and reports.

The Upsizing Wizard gives you a great start on migrating your application to a new server, but you still have some work to do. To get optimum performance, you must rewrite some portions of the application to take advantage of special server features.

Initialization Settings

In most cases, the default settings Access uses for a standard installation work best, but in some cases you might want to change the behavior of the program by using special settings. Table 20.2 shows the initialization settings for Access that relate to operation in client/server architecture.

TABLE 20.2. ACCESS INITIALIZATION SETTINGS FOR CLIENT/SERVER.

Setting	Default	Description
DisableAsync	0	When set to 1, forces synchronous query execution.
LoginTimeout	20	Specifies the number of seconds a login attempt can continue before timing out.
QueryTimeout	60	Specifies the number of seconds a query can run before timing out.
TraceODBCAPI	0	Shows whether ODBC API calls are traced in ODBCAPI.TXT. Default is 0 for No; 1 is for Yes.
ConnectionTimeout	600	Specifies the number of seconds that a cached connection can remain idle before timing out.
AsyncRetryInterval	500	For asynchronous processing, shows the number of milliseconds between polls to the server.
AttachCaseSensitive	0	Indicates whether table name matching is case sensitive. Defaults to 0 for No.
TraceSQLMode		When set to 1, inspects SQL statements sent to the server.
SnapshotOnly	0	When set to 0 (the default), forces all recordsets to be returned as snapshots.
AttachableObjects		Contains a list of object types that can be attached (such as tables, views, and so on).
TryJetAuth		When set to 0, prevents Access from attempting login with the default Admin account.

continues

TABLE 20.2. CONTINUED

Setting	Default	Description
PreparedInsert	0	When set to 1, inserts values in all columns.
PreparedUpdate	0	Similar to PreparedInsert, this setting determines whether all columns are affected by an update, or only the columns that have been changed in the updated record. PreparedUpdate can fire a trigger on a column that isn't changed.
FastQuery		When set to 1, speeds requerying by using more connections.
SQLTraceMode		Takes the same action as TraceSQLMode.

Summary

Access can be used to develop standalone and LAN applications, but it can also serve as a powerful and flexible front end for client/server applications. This means that you can upsize applications for dozens or hundreds of users or use Access as a data analysis tool for report writing, queries, and business graphics.

As this chapter has shown, Microsoft has included many special Access features specifically for client/server operations. The most important of them is probably the Pass-through query, which enables you to take advantage of stored procedures and other server features. You can expect even tighter integration of Access and database engines in the future.

To develop an efficient client/server application, you must master not only Access but also your database server software. You face many trade-offs in striving for the best performance from the application. Few fixed rules exist here; many things can be determined only by trial and error. Still, the rewards of using Access with client/server architecture are worth the effort.

Replication

One of the larger problems facing corporate IS teams today is the timely distribution of business information. As corporations become more dependent on information, centrally maintained databases can no longer keep up with the high volume of user requests for data. More and more systems are becoming decentralized or distributed, raising the issue of how to manage the distribution and synchronization of these satellite systems in a timely and accurate manner.

Replication came about as designers of large, distributed database systems found that there was too much time lag, and a certain level of fragility, in having systems rely on two-phase commits for making changes to databases. (A *two-phase commit* means that both the originating and target database agree that the proposed change is valid; therefore, the transaction must wait for both databases to allow it to be completed.) To get around this bottleneck, developers came up with the idea of putting the data closer to the end user by replicating the database.

This chapter covers how to create a replicable database. You can create replicated databases in several ways, including using the Tools menu, VBA code, and the Briefcase. After you learn how to replicate databases, you'll read about how to synchronize them. And finally, you'll learn how to troubleshoot possible conflicts and get some ideas on how to replicate a database set without causing too much trouble for the database administrator.

When to Use Replication

In some cases, replication is ideal; in others, it is not. Using replication creates advantages in the following three types of situations.

First, all databases have some kind of reports that must be run. When an Access database has a report running, the performance is hit hard because the report usually causes record locks. Therefore, to keep the performance at its maximum, creating a report database that is updated by replication is best. Consequently, all reports then run from this new report database.

Second, when users are located in different offices and are required to work across the wide area network (WAN), they operate at a slower rating than local users. To give these users the same performance as the local users, you need to set up a replicated database at each site, enabling the users to run from their new local database.

Third, when a database is required 24 hours a day, performing a backup becomes impossible. In most cases, when a database is required 24 hours a day, the data is vital. So to ensure that a backup is run without the database being taken down, you can use a read-only replica database that is updated at regular times. Then a backup can be performed on this new replica database.

Replication shouldn't be used in the following two situations. The first is a situation in which large numbers of transactions occur in a replication set. When the transaction numbers start to increase, so do the data conflicts. When the conflicts increase, it's likely that while the database administrator is trying to fix conflicts, the next synchronization should be run, making it impossible to resolve the conflicts. Also, the synchronization could take a long time to process all the transactions, causing a lot of network congestion or a synchronization call that never ends. In this type of situation, you should consider keeping all data local to the site and then, on a daily, weekly, or even monthly basis, running a batch job that updates the master database with the remote databases' records. After creating the updates, instead of exporting the data back out to the remote database, copying the master database would be a faster answer.

The second case is a situation in which it's absolutely crucial that data be consistent and up-to-date at all times. Because of possible delays and synchronization problems with the replication process, there is no way to guarantee this.

In these cases, and possibly many more, using replication is unwise because you can't do transactions between databases that would guarantee that the data is accurate and consistent.

Making a Database Replicable

The first step in making a database replicable is to create the master replication database. To do so, you must open the database you want to convert. You then can make the database replicable in two ways: by using the Access tool located in the Tools menu and/or by writing VBA code.

Using the Access Interface

To convert the database using the tool that comes with Access, simply choose Tools | Replication | Create Replica. The dialog box shown in Figure 21.1 appears.

FIGURE 21.1.
The prompt to continue with the replication.

Before the tool can create the Design Master database, it must close the database. If you are not a member of the Admins group, you are presented with a Cannot Open Database in Exclusive Mode dialog box. If you are a member of the Admins group for the database, you are asked whether you want to make a backup of the database before the database is converted. I strongly recommend that you have the replication tool create a backup. The default name is the original filename plus a .BAK extension. After the Design Master has been built, the dialog box shown in Figure 21.2 appears, prompting you for the name of the first replica database.

FIGURE 21.2.

The Location of New Replica dialog box.

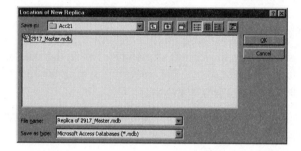

The replica database name defaults to "Replica of" plus the database name. You can change this name by clicking the File Name text box and typing the new name. I suggest that you keep some form of the Design Master's name to make the file easier to identify as a replicated database and to specify which database is the master. After you choose to create or not create the database, a confirmation dialog box opens for you to acknowledge.

Using VBA

To set the database to be a replica using VBA code, you must set its Replicable property to T. If the property Replicable is already in the database and you try to append this property to the database, an error occurs. The following code shows you how to set your current database and all its objects to be replicated.

```
Function make_replica_DB()
    Dim dbRep As Database
    Dim prpDB As Property

    'Open current database
    Set dbRep = CurrentDb

    ' Turn off error handling so that we can do our own error handling.
    On Error Resume Next
    Set prpDB = dbRep.CreateProperty("Replicable", dbText, "T")
```

```
    dbRep.Properties.Append prpDB

    If Err <> 0 Then
    MsgBox "Database is already replicated. The error ID is - " & _
        Err & Chr$(9) & Chr$(10) & " the error message is - " & Error
    Exit Function
    End If

    dbRep.Properties("Replicable") = "T"
    If Err <> 0 Then
    MsgBox "An unexpected error occurred the id was - " & _
        Err & Chr$(9) & Chr$(10) & " the error message is - " & Error
    Exit Function
    End If
    dbRep.Close
End Function
```

Remember that the database must be open in exclusive mode; otherwise, you receive an error. Also, in some cases you must close the database and reopen it for the replication to take effect. To see how this code works, check the module `Replicate` in the database `2917_Master_VBA.MDB` on the Web site for this book.

Changes to the Databases

When a database goes through the process of changing from a nonreplicated database to a replicated database, several changes are made to it. First, new system tables are added. Following is a list of system tables that are added to the database. These tables can't be changed by users or developers. It's a plus to know that they're available, but don't worry about them. They aren't all the tables that can be added to the database.

```
MSysErrors

MSysExchangeLog

MSysGenHistory

MSysOtherHistory

MSysRepInfo

MSysReplicas

MSysRepLock

MSysSchChange

MSysSchedule

MSysTableGuids

MSysTombStone

MSysTranspAddress
```

If these tables aren't visible when you open the database, choose Tools | Options, and on the View tab, click the Hidden Objects and System Objects check box.

The second change is that new system fields are added to each of your tables. Table 21.1 lists the fields and how they're used.

TABLE 21.1. THE NEW SYSTEM FIELDS THAT ARE ADDED.

Name	Description
s_Generation	A field that stores information about groups of changes
s_GUID	A new AutoNumber field that uniquely identifies the record
s_Lineage	A OLE Object field that contains information about changes

Also, for every OLE or memo field in the table, an additional system field is added. This field is named GEN_FieldName. It's a Long Integer Number field used to identify the object. Also, be aware that when you convert a table that has an AutoNumber in it, the field is changed from incremental to random. This change causes all your reports and forms that were sorting on this field now to malfunction. If you don't plan around this situation before you convert the database, it could come back to cause you problems. If you add a new AutoNumber field after the conversion to the database, you can select Incremental. So, to get around the conversion that occurs and possible problems, add all ID fields after you do the replication process of the database.

Lastly, three new properties are added to the database and are available only through the Microsoft Jet workspace: Replicable, ReplicableID, and DesignMasterID. The Replicable property is used to tell whether the database is replicated. After this field is set there is no going back, which is why it is strongly suggested that you make a backup. The ReplicableID property is a unique ID generated for each replicated database. The DesignMasterID property is used to identify the Design Master database. To change the Design Master, you set this value to On. Remember that you don't want two Design Masters in a set—this could cause data loss or data corruption.

You can calculate the total number of bytes available in a record in a replicable table by using this formula:

```
2048 bytes
       - (16 byte GUID value)
       - (4 bytes * the number of long value fields)
       - (4 bytes for the generation)
       - (4 bytes * the number of replicas that have ever made changes to
the record)
```

Access allows a maximum of 255 fields in a table, of which at least three fields are used by replication. You can calculate the total number of fields now available in a replicable table with this formula:

```
255 fields
    - (3 system fields)
    - (the number of long value fields)
```

Few applications use all the available fields in a table or characters in a record. If you have many memo fields or OLE objects in your table, however, you need to be aware of your remaining resources.

In addition to decreasing the available number of characters and fields, Access also imposes a limitation on the number of nested transactions allowed under replication. Whereas a nonreplicable database can have a maximum of seven nested transactions, a replicable database can have a maximum of six nested transactions.

Making Objects Local or Replicable

When you start working with replicated databases, you might want to make changes to objects without the objects being replicated out to the replica databases. To accomplish this, select the object and then right-click over it to open a menu, at the bottom of which is Properties. Click this option, and the dialog box shown in Figure 21.3 opens.

FIGURE 21.3.

The Properties dialog box for Access objects.

You're interested only in the attribute `Replicable`, located at the bottom of the dialog box. If a check mark appears in the check box, you have a replicated object; otherwise, you have a local object. To change the setting, click the check box. By default, all new objects are added as local objects. If this option is grayed out without a check mark in the box, the database isn't a replicated database. If it's grayed out with a check mark, it isn't the Design Master database.

NOTE

When you save new objects to the master database, the Save dialog box has a Make Replicable check box available for you to set the `Replicable` property.

What Can Be Replicated

System objects can't be replicated because they are unique to each Access database. All other Access objects—tables, queries, forms, reports, macros, and modules—can be replicated. Also, because you're using replication, using hidden objects can be a good idea. In this way, you still can replicate the objects while ensuring that the objects are out of sight of the users.

Database Security

When you create a replicated database, security becomes an issue because you don't want just anyone to get into the database. For information on how to create and set permissions on a database, refer to Chapter 23, "Security." The same rules for security apply to replicated databases as to nonreplicated databases. So, when you're setting up a replicated database, you also need to copy out a system database, or you need to make sure that the users have access to the share where the shared system databases are located. I recommend that you use the latter option if at all possible. The reason for making use of this option is simple—imagine having to add new users to all the system databases that are being used in the remote locations. For users who don't have access to the share, you need a way to replicate the system database out to them. The only side effect the users will run into is a slower login process.

Another security issue the database administrator needs to be aware of is how to stop users from making a database replicated. You can do this in two ways. The first is to set a database password on it. The second is to make sure that the user is signing in through a system database on which he or she doesn't have administrator privileges.

WARNING

Be aware that if you set a database password on a replicated database, it's impossible for other databases to synchronize with it.

Creating Additional Databases

After you create the Design Master, you need to create additional replicas of this database. Don't use the original to create replica databases because you'll just be creating new Design Masters. To create a replica database of the Design Master, use the tool supplied with Access or write VBA code that creates new replica databases.

Using the Access Tool

To use the Access tool, choose Tools | Replication | Create Replica. The dialog box shown in Figure 21.2 appears, prompting you for the name of the new replica database. After you set the location and name the new database, click OK. When the database has been created, the message shown in Figure 21.4 appears.

FIGURE 21.4.

The replica confirmation dialog box.

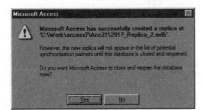

This dialog box confirms that the database has been created, and it shows you the name and the path where it was created. After you confirm the dialog box by clicking OK, the Database window reappears.

> **WARNING**
>
> One problem here is that when you create the replication database through the Access tool, you can't make a read-only replica database, which you would need for a report database or a backup database. The only way to create a read-only database presently is to use VBA code.

Using the VBA Code

Writing code that enables you to create a replica database is quick and simple. First, you need to open a connection to the database. Second, you must make a call to the `MakeReplica` function. This function needs to follow the database name, and it takes the following parameters. The first option is the new replica database name. The second option is the description that will be placed in the MSysReplicas system table under the Description column. The last option is optional, but if you want to create a backup database or a report database, the constant to use is dbRepMakeReadOnly. To make an additional replica database, you must call the MakeReplica method. Here is its syntax:

database.MakeReplica *replica, description*[,dbRepMakeReadOnly]

Set *database* to the master database of the replica set. *replica* is the name to be used for the new replica database. *description* is any valid string expression. dbRepMakeReadOnly and dbRepMakePartial are your two optional parameters. Here is an example of code that makes a read-only replica database:

```
Function MakeReadOnlyReplicaDatabase ()

     Dim dbMaster As DATABASE
     Set dbMaster = DBEEngine (0).OpenDatabase("DDE.MDB")
     Set dbMaster = OpenDatabase("2917_Master.MDB")
     dbMaster.MakeReplica "2917_Master_2.MDB", "Second of DDE.MDB",
dbRepMakeReadOnly
     dbMaster.Close
End Function
```

To check this code out, refer to the function MakeReadOnlyReplicaDatabase in 2917_Master_VBA.MDB on the Web site for this book.

Using Partial Replicas

To use partial replicas, you need to do three things. First, create a partial replica through VBA code by using the following:

```
dbMaster.MakeReplica "2917_Replica_3.MDB", "Third replica of DDE.MDB",
dbRepMakePartial
```

To see how this code works, refer to the function MakePartialReplicaDatabase in 2917_Master_VBA.MDB on the Web site for this book. After you create the partial replica, you need to set the filters on for the tables. To do so, you must open the Partial Replica in Exclusive mode. Then you need to set the ReplicaFilter property for each table. To do so, you can use any of the following code examples. The first example tells the table to load all rows:

```
dbNewPartial.TableDefs("Employees").ReplicaFilter = True
```

The next sample tells the table not to load any rows:

```
dbNewPartial.TableDefs("Categories").ReplicaFilter = False
```

The final example tells the table to load only the rows that match the criteria that is set. In this example, the table is set to load only rows that have a country equal to Germany:

```
dbNewPartial.TableDefs("Customers").ReplicaFilter = "Country = 'Germany'"
```

The last step is to tell the partial database to load the information. To do so, make the following call:

```
dbNewPartial.PopulatePartial "d:\FullReplica.mdb"
```

When you're making this call, remember that you can use only a full replica to receive your data, and that no other replicas can synchronize with this partial replica until this call has been made. To see how this code works, refer to the function `SetPartialDataSet` in `2917_Master_VBA.MDB` on the Web site for this book.

Synchronizing Replicated Databases

After all the databases are in place and on the users' machines or servers, you need to synchronize the data. To do this, use the tool that comes with Access or write VBA code that synchronizes the database, either at a certain time or after a certain number of records have been added. This choice depends on how important the data is to the users.

Using the Access Tool

To open the Access tool, choose Tools | Replication | Synchronize Now. The dialog box shown in Figure 21.5 opens, prompting you for the Synchronize Database name.

FIGURE 21.5.

The Synchronize Database dialog box.

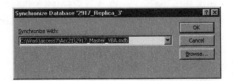

If you have synchronized the database before, the name defaults to the last database it synchronized with. Also, if you click the arrow to the right of the list box, a list of previously used synchronized database names appears. If the database you want to use isn't in the list, you can type the path plus the name into the list box. The synchronization process is capable of using the network path plus the database name, which saves you from having the share connected at all times.

Also, if you don't remember the path and database name, simply click Browse. This opens the file locator dialog box so you can locate the correct database.

After you locate the database, activate the database name and then click OK. This takes you back to the previous dialog box with the path plus filename you selected in the locator dialog box. If this is the file you want to synchronize with, click OK. A progress dialog box appears, showing the status of the update. After the synchronization is complete, the message shown in Figure 21.6 appears, explaining that the updates won't be effective until you close the database and reopen it.

FIGURE 21.6.

The confirmation of synchronization.

If you click Yes in this dialog box, the database is closed and reopened. If you click No, you're returned to the database, where you can continue with your work.

Remember, if you plan to use this method to keep the databases in sync, you must make sure that two tasks are completed. First, make sure that the users have access to Tools | Replication | Synchronize Now. Second, teach them how to use the tool.

Using VBA Code

To write VBA code to synchronize the database, you first need to have a list of all the database names and their locations. You can pull this list from `MSysReplicas`, but this method isn't recommended because this information was created when the replicas were first generated. In the master database, you should have a table that contains all the databases that are part of this set. This way, the replicas aren't doing the work to synchronize.

Now that you have a table set up with the names and paths, the next step is to run the `Synchronize` function. This function requires a database variable preceding it and then two parameters. The first parameter is mandatory, and the second is optional. The mandatory parameter is the database name, including the path you want to synchronize with. The optional parameter can be any of the items listed in Table 21.2.

TABLE 21.2. OPTIONAL PARAMETERS FOR THE SYNCHRONIZE FUNCTION.

Parameter	Description
dbRepImpExpChanges	Imports the data first, followed by the export of the local data that has changed
dbRepImportChanges	Imports the changes
dbRepExportChanges	Exports the changes
dbRepSyncInternet	Imports/exports the data through an Internet pathway

(For more information on using dbRepSyncInternet, refer to the next section.)

The following code uses a table that holds the database names plus the path. First, it sets up a variable that points to the database set. It then sets up a loop to go through this recordset, importing the data from each database from the recordset. It next resets the recordset to the first record. Then it calls the export function of Synchronize. Upon completion of the export, it closes down the snapshot and the database.

```
Function SynchronizeDB()
Dim db As Database, snpRepDB As Recordset

  Set db = CurrentDb

  Set snpRepDB = db.OpenRecordset("Select DBName from ReplicatedDBs;",
dbOpenSnapshot)
  snpRepDB.MoveFirst
  Do While Not snpRepDB.EOF
    db.Synchronize snpRepDB("DBName"), dbRepImportChanges
    snpRepDB.MoveNext
  Loop
  snpRepDB.MoveFirst
  Do While Not snpRepDB.EOF
    db.Synchronize snpRepDB("DBName"), dbRepExportChanges
    snpRepDB.MoveNext
  Loop
  snpRepDB.Close
  db.CloseEnd Function
```

The reason to import first and then export is to ensure that all the databases are current. If you don't take this step, the only up-to-date database is the last database called. If you have only one database to worry about, making the call to synchronize with a parameter of dbRepImpExpChanges works just fine. For more ideas on how to implement replication databases, refer to the section "A Better Way to Make Use of Replication" later in this chapter. When you finish entering the code, you can view the data changes right away, not after a restart, which makes this a more effective alternative. Also, when this type of code is implemented, you don't need to teach the user how to use the synchronization tool.

Synchronizing Databases Through the Internet

To synchronize a database through the Internet, you need to have the database set up on the Internet server. Then you can make the following call:

```
db.Synchronize "http://www.yourcompany_name.com/files/customer.mdb",
➥dbRepImpExpChanges + dbRepSyncInternet
```

This call performs a bidirectional synchronize from your database to `http://www.your-company_name.com/files/customer.mdb`.

Troubleshooting Replicated Databases

When you start working on three or more databases, and users are adding, editing, or deleting records from different databases, data conflicts always occur. With the replication capability of Access, when it has a conflict, it keeps the record with the most changes done to it.

After the decision has been made, a new table is created, named `table_Conflict`, in the database that had the conflict data. The `table` part of the name is the table that had the conflict. For example, say that you have a table named `Employee`, and when it is synchronized, it has a conflict; in this case, the new table is named `Employee_conflict`. The contents of this table are identical to the original, but it contains only the conflicting data.

Access provides two ways to resolve conflicts: by using the Access tool that is supplied and by using VBA code.

Using the Access Tool

When a database has been synchronized with another database and a conflict has occurred, you are asked if you would like to resolve the conflict when you open the database. If you answer Yes at this prompt, the dialog box shown in Figure 21.7 appears.

Here you are given a list of tables that have conflicts with the last synchronization. If you click Close, you're returned to the database without any conflicts being resolved. If Design has any errors, the View Design Errors button is enabled. To resolve the conflict, click Resolve Conflicts. This action opens the dialog box shown in Figure 21.8.

FIGURE 21.7.

*The Resolve
Replication
Conflicts dialog
box.*

FIGURE 21.8.

*The Resolve
Replication
Conflicts dialog
box.*

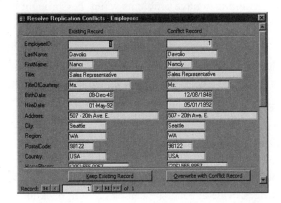

On the right side of this dialog box is the data that Access has decided is correct. On the
left side is the data you entered that was determined less likely to be valid. At the bottom
of the dialog box, you're given the choice of whether to keep the existing record or overwrite it with the conflicting data. If you aren't sure which choice to make or if more than
one record of conflict exists, you can navigate through each record, making this choice
for each record. After you fix all the records that have conflicts, the dialog box shown in
Figure 21.7 reappears. The other type of problem you can get is data errors. If you have
this type of problem, you are presented with a dialog to resolve it. The Replication Data
Errors dialog box gives you some ideas of how to repair the problem. Furthermore, if
more than one problem occurs, you can use the record navigation buttons located at the
bottom of this dialog box to scroll through the other problems.

Using VBA Code

To use VBA code in this case, you need to check whether any tables have a conflict
table. If a conflict does exist, you should create a recordset to the nonconflict table and
then create a second recordset to the conflict table. Before you can either fix the conflict
or delete it, you need to have a method in place to decide how to resolve conflicts. After
you have resolved the problems, you should then synchronize the database again to make
sure the data conflicts are replicated back out. After you fix all conflicts using the conflict resolution method, you should delete the conflict table.

Briefcase Replication

Another unique way to implement database replication is by using the Briefcase. As part of the usability studies that went into the design of Windows 95, Microsoft discovered that many people were copying their files and taking them home to work on them. The problem was that people could then have problems when they brought the files back to the original machine. People would forget to update files, or copy the original file over the modified one, or even clobber the changes someone else had made to a shared file.

For all these reasons, Microsoft designed the Briefcase as a tool for handling the distribution and updating of files. Even Access 95 was designed to take advantage of this capability with replicated databases.

You can use Briefcase replication in Access 97 to make special copies—called *replicas*—of an Access database. By doing so, users at different sites can all work on their own copies of the database at the same time, just as was proposed. Replication is different from simple copying because replicated databases can be synchronized with each other. This means that the changes made at each site can be brought back to the central database, and Access can take those changes and apply them to the original database. You can then make new replicas to distribute the changes to all the users.

Creating a Replication Database with Briefcase

Because Access relies on the Briefcase in Windows 95 to create replicated databases, the first step is to make sure that your system is set up with Briefcase. Figure 21.9 shows the default window when the Briefcase opens.

FIGURE 21.9.

A look at the Briefcase and its default window.

If you discover that Briefcase isn't installed, choose Start | Settings | Control Panel | Add/Remove Programs | Windows Setup, and then follow the onscreen instructions. You need to have your Windows 95 disks or CD-ROM available.

After you install Briefcase on your system, make sure that the database that will be replicated isn't protected by a database password. If it is, you must remove the password protection before replicating it.

You then need to open an Explorer window and find the .MDB file for the database. Using a previously replicated database file is best, if one exists; otherwise, use the Design Master database. (In the following text, you will see figures and examples of previously replicated databases.) Double-click the My Briefcase icon, which should be visible on your desktop. This action opens a window for the Briefcase, similar to the one shown in Figure 21.9.

Next, you simply click the .MDB file and drag the icon to the Briefcase window. After you drag and drop the icon, you're presented with a dialog box that looks somewhat like the one shown in Figure 21.10. This dialog box gives you a chance to abort in case you didn't mean to replicate this database.

FIGURE 21.10.

A verification dialog box for Briefcase replication.

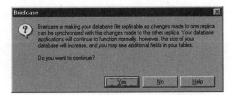

Assuming that you decide to continue, the next dialog box, shown in Figure 21.11, gives you the option of creating a backup of the database. If you have the disk space, making a backup is probably a good idea. Be sure to move the backup to a different directory to reduce the chance of confusing it with the current database.

FIGURE 21.11.

The backup verification dialog box.

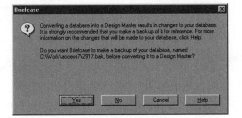

Either way, you end up spending time watching the screen while animated sheets of paper fly in both directions between the Briefcase and the folder.

You're then asked which database should be allowed to have design changes made to it. Although both the original and the replica database can have data inserted, updated, or deleted, only one of them can be allowed to accept changes to the structure of tables. Usually, you will want the original database to be the one that controls changes to the structure of the database. The exception would be if you create a database but are having someone else program changes to it, in which case the replica you give the other person needs to be able to have the changes made. The dialog box involved is shown in Figure 21.12.

FIGURE 21.12.

Briefcase's dialog box verification for an editable database.

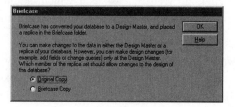

Finally, you end up with the process completed and a replica of the database in the Briefcase. Figure 21.13 shows what you see next.

FIGURE 21.13.

The result: a database in both places.

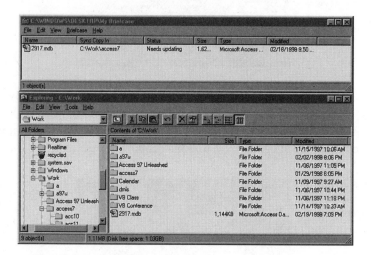

When you reopen the original database in Access, notice that the title for the database has changed. As shown in Figure 21.14, the open master (original) database appears.

However, the open replica shows a somewhat different title, as shown in Figure 21.15. The objects now have a new icon placed beside them, a yellow circle with a blue and red arrow inside.

21

FIGURE 21.14.

How the original (master) database looks after replication.

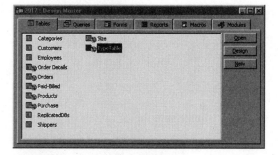

FIGURE 21.15.

The replica version of the same database.

After you convert a database into a replicable database, you can't convert it back to a nonreplicable database. However, you can create a new, nonreplicable database that contains all the objects and data from your replicable database without the additional system fields, tables, and properties associated with replication. This process requires the following steps:

1. Identify the replica that contains the objects and data you want to be in the new, nonreplicable database.

2. After choosing Tools|Options, click the View tab. On this tab, set the System Objects option to off (unchecked).

3. Create a new database and open it.

4. Import all the objects from the replica into the new database.

5. After choosing Tools|Options, click the View tab. Then check the System Objects option.

6. Open each table in the new database, and delete the fields labeled s_GUID, s_Lineage, and s_Generation.

7. Save your new database.

Taking the Database Home with You

The whole purpose of creating the replica is so you can take the database with you or distribute it to other people. After you create the replica, you can carry out the process of distributing it either by using disks (or other removable media that Windows 95 can recognize) or through a direct connection (such as a network).

In the case of a direct connection, make sure that the other computer is connected and then drag the Briefcase to the target machine. If you're using a disk, you can simply drag the Briefcase to the disk window in Explorer.

> **NOTE**
>
> If the Briefcase doesn't fit on a single floppy disk, you have a problem because it doesn't know how to span disks. In this case, you must create a direct connection via a network or through a dial-up RAS connection.

In either case, the Briefcase disappears from your desktop and resides on the new target. Figure 21.16 shows an example of moving the Briefcase to a floppy disk.

FIGURE 21.16.

The Briefcase has been moved to a floppy disk in drive A.

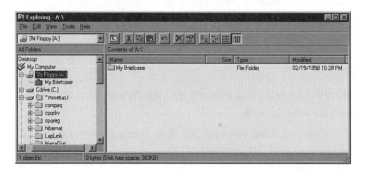

If you want to provide replicas to several people, you can right-click the desktop, choose New from the pop-up menu, and then select Briefcase from the drop-down list. By default, this Briefcase is called New Briefcase. After you create a new Briefcase, you need to create another replica of your original database. Remember that every time you replicate the original database, the three fields are added to allow for tracking the changes in each replica of the database. Even if you eventually delete one of the replicas, the tracking information remains on the original database.

You should work on the replicated database while it's still in the Briefcase. In other words, start Access and open the replica file where it is in the Briefcase. If you copy it to another machine from the Briefcase, you're essentially making a replica of a replica, and then you have to update the version in the Briefcase before you can bring it back and update the original version.

Bringing the Database Back and Synchronizing

When you are reattached to the computer that has the original copy of the database, or have the floppy disk in the drive of that computer, open the Briefcase window and click the database file. In the Briefcase window, choose Briefcase I Update Selection.

This process is what replication is all about. You no longer need to remember what you changed, just that you made a change. The Briefcase makes the necessary changes for you because it remembers what you have changed. This capability is referred to as the *power of replication*. After you have the database set up, keeping it synchronized is simple. If you have multiple replicas, they go through this process as each of them is attached to the machine again (or as the floppy disks come in).

You still need to select an administrator to monitor the four tables (mentioned earlier) for any errors that occur if more than two people are using the database. Along the same lines, you should develop a process ahead of time to handle any data disputes so that friction between people can be minimized when someone has to change his or her database because of a change made by someone else.

A Better Way to Make Use of Replication

Some of the biggest problems with replication in Access occur when a replica database set is poorly implemented. Following are some issues you should be aware of when thinking about using replication:

- The need to make backups of the Design Master.
- Resolving data conflicts without affecting the users of the database.
- Being able to synchronize the databases without causing poor performance for the users.
- The need to make backups without taking the database down and causing downtime for the users.
- Being able to resolve data conflicts without causing downtime for the users.

- Having users run reports off the database without causing performance problems for other users.

Any of these issues can cause a database administrator many headaches. The hierarchy depicted in Figure 21.17 is one way to implement a replica database set to try to make the database administrator's job that much easier.

At the top of the hierarchy is the Design Master. Make sure that when you create a Design Master, a backup of the original is created before conversion. Also make sure that no user can open or work on the Design Master.

The next level is the main synchronize database and the developer's database. The main synchronize database should be the only database that can actually add data to the Design Master, and the developer's database should be the only database that can change the structure of the Design Master.

The next level should be all read-only to ensure that no user can add data directly to these databases. The read-only status also ensures that most data conflicts will occur at this level. The main synchronize database imports the data from here, and then it exports data changes and any structural changes that need to be passed along. The main synchronize database and each main region database fall under the responsibility of the database administrator, and of course, the database administrator is responsible for the Design Master. The backup database is on this level because this database shouldn't directly access the Design Master. This database will be updated after the main synchronize database has been updated with the latest changes from the regions. Only three databases need to be backed up: the backup database, the Design Master (just in case), and the developer's database. The other databases can quickly be rebuilt from the main synchronize database if something goes wrong. So far, this chapter has concentrated on the responsibilities of the database administrator and the developer. The reason is that you want to make sure that this area is clean and easy for the administrator to administrate without much difficulty.

The hierarchy is made up of three regions; this discussion looks only at region 1. This region has a report database and a database that users can update. In any region, you could possibly find a report database and no user-updated database, as well as the reverse. What you find depends on the demands of the region. The reason for using a report database rather than just the update database is to keep performance at its best. The working database updates the regional master, and then the regional master database updates the main synchronizing database. The regional master database then imports all data changes that the main synchronize database has for it. After the updates have occurred, it then updates the working database, followed by the reporting database.

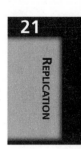

When and how often the databases are updated is up to the database administrator. But you shouldn't copy large numbers of records across the WAN if you can help it, and you don't want to call the synchronize routine too often if there is no data to be passed on. Also, you need to control the updates so the database administrator has enough time to fix any data conflicts, thus ensuring that the conflicts don't ripple their way down the hierarchy.

Summary

In this chapter, you learned what replication is, when you might want to use it, and how to use it. You also learned about some potential pitfalls and got some ideas for avoiding them. With this knowledge, you are ready to identify situations in which replication is the right answer, and you can design and implement the solution.

Performance and Security

PART
VII

IN THIS PART

Optimizing Your Application

Optimization: An Overview

In a world where hardware never seems to keep up with software, it's important to do everything you can to improve the performance of your application. This chapter helps you to optimize your applications for speed and reduce the memory and hard disk space required by your applications.

Optimization is the process of reviewing your operating environment, VBA code, application objects, and data structures to ensure optimum performance. In a nutshell, optimization is the process of making your application leaner and meaner. It's an ongoing process that starts at the beginning of the development process. Even after you design your application as carefully as possible, after it's in production, you will probably find that you need to fine-tune it further.

Users may become frustrated when an application runs slowly. In fact, if a user is not warned about a slow process, he or she may reboot or shut down the machine while a process is running. Doing so can have dire results on the integrity of the data.

> ### TIP
>
> To help reduce the chance of a user rebooting the computer during a lengthy process, it's generally a good idea to provide the user with some sort of indication that a process will take a while. You can do so by using a message box that appears before processing begins, or by providing a status bar that shows the progress of the task being completed.

You can do many things to optimize an application's performance. These things range from using a front-end tool such as the Performance Analyzer to fastidiously adhering to certain coding techniques. The following sections provide highlights of all the major ways you can optimize the performance of your applications.

Improving Application Performance by Modifying Hardware and Software Configurations

The Access environment refers to the combination of hardware and software configurations under which Microsoft Access is running. These environmental settings can greatly affect the performance of an Access application.

The easiest way to improve the performance of an Access application is to upgrade the hardware and software configuration on which it is running. This form of optimization requires no direct intervention from the developer. A side benefit of most of the environmental changes you can make is that any improvements made to the environment will be beneficial to users in all of their Windows applications.

Improving the environment involves more than just adding some RAM. It can also mean optimally configuring the operating system and the Access application.

Hardware, Hardware, More Hardware, Please!

The bottom line is that Windows 95 and Access 97 both crave hardware—the faster your users' machines and the more memory they have, the better. Additional hardware may not be the least expensive solution, but adding hardware certainly is the quickest and easiest way you can improve the performance of your application.

RAM, RAM, That's All I Need!

Memory is what Windows 95, NT, and Access crave most, whether you're running under the full version of Microsoft Access or using the runtime version. Microsoft Access requires 12MB of RAM just to run under Windows 95, its standard operating environment. Although 12MB of RAM is required, 16MB of RAM is recommended by Microsoft. Under Windows NT, Access requires a minimum of 16MB of RAM. Both requirements can climb dramatically if your users are running other applications or if your application uses OLE automation to communicate with other applications. The more RAM you and the users of your application have, the better. A great environment for Access 97 is 32MB of RAM. In fact, if every one of your users has at least 32MB of RAM, you can stop reading this chapter because everything else covered here is going to provide you with minor benefits compared to adding more RAM. If you are like most people and not every one of your users has a Pentium 120 with 32MB of RAM, read on.

> **NOTE**
>
> Developers should have a bare minimum of 24MB of RAM installed on their machines. Remember, this is a minimum. Most developers agree that 32MB of RAM is required if you intend to do any serious development work. Although you should develop with this configuration, it is important that you test the application with each build on the lowest-common-denominator machine. You may think that performance is great but later find that it is totally unacceptable on your users' machines.

Defragment Your Hard Disk

As your computer writes information to disk, it attempts to find contiguous space on the disk within which to place data files. As the hard disk fills up, files are placed in fragmented pieces on it. Each time your application attempts to read data and programs, it must locate the information scattered over the disk. This process is very time-consuming. Therefore, it is helpful to defragment the hard disk on which the application and data tables are stored by using a utility such as the Disk Defragmenter that ships with Windows 95 or Norton Utilities' Speed Disk.

> **TIP**
>
> You can easily automate the process of defragmenting a hard disk by using the System Agent included as part of the Microsoft Plus! package, which is sold as an add-on to Windows 95. The System Agent, one of the many components included with the Microsoft Plus! package, is a useful tool that enables you to schedule when and how often the defragmentation process occurs.

Compact Your Database

Just as the operating system fragments your files over time, Access itself introduces its own form of fragmentation. Each time you add and modify data, your database grows. The problem is that when you delete data or objects within your database, it does not shrink. Instead, Access leaves empty pages available in which new data will be placed, and these empty pages are not necessarily filled with data. You can free the empty space by using the Compact utility, which is part of the Microsoft Access software. The Compact utility frees excess space and attempts to make all data pages contiguous. You should compact your database frequently, especially if records or database objects (for example, forms and reports) are regularly added and deleted. You can access the Compact utility only when no database is open. To open it, choose Tools I Database Utilities. From this menu, you can find the Compact Database option.

Don't Use Compressed Drives

Regardless of the compression utility that you're using, disk compression significantly degrades performance with Access 97. This fact is documented in the Readme file.

Tune Virtual Memory: Tweak the Swap File

Although Windows 95 attempts to manage virtual memory on its own, you may find it useful to provide Windows 95 with some additional advice. To modify the size of the swap file, right-click My Computer. Select Properties and then select the Performance tab. Click Virtual Memory.

Changing the size of the swap file or moving it to a faster disk drive or a drive that is connected to a separate controller card might be useful. Any changes that you make might adversely affect performance. You therefore should evaluate whether any changes you make will help the situation—or, perhaps, make things worse!

> **TIP**
>
> If Access 97 or Windows is running on a compressed drive, you can improve performance by moving the swap file to an uncompressed drive. If possible, the swap file should be located on a drive or partition solely dedicated to the swap file, or a drive or partition that is rarely accessed by other applications. This way, you can ensure that the swap file remains in a contiguous location on disk.

Run Access and Your Application Locally

Installing both the Access software and your application objects on each user's local machine is best. Only the data tables should be stored on a network file server. Otherwise, you end up sending DLLs, OLE objects, help files, type libraries, executables, and database objects all over the network wire. If you want to get the worst possible performance out of an Access application, install it on a diskless workstation with 8MB of RAM!

> **TIP**
>
> If the application is a single-user application, place all databases on the local hard disk. Open the database for Exclusive use by marking the Exclusive check box in the Open dialog box.

Do Everything You Can to Make Windows Faster

It always amuses me that the users with the slowest machines and the least memory have the most accessories running. These accessories include multimedia, fancy wallpapers, and other nifty utilities. If performance is a problem, you may try experimenting to see whether eliminating some of these frivolous niceties improves the performance of your application. If it does, encourage the user to eliminate the frills, get more memory, or accept your application's slow performance.

Another tip to make Windows 95 run faster is to shut down and restart on a regular basis. Memory tends to get fragmented and applications run more slowly. Whereas I can go weeks or months in Windows NT without rebooting, I find it beneficial to reboot my Windows 95 machine a couple of times a day.

Change Access's Software Settings

In addition to the more obvious measures just outlined, some minor software tweaking can go a long way toward improving performance. Adjusting several settings in the Windows Registry can dramatically improve performance. These changes all involve the Registry's ISAM section. The properties that you might want to change include MaxBufferSize and ReadAheadPages, which determine how the Jet engine uses memory.

MaxBufferSize controls the maximum size of the Jet engine's internal cache. By default, it is set to optimize performance on most machines. It does so by reading data in 2KB pages, placing the data in a memory cache. The data in the cache is readily available to forms, reports, tables, and queries. Lowering the value for MaxBufferSize frees memory for other tasks. Changing the value might be helpful on a machine with a minimum memory configuration.

ReadAheadPages controls the number of 2KB data pages that the Jet database engine reads ahead when performing sequential page reads. This number can range from 0 to 31, with the default at 16. The higher the number, the more efficient Access is at reading ahead so that data is available when you need it. The lower the number, the more memory is freed up for other tasks.

As you configure any of these settings, remember that what is good for one machine is not necessarily good for the next. You need to optimize the settings for each machine with its unique hardware configuration in mind.

Understanding What Jet 3.5 Does to Improve Performance

Improvements have been made to the Jet 3.5 engine to dramatically improve performance over its predecessors. Some of these improvements appeared with the Jet 3.0 engine that shipped with Access 95, but many are new to Jet 3.5. The Jet 3.5 engine is thoroughly 32-bit. It takes advantage of multiple execution threads, providing significant performance benefits.

Specific improvements to Jet 3.5 include the following:

- Delete operations are faster. Portions of a page can be removed at once, rather than data being removed row by row.

- Multiuser concurrency on indexed columns is improved. More users can read and update indexed columns without experiencing locking conflicts. Furthermore, indexed columns no longer contain read locks.

- Transaction processing is now implicit. Whereas in earlier versions of Access, many users wrapped processing loops in the `BeginTrans…CommitTrans` construct so that they could limit the number of disk writes; the Jet 3.5 engine handles this job quite well on its own.

- Large queries run faster. This change is due to improvements in the transactional behavior of SQL data manipulation language (DML) statements, as well as new Registry settings that force transactions to commit when a certain lock threshold is reached.

- Queries containing the inequality operator (<>) run faster.

- Sequential reads are faster. Up to 64KB of disk space can be allocated at a time.

- Temporary queries run faster.

- Deleting a table is faster when you use SQL `DROP` or SQL `DELETE`.

- The amount of space occupied by indexes is reduced.

- When you compact a database, all indexes are optimized for performance.

- The page allocation mechanism is improved. This change better assures that data from a table is stored on adjacent pages and improves the read-ahead capability.

22

OPTIMIZING YOUR APPLICATION

- The cache is dynamically configured. The cache is configured at startup based on the amount of system memory available and contains the most recently used data, thereby enhancing performance.

- There is now ISAM support for HTML files.

- The `MaxLocksPerFile` Registry setting enables you to speed up the completion of large queries where data is stored on NetWare and Windows NT–based servers. It forces transactions to partially commit.

Letting the Performance Analyzer Determine Problem Areas

You can do many things to improve the performance of an application, and most of them require significant attention and expertise on your part. The Performance Analyzer is a tool that does some of the work for you. It analyzes the design of an Access application and suggests techniques that you can use to improve the application's performance. Many of these techniques can be implemented automatically.

To use the Performance Analyzer, choose Tools | Analyze | Performance. The dialog box shown in Figure 22.1 then appears.

FIGURE 22.1.

The Performance Analyzer dialog box.

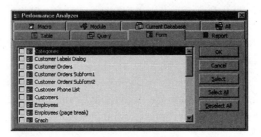

Select the individual tables, queries, forms, reports, macros, modules, and relationships that you want the Performance Analyzer to scrutinize. After you click OK, the Performance Analyzer analyzes the selected objects. Then the Performance Analyzer dialog box in Figure 22.2 provides you with a list of suggested improvements to the selected objects. These improvements are broken down into recommendations, suggestions, ideas, and items that were automatically fixed. Two suggested improvements are the addition of an index and conversion of an OLE object. For example, after analyzing the Northwind database that ships with Access, the Performance Analyzer suggests that the form called Customers should use a stored query as the row source for the control called Country. If you click the suggestion and then click Optimize, Access prompts you for a name for the query and then performs the change for you.

FIGURE 22.2.

The Performance Analyzer dialog box after you run the Performance Analyzer.

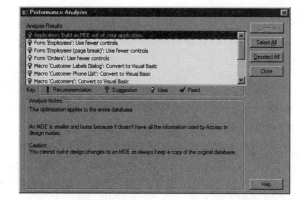

Designing Tables to Optimize Performance

Now that you have seen the changes you can make to your environment to improve performance, take a look at the changes you can make to your data structures. Such changes include eliminating redundant data, using indexes, selecting appropriate field datatypes, and using various query techniques.

Optimizing the Data Structure

Optimizing performance by tweaking the data structure is imperative for good performance. No matter what else you do to improve performance, poor data design can dramatically degrade the performance of your application. All other optimization attempts are futile without proper attention to this area.

You can spend days and days optimizing your data. These changes must be well thought out and carefully analyzed. You often can make these changes over time as problems are identified. Such changes can include those in the following sections.

Why Be Normal?

You should normalize your tables. Data that appears in multiple places can significantly slow down your application. An example is a company address appearing in both the Customer table and the Orders table. This information should be included only in the Customer table. Queries should be used to combine the address and order data when needed.

I Thought You Just Told Me to Normalize

When it comes to performance, unfortunately, there are no hard-and-fast rules. Although most of the time you can gain performance by normalizing your data structure, sometimes denormalizing can help. Generally, this is the case when you find yourself creating a particular join over and over again. You can try denormalizing the data to see if dramatic performance improvements result. Remember, denormalization has definite downsides regarding data integrity and maintenance.

Index, Index, Index!

It is amazing how far an index can go in improving performance. Fields on both sides of a join should be indexed. Any fields or combinations of fields on which you search should also be included in an index. You should create indexes for all columns used in query joins, searches, and sorts. You should create primary key indexes rather than unique indexes, and unique indexes rather than nonunique indexes. The performance improvements rendered by indexes are profound.

> **WARNING**
>
> Although indexes can dramatically improve performance, you should not create an index for every field in a table. Indexes do have their downsides. Besides taking up disk space, they also slow down the process of adding, editing, and deleting data.

> **TIP**
>
> In a multiple-field index, index on as few fields as possible. Multiple-field indexes can dramatically degrade performance.

Select the Correct Datatype

When you're defining a field, select the shortest datatype available for the storage of the data. For example, if you store a code between 1 and 10 within the field, you don't need to select double for a numeric field. It is recommend to use Long Integer wherever you were thinking of using Integer. The reason is that the Long Integer is what Windows 95 is based on.

Designing Queries to Optimize Performance

Optimizing your queries requires lots of practice and experimentation. For example, some queries involving a one-to-many relationship run more efficiently if the criteria is placed on the "one" side of the relationship. Others run more efficiently if the criteria is placed on the "many" side. Start with some basics that can go a long way toward improving the performance of your queries and of your application as a whole:

- Include as few columns in the result set as possible.
- Try to reduce the number of complex expressions contained in the query. Although including a complex expression in a query eliminates the need to build the expression into each form and report, the performance benefits gained may sometimes be worth the trouble.
- Use the Between operator rather than greater than (>) and less than (<).
- Use Count(*) rather than Count([column]).
- Group Totals queries by the field that is in the same table you're totaling. In other words, if you're totaling cost multiplied by price for each order in the Order Detail table, you should group by the Order ID within the Order Detail table, not the Order ID within the Orders table.
- When creating Crosstab queries, use fixed column headings.

Now that you have seen what you can do with the design of your queries to improve performance, take a look at a couple of simple techniques that you can employ to improve the performance of your queries.

A simple but often neglected method of optimizing queries is to deliver them compiled. A query compiles when you open it in Datasheet view and then simply close it. If you modify a query and then save it, it is not compiled until the query runs. Delivering pre-compiled queries ensures that they run as quickly as possible.

Also, you should compile your queries using the same amount of data that your application will contain, because Jet's query optimizer optimizes the query differently depending on the amount of data that it finds. If you build a query using 100 records that runs on a live table containing 100,000 records, the query is not properly optimized. You must rerun and resave your query using the correct quantity of data if you want the query to be optimized properly.

Making Coding Changes to Improve Performance

No matter what you do to optimize the operating system environment and improve your data design, poor code can continue to bog you down. A properly optimized application is optimized in terms of the environment, data design, and code. Just as poor table design can degrade performance, so can poor coding techniques. Changes to your code include the elimination of variants and dead code, the utilization of built-in collections, and the use of specific object types. An important code-related optimization is to deliver your modules precompiled.

The changes and techniques described in the following sections can all aid in the improvement of performance. Note that any one change does not make much of a difference; however, an accumulation of all the changes, especially where code is being reexecuted in a loop, can make a significant impact on the performance of your application.

Eliminate Variants and Use the Smallest Datatype Possible

Variant variables are the slowest. They carry a lot of overhead because they are resolved at runtime. Remember that the following statement declares a Variant type of variable:

```
Dim intCounter
```

To strong-type this variable as an integer, for example, you must modify your code to look like this:

```
Dim intCounter As Integer
```

Not only should you strong-type your variables, you should also use the smallest datatype possible. Remember that datatypes such as Boolean, Byte, Integer, and Long are the smallest and therefore the fastest. They are followed by Single, Double, Currency, and (finally) Variant. Of course, if you must store very large numbers with decimal points into a variable, you cannot pick Single. Just keep in mind that selecting the smallest datatype appropriate for the use of the variable is wise.

Use Specific Object Types

Just as the general Variant datatype is inefficient, generic object variables are also inefficient. The MakeItBold subroutine uses a generic object variable, as follows:

```
Private Sub cmdMakeBold_Click()
    Call MakeItBold(Screen.PreviousControl)
```

```
End Sub

Sub MakeItBold(ctlAny As Control)
    ctlAny.FontBold = True
End Sub
```

On the other hand, the `SpecificBold` subroutine uses a specific object variable, as follows:

```
Private Sub cmdSpecificBold_Click()
    Call SpecificBold(Screen.PreviousControl)
End Sub

Sub SpecificBold(txtAny As TextBox)
    txtAny.FontBold = True
End Sub
```

The difference is that the `SpecificBold` routine expects to receive only text boxes. It does not need to resolve the type of object it receives and is therefore more efficient.

This code is contained with a database called `271922.MDB` on this book's Web site in a module called `Sample`.

Use In-Line Code

There is a tendency to call out to procedures for everything. This tendency is good from a maintenance standpoint, but not from an efficiency standpoint. Each time VBA calls out to a procedure, additional time is taken to locate and execute the procedure. This extra time is particularly evident when the procedure is called numerous times. You need to decide how important maintainability is, as compared to speed.

Toggle Booleans Using Not

The following code is very inefficient:

```
If bFlag = True Then
  bFlag = False
Else
    bFlag = True
End If
```

You should modify it to look like this:

```
bFlag = Not bFlag
```

Besides requiring fewer lines of code, this expression evaluates much more quickly at runtime.

Use the Built-In Collections

The built-in collections are available whether or not you use them. By using For
Each...Next and a collection of objects, you can write efficient code. The following is an
example:

```
Sub FormCaption()
    Dim frm As Form
    For Each frm In Forms
        frm.Caption = frm.Caption & " - " & CurrentUser()
    Next
End Sub
```

Here, you are using the Forms collection to loop through each form quickly and efficiently, changing the caption on its title bar.

Use the Len Function

Using the Len function is more efficient than testing for a zero-length string. Here are the
options:

```
Sub SayNameZero(strName As String)
    If strName <> "" Then
        MsgBox strName
    End If
End Sub
```

or

```
Sub SayNameLen(strName As String)
    If Len(strName) Then
        MsgBox strName
    End If
End Sub
```

The second example is easier for VBA to evaluate, and therefore runs more quickly and
efficiently.

Use True and False Instead of Zero

Evaluating for True and False is better than evaluating for zero. Hence, the following
example is similar to the previous one:

```
Sub SaySalaryZero(lngSalary As Long)
    If lngSalary <> 0 Then
        MsgBox "Salary is " & lngSalary
    End If
End Sub
```

The following code runs more efficiently:

```
Sub SaySalaryTrue(lngSalary As Long)
    If lngSalary Then
        MsgBox "Salary is " & lngSalary
    End If
End Sub
```

Use Transactions... Sometimes?

In versions of Access prior to Access 95, transactions dramatically improved performance. Using explicit transactions, the data is written to disk only once, upon the CommitTrans. All changes between a BeginTrans and a CommitTrans are buffered in memory. Because disk access has the slowest throughput on a computer, this technique offered you major performance benefits in versions of Access prior to Access 95. The difference with Access 95 and Access 97 is that the Jet 3.0 and 3.5 engines implicitly buffer transactions. Most of the time, Jet's own transaction handling offers better performance than your own. At other times, you can improve on what Jet does on its own. The only way that you will know for sure is to do your own benchmarking. Each situation is different.

Eliminate Unused Dim and Declare Statements

As you modify your subroutines and functions, you may declare a variable and then never use it. Each Dim statement takes up memory and code space whether or not you're using it. Furthermore, Declare statements, which are used to call external library functions, also take up memory and resources. You should remove them if they're not being used.

Eliminate Unused Code

Most programmers experiment with various alternatives for accomplishing a task. This experimentation often involves creating numerous test subroutines and functions. The problem is that most people don't remove this code when they're done with it. This dead code is loaded with your application and therefore takes up memory and resources. Several third-party tools can help you to find both dead code and variable declarations. One that many people use is Total Access Analyzer by FMS, Inc. The Performance Analyzer, included as part of Access 97, can also assist you with the process of eliminating dead code and variables.

Use Variables to Refer to Properties, Controls, and Data Access Objects

If you're going to refer to an object repeatedly, you should declare the object and refer to the object variable rather than the actual control. Here's an example:

```
Forms!frmAny!txtHello.FontBold = True
Forms!frmAny!txtHello.Enabled = True
Forms!frmAny!txtHello.Left = 1
Forms!frmAny!txtHello.Top = 1
```

The following example is scaled down, but if numerous properties were being changed or if this code were being called recursively, you could use an object variable to make the code more efficient:

```
Private Sub cmdChangeObject_Click()
    Dim txt As TextBox
    Set txt = Forms!frmHello!txtHello1
    txt.FontBold = True
    txt.Enabled = True
    txt.Left = 100
    txt.Top = 100
End Sub
```

Use With…End With

Another way to optimize the code in the preceding example is to use a With…End With construct. The code looks like this:

```
Private Sub cmdChangeObjectWith_Click()
    With Forms!frmHello!txtHello2
        .FontBold = True
        .Enabled = True
        .Left = 100
        .Top = 100
    End With
End Sub
```

Use the Me Keyword

In the preceding example, you used Forms!frmHello!txtHello2 to refer to a control on the current form. Referring to the control as Me!txtHello is more efficient, however, because VBA searches only in the local name space. Although referring to the control this way makes your code more efficient, the downside is that the Me keyword works only within form modules. It does not work within code modules. You therefore cannot include the Me keyword in generic functions that are accessed by all your forms.

Use String Functions When Possible

Many functions come in two forms: one with a dollar sign ($) and one without. An example is `Left(sName)` versus `Left$(sName)`. Using the version with the dollar sign whenever possible is more efficient. Functions with the dollar sign return strings, rather than variants. When a string variable is returned, VBA does not need to perform type conversions.

Use Dynamic Arrays

Array elements take up memory whether they are being used. Therefore, using dynamic arrays is sometimes preferable. You can increase the size of a dynamic array as needed. If you want to reclaim the space used by all the elements of the array, you can use the `Erase` keyword, as follows:

```
Erase aNames
```

If you want to reclaim some of the space being used by the array without destroying data in the elements that you want to retain, use `Redim Preserve`, as follows:

```
Redim Preserve aNames(5)
```

This statement sizes the array to six elements. (It is zero-based.) Data within those six elements is retained.

> **WARNING**
>
> You need to be careful when using dynamic arrays with `Redim Preserve`. When you resize an array using `Redim Preserve`, the entire array is copied into memory. If you're running in a low-memory environment, virtual disk space may be used, slowing performance—or worse than that, the application can fail if both physical and virtual memory are exhausted.

Use Constants Whenever Possible

Constants improve both readability and performance. A constant's value is resolved upon compilation. The value that the constant represents is written to code. A normal variable has to be resolved as the code is running because VBA needs to obtain the current value of the variable.

Use Bookmarks

A bookmark provides you with the most rapid access to a record. If you plan to return to a record, set a variable equal to that record's bookmark. Then returning to that record at any time is easy. Here's an example:

```
Sub BookMarkIt()
    Dim db As DATABASE
    Dim rst As Recordset
    Dim strBM As String

    Set db = CurrentDb()
    Set rst = db.OpenRecordset("tblProjects", dbOpenSnapshot)
    strBM = rst.Bookmark
    Do Until rst.EOF
        Debug.Print rst!ProjectID
        rst.MoveNext
    Loop
    rst.Bookmark = strBM
    Debug.Print rst!ProjectID
End Sub
```

You can find the preceding code in the Sample module of 271922.MDB. The bookmark is stored in a variable before the Do Until loop is executed. After the Do Until loop executes, the recordset's bookmark is set equal to the value contained within the string variable.

Set Object Variables Equal to Nothing

Object variables take up memory and associated resources. Set their value equal to Nothing when you're done using them, as in the following statement. This way, you conserve memory and resources.

```
Set oObj = Nothing
```

Use Action Queries Rather Than Looping Through Recordsets

Besides being easier to code, executing a stored query is more efficient than looping through a recordset, performing some action on each record. Consider the following example:

```
Sub LoopThrough()
    Dim db As DATABASE
    Dim rst As Recordset

    Set db = CurrentDb()
    Set rst = db.OpenRecordset("tblProjects", dbOpenDynaset)
    Do Until rst.EOF
```

```
            rst.Edit
            rst!ProjectTotalEstimate = rst!ProjectTotalEstimate + 1
            rst.UPDATE
            rst.MoveNext
    Loop
End Sub
```

The preceding code, found in the Sample module of 271922.MDB, loops through a record-set, adding one to each project total estimate. Contrast this to the following code:

```
Sub ExecuteQuery()
    Dim db As DATABASE

    Set db = CurrentDb
    db.Execute "qryLowerEstimate"
End Sub
```

This code executes a stored query called qryLowerEstimate. The query runs much more efficiently than the Do Until loop.

Deliver Your Application with the Modules Compiled

Applications run more slowly when they are not compiled. Forms and reports load more slowly, and the application requires more memory. If you deliver your application with all the modules compiled, they do not need to be compiled on the user's machine before they are run.

To recompile all modules easily, choose Debug | Compile and Save All Modules with the Module window active. This command opens and compiles all code in the application, including the code behind forms and reports. It then saves the modules in the compiled state. This action preserves the compiled state of the application.

Retaining the Compiled State

Don't bother choosing Run | Compile All Modules if you plan to make additional changes to the application. An application becomes decompiled whenever the application's controls, forms, reports, or modules are modified. Even something as simple as adding a single control to a form causes the application to lose its compiled state. It is therefore important to choose Debug | Compile and Save All Modules immediately before you distribute the application.

> **WARNING**
>
> Renaming a database file causes the code contained in the database to decompile. Therefore, always choose the Compile and Save All Modules command after renaming a database.

Distribute Your Application as an MDE

The process of creating an MDE file compiles all modules, removes editable source code and compacts the destination database. All Visual Basic code runs but cannot be viewed or edited. Creating this file improves performance, reduces the size of the database, and protects your intellectual property. Memory utilization is also improved.

Organize Your Modules Well

You can theoretically place VBA code in any module within your application. The problem is that a module is not loaded until a function within it is called. After a single procedure in a module is called, the entire module is loaded into memory. Furthermore, if a single variable within a module is used, the entire module is loaded into memory. As you might imagine, if you design your application without much thought, every module in your application will be loaded.

If you place similar routines all in one module, that module is loaded and others are not. This means that if your user is using only part of the functionality of your application, he or she will never load other code modules. This way, you conserve memory and therefore optimize your application.

Designing Forms and Reports to Improve Performance

You can make several changes to forms and reports to improve your application's performance. These changes include techniques to load the forms and reports quickly, tips and tricks regarding OLE objects, and special coding techniques that apply only to forms and reports.

Designing Forms to Improve Performance

Because forms are your main interface to your user, making them as efficient as possible can go a long way toward improving the user's perception of performance within your application. Additionally, many of the form techniques are extremely easy to implement.

Form-optimization techniques can be categorized in two ways: those that make the forms load more quickly, and those that enable you to manipulate objects within the form more efficiently.

The larger the form and the more controls and objects that you have placed on it, the less efficient that form is. Make sure that controls on the form do not overlap. Grouping form data onto logical pages is also extremely beneficial. Grouping is especially important if your user has insufficient video RAM. Objects on subsequent pages should not be populated until the user moves to each page.

Forms and their controls should be based on saved queries. Include only fields required by the form in the form's underlying query. Avoid using `Select *` queries. Because Access is so efficient at internally optimizing the manipulation of query results, this improves the performance of your forms. To further take advantage of the power of queries, reduce the number of records that the query returns, loading only the records you need to at a particular time.

OLE objects take far more resources than images. If an OLE bitmapped object does not need to be changed, convert it to an image. To convert it, click the object and then choose Format | Change To.

Avoid the use of subforms whenever possible. Access treats a subform as a separate form. It therefore takes up significant memory. Make sure that all fields in a subform that are linked to the main form are indexed. If the data in the subform does not need to be edited, set its `AllowEdits`, `AllowAdditions`, and `AllowDeletions` properties to No, or set its `RecordsetType` property to Snapshot.

Make sure that the `RowSource` for a combo box includes only the columns needed for the combo box. Index on the first field that appears in the combo box. Indexing this field has a dramatic effect on the speed with which a user can move to an element of the combo box. Also, whenever possible, make the first visible field of a combo box a text field. Access converts numeric fields to text as it searches through the combo box to find a matching value. Finally, don't base list boxes or combo boxes on linked data if that data rarely, if ever, changes. Instead, make the static table local, updating it whenever necessary.

A general rule regarding the performance of forms is to place all database objects, except data, on each user's machine. This way, you can eliminate the need for Access to constantly pull object definitions over the network.

Close forms that are no longer being used. Open forms take up memory and resources, degrading performance.

22

OPTIMIZING YOUR
APPLICATION

Another tip that can help you to improve the performance of your forms dramatically is to use the default formatting and properties for as many controls as possible. This way, you can significantly improve performance because only the form and control properties that differ from the default properties are saved with the form.

> **TIP**
>
> If the majority of controls have a set of properties that are different from the default control for the form, you should change the default control for the form and then add controls based on the default. Access saves only the properties of the default control and does not need to store the properties for each control placed on the form. This change can result in dramatic performance improvements.

When users watch forms being drawn on the screen, they now perceive that the form is slow. One way to fix this is to make use of the `LockWindowUpdate` API. The declaration for the API is as follows:

```
Declare Function LockWindowUpdate Lib "user32" (ByVal hwndLock As Long)
As Long
```

Then, to make use of this API call, you would send in the form's `hWnd` like this:

```
LockWindowUpdate myForm.hWnd
```

Then you would send in 0 to release the form after you are sure it is fully loaded, like this:

```
LockWindowUpdate 0
```

Finally, eliminate the code module from forms that don't need it. A form without a form module loads more quickly and occupies less disk space. You can still call function procedures from an event property using an expression, or you can navigate your application from the form using hyperlinks. You can remove the module associated with a form by setting the `HasModule` property to No.

Designing Reports to Improve Performance

Many of the report-optimization techniques are the same as the form-optimization techniques. Reducing the number of controls, avoiding overlapping controls, basing reports on queries, and avoiding OLE objects are all techniques that improve the performance of reports as well as forms.

A few additional techniques specifically improve the performance of reports. Eliminate any unnecessary sorting and grouping expressions, and index all fields on which you sort or group. Base subreports on queries rather than on tables, and include only necessary fields in the queries. Make sure that the queries underlying the report are optimized and that you index all fields in the subreport that are linked to the main report.

A special technique that can be used to improve the performance of reports was introduced with Access 95. It involves the No Data event and HasData property. The No Data event is fired when a report is opened, and no data is returned by the record source of the report. The HasData property is used to determine if a report is bound to an empty recordset. If the HasData property of a subreport is False, you can hide the subreport, thereby improving performance.

Summary

The most attractive application can be extremely frustrating to use if its performance is less than acceptable. Because Access itself requires significant resources, you must make your code as lean and efficient as possible.

This chapter focused on several techniques for improving performance. One of the easiest ways to improve performance is to modify the hardware and software environment within which Access operates. The chapter covered how you can improve the performance of your applications dramatically by adding RAM, defragmenting a hard disk, and tuning virtual memory and other settings. The chapter also showed you how you can use the Performance Analyzer to identify problem areas in your application quickly and easily. Finally, the chapter focused on data-design fundamentals, coding techniques, and form- and report-optimization techniques.

By following the guidelines covered in this chapter, you can ensure that you don't inadvertently introduce bottlenecks into your application. Although any one of the suggestions included in this chapter might not make a difference by itself, the combined effect of these performance enhancements can be quite dramatic.

Security

CHAPTER 23

About Access Security

One of the most commonly overlooked features of an Access application is security. I have dissected shrink-wrapped software using the Jet Database Engine, and was able to break into system-level data and view details that I'm sure the developer had no intention of anyone viewing. What if this was corporate salary data or accounts receivable and billable data on a network file server? What if someone broke into a file and discovered that one of his colleagues had received a significant bonus that made his or her 2% raise pale in comparison, disenchanting him and leading to aggressive or passive-aggressive behavior? The fact is that unless a file is truly secure, anyone who can see the file on the network and has the knowledge can break into the database and view the information.

The Access security methods can be classified as direct and indirect security, and they are both equally important. Although this chapter is written primarily for the workgroup user on a local area network (LAN), most security features can be used with a standalone Access database.

Four direct methods of security are available in Access, and for LAN-implemented database files there is an additional, indirect method of security. Each method offers a different level of security, and each can be used independently or combined. Here are the four direct methods:

- Database password
- User-level security
- Database encryption
- Saving the application as an MDE file

Saving the application as a MDE file will not be presented here in detail. However, it is important to note that this is a form of security not for data, but for your design of forms, reports, and modules. See the section "Database Utilities" in Chapter 1, "Essentials for Creating New Databases," for details.

Database encryption is of no real value without one of the other two direct methods of security, since this only makes the file unreadable to a program other than Access.

A form of indirect security is when the database is located on a file server, available to other users via the LAN, and file-level security is applied. By "file-level security," I mean having the network administrator assign rights to the entire directory or database file on the network. These rights might allow the casual user to only read and modify the file without allowing them to copy, rename or delete it. However, the user can still create files (such as the LDB file when the database is opened and was not in use by anyone else prior to opening). Indirect file-level security is equally important to direct Access security using the Database password or user-level security. Why is that? Well, what good is the most secure database if any user on the network can delete the file or inadvertently replace it with an older version?

Plan for Security from the Start

When an Access application is started, one of the most forgotten parts of the development is security. Before you add your first object to the database, it's very important that you have already started planning the security that will be needed for the application.

One of the ways to do this is to have a table that will help you map the users to their groups, and then have another table that will help you map your groups to the objects in the database and to the types of permissions required to the object. When an object is added to the database, you then can map groups to the object, making sure that the users who need access to the object have it. And as a new user is added, you can add the groups to the user as required, making sure that the new user can do the required job in the database.

> **NOTE**
>
> Permissions should be added at a group level and not at a user level. This way, it is easier to add users because you tell the user to be part of this group, and automatically this user has the same permissions that the group has. It's easier to add or remove permissions because you just do it once for the group and not for each user. This in turn makes the application easier to support.

The Database Password

To add a database password, you select Tools | Security | Set Database Password. As shown in Figure 23.1, the Set Database Password dialog box is opened, prompting you for the password and a verification of the password. If you aren't logged onto the database in exclusive mode and you try to set the database password, an error will be displayed, telling you to reopen the database in exclusive mode.

FIGURE 23.1.

Setting the database password.

The level of security offered by a database password is very straightforward—either you know the password and can get into the database, or you don't know it and can't get in. This is the easiest security to implement and the most likely to have problems. One problem is that one user may tell another user, and then that user will tell others, and so on, until you have no security left on the database. The other problem comes about when everyone forgets the password. If you do forget the password, there is no way to recover the database.

If you're going to use replication, you can't use a database password because the synchronization becomes impossible. The calling database has no way to supply the database password. Also, if you try to import or link tables from this database, you will be required to enter the database password. The only other time the user will be prompted for the database password on a linked table is if the database password is changed.

User-Level Security Overview

User-level security for an Access application is always enabled, even if you don't sign into the application. Most users think that the security is turned off because they didn't need to enter a user name and password. In reality, security is on because, by default, Access logs you in as the default user. The default user is the Admin user, who has full permissions. One of the problems you face when setting up user-level security for your application is ensuring that the default user doesn't have permissions to the application.

There are two parts to user-level security: the workgroup file and the database file. The workgroup file maintains all user and group accounts and their passwords, while the database file maintains all of the permissions associated with each object within the database. This way passwords are managed in one place, allowing multiple databases associated with the same workgroup.

By default, when Access is opened, it logs into the default workgroup SYSTEM.MDW as the Admin user with a blank password. The Admin user is a member of the Admins group and the Users group. The SYSTEM.MDW workgroup is the file that is put on your computer during any type of Access installation. This SYSTEM.MDW file contains all groups and user account information. This is also where each user's preferences are stored. So before you add a new user to the database or groups, it's important to either create or join a new workgroup. To do this, you must use the Workgroup Administrator application.

The database file maintains the permissions associated with each object within the database. The idea behind permissions is to allow or disallow a user access to objects that are in the database, or even disallow access to the database itself. Permissions to the database are granted in two ways: to the user or to a group.

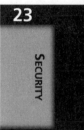

Using the Workgroup Administrator

The Workgroup Administrator application will help you join workgroup files or create them as needed. The first step in using the Workgroup Administrator is to open the application, WRKGADM.EXE. You can do this in two ways. The first method is to run the shortcut, MS Access Workgroup Administrator, in the folder where Microsoft Office is installed (typically, C:\Program Files\Microsoft Office). The second is to run WRKGADM.EXE directly. WRKGADM.EXE is located in the Windows\System directory. The Microsoft Installation program does not create an icon in the Start menu for this program. With this tool, you can join an existing workgroup or create a new workgroup.

Creating a New Workgroup

To create your own workgroup, carry out the following steps:

1. Now that Workgroup Administrator is open, click the Create button to open the Workgroup Owner Information dialog box. This dialog box is shown in Figure 23.2 with all information entered.

FIGURE 23.2.

The Workgroup Owner Information dialog box.

2. The first piece of information required goes into the Name text box. Enter your name here. The maximum is 39 alphanumeric characters.

3. The next text box is Organization. Enter the company name in this box. Again, the maximum is 39 alphanumeric characters.

4. Workgroup ID is the last piece of required information. Enter the ID, keeping in mind that the Workgroup ID is case-sensitive. The maximum is 20 alphanumeric characters.

5. Click OK.

6. The next prompt is the Workgroup Information File dialog box. Indicate the name of the workgroup and where to save it. If you aren't sure of the location, you can

click Browse and use the Select Workgroup Information File Locator to locate where you want to have your new workgroup created.

NOTE

The information used here to create the new workgroup file should be saved in a safe place in case you ever need to create a new workgroup file.

WARNING

Don't save the workgroup file with the same name as the application. Use a different extension, because Access must be capable of opening both the database file and the workgroup file. If the files are the same name when the application is opened, Access tries to create a .LDB file for both the Access database and the workgroup file. When it tries to create these files, you receive an "Error: unable to create file" message, and Access can't open the database.

For example, say that you have a database called Accounts.MDB, and you name the workgroup file Accounts.MDW. When Access is opened, it creates an Accounts.LDB file. Then, when the database Accounts.MDB is opened, Access tries to create another Accounts.LDB. It can't, though, because it will have a write conflict when it tries to use Accounts.LDB. The .LDB file is the Lock File that Access creates to keep track of who has what record locked. It defaults the file to *filename*.LDB. When the database is closed, it also removes all .LDB files for you. It's also suggested that you do not take the default setting, because it will overwrite the default SYSTEM.MDW that came with Access.

---

7. After you have entered the new workgroup name or path, click OK.

8. The dialog box shown in Figure 23.3 opens, prompting you to confirm the information you just entered. Click Change if you want to change any information.

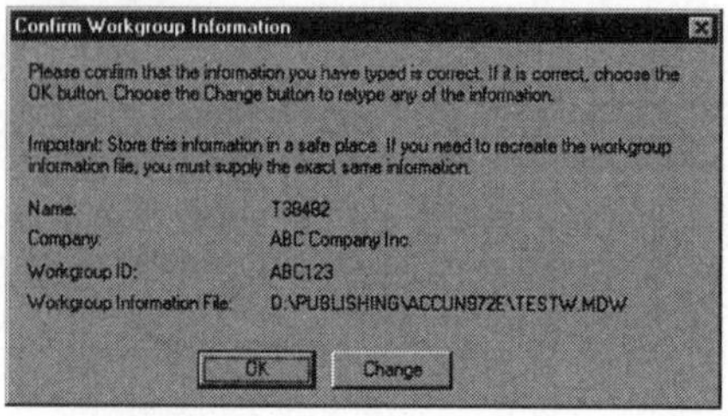

FIGURE 23.3.

The Confirm Workgroup Information dialog box.

9. Click OK to create the workgroup file. If the file already exists, you're prompted to confirm the overwrite of the existing workgroup file. When the file has been created, a confirmation dialog box is displayed, informing you that the workgroup was created.

10. Now you are back at the Workgroup Administrator dialog. Notice that the current default workgroup is the new workgroup just created. Click Exit to close this dialog and accept the new workgroup as the default workgroup for Access.

Joining an Existing Workgroup

If you have created a workgroup file, the next step is to have the users of the database application join this workgroup. First, open the Workgroup Administrator. Next, click the Join button to display the Workgroup Information File dialog box, shown in Figure 23.4.

FIGURE 23.4.

The Workgroup Information File dialog box.

In this dialog box, you can enter the path of the workgroup. This can be a drive letter, folder names, and filename, or it can be a network share name such as this:

\\MachineName\ShareName\Directory\WorkgroupName.mdw

If you aren't sure of the workgroup name and location, click the Browse button. This selection brings up the File Locator dialog box, which enables you to navigate your way through drives, folders, and network shares. When you have located your workgroup file, select it and then click OK. If you use a share name, rather than a physical drive or network drive that has been already connected to your machine, it's important to remember that this share name can never change unless you change each user's workgroup share information to reflect it.

> **NOTE**
>
> If you change the default workgroup by using the Workgroup Administrator to join an existing workgroup or a new workgroup, Access will always use this workgroup when opened, unless told otherwise by a command-line argument or switch.
>
> *continues*

23

SECURITY

You may not want a secured workgroup as your default workgroup. I prefer to keep the SYSTEM.MDW in the Windows\System directory as the default. Then, I keep each client's workgroup file in a project or company directory and log on to them as needed, using shortcuts and the Access command line switch /wrkgrp. The Target line for such a shortcut might look like this:

```
"C:\Program Files\Microsoft Office\Office\MSACCESS.EXE"
/wrkgrp "D:\Company X\Project Z\ProjZw.MDW"
/user John Doe
```

Running this shortcut would run Access and prompt you with the login dialog and John Doe as the user. You could add in the /pwd switch to the target, like /pwd Rumpelstiltskin. However, you may not want your password to a secured database buried in a shortcut, where anyone can view it.

User and Group Accounts

To do anything with users or groups, you first must open the User and Group Accounts dialog box, shown in Figure 23.5. To open this dialog box from within Access, select Tools | Security | User and Group Accounts.

FIGURE 23.5.

The User and Group Accounts dialog box.

In this dialog box, you can add new users, delete a user, add new groups, delete a group, add a user to a group, remove a user from a group, change the password for the current user, or clear a user's password.

Adding and Deleting Users

To add or delete a user, you must be a member of the Admins group. To add a user, follow these steps:

1. Click the New button.

2. In the dialog box that appears, enter the user name and personal ID. If you're on a network, it's suggested that you use the user's login name from the network. Otherwise, make sure that the name is unique for each user of the workgroup. Also be sure to use a unique personal ID.

3. Click OK.

To delete a user, follow these steps:

1. Select the user from the User list box. Transfer ownership of any objects the user may own to a new owner.

2. Remove all permissions from the user, either direct permissions or those implied through group membership. That is, remove the user from all groups (except Users, which cannot be removed), and then remove any permissions granted directly to the user.

3. Click the Delete button.

4. A Confirmation dialog box appears, making sure that you really want to delete the currently selected user. If you're sure, click Yes; otherwise, click No.

You're then returned to the dialog box shown in Figure 23.5.

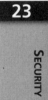

> **TIP**
>
> Follow common guidelines for creating a secure and unique personal ID. At minimum, use a mix of alphanumeric characters to create a string that isn't an actual word.

Adding and Deleting Groups

To add or delete a group, the first step is to click on the Groups tab, shown at the top of Figure 23.5. To add a group, follow these steps:

1. Click the New button.

2. Enter the new group name and personal ID for the group.

3. Click OK.

You're returned to the screen shown in Figure 23.5, and the active group is the group you just entered.

To delete a group, follow these steps:

1. Transfer ownership of any objects the group may own to a new owner.
2. Remove all permissions from the group.
3. Select the group you want to delete from the group list box.
4. Click the Delete button.
5. A confirmation dialog box appears, making sure that you really want to delete the currently selected group. If you're sure, click Yes; otherwise, click No.

You're then returned to the dialog box shown in Figure 23.5.

> **NOTE**
>
> When you're adding a new user or group, the name must be unique. You can't have a group and a user with the same name. If you do, a "Microsoft Access Account name already exists" message is displayed, and you're returned to the screen shown in Figure 23.5 after clicking OK.

> **NOTE**
>
> Deleting accounts (user or group) requires more rigor than creating accounts, if done properly. When an account is deleted, the associated security ID (SID) is also deleted in the workgroup. However, those permissions remain in all of the databases using this workgroup that have permissions assigned to that SID. The preceding strategy is to remove all implicit and explicit permissions prior to deleting the account. The database doesn't know the SID no longer exists. Therefore, if the same SID can be recreated by knowing the personal ID (PID) and user or group information, that new SID would have all the rights of the old one.

Adding or Removing a User from a Group

It's important to remember that not all users will belong to the same groups. So after you have added the groups, it's time to tell the users what group or groups they are members of. First, click on the Users tab if you aren't there already. To add a user to a group, you then carry out the following steps:

1. Select the user you want to work with from the User list box.

2. In the Group Membership area, click on a group in the Available Groups list box and then click the Add button. This adds the user to the currently selected group.

To remove a user from a group, carry out the following steps:

1. Select the user you want work with from the User list box.

2. In the Group Membership area, click on a group in the Member Of list box and then click the Remove button. This removes the user from the currently selected group.

> **NOTE**
>
> A user cannot be deleted from the Users group using the Access user interface to Jet security. Using DAO, a user can be programmatically removed from the Users group, or never added to this group upon creation of the user. However, they will not be able to log on to the database using the Access UI.

Changing Your Logon Password

To change your password, you need to click on the Change Logon Password tab. Here you're required to enter the following three pieces of information:

- The old password
- The new password
- A verification of the new password

If the old password doesn't match the current password, you can't change the password. Nor can you change it if the new password and the verify password don't match. After you have typed the old, new, and verify passwords, you can click either Apply or OK. The Apply button leaves you at the screen shown in Figure 23.5, and the OK button returns you to Access.

Clearing a User Password

To clear a user password, the first step is to make sure that you're on the Users tab. Then select the user from the User list box, and click the Clear Password button. Before clicking the Clear Password button, make sure that you've selected the correct user because there is no confirmation—the password is just reset.

NOTE

If you aren't a member of the Admins group, the only available option is Change Logon Password.

WARNING

If you clear the Admin user's password, you will no longer be required to sign into the database, unless you logon via command line switches; all users will be entering the application as Admin and will have the permissions granted to the Admin user. If the Admin user was not removed from the Admins group, this effectively eliminates security. On the other hand, this would give the casual user access to the level of permissions assigned to the Admin user, while for the true administration users a command line logon would be required, giving them greater security access to the database.

User and Group Permissions

After you have added the users and their groups, it's time to define the permissions that these groups or users will have on the objects in the database. To do this, you must be signed in as a member of the Admins group. After you're in the database, you need to open the dialog box shown in Figure 23.6 by selecting Tools I Security I User and Group Permissions. This dialog box has two tabs: Permissions and Change Owner.

FIGURE 23.6.

The User and Group Permissions dialog box with the Permissions tab active.

The Permissions tab is the active tab shown in Figure 23.6. This tab has three components. The first is the User/Group Name area, which contains a list of users or groups, depending on which List option button is active. The second is an Object Name list box, which is composed of all objects that match the object type currently selected in the Object Type combo box. The Object Name list box is a multiselect list box, meaning that you can select more than one object in the list at a time. To do this, hold down the Shift or Ctrl key while selecting the objects with the mouse. The third component is the Permissions area, with the permissions for the currently selected user or group and the selected object.

Following is a step-by-step process for changing the permissions on an object in the database:

1. Select the user or group from the User/Group Name list box. If you want to change from a user list to a group list, click the List option button named Groups.

2. Select the object from the Object Name list box. To change the list to a different type of object, click the arrow at the side of the Object Type combo box and select the object for which you want to change the permissions.

3. Based on the type of object and the user or group selected, the Permissions check boxes fill in automatically. To add or remove a permission manually, click on the corresponding Permissions check box.

4. Either click Apply, which applies the permissions without prompting for confirmation, or select a new object. If you select a new object, you're prompted as to whether you want to apply your changes. If you have made a change and you try to close the dialog box or try select a new object, a Change dialog box appears, asking whether you want to save the permissions changes.

Different permissions are available for each object type in the database, depending on the active object type. The following list gives you some notes to remember when trying to turn on or off permissions on a Table object:

- If you mark any of the data options—Read Data, Update Data, Insert Data, or Delete Data—Read Design is selected by default.

- If you select any data option other than Read Data, Read Data is selected by default.

- If you deselect Read Data, all other data options and design options are turned off, except for Read Design.

- If you select Modify Design, the Read Data, Update Data, and Delete Data options are selected by default.

- If you select Administer, all design and data options are selected by default.

The following list gives you some notes to remember when trying to turn on or off permissions on a Queries object:

- If you mark any of the data options—Read Data, Update Data, Insert Data, or Delete Data—Read Design is selected by default.
- If you select any data option other than Read, Read Data is selected by default.
- If you deselect Read Data, all other data options and design options are turned off, except Read Design.
- You can select Read Design with all or none of the data options.
- If you select Administer, all design and data options are selected automatically.

For Form objects, four permissions options are available:

- If you select Open/Run, the user or group can open and run the form.
- If you select Read Design, the user or member of a group can view the form design.
- If you select Modify Design, the user or member of the group can make changes and delete the form.
- If you select Administer, all permissions are selected automatically.

For Report objects, four permissions options are available:

- If you select Open/Run, the user or group can open and run the report.
- If you select Read Design, the user or member of a group can view the report design.
- If you select Modify Design, the user or member of the group can make changes and delete the report.
- If you select Administer, all other permissions are selected automatically.

For Macro objects, four permissions options are available:

- If you select Open/Run, the user or group can open and run the macro.
- If you select Read Design, the user or member of a group can view the macro design.
- If you select Modify Design, the user or member of the group can view, make changes to, and delete the macros.
- If you select Administer, all other permissions are selected automatically.

For Module objects, three permissions options are available:

- If you select Read Design, the user or member of a group can view the module design.
- If you select Modify Design, the user or member of the group can make changes and delete the module.
- If you select Administer, all other permissions are selected automatically.

The last database object you can set permissions on is the database itself. To do this, select Database from the Object Type list box. Notice that in the list of object names, only one option is available: Current Database. Also, only three permissions options are available:

- If you select Open/Run, the user or member of the group can open and run the database.
- If you select Open Exclusive, the user or member of the group can open the database exclusively. If you want to make sure that no user opens the database exclusively, this is the best way to do it.
- If you select Administer, all other permissions are selected automatically.

If a group needs to be able to open the database to use forms and run reports, these are the minimum permissions you need to give this group:

- Tables—The group needs Read/Design and Read Data to be selected, or else forms and reports won't be able to open.
- Queries—The group needs Read Design and Read Data to be selected for the queries to operate.
- Forms—For the forms to be opened by the group, Open/Run needs to be selected.
- Reports—For the reports to be run or printed, Open/Run needs to be selected.
- Macros—If any macros will be run by the forms or reports or on open, Open/Run needs to be selected.
- Modules—You need not select anything for the modules to function correctly.
- Database—The group needs to have Open/Run selected, or else the group's users won't be able to open the database.

Ownership

Figure 23.7 shows the User and Group Permissions dialog box with the active tab set to Change Owner. The Change Owner tab has three components. The first part is the Object and Current Owner list box. This area derives its list from the Object Type combo box, whose default is Form. The second part is the New Owner combo box, which is derived from the List item that is selected (either Users or Groups). The last part is the Change Owner button. This button takes the currently selected object and changes the owner to the selected New Owner. If you have permissions to change the owner, the object is updated to the new owner; otherwise, an Error dialog box appears, indicating that you can't change the owner of this object.

Three buttons are available to select here: the OK and Cancel buttons, which return you to the screen shown in Figure 23.5, and the Help button, which opens Help and gives you some information on how to fix the problem. You can change all objects in the database this way, except for the actual owner of the database. There is no way to change the owner of a database, other than creating a new database and importing the other objects from the original database into the new one.

FIGURE 23.7.

The User and Group Permissions dialog box with the Change Owner tab active.

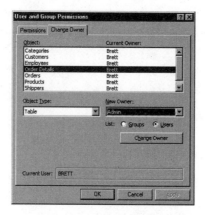

The following process explains how to change the owner of a database, if the intended workgroup is the same as the workgroup of the database to be imported. (If the workgroup needs to be different, see the section on removing security.)

1. Start Access using the New Owner, and create a new database.

2. Select File | Get External Data | Import.

3. In this dialog box, first make sure that the File of Type box is set to Microsoft Access. Then navigate through the folders until you locate the database for which you want to change the owner. Select the database and then click OK.

4. Make sure that you select all objects under each of the six tabs. Notice the Options button within this dialog. By default, the table relationships will be imported.

However, menus and toolbars will not be imported, nor will import/export specifications. If applicable, you may want these items to be imported, too.

5. Click OK.

The dialog box changes from the list of objects to the status of the import. For more details on how to import and export data, refer to Chapter 2, "Using Alternate Data Sources." When you're finished importing all the objects, you have successfully changed the database owner.

> **NOTE**
>
> When you're assigning ownership of objects, it's possible to assign the ownership to groups. But the database object must always be assigned to a user.

The Security Wizard

To run the Security Wizard, you select Tools | Security | User-Level Security Wizard. But before you do this, it's important to open Access as the new Admin user of a secured workgroup, created with a non-blank Workgroup ID. The reason is that the new database will be created using the current user as the owner. After you have signed in as the new Admin user for the database and have opened the Security Tool, the dialog box shown in Figure 23.8 is opened, prompting you for which objects you want to secure in the new database.

FIGURE 23.8.

The User-Level Security Wizard dialog box.

> **NOTE**
>
> The User-Level Security Wizard creates a new database and doesn't affect the current database.

23

SECURITY

After you have selected the objects that you want to be secured, click OK. If you want more information on the process, click the Help button. The Cancel button returns you to the Database window. If you didn't sign in as the new Admin user, but as Admin, the message shown in Figure 23.9 is displayed.

FIGURE 23.9.

The User-Level Security Wizard's Admin warning dialog box.

This dialog box tells you that the database can't be successfully secured when you're signed in as user Admin. You can carry on, but the database won't be secured the way that the User-Level Security Wizard is designed to secure it. It's suggested that you sign out and then sign in again as the new Admin user. Otherwise, the Destination Database dialog box shows up next and wants to know the new name for the secured database. The default name is Secure + *DatabaseName*.MDB. After you have entered the new database name and its new location, click the Save button. If you watch the Status bar, you can see the progress as the database is secured. When the secured database has been created, the dialog box shown in Figure 23.10 is displayed.

FIGURE 23.10.

The User-Level Security Wizard acknowledgment dialog box.

This dialog box announces that your new database has been created successfully. If you acknowledge the dialog box by clicking OK, you're returned to the UnSecure Database window.

Database Encryption

After you have secured the database, you can take one more step to make sure that no user can view its data. That step is to encrypt the database so that it can't be read by a utility program or a word processor application. A database that's undergoing encryption or decryption cannot be open. You can encrypt and decrypt a database with or without another database being open, but the open database cannot be the encrypted or decrypted.

I highly recommend that you close all databases first and then encrypt or decrypt them. To do this, follow these steps:

1. Open Access without any databases being open.

2. Open the Encrypt Tool by selecting Tools | Security | Encrypt/Decrypt database.

3. The Encrypt/Decrypt Database Locator dialog box opens. Navigate through folders on your local machine or network share until you locate the database you want to encrypt or decrypt, and select that database.

4. Click OK.

5. The Encrypt Database dialog box appears. Type the new database name and the location in which to save it. I suggest that you do not delete the original, in case something goes wrong with the new database.

6. Click OK.

> **NOTE**
>
> Only members of the Admins group or the database owner can encrypt or decrypt a database, and no users can be using the database.

After the encryption process has finished, you're returned to Access. If you want to decrypt a database, you follow the same steps, except that you're prompted for the decrypt database name rather than the encrypt database name in step five of the preceding six-step process.

A Walkthrough of Securing a Database

To secure your database using user-level security, follow these steps:

1. Create a new workgroup using the Workgroup Administrator Tool. Be sure the Workgroup ID is populated and that it is not something simple. Save this information on paper and keep it in a safe place.

2. Open Access using this new workgroup, signing in as Admin user.

3. Open the database you're securing.

4. Add a new Admin user. I suggest that you use a name convention like *Application Name* + Admin.

5. Add the Admins group to the new Admin user.

6. Change the Admin password. This change will force you to sign in the next time you open Access.

7. Change Users group permissions to be No Run/Open, No Open Exclusive, and No Administer on the Database Object. To be extra conservative, you could remove all rights from all objects for the Users group.

WARNING

Any user of a database that has Open/Run permissions can create new tables, queries, forms, reports, macros, or modules. So if you leave the Users group with Open/Run on the database, the Admin user can open your secured database and create any new object he wants. The creator retains administrator privileges on this new object. For a secure database, make sure that the Users group has no permissions on that database.

---

8. Close Access.

9. Reopen Access, this time signing in as the new Admin user.

10. Open the database you're securing.

11. Run Security Wizard on the database, making sure that you select all objects in the first dialog box.

12. When the Security Wizard has finished, close Access again.

13. Reopen Access, this time signing in as the new Admin user.

14. Open the database you're securing.

15. Remove the Admins group for the Admin user. This action ensures that any user who opens that database without using the correct workgroup file can't see any of the database objects.

16. Add the groups that will be required for the database.

17. Add all users to their correct groups.

18. Assign permissions to the groups as required.

19. As new objects are added, add or remove the permissions as required.

Removing Security

The first step of creating a user-level secured database is creating the unique workgroup and a non-blank workgroup ID. The final step in removing Jet security is to import the database objects into a database owned by the admin user, with a workgroup file having a blank workgroup ID. Before this can be done, though, the database must be unlocked to the Users group.

To remove the security of a database or transfer a secured database of one workgroup to another workgroup, do the following:

1. Backup your secured database or copy it to a temporary file for this conversion process.

2. Open the database, logging on as the database owner or a member of the Admins group.

3. For the database object, grant the Users group at least Open/Run permission; for all table objects, grant the Users group at least Read Design and Read Data permissions; and for all other objects of interest, grant the Users group at least Read Design permissions.

4. Close this session of Access.

5. Reopen Access using the either the default SYSTEM.MDW or some other secured workgroup that you want this database transferred to, and log on as the user you want to be the owner of this new database. If you want to remove security and not transfer it to a different workgroup, log on as the Admin user.

6. Create a new database and import all of the objects from the temporary database into this new database. This is done using the File|Get External Data|Import command.

7. If the security of this database were being transferred to a different workgroup, the appropriate permissions for all objects would need to be assigned.

Jet Security Through Other Programming Interfaces

Access is just one method of interfacing with the Jet database engine. Other development tools can use it very successfully as well. These tools include Visual Basic, Delphi, PowerBuilder, and many others. Jet security is the same, no matter what interface is used.

The user interface provided by Access for security features is very functional. I have found no reason to attempt to re-create the functionality provided by Access in some other language for the purpose of developing the security for a particular workgroup and database. At most, I have found the need to only develop an interface to manage users and groups; specifically, the ability to create new users and add them to, or delete them from, existing groups. For the more serious security maintenance activities, I will use Access to log on to the workgroup and database and perform the tasks. All of the functionality Access provides can be programmed, but I just have not found a reason to do so.

If you do use a development tool other than Access, you will find this section invaluable and not readily documented. In Listing 23.1, you see what it takes to log on to a secured database and workgroup using DAO in a programming tool other than Access. This code is specifically for Visual Basic, and the DAO Object Library must be referenced.

Listing 23.1. Example log on function for a Jet database.

```
Option Explicit
  Dim dbe As PrivDBEngine
  Dim wsp As Workspace
  Dim db As Database

Function bolLogon(strUserName As String, strPassword As String) As Boolean

  ' This function returns True if the log on was successful
  '    and False otherwise.

  On Error GoTo ErrorHandler
  Dim intResponse As Integer

  Set dbe = New PrivDBEngine

  'Associate the database engine with the desired workgroup
  dbe.SystemDB = "C:\CompanyXX\ProjZw.mdw"

  On Error Resume Next

  Set wsp = dbe.CreateWorkspace("WorkgroupXX", strUserName, strPassword)
  Set db = wsp.OpenDatabase("C:\CompanyXX\ProjZ.mdb")

  If Err Then
    intResponse = MsgBox( _
      "Incorrect Password, User ID, or you are not a registered user." & _
      "Please try again.", vbOKOnly, "Login Failure")
    GoTo ErrorHandler
  End If

  On Error GoTo ErrorHandler

  ' Other Processing............
  ' Other Processing............
  ' Other Processing............
```

```
    bolLogon = True
    Exit Function

ErrorHandler:

    bolLogon = False
End Function
```

The key to Listing 23.1 is the `PrivDBEngine` object, a copy of the top-level `DBEngine` object. If you used the `DBEingine` object, you would find that attempting the line `dbe.SystemDB = "C:\CompanyXX\ProjZw.mdw"` would be useless, and the value of `dbe.SystemDB` would still be set to the default after execution of this line of code.

Summary

Security is often neglected as an aspect of database and workgroup administration. This chapter has armed the administrator (and user) with information on creating workgroups and adding users to them. Creating users and assigning user permissions and passwords were detailed. The coverage of the User-Level Security Wizard and database encryption showed additional methods for adding security features to Access applications. Finally, Jet database security through other programming interfaces was introduced.

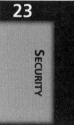

23

SECURITY

Implementing Web Publishing

PART VIII

Configuring a
Web Site for
Access

CHAPTER 24

Whether you are publishing real-time data to a Web site or using static HTML pages, one thing is for sure—you need a Web site. You also need one in order to publish Access 97 data so that others can see it. Web sites come in many flavors: intranet sites, World Wide Web sites, personal home page directories on a host, and local computer HTML publishing. Having a Web site also requires a Web server. This chapter discusses how to prepare your Web site and Web server for Web database publishing with Microsoft Access 97. If you do not have access to a Web site and still want to practice Web database publishing, you can use the Personal Web Server that is included with Office 97 and FrontPage 97/98, and is also available free on the Internet.

> **NOTE**
>
> There are many Internet Service Providers (ISPs) that support Access 97-based Web Publishing and Active Server Pages. Browse the Web and check them out.

If you have no control over the Web server you will be using, you should still read this chapter so you will know the limitations and capabilities of the server. If you are a database developer, a Web administrator will probably take care of the most basic configuration issues (like setup), so we will not discuss the basic configuration here at any great length.

Deciding What Type of Server to Use for Web Database Publishing

There are many types of Web servers out there. We will be discussing why to use certain types of servers in this section, including:

- Non-Microsoft Web servers
- Personal Web Server
- Peer Web services
- Internet Information Server 3.0/4.0

Using Non-Microsoft Web Servers

Publishing your Access 97 data on a Web site can be done on any Web server. You can use an online service like AOL that gives you several megabytes for HTML pages, or an ISP to give you a "Virtual Server."

If you just have a directory on someone else's server, you are limited to publishing static HTML documents. There is no configuration to be done to your Web site, except creating the HTML pages that will link to your Access-generated HTML pages.

To publish static HTML pages, have Access 97 generate the HTML for you (as we will discuss in Chapter 25, "Using Access 97 with Static HTML Pages"). All you have to do after you create your pages is upload them to your directory on the Web server. People have told me that when they use a non-Microsoft Web server through a dial-up account, they can't use Access databases for real-time Web publishing. Even though you cannot use 100% real-time publishing, some degree of automation can be performed. You can automate the export of HTML pages from Microsoft Access and then use the Internet Transfer ActiveX Control (ITC) to transfer the files to your server. The process of sending the files to your server can be automated on a timer from within Access.

To use the ITC, make sure you have a license for it. (A license comes with Visual Basic 5.0 or Office 97 Developers' Edition.) Then all you have to do is drop the ITC onto a form with a timer and leave the database open with a connection to the Internet or your intranet. You will have to use the POST action of the ITC. Listing 24.1 shows POST in action.

LISTING 24.1. USING THE POST ACTION OF THE ITC.

```
With ActiveXITC
    .URL=" ref hyperlink "ftp://ftp.nycaccessvb.com"
ftp:\\ftp.accessvb.com"
    .UserName="Stevef"
    .Password="password"
    .Execute , "DIR"   ' Will return the current directory
    .Execute , "POST" "C:\accessdocs\default.htm
    .Execute, "Close"
End With
```

Listing 24.1 uses an ITC ActiveX control named ActiveXITC and sets the URL property to the desired FTP address. Next the username and password are entered. Listing 24.1 then uses the Execute method of the ITC three times: first to return the current directory, next to POST a document to the FTP site, and lastly to close. Although this is a very basic example, you can easily turn it into a very useful automated procedure. Attaching this code to a timer event after some code to generate HTML pages to a location on your hard drive, can simplify automated FTP transmissions. (See the next chapter for a discussion of the OutputTo method.)

If you have access to your Web server, but it is not a Microsoft Windows Web server, you can still use Access 97 with Web publishing. Using a non-Microsoft Web server will currently make Active Server pages and the Internet Database Connector unavailable

24

CONFIGURING A WEB SITE FOR ACCESS

You cannot use the techniques described in this book, so you will have to use the Common Gateway Interface (CGI) approach. The CGI approach is very difficult for the database developer because users change their minds very often, and you have to change the code in CGI scripts manually. Because Active Server Pages and IDC support is built right into Access 97, a non-Windows Web server is not recommended at this time.

Although the advanced features discussed in the later chapters of this book are not available, you can write a CGI script to fetch data from an Access 97 database. Access will not run on a non-Windows machine, so the database will have to reside on a Windows NT machine on the network. The database will also have to be set up as an ODBC system data source, and your script will need to use ODBC to fetch the data and generate an HTML page.

Personal Web Server

If you want to produce some low-volume Web sites that will be displayed locally, over an intranet, or even over the Internet with Windows 95, the Personal Web Server is your natural choice. It's also a great tool for learning Web database publishing. All the material presented in this book can be used and tested using the Windows 95 Personal Web Server. The Personal Web Server can:

- Publish Web pages on the Internet, an intranet, or a LAN by using the HTTP service.

- Include support for ActiveX controls (IE 3.0 and later is required to view ActiveX controls).

- Provide an FTP site for you.

- Give you access to the Internet Server API (ISAPI), allowing you to use Active Server Pages and the Internet Database Connector.

- Use Secure Sockets Layer.

As long as you have a network connection and TCP/IP installed, you can use the Personal Web Server. If you are using the Personal Web Server on a standalone machine that's not hooked up to any network, PWS will install TCP/IP for you as part of its installation. You may already have the Personal Web Server installed on your machine. To check for it, open Control Panel and look for Personal Web Server, as shown in Figure 24.1. Some versions of Windows include the Personal Web Server, and some Microsoft products include it on their installation CDs.

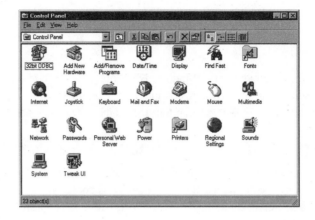

FIGURE 24.1.
Windows 95 Control Panel, showing that the Personal Web Server is set up.

If you are just starting out and have no access to a Web server, the Personal Web Server is the best choice. If you have access to Windows NT or need to publish large-volume sites over the Internet, Personal Web Server is not the best option.

> **WARNING**
>
> If you install Microsoft Personal Web Server 4.0, which is compatible with IIS 4.0, you will lose the ability to use FTP Server.

Obtaining Personal Web Server

If you do not have Personal Web Server installed on your machine, getting it is easy. The FrontPage 97 and Office 97 CD-ROMs have the Personal Web Server setup files, and you can find them on the Internet at

```
http://www.microsoft.com
```

Peer Web Services

Peer Web Services is a superset of Personal Web Server and runs only on Windows NT Workstation 4.0. In addition to all the benefits the Personal Web Server provides, Peer Web Services includes the following:

- Remote administration
- Capability to use pass-through security with Windows NT Server and Novell NetWare

- Capability to use local-user security if Microsoft file- and print-sharing are not installed

- Gopher services

Peer Web Services is included with Windows NT Workstation 4.0. If you plan to do low-level Web publishing, or are just interested in learning the material in this book and use Windows NT Workstation 4.0, Peer Web Services is the server for you.

Microsoft Internet Information Server 3.0

Just over two years old, Microsoft's Internet Information Server (IIS) is already the most popular Web server for commercial Internet sites. IIS is chosen over its bitter rival Netscape Enterprise Server by a ratio of over 4 to 1. (Source: Netcraft Web Server Survey at http://www.netcraft.com.) On the intranet scene, IIS has a complete dominance over Netscape and Lotus Domino.

After Microsoft made version 1.0 of IIS available in February 1996, over 50,000 people downloaded it in the first two months, an unprecedented number for a Web server. Version 2.0 was included with Windows NT Server version 4.0. In the three months after version 3.0 was made available in December 1996, over 150,000 people downloaded it. IIS Version 4.0 is an add-on to NT 4.0 via the NT 4.0 Option Pack, and is supposed to be included with Windows NT 5.0. If your Web site is currently using Windows NT, you will want to use the most current version of IIS. If you're going to be responsible for tasks other than those discussed in this chapter, or if you're looking for a more complete reference to IIS, make sure to read the documentation included with IIS after installing. Documentation is displayed in HTML format, as shown in Figure 24.2.

IIS's competition uses CGI. CGI scripts are programs that must be called and executed each time they are called. That means each time a CGI program is called, a separate instance of the program has to run on the server! This approach is not too efficient on a big Web site. IIS exposes its API, ISAPI, as an in-process DLL. IIS and ISAPI are known for high performance because when IIS is loaded, it loads the DLLs into memory and simply creates a new thread in the same address space for each subsequent client request. Because the DLL is already running, IIS is much faster. In addition, ISAPI is assessable like any standard Windows API call. If you are familiar with Microsoft Windows programming with VBA, Visual Basic, or C++, you will feel right at home using ISAPI.

If you are running a high-volume site from Windows NT, Microsoft IIS is for you. IIS is part of the Windows NT operating system as of version 2.0. Because Microsoft built NT and IIS, all of the new developments discussed in this book, like Active Server Pages and the Internet Database Connector, work with IIS.

FIGURE 24.2.

IIS's documenta-tion.

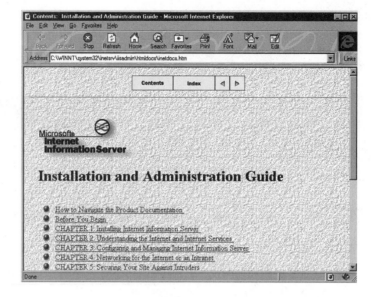

Obtaining IIS

IIS 2.0 is part of Windows NT Server 4.0. To upgrade, you need NT Service Pack 1a or later and the most recent version of IIS, located at

`http://www.microsoft.com/iis`

To upgrade to IIS Version 4.0, you will want to obtain the NT 4.0 Option Pack, which includes the following:

- Microsoft IIS 4.0
- Microsoft Personal Web Server 4.0
- Microsoft Transaction Server 2.0
- Microsoft Message Queue Server 1.0
- Microsoft Virtual Meeting

Registered users of NT 4.0 can download the Option Pack for free or can order the CD for $99 from Microsoft's Web site.

24

CONFIGURING A
WEB SITE FOR
ACCESS

Which Web Server to Use?

By now you should have some idea of which Web server is the best to suit your needs. If you are using just static HTML pages, a non-Microsoft Web server is fine. If you are de-pendent on an ISP, use Personal Web Server and just upload the files via FTP or FrontPage. If you are running a full-blown Web site yourself, you need to use

IIS 3.0 or 4.0. Although we recommend IIS 4.0, there are one or two differences between IIS 3.0 and 4.0. You will need a further understanding of dynamic Web publishing with IDC and ASP technology, discussed in Chapter 26, "Publishing Dynamic Web Pages," before you decide.

> **NOTE**
>
> The examples in this book use IIS 3.0 and PWS 2.0 because we consider them the least common denominator and largest installed base.

Understanding the Structure of a Web Site

Your Web site is located on a Web server, which controls all aspects of the site. Web site administration can be broken down into three parts:

- Directories
- Logging
- Services

There are other issues that come into play when you are talking about Web sites, such as domains, IP addresses, and security. If you are setting up a Web server on a test machine for development and testing only, you do not need to be concerned with IP addresses and security. If you are working on a public site, however, you will need an administrator.

This chapter assumes that you will have a site administrator who is separate from the database administrator. The information presented here will give you a working knowledge of Web sites so you can configure an existing Web site or check that your site was configured correctly for Web database publishing. This chapter makes no assumptions about your knowledge of Web servers and will also help the programmer new to Web servers set up Personal Web Server or a test IIS server in a short time.

> **NOTE**
>
> All of the examples in this book will be done on Personal Web Server running Windows 95 to demonstrate that the lowest common denominator, Personal

Web Server, has the same power as IIS. This book also has a Web site, located at http://www.orcs.com/access97, where you can see the examples from Chapter 26 in action. The Web site uses IIS 3.0. To prove that you can learn everything on Personal Web Server, all I did was copy the files from my local computer running Personal Web Server to the computer running the Web site using IIS, with no modification.

Directories

Each Web site is made up of directories consisting of files and subdirectories. The directories and files that make up your Web site may be located on the same physical machine that the Web server is on, or they may be located on another server on the network.

When you install your Web server, it will create a default directory on your hard drive, usually called INetPup or WebShare. Within that directory will be a root directory for FTP and World Wide Web services. The default name is WWWRoot. Figure 24.3 shows WWWRoot on my machine in Windows Explorer.

FIGURE 24.3.

The WWWRoot *directory.*

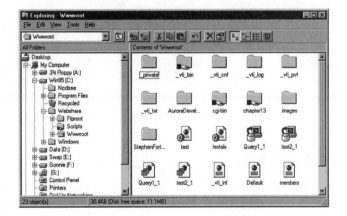

The Root Directory

The WWWRoot directory is the home directory for your Web site. When users on the Web or an intranet type in your URL or IP Address, they will be directed to this directory. As shown in Figure 24.4, your default document is called default.htm, so users will be directed there when they type in your URL. default.htm is your site's home page.

FIGURE 24.4.

*Web server
administration on
Personal Web
Server.*

Many sites use `index.htm` or `index.html` as their default location. Microsoft servers use `default.htm`. There is no difference between the two, and IIS lets you change the default document for all directories, as shown in Figure 24.5.

Even though your WWWRoot may be located a few levels down on your own physical file system, it is considered the topmost level for your Web or FTP site. All files and subdirectories located in WWWRoot are available to your Web site. As described in the next section, you can also set up virtual directories that will contain files for your Web site anywhere on your file system.

Virtual Directories

The process of setting up a particular directory on your local file system to make it a directory on your Web site is called *aliasing* or creating a *virtual directory*. When you create an alias, the physical directory becomes a directory on your Web site.

To set up an alias, go into your Web server's administration program and choose the option to manage directories, as shown in Figure 24.5 for IIS and Figure 24.6 for Personal Web Server. (Personal Web Server for Windows 95 does its administration via ISAPI scripts through a browser. IIS has its own separate executable to manage administration.)

FIGURE 24.5.

Directory alias administration on IIS.

FIGURE 24.6.

Directory alias administration on Personal Web Server.

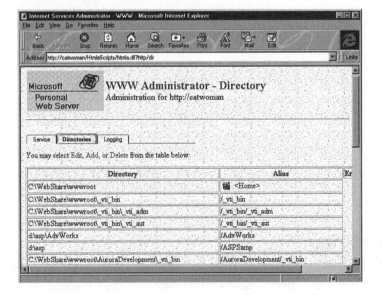

The Directories dialog lets you add, remove, and edit virtual directories at your site. Add a virtual directory by clicking Add and then providing the actual path to the physical directory on your file system. Then give it an alias name. Make sure the name you give fully describes what the Web pages in the directory will contain. Also remember not to give it too long a name or the site's URL will become very long. Once a virtual directory is created, you can access it from the Web by typing in `http://www.yourserver.com/VirtualDirectoryName`. Place a `default.htm` and any other files you need for this virtual directory in the physical directory to make it available to your Web site.

To delete a virtual directory, select the directory and click Delete. All this does is remove the virtual directory from the directory tree of your Web page. The directory still exists in your physical file system. To remove it from your file system completely, delete it in Windows Explorer.

To edit a virtual directory, select it and click Edit. This brings up the Edit dialog shown in Figure 24.7. Here you can change the physical directory of a virtual directory, its alias, and other properties that we will look at in the "Configuring Your Web Site for Access 97 Web Database Publishing" section later in this chapter.

FIGURE 24.7.

The edit feature of a Web server administration program.

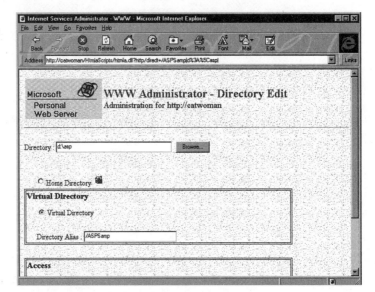

Logging

All Microsoft Web servers let you log information about the users that come to your Web site. To set up logging capabilities on your Web server, go to the administration tools and select Logging. The result for Personal Web Server is shown in Figure 24.8, and the result for IIS is shown in Figure 2.9. Both IIS and Personal Web Server let you log your access records to a text file. Figure 24.10 is an example of a text log file that is generated by the Web server's logging capabilities. The log shows various things, including the date and time of the request, the IP address that requested the page, and what action was taken.

FIGURE 24.8.

The logging dialog for Personal Web Server.

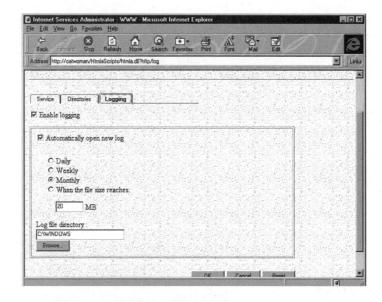

FIGURE 24.9.

The logging dialog for IIS.

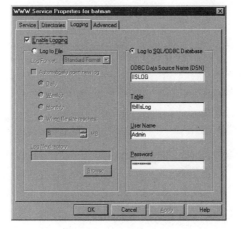

In addition to a text file, IIS also allows you to log the information on your Web site directly to an ODBC data source. As you can see in Figure 24.10, I have IIS set up to log the Web site data directly to a database. In this situation, it is an Access 97 database. Although logging to a database is quite convenient, if your site has a tremendous amount of traffic you should log to a text file and import the text to your database at a later time. This will decrease the workload of your server and improve its overall performance. Because the text file always produces the log with the same structure of information, it is safe to import into a database. If your site gets an average amount of data, logging directly to an ODBC database is a perfect option.

FIGURE 24.10.

A sample text log generated by the Web server.

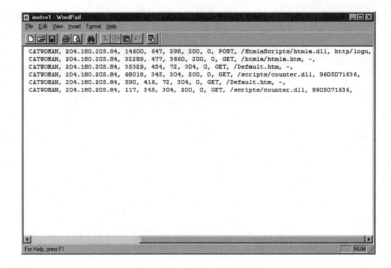

Services

A Web server will provide a number of different services for you. Figure 24.11 shows the IIS service manager, and Figure 24.12 shows the Personal Web Server service manager. Web servers provide an HTTP or Web service, FTP service, and usually Gopher service. FTP and Gopher follow the same rules as the directory and virtual directories. For FTP, the root directory is usually FTPRoot. You can set up virtual directories for your FTP users.

FIGURE 24.11.

IIS's service manager.

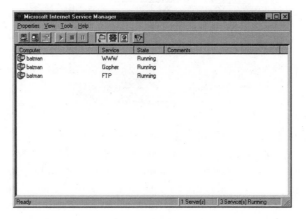

FIGURE 24.12.

Personal Web Server's service manager.

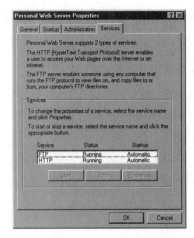

In addition to these services, a Web server must provide some layer of security. IIS provides you with similar security features found in Windows NT. IIS will assign your default Web or FTP user with a login account, `IUSR_MachineName`. This user becomes a member of the Guests group in NT, so if you change the permissions to this group, you change the permissions for the users of your Web site and FTP site. IIS also lets you set up individual access rights and prevent certain users from accessing your site. Figure 24.13 shows the Advanced tab of the IIS administrator. You can specify a certain IP address to grant or deny access to.

FIGURE 24.13.

The Advanced tab of the IIS administrator.

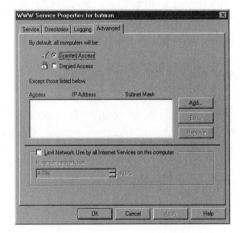

24

CONFIGURING A
WEB SITE FOR
ACCESS

Configuring Your Web Site for Access 97 Web Database Publishing

A Web site can be a very complex place. As you saw in the previous section, the Web server is not the only component. The network attached to your Web server can also play an important role. For example, you may have connected network drives set up as virtual directories for each department in your organization. This section discusses configuration issues that come into play when you implement Access Web publishing.

Directories

Setting up your virtual directory for Web publishing is very important. You want to set up a virtual directory that is dedicated to your Web publishing because it is much easier to maintain. Your Access database should not be in this directory. It should be in a separate directory, on a separate partition of the hard drive if possible.

When setting up a virtual directory, it is extremely important that you grant Execute access to the directory. Execute access will grant the Web client's request to execute scripts in that virtual directory and that directory alone. In order for Active Server Pages and IDC files to run properly, they must be placed in a directory where Execute access is allowed. This is why it is important to have the Access database in a directory that the Web server has no access to. You do not want to place the database in a directory that is exposed to the Web. Figure 24.14 shows a sample virtual directory set up on a network drive with Execute access granted.

Where to Put the Access Database

It is advantageous to put the Access database on the same computer as the Web server, because all Access databases' processing is done locally. You want to place the database in a local directory that is not part of the virtual directory system. This is to prevent unauthorized users from downloading your database. If you were using an SQL Server, you would want to place the SQL Server database on its own machine. Place the Access database on the same machine as the Web server, but place it on a separate partition for better performance.

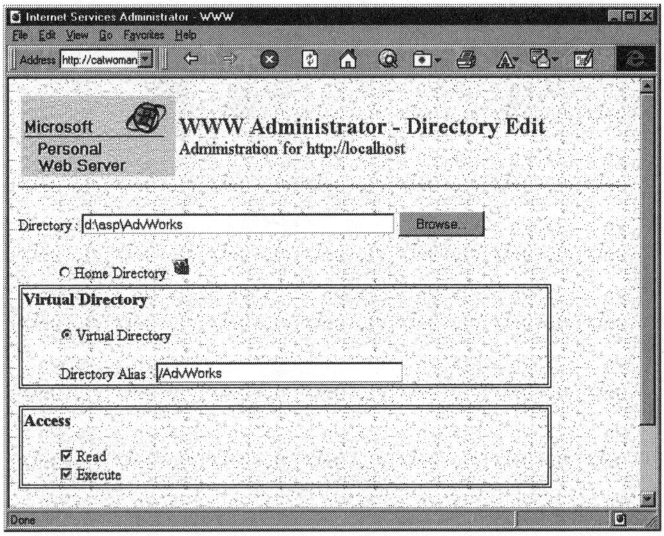

FIGURE 24.14.

Setting up a virtual directory with Execute access.

> **NOTE**
>
> There are many great third-party partition tools out on the market as an alternative to FDISK, like Partition Magic. Remember to always make a complete backup of your disk before you use any third-party partition tool.

You will have to set up any Access database that you will be using for Web publishing as a System DSN ODBC Datasource. The steps for doing so are laid out in the next section.

Setting Up Your Access Database as an ODBC Datasource

In order for Active Server Pages and IDC files to communicate with your Access 97 database, they must use ODBC. ODBC is a set of drivers that let databases of different formats talk to each other. If you did a full install of Access 97, the ODBC driver will be installed on the machine you are running. If not, reinstall Access 97 and then follow these steps:

1. Enter Control Panel and click the 32-bit ODBC icon, as shown in Figure 24.15.

FIGURE 24.15.

The 32-bit ODBC option in Control Panel.

2. Open the ODBC Data Source Administrator applet from Control Panel and select the System DSN tab, as shown in Figure 24.16.

FIGURE 24.16.

ODBC Data Source Administrator.

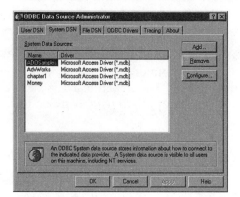

3. Click Add to bring you to the Create New Data Source dialog box, as shown in Figure 24.17.

FIGURE 24.17.

The Create New Data Source dialog.

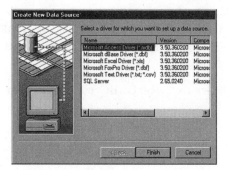

4. Select Microsoft Access driver and click Finish. This brings you to the ODBC Microsoft Access 97 Setup dialog, as shown in Figure 24.18.

FIGURE 24.18.

The ODBC setup for your Access database.

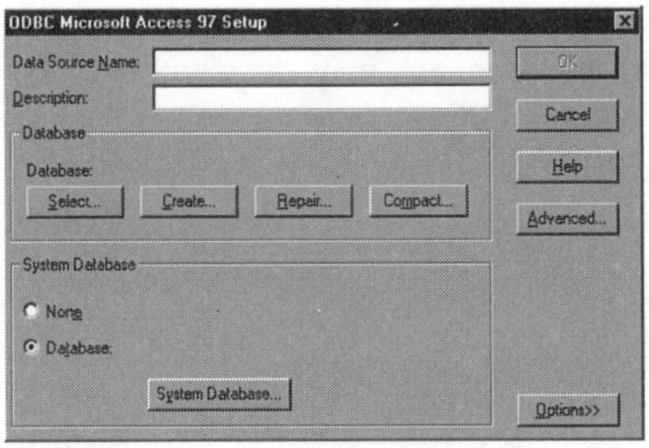

5. Enter the data source name of your database. This is the name that the Publish to the Web Wizard, discussed in Chapters 25 and 26, will ask you for. Give it a descriptive name and fill in the description, as shown in Figure 24.19.

FIGURE 24.19.

Setting up the data source name.

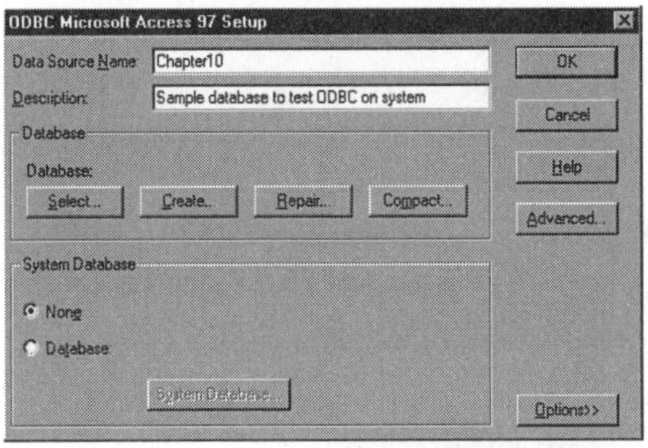

6. In the Database section of the ODBC Microsoft Access 97 Setup dialog, click the Select button to bring up the Select Database dialog shown in Figure 24.20. Select the database you will be using for Web publishing and click OK. When you are back to the ODBC Microsoft Access 97 Setup dialog, click OK to go back to Control Panel. Now your Access 97 database is set up for Web database publishing.

Setting Up the OLE DB Provider for Microsoft Access

In addition to using the ODBC data source, you may still want to use Access 97 with Active Server Pages and ActiveX Data Objects (ADO). If so, you will want to use the

OLE DB Provider for Microsoft Access. (See Chapter 26 for more details on ADO and OLE DB.) The OLE DB Provider for Access is available for download as part of the OLE DB SDK at `http:\\www.microsoft.com\data`. To install the provider, first make sure that ADO 1.0 or later is installed. (To get ADO 1.0 or higher, you can download it from `http:\\www.microsoft.com\data`. You may already have a version of ADO installed on your machine if you have Visual InterDev, ASP, IIS 4.0, or Visual Studio 98 beta installed.) It is recommended that you use the latest version of ADO available, since later versions of ADO are faster than earlier ones. However, JP will work with any version of ADO.

FIGURE 24.20.

The Select Database dialog.

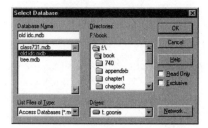

Once you install ADO and download the SDK (it is a big download, so you may want to order the CD-ROM), look for the `Jet/Access` directory. There will be a DLL file called `MSJTOR35.DLL` on the CD or your download directory. (If you cannot find it, search for `MSJTOR35.DLL`.) To install the provider, copy `MSJTOR35.DLL` to either your system directory or `\Program Files\Common Files\system\ole db` and run `regsvr32` on it, as shown in Figure 24.21.

FIGURE 24.21.

Running `regsvr32` on the DLL from Windows 95 Start menu's Run option.

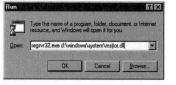

Summary

This chapter showed you to the basics of a Web site, including how to configure a Web server. You learned how to set up your file system directories to become virtual directories in your Web site. Lastly, you learned in detail how to set up an Access 97 database to be an ODBC data source for Web publishing.

Using Access 97 with Static HTML Pages

One of the greatest features of Microsoft Access 97 is its capability to output database objects and convert them to another format. For years Access users have been converting database objects to text, Microsoft Excel, Word, RTF, and many other formats. With Access 97, the Internet has been added to the output functionality. This great new feature will enable you to publish static Web (HTML) pages from your Access 97 database.

Static HTML is an HTML document that is a snapshot of your data at the time it was created. This chapter will look at the static HTML output, and the next chapter will look at dynamic data HTML using IDC and Active Server Pages.

> **NOTE**
>
> All of the techniques in this chapter apply to Access 97. However, when you're using the HTML and IIS wizards for Access 95, most of the techniques discussed in this chapter apply. For all other versions of Access, only the section "An Alternative HTML Generation Technique" will apply.

Saving Database Objects as HTML Documents

The most basic and least flexible method of generating an HTML document from an Access 97 database object is to save the database object as HTML using the Access User Interface menus. This captures a one-time snapshot of the database object in an HTML document. To save a database object as HTML, you must do the following:

1. Select the individual database object and choose File | Save As/Export from the main menu. This brings you the Save As dialog box, as shown in Figure 25.1.

FIGURE 25.1.
Save As dialog box.

2. In the Save As dialog box, select the option To an External File or Database and click OK.

3. In the Save Form 'Categories' As dialog box shown in Figure 25.2, select HTML in the Save as type combo box and choose the directory in which you want to save the HTML document in the Save in combo box.

FIGURE 25.2.

Save Form 'Categories' As dialog box.

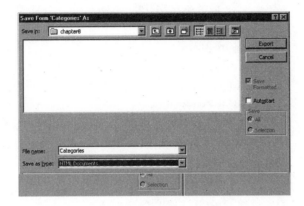

Save As HTML allows the user who is not familiar with the advanced features of Access 97 and the Internet to easily create a form or report and save it as an HTML document. Because you're a more advanced user or someone who develops Access 97 databases for others to use, you will want more control over the process. The rest of this chapter shows you more of the options you have to create a static HTML document based on an Access 97 database object.

Using Visual Basic for Applications to Output Database Objects as HTML

As with everything else available to the users, you have programmatic access to the Save As HTML feature. Access gives you access to this feature through the OutPutTo method of the DoCmd object. The syntax for the OutPutTo method is as follows:

```
DoCmd.OutputTo objecttype[, objectname][, outputformat][, outputfile][, autostart][, templatefile]
```

Table 25.1 lists the parameters the OutPutTo method accepts.

TABLE 25.1. THE PARAMETERS OF THE OUTPUTTO METHOD.

Argument	Description
objecttype	An indicator of the type of object to be exported. You should use one of the built-in constants:

continues

TABLE 25.1. CONTINUED

Argument	Description
	acOutputForm
	acOutputModule (HTML not allowed, text export only)
	acOutputQuery
	acOutputReport
	acOutputTable
objectname	A string expression that contains the object name you want to export. For example, Form1.
outputformat	A constant representing the type of format to export to:
	acFormatActiveXServer
	acFormatHTML
	acFormatIIS (for IDC files)
	acFormatRTF (Rich Text Format)
	acFormatTXT (MS-DOS text)
	acFormatXLS (Microsoft Excel)
	If this parameter is left blank, Access 97 will prompt the user.
outputfile	A string expression representing the filename for your new document. For example, C:\Customers.htm.
	If you leave this argument blank, Access 97 prompts you for an output filename.
autostart	If True (-1), Access 97 will start the associated application, like Internet Explorer, after the output is completed. This is ignored for ASP and IIS.
templatefile	A string expression that's the full name, including the path, of the file you want to use as a template file for the conversion. There will be more on templates later in this chapter.

Using the OutPutTo Method in Your Applications

Calling the OutPutTo method is easy. Just use the syntax described in the previous section, for example:

```
DoCmd.OutputTo acOutputForm, "Categories", acFormatHTML,
➥"c:\Categories.htm", True
```

This will output the Categories form to c:\categories.htm and start up the default browser when it is done.

As with all Visual Basic actions, it is much better if you can reuse your code in another applications or multiple times in one application. I created a reusable function called `OutPutHTML()` that is included in the `chapter25.mdb` database on the Web site for this book. The syntax to call `OutPutHTML` is as follows:

```
fSuccess= OutputHTML(strObjectType , strObject, strpath[, fPreview]
➥[, strTemp])
```

The `OutPutHTML()` function accepts five parameters, three of which are required. Table 25.2. explains the parameters of the `OutPutHTML()` function.

TABLE 25.2. THE PARAMETERS OF THE `OUTPUTHTML()` FUNCTION.

Parameter	Description

strObjectType	A string value representing the type of object you need to export. The function will accept the following:
	
	`Form`
	
	`Report`
	
	`Table`
	
	`Query`

strObject	A string value representing the name of the object you are exporting, for example, `Form1`.
strpath	A string value representing the new file's name including its full path, for example, `c:\test.htm`.
fPreview	An optional Boolean (True/False) value that indicates if you want to preview the document in your default browser after the conversion is complete. If left blank, False is assumed.
strTemp	A string value representing the full path to a template HTML document to use in the conversion process, for example, `C:\templates\green.html`.

The `OutPutHTML` function, shown in Listing 25.1, will determine which type of object to output using the `strObjectType` and perform the `OutPutTo` method using the supplied variables. Here's an example of calling the function:

```
Dim fOK as Boolean

x= OutPutHTML("Form","Categories","C:\help.htm",-1)
```

The `OutPutHTML()` function, shown in Listing 25.1, is an example of a reusable piece of code. You can import the module from `chapter25.mdb` on the Web site for this book into your own applications to use.

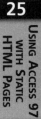

25

USING ACCESS 97 WITH STATIC HTML PAGES

LISTING 25.1. THE OUTPUTHTML() FUNCTION.

```
Function OutputHTML(strObjectType As String, strObject As String, _
            strpath As String, Optional fPreview As Boolean = False, _
            Optional strTemp As String) As Boolean
'''''''''''''''''''''''''''''''''
'Purpose: To output a database object to HTML
'Accepts:strObject: Object Name, strpath: New File name & path
'strObjectType can be "Forms,Queries, Reports, or Table"
'fPreview: boolean to see if you want to preview in browser
'strTemp: the template File to use if desired
'Returns: A boolean value to know if it worked
'Calls: None
'Date:4/15/97
'Developer:Stephen Forte
'Notes:Chapter 25
'''''''''''''''''''''''''''''''''
'Set up Error Trap
On Error GoTo OutHTML_Err

'Used for the "Object type"
Dim intObjType As Integer

'Determine what was passed
Select Case strObjectType

    Case "Forms"
        intObjType = acOutputForm
    Case "Queries"
        intObjType = acOutputQuery
    Case "Reports"
        intObjType = acOutputReport
    Case "Tables"
        intObjType = acOutputTable
    Case Else
    'Incorrect Database Object passed
        MsgBox "You did not pass a valid DB object for this procedure _
to work", vbCritical, "HTML Output"
    'Set to False and Exit
    OutputHTML = False
    GoTo OutHTML_Exit

End Select

'Do the Actual HTML Conversion
DoCmd.OutputTo intObjType, strObject, acFormatHTML, _
 strpath, fPreview, strTemp

'Set to True
OutputHTML = True
```

```
OutHTML_Exit:
Exit Function

OutHTML_Err:
OutputHTML = False
MsgBox "Error: " & Err.Description, _
    vbCritical, "HTML Output"
Resume OutHTML_Exit

End Function
```

Using a Macro to Export a Database Object as HTML

Although a macro is not the preferred method of exporting a database object as static HTML, it is something you can teach the average user to do. (So you will not have to do it for them!)

> **NOTE**
>
> Because macros cannot be error-handled and cannot accept parameters, they are not flexible enough for application development. I highly recommend learning the basics of VBA, and most examples in the book are in VBA-only, but some examples are given of macros because you can teach the average or beginning user to do them. This comes in handy if you are developing an application that users will be creating objects in. You will not have to constantly create procedures or macros for users if they know how to do them themselves.

To save a document to HTML using a macro, create a new macro and select OutPutTo in the Action box, as shown in Figure 25.3. In the macro arguments, choose the correct object type and object name from the combo boxes. Make sure you select HTML as the format and the filename you want to output to. Additionally, you can set autostart to Yes to view the document in your browser, and you can provide a template file to use if desired.

As you can see, there is no flexibility at all with using a macro. You have to hard-code the macro with the object and filename.

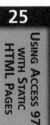

25

USING ACCESS 97
WITH STATIC
HTML PAGES

FIGURE 25.3.

OutPutTo *macro.*

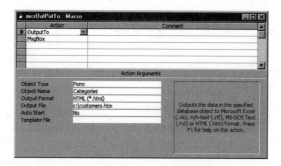

Using the Publish to the Web Wizard to Publish Static HTML Documents to the Web

An exciting new tool included with Access 97 is the Publish to the Web Wizard. This customizable wizard will walk the user through creating Web pages for her database objects. Using the Publish to the Web Wizard is very easy. This section discusses how to use it, and the next section discusses how to customize it.

To use the Publish to the Web Wizard, first make sure all wizards are installed. If you choose the minimum setup, sometimes the wizards are unavailable. If you have errors trying to get to the wizard as described in the following section, reinstall Microsoft Access 97 from the Office CD-ROM. If you are sure the wizards are installed, continue on.

The steps to take when publishing your database to the Web are as follows:

1. From the Access 97 main menu, choose the File | Save As HTML menu option shown in Figure 25.4.

2. After choosing the File | Save As HTML selection, you should see the first screen of the Publish to the Web Wizard. Figure 25.5 shows the first page of the wizard. Although this page may seem unimportant, it'll be vital later on when you begin to customize the wizard. To continue, click Next.

3. The next page of the wizard is a database explorer with check boxes next to each database object, as shown in Figure 25.6. Go through the tabs and select the objects that you want to export. You can take advantage of the Select All option, as well as choosing the All Objects tab and using the Select All button if you want to export your whole database to the Web quickly. To continue, click Next.

FIGURE 25.4.

Save As HTML menu option.

FIGURE 25.5.

Page 1 of the Publish to the Web Wizard.

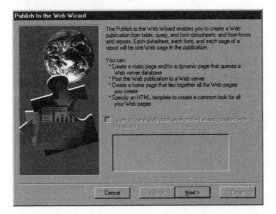

FIGURE 25.6.

Page 2 of the Publish to the Web Wizard.

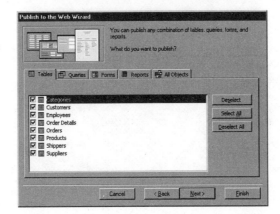

4. The next page, shown in Figure 25.7, asks you which template you want to use for your HTML page, if any. Access 97 ships with ten prebuilt templates that are customizable. (Details on how to customize the templates are in the next section. If you are not happy with the Access templates, you can create your own.) Select a template and click Next to continue.

FIGURE 25.7.

Page 3 of the Publish to the Web Wizard.

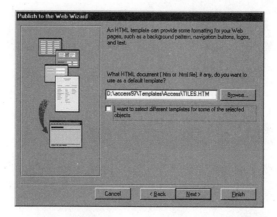

5. The next page, shown in Figure 25.8, asks you how to export the objects, giving you the opportunity to have some static pages and some dynamic pages. Because this chapter is on static HTML, choose Static HTML and click Next. (The next chapter covers Active Server Pages and IDC in detail. ASP and IDC also require access to a Web server, while static HTML does not.)

FIGURE 25.8.

Page 4 of the Publish to the Web Wizard.

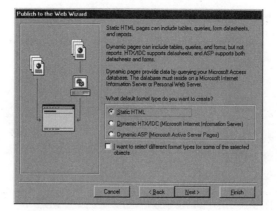

6. The next page of the Wizard, shown in Figure 25.9, asks you where you want to save your HTML documents. As you remember from the discussion of directories in Chapter 9, "Reacting to Events in the Interface," a directory in your file system may be a virtual directory on your Web server. Navigate to the appropriate directory with your browser if necessary. Below the file location is an option to integrate the wizard with the Microsoft Office 97 ValuPack. If the ValuPack is installed on your computer, and you have virtual directories set up with the Personal Web Server or IIS through the ValuPack, you can directly publish them there from the wizard page here. To continue, click Next.

FIGURE 25.9.

Page 5 of the Publish to the Web Wizard.

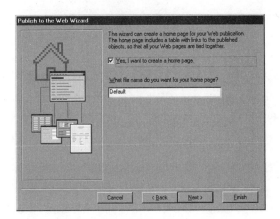

7. The next-to-last page of the Wizard, shown in Figure 25.10, asks you if you want Access 97 to create a home page for you and what title it should have. If you select Yes, remember what you learned about the Switchboard in Chapter 8, "Working with Command Bars." Access will create a default home page for you and export the database object's properties as a description. In addition, if you want the home page to be the default document in the virtual directory, as discussed in Chapter 9, remember what you assigned as the default document. Your server may be configured for either default.htm or index.htm, so check with your Webmaster if you are not sure.

8. The last page of the wizard, shown in Figure 25.10, asks if you want to save the questions you answered as a Web Publishing Profile. This is discussed later in the "Customizing the Publish to the Web Wizard" section, so if you choose to save the specifications of the wizard for reuse later on, give it a descriptive name. Click Finish and the wizard will begin its work. With large databases, the wizard may take a while because it is exporting many database objects at once.

FIGURE 25.10.

Page 6 of the Publish to the Web Wizard.

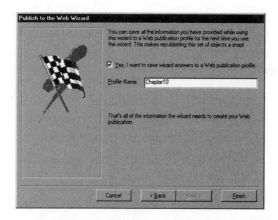

The Results of the Publish to the Web Wizard

The Publish to the Web Wizard creates a Web page for each object you asked it to, and a home page if you requested it to do so. Figure 25.11 shows the results of the Publish to the Web Wizard.

FIGURE 25.11.

The results of the Publish to the Web Wizard.

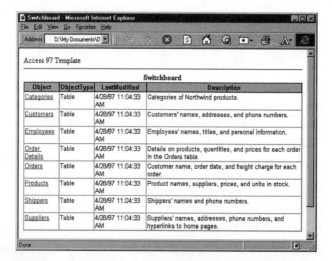

> **NOTE**
>
> The Publish to the Web Wizard is very helpful. However, when you're using a template, your results may not be exactly what you expected. The wizard is not

"smart" enough to copy the background images specified by the template `.htm` file to the directory you specified, making your Web pages display the standard gray background. To get around this, just copy the images from the `Template` folder in your Access directory to the virtual directory where you saved the HTML file.

Customizing the Publish to the Web Wizard

Did you think the Publish to the Web Wizard was a little too much work for your users? Or maybe you would always export the same database objects with the same specifications on a weekly basis, and wouldn't want to go through the same wizard questions again and again. Well, help has arrived! When you use the Publish to the Web Wizard for the first time on a specific sequence that you know you will be doing over and over again, the last page lets you save your specification, as shown in Figure 25.10. The wizard asks you to provide a name for your specification so you can use it again later on. The next time you use the wizard, you will have the option to use your saved specification. You can either click the Finish button to skip the steps, or you can go through the steps one by one and your previous answers will be there. Figure 25.12 shows the first page of the wizard, where you can use a presaved wizard specification.

FIGURE 25.12.
Saved specifications of the Publish to the Web Wizard.

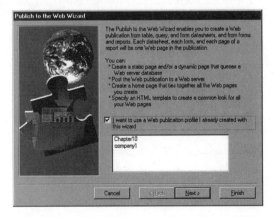

Customizing the HTML Template File

Access 97 ships with ten HTML template documents for your use with the `OutPutTo` method or the Publish to the Web Wizard. If you do not like them or feel that they are a little too basic, you can customize them or create your own. This is great if you want to include your company's logo and some header or footer information, like an email address. Listing 25.2 shows you one of Access 97's HTML templates:

LISTING 25.2. ACCESS 97 HTML TEMPLATE FILE.

```
<HTML>

<TITLE><!--ACCESSTEMPLATE_TITLE--></TITLE>


<BODY background = tiles.jpg>


<!--ACCESSTEMPLATE_BODY-->

</BODY>

<BR><BR>

<IMG SRC = "msaccess.jpg">

</HTML>
```

Note that the <!--AccessTEMPLATE XXX --> tag is where the wizard will place certain information, like the data or document title. This placeholder tells Access 97 where to insert the data that matches the placeholder. When Access saves your data as HTML, the placeholders are replaced with the correct data. Table 25.3 lists all the placeholders available to you in the HTML template file.

TABLE 25.3. ACCESS 97 HTML PLACEHOLDERS.

Placeholder	Description	Location
<!-- AccessTemplate_ Title-->	Name of database object being saved.	Between <Title> and </Title> tags.
<!-- AccessTemplate_ Body -->	Data output to HTML document.	Between <Body> and </Body> tags.
<!-- AccessTemplate_ FirstPage -->	Anchor tag to jump to first page.	Between <Body> and </Body> or after </Body> tags.

Placeholder	Description	Location
`<!-- AccessTemplate_ PreviousPage -->`	Anchor tag to jump to previous page.	Between `<Body>` and `</Body>` or after `</Body>` tags.
`<!-- AccessTemplate_ NextPage -->`	Anchor tag to jump to next page.	Between the `<Body>` and `</Body>` or after `</Body>` tags.
`<!-- AccessTemplate_ LastPage -->`	Anchor tag to jump to last page.	Between `<Body>` and `</Body>` or after `</Body>` tags.
`<!-- AccessTemplate_ PageNumber -->`	Displays current page number.	Between the `<Body>` and `</Body>` or after `</Body>` tags.

Now that you have all the placeholders down, create your own template! Open a text editor and copy Listing 25.2 into it. You will want to use a text editor to edit your HTML template because most visual HTML editing tools do not understand Access's template placeholders. Edit your template however you see fit. Listing 25.4 shows the HTML code I created. I put in my company logo, along with an email link to the Webmaster and a page number indicator.

LISTING 25.3. CUSTOM HTML TEMPLATE.

```
<!DOCTYPE HTML PUBLIC "-//IETF//DTD HTML//EN">
<html>

<head>

<title></title>
</head>

<body background="company1.jpg">

<p><img src="aurora.gif" width="460" height="55"> <!--ACCESSTEMPLATE_BODY-
-> </p>

<br>
Page#: <!--ACCESSTEMPLATE_PageNumber-->


<p><em>Copyright 1997, Aurora Development Group, LTD. </em></p>
```

continues

LISTING 25.3. CONTINUED

```
<p><strong>Contact the webmaster with problems: </strong><a
href="mailto:webmaster@auroradev.com"><strong>webmaster@auroradev.com</str
ong></a></p>
</body>
<hr>
<A HREF=<!--ACCESSTEMPLATE_FirstPage-->>[First] </A>
<A HREF=<!--ACCESSTEMPLATE_PreviousPage-->>[Previous] </A>
<A HREF=<!--ACCESSTEMPLATE_NextPage-->>[Next] </A>
<A HREF=<!--ACCESSTEMPLATE_LastPage-->>[Last] </A>
<hr>
</html>
```

The HTML template in Listing 25.3 produces an HTML document that looks like the one in Figure 25.13.

FIGURE 25.13.

HTML document created by Access 97 based on the template.

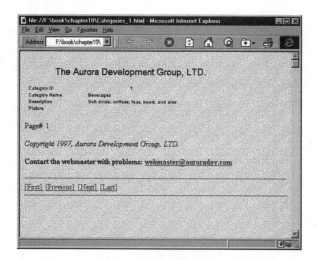

If you experiment with the Publish to the Web Wizard's saved specifications and the custom template HTML file, you can gain a lot of control over the process of exporting to HTML. These techniques can help you to create some very nice Web pages that are ready to be published right away, or at least with very little touch-up. With Access 97, anyone can be a Webmaster!

Gaining More Control over the HTML Conversion Process

The techniques discussed in Chapter 8 and this chapter should satisfy most users. Sometimes you need complete customization of a Web page generated by Access, or your users might not be familiar with Access enough to use the Publish to the Web Wizard.

Creating Your Own Publish to the Web Wizard

What happened to "If it ain't broke, don't try to fix it"? Microsoft did an excellent job with the Publish to the Web Wizard, but because it *is* a wizard, you cannot distribute it with your runtime applications shipped with the Office Developers Edition Setup Wizard (formerly known as the Access Developers Toolkit). In addition, you might want to directly control what your users see, and hard-code some information like the template file and output directory. If situations like these arise, you will have to take matters into your own hands.

If you use the OutPutTo method of the DoCmd object, you can create automated HTML generation features in your applications that respond to either a click of a button or a timer event. Using the OutPutHTML() function discussed in Listing 25.1, you can generate some advanced automated HTML conversion features for your users. For example, in Figure 25.14, I created the Simple Publish to the Web Tool to get you started. The chapter25.mdb file on the Web site for this book contains all the code and the form that make up this simple tool.

FIGURE 25.14.

A Simple Publish to the Web tool.

The form in Figure 25.14, frmPubWiz, uses two list boxes and two text boxes to gather the necessary information to do its work. The user can select multiple database objects of the same type to output to a specified path using a specified template. You can redesign this form to hard-code the paths, or even the objects if need be.

25

USING ACCESS 97 WITH STATIC HTML PAGES

Listbox1 contains the types of database objects you can publish to the Web. When you select an object type from Listbox1, it will call a function to fill Listbox2. This is a very powerful feature of Access, using a callback function to fill a list box programmatically. When you select Listbox1, it will requery Listbox2. Listbox2 will then display the database objects of that type, allowing the user to select as many of them as they want.

Listbox2 is a multiselect list box, a new feature added to Access 95 and Access 97. To allow users to select multiple items in a list box, you need to set the list box's Multi Select property to Simple or Extended, as shown in Figure 25.15. Simple will allow users to select as many items with the mouse. Extended will do the same, but the user must hold down the Ctrl key while clicking the mouse button. Simple is the preferred way because users might already be familiar with this method.

FIGURE 25.15.

The Multi Select *property of a list box, set to* Simple.

Referring to the selected items in the Multi Select list box is not as straightforward to most Access 97 users. When you select Simple or Extended, an ItemsSelected collection becomes available to you. You need to loop through the items in the ItemsSelected collection with a For…Each loop, as shown in the following example taken from Access 97 help:

```
Sub BoundData()
    Dim frm As Form, ctl As Control
    Dim varItm As Variant
    Set frm = Forms!Contacts
    Set ctl = frm!Names
    For Each varItm In ctl.ItemsSelected
```

```
        Debug.Print ctl.ItemData(varItm)
    Next varItm
End Sub
```

The Simple Web Publishing tool works by using the For...Each loop in Listbox2 and calling the OutPutHTML() function from Listing 25.1 on each item selected in Listbox2, using the information on the form to supply the function's parameters. The code to do this is shown in Listing 25.4.

LISTING 25.4. THE SIMPLE WEB PUBLISHING TOOL.

```
Sub PublishWiz()
''''''''''''''''''
'Purpose: Loop through the selected items and
'output them to HTML
'Calls:OutPutHTML
''''''''''''''''''

On Error GoTo Pub_Err

    Dim varItm As Variant
    Dim fOK As Boolean

'Begin the For...Next Loop
    For Each varItm In Me!Listbox2.ItemsSelected
        'Call the OutPutHTML function
        fOK = OutputHTML(Me!ListBox1, Me!Listbox2.ItemData(varItm), _
            Me!txtOutPutpath & Me!Listbox2.ItemData(varItm) & ".htm", _
            False)

    Next varItm

Pub_Exit:
Exit Sub

Pub_Err:
MsgBox Err.Description, vbInformation
Resume Pub_Exit

End Sub
```

Using the techniques described in this section, you can easily create your own HTML output functions that you can control in situations where the Publish to the Web Wizard is inadequate.

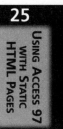

25

USING ACCESS 97
WITH STATIC
HTML PAGES

An Alternative HTML Generation Technique

For complete control over your HTML output, there is still another way to do it. You can use standard file I/O to build an HTML page in code and then save the file as *something*.htm. This way is the most flexible because you have total control over what is output to HTML. You can specify spacing, fonts, and attributes, and make decisions on what to export in your Visual Basic code.

The file I/O technique will work in any version of Access and any product supported by VBA. I've been using this technique for quite some time in Access 2 and 95 but rarely use it today in Access 97 because it is so time-consuming. As with anything that gives you 100% control, you will always pay the price with your time.

If you have an HTML page that has to be layed out in an exact way, and all the techniques that you have learned in this book have not helped you customize Access's output, you might want to use this method. File I/O has been around for years. Many languages use it to do text file reading and writing. Because HTML is just standard text (and so are Active Server Pages and IDC files), you can use all of the methods of file I/O with an HTML page.

File I/O works by opening a file for input or append, from which you read or write literal strings, for example:

```
Open "c:\hello.txt" For Output As 1
Print #liFileNu1, "Hello World!!"
Close #1
```

This opens a file named hello.txt on your C drive and writes "Hello World" into it. To use file I/O to generate an exact Web page, first create the Web page in your favorite HTML editor and then switch to source view. Then you will have to make sure there are no quotation conflicts. Quotation conflicts are the hardest thing about file I/O HTML generation. Because the Visual Basic code that writes into a file is within quotes itself, your string value must not contain any embedded quotation marks, for example:

```
<img src="title.gif" alt="[Access]" align=bottom width=54 height=59>
```

This HTML code must take care of the quotes around the words title.gif and [Access]. To do so, you must define a constant in your code for the quotation mark. I usually declare a string variable and set it equal to Chr(34), the ASCII value for a quote, for example:

```
Dim Quote As String
Quote = Chr(34)
```

Now that you have the quote defined in your code, you can concatenate the string value whenever you need a quote in your code, for example:

```
<img src="title.gif" alt="[Access]" align=bottom width=54 height=59>
```

The preceding would look like this in Visual Basic code:

```
"<img src=" & quote & "title.gif" & quote & " alt=" & quote & "[Access]" _
& quote & " align=bottom width=54 height=59>"
```

After you generate your code, you need to use Data Access Objects (DAO) code to provide data from your application to your HTML document. This is where you can use logic in your code to create pages based on only the data you need.

When I was responsible for my Access User Group's Web page, in the Access 2.0 days when there was no Publish to the Web Wizard, I used code like this to produce an "active members" page. (Now it is an Active Server Page.) I would use a query to show all the active members, and then use DAO to loop through the recordset and add the names to the Web page. Other variables, like the date and time, were easily added to the bottom of the page to produce a "last updated" line.

Listing 25.5 is the function PRINTHTML() from chapter25.mdb, which loops through the Customer table in the Northwind database and prints the records to an HTML file. The result is shown in Figure 25.16. You can use this technique to include JavaScript and VBScript functions, ActiveX controls, and Java applets. You have complete control over the process. All you have to do is manipulate the code in Listing 25.16 to suit your needs.

NOTE

If you plan to use the code in Listing 25.5 in Access 2.0, you must make the function return an integer. Access 2.0 does not support the Boolean data type. In addition, you must replace the line Set db=CurrentDB with Set db= DBEngine (0)(0).

LISTING 25.5. THE PRINTHTML() FUNCTION.

```
Function PrintHTML() As Boolean
''''''''''''''''''''''''''''''''''
'Purpose: Generate a manual HTML page
'Using File I/O
```

continues

LISTING 25.5. CONTINUED

```
'Accepts: Nothing
'Returns:True or False
'Date: 07/22/95
'Notes: Converted to Access 95: 12/04/95
'Converted to Access 97: 11/28/96
'''''''''''''''''''''''''''''
On Error GoTo HTMLIO_Err

'Constant for Quote
Dim quote As String
quote = Chr(34)


Dim liFileNum As Long
Dim db As Database, rst As Recordset
'Change to Set db=DBEngine(0)(0) in Access 2.0
Set db = CurrentDb()
Set rst = db.OpenRecordset("Customers")
rst.MoveFirst

  liFileNum = FreeFile
    Open "c:\windows\desktop\members.htm" For Output As liFileNum
    Print #liFileNum, "<!doctype html public " & quote & "-//IETF//DTD_
HTML//EN" & quote & ">"
    Print #liFileNum, "<HTML>"
    Print #liFileNum,
    Print #liFileNum, "<HEAD>"
    Print #liFileNum, "<title>NorthWind Customer Listing</title>"
    Print #liFileNum, "</HEAD>"
    Print #liFileNum,

    Print #liFileNum, "<p align=center><img src=" & quote & "title.gif" &
quote & " alt=" & quote & "[Access]" & quote & " align=bottom width=54
height=59> </p>"
    Print #liFileNum, "<h1><center><font color=" & quote & "#000000" &
quote & " > NorthWind Traders <BR> Customer Information Page"
    Print #liFileNum, "</font></center></h1>"
    Print #liFileNum, "<HR>"

        Do Until rst.EOF
            Print #liFileNum, "<BR>" & rst!CompanyName & "<BR>"
          rst.MoveNext
        Loop

    Print #liFileNum, "<hr>"
    Print #liFileNum, "This page last updated: " & Now()
    Print #liFileNum, "</BODY>"
    Print #liFileNum,
    Print #liFileNum, "</HTML>"
```

```
    Close #liFileNum

    MsgBox "File Done!"
    rst.Close
    PrintHTML = True

HTMLIO_Exit:
Exit Function

HTMLIO_Err:
PrintHTML = False
MsgBox Err.Description, vbInformation, "HTML I/O"
Resume HTMLIO_Exit
End Function
```

FIGURE 25.16.

The results of the PrintHTML() *function.*

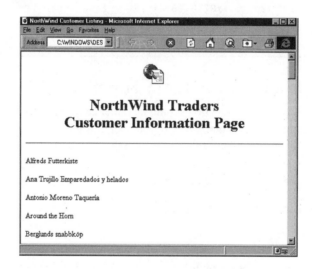

The HTML code generated by the PrintHTML() function is shown in Listing 25.6.

LISTING 25.6. THE HTML GENERATED BY THE PRINTHTML() FUNCTION.

```
<!doctype html public "-//IETF//DTD HTML//EN">
<HTML>

<HEAD>
<title>NorthWind Customer Listing</title>
</HEAD>

<p align=center><img src="title.gif" alt="[Access]" align=bottom width=54
height=59> </p>
```

continues

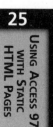

25

USING ACCESS 97
WITH STATIC
HTML PAGES

LISTING 25.6. CONTINUED

```
<h1><center><font color="#000000" > NorthWind Traders <BR> Customer
Information Page
</font></center></h1>
<HR>
<BR>Alfreds Futterkiste<BR>
<BR>Ana Trujillo Emparedados y helados<BR>
<BR>Antonio Moreno Taquería<BR>
<BR>Königlich Essen<BR>
<BR>La corne d'abondance<BR>
<BR>La maison d'Asie<BR>
<BR>Wilman Kala<BR>
<BR>Wolski  Zajazd<BR>
<hr>
This page last updated: 5/1/97 3:18:21 PM
</BODY>

</HTML>
```

Customizing the `HTMLPrint()` Function

Customizing the `HTMLPrint()` function should be rather easy. Just add the HTML tags that are needed to make it suit your needs. If you plan to use the this type of HTML generation, also plan to spend a good deal of time with the Web page in an editor to generate the HTML for you beforehand. Then you can pretty much copy and paste the HTML into your Access function, except for the quotation marks, which you will have to pay special attention to.

Summary

This chapter showed you how to publish static data to HTML files. This is a good technique if you do not have access to your Web server and need to upload the HTML files server or your ISP supports IIS 3.0 or 4.0 (many do and are as cheap as $25 a month), you will want to publish dynamic data on a Web site using the Internet Database Connector and Active Server Pages, the focus of the next chapter.

Publishing Dynamic Web Pages

If you want to move past static Web pages and publish your data "on-the-fly" to create an interactive Web site, you will want to learn about the Internet Database Connector (IDC) and Active Server Pages (ASP).

Static Web pages, discussed in Chapter 25, "Using Access 97 with Static HTML Pages," are only good if you do not want the Internet or intranet users to have access to the most up-to-date information. Using the Internet Database Connector, you can always guarantee that your Web site provides the user with the latest information.

The IDC eliminates a lot of the maintenance of your Web site. For example, if you were the Webmaster for any site that has a "User Listing" page, you would want to maintain the page with an interactive database. In the old days, you had to manually update the user's information on the HTML page itself every time the information changed. With the IDC the members can make changes over the Web, and the User Listing page will automatically update itself when the next visitor hits your Web site because the data is stored in your Access 97 database.

This chapter will cover how to use the IDC by using the Publish to the Web Wizard, and how to get the most flexibility from your Web pages by creating them by hand. Next, we will look at some advanced features of the IDC and a real live example. The next generation of Web technology, Active Server Pages, is the topic of the second part of this chapter.

Introducing the Internet Database Connector (IDC)

The Internet Database Connector (IDC) is a part of the Internet Information Server (IIS) 1.0 to 3.0 that allows standard HTML pages to interact with any ODBC data source. A major benefit is that IDC works independently of the Web browser. All you need is to use Microsoft IIS or Personal/Peer Web Server for internal sites on Windows 95/NT Workstation.

IDC is an older technology, but it is still widely in use today. You can use the information in this chapter to enhance your current IDC applications, but if you are starting new Web applications, use the ASP technology discussed in the second part of the chapter.

> **CAUTION**
>
> IDC is not supported by IIS 4.0.

Publishing Dynamic Web Pages

CHAPTER 26

771

26

PUBLISHING
DYNAMIC WEB
PAGES

IDC works by having an IDC file and an HTX file located on your Web server. When the user requests the IDC file, it runs the SQL statement located in the IDC file against the ODBC data source and shows the user the results in the corresponding HTX template file. Although the IDC file may be new to you, the HTX file is very similar to the HTML template file discussed in Chapter 25, with some special modifications. Later in this chapter we'll dissect the IDC and HTX files to show you how to get the best results.

> **NOTE**
>
> Because the IDC uses ODBC to talk to your database, the techniques used here can work on any ODBC-compliant database, including but not exclusive to Access (any version), Microsoft SQL Server, Oracle, and Sybase. The focus of this book is Access 97, so the techniques discussed here may not be applicable to the other IDC-compatible databases. Additionally, Access 97 is the only database system that has a built-in wizard to create the IDC and HTX files for you. Access 95 has a downloadable IIS wizard add-in that is similar to the Publish to the Web Wizard discussed throughout this book. You can download it from the Microsoft Web site at `http://www.microsoft.com`.

Creating Interactive Web Pages with the IDC Using Wizards

Once again, Microsoft has created something very powerful and enabled the average user to use it with wizard technology. The Publish to the Web Wizard that you became familiar with in Chapter 25 can also create IDC dynamic Web pages very quickly. Because you mastered this wizard in the last chapter, using it to produce IDC files will be very easy for you.

Getting Started: What to Do Before You Use the Wizard

You need to do two things before you get started. The first is a to set up a location on your Web server. You need to set aside a physical directory and create a virtual directory in IIS or Personal Web Server with execute permissions. Please refer to Chapter 24 to find out how to set up a virtual directory and set permissions for it.

Because the IDC uses ODBC to talk to your Access 97 database, you will need to set it up as a system ODBC data source and remember the name you assign it. Please refer to Chapter 24, "Configuring a Web Site for Access," to find out how to set up your Access 97 database as an ODBC data source.

After you have your directory and your ODBC data source set up, you are ready to publish interactive Web pages.

Using the Publish to the Web Wizard to Publish Interactive Web Pages

Using the Publish to the Web Wizard is similar to what was described in Chapter 25. Invoke the wizard by going to the main menu and choosing File | Save As HTML. As shown in Figure 26.1, you can choose the database object you want to publish. Using the IDC is best for publishing lists of data from a table and a query. For best results, you should use tables and queries with the IDC, and forms and reports with Active Server Pages.

FIGURE 26.1.

The Publish to the Web Wizard object listing.

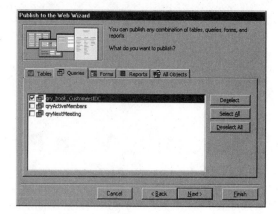

After selecting the database objects you want to output as dynamic Web pages, select a template from page 3 of the wizard. Move on to page 4 of the wizard, as shown in Figure 26.2. Choose the Dynamic HTX/IDC (Microsoft Internet Information Server) option and click Next.

On page 4 of the Wizard, as shown in Figure 26.3, enter the data source name that you gave your database in the ODBC Data Source administrator. If you have implemented Microsoft Access (Jet) security on your database, enter the user name and password that you want the users to use when accessing the database object.

On page 5 of the Publish to the Web Wizard, type the physical path to the virtual directory on your Web server, as shown in Figure 26.4. Remember that this directory needs to have execute permissions, as described previously. Go through the rest of the wizard and click Finish when you are ready. Access will create the IDC and HTX files for you.

Publishing Dynamic Web Pages

CHAPTER 26

773

26

PUBLISHING
DYNAMIC WEB
PAGES

FIGURE 26.2.

The Publish to the Web Wizard IDC dialog.

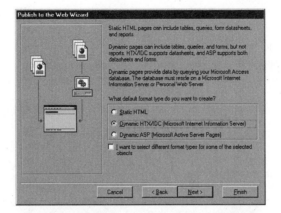

FIGURE 26.3.

Page 4 of the Publish to the Web Wizard, with the IDC data source name, user name, and password.

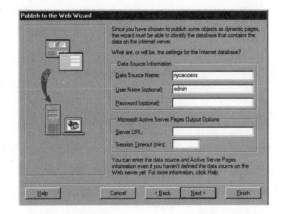

FIGURE 26.4.

The Directory dialog box of the Publish to the Web Wizard.

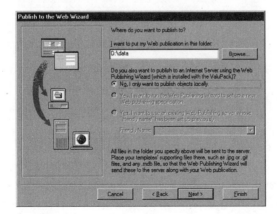

After the wizard creates the IDC file for you, you need to access the IDC file through the HTTP protocol. You cannot view these files through Windows Explorer because the Web server needs to process them first. The wizard creates an IDC file and an HTX file for each database object that you choose to export. When the user jumps to the IDC file, the server will run the IDC script and produce a Web page on-the-fly. To link to an IDC file, you must follow the following format:

```
http://yourcomputername/yourfilename.idc?
```

For example:

```
http://localhost/chapter26/test1.idc?
```

This will query the Customer table and export the whole table on-the-fly to the Web browser as standard HTML. Because this is done in real time, when you update your data, your Web page will reflect these changes. Figure 26.5 shows the results of the preceding query.

FIGURE 26.5.

The results of an IDC file query over the Internet.

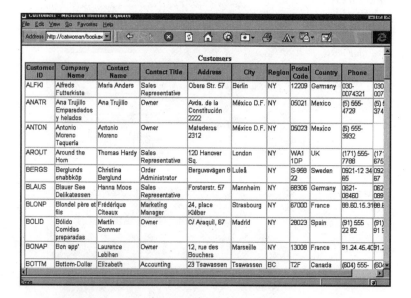

Exporting Parameter Queries to IDC Files

What makes the IDC so powerful is that it will query your database each time the user clicks on the link to the IDC file, so the Web page will always be up to date. However, you can produce dynamic Web pages based on select queries or parameter queries. Using a standard query is the same as using a table in the Publish to the Web Wizard.

To export a parameter query, first create a parameter query as I did in Figure 26.6. All I did was place the parameter as the criteria for the Country field in the Customer table in Northwind. Make sure you explicitly declare your parameter, because the IDC file will not work otherwise. As shown in Figure 26.6, to declare a parameter in a query, type the parameter prompt in brackets as the criteria in the QBE grid. Then choose Query | Parameters from the main menu and enter the text in the parameter prompt exactly the same way you did in the criteria. Also tell Access which data type it will be expecting and the data type of the field you are placing the parameter on. Make sure you get it right, because if you type text and have an integer field, you will get a "Type Mismatch" error at runtime.

FIGURE 26.6.

Creating a parameter query.

Save your query and run it. Access will ask you to supply a parameter in the "Enter Parameter" Value dialog box, as shown in Figure 26.7. Typing in "Germany" will get you all the records in the Customer database where the field name Country contains the word "Germany".

FIGURE 26.7.

The Enter Parameter Value dialog box.

Exporting the parameter query is simple. Just run the Publish to the Web Wizard and select the query to be exported. Follow the wizard as normal. However, the wizard will export the query as one HTML file, one IDC file, and one HTX file. The HTML file is the one you want to place your link to, because this is where you will ask the user for the parameter. This HTML file, shown in Figure 26.8, will contain an HTML form that you can use independently, or you can copy and paste it to another HTML page. The button on the HTML form will call the IDC file and pass it the value your user typed in to run the query.

FIGURE 26.8.

The HTML para-meter file.

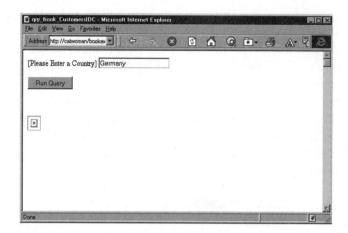

After typing in your parameter, just as you would in Access, click on the Run Query button. The query will run against the database and the results will be sent to your Web browser, as shown in Figure 26.9.

FIGURE 26.9.

The results of an IDC parameter query over the Internet.

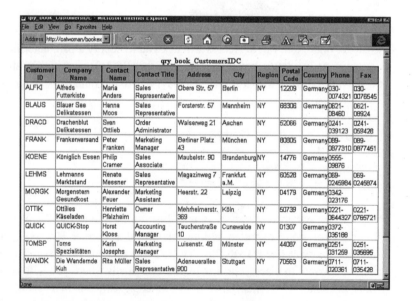

Limitations of the Publish to the Web Wizard

There are a few things that, by design, the Wizard will not do for you:

- IDC is not supported by IIS 4.0.
- Wizard will not export action queries.

Publishing Dynamic Web Pages

CHAPTER 26

777

26

PUBLISHING
DYNAMIC WEB
PAGES

- Exported HTML is very basic.
- Expressions in forms and reports are not exported.
- Hyperlinks show up as text in IDC results.
- `FilterBy` and `OrderBy` properties are ignored in forms and reports.
- Queries exported to IDC/HTX lose the table's formatting.

Publish to the Web Wizard Does Not Export Action Queries

The ability to export action queries to IDC files has been left out of the Publish to the Web Wizard. As you will see later on in this chapter, the IDC can update, delete, and insert data into your Access database over the Web. To create action IDC files, you will have to do them manually. This process is covered later in the chapter in the section called "Advanced Techniques of the IDC."

The HTML Pages Exported by the Wizard Are Very Basic

As you will remember from Chapter 25, the Publish to the Web Wizard produces some very standard HTML when it exports your data. By customizing the Template file you use in the wizard with the techniques discussed in Chapter 25, and by customizing the HTX file discussed later in this chapter, you can create some very professional-looking Web pages.

Expressions in Forms and Reports Are Not Exported

Expressions in forms and reports are very common in Microsoft Access. When you are exporting an Access 97 form that contains an expression, the field will appear blank in your Web browser when you run the query. This is because when Access 97 exports a form, it only exports a table based on the form's recordset. So an expression on a form that looks like this:

```
=[FirstName] & "   " & [LastName]
```

will not show up in your browser. To get around this problem, move the expression to the query that is the recordset of the form and make the form's field control source the field in the query. Using this technique, your expressions will appear in the IDC/HTX files. The only disadvantage to this is that expressions in queries cause Jet to run the query at a slower rate. This is an example where you should have two queries, one for your user's form and another in your "Web" database.

Hyperlinks Show Up as Text in IDC Results

When exporting static data to HTML, Access knows to convert hyperlinks to the proper HTML `"<A HREF>"` tag. However, IDC files are not controlled by Access—the ODBC driver controls them. Jet stores the hyperlink data type internally, with all three parts— the hyperlink address, subaddress, and display text—separated by a pound sign (#). When the hyperlink is exported, this internal structure is returned as text, complete with the # values separating the hyperlink parts. In addition, since the field is not stored internally with the `"<A HREF>"` tag, ODBC does not know that the field should become a hyperlink.

Fortunately, you can fake out ODBC by writing a complex function as the control source of your hyperlink field in your query. You cannot write a reusable function in an Access VBA module to do this for you, because ODBC does not recognize user-defined functions. (Not that I didn't waste an hour on one!) To create a query that will show valid hyperlinks when exported in IDC format, enter an expression like this for the field that is a hyperlink:

```
 "<A HREF=""" & Right([fieldname],Len(IIf(IsNull _
([fieldname]),"",[fieldname]))-
➡InStr(IIf(IsNull([fieldname]), _ "",[fieldname]),"#")) & """>" &
IIf(Left([fieldname], _
➡IIf(InStr(IIf(IsNull([fieldname]),"",[fieldname]),"#")>1, _
➡InStr(IIf(IsNull([fieldname]),"",[fieldname]),"#")-1,0))="", _
➡ [fieldname],Left([fieldname],IIf(InStr(IIf(IsNull _ ([fieldname]),
➡"",[fieldname]),"#")>1,InStr(IIf(IsNull _
([fieldname]),"",[fieldname]),"#")-1,0))) & "</A>"
```

The expression is so long because it must account for nulls in the hyperlink field, and the `NZ()` function cannot be used with IDC. The expression must also handle hyperlinks that do not contain the displaytext or caption portion of the hyperlink field.

When you're exporting a table that contains a hyperlink field, you will encounter this same problem of hyperlinks displaying as text. The only solution is to create a query that returns all the rows as the table and alias the hyperlink field(s) with the preceding example.

FilterBy and OrderBy Properties Are Ignored in Forms and Reports

If you are exporting tables, queries, or forms that contain `OrderBy` or `Filter` properties to IDC format, the recordset will not be filtered on the Web output. This is because the

Publishing Dynamic Web Pages

CHAPTER 26

779

26

PUBLISHING
DYNAMIC WEB
PAGES

IDC file will use the SQL statement associated with the form or query when exporting a table, and all records are returned. ODBC does not understand the OrderBy and Filter properties, just as it does not understand user-defined functions.

To work around this, create a new query that uses the new sort or filter criteria, or use a parameter query. Then export the new query to IDC format using the Publish to the Web Wizard.

Queries Exported to the IDC/HTX Format Lose the Table's Formatting

When you export a query based on a table that has a formatted field, some of the data's formatting is lost. This will happen in the formatting of the following data types:

- Currency
- Date/time
- Percent
- Boolean (True/False)

The Format property is used for display purposes only, and the ODBC driver ignores it, exporting just the raw value of the field. To work around this problem, you must use the Format() function in your query. For example, to format a currency field to display the dollar signs, use this function in your query:

```
Price: Format([Orders].[Price],'Currency')
```

Export this new formatted query to an IDC/HRX file using the Publish to the Web Wizard.

> **NOTE**
>
> If you are new to the Format function in queries, check out Access 97's online help for more details.

Customizing the IDC and HTX Files

The Publish to the Web Wizard will produce an IDC file and an HTX file with the same name. These two files work hand-in-hand in producing your interactive Web pages. Understanding what makes up the IDC and HTX files is crucial to developing customized interactive Web pages.

The IDC is a built-in feature of Microsoft IIS or any Web server built on its architecture, like Personal/Peer Web Server for Windows 95/NT. Understanding the architecture of IDC and HTX will also help you in non-Access Web development. The first part of this section explains what makes up the IDC and HTX files so you will be able to customize them. The second part of this section shows you how to customize the output of your data.

The IDC File

Simply put, the IDC file is a text file script that the Web server reads and executes. To edit an IDC file, just open it up with Notepad as shown in Figure 26.10.

The contents of an IDC file are as follows:

Datasource—Your system DSN name

Template—The name of your HTX file

SQLStatement—The SQL statement to return to your HTX file

Password—Password to your database if security is used

Username—User name if security is used

FIGURE 26.10.

The contents of a typical IDC file.

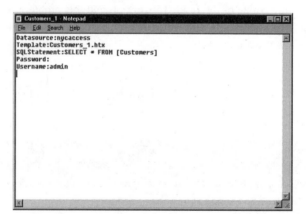

If the Publish to the Web Wizard made your IDC file for you, the wizard will fill in the data source, SQL statement, and template for you automatically. The wizard will also prompt you for your password and username if it's a secured database.

If you want to change any of the components of the IDC file, just open it up in Notepad and change the component you are interested in. If you want to alter the SQL statement and you go over one line, make sure to use a plus sign (+) to continue.

In addition, you can pass a variable from the calling HTML form to your IDC file to use in your SQL statement. To do this, you need to place the HTML form field's name inside

Publishing Dynamic Web Pages

CHAPTER 26

781

26

PUBLISHING
DYNAMIC WEB
PAGES

two percent signs (%). In our example of using a parameter query with an IDC file, where we asked you for a country name, there was an HTML form named "Please Enter a Country". Here is the HTML of the calling form:

```
<FORM METHOD="GET" ACTION="qry_book_CustomersIDC_1.IDC">
[Please Enter a Country] <INPUT TYPE="Text" NAME="[Please Enter a
Country]"><P>
<INPUT TYPE="Submit" VALUE="Run Query">
</FORM>
```

To include what the user typed into the Please Enter a Country field, the IDC must look like this:

```
Datasource:nycaccess
Template:qry_book_CustomersIDC_1.htx
SQLStatement:SELECT Customers.*
+FROM Customers
+WHERE (((Customers.Country)='%[Please Enter a Country]%'));
```

This is the same as creating a parameter query in Access, except that you are using the field name as your parameter name prompt. As you can see, an understanding of SQL is important in customizing an IDC file. Techniques for customizing the SQLStatement in an IDC file will be discussed in the next section.

Customizing the SQL Statement of an IDC File

If you want to change the SQL statement in your IDC file around to customize your needs, just open the IDC file in a text editor and modify the SQLStatement portion of the IDC file. Because IDC files use ODBC drivers to communicate with your Access 97 database, in some situations you may have slightly different syntax. ODBC uses a percent sign (%) as a wildcard, while Access 97 uses an asterisk (*). To use the wildcard with this example:

```
SQLStatement:SELECT Customers.*
+FROM Customers
+WHERE (((Customers.Country)='%[Please Enter a Country]%'));
```

You can place a wildcard after the Please Enter a Country field so users can enter a letter such as "U" and the query will return all the countries beginning in the letter "U", like the United Kingdom and the United States. To do this, you must add two percent signs (%%) after the parameter name in your SQL statement and change the equal (=) predicate to Like. Here is the new SQL:

```
SQLStatement:SELECT Customers.*
+FROM Customers
+WHERE (((Customers.Country)Like '%[Please Enter a Country]%%'));
```

You can use this technique to create search engines by placing the wildcard before and after the parameter. Once you become familiar with SQL, you can optimize your SQL statement in any way you see fit.

The HTX File

The HTX template file is very much like the template files Access 97 uses in static HTML output, as discussed in Chapter 25. The main difference between the HTML template and the HTX template is the placeholders. An HTX template is a simple HTML file that you can edit, with a detail section for the Web server to insert the data. All of your data returned by the IDC script is placed between the following tags:

```
<%BeginDetail%>
...
*Your Data*
...
<%EndDetail%>
```

When the IDC script runs, it will iterate through all the records and place the data within the BeginDetail and EndDetail tags. There must be placeholders for the data to be stored. The placeholder for the data is <%FieldName%>. The HTX file gets the name of the fields from the IDC file. For example, an IDC file like

```
Datasource:Chapter26
Template:Test.htx
SQLStatement: Select Fname, Lname, Birthday from Customers
```

can support an HTX template like

```
<%BeginDetail%>
<PRE>
First Name: <%Fname%>
Last Name: <%Lname%>
Birthday: <%Birthday%>
</PRE>
<%EndDetail%>
```

Notice that in the preceding example, the three field names, Fname, Lname, and Birthday, were all from the IDC file's SQL statement.

Customizing the IDC and HTX Files for Better HTML Output

The Publish to the Web Wizard produces an IDC and HTX template. Most of your customizations will take place in the HTX file. The only thing you may want to change in the IDC file is the SQL statement.

The HTX file's HTML section can be customized any way you see fit. You can use an HTML editor to add graphics and your company logo. Access 97 will only create an HTX file that displays your data in a table. As you will soon see, there is much more power available to you in an HTX template.

Publishing Dynamic Web Pages

CHAPTER 26

783

26

PUBLISHING
DYNAMIC WEB
PAGES

When using an HTX template, you may want to display a message if there were no matching records or reformat the result set.

Customizing the Results

Open the HTX file and look where Access 97 created the `<%BeginDetail%>` and `<%EndDetail%>` tags. You can use a text editor or an HTML editor like FrontPage to modify the HTML tags between the tags. Access formats the results in a simple table. If you want to add some jazz to that output, just add what you think is necessary. In the following example, I add some preformatted text and a horizontal line after each record:

```
<%begindetail%>
<pre>
<strong>Company Name</strong>    : <%CompanyName%>
<strong>Contact Person</strong> : <%ContactName%>
<strong>Phone Number</Strong>    : <%Phone%>
<strong>Company Country</strong>: <%Country%>
</pre>
<hr>
<%enddetail%>
```

What to format is totally up to you. If you are not going to use the HTML table that Access created for you, just remember to delete all the table tags in the HTX file.

In addition to being able to display the field names, your IDC file can also display the IDC's parameter. For example, the `[Enter a Country Name]` parameter in the IDC file can be used in your HTX template. The way to refer to an IDC variable in your HTX file is by using the `IDC.ParameterName` syntax. For example:

```
Matching Records from Country: <%IDC.[Please Enter a Country]%>
```

You can further customize your page to display "Matching Records for:" on the top of your page and use the result as the title of your HTML results document. For example:

```
<html>
<head>
<title>Search Results: <%IDC.[Please Enter a Country]%></title>
</head>
<body background="tiles.jpg">
<Center><strong>Matching Records from Country: <%IDC.[Please Enter a
Country]%></strong></center><br><hr>
<%begindetail%>
<pre>
<strong>Company Name</strong>    : <%CompanyName%>
<strong>Contact Person</strong> : <%ContactName%>
<strong>Phone Number</Strong>    : <%Phone%>
</pre>
<hr>
<%enddetail%>
```

This will display the result shown in Figure 26.11.

FIGURE 26.11.

*A customized
HTX result set.*

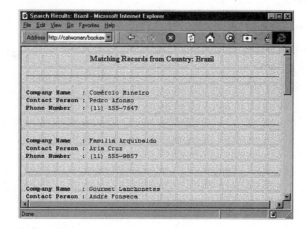

Conditional HTML Generation in the HTX File

The IDC also supports conditional HTML generation based on logical predicates you can place in the HTX template file. For example, you may want to display a message if there are no matching records. To use conditional HTML generation, you must use the If construct, as shown here:

```
<%If Condition>
```

Here's the HTML generated if the condition is true:

```
<%Else%>
```

Here's the HTML generated if the condition is false:

```
<%EndIf%>
```

The syntax for the If condition is

```
<%IF value1 IDC-Operator value2%>
```

The IDC operator is one of four conditional operators you can use to compare two values, as shown in Table 26.1.

TABLE 26.1. THE IDC OPERATORS FOR CONDITIONAL HTML GENERATION.

Operator	Description	Example
EQ	Equals: Value 1 = Value 2	`<%IF City EQ 'Berlin'%>`

Publishing Dynamic Web Pages

CHAPTER 26

785

26

PUBLISHING
DYNAMIC WEB
PAGES

Operator	Description	Example
LT	Less than: Value 1 < Value 2	`<%IF Age LT 21%>`
GT	Greater than: Value 1 > Value 2	`<%IF Age GT 21%>`
CONTAINS	Contains: If Value 2 is a substring of Value 1	`<%IF Lname CONTAINS CompanyName%>`

When there are no matching records, you may want to display a message to the user. To do this, you must use the `If` construct, comparing the internal IDC constant `CurrentRecord` to 0. For example, you can put this into your HTX file:

```
<%IF CurrentRecord EQ 0%>
No Records Found!
<%Endif%>
```

This HTML code will only be output if there are no records. You can even put links back to the original page so the user can try again. The following example shows the `If` construct in action, producing a message to the user and a link back to the question page:

```
<%If CurrentRecord EQ 0%>
<p align="center"><font size="4"><strong> No
Matching Records</strong></font></p>
<p>Sorry, there are no matching records from your selection: <font
color="#FF0000"><strong><%IDC.[Please Enter a
Country]%></strong></font><br>
Please Try again.<br>
<a href="qry_book_CustomersIDC_1.html">Click Here to Try again</a>
<%endif%>
```

The HTML output of this is shown in Figure 26.12.

FIGURE 26.12.

*A conditional
HTX result set.*

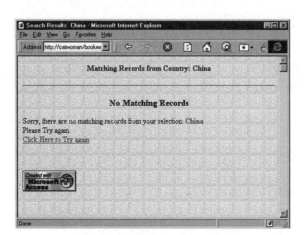

Advanced Techniques of the IDC

So far you have learned about the power of the IDC by using select queries with wildcards and parameters. But the IDC's power is much greater than just select queries. You can also manipulate data with the IDC, as well as provide a filter for your users to aid them in their selection of a parameter.

Using Action Queries with the IDC

The Publish to the Web Wizard will not export any action queries to IDC/HTX format. If you want to provide the ability to insert, delete, and update records, you must write the IDC file and HTX script yourself.

If you want to update records in a table when the user clicks the Submit button, you will have to use the SQL syntax Update statement. You need to write the IDC file manually, as shown:

```
Datasource:nycaccess
Template: inserted.html
SQLStatement:
+Update DistinctRow Customers
+Set Customers.ContactName= '%Contact%'
+WHERE ((Customers.CustomerID= '%[ID]%'));
Password:
Username:admin
```

Remember that an action query returns no rows, so you have to provide a regular HTML file in the Template field of the IDC file. The form that calls this IDC file has two fields, ID and Contact, that are passed to the IDC file:

```
<Form Name="UpdateDB" form action="update.IDC" method="POST">
    <p>Please Enter Your Customer ID <input type="text" size="20"
    name="[ID]"></p>
    <p>Please enter a new Contact Person <input type="text"
    size="20" name="Contact"></p>
    <p><input type="submit" value="See Results"> </p>
</form>
```

Figure 26.13 shows the HTML form calling the IDC file. When run, the query will return the user to a page where he can query the database and view the results. The results are shown in Figure 26.14.

FIGURE 26.13.

HTML form to call the update.IDC *file.*

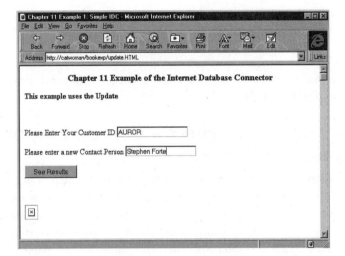

FIGURE 26.14.

The Access 97 database displaying the result of the update over the Web.

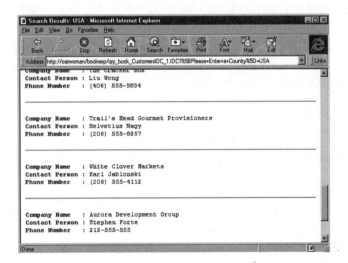

Even though you probably would not want to give access to delete queries, you can perform them by using the SQL `Delete` syntax. Most likely you will want the ability to add a record into an Access 97 database over the Web. This can be accomplished easily using the SQL `Update` syntax. If you wanted to provide an HTML form to add a record to the Customers table, allowing the customer to add a customer ID and name, the IDC file would look like this:

```
Datasource:nycaccess
Template:newrecord.html
```

```
SQLStatement:
+INSERT INTO Customers CustomerID,CustomerName VALUES('%ID%','&Name%')
Password:
Username:admin
```

Remember that an insert will not return any records, so the HTML template can bring a user to a normal HTML file.

Using the IDC to Filter a Combo Box on Another HTML Page

When you export a parameter query to the Web, the HTML search field is a freeform text field. The users of your Web page may not know what all of the possible criteria are. For example, the database stores the United Kingdom as "UK", so a user entering "United Kingdom" will not get any results. You may want to convert the freeform parameter field to a dynamic combo box with all the values that are possible choices. Then use that combo box to query the database. In order to do this you need to use two IDC files, the first to produce the combo box and the second to process the results.

There are a total of four files that you need. The first is an IDC file that will run a query against the database and return all possible cities in a Groupby query. Here are the contents of the IDC file:

```
Datasource:nycaccess
Template:city.htx
SQLStatement:SELECT Customers.City
+FROM Customers
+GROUP BY Customers.City;
Password:
Username:admin
```

The template file used by this IDC uses the BeginDetail/EndDetail loop to fill a combo box, called a Select in HTML. The HTML of city.htx is shown here, and the results are shown in Figure 26.15.

```
<html>
<head>
<title>Chapter 26 Example</title>
</head>
<body background="mcst.jpg" leftmargin="185">
<p align="center"><font size="4"><strong>Chapter 11 Example:
</strong></font></p>
<p align="center"><font size="4"><strong>Dynamic Combo Box
</strong></font></p>
<p><strong>Using an IDC file to Filter another IDC file </strong></p>
<form action="city_1.IDC" method="GET">
```

```
Please Choose a City:
<select name="[Please Choose a City]" size=1>
<%BeginDetail%>
        <option value=<%City%>><%City%>
<%EndDetail%>
</select>
<input type="submit" value="Run Query"> </p>
</form>
<p><img src="msaccess.jpg" width="114" height="43"></p>
</body>
</html>
```

FIGURE 26.15.

The results of running an IDC file to fill a combo box.

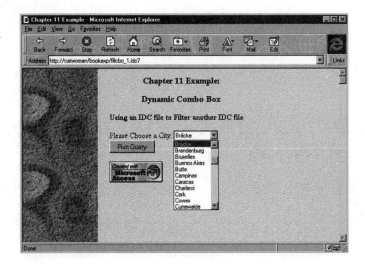

By including a form with a submit value equal to `city_1.idc` and a combo box field named Please Choose a City, you can write an IDC file that will fetch the matching records. The IDC file to do that is shown here:

```
Datasource:nycaccess
Template:city_1.htx
SQLStatement:SELECT Customers.*, Customers.City
+FROM Customers
+WHERE (((Customers.City)='%[Please Choose a City]%'));
Password:
Username:admin
```

This IDC file uses the Please Choose a City field from the `city.htx` output results and produces the results from `city_1.htx`, as shown in Figure 26.16.

FIGURE 26.16.

The results of running the IDC file from the combo box.

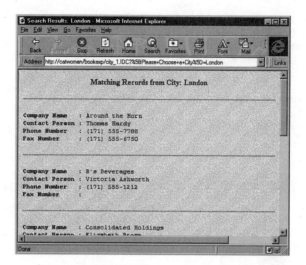

Sample Application: Web Page Guestbook Application

To bring all of the topics together, I created a sample application using the IDC. It's a guestbook application powered by Access 97. If you have ever signed a guestbook on a Web page, chances are that it was created with a complex Common Gateway Interface (CGI) script. With just a few IDC and HTX files, you can create a working guestbook in only a few minutes.

First we need to create a table in our database, which will be called `tblGuestbook`. Table 26.2 displays all the fields we need for our guestbook application.

TABLE 26.2. THE FIELDS OF `TBLGUESTBOOK`.

Field Name	*Data Type*	*Notes*
`ID`	AutoNumber	Used for primary key
`strName`	Text	Used for name
`strEMail`	Text	Used for email
`strURL`	Text	Used for URL
`memComment`	Memo	For the comment
`dtmDate`	Date/Time	Date of the comment (default value set to `NOW()`)

The guestbook application will give a visitor the opportunity to comment on the site. The guestbook page is shown in Figure 26.17. Clicking the Submit button will run the IDC file in Listing 26.1. This IDC file will insert a record with the user's comments about the site into the Access 97 database we placed on the Web.

FIGURE 26.17.

The guestbook page.

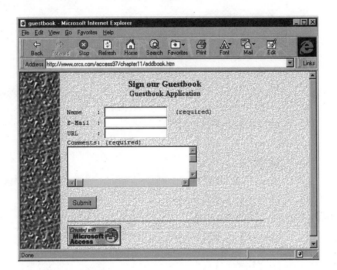

LISTING 26.1. THE INSERT GUESTBOOK IDC FILE.

```
Datasource:nycaccess
Template:searchgb.HTML
SQLStatement:
+INSERT INTO tblGuestbook (strName,strEMail,strURL,memComment) values
+('%txtName%','%txtEMail%','%txtURL%','%memComment%');
Password:
Username:admin
```

After the user successfully makes an entry into the guestbook and the IDC file in Listing 26.1 is run, the result page is `searchgb.html`, shown in Figure 26.18. Users can also get to this page by going to the main menu.

The search guestbook page gives the user three different opportunities to view data in the guestbook. All three choices point to a different IDC file. However, each IDC file uses the same HTX template, shown in Listing 26.2.

FIGURE 26.18.

The search guest-book page.

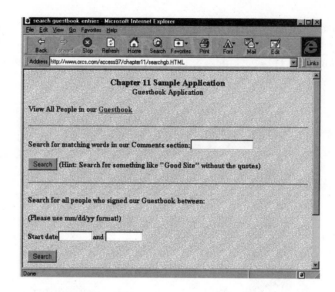

LISTING 26.2. THE SEARCH RESULTS IDC FILE.

```
<HTML>

<TITLE>guestbook entries</TITLE>

<BODY background = "/access97/images/gray.jpg">
<strong></Center>Guestbook Entries</strong></center>

<%BeginDetail%>
<Pre>
<strong>Name       </strong>:<%strName%>
<strong>E-Mail     </strong>:<%strEMail%>
<strong>Web Site   </strong>:<%strURL%>
<strong>Comment    </strong>:<%memComment%>
<strong>Date Signed</strong>:<%dtmDate%>
</Pre>
<HR>

<%EndDetail%>

<%If CurrentRecord EQ 0%>
<p align="center"><font size="4"><strong> No
Matching Records</strong></font></p>

<p>Sorry, there are no matching records from your selection.<br>
Please Try again.<br>
<a href="searchgb.html">Click Here to Try again</a>
<%else%>
<a href="index.html">Chapter 11 Home</a> <br>
```

```
<a href="/access97/index.html">Main Menu</a>
</BODY>

<BR><BR>

<IMG SRC = "/access97/images/msaccess.jpg">

</HTML>
```

There are three ways a user can search. The first way is to just view the entire contents of the whole guestbook. Figure 26.19 shows a sample of the results HTX template from Listing 26.2. This is the result of doing a search of the entire guestbook.

FIGURE 26.19.

The search guest-book page results.

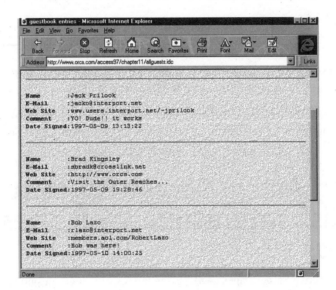

The second way is to search for specific words in all of the comment sections. A user can look for the words "great site," "bad site," or whatever from all the guestbook entries. This can be done by placing the wildcard operator before and after the word the user typed into the text box. The IDC file to do this is shown in Listing 26.3.

LISTING 26.3. THE SEARCH IDC FILE.

```
Datasource:nycaccess
Template:restultbook.htx
SQLStatement:SELECT tblGuestbook.*
+FROM tblGuestbook
+WHERE ((tblGuestbook.memComment) Like  '%%%Enter Search%%%'));
Password:
Username:admin
```

Notice that the Where clause in Listing 26.3 uses the % wildcard, which is ODBC's wildcard, not Access's.

Lastly, the user can view the guestbook entries entered between two dates. The IDC file to do this is shown in Listing 26.4.

LISTING 26.4. THE SEARCH BY DATES IDC FILE.

```
Datasource:nycaccess
Template:restultbook.htx
SQLStatement:SELECT tblGuestbook.*
+FROM tblGuestbook
+WHERE (((tblGuestbook.memComment) Like  '%%%Enter Search%%%'));

Password:
Username:admin
```

Although this application is generic, you can use the techniques discussed here to build huge order-entry or information-centric Web sites rather easily.

As you can see, the IDC is a great way to create dynamic, data-driven Web pages. If you crave even more power and flexibility, Microsoft has provided Active Server Pages technology.

Using Active Server Pages to Publish Interactive Web Sites with Access 97

Microsoft's Active Server Pages (ASP) is the latest technology for publishing your data dynamically on the Web. ASP is a component of Internet Information Server 3.0 and 4.0, and is available to Personal/Peer Web Server as well. With ASP, you can develop the next generation of Web pages that go beyond the limited functionality of the Common Common Gateway Interface (CGI) and the Internet Database Connector. Interactive sites can be built easily with Active Server Pages and can include personalized customer service, order entry, "shopping cart" applications, and many more interactive sites. Web pages can be customized by the user and can be re-created the next time the user visits your site, providing a much more personal experience.

With Active Server Pages you can build interactive sites that keep global variables during a user's visit for you to use. Traditionally, client/server systems could keep state between screens with global variables and classes. Maintaining state on a Web page had never been done before, but with Active Server Pages it is a very easy process. Prior to

Publishing Dynamic Web Pages

CHAPTER 26

795

26

PUBLISHING
DYNAMIC WEB
PAGES

Active Server Pages, you needed very complex CGI scripts using cookies to remember who was at your site as they navigated through it. This functionality is built into Active Server Pages, requiring not a single line of code.

Like its predecessor IDC/HTX, Active Server Pages are browser-independent and pretty easy to implement and customize. It gives you extreme flexibility in publishing your Web site using Access 97. This section will explain what Active Server Pages are and show you how to create Active Server Pages, both with the Publish to the Wizard and on your own.

What Are Active Server Pages?

Have you ever gone to a Web site and saw that the URL was something like `http://www.nycaccessvb.com/default.asp`? A file with the `.asp` extension is an Active Server Page and is accessed just like any HTML page through the HTTP protocol. The big difference between HTML and ASP is how the Web server treats the page. Active Server Pages contain standard HTML and instructions for the Web server. These instructions are server-side scripts that will conditionally output HTML based on conditions you set up or on records in a database. The Web server will process Active Server Pages' instructions, and then the Web server sends plain HTML to your browser.

An Active Server Page is a file that contains HTML or HTML and server-side scripting. When the server processes the ASP file, it will carry out the script on the server and send the browser plain HTML. Because all script is processed on the server, ASP files are browser-independent. If there is no server-side script in the ASP file, the Web server will just output the HTML directly. For example, you can take a normal HTML page and change its extension to `.asp` to create an Active Server Page. When you request the ASP file, you will be sent plain HTML, because the server will write the HTML out from the ASP file. If you add some script to the page, such as to change the background color based on the day of the week, this script will be run on the server and you will only receive HTML with the correct `<Backcolor="XXX">` tag.

VBScript is the default script language of Active Server Pages and will be the focus of the second part of this section. It's a subset of Visual Basic and Visual Basic for Applications. If you are already familiar with VB and VBA, you should be at home with VBScript. If you are already familiar with JavaScript, ASP supports that as well. If you currently use another scripting language, like Perl, you can use it with Active Server Pages if you obtain a plug-in from the vendor of the scripting language.

Because your script executes on the server and only HTML is generated for the Web browser, any complex code and business rules contained in your script are protected. If a user chooses to view the source of the document, all she will see is the HTML sent to the browser. Your code will not be visible to the browser.

Active Server Pages Versus CGI

Active Server Pages are an integrated part of the operating system and is compile-free. A CGI program must be compiled every time a change is made, whereas when you change an ASP file and save it, the script is automatically compiled the next time it is requested. This means that when you're developing an ASP Web application, you can save the page and immediately preview it in a browser.

The structure of a CGI program was described in the previous chapter, and when it's compared to an in-process Active Server Page, performance is vastly improved. ASP will maintain state for you automatically for each user who hits your Web site. ASP can easily integrate to legacy data as well as your Access 97 database. Although it is quite an effort to access ODBC data with CGI, ODBC access is built into Active Server Pages with a powerful data access component called ADO.

Obtaining Active Server Pages

Before converting all of your application's objects, you need to make sure that you have Active Server Pages installed and working, an ODBC data source set up for your database, and a virtual directory with execute permissions set up for your application. Please refer to the sections in Chapter 24 titled "Virtual Directories" and "Setting Up Your Access Database as an ODBC Data Source" for further reference. Information on installing and verifying Active Server Pages is in the next section.

Installing Active Server Pages on Your Machine

Active Server Pages are a free add-in for Microsoft Web servers. To install ASP with Windows NT 4.0, you need to make sure you are running IIS 2.0 and Windows NT 4.0. Then download IIS 3.0 from the Microsoft Web site. You do not need NT 4.0 Service Pack 2.0, but it is recommended. You will need Service Pack 1a, which is included with the ASP download. If you are using Personal/Peer Web Server for Windows 95/NT WS 4, you can download the IIS 3.0 ASP piece from the Microsoft Web site. (For IIS 4.0, you will need to have NT 4.0 Service Pack 3 installed.) When you install IIS 4.0, ASP will be installed by default.

After installing Active Server Pages to your Windows Web server, you should verify that it is working properly. In Knowledge Base article ID# Q162976, Microsoft recommends the following steps to verify that Active Server Pages is installed correctly:

1. After installation and reboot, click the Start button, point to Programs, point to Microsoft Internet Server or Personal Web server, and click Active Server Pages Roadmap. This is illustrated in Figure 26.20.

FIGURE 26.20.

The Active Server Pages roadmap from the Start menu.

2. As shown in Figure 26.21, select the More Samples hyperlink from the ASP in action column.

FIGURE 26.21.

The Active Server Pages roadmap.

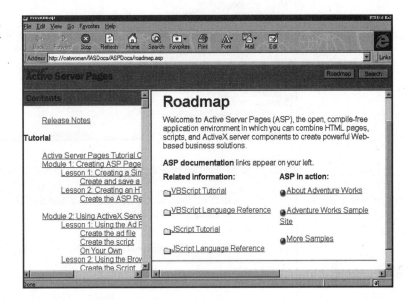

3. Click the ADO Using Server.CreateObject hyperlink shown in Figure 26.22.

You should see a table with order information. If you see the same table shown in Figure 26.23, both Active Server Pages and ADO (a data-access component of Active Server Pages that is discussed later in this chapter) are working correctly. If you did not see the table, you will have to reinstall ASP from setup.

Once you have Active Server Pages set up and your Web server configured, you are ready to create ASP applications. The next section will show you how to generate some simple Active Server Pages quickly with the Publish to the Web Wizard. The second part of this section explains the ASP engine more in-depth, and shows you how to create some custom solutions with Active Server Pages.

FIGURE 26.22.

The Active Server Pages samples.

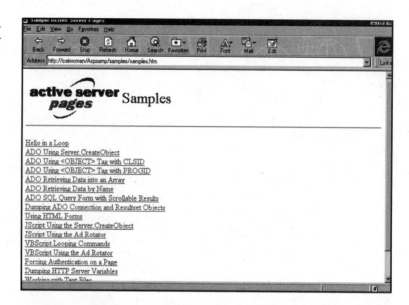

FIGURE 26.23.

The Active Server Pages test results.

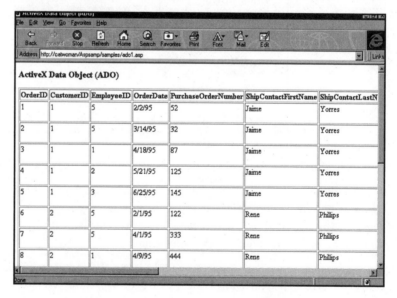

Publishing Dynamic Web Pages

CHAPTER 26

799

26

PUBLISHING
DYNAMIC WEB
PAGES

Creating Active Server Pages with the Publish to the Web Wizard

With the Publish to the Web Wizard, you can save a Microsoft Access 97 form as an Active Server Page. When you do so, the ASP will emulate most of the Access form's navigational functionality. Users will have the ability to browse records, update or delete existing records, and add new records by using a Web browser. The ASP wizard is *not* an Access-form-to-ASP conversion. Only the form navigation will be preserved. Any functions, controls, and formatting that you provided for the form will be lost.

> **NOTE**
>
> Access 97 will allow you to export reports, queries, and tables to an Active Server Page. However, the best resource for an ASP is a form because of the form's functionality. By nature, a form will allow you to add, delete, and edit records. Tables, queries, and reports exported to ASP will just be dynamic snapshots of your data, like an IDC file using a `Select` statement.

To convert a form or group of forms to Active Server Pages using the Publish to the Web Wizard, start the Wizard by choosing File | Save As HTML from the main menu. By now you should be very familiar with this wizard. Choose the database objects you want to export and the HTML template you also want to use. (Remember from Chapter 24 that these templates are fully customizable.) When you get to the format type question page of the wizard, shown in Figure 26.24, choose the Dynamic ASP (Microsoft Active Server Pages) option.

FIGURE 26.24.

The format type page of the Publish to the Web Wizard.

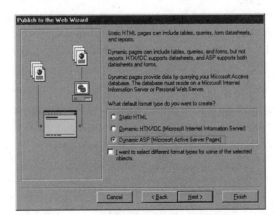

The next page of the wizard, shown in Figure 26.25, asks you for the ODBC data source name, password of your database, URL, and session timeout. Enter the correct information for the ODBC data source and user name and password. For URL, put the URL of the Web server where the ASP file will reside. (See `http://www.mcp.com`.) A session timeout is how long the Active Server Pages will wait before breaking the connection and destroying the session state information for your user, releasing this memory back to the server. ASP files use the default of 20 minutes, so use that.

FIGURE 26.25.

Publish to the Web Wizard session state and data source information.

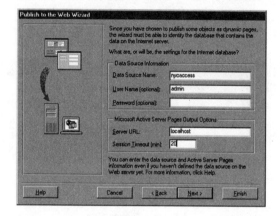

Figure 26.26 shows the final result of your Active Server Page conversion. You have to open your ASP in your browser using its correct URL. For example, you can get to an ASP file on your computer by using

`http://computername/virtualdirectorynam/filename.asp`.

Understanding the Wizard's ASP Output

As you can see in Figure 26.26, the Active Server Page created by the Wizard can browse through records and preserves as much of your form as possible. The wizard does this by using the HTML Layout Control, which is contained in the ALX file created by the wizard. The HTML Layout Control is a 2D control that will allow you to place ActiveX controls on your form in an exact location.

When you're exporting forms to Active Server Pages, the Publish to the Web Wizard follows some basic rules. When the form is converted to an Active Server Page, Access 97 will replace your standard Access controls with ActiveX controls. (For more on ActiveX and ActiveX controls, see Chapter 7, "Using ActiveX Controls for Interactivity.") Table 26.3 lists all the controls exported and their ActiveX equivalents. All of your form's code will not be converted to the Active Server Page; you will have to write the equivalent VBScript in the ASP file. (VBScript is covered in the next section.) All formatting and input masks are also lost.

FIGURE 26.26.

Publish to the Web Wizard's converted Active Server Page.

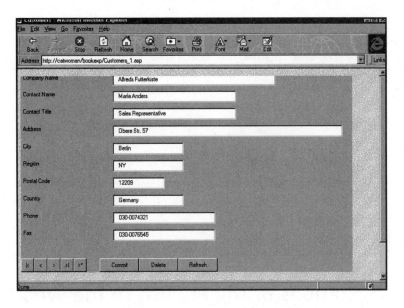

TABLE 26.3. ACCESS CONTROLS CONVERTED TO ACTIVE SERVER PAGES (ACTIVEX CONTROLS).

Microsoft Access 97 Control	*ActiveX Control*
Text box	Text box.
Text box control bound to a hyperlink field	A text box that will display the hyperlink as text. The hyperlink can't be followed.
List box	List box.
Combo box	Combo box.
Label	Label (unless the label has a hyperlink, in which case an HTML hyperlink is created for the label).
Command button	Command button, without any code. If the command button has a hyperlink, an HTML hyperlink is created for the command button.
Option group	A frameless option group.
Option button	Option button.
Check box	Check box.
Toggle button	Toggle button.
ActiveX control	The same ActiveX control, but any code behind the control is lost.
Subform	A datasheet-only representation of the subform.

Table 26.4 lists all of the controls not supported by the Active Server Page conversion.

TABLE 26.4. CONTROLS THAT ARE NOT CONVERTED TO ACTIVE SERVER PAGES.

Control Name
Tab control and all of its contents
Rectangle
Line
Page break
Unbound object frame
Bound object frame
Image control
The form's background `Picture` property

Limitations of the Publish to the Web Wizard

Although the Publish to the Web Wizard does a great job converting your forms to Active Server Pages, it is not as flexible as we would like it to be. All of your form's code is lost, as well as any validation, input masks, and formatting you may have applied. The wizard also uses the ActiveX HTML Layout Control and ActiveX controls on your Active Server Page. This is the biggest limitation of the wizard, because not all browsers support ActiveX controls.

You can use the Publish to the Web Wizard to create some quick-and-dirty Active Server Pages. But if you want robust Active Server Pages that are browser-independent, you will have to learn the basics of ASP.

Active Server Pages 101

In order to create your own Active Server Pages applications with Access 97 as your database back-end, you need to learn the basics of Active Server Pages. Although this topic can fill a whole book, this section will give you the basics to get started. We will cover:

- The ASP engine
- Server-side VBScript
- Application and session objects
- Response and request objects
- The `Global.asa` file

The Active Server Pages Engine

Active Server Pages are a single Internet Server Application Programming Interface (ISAPI) that has been added to IIS 3.0 and 4.0. When a browser requests a file from the Web server, the ISAPI filter checks if the request is for an Active Server Page. If the Web browser requested an Active Server Page, the ASP engine takes over. It parses out the entire ASP file, runs the server-side script from top to bottom, and returns HTML back to the Web browser. The following section describes the server-side script.

Server-Side Scripting

Your ASP file contains server-side script and HTML. The server-side script is written in VBScript by default, and that is what we will focus on in this section. Visual Basic Scripting Edition, better known as VBScript, is a very powerful server- and client-side scripting language.

VBScript is a subset of Visual Basic and shares the same syntax and language features as VBA. If you have been using VBA, you can learn VBScript very quickly. VBScript leaves out some important features of VBA, so it will be small and safe to run over the Internet. For example, file I/O, DLL calling, and the ability to call OLE automation have been left out. All data types (`Long`, `String`, and so on) have been left out, and all data variables use the data type of `variant`. Table 26.5, taken from the VBScript documentation, lists all of the features of VBA that were left out VBScript.

TABLE 26.5. ALL FEATURES OF VBA NOT SUPPORTED BY VBSCRIPT.

Category	*Omitted Feature/Keyword*
Array Handling	Option base
	Declaring arrays with lower bound <> 0
Collection	Add, Count, Item, Remove
	Access to collections using ! character (such as `MyCollection!Foo`)
Conditional Compilation	`#Const`
	`#If...Then...#Else`

continues

TABLE 26.5. CONTINUED

Category	Omitted Feature/Keyword
Control Flow	DoEvents
	GoSub...Return, GoTo
	On Error GoTo
	On...GoSub, On...GoTo
	Line numbers, Line labels
	With...End With
Conversion	CVar, CVDate
	Str, Val
Data Types	All intrinsic data types except Variant
	Type...End Type
Date/Time	Date statement, Time statement
	Timer
DDE	LinkExecute, LinkPoke, LinkRequest, LinkSend
Debugging	Debug.Print
	End, Stop
Declaration	Declare (for declaring DLLs)
	New
	Optional
	ParamArray
	Property Get, Property Let, Property Set
	Static
Error Handling	Erl
	Error
	On Error...Resume
	Resume, Resume Next
File Input/Output	All traditional Basic file I/O
Financial	All financial functions
Object Manipulation	TypeOf
Objects	Clipboard
	Collection

Category	Omitted Feature/Keyword
Operators	Like
Options	Deftype
	Option Base
	Option Compare
	Option Private Module
Strings	Fixed-length strings
	LSet, RSet
	Mid Statement
	StrConv
Using Objects	Collection access using !

VBScript is kept small to ensure that the VBScript compiler will be very quick and efficient. Another reason VBScript has limited functionality is because it can run on the browser as well as the server. If you are running a script on the browser, you do not want to give that script access to the underlying file system. So unscrupulous VBScript developers can't develop a script to reformat your hard drive!

Although some features were left out of VBScript, Table 26.6 (from the VBScript documentation) lists all the features still included.

TABLE 26.6. ALL THE FEATURES INCLUDED IN VBSCRIPT.

Category	Keywords
Array Handling	Array*, Dim, Private*, Public*, ReDim, IsArray, Erase, LBound
Assignments	Set
Comments	Comments using ' or Rem
Constants/Literals	Empty, Nothing, Null, True, False
Control Flow	Do . . .Loop, For. . . Next, For Each. . .Next*, If. . .Then. . .Else, Select Case, While. . . Wend

continues

TABLE 26.6. CONTINUED

Category	Keywords
Conversions	Abs, Asc, AscB, AscW, Chr, ChrB, ChrW, CBool, CByte, CCur, CDate, CDbl, CInt, CLng, CSng, CStr, DateSerial, DateValue, Hex, Oct, Fix, Int, Sgn, TimeSerial, TimeValue
Dates/Times	Date, Time, DateAdd*, DateDiff*, DatePart*, DateSerial, DateValue, Day, Month, Weekday*, Year, Hour, Minute, Second, Now, TimeSerial, TimeValue
Declarations	Const*, Dim, Private*, Public*, ReDim, Function, Sub
Formatting Strings	FormatCurrency*, FormatdateTime* FormatNumber* FormatPercent*
Error Handling	On Error, Err
Input/Output	InputBox, LoadPicture*, MsgBox
Literals	Empty, False, Nothing, Null, True
Math	Atn, Cos, Sin, Tan, Exp, Log, Sgr, Randomize, Rnd

Category	Keywords
Objects	`CreateObject*,` `Dictionary*, Err,` `FileSystemObject*,` `GetObject*, TextStream*`
Operators	Addition (`+`), Subtraction (`-`), Exponentiation (`^`), Modulus arithmetic (`Mod`), Multiplication (`*`), Division (`/`), Integer Division (`\`), Negation (`-`), String concatenation (`&`), Equality (`=`), Inequality (`<>`), Less Than (`<`), Less Than or Equal To (`<=`), Greater Than (`>`), Greater Than or Equal To (`>=`) `Is, And, Or, Xor, Eqv, Imp`
Options	`Option Explicit`
Procedures	`Call, Function, Sub`
Rounding	`Abs, Int, Fix,` `Round*, Sgn`
Script Engine ID	`ScriptEngine*` `ScriptEngineBuildVersion *` `ScriptEngineMajorVersion *` `ScriptEngineMinorVersion *`

continues

TABLE 26.6. CONTINUED

Category	Keywords
Strings	Asc, AscB, AscW, Chr, ChrB, ChrW, Filter*, Instr, InStrB, InstrRev*, Join*, Len, LenB, Lcase, Ucase, Left, LeftB, Mid, MidB, Right, RightB, Replace*, Space, Split*, StrComp, String, StrReverse*, LTrim, RTrim, Trim
Variants	IsArray, IsDate, IsEmpty, IsNull, IsNumeric, IsObject, TypeName*, VarType

* Denotes New Keywords

You can learn VBScript through trial and error by just experimenting with some VBA code and seeing if it will work in VBScript. In addition, Microsoft has made VBScript's documentation available to help you learn and use it. Downloadable from http://www.microsoft.com/vbscript, the documentation is available for free. Once you download and install the documentation, a full language reference and tutorial are installed on your machine, as shown in Figure 26.27.

FIGURE 26.27.
VBScript's documentation.

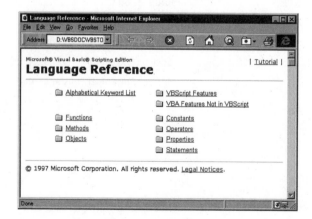

Using VBScript with Active Server Pages

Although you can create great-looking sites that incorporate VBScript on the client side (VBScript actually runs in the Web browser on the local machine), we are only concerned with the server-side script because that is how the ASP engine will generate HTML for you. Here are a few things you can do with VBScript on the server:

- Create a variable and assign a value to it, make decisions to it, or include it in the HTML output.

- Perform operations on variables using If…Then, Select Case, and many other operators.

- Create procedures that only run on the server to do log-ins, data validation, and formatting.

- Dynamically create client-side VBScript to execute on the client in the outputted HTML.

All VBScript that runs on the server is written between <%> tags. You can incorporate pieces of script mixed with HTML. For example, Listing 26.5 is an ASP file that assigns my name to the variable strName and then combines it with HTML to produce a Web page.

LISTING 26.5. A SAMPLE ASP FILE USING A VARIABLE.

```
<HTML>
<HEAD><TITLE>Variables</TITLE></HEAD>
<BODY BGCOLOR=#FFFFFF>
<% strName="Stephen Forte" %>
Hello <%=strName%>
</BODY>
</HTML>
```

When a user requests an ASP file with the code in Listing 26.5, the Web server will run the script between the <%> delimiters and produce a Web page in HTML, as shown in Figure 26.28.

Listing 26.6 shows the HTML source of the Web page in Figure 26.28.

LISTING 26.6. THE HTML SOURCE OF THE WEB PAGE IN FIGURE 26.28.

```
<HTML>
<HEAD><TITLE>Variables</TITLE></HEAD>
<BODY BGCOLOR=#FFFFFF>
Hello Stephen Forte
<BR>
</BODY>
</HTML>
```

FIGURE 26.28.

The Web page produced by the ASP file in Listing 26.5.

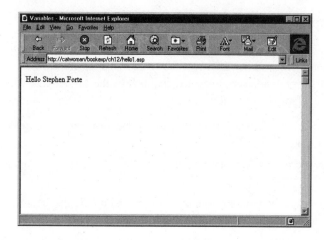

Compare the ASP file in Listing 26.5 and the HTML that the ASP file generated in Listing 26.6. Notice that the VBScript code inside the <%> code is not in the HTML, because that VBScript produced the HTML final result. The code <%=strName%> was replaced in the HTML output with the value of the variable.

In addition to variables, the ASP file in Listing 26.7 uses a loop to increase the value of the variable to produce HTML.

LISTING 26.7. ASP FILE USING SERVER-SIDE SCRIPTING.

```
<HTML>
<HEAD><TITLE>Creating Hello World with Incremental Text Size
Increase</TITLE></HEAD>
<BODY BGCOLOR=#FFFFFF>
<% for i = 3 to 7 %>
    <FONT SIZE=<% = i %>>Hello World</FONT><BR>
<% next %>
<BR>
<BR>
</BODY>
</HTML>
```

When a user requests the ASP file in Listing 26.7, the VBScript will loop five times and increase the font size by one on each loop, producing the Web page in Figure 26.29, with the HTML source shown in Listing 26.8.

Publishing Dynamic Web Pages

CHAPTER 26

811

26

PUBLISHING
DYNAMIC WEB
PAGES

FIGURE 26.29.

The Web page produced by the ASP file in Listing 26.7.

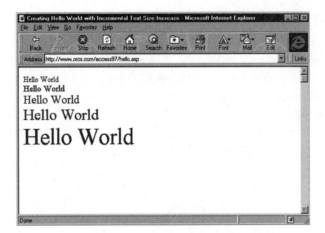

LISTING 26.8. HTML SOURCE FROM THE WEB PAGE GENERATED BY THE ASP IN LISTING 26.7.

```
<HTML>
<HEAD><TITLE>Creating Hello World with Incremental Text Size
Increase</TITLE></HEAD>
<BODY BGCOLOR=#FFFFFF>
    <FONT SIZE=3>Hello World</FONT><BR>

    <FONT SIZE=4>Hello World</FONT><BR>

    <FONT SIZE=5>Hello World</FONT><BR>

    <FONT SIZE=6>Hello World</FONT><BR>

    <FONT SIZE=7>Hello World</FONT><BR>
<BR>
<BR>
</BODY>
</HTML>
```

As you can see in the prior two examples, Active Server Pages use VBScript on the server and produces standard HTML based on your script.

The Application, Session, Response, and Request Objects

Active Server Pages have some built-in objects available for you to use in your application. The following section is only an introduction. For a more in-depth discussion on these objects, see the Active Server Page documentation that is included with IIS or PWS.

The `Application` Object

When developing Active Server Pages, each virtual directory on your Web server is considered an *application*. ASP will refer to each application as an *object*. The `Application` object can be used to maintain application-wide information that can be accessed by all users within an application. The `Application` object comes to life when the first user comes to your directory since your Web server was last started. The `Application` object will be available to all users who visit your site, and lives on until all user sessions time out or the Web server is restarted.

Properties can be added to the `Application` object dynamically that are considered global variables available to each page in your application and each user in your application. Using a property of the `Application` object is easy. The syntax in ASP is

```
<%Application("propertyname")=value %>
```

For example, let's say that you want to determine how many users have logged in at the same time. You can set up a property called `VisiterNum` like this:

```
<%Application("VisiterNum")=0 %>
```

Then, as each user logs into your system, either through a prompt or by going to your default page, you can increase this global variable by one and display the total number of current users. You will also want to decrease the variable by one when a user leaves to keep the number accurate. You would increase the property by one when a new user logs in like this:

```
<%Application("VisiterNum")=Application("VisiterNum")+1
```

When a user logs off, you would use

```
<%Application("VisiterNum")=Application("VisiterNum")-1
```

Displaying the concurrent users your application has at any given point is very easy with Active Server Pages. Just use the following in your ASP file:

```
We have <%=Application("VisiterNum")%> Concurrent users!
```

In summary, the `Application` object stores global variables for use with each page in your application, and can be accessed by every user. To maintain state with individual users, or use global variables for each individual user, you must use the `Session` object.

The `Session` Object

Perhaps the most important object you can learn in Active Server Pages development is the `Session` object. ASP will maintain state for you, and the `Session` object will keep its scope for the current user automatically. If you have 200 users at your page at a time, you will have 200 `Session` objects running.

The `Session` object enables you to create custom properties that will be globally scoped for the specific user that comes to your Web site. `Session` objects are what enable you to provide a unique and personalized experience for your users. For example, you can ask your user what colors she likes and what her name is. You can use the `Session` object to create pages using her favorite colors and refer to her by name for the duration of her visit.

A new `Session` object comes to life every time a new user comes to your Web site, and gets destroyed when the user leaves your Web site or there is a time of inactivity (called the session timeout). To refer to a `Session` object's custom property, you use the identical syntax as the `Application` object:

```
<%Session("propertyname")=value %>
```

Once this property is set, you may refer to it from every page in your Web site.

Using the Response and Request Objects

The `Application` and `Session` objects outlined in the previous section could to create custom properties that maintained state for you. Two more objects, `Response` and `Request`, have methods that enable you to take certain actions or collect data through server-side scripting.

The Response Object

To manage the interaction between the server and the browser, you will use the `Response` object. There are eight methods of the `Response` object available to you, but for our discussion of ASP and Access 97, we will be looking at the `Response.Redirect` and `Response.Write` methods.

Response.Redirect

When you want to display a certain page in the browser, you should use the `Redirect` method of the `Response` object from within your server-side script. For example, let's say you have a log-in screen, and your user is brought to a sign-in screen that will authenticate his user ID against an Access 97 database. If the ID exists, the user goes to your main page. If not, the user goes to a new member sign-up page. You can use an `If...Then` construct along with the `Response.Redirect` method, as shown here.

```
<%If fLogin=True then
    'User Passed login Test
    Response.Redirect "welcome.html"
Else
    'User not in system
    Response.Redirect "newmember.asp"
End if%>
```

Response.Write

When you are constructing an ASP file to output HTML to the Web browser, you will want to write text for the HTML. The way to do this is with the `Write` method of the `Response` object. `Response.Write` has a very simple syntax:

```
Response.Write("string value")
```

For example, you can conditionally create messages for your users based on information they provide. You may ask the user how old she is and then use the `Write` method to give her some feedback when constructing a new page. The following code will use the `Response.Write` method to give the user feedback:

```
<%If intAge < 21 Then
Response.Write("The Drinking Laws in New York")
Response.Write ("State that you cannot buy any")
 Response.Write("alcohol until you reach the age")
Response.Write(" of 21. Sorry!")
Else
Response.Redirect "buy.asp"
End If%>
```

The Request Object

You may have been wondering, "How can you determine what a user typed into a text box on a particular HTML page?" Enter the `Request` object. This is your link to what the user typed into the Web browser. The `Request` object can pass the information from many different places on your user's Web page, but we will only concern ourselves with the calling HTML form on your user's Web page. Each form that calls an ASP will have HTML controls inside of it, like text boxes and combo boxes, as discussed earlier. If you name these controls and then call an ASP file, the ASP file has access to the values inside of these controls with the following syntax:

```
Request.Form("controlname")
```

You can use the `Request.Form` object to capture the user's information and insert it into an Access 97 database or construct a SQL statement. You can also assign a variable to something the user typed, as seen here:

```
<% intAge=Request.Form("txtAge")%>
```

The Global.asa file

There is a special file used with Active Server Pages called the `Global.asa` file. This file is placed in the root of your virtual directory and manages the events of the `Application`

Publishing Dynamic Web Pages

CHAPTER 26

815

26

PUBLISHING
DYNAMIC WEB
PAGES

and Session objects. Global.asa is also used to create Application and Session variables. The Application and Session objects have events that fire off at the start and end of the object's creation:

- Application_OnStart
- Application_OnEnd
- Session_OnStart
- Session_OnEnd

You can use these events to create variables, insert or look up records in a database, and make sure the user has logged on. Global.asa is not like the default document in your virtual directory. It's accessed the first time your user enters any page in your virtual directory. Global.asa produces no HTML like ASP files do, but instead has code that will execute the events associated with the Application and Session objects. As ASP becomes more popular and Microsoft adds a richer event model to it, Global.asa will be the location where these events' code handlers will be placed.

The code in Listing 26.9 is an example of Global.asa using the Session and Application OnStart events. An Application OnStart event fires the first time someone visits your Web site after a stop in the WWW Service in IIS. The Session OnStart event fires once for each visitor when they first arrive. With the Application object, we set a global variable called VisitorNum to keep track of the number of concurrent visitors to our site, as described in a previous section. Inside the Session OnStart event we set a connection to the sample database, so each page can use the connection object created here. (There is more on the database connection features in the section "Introduction to ActiveX Data Objects (ADO)" later on in the chapter.) Inside the Session OnStart event handler, we create five session-wide variables based on the database information.

LISTING 26.9. THE GLOBAL.ASA FILE FOR THE ACCESS97 VIRTUAL DIRECTORY.

```
<SCRIPT LANGUAGE="VBScript" RUNAT="Server">
'Global ASA file for www.orcs.com/access97
'Purpose: Set up Application and Session Properties
'May 1, 1997
'Stephen Forte

</SCRIPT>
<SCRIPT LANGUAGE=VBScript RUNAT=Server>

Sub Application_OnStart
'Set up for Global
Application("VisitorNum")=0
```

continues

LISTING 26.9. CONTINUED

```
Application("Start")=Now
End Sub

Sub Session_OnStart
'This is setting the database connection for the user
'Also This is sets the connection time-out, etc
Session("Start")=Now
        Session("DataConn_ConnectionString") =
"DSN=nycaccess;DBQ=D:/wwwroot/access97/data/nyc.mdb;DriverId=25;FIL=MS
Access;MaxBufferSize=512;PageTimeout=5;"
        Session("DataConn_ConnectionTimeout") = 15
        Session("DataConn_CommandTimeout") = 30
        Session("DataConn_RuntimeUserName") = ""
        Session("DataConn_RuntimePassword") = ""
End Sub
</SCRIPT>
```

Examples of Active Server Page Objects

The example at the end of this chapter will show ASP objects in action. Figure 26.30 also shows an example of ASP objects printed to HTML.

FIGURE 26.30.

ASP objects.

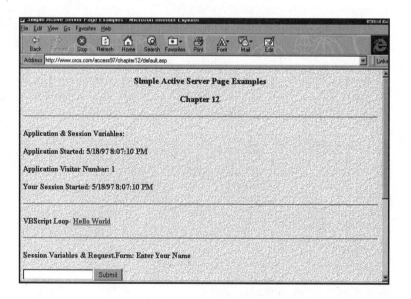

The sample Web page takes advantage of Application and Session custom variables. I created start and VisitorNum variables of the Application object and assigned the current time to the start variable during the Application OnStart event. During the

Publishing Dynamic Web Pages

CHAPTER 26

817

26

PUBLISHING
DYNAMIC WEB
PAGES

OnStart event of the current user's session, I also assigned the session's Start property to the current time. A user's session start time may not be the current time, because the Session OnStart event fires off when the user goes to any page in the /access97 directory. Listing 26.10 shows how we refer to these variables in the sample Web page.

LISTING 26.10. APPLICATION AND SESSION VARIABLES.

```
<hr>
<%Application("VisitorNum")=Application("VisitorNum")+1%>
<p align="left"><strong>Application &amp; Session Variables:</strong></p>
<p><strong>Application Started: <%=Application("Start")%> </strong></p>
<p><strong>Application Visitor Number: <%=Application("VisitorNum")%>
</strong></p>
<p><strong>Your Session Started: <%=Session("Start")%> </strong></p>
<hr>
```

Introduction to ActiveX Data Objects (ADO)

The previous section gave you a through introduction to Active Server Pages. To really make your ASP applications more powerful, include access to an Access 97 database. Within Visual Basic for Applications, the developer has access to programmatic data access object models called Data Access Objects (DAO) and Remote Data Objects (RDO). The next generation of data access is called ActiveX Data Objects or ADO.

ADO enables you to write a client application to access and manipulate data in a database through a "provider." ADO's primary benefits are ease of use, high speed, low memory overhead, and a small disk footprint. ADO can be implemented using VBScript or JScript inside your ASP application.

Using ADO in Your ASP Applications

If you are already familiar with DAO or RDO, you will be right at home with ADO. It works by communicating with an ODBC data source via the new OLEDB application programming interface. To gain access to your data, first set up a Connection object to an ODBC data source. Then open a recordset to hold your data and incorporate the data into your ASP file. When the server processes the ASP file, it will query the data source in real time and provide you a current view of the data.

The object model and advanced techniques of ADO have filled whole books, so we will just cover enough for you to build a robust ASP application. We will look at two objects, the Connection and Recordset objects. Connection and Recordset will give you enough power to create just about any type of ADO application you want.

> **NOTE**
>
> The most basic and powerful parts of the object model are discussed here, but you may want to learn more on your own about ADO because it is the way of the future of data access. For more on ADO, refer to the Microsoft Web site. There are many white papers and help files that you can download to help you learn the object model very quickly. If you also check out the OLEDB SDK available at the Microsoft Web site, there are a few sample applications using ADO as well. If you own Visual Studio or have access to the MSDN Visual Tools CD-ROM library, the ADO object model is fully referenced.

The Connection Object

A Connection object represents a unique session with a data source. In the case of a client/server database system, it may be equivalent to an actual network connection to the server. The Connection object is very similar to the Workspace object in DAO. Before you work with a Connection object, you must set it up as an object variable equal to a valid connection. The syntax is

```
Set dbconn=server.createobject("adodb.connection")
```

Once you have set up a Connection object, you will want to open a connection to an ODBC data source so you can fetch or update data using the Open method. The syntax for the Open method of the Connection object is

```
connection.Open ConnectionString, UserID, Password
```

ConnectionString is a valid ODBC connection string, as shown here:

```
dbconn.open "dsn=NYCACCESS ;uid=Admin"
```

Once you have a valid connection set, you can use the Execute method of the Connection object to create a valid recordset. The syntax is

```
Set recordset = connection.Execute(CommandText, RecordsAffected, Options)
```

Table 26.7 describes the parameters of the Execute method.

TABLE 26.7. THE PARAMETERS OF THE EXECUTE METHOD.

Parameter	Description
CommandText	A string containing the SQL statement, table name, or stored procedure to execute.
RecordsAffected	Optional. A long variable to which the provider returns the number of records that the operation affected.

Parameter	Description
Options	Optional. A `CommandTypeEnum` value that indicates how the provider should evaluate the `CommandText` argument. Can be one of the following constants:
adCmdText	Evaluate `CommandText` as a textual definition of a command.
adCmdTable	Evaluate `CommandText` as a table name.
adCmdStoredProc	Evaluate `CommandText` as a stored procedure.
adCmdUnknown	The type of command in the `CommandText` argument is not known.

The `Recordset` Object

A `Recordset` object is a representation of an entire set of records from a table, or the results of an executed SQL statement. It's your hook to manipulating data at the record level. Just like in DAO and RDO, at any time the `Recordset` object only refers to a single record within the set as the current record. When you use ADO, you manipulate data almost entirely using `Recordset` objects. All `Recordset` objects are constructed using records (rows) and fields (columns).

There are many properties and methods of the `Recordset` object that are available to you. We are going to look at the `EOF` (for End of File) property in the next example. `EOF` will allow you to move through a recordset inside of a loop from the first record to the last. Listing 26.11 opens a connection and a recordset, loops through all the records, and writes then to the HTML output of the ASP file.

LISTING 26.11. THE ADO.ASP FILE.

```
<!DOCTYPE HTML PUBLIC "-//IETF//DTD HTML//EN">
<html>
<head>
<title>Chapter 26: ADO Example</title>
</head>
<body>
<h2 align="center">Northwind Traders Customer Listing </h2>
<p align="center">Chapter 12 ADO Example</p>
<hr>
<% 'Begin VB Server-Side Script
Dim x
Dim dbconn
Dim rst
'Set up connection
```

continues

LISTING 26.11. CONTINUED

```
Set dbconn=server.createobject("adodb.connection")

'Set up database
dbconn.open "dsn=NYCACCESS"

'Set up the recordset
set rst=dbconn.execute ("Select * from Customers")

'Use for a counter
x=1
Do Until rst.eof
    response.write x & ". " & rst("CompanyName")%>
<br>
<%rst.movenext
x=x+1
loop
dbconn.close
'End All Server-Side Script%>
<hr>

<p>Chapter 26 <a href="default.asp">Home</a></p>
</body>
</html>
```

Figure 26.31 demonstrates the result of the ASP file in Listing 26.11.

FIGURE 26.31.

The results of the ado.asp *file.*

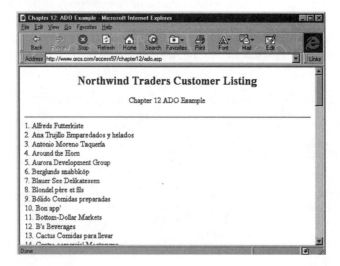

As you can see with the combination of ASP, VBScript, and ADO, you can create very powerful data-driven Web pages with Access 97 databases as an engine. The last section of this chapter describes a real-life example.

Real-Life Example: Establishing a Self-Maintaining, Membership-Based Web Page

If you run a Web site that needs to keep track of members and provide a log-in, Access 97 and ASP are your answer. I run a local Access and Visual Basic Users Group in New York City. We have a Web site located at http://www.nycaccessvb.com that uses ASP to display a member listing, meeting finder, and a code library, all created by ASP files that hit our Access 97 database. In addition, we want a member to be able to update his or her own information via a login and see some Web site content that is available to only the members, like a job forum.

This application should only let people with a valid user ID and password enter the system. After a user logs on, we set a session variable to the user ID so the user will not have to keep typing in his name at every subsequent page in the system. Lastly, the system will write to the database the current date as the last login time.

The application starts when the user visits the NYC Access VB Web site with a prompt to log in, as shown in Figure 26.32.

FIGURE 26.32.

The login prompt.

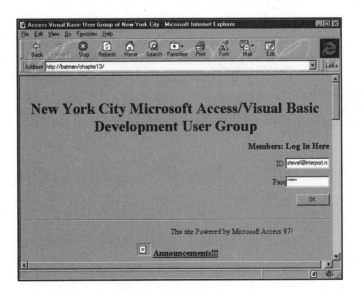

The login page is just an HTML form that calls an ASP file as its action. Listing 26.12 shows the HTML code to create the login form.

LISTING 26.12. HTML CODE TO CREATE A LOGIN CODE.

```
<form action="login.asp"
method="post" name="frmLogin">
    <p align="right">ID <input type="text" size="15" name="txtID"></p>
    <p align="right">Pass<input type="password" size="15"
    name="txtPass"></p>
    <p align="right"><input type="submit" name="cmdOK"
    value="    OK    "> </p>
</form>
```

When the user clicks the Submit button, the ASP `Login.asp` runs. `Login.asp` looks at the membership Access 97 database. This table has a field for the user ID, password, last login date, and other fields. Listing 26.13 shows the contents of the `Login.asp` file.

LISTING 26.13. ASP FILE LOGIN.ASP.

```
<%@ LANGUAGE="VBSCRIPT" %>

<HTML>
<HEAD>
<META NAME="GENERATOR" Content="Microsoft Visual InterDev 1.0">
<META HTTP-EQUIV="Content-Type" content="text/html; charset=iso-8859-1">
<TITLE>Login Form</TITLE>
</HEAD>
<BODY>
<BODY BGCOLOR=#FFFFFF>


<%
'Purpose: All users to login
'Will kick back if user did not enter a UserID or pwd
'Also will kick back if incorrect pwd

'Variables
Dim rst
Dim strUserID
Dim strPass
Dim strSQL

Dim ado_OpenKeyset
Dim ado_LockOptimistic

'For the recordset open arguments
ado_OpenKeyset=1
```

Publishing Dynamic Web Pages

CHAPTER 26

823

26

PUBLISHING
DYNAMIC WEB
PAGES

```
ado_LockOptimistic=3

'Pass the form info into the variables
strPass=request.form("txtPass")
strUserID=request.form("txtID")

'Build SQL String
strSQL="SELECT FName, LName, Email, lastLogin, pass, Status FROM
tblMembers WHERE (Email =" & "'" & strUserID & "'" & ")"

'set up rst
Set rst=server.createobject("ADODB.RECORDSET")

'Open rst
rst.open strSQL, _
    "DSN=nycaccess",ado_OpenKeyset,ado_LockOptimistic

'First test to See that the User Entered a UserID and a Password
If strUserID="" or strPass="" then
    Response.Write "You did not enter a User ID or a Password, please do."

else

'If rst is at the end of file (EOF) then there is no match
if rst.eof then
    response.write "Your User ID is not in the System!!!"

else
'OK a match, see if correct pass

    If rst("pass")= strPass Then
'Pass OK
'Begin to Build the WWW page

        Response.Write "Welcome " & rst("FName") & " " & rst("LName")
        Response.Write "<br>"
        Response.Write "You last logged on " & rst("lastLogin")
        Response.Write "<br><br> <a href=" & chr(34) & "admin.htm" &
chr(34) & ">Update </a>Account profile "
        Response.Write "<br>  <a href=" & chr(34) & "job.htm" & chr(34) &
">Members </a> Only Job Forum"

'Set the Last Update Time to Now

rst.update ("lastlogin"),Date()


'Set a "Global" or Session Variable
Session("User") = strUserID

Else
```

continues

LISTING 26.13. CONTINUED

```
'Incorrect pass
    response.write "Your User ID: <strong>" & strUserID & "</strong> is
OK, Wrong Password!!!"
end if


end if
end if
'Close rst
rst.close
%>
</BODY>
</HTML>
```

The `Login.asp` file shown in Listing 26.13 will first set up variables for use in the script. Then a SQL statement is built using the information the user input into the form as part of the `Where` clause. The variable `strUserId` is used to hold the user's ID. The SQL statement looks like this:

```
strSQL="SELECT FName, LName, Email, lastLogin, pass, Status FROM
tblMembers WHERE (Email =" & "'" & strUserID & "'" & ")"
```

As you can see, the primary key of `tblMembers` is the field `Email`. A user's email address is also his user ID. If the user did not enter a user ID or password, he gets a warning with a `Response.Write` method, as shown in Figure 26.33.

FIGURE 26.33.

The prompt when no password or user ID is entered.

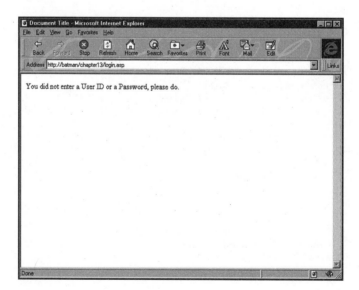

If the user did enter a password and a valid user ID, the script looks to see if the user entered the correct password. Here's the VBScript code to determine if a password is correct:

```
If rst("pass")= strPass
```

If the password is incorrect, the user is prompted with a Response.Write, as shown in Figure 26.34.

FIGURE 26.34.

The incorrect password prompt.

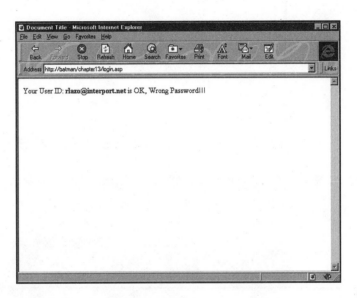

If the user enters the correct password, we must set a session variable to the user ID and update the Access 97 database field called lastlogin, as shown here:

```
'Set the Last Update Time to Now
rst.update ("lastlogin"),Date()
'Set a "Global" or Session Variable
Session("User") = strUserID
```

After the user is validated, you use the Response.Write to build the members-only Web page. You may choose to use a Response.Redirect to show the user a completely different HTML members only page. The members-only page is shown in Figure 26.35.

Now that the user is logged into the system, you will want to provide all of the member-specific content here. In addition, one of the key selling points of ASP is that you can give users the ability to maintain their own account information. In this situation, you are only concerned with giving the user the ability to change his own password. After the user logs into the members-only site, there is an option to update his own account information, as shown in Figure 26.36.

FIGURE 26.35.

The members-only page.

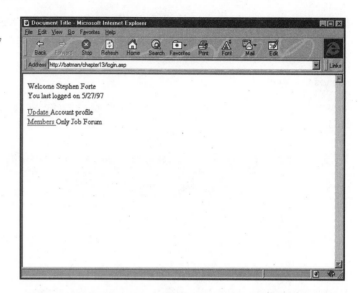

FIGURE 26.36.

The members-only change password page.

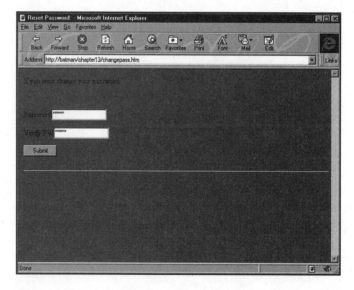

There is an HTML form available for the user to enter a new password into the system and verify it. Listing 26.14 shows the HTML code needed to create this form.

Publishing Dynamic Web Pages

CHAPTER 26

827

26

PUBLISHING
DYNAMIC WEB
PAGES

LISTING 26.14. THE CHANGE PASSWORD FORM.

```
<form action= "changepass.asp" form method="POST" name="frmNew">
    <p>Password<input type="password" size="20" name="txtPass"></p>
    <p>Verify PW<input type="password" size="20" name="txtVerify"></p>
    <p><input type="submit" name="cmdOK" value="Submit"></p>
</form>
```

The form in Listing 26.14 calls the changepass.asp file, which does the actual password change for the user and confirms the password change. Listing 26.15 shows the source code for the changepass.asp file.

LISTING 26.15. THE CHANGEPASS.ASP FILE.

```
<%@ LANGUAGE="VBSCRIPT" %>

<HTML>
<HEAD>
<META NAME="GENERATOR" Content="Microsoft Visual InterDev 1.0">
<META HTTP-EQUIV="Content-Type" content="text/html; charset=iso-8859-1">
<TITLE>Document Title</TITLE>
</HEAD>
<BODY>

<%
'Purpose: Check for password confirmation and update database
'If the password is not the same in each box, abort

'Dims
Dim rst
Dim strPass
Dim strVerify
Dim strSQL

Dim ado_OpenKeyset
Dim ado_LockOptimistic

ado_OpenKeyset=1
ado_LockOptimistic=3

'Get the values the user entered in the form
strPass=request.form("txtPass")
strVerify=request.form("txtVerify")

'Check to see if the text boxes match
```

continues

LISTING 26.15. CONTINUED

```
If strpass <> strVerify then
    response.write "You did not enter the correct password in the verify
box! <br>"
    response.write "Please do"

else

    strSQL="SELECT  pass, Status FROM tblMembers WHERE (Email =" & "'" &
Session("User") & "'" & ")"

    'set up rst
    Set rst=server.createobject("ADODB.RECORDSET")

    rst.open strSQL, _
        "DSN=nycaccess",ado_OpenKeyset,ado_LockOptimistic




    if rst.eof then
        response.write "Your User ID is not in the System!!!"

    else


        rst.update ("pass"),strVerify
        Response.Write "You password has been changed, please remember
it!!"

    end if
    rst.close
end if%>

</BODY>
</HTML>
```

The code in Listing 26.15 is not all that different than the code in Listing 26.13. In Listing 26.15, we first make sure that the user typed in a matching password in the Confirmation box, and only proceeds if she did. Then Listing 26.15 builds a SQL string using the global session variable User, which we defined at login as the user ID in the Where clause. This is an example of maintaining state at a Web site. There is no need to ask the user to retype in his user ID or call a complex and server intensive CGI-BIN program to maintain state.

After the recordset is opened, we use the `Update` method of the `Recordset` object to update the user's password in the database on the Web server. The next time the user logs in, the new password will be in effect. Figure 26.37 shows the confirmation screen that the password has changed.

FIGURE 26.37.
The members-only change password page.

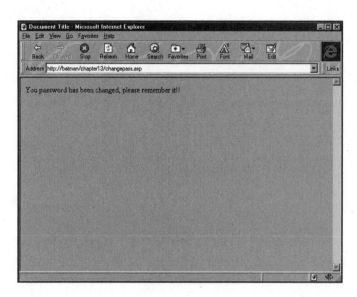

This concludes our real-life example. For some more ideas and examples, you can go to `http://www.orcs.com/access97` for a listing of all Web sites that are using Access 97 as a data engine.

I hope that this example and this chapter can get you started with building great Internet-based Access 97 applications!

Summary

This chapter showed you how to use all aspects of Access 97 Web publishing, from first generation IDC creation to the most current OLEDB-Access provider-based Web site. It is now up to you to take the knowledge you gained in this chapter and build some killer Web applications powered by Access 97.

APPENDIX A

Operators, Functions, and Expressions

IN THIS APPENDIX

Constants

Constants are somewhat like Access 97 reserved words in that the numeric or string value doesn't change during program execution. Constants can be divided into three groups: predefined VBA constants, intrinsic constants, and system-defined constants.

Predefined Constants

Predefined constants are constants that the developer creates, usually in modules. A predefined constant begins with the letters CONST. For example:

```
CONST C = 186,000           Speed of light
CONST Dearth = 7926.68      Diameter of the Earth
CONST Pi = 3.14159          Pi is 3.14159
```

These things hold true no matter the circumstances. After constants are loaded, they can be used anywhere.

Intrinsic Constants

Intrinsic constants, such as VbString and VarType, are constants supplied by Visual Basic. They don't have to be loaded or declared separately. *Intrinsic constants* can be divided into five categories: data access constants, macro action constants, security constants, variant constants, and miscellaneous constants. Because these can't be disabled, other constants can't use the same names. Intrinsic constants can be used only in modules.

System-Defined Constants

Only five system-defined constants exist: Yes, No, On, Off, and Null. They can be used in every object of the database container except modules.

Operators

An *operator* is a word or symbol representing an operation that needs to be performed on one or more elements of an expression. Access 97 includes several different classes of operators that you can use in your expressions, including arithmetic, concatenation, comparison, and logical operators. The following sections detail the operators included in each of these classes.

Arithmetic Operators

The first of the four groups of operators is the arithmetic operators. These operators are used to execute mathematical calculations between two or more numbers:

^	Raises one number to the power of another number.
*	Multiplies one number by another number.
/	Divides and returns a floating-point result.
\	Divides and returns an integer result.
MOD	Stands for *modulus*; it returns the remainder of two divided numbers.
+	Adds one number to another number.
-	Subtracts one number from another.

Concatenation Operators

The second group of operators is the concatenation operators. These operators are used to bring strings together. The word "concatenation" actually means "to unite or bring things together." In Access 97, *concatenation* refers to "a family of operators found in expressions." The Access 97 concatenation operators are used to unite or bring strings together. There are two types of concatenation symbols:

&	Brings two string fields together as one field.
+	Brings two variable number fields together and sums them. It can also be used to bring two text strings together; however, it doesn't sum these text strings.

An example of this is

```
String = "Hello " & "World"
```

This will produce the string "Hello World." The same result can be obtained by using + instead of &.

TIP

It is generally recommended that you use the & operator instead of the + operator to concatenate strings to avoid any confusion with the addition sign.

Comparison Operators

Comparison operators make up the third group of operators. They utilize Boolean symbols and are used to perform comparisons between two or more fields or expressions. The comparison operators are shown in the following list:

=	One field is equal to another field.
<>	One field is not equal to another field.
<	One field is less than another field.
>	One field is greater than another field.
<=	One field is less than or equal to another field.
>=	One field is greater than or equal to another field.
Like	Pattern-matching similar to the Find feature; for example, Like abc* finds all records that start with abc.
Is	Object-reference comparison that checks whether two object references refer to the same object.

Logical Operators

The final group of operators is the logical operators. They perform logical actions between two fields or expressions. The logical operators are listed here, along with examples of their usage:

Not   Negation between two fields or expressions.

The following example illustrates the use of the Not operator:

```
A = 10: B = 8: C = 6      ' Initialize variables for comparison examples.
MyValue = Not(A > B)      ' Returns False.
MyValue = Not(B > A)      ' Returns True.
```

And   Conjunction between two fields or expressions.

The use of the And operator is illustrated here:

```
MyValue = A > B And B > C      ' Returns True.
MyValue = B > A And B > C      ' Returns False.
```

Or   Disjunction between two fields or expressions.

The use of the Or operator is shown here:

```
MyValue = A > B Or B > C      ' Returns True.
```

Between…And   Midsection between two fields or expressions.

You use the Between…And operator to evaluate whether the value of an expression falls within a range of values. You cannot use wildcard characters with the Between…And operator:

```
Xor     Exclusion between two fields or expressions.
```

The following example illustrates the use of the Xor operator:

```
MyValue = A > B Xor B > C      ' Returns False.
```

```
Eqv   Equivalence between two fields or expressions.
```

The following example illustrates the use of the Eqv operator:

```
MyValue = A > B Eqv B > C       ' Returns True.
```

```
Imp   Implication between two fields or expressions.
```

The use of the Imp operator is shown here:

```
MyValue = A > B Imp B > C       ' Returns True.
```

System Functions

A *function* is a procedure that returns a value. You can use a function as part of an expression. If you are declaring a function, you begin with the Function statement and end with the End Function statement. Functions operate similarly to operators; however, they aren't represented by symbols. For example, the + operator and the SUM function perform the same action: they add. The difference between the two is that the + operator can add only two items at a time, whereas the SUM function can total all the items. Of course, you could have *one item + another item + another item* and so on, but it might be easier to SUM all the items.

Altogether, Access 97 provides more than 160 functions of various types.

Types of Functions

Some of the types of functions that are included in Access 97 are

- Conversion
- Date/Time
- Financial
- Mathematical
- String Manipulation
- Datatype Conversion
- Domain
- Miscellaneous

This section contains definitions and examples of the many types of functions in this list.

Conversion

The Asc function returns a character code corresponding to the ASCII value of the character that is passed to it. An example is shown here:

```
NewNumber = Asc("A")     ' Returns 65.
```

The Hex function returns the hexadecimal value of a number that is passed to it as an argument:

```
NewHex = Hex(10)     ' Returns the value A.
```

The Oct function returns the octal value of a number that is passed to it as an argument:

```
NewOct = Oct(459)     ' Returns the value of 713.
```

Date/Time

The Date function returns the current system date:

```
NewDate = Date     ' NewDate now contains the current system date.
```

The DateAdd function adds x number of months to a date to display a date x months in the future. The DateDiff function displays the number of days between today and a given date. The DatePart function takes a date as an argument and returns the quarter of the year in which the date occurs. The DateSerial function returns a date datatype for a specified year, month, and day. The DateValue function converts a string value to a date datatype.

The Day function returns an integer that represents the day of the week of a date that is passed to the Day function as an argument. The FileDateTime function shows the date and time that a file was created or was last modified. The IsDate function is used to evaluate whether an expression can be converted to a date. The Month function takes a date as an argument and returns a value that is the number of the month in the date argument. The Now function returns the current system date and time. The TimeSerial function returns a time value for an hour, minute, and second that are passed in as an argument to the TimeSerial function. The TimeValue function converts a string to a time value. The Time function returns the current system time. The Weekday function takes a date as an argument and returns a numerical value representing the day of the week that is held in that date. The Year function takes an argument that is a date and returns the year contained in the date argument.

Financial

The DDB function is used to indicate the potential depreciation of an asset over a specified period of time. The DDB function uses the double-declining balance method. An example of the syntax for the DDB method is

```
DDB(cost, salvage, life, period[, factor])
```

cost is the initial cost of the asset, salvage is the value of the asset at the end of the evaluation period, life represents the useful life of the asset, period is the period for which the depreciation is calculated, and factor is an optional value that specifies the rate at which the balance declines.

The SLN function is used to specify the straight-line depreciation of an asset for a single period of time. An example of the syntax for the SLN function is

```
SLN(cost, salvage, life)
```

cost is the initial cost of the asset, salvage is the value of the asset at the end of the evaluation period, and life is the useful life of the asset.

The SYD function is used to return the sum-of-years' digits depreciation of an asset. The syntax for the SYD function is

```
SYD(cost, salvage, life, period)
```

cost is the initial cost of the asset, salvage is the value of the asset at the end of the evaluation period, life is the useful life of the asset, and period is the period for which depreciation is calculated.

The FV function returns the future value of an annuity and is calculated based on fixed payments and interest rate. The syntax for the FV function is

```
FV(rate, nper, pmt[, pv[, type]])
```

rate is the interest rate, nper is the total number of payments, pmt is the payment that is made, pv is an optional value that represents the present value of the future payments that will be made, and type is an optional value that specifies when the payments are due.

The Rate function returns the interest rate per period for an annuity. An example of the syntax for the Rate function is

```
Rate(nper, pmt, pv[, fv[, type[, guess]]])
```

nper is the total number of payments, pmt is the amount of each payment, pv is the present value of the future payments that will be made, fv is an optional value that represents the future value that will be there after the last payment, type is an optional value that indicates when the payments will be made, and guess is an optional value that represents the value you estimate will be returned.

The IRR function returns the internal rate of return for a series of payments. A sample of the syntax for the IRR function is

IRR(values()[, guess])

values() is an array of values that represent cash flow values, and guess is an optional value that represents the value you estimate will be returned.

The MIRR function returns the modified internal rate of return for a series of payments. An example of the syntax is

MIRR(values(), finance_rate, reinvest_rate)

values() is an array of values that represent cash flow values, finance_rate is the interest paid as finance charges, and reinvest_rate is the interest rate that comes from cash reinvestment.

The NPer function returns the number of periods for an annuity based on fixed payments and interest rate. An example of the syntax for the NPer function is

NPer(rate, pmt, pv[, fv[, type]])

rate is the interest rate per period, pmt is the payment made each period, pv is the present value of the future payments to be made, fv is an optional value representing the future value of the cash balance after the last payment, and type is an optional value that represents when the payments are due.

The IPmt function returns the interest payment for a specified period of an annuity based on fixed payments and interest rate. An example of the syntax for the IPmt function is

IPmt(rate, per, nper, pv[, fv[, type]])

rate is the interest rate per period, per is the payment period that is being calculated, nper is the total number of payments, pv is the present value of the future payments, fv is an optional value that represents the future value of the balance after the last payment, and type is an optional value that represents when the payments are due.

The Pmt function returns the payment for an annuity based on fixed payments and a fixed interest rate. An example of the Pmt function syntax is

Pmt(rate, nper, pv[, fv[, type]])

rate is the interest rate per period, nper is the total number of payments, pv is the present value of the future payments, fv is an optional value that represents the future value of the balance after the final payment, and `type` is an optional value that represents when the payments are due.

The `PPmt` function returns the principal payment of an annuity based on fixed payments and interest rate. The syntax for the `PPmt` function is

`PPmt(rate, per, nper, pv[, fv[, type]])`

`rate` is the interest rate, *per* is the period of payments that is being calculated, `nper` is the total number of payments, *pv* is the present value of the future payments, *fv* is the future value of the balance after the final payment, and *type* represents when the payments are due.

The `NPV` function returns the net present value of an investment based on payments and a discount rate. An example of the syntax is

`NPV(rate, values())`

`rate` is the discount rate, and `values()` is an array of values that represent payments.

The `PV` function returns the value of an annuity based on fixed payments and interest rate. An example of the `PV` function is

`PV(rate, nper, pmt[, fv[, type]])`

`rate` is the interest rate, `nper` is the total number of payments, `pmt` is the payment amount, `fv` is an optional value that represents the future value of the balance after the last payment, and `type` is an optional value indicating when the payments are made.

Mathematical

The `Atn` function returns the arctangent of a number:

`Atn(number)`

The `Cos` function returns the cosine of a number:

`Cos(number)`

The `Sin` function returns the sine of a number:

`Sin(number)`

The `Tan` function returns the tangent of an angle:

`Tan(number)`

The `Exp` function returns the base of a natural logarithm raised to a power:

`Exp(number)`

The `Log` function returns the natural logarithm of a number:

```
Log(number)
```

The `Sqr` function returns the square root of a number:

```
Sqr(number)
```

The `Rnd` function returns a random number. The optional number argument to the `Rnd` function is a numeric expression to use as a seed:

```
Rnd[(number)]
```

The `Abs` function returns the absolute value of a number:

```
Abs(number)
```

The `Sgn` function returns the sign of a number:

```
Sgn(number)
```

The `Int` and `Fix` functions remove the fractional part of a number and return the integer value that remains. `Int` rounds the value it returns up to the nearest number if the number is negative, while `Fix` rounds the value it returns down to the nearest number if the number is negative. An example of the syntax for both of these functions is

```
Int(number)
Fix(number)
```

String Manipulation

The `StrComp` function returns the results of a string comparison. The syntax for the `StrComp` function is

```
StrComp(stringone, stringtwo,num)
```

`stringone` represents the first string of the comparison, `stringtwo` represents the second string of the comparison, and `num` is an optional argument that indicates whether to use a textual comparison or a binary comparison.

The `StrConv` function returns a string that has been converted according to a specified manner. An example of the syntax is

```
StrConv(string, conversion)
```

`string` is the string to be converted, and `conversion` can be any of the following constants:

- `vbUpperCase` has a value of 1 and converts the string to uppercase characters.
- `vbLowerCase` has a value of 2 and converts the string to lowercase characters.

- vbProperCase has a value of 3 and converts the first letter of every word in the string to an uppercase character.

- vbWide has a value of 4 and converts single-byte characters in the string to double-byte characters. This constant only applies to Far East locales.

- vbNarrow has a value of 8 and converts double-byte characters to single-byte characters. This constant only applies to Far East locales.

- vbKatakana has a value of 16 and converts all the Hiragana characters in the string to Katakana characters. This constant only applies to Japan.

- vbHiragana has a value of 32 and converts Katakana characters in the string to Hiragana characters. This constant only applies to Japan.

- vbUnicode has a value of 64 and converts the string to Unicode. This constant forces the function to use the default code page of the system that it is run on.

- vbFromUnicode has a value of 128 and converts the string from Unicode to the default code page of the system that it is run on.

The LCase function converts a string to lowercase characters.

The UCase function converts a string to uppercase characters.

The Space function returns a string that consists of a series of spaces. You can specify the number of spaces as a parameter to the Space function call. The following example shows the syntax for the Space function:

```
NewString = "Hello" & Space(10) & "World"
```

The String function operates in much the same way as the Space function. You pass it a character to repeat and the number of times that you want the character repeated, and the String function returns a string of repeating characters of the length that you have specified. An example of the String function is

```
NewString = String(5, "~")
```

This sample code will return the following string: ~~~~~.

The Len function returns the number of characters in a string.

The InStr function returns the position of a string within another string. It returns the position of the first occurrence of the string that it is searching for. The following example shows the syntax for the InStr function:

```
NewPosition = Instr(4, StringToSearch, CharToSearchFor, 1)
```

The Left function returns a specified number of characters from the left of the string that is passed to the function as a parameter. The following code example shows the syntax for the Left function:

```
AString = Left(SearchString, num)
```

SearchString is the string to be searched, and num is the number of characters to be returned as a result of running the Left function.

The LTrim function strips leading spaces from a string that is passed as an argument to the function. The following example shows what happens to a string that is passed to the LTrim function:

```
OldString = "    This is the string    " 'initialize the string
NewString = LTrim(OldString)
```

After the LTrim function, OldString contains the following string:

```
"This is the string"
```

The RTrim function strips the trailing spaces from a string that is passed as an argument to the function. The following example shows what happens to a string that is passed to the RTrim function:

```
NewString = RTrim(OldString)
```

After running the RTrim function, OldString contains the following string:

```
"    This is the string"
```

The Trim function strips both leading and trailing spaces from a string that is passed as a parameter to the function. The following example shows what happens to a string that is passed to a Trim function:

```
NewString = Trim(OldString)
```

After the Trim function, OldString contains the following string:

```
"This is the string"
```

The Mid function returns a specified number of characters from a string that is passed to the Mid function as a parameter. The following code example shows the usage of the Mid function:

```
NewString = Mid(OldString, 1, 3)
```

After running the Mid function, NewString contains the following string: Thi.

The `Right` function returns the specified number of characters from the right side of a string that is passed to the `Right` function as a parameter. The following code example shows the syntax of the `Right` function:

```
NewString = Right(OldString,2)
```

After running the `Right` function, `NewString` contains the following string: ng.

The `Option Compare` statement sets the default string comparison method that is used. The `Option Compare` statement can take one of two values, either `Option compare Binary` or `Option compare Text`. If the method is `Option compare Binary`, the comparison is made with the binary values of each string in the comparison. If the method used is `Option compare Text`, the comparison is made with the actual text value of each string in the comparison.

Datatype Conversion

The following functions are used to force datatype conversions. These functions are described and examples of their syntax are found in "Conversion" earlier in this chapter.

The `CBool` function is used to convert an expression to a Boolean value. If the expression evaluates to a nonzero value, `CBool` returns True; otherwise, it returns False.

```
A = 5: B = 5    ' Initialize test variables.
NewBool = CBool(A = B)    ' NewBool evaluates to True.
```

The `CByte` function converts an expression to a byte value:

```
ThisDouble = 123.4567    ' A double value
NewByte = CByte(ThisDouble)    ' The value in NewByte is 123.
```

The `CCur` function converts an expression to a currency value:

```
NewCurr = CCur(ThisDouble)
```

The `CDate` function converts a string to a date datatype:

```
OldDate = "February 24, 1998"    ' Define a date.
NewDate = CDate(OldDate)    ' Convert OldDate to a Date data type.
```

The `CDbl` function converts an expression to a double value:

```
NewDouble = CDbl(123.2587458965)    ' Convert value to a Double.
```

The `CInt` function converts a value to an integer value:

```
OldValue = 1234.5678    ' OldValue is a Double.
NewValue = CInt(OldValue)    ' NewValue contains 1234.
```

The CLng function converts values to long values:

```
OldValue = 123.45
NewValue = CLng(OldValue)      ' MyLong1 contains 123.
```

The CSng function converts values to single values:

```
OldValue = 12.3456789
NewValue = CSng(OldValue)      ' NewValue now contains 12.34567.
```

The CStr function converts numeric values to strings:

```
OldValue = 123.456     ' A double value.
NewValue = CStr(OldValue)      ' NewValue now contains "123.456".
```

The CVar function converts an expression to a variant:

```
OldValue = 1234      ' An Integer value.
NewValue = CVar(OldValue & "22")     ' NewValue now contains the string
          ' 123422.
```

The CVErr function is used to create a user-defined error in the procedures that you create. The CVError function takes one argument, errornumber, which can be any valid error number. The following is an example of the syntax of the CVError function:

```
CVErr(errornumber)
```

The Fix and Int functions are both used to remove the fractional part of a number and then to return the resulting value. Where the Fix and the Int functions differ is in the way they handle negative numbers. The Int function rounds the number down, and the Fix function rounds the number up. The syntax for both the Int and the Fix functions is the same. The syntax for the Int function is shown here, where number is any valid numeric expression:

```
Int(number)
```

Domain

A *domain* is another name for a set of records. You use aggregate functions to describe certain properties of a domain. You can also use aggregate functions to provide information about the records in a domain. There are two types of aggregate functions: the domain aggregate functions and the SQL aggregate functions. Both of these functions provide much the same result, but they are used in different ways in different situations. One of the main differences is that you can call the SQL aggregate functions from within a SQL statement. However, you cannot access the SQL aggregate functions from within Visual Basic. On the other hand, the domain aggregate functions can be used from within Visual Basic but also in a SQL function.

The domain aggregate functions include the following:

> The DAvg function is used to find the average of a set of values in a set of records that you specify.

> The DCount function is used to find the number of records that exist in a range of records that you specify.

> The DLookup function is used when you want to retrieve the value of a particular field from a set of records that you specify.

> The Dfirst and the DLast functions are used to return the first and last record of a field that you specify. These functions are typically used to retrieve random records.

> The DMin and the DMax functions are used to calculate the minimum and maximum values of a set of records that you specify.

> The DStDev and the DStDevP functions are used to calculate the standard deviation in a set of values that is included in a set of records that you specify.

> The DSum function is used to calculate the sum of a set of values that is pulled from a set of records that you specify.

> The Dvar and the DVarP function are used to calculate variance across a set of values that is included in a set of records that you specify.

> The DAvg function is used to calculate the average of a set of values in a set of records that you specify.

Miscellaneous

The DoEvents function allows the operating system to process other events. The DoEvents function passes control to the operating system. After the events have been processed, the operating system will return control to your Access 97 application. The following example illustrates the use of the DoEvents function:

```
DoEvents( )
```

> **WARNING**
>
> Do not use the DoEvents function if other applications will be able to interact with your application in unforeseen ways while you're yielding control to the operating system.

The AppActivate statement activates an application window by changing focus to the application whose title is passed as a parameter to the AppActivate statement. The focus moves back to the Access 97 application when the user either changes the focus back manually or closes the application window. The AppActivate statement decides which application to activate by comparing the title that is passed to it with the titles of the applications that are currently running on the user's machine. If there is no match, the AppActivate statement changes the focus to the first running application whose title begins with the title that was passed as a parameter. If there is more than one application running whose title matches the title that is passed to the statement, the AppActivate statement chooses to change the focus to the first application whose title matches the title that is passed to it. The following example illustrates the correct syntax for the AppActivate statement:

```
AppActivate title[, wait]
```

title is a string representing the title of the application that you want to set the focus to, and *wait* is an optional value that specifies whether the calling application must have focus before it can call the application that is specified by title.

The Shell function exits the calling Access 97 application and runs an executable program before returning to the calling Access 97 application. If the Shell function is successful, it returns a double value that indicates the executable program's task ID. If the Shell function is not successful, it will return a zero to the calling Access 97 application. The following example illustrates the syntax of the Shell function:

```
Shell(pathname[,windowstyle])
```

pathname is a string that represents the name of the executable program that is to be executed. The pathname string also includes any command-line switches or arguments that need to be sent to the executable program. The windowstyle parameter is an optional integer constant that indicates how the executable program is to be started. If the windowstyle parameter is not sent to the Shell function, the executable program is started minimized with focus by default. The following list is composed of the constants that are valid parameters to the Shell function:

- vbHide has a value of 0 and indicates that the executable program is started as a hidden window that has focus.

- vbNormalFocus has a value of 1 and indicates that the executable program is started at its original size and window position and has focus.

- vbMinimizedFocus has a value of 2 and indicates that the executable program is started as an icon and that the executable program has focus.

- vbMaximizedFocus has a value of 3 and indicates that the executable program is opened as a maximized window with focus.

- vbNormalNoFocus has a value of 4 and indicates that the executable is opened to its most recent size and window position, but the currently active application retains focus.

- vbMinimizedNoFocus has a value of 6 and indicates that the executable program is opened as an icon and that the currently active application retains focus.

The SendKeys statement sends a string of keystrokes to the currently active application as if those keystrokes were typed at the keyboard. The following code is an example of the syntax for the SendKeys statement:

```
SendKeys string[, wait]
```

string is composed of the keystrokes to send to the application, and wait is an optional value that indicates whether the keystrokes must be processed before control is returned to the calling application.

When you send keystrokes to the application, you represent characters on the keyboard by using the characters themselves as part of the sending string. To send more than one character, merely append each additional character to the string that you are sending. For example, if you want to send the keystrokes that represent the characters h, e, l, l, and o, you would use "hello" for the sending string. To send the following special keyboard characters with the SendKeys statement, you must enclose the characters in braces. This applies to the following characters: +, ^, %, ~, (,), [,], {, and }. You cannot use the SendKeys statement to send keystrokes to any application other than a Windows application.

The Beep statement uses the computer's built-in speaker to sound a beep.

The CreateObject function is used to create and return a reference to an ActiveX object. The following example illustrates correct syntax for the CreateObject function:

```
CreateObject(class)
```

class uses the syntax appname.objecttype, appname represents the name of the application that is providing the object to be created, and objecttype is the type of object to create.

The GetObject function is used to return a reference to an ActiveX object from a file. The GetObject function uses the following syntax:

```
GetObject([pathname] [, class])
```

pathname is a string that contains the full pathname of the object that is supposed to be retrieved. If you include the class parameter, you can omit the pathname parameter. The class parameter represents the class of the object that is to be retrieved. class uses the syntax appname.objecttype; appname represents the name of the application that is providing the object to be created, and objecttype is the type of object to create.

The QBColor function returns a value that represents an RGB color code. The QBColor function uses the following syntax:

```
QBColor(color)
```

color is a whole number in the range of 0–15. These numbers represent various RGB color codes.

The RGB function returns a value that represents an RGB color value. The RGB function makes use of the following syntax:

```
RGB(red, green, blue)
```

red is a number in the range of 0–255 that represents the red component of the color. The parameters green and blue also are numbers in the range of 0–255 that represent the green and blue components of the color, respectively.

Working with Dates and Times

Expressions can contain dates and times. A date expression is any expression or part of an expression that can be interpreted by Access as a date. It can be a literal date, numbers and strings that look like dates, or dates returned by functions. The range represented can be any date from January 1, 100 A.D. to December 31, 9999, inclusive. A time expression works in conjunction with a date expression and can't exist without one. Dates and times are stored as real numbers. These real numbers are broken down into two halves separated by a decimal. The value that appears to the left of the decimal represents the date. The value that appears to the right of the decimal represents the time. The time is represented in increments between 0:00:00 and 23:59:59, inclusive.

NOTE

Date/time values can appear as negative numbers. Negative values represent dates before December 30, 1899. The left side is the number of whole days that have expired since December 30, 1899. Midnight is represented by 0, and midday is represented by .5. So if today were January 1, 1900, at noon, the number stored would be 0.5. A full day would not have been completed; only exactly one half of a day would have been completed. The time would be .5, and the day would still be 0. At one second before midnight on January 1, 1900, the time stored would be 0.9999999999. At the stroke of midnight, the time stored would be 1.0. Even though the time is stored like that, it's displayed according to the time format as set on the computer (either 12-hour or 24-hour format).

Dates are stored as 64-bit floating-point numbers. When a date/time string is entered into an expression, Access 97 recognizes the literal format of a date/time during its parse and places the pound sign (#) on either side of the date/time. Access 97 converts `January 1, 1995` to `#1 Jan 95#`.

Date and Time Formats

The date/time data has several predefined display formats. These formats usually appear in forms and reports and datasheets. They can appear in tables; however, the data is stored in a 64-bit floating-point number. Table A.1 lists the predefined formats visible in the date/time datatype of a field in a table.

TABLE A.1. THE PREDEFINED DATE/TIME FORMATS PROVIDED BY ACCESS 97.

Format	Display
General	`01/01/95 12:00:00 AM`
Short Date	`01/01/95`
Medium Date	`1-Jan-95`
Long Date	`Sunday, January 1, 1995`
Short Time	`00:00:00 (Midnight)`
Medium Time	`12:00 AM`
Long Time	`12:00:00 AM`

> **TIP**
>
> If the numbers being returned don't coincide with the preceding chart, check the machine's Control Panel for the predefined number and date/time formats. They can be found under the Regional Settings in the Date and Time tab.

Through expressions, it's possible to customize the display of the date/time formats. Table A.2 shows the different formats you can use to customize the display of date/time formats.

A

OPERATORS,
FUNCTIONS, AND
EXPRESSIONS

TABLE A.2. THE CUSTOM DATE/TIME FORMATS.

Format	Display
d	Day of the month between 1 and 31
dd	Day of the month between 01 and 31
ddd	Day of the month between SUN and SAT (displays only three letters)
dddd	Day of the month between Sunday and Saturday (displays the whole word)
w	Day of the week between 1 and 7
ww	Week of the year between 1 and 52
m	Month of the year between 1 and 12
mm	Month of the year between 01 and 12
mmm	Month of the year between JAN and DEC (displays only three letters)
mmmm	Month of the year between January and December (displays the whole word)
q	Quarter of the year between 1 and 4
y	Number of the day in the year between 1 and 365
yy	Number of the year between 00 and 99
yyyy	Number of the year between 0100 and 9999
h	Number of the hour between 1 and 23
hh	Number of the hour between 01 and 23
n	Number of the minute between 1 and 59
nn	Number of the minute between 01 and 59
s	Number of the second between 1 and 59
ss	Number of the second between 01 and 59
AM/PM	Uppercase AM/PM on a 12-hour clock
am/pm	Lowercase am/pm on a 12-hour clock
A/P	Uppercase A/P on a 12-hour clock

A slash (/) is used as a date separator. This might vary according to the time separator established in the Regional Settings of Control Panel.

A colon (:) is used as a time separator. This might vary according to the time separator established in the Regional Settings of Control Panel.

By using these custom formats, it's possible to create expressions that return values such as this:

```
Day Hired was Saturday.
```

Using the IIF Function

The IIF statement is a function that helps control the program flow of a database. It can be found in the Expression Builder under the Built-In Functions in a grouping called Program Flow. In the following example, IIF is a statement that is executed on every record in a query. This statement has two parts: a true part and a false part. Here is the syntax:

```
Status: IIF([StateOrProvince]="NC","VAC Employee","XYZ Employee")
```

The beginning of the statement starts with IIF; Status: is the name of the new field. The expression [StateOrProvince] = "NC" follows the IIF. The true part and the false part of the IIF statement are separated by commas. The true part is "VAC Employee", and the false part is "XYZ Employee".

This IIF function evaluates every record in the query. If the record's StateOrProvince field equals NC (true), the value in the new field called Status will be VAC Employee. If the record's StateOrProvince field doesn't equal NC (false), the value in the new field called Status will be XYZ Employee.

IIF functions can have only one of two answers. The expression equals either true or false. There are no maybes. Both parts of the expression are evaluated for every record. Be careful when using the IIF function on numbers. If the false part of an IIF statement results in a division-by-zero error, an error occurs even if the expression is true.

Expressions Defined

An *expression* is a tool utilized by the developer to give power to applications, and is a combination of operators, constants, literal values, and functions that evaluates to a single value. Expressions can be found in queries, forms, reports, and controls on forms and reports.

Expressions are used in Access 97 anywhere you can use a column or field from a table, such as forms, reports, and queries. They can even be used as a property within a field itself in a table. For example, the following expression can be entered into the Default property of a Date/Time field in a table so that the data that is stored pertains to a period from now until one year from today (this is just a simple example; in reality, it obviously wouldn't work in leap years):

```
=Now() + 365
```

Because the `Default` property appears for just about all fields in tables, forms, and reports, this expression could be entered anywhere. Depending on the location, the expression would be executed on the opening of that table, form, or report. Expressions can also be located in the `Criteria` line of a field in a query. With a slight modification to the preceding code, the following expression, when entered in the `Criteria` cell of a `Date/Time` field in a query, returns all the records with a date earlier than now:

```
<Now()
```

Because expressions are pieces of code that contain a combination of operators, constants, and variables, expressions can appear in macros and modules too. In essence, expressions can appear in all six objects of the database container: tables, queries, forms, reports, macros, and modules. They can be used to calculate fields or set criteria, or they can be used as a validation rule.

An Example of an Expression

Earlier, expressions were summed up to be mathematical sentences that make logical sense. The parts of an expression must be combined in such a manner that they make sense when Access 97 tries to execute the expression. The following is an example of an expression:

```
TotalCost: [delivery charge] + (([quantity]*[price]) +
(([quantity]*[price])*[tax]))
```

To explain the preceding expression, it's necessary to assign each item a value. For this example, assign the following values to the items:

> `TotalCost` is the field name of the expression.
>
> `delivery charge` is $35.
>
> `quantity` for the first record is 100.
>
> `price` for the first record is $50.
>
> `tax` is 6 percent.

The symbols such as * and + are operators. `TotalCost` is a variable name. The items `delivery charge`, `quantity`, `price`, and `tax` are field names. These are the parts of the preceding expression.

Which answer is returned by Access 97 for the preceding expression: 405 or 5335? The correct answer is `5335`. Expressions are read from left to right; however, any part of the operation that is contained in parentheses is performed first. The correct way to read the preceding expression is

```
([quantity]*[price]) = 5000
([quantity]*[price])*[tax] = 300
(([quantity]*[price]) + (([quantity]*[price])*[tax])) = 5300
[delivery charge] + 5300 = 5335
TotalCost = 5335
```

Parts of an Expression

An expression can be summed up as a kind of mathematical sentence. Many different parts can be combined to make up this sentence. The parts of this mathematical sentence must be presented in such a way as to make logical sense. The result of this mathematical sentence is that it returns a value.

The parts of an expression can stand either alone or in combination. As with real sentences, one word or several words can make up the sentence. Real sentences are made up of parts called subjects, verbs, adverbs, adjectives, and so on. Expressions are made up of these parts:

- Operators—Symbols that are prevalent in Boolean algebra, as well as other symbols.
- Constants—Numeric or string values that don't change.
- Literal values—Exact representations, such as numbers, strings, and dates.
- Functions—Procedures that return a value; for example, Now returns the current date.
- Field names—Names given to fields in a table. Must be surrounded by brackets if the name is made up of two or more words.

Most expressions perform calculations that return a value. Usually, calculations are performed with operators. Operators play a big part in expressions. There are many different operators, but all are usually part of one of the following four groups.

Order of Operation

At times, several different operations might need to take place in an expression. Operations must be performed in a predetermined order as designated by Access 97. When operations from the same group appear in an expression, the predetermined order takes place. Within each group listed previously, the operators are listed in that predetermined order. If two or more groups are involved in an expression, these groups also are performed in a predetermined order. The arithmetic operators are first, followed by the concatenation, comparison, and logical operators. This is called *operator precedence*.

If it's necessary to perform a certain operation before others in the preordained order, place that operation in parentheses. Parentheses override Access's operator precedence. If more than one operation is enclosed in parentheses, however, operator precedence again is maintained.

Making Calculations

The reason for calculations in queries, forms, and reports is to return values that are useful to the user. Calculations can't be discussed without a mention of datatypes. The precision of the results from a calculation depend a lot on the number datatype of the field in the expression. Six types of data concern numbers, and they are listed in Table A.3.

TABLE A.3. THE NUMBER DATATYPES.

Datatype	What It Stores
Byte	Can handle 0 to 255
Integer	Can handle –32,768 to 32,767
Long	Can handle –2,147,483,648 to 2,147,483,647
Single	Can handle –3.402823E38 to –1.401298E-45 and 1.401298E-45 to 3.402823E38
Double	Can handle –4.94065645841247E-324 to –1.79769313486232E308 and 1.79769313486232E308 to 4.94065645841247E324
Replication ID	Global Unique Identifier
Currency	Can handle –922,337,203,685,477.5808 to 922,337,203,685,477.5807

Remember, the precision of the data resulting from the calculations that are performed depends on the number datatype. The more precise the datatype, the more precise the result.

Creating Calculations

The equal sign (=) constitutes the beginning of a calculation. When the calculation expression has been entered into the field, Access converts the field to an alias name, such as Expr1. Calculations can sum, average, count, or total all the records in a query.

Custom calculations can be performed on numeric, text, and date calculations. Several aggregate functions can be performed using information from one or more fields in a query. These custom calculations need to be created in a new field cell entered as an expression. Through the logical combination of several literals, field names, functions, and operators, complex calculations can be performed.

Summary

This appendix covered operators, functions, and expressions. The different parts of an expression were identified and described. Expressions can contain operators, constants, literal values, functions, field names, and variable names. Several functions that are included with Access 97 were defined, and examples were given of many of the functions.

Operators are the symbols used in an expression. There are four groups of operators: arithmetic, comparison, concatenation, and logic.

Expressions can be used in tables, queries, forms, reports, and macros. Expressions can be used to set the value of properties and to calculate fields and conditions in queries. They can also be used as record sources for forms and reports.

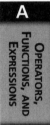

A

OPERATORS, FUNCTIONS, AND EXPRESSIONS

Access 97 Specific Features

APPENDIX B

What's New?

The most noticeable difference between Access 95 and Access 97 is the Internet support that is built into the application. This Internet support is a common theme throughout Microsoft's Office 97 suite of applications. There are several new wizards included in the Access 97 application, including a Chart Wizard that allows you to create over 20 different types of charts. In this version of Access, you can use the database utilities on a database that you have open currently. These database utilities are the Compact Database and the Repair Database utilities, which used to require you to close the database before attempting database maintenance. Access 97 has new command bars and class modules, in addition to several other new features. This appendix describes in detail some of the differences between Access 95 and Access 97.

> **NOTE**
>
> Access 97 now supports the IntelliMouse, a mouse that comes with a scrolling wheel mounted on the top. If you have an IntelliMouse, you can scroll through your datasheets and forms with it.

Performance Enhancements

Access 97 has been reworked to provide significant performance improvements over Access 95. Access 97 loads its databases faster because it does not load Visual Basic and DAO objects until they are needed. In Access 97, a form or a report does not automatically have an associated module. Instead, Access 97 doesn't load any modules until the VB code in the module is requested. This can result in your application having fewer modules to compile, thus enabling a faster compile time. Access 97 even allows you to speed up queries when you are using an ODBC data source. It also allows you to send bulk update queries to the server, in which all the records are processed at once instead of one record at a time.

Tab Control

Access 97 introduces a new control to the Access toolbox: the Tab control. It's a dialog box with *dividers*, called *tabs*, that separate the information into groups. The tab dividers are called *pages* and are stored as Page objects in the Tab control's Pages collection. Each page has a Controls collection to list the Control objects that are on that page. Each page can contain one or more controls. The Tab control has a Value property that shows which Page object of the Tab control is selected. The pages are indexed as integers starting with 0. For example, when the first page in a Tab control is selected, the Tab control's `Value` property will be equal to 0. If the third page in the Tab control is selected, the Tab control's `Value` property will be equal to 2.

You can add a new page to a Tab control by using the Add method of the Pages collection. In the same manner, you can delete a page from a Tab control by using the Remove method of the Pages collection. You can also adjust the height and width of the tabs on the Tab control by using the `TabFixedHeight` and `TabFixedWidth` properties of the Tab control.

Jet Database Improvements

Access 97 uses an updated version of the Microsoft Jet database engine. Access 95 used version 3.0; Access 97 uses version 3.5. The new Jet engine is faster at processing large queries and queries that include the inequality operator (<>). Sequential database reads and temporary queries run much faster, and even deleting tables is faster than in the 3.0 version of the Jet engine.

There is a new Registry setting that allows you to speed up large queries that are run against NetWare and Windows NT servers. The setting does this by forcing transactions to partially commit. You can set this Registry setting, `MaxLocksPerFile`, by using the DAO `SetOption` method to give the setting a new value at runtime. This method does not replace the value of `MaxLocksPerFile` in the Registry, but only overrides it for the current application. If you open up the Registry with RegEdit or another utility while this is in effect, you will still see the original value of the Registry key.

Access 97 Internet Support

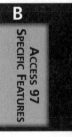

Microsoft Access 97 now includes extensive support for using the Internet. Users can incorporate hyperlinks to a site on the Internet or an intranet, or files on a local or remote computer, inside an Access form. Using the new Publish to the Web Wizard, you also can convert an existing form datasheet, table, or query to Hypertext Markup Language (HTML) or Microsoft Internet Information Server IDC/HTX or ASP files. If using a wizard is not your style, you can use the new Save to HTML/Web Formats command, which enables you to save your form datasheets, reports, queries, or tables to their HTML equivalents.

Hyperlinks

Access 97 includes a new datatype: the hyperlink datatype. You can now store hyperlink information in a field in an Access 97 database, the same way that you store strings and numbers. Access 97 allows you to use hyperlinks in your database to jump from one datasheet to another, or from one form or report to another, the same way that you would use a hyperlink on a Web page to jump to another Web page. You can also use a hyperlink to jump to a document that was created by another Microsoft Office application, such as Word or Excel. You can enable hyperlinks on labels, image controls, or command buttons on the forms within your Access 97 application.

A hyperlink field in an Access 97 database can contain up to three parts: `displaytext`, `address`, and `subaddress`. The parts of a hyperlink field are separated by the pound sign (#). The syntax for a hyperlink field would be

```
displaytext#address#subaddress
```

The `HyperlinkPart` function returns information about the parts of the hyperlink datatype. It can be used to return the actual value of one of the three parts of a hyperlink field.

The `Follow` method is used with a hyperlink field that is associated with a control on a form or report in your Access 97 application. The `Follow` method jumps to the document that is listed in the hyperlink field. It works exactly the same as clicking a hyperlink on the Web. The syntax for the `Follow` method is

```
object.hyperlink.Follow[([newwindow],[addhistory],[extrainfo],[method],
⮕[headerinfo])]
```

`object` is the name of the object that the hyperlink field is bound to. The objects can be labels, command buttons, and image controls. `hyperlink` is the hyperlink that is associated with the object. `newwindow` is a Boolean value that defaults to False. A value of True for `newwindow` will result in the document being sent to a new window, and a value of False results in the document opening in the current window. The default value of `addhistory` is True, and this value adds the hyperlink to the History folder. Setting this value to False results in the link not being added to the History folder. The `extrainfo` argument is a string or array that contains the extra information that is sent to the hyperlink. The `method` argument contains an integer that specifies whether the method of posting is `GET` or `POST`. And the `headerinfo` argument is a string that can contain extra header information.

The following code example binds a hyperlink to a command button, and then opens the hyperlink when the form that the command button is housed on is loaded:

```
Private Sub Link_Load()
    Dim ctrl as CommandButton
    Set ctrl= Me!Command1
    With ctrl
        .Visible  = False
        .HyperlinkAddress = "http://www.mcp.com/"
```

```
        .Hyperlink.Follow
    End With
End Sub
```

You can use the `FollowHyperlink` method to allow your Access 97 application to jump to a hyperlink that has been supplied by the user of your application. You can prompt the user for a hyperlink, and then use the `FollowHyperlink` method to jump to the document represented by that hyperlink. When using the `FollowHyperlink` method, you can use the extra info and the method arguments to query a search engine or send parameters to another CGI script. The syntax for the `FollowHyperlink` method is

```
[application.]FollowHyperlink
address,[subaddress],[newwindow],[addhistory],[extrainfo],[method],[header
➥info]
```

`application` is the name of the application object, and `address` is a string that contains a valid hyperlink address. The following listing shows the arguments to the `FollowHyperlink` method, along with their default values:

- The `subaddress` argument is a string that contains a location in the document, such as a bookmark in a Word document or an anchor in an HTML document.

- If the Boolean value of the `newwindow` argument is True, the document is opened in a new window. If the value is set to False, the document is opened in the current window. The default value is False.

- A True value for the `addhistory` argument results in the hyperlink being added to the History folder. A False value results in the hyperlink not being added to the History folder. The default value for the `addhistory` argument is True.

- The `extrainfo` argument is a string that allows you to specify parameters to pass to a CGI script or an ASP page. The information that is contained in the `extrainfo` argument is typically shown after the hyperlink address and is preceded by a question mark (?) in your Web browser.

- The `method` argument is an integer that specifies whether your hyperlink addresses the server using the GET or the POST method.

- The `headerinfo` argument is a string that contains extra header information.

An example of using the `FollowHyperlink` method is shown in the following function, which gathers a hyperlink from the user of your application and jumps to the document indicated by the hyperlink:

```
Function GoSurfing() As Boolean
    Dim userinput As String
    userinput=InputBox("Please enter a valid URL")
    Application.FollowHyperlink userinput,,True
```

B

SPECIFIC FEATURES

ACCESS 97

```
        GoSurfing=True
Exit_GoSurfing:
    Exit Function
```

Using Access 97, you can specify the hyperlink that you want to jump to via two new properties that appear in the command button, image control, and label controls. These properties are as follows:

HyperlinkAddress	Specifies the path to an object, document, or Web page.
HyperlinkSubAddress	Specifies a subaddress within the linked object. This subaddress can be an object (form or report) in an Access database, a bookmark in a Word document, a named range in an Excel spreadsheet, a slide in a PowerPoint presentation, or an anchor on an HTML document.

The HyperlinkAddress property is used with a control that has a hyperlink associated with it, and is a string that contains the UNC path to a file such as a Word document or an Excel spreadsheet. You can also store an URL to a Web page in the HyperlinkAddress property. You can only access the HyperlinkAddress property with Visual Basic within Access 97 or by using the control's property sheet.

When you move your mouse over a control that has the HyperlinkAddress property set, the mouse cursor will change into a pointing hand in the same way that it does inside your Web browser. To jump to the hyperlink represented by the HyperlinkAddress property, click the control. If you are pointing to an object inside your current Access 97 database, you should leave the HyperlinkAddress property blank and indicate the object that you want to open in the HyperlinkSubAddress property. You should also indicate the object type. The syntax for this is

```
objecttype objectname
```

objecttype is the type of object you are pointing toward, and objectname is its name. If you intend to open an object that is stored in another Access database, you should enter the UNC path to the database and the name of the database in the HyperlinkAddress property, and indicate the object within that database in the same way that you indicate the object inside the current database.

You can enter hyperlinks in the Properties window for the particular control, or insert them by choosing Insert|Hyperlink.

Publish to the Web Wizard

The Publish to the Web Wizard allows for the automatic creation of a Web page from an Access 97 form datasheet, table, query, or report. To use the wizard, choose File|Save As HTML. Using the wizard, you go through several steps, supplying information needed to create a Web page. Figure B.1 shows the second step in the Publish to the Web Wizard. One of the final steps prompts you to choose between a static HTML page or a dynamic HTX format that queries data residing in an Access database on a Microsoft Internet Information Server or personal Web server. In the last step, the wizard asks if it should create a default page and, if so, what template it should use.

FIGURE B.1.

A step from the Publish to the Web Wizard.

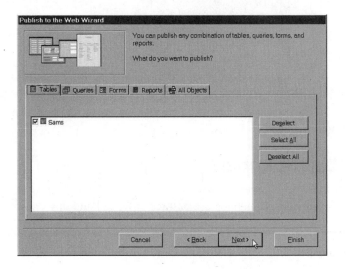

The File Menu's Save As HTML Command

In addition to the Publish to the Web Wizard, Access also offers a generic Save As HTML command to convert a single object to HTML, IDC/HTX, or ASP format. To use the command, highlight a form, datasheet, table, query, or report and choose File|Save As HTML. If you choose the HTML format, notice that the Internet Explorer opens with the new page displayed. Figure B.2 illustrates the Save As HTML menu item.

IDC/HTX and ASP Files

Using Access 97, you can output table, query, and form datasheets as Microsoft Internet Information Server IDC and HTX files. The IDC file includes the data source information, such as username, password, server, database, and the query that returns the data. The HTX file is an HTML file that maps the returning data to the field merge codes.

FIGURE B.2.

*The Save As
HTML menu item.*

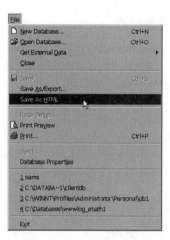

You can also output tables, queries and forms as Microsoft Internet Information Server version 3.0/4.0 ASP pages. ASP pages are the descendants of the IDC/HTX pages that were used by IIS version 2.0. For more information about ASP, see Chapter 26, "Publishing Dynamic Web Pages."

AutoList Members

Access 97 makes it very easy to write Visual Basic code to use in your application. It provides coding help through the use of three different Auto tips:

- Auto List Members
- Auto Quick Info
- Auto Data Tips

The Auto List Members option lists the relevant objects, properties, methods, and constants that can follow an object name when you type it into the statement. You can click an item in the list that is offered, or you can continue typing your code. If you continue typing, the list changes to display the item that is closest to what you have typed. When an item is selected, you can enter it by pressing Ctrl+Enter or the Tab key. To close the list, press the Esc key.

The Auto Quick Info option helps you enter code by suggesting syntax information about procedures and methods that you type into the Module window. This option will even list the arguments that you need to use with the procedure or method that you are calling.

You can check the value of a variable or an expression while the code is in break mode by using the Auto Data Tips option. When the code is in break mode, just place your mouse over a variable or expression, and a tip will pop up with the variable or expression's current value.

Class Modules

Access 97 now includes support for form, report, and basic-level class modules. A *class module* serves as a template for the building of an object. Just as a building has blueprints to specify how it is to be built, an object has a template (class module) that specifies what an object will be once it is created. A class module consists of properties and methods. After a module is available, you can create an object in memory; then you can set its properties and call its methods to perform functions. This approach is powerful because it enables you to build standard modules that you can use over and over throughout the program.

You can build an object that performs certain tasks. Say that you need an object that returns the zip code for a specified city. You can construct an object with a property that stores a specific city, and you then can write a method that returns to a caller the zip code for that city. You don't have to know anything about the code inside the module except for the property name to accept the city and the method to return the zip code; then every form or report in the database can use this module.

Be aware that class module data exists independently for each object that you create from a class. That means that class module data has a lifetime only as long as the life of the object. It is created at the same time as the object, and is destroyed at the same time as the object.

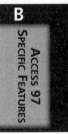

Partial Replication

Access 97 allows you to create a partial replica of your database that contains a subset of the database's records. You use a filter to restrict the data for your partial replica. The benefits of partial replication include reduced network traffic, smaller replicated databases, and increased security. By using a partial replica, you are replicating only the data that you need at the remote site.

For example, you could keep a database of all employees of a multistate company at the main corporate headquarters and replicate only those employees that actually work in each state to the various state headquarters. This way, the state headquarters are not burdened with replicating data that they will never use. Instead, they only replicate the data that is actually useful. This also means that the replication takes less time and that the remote databases take up much less space on the state headquarters' servers.

Access 97 MDE Files

Access 97 introduces a new file format called *MDE*. This format is best used when your database includes Visual Basic code. When a database is saved in this format, Access 97 compiles all modules, removes all editable source code, and compacts the destination database. The application still runs all the Visual Basic code, but the code cannot be viewed or edited. This removal of the Visual Basic code also reduces the size of the file and improves memory usage for faster performance.

The following is a list of tasks that you cannot perform once the MDB is converted to an MDE file:

- You cannot create, modify, or view forms, reports, or modules.
- You cannot add, delete, or modify references to object libraries or databases.
- You cannot change code using the properties or methods of Access objects.
- You cannot change the database's VBA project name via the Options dialog box.
- You cannot import or export forms, reports, or modules.
- You can export and import tables, queries, and macros, but only to and from non-MDE file databases.

If you save your database as an MDE file, be sure that you have saved a copy of your original database. If you need to modify the format of any modules, reports, or forms in your database, you must open the original version of your database, make the modifications, and then resave the file as an MDE file.

Command Bars

Access 97 introduces a new feature called *command bars*. These command bars are a combination of the separate menus and toolbars that were used in previous versions of Access. In Access 97, shortcut menus, toolbars, and menu items are now considered command bars. They are programmable and can be customized to meet your specific needs.

You must set a reference to the Microsoft Office 8.0 Object Library to be able to program with command bars. To set this reference, go to the module Design view, click References in the Tools menu, and click the check box next to Microsoft Office 8.0 Object Library. All command bars are a member of the `CommandBars` collection, which belongs to the Access application object. The `CommandBars` collection includes, by default, all the command bars that exist within your application. You can easily add and delete new bars from the collection, as well as the controls (which are part of the `CommandBarControls` collection) that reside on these bars.

Command bars can be one of three types: toolbar, menu bar, or pop-up menu. Each type can consist of built-in and customized commands. All previous menu bars, shortcut menus, and toolbars are converted automatically when you convert a database to Access 97. The following lists some of the new objects introduced with command bars:

- `CommandBars` collection object
- `CommandBar` object
- `CommandBarControls` collection object
- `CommandBarControl` object
- `CommandBarButton` object
- `CommandBarComboBox` object
- `CommandBarPopup` object

These new objects allow much greater control of the tools available in Access. The following code, for example, shows how you can make visible a specific command bar called `MyCommandBar`:

```
For Each cb In CommandBars
    If cb.Name = "MyCommandBar" Then
        cb.Visible = True
    End If
Next cb
```

You can easily add a command bar of your own to the collection by using the `Add` method of the collection. You can also add a control to an existing command bar by using the `Add` method of the `CommandBarControls` collection. The `CommandBars` collection and the other collections that make it up are unique in that they are indexed beginning with a 1. Most other collections in Access 97 are indexed beginning with a 0.

The Office Assistant

The most significant change to the Access 97 help system is the introduction of the Office Assistant, which is a combination of the Help system's Search function and an online tutorial. The Office Assistant, opened by pressing F1, is represented by an animation, called an *actor*, in the lower-right portion of the screen. The program ships with several actors, and you can choose which actor you want to be the assistant.

When you open the assistant, it presents you with a pop-up balloon that displays several choices. Your location in the program when you open the assistant determines the choices that are listed in the balloon. If a topic of interest does not appear, you can type in a search topic (the assistant can understand conversational English) and click the Search button. The Office Assistant demonstrates how a task can be accomplished when you click the Show Me button. It also can display tips.

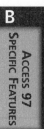

The Office Assistant is a part of all the applications that make up the Office 97 suite. Any changes that you make to the way the Office Assistant works are reflected to all the applications that make up the Office 97 suite.

ODBCDirect

Access 97 includes new technology that allows you to access ODBC databases without using the Jet database engine. This technology is called ODBCDirect, and it uses the DAO 3.5 object model. ODBCDirect can speed up the access to your ODBC database because it doesn't require Access 97 to load the Jet database engine. ODBCDirect gives you faster database access and increased control over some server-specific features by letting you do the following:

- Specify the location of cursors, locally or on the server.
- Specify input values and check return values from stored procedures on the server.
- Perform asynchronous queries that allow you to start another query while one is still running.
- Cache Recordset object changes locally and submit them to the server in batches.

> **WARNING**
>
> If your Access 97 application requires that forms or controls in your application be bound to data that comes from an ODBC data source, you must use the Jet engine to access the data. Data that is accessed through the use of ODBCDirect cannot be bound to a form or a control.

Converting a Prior-Version Access Database to Access 97

Access 97 lets you share your Access database with users who have not upgraded to Access 97. You can upgrade parts of your database so that users of any version can share the data that makes up the application. You can either keep your database in one file, or you can split your database into a front-end/back-end application. Access 97 comes with a Database Splitter Wizard that will automate this process.

A front-end/back-end application is an Access database that is really two databases. The back-end database contains the application's data tables and is usually located on a network server to give multiple users access to its data. The front-end database contains all the other components that make up the Access application and is usually installed on the user's computers. The front-end database contains links to the tables that are stored in the back-end database.

When you have a multiuser database in a situation where you cannot upgrade all the users at the same time, the need will arise for all the users to use the database at the same time without converting it to Access 97 format. To do this, have your Access 97 users enable the database without converting it. They will be prompted to make this choice when they open the database. If the database is merely enabled and not converted, the original users can still access the database along with the Access 97 users. The only caveat is that the Access 97 users cannot modify or design any objects that make up the database. If you need to modify or design the objects, you must open up the database in the version of Access that it was created in. You can enable Access databases from versions 1.x, 2.0, or 95 to work with Access 97, but you cannot open an Access 97 database with a previous version of Access.

If you do not want to enable the database in Access 97, you can create a front-end/back-end application as long as the back-end portion of the application that contains the databases remains the oldest version of Access that is used.

> **TIP**
>
> In Access 97, the `DoMenuItem` command is replaced with the `RunCommand` command, but the `DoMenuItem` command is still supported for the purposes of backward-compatibility. If you do a database conversion, the `DoMenuItem` command is automatically replaced by the `RunCommand` command.

If you are converting a secured database from a previous version of Access to an Access 97 database, you must ensure that you have joined the workgroup that defines the user accounts accessing the database that you intend to convert to Access 97. The user account that you use during the conversion must have the following permissions for the database that you want to convert:

- Open/Run
- Open Exclusive
- Modify Design or Administer permissions for all tables in the database
- Read Design permissions for all objects in the database

B

ACCESS 97
SPECIFIC FEATURES

> **TIP**
>
> If you attempt to convert a database to Access 97 and it doesn't work, you can accomplish the same results by creating a new database in Access 97 and importing all the objects from your older Access database into the Access 97 database.

Summary

This appendix has introduced you to several new features of Access 97. These features are dealt with in detail within the chapters of this book. The main additions to Access 97 involve the Internet, which enable you to integrate your Access 97 database application with the Internet rapidly and easily.

INDEX

Access 97 Programming Unleashed

Scott Billings, Joe Rhemann, et al.

Access 97 solves all the development problems within Access 95, which will lead to more developers adopting Access 97 as their preferred database application development environment. Using hands-on, real-world examples, this book teaches users key programming and development concepts and provides extensive coverage of the most widely used topics in database programming.

Covers key topics, including VBA, Active Data Objects, OLE DB, ODBCDirect, jet replication, code libraries, performance optimization, security, Visual SourceSafe, and Web connectivity.

CD-ROM is loaded with sample database applications and source code that can be adapted to the developer's everyday, real-world programs.

Covers Access 97

$49.99 USA/$70.95 CAN	*User Level: Accomplished - Expert*
ISBN: 0-672-31049-X	*1,000 pp.*
Sams Publishing	

SE Using Access 97, 2nd Edition

Roger Jennings

Special Edition Using Access 97, 2nd Edition is a tutorial. Readers will learn to how to build an Access 97 database from scratch and how to work with existing databases. They will learn to build forms, reports, and program more complex applications as they develop their skills. *Special Edition Using Access 97, 2nd Edition* is a reference. After readers have built their database, they will refer back to the text for daily troubleshooting or to install new features. The one true "must have" Access 97 resource with start to finish coverage. Making the best even better: All new coverage for the #1 Access book on the market. Over 300,000 units of Special Edition Access have been sold within the past 3 years. Expanded coverage of VBA and Office integration.

$49.99 US/$71.95 CDN	*All User Levels*
ISBN: 0-7897-1452-3	*1,312 pp.*
Que	

Alison Balter's Mastering Access 97 Development, Second Premier Edition

Alison Balter

One of the premier corporate database applications, Access, is a powerful application that can be programmed and customized. This book shows users how to develop simple and complex applications for Access 97.

Shows how to create tables, forms, queries, reports, and objects.

Teaches how to program Access applications for a client/server environment.

CD-ROM includes source code, reusable functions, forms, and reports.

Covers Access 97

$49.99 USA/$70.95 CDN   *User Level: Accomplished - Expert*
ISBN: 0-672-30999-8   *1,100 pp.*

Access 97 Power Programming

F. Scott Barker

Written by one of the most well-known Access developers and trainers, this is the ultimate authority for the Access programmer, providing great insight into the inner workings of Access. Programmers will use this guide to become more proficient in many important areas, including 32-bit OLE controls, OLE/DDE automation, and more. No Access power user or programmer should be without *Access 97 Power Programming*. Contains valuable routines that Access programmers can use in their own programs to save time. Filled with practical examples that give direct explanations of tough concepts. Previous edition of this book won a Reader's Choice award from *Visual Basic Programmer's Journal.*

$59.99 US/$85.95 CDN   *User Level: Accomplished - Expert*
ISBN: 0-7897-0915-5   *1,024 pp.*
Que

Add to Your Sams Library Today with the Best Books for Programming, Operating Systems, and New Technologies

The easiest way to order is to pick up the phone and call

1-800-428-5331

between 9:00 a.m. and 5:00 p.m. EST.
For faster service please have your credit card available.

ISBN	Quantity	Description of Item	Unit Cost	Total Cost
0-672-31049-X		Access 97 Programming Unleashed	$49.99	
0-7897-1452-3		Special Edition Using Access 97, Second Edition	$49.99	
0-672-30999-8		Alison Balter's Mastering Access 97 Development, Second Premier Edition	$49.99	
0-7897-1117-6		Access 97 Power Programming	$59.99	
		Shipping and Handling: See information below.		
		TOTAL		

Shipping and Handling: $4.00 for the first book, and $1.75 for each additional book. Floppy disk: add $1.75 for shipping and handling. If you need to have it NOW, we can ship product to you in 24 hours for an additional charge of approximately $18.00, and you will receive your item overnight or in two days. Overseas shipping and handling adds $2.00 per book and $8.00 for up to three disks. Prices subject to change. Call for availability and pricing information on latest editions.

201 W. 103rd Street, Indianapolis, Indiana 46290

1-800-428-5331 — Orders   1-800-835-3202 — FAX   1-800-858-7674 — Customer Service